THE OXFORD HANDBOOK OF

RELIGIOUS PERSPECTIVES ON REPRODUCTIVE ETHICS

THE OXFORD HANDBOOK OF

RELIGIOUS PERSPECTIVES ON REPRODUCTIVE ETHICS

Edited by
DENA S. DAVIS

OXFORD
UNIVERSITY PRESS

OXFORD
UNIVERSITY PRESS

Oxford University Press is a department of the University of Oxford. It furthers
the University's objective of excellence in research, scholarship, and education
by publishing worldwide. Oxford is a registered trade mark of Oxford University
Press in the UK and certain other countries.

Published in the United States of America by Oxford University Press
198 Madison Avenue, New York, NY 10016, United States of America.

© Oxford University Press 2024

All rights reserved. No part of this publication may be reproduced, stored in
a retrieval system, or transmitted, in any form or by any means, without the
prior permission in writing of Oxford University Press, or as expressly permitted
by law, by license, or under terms agreed with the appropriate reproduction
rights organization. Inquiries concerning reproduction outside the scope of the
above should be sent to the Rights Department, Oxford University Press, at the
address above.

You must not circulate this work in any other form
and you must impose this same condition on any acquirer.

Library of Congress Cataloging-in-Publication Data
Names: Davis, Dena S., 1947- editor.
Title: The Oxford handbook of religious perspectives on reproductive ethics/
Dena S. Davis.
Description: New York, NY : Oxford University Press, [2024] |
Includes bibliographical references and index.
Identifiers: LCCN 2023041601 (print) | LCCN 2023041602 (ebook) |
ISBN 9780190633202 (hardback) | ISBN 9780190633219 |
ISBN 9780190633233 (epub)
Subjects: LCSH: Human reproduction—Moral and ethical aspects. |
Human reproduction—Religious aspects.
Classification: LCC QP251 .O928 2023 (print) | LCC QP251 (ebook) |
DDC 176—dc23/eng/20231122
LC record available at https://lccn.loc.gov/2023041601
LC ebook record available at https://lccn.loc.gov/2023041602

DOI: 10.1093/oxfordhb/9780190633202.001.0001

Printed by Sheridan Books, Inc., United States of America

For B.K.H.

Contents

Notes on Contributors   xi

Introduction   1
Dena S. Davis

PART I THE ABRAHAMIC RELIGIOUS TRADITIONS

1. Jewish Ethics: Theological Foundations, Classical Sources, Hermeneutical Challenges   7
   Louis E. Newman

2. Sources of Catholic Moral Theology   22
   Dolores L. Christie

3. Protestant Sources of Moral Knowledge   37
   Karen L. Lebacqz

4. Muslim Reproductive Ethics: Sources and Methodology   59
   Abdulaziz Sachedina

5. The Role of Authority in Understanding Religious Ethics   83
   Dena S. Davis

6. Natural Law and Reproductive Ethics   90
   Bethany Kieran Haile

PART II THE ETHICS OF BEING A PARENT

7. Beyond the "First Commandment": Procreation and Parenting in Judaism   115
   Seth Goren

8. A Long Road to a Catholic Theology of Parenthood   136
   Ann Shepard Feeley Swaner

9. Protestant Perspectives on Procreation and Parenting 156
   Joel James Shuman

10. Parents and Children in the Qur'an and Premodern Islamic Jurisprudence 172
    Janan Delgado and Celene Ibrahim

11. Religious Perspectives on Gay Parenting 191
    Brett Krutzsch

12. Religious Perspectives on Population Justice 204
    Daniel C. Maguire

PART III DIFFERENT WAYS OF MAKING FAMILIES

13. Adoption, Personal Status, and Jewish Law 221
    Michael J. Broyde

14. Islamic Perspectives on Adoption 239
    Faisal Kutty

15. Adopting Embryos 261
    John Berkman

16. Biblical Contexts for Adoption and Surrogacy 284
    David M. Smolin

17. Jewish Perspectives on Gamete Use, Donation, and Surrogacy 320
    Elliot N. Dorff

18. Islamic Perspectives on Gamete Donation and Surrogacy 337
    Ayman Shabana

PART IV CONTRACEPTION AND ABORTION

19. Catholic Teaching on Contraception: An Unsettled Business? 355
    Aline H. Kalbian

20. Contraception: Protestant Evangelical Perspectives 372
    David B. Fletcher

21. Abortion in the Jewish Tradition of Religious Humanism   388
    NOAM ZOHAR

22. The Roman Catholic Position on Abortion   403
    PATRICK LEE

23. Talk Less: Why Protestants Will Never Agree on Abortion
    (and That's OK)   421
    KATHRYN D. BLANCHARD

24. Islamic Perspectives on Abortion   443
    THOMAS EICH

25. Public Opinion and Attitudes toward Abortion: Patterns across
    Religious Traditions   459
    TED G. JELEN

PART V PRENATAL DIAGNOSIS

26. Pregnancy and Piety: The Situated Ethics of Prenatal Diagnostic
    Technologies for Ultra-Orthodox Jewish Women   477
    ELLY TEMAN AND TSIPY IVRY

27. Christian Perspectives on Prenatal Diagnosis   498
    KAREN PETERSON-IYER

28. Evangelical Perspectives on Prenatal Testing   526
    PAIGE COMSTOCK CUNNINGHAM

Index   549

Notes on Contributors

John Berkman is professor of moral theology at Regis College, University of Toronto, at the Graduate Centre for Theological Studies in the Toronto School of Theology, and a fellow of the International Society for Science and Religion. He previously taught at the Dominican School of Philosophy & Theology in Berkeley, California, and was director of the Division of Moral Theology/Ethics at the Catholic University of America. He has been a visiting professor at Duke Divinity School, a visiting fellow at Christ Church College, Oxford, and a visiting research scholar at the Aquinas Institute at Blackfriars, Oxford. He teaches and writes in the areas of Thomistic ethics, healthcare ethics, and animal ethics. He recently published "G.E.M. Anscombe's 'I am Sadly Theoretical: It Is the Effect of Being at Oxford' (1938): A Newly Discovered Article by Anscombe Edited and with an Editor's Introduction" in *New Blackfriars* in September 2021, and is editing *The Oxford Handbook of Theological Bioethics*. Many of his publications can be found at his academia.edu and researchgate.net webpages.

Kathryn D. Blanchard is Charles A. Dana Professor of Religious Studies Emerita at Alma College in central Michigan. She is the coauthor of *An Introduction to Christian Environmentalism* (Baylor, 2014) and coeditor of *Lady Parts: Biblical Women and "The Vagina Monologues"* (Wipf & Stock, 2012). She has also written for online venues including *Religion Dispatches*, *Killing the Buddha*, and *Women in Higher Education*.

Michael J. Broyde is a professor of law at Emory University School of Law and the Berman Project Director of the Center of the Study of Law and Religion at Emory University. He has served in many rabbinic capacities over the years, both as a synagogue rabbi and as a member of various rabbinical courts.

Dolores L. Christie is retired executive director of the Catholic Theological Society of America. Dr. Christie has taught college and graduate school for almost forty years. She serves on the ethics committee of the Hospice of the Western Reserve and the chemical dependency committee of the Ohio Solid Organ Transplant Consortium. She has authored several books, chapters, and articles, including *Last Rights: A Catholic Perspective on End-of-Life Decisions*, and *It's Time: Narratives on Illness, Aging, and Death* (Cascade Books, 2019).

Paige Comstock Cunningham, PhD, JD, is a consultant in higher education administration, board governance, and strategic planning, and a lecturer in bioethics and public policy. Cunningham is an affiliate professor of law and bioethics at Trinity Law

School and Trinity Graduate School. She is executive director emeritus of The Center for Bioethics & Human Dignity at Trinity International University and served as Interim President of Taylor University from 2019 to 2021.

Dena S. Davis is Presidential Endowed Chair in Health, professor of religion studies, and professor of bioethics, emerita, at Lehigh University. Before that she taught for twenty-one years at Cleveland-Marshall College of Law. She was a fellow in bioethics at the Cleveland Clinic, and has been a visiting scholar at the National Human Genome Institute, Arizona State University, the Hastings Center, and the Brocher Foundation. She has been a Fulbright Scholar in India, Israel, Indonesia, Italy, and Sweden. Her research interests in bioethics include reprogenetics, genetic research, and end-of-life issues around dementia.

Janan Delgado earned her PhD in the study of religion at Harvard University in 2022. Her research examines the progress and evolution of child custody law within the Mālikī school of Islamic jurisprudence in al-Andalus between the ninth and the twelfth century and highlights notions of womanhood, motherhood, fatherhood, stepfatherhood and childhood in Islamic jurisprudence.

Elliot N. Dorff, rabbi (Jewish Theological Seminary, 1970), PhD in philosophy (Columbia University, 1971), and four honorary doctorates, is rector and Distinguished Service Professor of Philosophy at American Jewish University and visiting professor at UCLA School of Law. He served on three federal commissions—on the distribution of healthcare, stopping the spread of sexually transmitted diseases, and revising the guidelines for research on human subjects—and he currently serves on the state of California's ethics committee governing stem cell research within the state. Author of fourteen books and over two hundred articles on Jewish thought, law, and ethics, and editor or coeditor of fourteen more books on those topics, his book on medical ethics is *Matters of Life and Death: A Jewish Approach to Modern Medical Ethics*.

Thomas Eich is professor for Islamic studies at the Asia Africa Institute at the University of Hamburg. He earned his PhD at Bochum University in 2003 with a work on the writings and personal networks of Abu l-Huda al-Sayyadi, a late Ottoman sufi. Afterward he has developed a focus on Contemporary Muslim Medical Ethics, especially beginning of life issues. He developed this research further into the analysis of the historical development of imaginations of the unborn. His current ERC project, "Contemporary Bioethics and the History of the Unborn," is devoted to this field.

David B. Fletcher is in the philosophy department of Wheaton College, Illinois, and has been adjunct professor of bioethics at Trinity Graduate School, Illinois. He serves on the Ethics Advisory Committee of Northwestern Medicine Central DuPage Hospital. He writes and speaks primarily on bioethical topics and is the author of various journal articles, contributions to a number of books, and *Social and Political Perspectives in the Thought of Soren Kierkegaard* (University Press of America, 1982).

Seth Goren lives in Toronto and is Hillel Ontario's chief executive officer, as well as a PhD student at the Ontario Institute for Studies in Education of the University of Toronto. After earning a BA and MA in linguistics from the University of Pennsylvania and teaching English in the Czech Republic, Seth received his JD from the University of Pennsylvania Law School and practiced human rights, commercial, and consumer protection law. His commitment to interfaith community, LGBTQ2SIA+ advocacy, and Jewish communal work led him to Hebrew Union College-Jewish Institute of Religion's rabbinical school as a Wexner Graduate Fellow. He served previously as the executive director of Repair the World: Philadelphia and as the first director of Jewish Student Life and associate chaplain at Lehigh University, where he also taught courses on interfaith dialogue and Jewish law.

Bethany Kieran Haile (1984–2019) received her doctorate in theological ethics from Boston College. She was a regular contributor to the magazine *U.S. Catholic* and to CatholicMoralTheology.com. Haile lived in Iowa with her husband and four children until her untimely death.

Celene Ibrahim is the author of *Women and Gender in the Qur'an* (Oxford University Press, 2020) and *Islam and Monotheism* (Cambridge University Press, forthcoming). Ibrahim completed a PhD in Arabic and Islamic civilizations at Brandeis University. She is a faculty member in religious studies and philosophy at Groton School.

Tsipy Ivry is a senior lecturer in the department of anthropology at Haifa University. Her research specializes in the anthropology of reproduction and medical anthropology as well as Japanese studies. Her comparative ethnography of pregnancy in Israel and Japan, *Embodying Culture: Pregnancy in Japan and Israel* was published in 2010 by Rutgers University Press.

Ted G. Jelen (1952–2017) was a professor of political science at the University of Nevada, Las Vegas. Jelen received his PhD from Ohio State University. He joined the UNLV faculty in 1997, and also taught at Benedictine University, DePauw University, Ipek University in Turkey, and Georgetown University. He published fourteen scholarly books and over one hundred articles and chapters in academic outlets. He was editor of the *Journal for the Scientific Study of Religion* and was a founding coeditor of *Politics and Religion*.

Aline H. Kalbian (PhD, University of Virginia, Religion and Ethics) is an associate dean of the College of Arts Sciences at Florida State University. Her areas of research are religious ethics, medical ethics, Catholic moral theology, and gender and sexuality. She is the author of numerous articles and two books: *Sexing the Church: Gender, Power, and Ethics in Contemporary Catholicism* (Indiana University Press) and *Sex, Violence, Justice: Contraception and the Catholic Church* (Georgetown University Press). Kalbian co-edited the *Journal of Religious Ethics* from 2011 to 2021.

Brett Krutzsch is a scholar of American religion and LGBTQ history at NYU's Center for Religion and Media where he serves as editor of the *Revealer*, an online magazine about religion and society, and where he teaches in NYU's department of religious studies. He is the author of *Dying to Be Normal: Gay Martyrs and the Transformation of American Sexual Politics* (Oxford University Press, 2019), a 2020 Lambda Literary Award finalist for best LGBTQ nonfiction book of the year.

Faisal Kutty is a lawyer and an associate professor at Southwestern Law School. He holds a JD (cum laude) from the University of Ottawa, an LLM from Osgoode Hall Law School of York University, where he is also a PhD candidate in law. He has previously taught at Osgoode, Valparaiso University Law School, and Barry University Law School. His articles and chapters on law and religion, legal pluralism, national security, Islamic law, comparative law, and international law have appeared in numerous law reviews and peer-reviewed books.

Karen L. Lebacqz taught ethics and bioethics for three decades in the Graduate Theological Union in Berkeley, California. A former member of the National Commission for the Protection of Human Subjects of Biomedical and Behavioral Research, she has also served as consultant to the director of health for California, as bioethicist in residence at Yale University, and as chair of the ethics advisory committee of the Geron Corporation, which pioneered in stem cell research. She is ordained in the United Church of Christ.

Patrick Lee holds the John N. and Jamie D. McAleer Chair of Bioethics, and is the director of the Center for Bioethics, at Franciscan University of Steubenville. He is the author of three books (*Body-Self Dualism in Contemporary Ethics and Politics*, with Robert P. George, 2008; *Abortion and Unborn Human Life*, 2010; and *Conjugal Union: What Marriage Is and Why It Matters*, with Robert P. George, 2014), and of numerous scholarly and popular articles.

Daniel C. Maguire is the author of fourteen books and editor of three anthologies, as well as 250 articles in various journals. His most recent book is *Christianity without God: Moving Beyond the Dogmas and Retrieving the Epic Moral Narrative* (SUNY Press, 2014). He is past president of the Society of Christian Ethics and the Religious Consultation on Population, Reproductive Health, and Ethics.

Louis E. Newman is the John M. and Elizabeth W. Musser Professor of Religious Studies, Emeritus, at Carleton College. He was formerly associate vice provost for undergraduate education and dean of undergraduate advising at Stanford University. A leading figure in the field of Jewish ethics, he is the author of several books, including *An Introduction to Jewish Ethics* and *Past Imperatives: Studies in the History and Theory of Jewish Ethics*, as well as coeditor (with Elliot N. Dorff) of *Contemporary Jewish Ethics and Morality: A Reader*.

Karen Peterson-Iyer is an associate professor of theological and social ethics in the religious studies department of Santa Clara University. She is the author of *Designer Children: Reconciling Genetic Technology, Feminism, and Christian Faith*. Her various articles have appeared in the *Kennedy Institute of Ethics Journal*, *Second Opinion: Health*,

Faith, and Ethics, Journal of Moral Theology, Journal of the Society of Christian Ethics, and *Journal of Feminist Studies in Religion.* Her research interests lie primarily in the fields of bioethics, sexual ethics, and political/social ethics. She also serves on the ethics committee of the Stanford Hospital and Clinics at Stanford University. She earned her PhD from Yale University, her MDiv from Pacific School of Religion, and her BA from Stanford University.

Abdulaziz Sachedina is professor and Endowed IIIT Chair in Islamic Studies at George Mason University in Fairfax, Virginia. Dr. Sachedina, who has studied in India, Iraq, Iran, and Canada, obtained his PhD from the University of Toronto. He has been conducting research and writing in the field of Islamic Law, Ethics, and Theology (Sunni and Shiite) for more than four decades. In the last twenty years he has concentrated on social and political ethics, including interfaith and intrafaith relations, Islamic biomedical ethics, and Islam and human rights. Dr. Sachedina's publications include *Islamic Messianism* (State University of New York, 1980); *Human Rights and the Conflicts of Culture,* coauthored (University of South Carolina, 1988); *The Just Ruler in Shiite Islam* (Oxford University Press, 1988); *The Prolegomena to the Qur'an* (Oxford University Press, 1998); *The Islamic Roots of Democratic Pluralism* (Oxford University Press, 2002); *Islamic Biomedical Ethics: Theory and Application* (Oxford University Press, 2009); *Islam and the Challenge of Human Rights* (Oxford University Press, 2009); and *Islamic Ethics: Fundamental Aspects of Human Conduct* (Oxford University Press, 2022), in addition to numerous articles in academic journals.

Ayman Shabana is associate research professor at Georgetown University's School of Foreign Service in Qatar. His teaching and research interests include Islamic legal history, Islamic law and ethics, human rights, and bioethics. He is the author of *Custom in Islamic Law and Legal Theory* (Palgrave, 2010) in addition to several academic journal articles, which appeared in *Islamic Law and Society, Journal of Islamic Studies, Zygon: Journal of Religion and Science,* and *Medicine, Health Care and Philosophy.*

Joel James Shuman is professor of theology at King's College in Wilkes-Barre, Pennsylvania. A native West Virginian, he attended Bethany (WV) College. He is a graduate of the program in physical therapy at the Medical College of Virginia in Richmond, and practiced physical therapy for ten years in Wisconsin, West Virginia, and Virginia. He earned the MTS from Duke University Divinity School and the PhD in religion, specializing in theological ethics, from the Graduate School of Arts and Sciences at Duke University. He writes about theology and the applied biological sciences, especially medicine, and is the author, coauthor, or coeditor of four books and numerous articles and book chapters. During the 2018–2019 academic year he was the scholar in residence with the Theology, Medicine, and Culture Initiative at Duke Divinity School, where he did research on the opioid crisis.

David M. Smolin is the Harwell G. Davis Professor of Constitutional Law, and the director of the Center for Children, Law, and Ethics at Cumberland Law School, Samford University. He serves as an independent expert for the Hague Conference on Private International Law (HCCH) on intercountry adoption issues, and serves as an external expert for the International Reference Centre for the rights of children deprived of their family, of the International Social Service (ISS/IRC), on adoption and surrogacy issues. Most of his adoption and surrogacy-related writings are available at http://works.bepress.com/david_smolin/.

Ann Shepard Feeley Swaner is associate professor of theology, emerita, in the School of Professional and Career Education at Barry University in Miami Shores, Florida. She earned a BA degree from the University of Saint Michael's College in the University of Toronto and a PhD in religion from the University of Iowa School of Religion. Her professional interests include theology of marriage, history of Christianity, and history of religion in the United States.

Elly Teman is a medical anthropologist specializing in the anthropology of reproduction. She is a senior lecturer at Ruppin Academic Center in the department of behavioral sciences. Her ethnography of gestational surrogacy in Israel, *Birthing a Mother: The Surrogate Body and the Pregnant Self*, was published in 2010 by University of California Press.

Noam Zohar is professor of philosophy in Bar Ilan University, and director of its graduate program in bioethics. He has received visiting fellowships at Harvard University and at the Institute for Advanced Study in Princeton. His research and teaching are in the fields of moral and political philosophy, with an emphasis on applied ethics—particularly bioethics and the ethics of warfare; as well as the fields of rabbinics and philosophy of *Halakhah*. His publications include essays and books in those fields, including *Alternatives in Jewish Bioethics* (SUNY Press, 1997); *Quality of Life in Jewish Bioethics* (ed., Lexington Books, 2006). With Michael Walzer and Menachem Lorberbaum he is editor of the series *The Jewish Political Tradition* (Yale University Press: Volume 1: Authority [2000]; Volume 2: Membership [2003]; Volume 3: Community [2018]; and Volume 4: Politics in History [forthcoming]). He has served in various bioethics commissions and advisory boards, including Israel's national bioethics council.

INTRODUCTION

DENA S. DAVIS

As I write this introduction, the third season of the Israeli series, *Schtisel*, has arrived on Netflix, eagerly awaited by viewers around the world who would never have imagined how caught up they would get by this family drama of four generations of ultra-Orthodox Jews living in Jerusalem. One episode focuses on Ruchami and Hanina, a young couple who have been married for five years, but without children. It turns out that pregnancy and childbirth would threaten Ruchami's life. She is using an IUD, but she keeps threatening to have it removed, risking her life to become a mother. Finally, with great reluctance, Hanina visits the *rebbe*, the spiritual authority in their community, to discuss the possibility of using a surrogate. They are, says the rebbe, caught between two "non-ideal" situations: surrogacy, normally forbidden, is non-ideal, but so is Ruchami's unhappiness and the possibility that she might go ahead and take the risk, which is also forbidden.

Ultra-Orthodox Jews themselves rarely own or watch television, so this show is clearly pitched to an audience of outsiders. What are they to make of this abstruse conversation, and why are they so riveted by a conundrum they do not share? The answer, I believe, is that issues of reproduction and procreation and family-building in general, are universally compelling. People for whom reproduction used to be out of bounds or a least problematic, e.g., gay and lesbian people, and people facing infertility, are now also making use of new technologies and expanded societal opportunities to create their families. The "test-tube babies" that made such a stir in 1978, are now routine, and gestational/genetic surrogacy has supplanted what has ironically come to be called "traditional surrogacy."

At the same time that assisted reproductive technologies open parenthood to more people, birth rates are going down around the world, as remaining single and "child-free" becomes another acceptable option. The choice of whether to become a parent highlights questions of why we have children, and how we perceive our parental obligations.

People's reproductive choices are all around us, and the results, at least, are obvious to the naked eye in the shape of their families, even if the details are discreetly hidden from view. For many people, reproductive choices are guided or at least influenced by the religion they were raised in, or the ones they adopt. Often, religious views on reproductive choices have an impact on politics and law. Access to abortion, contraception, and surrogacy, tax credits for children, subsidized childcare: all express societal attitudes toward sex, reproduction, and the shape of modern families.

This *Handbook* addresses the broad sweep of religious attitudes toward reproductive ethics, in the Abrahamic traditions (that is to say, Judaism, Christianity, and Islam). To some extent, it aims to provide a parallel to the *Oxford Handbook of Reproductive Ethics* (Francis, 2017), which confined itself to nonreligious perspectives. The present work is not an encyclopedia, nor does it attempt to cover comprehensively every possible issue from the perspective of every possible scholar. The latter would be quite impossible, even if we confined ourselves to one religious tradition, much less three. Rather, as editor I have invited some of the sharpest, most interesting scholars I could find, to write cutting-edge papers about some of the most interesting issues in reproductive ethics.

Some of these topics are obvious, not to mention newsworthy. But behind the issues of contraception, abortion, and prenatal diagnosis are more foundational questions. What does it mean to be a parent? Why do different religious traditions view procreation as more or less obligatory, and how do those differences manifest themselves? Can authentic parenthood exist without biological connection?

The *Handbook* begins with chapters that lay out the basic sources for thinking about morality in the Jewish, Catholic, Protestant, and Muslim traditions, complemented by a brilliant discourse on natural law and its implications for reproductive ethics. This section is capped by a piece on the role of authority in the different religious traditions.

The next section tackles the meaning of parenthood itself, from different religious perspectives. Do we have children for our own pleasure, or from some sense of religious necessity? Do we raise children to be their best selves, or to strengthen their religious community, or to bring glory to God? This section is rounded out by a piece on gay and lesbian parenting, surely one of the great familial revolutions of our time, and by a cautionary paper on population justice.

The following chapters consider different ways of forming families, including adoption of children, "adoption" of embryos, gamete donation, and surrogacy. One way or another, what all these strategies have in common is that they expand the traditional parental dyad to include a third person or more: the person who donates their sperm or egg; parents who are unable to care for their own children and give them into the care of others; women who carry children for others; couples who choose to donate "spare" embryos from in vitro fertilization to infertile couples. Some form of this practice goes back to Biblical times, when Sarah, being infertile, encouraged Abraham to have a child with her slave, Hagar, so that Abraham could have an heir. As readers of the Bible will remember, that did not turn out so well. Does that early story damn third parties forever in the eyes of the Abrahamic religions, or can families be created by more than two adults?

The next section, addressing contraception and abortion, takes the opposite tack of considering religious perspectives on *avoiding* conception. It ends with an intriguing look from a social scientist on how public opinion and attitudes toward abortion correlate—or don't correlate—with religious identities. Finally, in the concluding section, scholars look at the complex question of prenatal testing and diagnosis.

I am especially pleased at the mix of authors represented in this book. Some are senior scholars whose names are well known to the sophisticated reader. Some are new scholars whose fresh approaches to old questions are surprising and intriguing. One or two have academic training but don't come from academia. Within the religious traditions, we have scholars from a wide range of perspectives, for example, evangelical as well as mainstream Protestants. No attempt has been made to check off every box, that is, to approach every topic from every possible religious perspective. That would make for a doorstop rather than a one volume book. But within these twenty-nine chapters, there are challenging and thought-provoking ideas that will, I hope, lead to even more dialogue.

Bibliography

Francis, Leslie. *The Oxford Handbook of Reproductive Ethics*. New York: Oxford University Press, 2017.

PART I
THE ABRAHAMIC RELIGIOUS TRADITIONS

CHAPTER 1

JEWISH ETHICS

Theological Foundations, Classical Sources, Hermeneutical Challenges

LOUIS E. NEWMAN

JEWISH ethics, like all systems of religious ethics, is grounded in certain religious convictions, practices, and traditions. The goal of this chapter is to provide an overview of those religious parameters that have defined Jewish ethics over its long history. I will also briefly introduce the literary sources that both traditional and contemporary Jewish ethicists draw upon and the key theological concepts that shape this moral tradition. In short, this introduction to Jewish ethics will provide a broad conceptual and historical framework for understanding Jewish approaches to both theoretical and practical moral issues, including those related to human reproduction. The central question I address here, then, is not "What does Judaism say about a particular moral issue," but "What does it mean for Jewish ethicists to take positions about that issue (or any other), what are the resources upon which they can draw in doing so, and what are the challenges they face in speaking on behalf of this religious tradition regarding the moral issues of our day?"

THEOLOGICAL FOUNDATIONS

Despite many methodological disputes among Jewish authorities, Jewish ethics rests upon a shared foundation of classical sources and religious beliefs. The Hebrew

Bible, especially its first five books (the Torah, or Pentateuch), have traditionally been understood as the revealed word of God to the Israelites. As such, it is the pre-eminent source of moral and religious truth and provides the blueprint for Jewish religious life. The views of God as the sole and unique creator of the world; of humans as being created "in the image of God" and so having a special place at the pinnacle of creation; of God as the author of human history and of the Jewish people as singled out for a special destiny and especially for distinctive obligations; of human history as purposeful, leading to a final culmination usually envisioned as a redemption from interpersonal and international conflict—all these beliefs are at the heart of Jewish religious life. At the center of this grand religious narrative is the story of the Israelites' enslavement in Egypt, God's miraculous deliverance of them, and God's leading the people to Mt. Sinai (the location of the revelation of Torah) and then to the Promised Land. All subsequent Jewish practice was understood as a "remembrance of the exodus from Egypt" and all future acts of divine intervention in history were patterned on God's past deliverance of the Jews from slavery. Until the modern period when these classical beliefs were radically challenged, these core beliefs defined the parameters of Jews' cosmology, anthropology, theory of history, and self-understanding.[1]

These fundamental beliefs find expression most prominently in the traditional liturgy of Jewish practice. In daily prayers, Jews reaffirmed each of these core beliefs about creation, revelation, and redemption. Moreover, weekly practices such as refraining completely from work on the Sabbath, to honor that God created the world in six days and rested on the seventh (Genesis 1:1–2:3), affirms God's dominion over nature. Similarly, the annual recitation of the exodus narrative on Passover reinforces the view that "in every generation one must see oneself as if he/she was personally redeemed" from Egyptian slavery. The close connection between narrative and practice is further concretized in the ritual of reading through the Torah in its entirety on an annual cycle, so that stories of God's creation, revelation, and redemption are woven into the rhythms of weekly worship services. In short, this narrative provides the ritual structure for all of Jewish religious life, the scaffolding, as it were, around which all subsequent religious views and practices are built.

It follows that Jews for the most part have simply assumed that the natural world is orderly and "good," created for a divine purpose, even if that purpose remains elusive and/or specific natural events appear to be malevolent. They likewise assumed that, while God has moral expectations of all human beings (prohibitions against murder, adultery, and stealing, among others, are universal), God imposed a much more extensive set of obligations on the Jews. These religious commandments were given as a sign of God's love for the people of Israel, as a way of creating an intimate relationship; by observing these rules the Jews, in turn, demonstrate their devotion and gratitude to God. That relationship was typically conceived as a covenant, frequently imagined by later Jewish authorities as a kind of exclusive marriage between God and Israel. As such it establishes a framework of mutual obligations and it was assumed that if the Jews observed God's law, then God would reward the people, protecting them from both natural disasters and historical misfortunes. Moreover, by observing the law and being an example to the world of how to lead a life of holiness and devotion, the Jews were bringing the world as a whole closer to its ultimate redemption.

It should be noted that this religious mythology has both universalistic and particularistic elements that are closely interconnected. All people are created in the divine image, but the Jews have an especially close relationship to God; all human beings are called to be moral, but only the Jews have been given a very detailed set of obligations; God's concern is with all of human history, but in that historical drama the Jews play a central role. The tension between these two elements of Jewish theology is never entirely resolved and represents one of the sources of divergent tendencies within Jewish ethics.

Textual Sources

Jewish ethics is grounded in a textual tradition that, as noted above, begins in the Hebrew Bible. But because the meaning of Scripture is often not self-evident, Jewish teachers over the centuries have written hundreds of linear commentaries to the Biblical text. Through these commentaries (among other writings), Jewish teachers articulated their values and beliefs, including many that depart substantially from the superficial sense of the text. All this commentary was understood as an extension of the text itself, sometimes as revealing hidden meanings in the Biblical text that are accessible only to deeply learned rabbis. Indeed, classic editions of the Hebrew Bible are printed with the Biblical text in the center of the page and some of the most prominent commentaries arranged around it. This is not merely a convention adopted by printers; it reflects a basic set of theological and conceptual assumptions—that the Biblical text is at the center of this tradition, but that it is never encountered on its own terms; rather, it is read through the lenses of earlier generations of scholars who have tried to make sense of its teachings. Each of these commentaries builds upon earlier ones, alternately affirming or disputing the insights of earlier rabbis in the chain of tradition. And all of these intersecting and conflicting views, including disputes between rabbis who lived centuries apart, are preserved on the pages of classical Jewish texts.

But there is a still more profound set of assumptions at work here. Each new commentary is an extension of that original revelation, not merely a gloss on it. As Gershom Scholem observed in a classic essay,

> All this [commentary] was somehow part of revelation itself—and more: not only was it given along with revelation, but it was given in a special, timeless sphere of revelation in which all generations were, as it were, gathered together; everything really had been made explicit to Moses, the first and most comprehensive recipient of Torah. The achievement of every generation, its contribution to tradition, was projected back into the eternal present of the revelation at Sinai.[2]

Or, in the words of a second-century Jewish sage about Torah, "Turn it and turn it, for everything is in it."[3] This idea of revelation has far-reaching implications: that revelation did not end at a given point in Israel's past; that each rabbi's new insight into Torah, or new interpretation of an ancient rule, was part of the Torah all along, just waiting to be discovered; that even when rabbis reach diametrically opposed positions on some matter of ethics or religious practice, "both these and those are the words of the living God"[4]; and that the quintessential form of devotion to God is immersing oneself in the study of this ever-expanding body of texts, for this is how one encounters the voice of God and discerns what is right.

Yet, the textual tradition is even more complex than this. For in addition to all this commentary, the rabbis in the second century CE codified a body of legal rulings that had previously been transmitted orally for generations. These rulings frequently explained what in the Torah were very general rules. For example, where the Torah simply says that on the Sabbath one should refrain from work, later rabbis defined in great detail what constitutes forbidden labor; where the Torah simply instructs us to honor our parents, rabbis specified precisely how one does this, as well as the circumstances under which one might be exempt from doing so. These collected rulings were known as the *Mishnah*, consisting of thousands of rabbinic rulings organized in sixty-three separate treatises, and constitute the first post-Biblical collection of Jewish law.[5]

But—as the reader might by now have suspected—the Mishnah itself then becomes the scaffolding upon which subsequent generations of rabbis compose their commentaries. For the rules of the Mishnah are often very spare, just a legal opinion without any legal reasoning to justify it. And the Mishnah frequently records disputes between rabbis who held different opinions about the same issue, without any apparent resolution. This left ample room for rabbis from the second to the sixth centuries to develop their own interpretations of these Mishnaic treatises. What comes to be known as the Talmud is the record of approximately four centuries of wide-ranging rabbinic discussion of the Mishnah. And, again not surprisingly, the Talmud, once published, itself becomes the springboard for further generations of commentary.[6]

This expansive literature has defined the curriculum for the education of rabbis throughout Jewish history. In the aggregate, it has also been the main source to which those rabbis have turned when they sought answers to any moral or religious question they faced. For what mattered to them was not "What do *I* think is the right answer to this question, based on my own conscience or my own understanding of what God is calling us to do?" Rather, rabbis traditionally addressed moral issues by asking "What has this tradition, as encapsulated in this ever-expanding body of texts and tradition, already said about this matter and how do those views apply to the question at hand?" In short, Jewish ethics has always been deeply tied to a tradition of texts, to the study of those texts, and then to their application to new issues as they arise.

In precisely this sense, Jewish ethics has generally been casuistic in nature, drawing legal principles from cases and then applying them to new sets of facts. But it would be a mistake—though a mistake that has commonly been made—to think of Jewish ethics as exclusively legal in nature.[7] The Torah, broadly understood, contains much more than just law; there is also narrative, prophecy, proverbs, psalms, and much more. The Talmud, too, contains anecdotes about the rabbis, fanciful extrapolations from Biblical texts that have no legal import whatsoever, but nonetheless often explore important values and contain much wisdom. During the medieval period, Jewish scholars also produced law codes, philosophical treatises, and pietistic literature that frequently touch on issues of moral development, ethical theory, and the challenges and rewards of living righteously. All this, too, is part of that immense body of Jewish tradition upon which rabbis over the centuries have drawn whenever they sought to speak on behalf of this tradition and offer guidance to the Jewish community. Indeed, as we'll see, the relationship between the legal and nonlegal dimensions of this tradition has been one of the key issues in Jewish ethics over the centuries.

Contemporary Challenges to Tradition

The period of the Enlightenment in Europe profoundly challenged Jewish traditional norms and beliefs. The new emphasis on scientific and historical inquiry undermined the belief that God had revealed the Torah to the Jews at Mt. Sinai in precisely the form in which we have it today. New scholars developed theories that could explain discrepancies in Scripture as resulting from a complex process by which multiple documents, written at different times and by different groups of ancient Israelites, had been combined into the text we have now. Moreover, the Age of Reason was skeptical of the Biblical accounts of miracles, including those that were central to the Jews' understanding of themselves. These intellectual currents were powerful and, as Jews were exposed to them in increasing numbers in the seventeenth and eighteenth centuries, they found it difficult to simply affirm the veracity of the Torah, as their ancestors had. But if God had not revealed the Torah to the Jews in this way, then in what sense was Torah a unique source of moral and religious truth? Why would one feel compelled to observe Jewish law? And why devote oneself to studying this body of traditional texts, or assume that the moral insights found there were of any greater value than those to be found in the works of secular philosophers?[8]

In addition to these theological and philosophical challenges, Jews faced sociological pressures to assimilate into the mainstream of European society. Throughout the nineteenth century Jews were granted civil rights—including the right to attend universities, hold public office, own land, and enter various professions—all of which had traditionally been denied to them. These greatly expanded opportunities brought Jews into far more extensive contact with their non-Jewish neighbors, for whom many of these traditional Jewish practices seemed arcane and out of step with modern culture.

Jews could far more easily leave their own relatively self-contained communities and assimilate into the general society. As they did, often in very large numbers, they jettisoned both traditional practice and any allegiance to the norms of the traditional communities they left behind.

Those Jews—and there were many—who remained committed to preserving a distinctive Jewish identity and to the value of their religious tradition, began to reform that tradition in light of these new intellectual currents and sociological realities. The Reform movement, which was born in Germany in the early nineteenth century, focused initially on liturgical reforms, but quickly began to articulate a philosophical basis for the changes it embraced. The Torah in its current form included ancient myths that were no longer believable and detailed laws that were not applicable to the contemporary situation in which Jews found themselves. But the Torah, they argued, also contained timeless, eternal truths—especially that God was a benevolent creator, that there was a moral law, akin to natural law, that was best articulated in the Torah and that the Jews had a duty to spread these moral truths to the rest of humankind. Once all people had come to believe in "the fatherhood of God and the brotherhood of man," then the messianic age long predicted by the Biblical prophets would indeed become a reality. This position, often called "ethical monotheism," had the virtue of bringing Jewish belief in line with the scientific and historical thinking of the time, but also of preserving a central role for Jews to play in the unfolding drama of God's relationship with humanity. It also led to a prioritizing of the moral dimensions of Judaism over its ritual dimensions. Some Reform thinkers insisted, in fact, that "its [Judaism's] predominant aspect from the very beginning was its ethical character, the importance it attached to the moral law. Ethics constitute its essence."[9]

The Reformers' radical reconceptualization of Judaism evoked strong counterforces within the Jewish community among those who either believed that modernity should be judged by the standards of tradition (rather than the other way around) or that reforming Judaism was inevitable, but that the early proponents of these changes had taken them too far. Thus, there emerged a wide spectrum of subgroups within the Jewish community, which persist to this day. The most traditional among them are most skeptical of scientific or philosophical challenges to the tradition, maintain allegiance to Jewish law as the centerpiece of Jewish moral and religious life, and continue to see classical Jewish texts as the primary, if not the only, source of Jewish moral guidance. Other groups seek more nuanced ways of combining elements of modern thought and practice with Jewish tradition, arguing that Judaism has always evolved in response to changing historical circumstances. Precisely which components of Jewish practice and doctrine are essential and which are subject to change (and how) remains a primary focus of intellectual debate within the contemporary Jewish community.[10]

Of course, where one falls on this spectrum will have implications for how one balances the universalistic and particularistic elements of the tradition noted above. It will also inform the degree of authority one ascribes to the Torah and all the traditional texts that flow from it, just as it will influence how one thinks about the degree of autonomy individuals have in relation to the community. The modern era ushered in dramatic changes in Jewish life and thought that continue to reverberate as ideological tensions within the Jewish community intensify. This has also been a period of great intellectual vitality, as many rabbis and scholars, committed to blending the best of tradition and modernity, generate creative new work in Jewish philosophy, ethics, liturgy, and Biblical interpretation. Most recently, feminism and post-modernism have unleashed yet other intellectual forces that have generated new work in Jewish ethics.[11]

LAW AND ETHICS IN JUDAISM

It is sometimes claimed that Judaism is a legalistic religion and that, therefore, there really is no ethic separate from the legal tradition. And while these claims are not baseless, the issue is far more complicated than such simple pronouncements would suggest. Understanding the complex relationship of law and ethics in Judaism provides one important window into the nature of Jewish ethics.[12]

Alongside the vast legal tradition described above—encompassing Scripture, Mishnah, Talmud, legal codes, and much more—there are also other strands of ethical reflection in Judaism. Some of these I have already alluded to in terms of the narrative elements of the tradition, including the narratives found within the Torah as they were embellished by the rabbis, but also narratives of the rabbis themselves—how their lives embodied righteousness and piety, how they served as moral exemplars for their communities, and so forth. These stories have, in fact, sometimes found their way into rabbinic discussions that are otherwise framed in legal terms. But even when they stand alone, they represent an important dimension of ethical thought, akin to what we now think of as virtue ethics. Indeed, there is a very substantial Jewish pietistic literature that is built on the assumption that there is far more to living righteously than observing the law alone. Righteousness is a matter of inward intention, purity of heart, cultivating qualities of generosity and compassion, among other things. These are not necessarily required by the law, which more often focuses on external behaviors, but they are part and parcel of what God expects of us.[13]

It is worth noting that within the Torah itself we find passages that seem to gesture toward some open-ended moral norms that are not (or perhaps cannot be) captured in legal injunctions. "Do the right and the good in the eyes of the Lord" (Deuteronomy 6:18) is one classic example. Classical Jewish commentators linked this verse with the concept of supererogation, that is, going beyond what the law explicitly requires. The rabbis had a number of ways of referring to such moral standards, but the key concept appears to have been that the law may establish the "floor," the minimum standards of behavior that all must follow, but that truly righteous people do not stop there. Indeed, there are even discussions in the Talmud that appear to suggest that at times the rabbis invoked such extralegal norms in their determination of what the law should be.

Finally, but not insignificantly, Jewish authorities over the ages were influenced by the intellectual and philosophical currents of their day. In medieval times, Maimonides presented the essence of Jewish ethics in ways that mirrored Aristotelian notions of the "golden mean,"[14] and in the early twentieth century Hermann Cohen's Jewish ethics was explicitly neo-Kantian.[15] In these ways, among others, Jewish thinkers have drawn on what they regarded as the best moral thinking of their time and attempted to blend it with—or, some might argue, impose it on—Jewish tradition.

From these examples, it might appear to be clear that there is a vibrant ethical tradition in Judaism separate from and/or intertwined with Jewish legal ethics. And yet some have argued that what appears to be separate is actually what the law itself requires. For if, as the Psalmist says, "the law of the Lord is perfect, restoring the soul" (Psalm 19:7), then it can hardly be the case that the law is deficient in relation to some external moral norms. In fact, some authorities claimed that the very standard referred to as "beyond the line of the law" was, in fact, legally enforceable. So, the evidence within the tradition is itself ambiguous as to the relationship between law and ethics. The question is what this tells us about our subject matter.

I suggest that these fuzzy lines between law and ethics are emblematic of the fact that Jewish law is a religious system whose goal, in the words of Leviticus 19:17, is "to be holy, as I the Lord your God am holy." In this sense, anything which enhances the holiness of the people is immediately assimilated into the law. But at the same time, Jewish law was a functioning system in which rabbis served as judges and had to adjudicate real disputes. It could not realistically impose the highest standards of righteous behavior on everyone. And so it necessarily distinguished between actionable legal rules and supererogatory moral ideals.

The import of this ambiguous distinction between law and ethics is simply this: because of the religious, but also pragmatic, character of Jewish law, ethics must be situated both within and beyond the law. And because Jewish ethics straddles these two domains, it represents a kind of contested terrain. It is always both law and not-law, always about what is practicable and also what is ideal, always being pulled toward one pole by those who wish to draw firm distinctions between the two domains, but pulled toward the opposite pole by those who wish for Jewish ethics to be as expansive and encompassing as possible.

Jewish Ethics: Legal, Covenantal, and Narrative

As contemporary Jewish ethicists have attempted to provide guidance on the moral issues of our day, they have faced the problem of how to apply the vast literary and conceptual resources of this tradition to specific and sometimes unprecedented problems. What parts of this tradition are pertinent to the questions at hand? How exactly should we connect these moral teachings—frequently written in a very different idiom and reflecting very different historical circumstances—to questions such as contraception, surrogacy, and genetic engineering? This challenge is at the heart of the enterprise of contemporary Jewish ethics and it, too, is contested terrain.

A simple survey of the literature in the field[16] suggests that most Jewish ethicists over the past fifty years have adopted what we might call a *legal* approach to this problem. They regard the law as the central resource for Jewish ethics and so approach any contemporary moral problem as would a lawyer in an American legal context. What statutes (that is, laws in the Torah, Talmud, or codes of Jewish law) appear to be precedents for this matter? What circumstances shaped the development of those rules and how relevant are they to the circumstances we face today? What principles can be extracted from this series of precedents to guide our moral judgments, even if those principles were not articulated explicitly in the past? In short, ethicists of this persuasion view moral problems through the lens of a legal process, one that offers them a vast body of cases, rules, and principles that can be marshalled to construct "a Jewish view" of whatever moral issue we may be facing. This legal methodology is perhaps most akin to the way Jewish authorities proceeded in pre-modern times and continues to be most prevalent among contemporary Orthodox rabbis, though not only among them.

Others, however, have adopted an approach that places *covenant*, rather than law, at the heart of this enterprise.[17] Without overlooking the centrality of law and legal reasoning within Judaism, they regard the law alone as too confining a framework. From their perspective, the covenant between God and Israel represents the foundation of Jewish moral duty. This bond, often analogized to a marriage, is more fluid and open-ended than the system of Jewish law. The goal is to live in a way that is faithful to this covenantal relationship, giving due consideration to the ways in which earlier generations of Jews have understood their obligations with that same relationship. Faced with a contemporary moral question, then, they are apt to ask not "What legal precedents apply here?" but rather "what choice(s) here will enable us to live most authentically as a community in relationship to God?" In framing the question in these terms, they affirm that Jewish moral life is lived in the context of a dynamic partnership, one in which God's commands and expectations are in dialectical relationship with the needs and goals of God's people.

Yet a third approach to contemporary Jewish ethics, adopted by a somewhat smaller but still influential group of scholars, places *narrative* at the core of this process.[18] Neither law nor covenant provides an adequate frame for considering Jewish moral obligations, which are captured in far richer and more nuanced ways through stories. For narrative ethicists, these stories—whether "master narratives" like the story of the Israelites' exodus from Egypt, or the stories of Biblical characters like Ruth, or the stories of individual rabbis' lives related in the Talmud—provide moral guidance by describing for us in rich detail how moral life is lived. The goal is to live in and through those stories in ways that will shape our character and tutor our moral imagination, as much as (perhaps more than) they will guide us toward specific moral choices. In contrast to legalists, narrative ethicists will often find relevant moral guidance in narratives that are far removed from the details of the ethical question at hand. For what matters to them is the moral arc of one's life, and how the arc of particular narratives can be instructive in helping us to reimagine our moral capacities, or attend to otherwise overlooked dimensions of a moral situation. This approach to contemporary Jewish ethics tends to focus less on rules or discrete decisions than on cultivating moral virtues and deepening one's moral insight.

What are we to make of these radically different approaches to contemporary Jewish ethics? First, it must be noted that these methods are not mutually exclusive. It is possible to find within the same article some combination of reasoning from legal precedent, appeal to covenantal responsibility, and lessons drawn from narratives. And this should not be surprising. All of these—law, covenant, and narrative—are important components of Jewish tradition. Each can be a tool or resource for unraveling the complexities of a particular moral issue. What matters to most thinkers is less the purity of their approach than the sense that they have attempted to glean from the tradition whatever it can offer us—whether in the form of precedents, concepts, or lived experience.

That said, these approaches do represent quite different ways of thinking about Judaism, and also about ethics. Those who focus largely on the legal dimensions of Judaism do so out of the conviction that the law is the essence of Judaism, that Torah in its broadest sense encapsulates God's instruction to the Jews regarding how to live a holy life. Ethics, accordingly, is a rule-based system of behavior. For them, the challenge in any ethical situation is to determine which rule applies and then to connect the ruling in this specific case to other rulings in similar cases across time. Constructing a moral life is somewhat akin to building a physical structure. The divine architect has given us the blueprints, and where the schematic designs (that is, the body of precedents) are insufficient on their face to help us make a particular decision, we need to study them even more closely to determine the Architect's intent.

Covenantal ethicists, by contrast, think of Judaism as essentially about a mutual, loving relationship between God and Israel. Law plays a role in defining the terms of that relationship, to be sure, but the relationship is not reducible to the terms of the law. Because they think of the goal of Jewish life as that of maintaining this relationship, they will frame ethical decisions as questions of the demands of living authentically and faithfully in that relationship. And just as the rabbis often analogized the covenant to a marital relationship between God and Israel (with Torah cast in the role of the *ketubbah*, or marriage contract), these ethicists will turn to the text of the Torah for guidance about the values embedded in this relationship, more than for specific rules that tell us what we should do. After all, marriage contracts define the obligations of the two partners in terms of love and trust, honor, and fidelity, but make no effort to spell out the specific obligations that will arise in daily marital life. Any pertinent legal rules that may be identified from the textual tradition are valuable primarily insofar as they capture one way of understanding what one earlier religious authority thought was required for living covenantally.

Finally, narrative ethicists regard Torah as most fully conveyed through story, and so too living ethically is fundamentally about writing the story of who we are and who we wish to become over the course of our lives. It is about cultivating character, and so the characters we encounter within the tradition (including the character of God and of Israel) instruct us about the sort of life we should be striving to live. Such an ethic will emphasize virtues over rules, the textual of one's moral life over the individual moral choices. Torah, on this view, is akin to a work of art, which inspires us to see ourselves and the world through a new and more expansive lens. By internalizing these stories and living through them we come to embody Torah most fully.

The Problem of Interpretation in Jewish Ethics

Notwithstanding the differences in approach that characterize contemporary Jewish ethicists, all face the common challenge of interpreting Torah (however conceived) in relation to ethical questions that confront us. All must build a bridge between the resources they find within Jewish tradition and our moral questions, however implicitly or explicitly they identify their methods for doing so. In closing, then, I wish to explore this challenge with some attention to the issues of reproductive ethics covered in this volume.[19]

Given the vast literary output of Jewish authorities over the centuries, there is a virtually limitless body of material upon which to draw when considering any contemporary ethical issue. The possibilities are constrained only by the erudition and imagination of the contemporary ethicist. And yet, there are intrinsic challenges to this enterprise that readers should appreciate when reading and evaluating the specific positions that they will encounter in this collection of essays.

Some contemporary moral issues are genuinely unprecedented. Until fairly recent times, prenatal testing and genetic engineering were unknown. Accordingly, there are simply no traditional texts that speak directly and explicitly about these matters. Under such circumstances, the ethicist must attempt to derive moral guidance from the materials that do exist, and this often requires drawing quite extended inferences from ancient or medieval sources to modern technologies. To be sure, modern authorities can find sources that touch on issues that are also pertinent to these matters, but often only in a rather indirect way.

How do Biblical stories about Jacob's efforts to manipulate the breeding of his uncle Laban's flocks (see Genesis 30) pertain to the question of whether other sorts of genetic manipulations are permissible? How do rabbinic sources about the blessing traditionally recited that praises God when one sees someone with physical deformities inform our attitude toward eugenics? On their face, these questions might appear absurd, yet the utterly unprecedented nature of the issues at hand requires Jewish ethicists to search for the closest analogs they can find, or at least for sources that invoke values that might reasonably be extended to such cases. Of course, there are no rules for drawing such inferences, at least none that are universally accepted among contemporary Jewish writers on these subjects. One ethicist's reasonable inference is another's illegitimate or illogical leap. But contemporary writers can take some solace, at least, in the fact that Jewish tradition is replete with disputes among authorities, who differed both in their conclusions and in means by which they justified them.

Other challenges faced by contemporary Jewish ethicists are slightly less radical. For there are issues, such as contraception and abortion, that have analogs in ancient times. Using the methods available to them, people attempted to practice birth control, though without the sophisticated ability to alter a woman's natural menstrual cycle. Similarly, the practice of intentionally ending a pregnancy was familiar to the ancient and medieval rabbis. The question here is whether advances in our scientific understanding of human fertility, hormones, and fetal development change the ethical landscape in which such decisions are made.

Does our medical technology, which enables us to combine eggs and sperm in a test tube and implant them in a human womb, or to freeze fertilized eggs and implant them years later, fundamentally change the ethics of reproduction? In what ways can the pronouncements of earlier generations on fertility and contraception guide us in a time when scientific developments make our interventions so much more reliable? The answers to these questions require ethicists to consider whether traditional ethical views were limited by the state of science at that time, or whether they reflect values that are timeless. Or to put it in the starkest terms, if the same authorities whose views we cite had access to the medical knowledge that we have, would they hold the same views? We cannot know for certain, of course, but we can do our best to extrapolate from what they knew and how they explained their views.

Yet another sort of challenge is reflected in the discussions that follow. Some contemporary ethical questions are essentially unchanged since ancient times. What are the obligations of children to parents, or of parents to their children? Parenting does not pose fundamentally unprecedented issues, nor are there scientific advances that alter the very nature of this relationship. Even surrogacy of a sort was known in ancient times, as many Biblical characters had concubines who bore children for them when their wives were unable to do so (see Genesis 16, 30). The challenges of building a bridge from classical sources to contemporary realities here are less dramatic, though still significant. Parenting today may have a rather different cultural significance, given the ways in which society has changed—that people move many times over the course of their lives and rarely live in the same communities as their children and grandchildren, that people live longer, that child mortality rates are far lower, and that there are government-provided safety nets that may make parents less dependent on their children in old age. How relevant are these social and cultural changes? Regarding surrogacy, does it matter that today surrogate parents, unlike concubines of old, are financially compensated for their services? Or that they typically don't have an established status within the patriarch's family (or, for that matter, that married men today occupy a very different place within the family structure than did ancient patriarchs)?

These are but a few of the sorts of challenges that contemporary ethicists face, particularly those who wish to do ethics in the context of an ongoing religious tradition. In such contexts, every ethical judgment requires addressing a wide range of meta-issues—where does moral authority reside, what are the core religious and moral truths that one wishes to preserve, what methods should be employed in applying those truths to contemporary moral questions, and which dimensions of the contemporary context must be taken into account, and how, in this process. These issues are as difficult to resolve as they are inescapable. They are also the cause for much lively debate among ethicists and, I would argue, they are what makes contemporary religious ethics such a dynamic field.

In the face of such formidable challenges, one might well wonder what motivates contemporary Jewish ethicists to persist in this endeavor. The answer can only be the conviction that Judaism can and must speak to the moral challenges of our times. It *can* because it encompasses centuries of accumulated ethical insight and wisdom; it *must* because otherwise it risks lapsing into irrelevance. And yet, as the foregoing analysis has shown, this endeavor is intrinsically fraught with intellectual risks. There is no firm or immutable methodological ground on which to stand. Jewish ethics, then, is the courageous effort, despite these challenges, to interpret the multitude of diverse sources bequeathed by earlier generations of religious authorities and thereby extracting from them the rules, values, and virtues that enable us to address the moral questions we face today. This is arduous and precarious intellectual work. It is also of the utmost significance for the survival of this religious tradition. Some might argue that it is equally significant for ours.

Notes

1. For contemporary reflections on the classical themes of Jewish theology, see Arthur A. Cohen and Paul Mendes-Flohr, eds., *Contemporary Jewish Religious Thought* (New York: Charles Scribner's Sons, 1987); and Elliot N. Dorff and Louis E. Newman, eds., *Contemporary Jewish Theology* (New York: Oxford University Press, 1998).
2. Gershom G. Scholem, "Revelation and Tradition as Religious Categories in Judaism," in *The Messianic Idea in Judaism and Other Essays on Jewish Spirituality* (New York: Schocken, 1971), 288–289.
3. Pirke Avot 5:22. See Leonard Kravitz and Kerry M. Olitzky, eds. and trans., *Pirke Avot: A Modern Commentary on Jewish Ethics* (New York: UAHC Press, 1993), 89.

4. Babylonian Talmud, Tractate Eruvin 13b. The statement refers to the perennial disputes between the disciples of Hillel and the disciples of Shammai, two pre-eminent first-century CE Jewish sages.
5. For a complete English translation of the Mishnah, see Jacob Neusner, *The Mishnah: A New Translation* (New Haven, CT: Yale University Press, 1988).
6. There are, in fact, two Talmuds that record the explications of the Mishnah by rabbis from approximately 200–450 CE, one in Babylonia and the other in Palestine (also known as the Jerusalem Talmud). The Babylonian Talmud is considerably larger and more frequently cited by subsequent authorities.
7. This mischaracterization is common among many Christian thinkers going back to antiquity, who have contrasted Judaism as a religion of "law" with Christianity as a religion of "love." But it has also been common among contemporary Orthodox Jewish authorities. See, for example, J. David Bleich, "Introduction: A Priori Component of Bioethics," in *Jewish Bioethics*, ed. Fred Rosner and J. David Bleich (New York: Hebrew Publishing Co., 1979), xix: "A person who seeks to find answers within the Jewish tradition ... must examine them through the prism of *Halakhah* for it is in the corpus of Jewish law as elucidated and transmitted from generation to generation that God has made His will known to man."
8. For a fuller discussion of the Jewish Emancipation and its aftermath, see Michael A. Meyer, *The Origins of the Modern Jew: Jewish Identity and European Culture in Germany, 1749–1824* (Detroit, MI: Wayne State University Press, 1972).
9. Leo Baeck, *The Essence of Judaism* (New York: Schocken, 1948), 59.
10. For one prominent Conservative Jewish position on these matters, see Elliot N. Dorff, *The Unfolding Tradition: Jewish Law after Sinai* (New York: Aviv Press, 2005), especially Dorff's lively and insightful exchange with Eugene B. Borowitz, a prominent Reform thinker, 463–480.
11. See, for example, Laurie Zoloth, *Health Care and the Ethics of Encounter* (Chapel Hill: University of North Carolina Press, 1999), and Steven Kepnes, Peter Ochs and Robert Gibbs, *Reasoning After Revelation: Dialogues in Postmodern Jewish Philosophy* (Boulder, CO: Westview Press/Perseus, 1998).
12. For a fuller explication of these issues, see my essay, "Ethics as Law, Law as Religion: Reflections on the Problem of Law and Ethics in Judaism," in *Past Imperatives: Studies in the History and Theory of Jewish Ethics* (Albany, NY: State University of New York Press, 1998), 45–62.
13. The first classic work in this tradition, from the eleventh century, is Bachya ibn Paquda's *Duties of the Heart*, 2 vols., trans. Moses Hyamson (Jerusalem: Feldheim Publishers, 1970). The modern pietistic (*mussar*) movement was founded by Israel Salanter in Lithuania in the nineteenth century. This movement has recently experienced a significant revival in North America through the work of Alan Morinis; see *Everyday Holiness: The Jewish Spiritual Path of Mussar* (Boston and London: Trumpeter, 2007), and the work of the Mussar Institute, which he founded (http://www.mussarinstitute.org).
14. Moses Maimonides, "Eight Chapters (Shemoneh Perakim)," trans. Isadore Twersky, *A Maimonides Reader* (New York: Behrman House, 1972), 361–386.
15. Herman Cohen, *Religion of Reason Out of the Sources of Judaism*, trans. Simon Kaplan (Atlanta, GA: Scholars Press, 1995).
16. For a still helpful, if somewhat dated, survey of the field, see S. Daniel Breslauer, *Modern Jewish Morality: A Bibliographical Survey* (Westport, CT: Greenwood Press, 1986).
17. Eugene B. Borowitz championed this approach throughout his life; for his most complete articulation of this position, see *Renewing the Covenant: A Theology for the Postmodern Jew* (Philadelphia: Jewish Publication Society, 1991).

18. See Michael Goldberg, *Jews and Christians: Getting Our Stories Straight* (Eugene, OR: Wipf and Stock, 2001; originally published by Trinity Press International, 1991).
19. I elaborate on this fundamental problem in my essay, "Woodchoppers and Respirators: The Problem of Interpretation in Contemporary Jewish Ethics," in *Past Imperatives*, 161–183.

Bibliography

Adler, Rachel. *Engendering Judaism: An Inclusive Theology and Ethics*. Philadelphia, PA: Jewish Publication Society, 1998.

Borowitz, Eugene B. *Exploring Jewish Ethics*. Detroit, MI: Wayne State University Press, 1990.

Breslauer, S. Daniel. *Toward a Jewish (M)Orality: Speaking of a Postmodern Jewish Ethics*. Westport, CT: Greenwood Press, 1998.

Dorff, Elliot N., and Jonathan K. Crane, eds. *The Oxford Handbook of Jewish Ethics and Morality*. New York: Oxford University Press, 2012.

Dorff, Elliot N., and Louis E. Newman, eds. *Contemporary Jewish Ethics and Morality*. New York: Oxford University Press, 1995.

Gordis, Robert. *Judaic Ethics for a Lawless World*. New York: Jewish Theological Seminary of America, 1986.

Mittleman, Alan. *A Short History of Jewish Ethics: Conduct and Character in the Context of Covenant*. Chichester, UK: Wiley-Blackwell, 2012.

Newman, Louis E. *An Introduction to Jewish Ethics*. Upper Saddle River, NJ: Pearson Prentice-Hall, 2005.

Newman, Louis E. *Past Imperatives: Studies in the History and Theory of Jewish Ethics*. Albany: State University of New York Press, 1998.

Novak, David. *Jewish Social Ethics*. New York: Oxford University Press, 1992.

Sherwin, Byron L., and Seymour J. Cohen. *How to Be a Jew: Ethical Teachings of Judaism*. Northvale, NJ: Jason Aronson, 1992.

Telushkin, Joseph. *A Code of Jewish Ethics*. New York: Bell Tower, 2006.

Teutsch, David A. *A Guide to Jewish Practice*, vol. 1. Wyncote, PA: Reconstructionist Rabbinical College Press, 2011.

CHAPTER 2

SOURCES OF CATHOLIC MORAL THEOLOGY

DOLORES L. CHRISTIE

CATHOLIC moral theology is a complex topic; its sources multilayered. Each will be considered in turn. The Catholic Church begins with the Bible and what is called "Tradition." First, the Biblical canon offers a nonnegotiable starting place for any Christian theological work. Nevertheless Catholics believe that divine counsel continues beyond the Biblical period, within the institutional church. Second, Tradition represents both the continuity and novelty of Catholic thinking. As history proceeds and human knowledge grows, novelty—particularly in morals—is sometimes embraced and sometimes rejected by church authority.

Third, beyond the content of specific documents both the natural law Tradition and conscience are sources for Catholic thinking. Natural law theory has been central to Catholic teaching for centuries, particularly in sexual issues. Fourth, personal conscience is important both in individual decision-making and in development of doctrine and moral teaching.

Fifth, theologians respect various levels of official teaching. Not every utterance of a bishop, an episcopal conference, or even of the pope, has the same level of authority. Some documents have a scope limited to a particular venue and/or a particular issue.

Sixth, it is important to include a brief summary of the contemporary conversation on reproductive technology. Since the Second Vatican Council (1962–1965), the focus of Catholic theological reflection has moved from a derivative methodology—an *interpretation* of precipitated teaching—to a *more historical and developmental method*—discernment of what God reveals today and what new teaching might result. Let us consider these topics in order.

Scripture

Major religions have stories that capture seminal insights, their understanding of their experience of the divine. A devout Muslim turns to the Qu'ran, a pious Hindu consults the Vedas, Jews revere the Torah, Christians the Gospels. Like other Christians, Catholics reference a Scriptural canon that includes both the Jewish and Christian experience. Although foundational religious stories are different, their concept of what is good often overlaps. Believers, as well as those who do not believe, see life, fidelity, and justice as important values. They are incorporated in both secular and religious codes. While Catholic Tradition highlights some goods, even connects them to the following of Christ, what is of value is not parochial. Human values are, Catholics believe, universal, and not unique to a particular religious Tradition. Nevertheless, application may vary.

Most Western believers, including Catholics, speak of the Bible as "inspired." The Second Vatican Council affirmed: "Those divinely revealed realities which are contained and presented in Sacred Scripture have been committed to writing under the inspiration of the Holy Spirit" (*Dei verbum*, 11). This is a statement of faith more than one of science, but the Scriptural books endure with good reason. Authentic religious experience captures not only the minds but the hearts of listeners.

A good example is found in the fourth chapter of John's gospel. A Samaritan woman of bad reputation comes in the heat of the day to draw water from the communal well. Jesus, parched, asks her for a drink. The multi-meaning conversation that follows inspires the woman to radical change. She is so affected that she—who avoided the critical townspeople by coming for water when no one else is there—runs to tell those same people about her encounter. Her message is compelling. The townsfolk rush to "see for themselves." They do, and they, too, are inspired. And then someone preserved and passed on the story. The question is, why?

Persons and events that inspire generally touch deeply a common yearning or value. The speaker evokes something that is already there, perhaps dormant in the listener, much like a tuning fork awakens a matching sound in objects in its orbit. A particular faith—expressed in foundational religious writings—survives because it is congruent with people's yearnings. It survives—usually in written form—because it serves people's needs and hopes.

To consider Scripture a source for moral direction is to begin a priori with the assumption that there is a God and that God communicates with human beings. No scientist can prove the connection between God and the words of Scripture. No scientist can prove even that God exists. Nevertheless, inspirational stories resonated with the collective experience of the people who composed, collected, and preserved the corpus for centuries. For them, and for those through centuries, the words speak to their hearts with truth and trust.

Although Catholics take the Bible to be inspired, they reject a literal reading of sacred texts. The work is not a definitive account of historical events—a grainy newsreel of a singular occasion. Rather, inspiration refers to the *purpose* of Scriptural texts: to record the essence of the religious experience of the person or persons who testify to encounters with God and the conclusions that derive from those experiences. Since these happenings are ecstatic, that is, outside normal describable experience, communication beyond the actual events must be metaphoric. The metaphors and language, though, are drawn from the cultural context of the narrators, who translated as best they can. It is always difficult to capture nuance in a translation. "Sad," the English translation from St. Exupery's French novel, can never completely convey the *triste* that his Petit Prince felt.

Dei verbum goes on to say, "However, since God speaks in Sacred Scripture through men in human fashion, the interpreter of Sacred Scripture, in order to see clearly what God wanted to communicate to us, should carefully investigate what meaning the sacred writers really intended, and what God wanted to manifest by means of their words" (*Dei verbum*, 12). These words task the Scripture scholar with the duty to search out the intention of the sacred writers in their own historical context. First, they must pay attention to literary forms.

> For the truth of faith is set forth and expressed differently in texts which are variously historical, prophetic, poetic, or of other forms of discourse. The interpreter must investigate what meaning the sacred writer intended to express and actually expressed in particular circumstances by using contemporary literary forms in accordance with the situation of his own time and culture. (*Dei verbum*, 12)

Second, scholars must investigate the cultural context of the Biblical pericope, even beyond the verisimilitude of its historical placement. It is no accident, for example, that the triumph of younger sons is featured in stories written during the tenure of a "younger son" on Israel's throne (both David and Solomon); although the incident described—even if it actually happened—takes place much earlier. (See Gen. 4, Gen. 25, and Gen. 37, for example.)

The same meticulous care must be taken to discover behavioral norms. Culture, past and present, shapes the mores and moral prohibitions that influence conduct. Institutional narratives and behavioral norms are impacted by political realities, contemporary science, custom, and sometimes even by ignorance. Were not children of the twentieth century instructed by trusted teachers that toilet seats were possible vectors for pregnancy, and that left-handedness was the result of student stubbornness? Did not Thomas Aquinas believe that the soul of the male child was infused into the fetus months earlier than that of the (inferior) female child?

The scholar's mission is to study the literary forms, the context and cultural presuppositions of a particular Scriptural text and to sift the essence of the divine message from the accidental scraps that are cultural garnish—Scriptural parsley or fruit puree—and not the essence of an elegant literary meal. God's revelation is the meat, not the decoration.

The Biblical text, like church teaching, has accumulated over time—a snowball rolling over the cluttered landscape of history. As it moves, it continues to be mostly snow. Nevertheless, as the ball becomes larger and larger it picks up irrelevant debris—a dead leaf or two, a stick that someone left on the grass, a bit of dirt that shadows its pristine whiteness. It is up to the people who are, in a sense, keepers of the snowball (those who lead the faith community as well as its members), to pick out the debris while preserving the accumulating snow. Point? A rolling snowball can pick up cultural debris that has little to do with its "snowball-ness." Cultural shifts may even change the resulting snow figures from exclusively snow *men* to inclusion—now recognizing the equal personhood of women—of an occasional snow *woman*.

To understand the inspired message of the Scriptural "snowball" requires distinguishing the essential snow from the debris acquired along the way. This is particularly important in moral matters, since behavioral norms—both personal and communal—are shaped by the culture from which they come. Sometimes they transcend bias or ignorance; sometimes they do not.

For example, the God-sanctioned dominance of the Israelites over the Canaanites was legitimized by a concocted tale of a divine curse on Ham, son of Noah and supposed ancestor of the Canaanite people, because he mocked the nakedness of his drunken father. The story has been used throughout history to oppress people of color (the presumed progeny of Ham's black offspring). The Ham story adds credence to the people-of-color-are-inferior-to-whites narrative used to justify slavery. This is not today's morality.

A search for Biblical passages on reproductive technology reveals very little. Genesis suggests that human couples be "be fruitful, and multiply, and replenish the earth" (1:28). The text is silent on condoms and cloning.

One must concede that there are some passages that appear to condemn specific sexual practices. The story of Onan (Gen. 38:6–10) ends with God slaying Onan, presumably for "spilling his seed" (considered a contraceptive or even abortive act at the time). Modern scholars debunk this common belief, that the sin was masturbation or *coitus interruptus*. *The New Jerome Biblical Commentary* states unequivocally: "Onan's offense is obvious: he selfishly refuses the responsibility of fulfilling his duty to his brother [to marry his brother's widow and produce children], as the law provided."

Which is correct? Is Onan's sin sexual misconduct or refusing a religious duty? Today are we to condemn sexual intercourse that disallows the "natural" completion of the marital act? While the realities of ancient times provided a reason for such a law, does today's overpopulated world require the fathering of children for a brother's widow?

The passage recounting the story of Lot and his angelic visitors (Gen. 19) is even more puzzling. After cajoling some "angels" to stay at his house, Lot is accosted by a crowd of townsmen who want to have homosexual relations with his visitors. Lot, in his attempt to protect the guests from rape, instead offers the crowd his virgin daughters. God's wrath follows, destroying the town. Does God really condemn the town for the attempted actions of libidinous men and spare the guy who willingly offers his daughters for sex?

While the Decalogue requires "Thou shalt not kill," this rule did not prevent a future King of Israel from the slaughtering women and unborn children (2 Kings 15:16). No divine punishment followed. Other passages in the Hebrew Scriptures that appear to prohibit certain sexual actions are similarly confusing. Many of them assign guilt specifically to women. All of them reflect mores of the times.

The Christian Scriptures speak generously of repentance and resurrection, but they are generally silent about reproduction. Beyond the gospels, which consider divorce, the Letter to the Hebrews cautions that "Marriage [is] honorable in all, and the bed undefiled: but whoremongers and adulterers God will judge" (13:4). Ephesians counsels wives to submit to their husbands, but seems to soften that message with the next statement telling husbands to love their wives as Christ loved the church (5:22–38). Aside from these, almost nothing is said about marital relations, let alone contraception or assisted conception.

If the Bible does not address modern reproductive issues specifically, how does one proceed? First, the researcher must pay close attention to the ancients' ignorance of human biology, which contributes to inaccurate conclusions. People of the Book did not realize even that women made a contribution to baby making beyond a nice resting place or that homosexuality was hard-wired into some persons.

Second, for the most part ancient people saw women as property, and only as receptacles for male sperm. As late as the sixteenth century the sperm was identified (wrongly) as a "homunculus," a tiny but complete human being. The woman provided only nourishment for the child, much as the earth contributes nutrients to rich grain seed. The moral conclusion from the inaccurate belief is that interference with the "natural" act of human sexual intercourse is akin to abortion. Without doubt that mistaken belief influenced for centuries even Catholic philosophers like Thomas Aquinas. To use sacred texts to condemn interference with intercourse as abortion, or to relegate women to a secondary role in procreation is to base divine command in factual error.

In its 2008 document, *The Bible and Morality: Biblical Roots of Christian Conduct*, the Pontifical Biblical Commission directly addressed the difficulty of trying to find moral laws in Scripture. After five years of discussion, and one might assume a level of frustration in trying to define specifics, the committee concluded that the Bible has little of substance to say about sexual morality.

With this in mind, the committee suggested the Decalogue from the Hebrew Scripture and the Beatitudes from the Christian corpus as paradigmatic examples of essential values such as life, dignity, justice, and community. If followed, they formed the ground of proper human response to God's call.

From the Decalogue they inferred a duty to respect human life in all its stages. While not addressed in so many words—the text is centuries old—the fifth commandment can be seen as a cautionary tale for treatment of embryos and for thinking broadly about such new technologies as genetic engineering. The Beatitudes call humanity to a more perfect living, but without norms for concrete situations. Its model of perfection is shaped by social concerns: poverty, persecution, injustice. Reproductive issues do not make the list. In the next section the place of Tradition in filling that void will be discussed.

Tradition: Development and Stagnation

Catholics affirm that God's communication occurs beyond the first century. Jesus Christ *is* Emmanuel, that is, "God with us." Not all moral truth is contained in the Biblical canon. The institutional church, embodied in its leaders and members, is responsible for preserving, passing on, and evaluating the insights of the past as well as those of the present. The Tradition recognizes even secular and scientific knowledge as part of God's revelation.

There is much that human beings do not know, so much to discover. New knowledge is to be embraced and examined within the church community. That is why doctrine can develop over time. With new insight, new conclusions are possible. Just as people no longer see the world as flat and must adjust their maps accordingly, so must new understanding about God's revelation confront moral precepts. When we understand the sperm as less than a complete human being, we must rethink conclusions that discarding "homunculi" is murder.

In teaching, too, there are criteria to judge what to keep and what to leave behind. First, it is important to identify the portions of revelation that have a basic, unchanging meaning. That is a constant that the exigent discoveries over time and culture cannot change. The major message of Christian faith is that God enters into history, to announce God's love and to bring hope: "I will be your God; you will be my people." As noted above, the message is simple. It is left to those who shepherd the community of faith to derive from this message a code of responsive behavior for believers.

Second, any new knowledge or insight must ring true with the magisterium—both those who comprise the official teaching authority (generally bishops) and those who do theology. Catholic thinking postulates a two-faceted magisterium. On the one hand the magisterial task is to teach. On the other hand, the magisterium does theological work that both interprets past teaching and develops doctrine. When the church functions ideally there is a reciprocity between the conclusions of the leaders who instruct and the insights of the faithful, the people in the pews. In its 2014 document, *Sensus fidei in the Life of the Church*, the International Theological Commission made what some would consider radical statements:

> Alerted by their *sensus fidei*, individual believers may deny assent even to the teaching of legitimate pastors if they do not recognize in that teaching the voice of Christ, the Good Shepherd. (63)
>
> What is less well known, and generally receives less attention, is the role played by the laity with regard to the development of the moral teaching of the Church. It is therefore important to reflect also on the function played by the laity in discerning the Christian understanding of appropriate human behavior in accordance with the Gospel. In certain areas, the teaching of the Church has developed as a result of lay people discovering the imperatives arising from new situations. The reflection of theologians, and then the judgment of the episcopal magisterium, was based on the Christian experience already clarified by the faithful intuition of lay people. (73)
>
> Not only do they have the right to be heard, but their reaction to what is proposed as belonging to the faith of the Apostles must be taken very seriously, because it is by the Church as a whole that the apostolic faith is borne in the power of the Spirit. (75)

It is not only the jurisdiction but the responsibility of the lay members of the church to exercise this function. If the anthropology that the church teaches is true (that all human beings are capable of knowing and doing the good) then the acceptance or rejection of church teaching is a titer of whether the teaching is truly orthodox. Some have claimed that the wide non-acceptance of *Humanae vitae*, the encyclical that reaffirmed the Traditional teaching ban on so-called "artificial" prevention of conception, is a sign that the teaching is invalid. Further, as the commission document notes, the voice of the faithful must be taken seriously in the formation of new teaching. This is particularly important in moral teaching.

One can see gradual changes in church teaching in response to what Vatican II called "the signs of the times." These changes are most apparent in social ethics, as indicated below. Prohibitions in medical matters have been revised. It is no longer considered immoral to charge money for lending money, but in the area of sexual morality there has been resistance to development. Part of the reason for this is an argument drawn from natural law.

Natural Law Theory

Before the Second Vatican Council and particularly before the publication of the encyclical letter *Humanae vitae* (1968), norms on sexual issues were based on an interpretation of natural law. The ground swell of dissent after its publication changed that. In large measure it was the insights of Catholic theology beyond the official magisterium that have been responsible for a gradual change in thinking.

Natural law has two meanings. On the one hand, it refers to the inherent property of human beings, an ability belonging to people *by their nature* to know and to do what is good. As Thomas Aquinas affirms: "Therefore, the first precept of the natural law is that we should do and seek good, and shun evil." Thomas affirms that human beings can discern good and evil by an inherent human quality: practical reason, a "natural law" that provides the basis both for trusting decisions of conscience as inviolable and for inviting consultation from the community of faith to affirm or critique emerging church teaching. Most Catholic thinkers accept this positive anthropology, the first meaning of natural law.

The second meaning is not as simple. Thomas goes on to say:

> And all the other precepts of the natural law are based on that precept....
>
> And since good has the nature of end, and evil the nature of the contrary, reason by nature understands to be good all the things for which human beings have a natural inclination, and so to be things to be actively sought, and understands contrary things as evil and to be shunned.

Therefore natural law is also taken to be a set of principles, laws within all nature from inanimate reality to human beings. In this sense, natural law is not only a human *faculty* (Meaning 1), it has *moral content* (Meaning 2).

As a philosopher, Aquinas saw a teleology in all creation, including in the functions of the human body. As a theologian, he saw this teleology as divine law as well. To violate or restrain a natural function's purpose is to commit sin. This static interpretation of natural law survives into this century. One may not eat and then vomit in order to enjoy a second sumptuous meal. One may not enjoy the pleasure of sexual intercourse and thwart the natural teleology of the act to procreate.

In such a fixed world view, there is no room for novelty, no room for deviating from God's intended purpose. Aquinas concludes his discussion with a firm statement:

> The natural law as consisting of general precepts, which are never wanting, cannot be dispensed.... [E]very human being is subject to the divine law as private persons are subject to public law. And so, as only rulers or their representatives can dispense from human laws, so only God or his special representatives can dispense from precepts of the divine law.

Following this position, the church designates certain actions as "intrinsic evil," that is, no circumstance can mitigate their sinfulness. Included are such actions as abortion, prostitution, lying, and murder. In the 1993 encyclical *Veritatis splendor*, John Paul II lists acts considered to be intrinsically evil and then in the next paragraph especially underlines contraception and weds it to the same criteria. Quoting his predecessor, the pope notes:

> With regard to intrinsically evil acts, and in reference to contraceptive practices whereby the conjugal act is intentionally rendered infertile, Pope Paul VI [in *Humanae*

vitae] teaches: "Though it is true that sometimes it is lawful to tolerate a lesser moral evil in order to avoid a greater evil or in order to promote a greater good, it is never lawful, even for the gravest reasons, to do evil that good may come of it (cf. Rom. 3:8)—in other words, to intend directly something which of its very nature contradicts the moral order, and which must therefore be judged unworthy of man, even though the intention is to protect or promote the welfare of an individual, of a family or of society in general." (*Veritatis splendor*, 80)

Note two things. First, the pope refers to "the natural order." In his mind, the "natural" function for human intercourse is to produce offspring. Second, the pope condemns contraception (above) precisely when "the conjugal act is intentionally rendered infertile." Does that imply that only those who employ "unnatural" (read: pills, condoms, IUDs) means have a direct and singular intention to prevent conception?

When it has spoken on the issue of conception prevention, Catholic teaching has applied this static natural law model consistently. Two twentieth-century encyclicals speak to this. *Casti connubii* (1930), which affirmed the primary end of marriage as bearing children (11). After the Second Vatican Council another document moved the needle just a bit. *Humanae vitae* (1968) elevated the mutual sharing of husband and wife to a par with but inseparable from the reproductive end. Both encyclicals speak teleologically, of the "ends" of marriage. Official church teaching continues to condemn any action which frustrates the natural teleology of the marital act to avoid pregnancy or that separates fertilization from the marital act.

In past church teaching even the structures of society were seen as predetermined by God's natural law. God is the author of the universe and—being God—what God has made is absolute. It must not be violated. This belief had significant impact on Catholic teaching over the centuries, including some that today would be considered oppressive to human dignity. Much of Catholic teaching remained consistent, from Christian Scripture—which not only acknowledged the existence of slavery but accepted it—to the structures of family, economic, and political life that were not questioned seriously until the twentieth century.

Over time, many "natural law" assumptions have been questioned: some abandoned or even condemned by Catholic teaching. Women got the vote and equal status with men, even in marriage. Within the church, more leadership roles have become available to women, although priesthood is still denied. For more than a century church leaders have promoted labor unions vigorously, giving a voice to those who do not own the means of production. Theological arguments that supported capital punishment were discarded. Religious freedom was embraced by the church. Official teaching reflects these changes.

In the area of sexual ethics, however, change in official church teaching has been slow or nonexistent. The commission established by the Pope John XXIII in 1963 (and expanded after his death by Pope Paul VI) to consider the issue of birth control recommended a change in teaching. (Its composition reflected the lived experience of married couples who served on it.) Nevertheless the encyclical which followed in

1968 (*Humanae vitae*) reiterated previous teaching that prohibited even the use of the Pill. Ironically the doctor who helped develop the Pill was a practicing Catholic, who was trying to find a method that did not pose a physical barrier to achieve contraception. He, as did others, saw the Pill as just as a "natural" alternative to other methods.

After *Humanae vitae* reaffirmed the inseparability of the ends of marriage and its past teaching regarding contraception, Catholic couples and theologians responded collectively in dissent. The former ignored the document; the latter took on the document to defend it strongly or to critique its natural law conclusions.

The dialogue resulted in a different approach to natural law as well as a split in Catholic theological thinking. Those who believed that the teaching should be changed looked at natural law through a new historical lens. If nature is not static, as church documents on regulation of birth have consistently taught; perhaps change in teaching is required. Perhaps God was telling the church something new, based in historical change. Some theologians incorporated this new understanding in their work; others continued to apply a static world view to sexual issues. Certainly the norms for sexual ethics were not embedded in what comprises essential church teaching. And not all church teaching is created equal.

Levels of Church Authority

It is important to understand how church documents are ranked. Catholic sources for moral wisdom are not all equal in level of authority or importance. Certainly the Biblical text and the creeds, which summarize essential beliefs, rank first. They contain the core of the Christian message.

The next level derives from the universal teaching authority of the church in the body of bishops, led by the elected bishop of Rome, the pope. Generally the bishops speak together through ecumenical councils, such as Vatican II. In the history of the Catholic church there have been twenty-one such events. Catholics believe in the authenticity of teaching that flows from this collective episcopal voice and/or the statements of the pope made *ex cathedra*, that is speaking infallibly from the chair of Peter.

What does infallible mean? Consider a Montessori teacher instructing her class in how to wash a table. The lesson shows young children a method that results "infallibly" in a clean table. That is not to say that a table cannot be cleaned in other ways. Catholics believe certain teaching is infallible in that it articulates essential doctrine and/or a certain path of behavioral response to God's covenant call. Like producing a clean table, a statement of infallibility does not assume that there may not be a clearer instruction as to how to get a table clean.

Lesser church documents generally are written in response to particular concerns within an historical context. The term used is "ordinary magisterium," to distinguish from those types listed above. Usually it is in these types of documents that moral concerns are addressed. They include papal encyclicals, statements of regional synods of bishops, or of individual bishops to their own dioceses.

Commissions and committees of theological experts serve in an advisory capacity. While documents generated by the ordinary magisterium of the church do not carry the weight of official church teaching, they are congruent with more important writings and should be taken seriously. There is one further factor to consider.

The Importance of Conscience

The groundbreaking Vatican II document, *Gaudium et spes*, affirmed the preeminence of conscience in decision-making:

> Conscience is the most secret core and sanctuary of a man. There he is alone with God, Whose voice echoes in his depths. In a wonderful manner conscience reveals that law which is fulfilled by love of God and neighbor. In fidelity to conscience, Christians are joined with the rest of men in the search for truth, and for the genuine solution to the numerous problems which arise in the life of individuals from social relationships. Hence the more right conscience holds sway, the more persons and groups turn aside from blind choice and strive to be guided by the objective norms of morality. (*Gaudium et spes*, 16)

The human conscience is respected as a sacred place where God speaks. Catholic anthropology admits the muddy nature of reality, but it affirms that the dignity of human persons requires that the conscience be the final arbiter of personal human action. Nevertheless a healthy conscience is not solitary or uninformed. The wisdom of the community, including church teaching, comprises the sounding board that validates personal decisions. If a person takes only his or her own counsel, morality devolves into subjectivism—which holds that no value is universal.

Counsel comes from many sources. As a person moves through life, he or she forms the conscience to think clearly, consider the values at stake in any decision, and to act according to those values. Moral narratives from family and communal institutions become part of the reference library each person carries. Flemish theologian Louis Janssens called this the "objective culture." This refers to the collective wisdom humanity has gathered as its moral snowball moves through time. It is the bundled set of narrative, values, and procedures derived from sacred texts and cultural trial and error. For Catholics some of this wisdom is preserved and passed on in the Tradition. It represents a communal ecclesial consensus of what is good and sometimes concrete advice on how to make value real.

There is another element, however, which Janssens called "subjective culture." Each individual has a unique set of experiences which guide their particular actions. The set is rather like a personal "snowball." Sometimes detritus which others cherish or overlook is sensed by a person as not of value. The fungible subjective culture of the person ideally is always in dialogue with the evolving objective culture, including the sources which the church provides. Such dialogue provides an antidote to ignorance, self-delusion, and relativism.

In his stages of moral development Lawrence Kohlberg observed that sometimes consensus—even strongly-held beliefs of the culture—can be wrong. Sometimes it is the novel insight of an individual person that causes change. Giants of history—Jesus, Mohammad, Gandhi, even Martin Luther King—have stood against accepted cultural narratives and norms. Their moral gravitas, their sensitive consciences, afforded them a clearer vision of what the good is. What they saw, in turn, changed how others saw. The important task for all persons is to navigate the oscillating sea between their experience and the common understanding of the dominant culture, including what is taught by the church. And then to speak.

Contemporary Catholic Debate on Reproductive Issues

Since Vatican II and the vigorous debate following the encyclical *Humanae vitae*, there has been an expanding theological dialogue on reproductive issues. The Council invoked the "signs of the times," legitimizing in a formal way the process of listening to what new is being said in and to the culture. Vatican II emphasized not a-historical laws but the human person as the central consideration in moral decision-making, including reaffirmation of conscience as central and sacrosanct to the ethical project.

Humanae vitae provoked a healthy re-evaluation of the understanding of natural law theory—at least in theological circles. An historical approach to natural law understands that nature as well as our understanding of nature, is not fixed but evolving. Swift progress in reproductive technology has made the conversation even more urgent.

We see some crumbling of the edges of past thinking in official documents such as *Donum vitae* (1987), which struggled (not too successfully) with how to incorporate past thinking on assisted reproduction with modern methods. It draws its conclusions more on principles than on prescriptions for behavior: the dignity of persons, respect for the embryo and the marital bond, and the dignity of procreation.

Today Catholic theology strains to move beyond past thinking on sexual issues. Catholic believers, particularly theologians, have a responsibility to pursue this project. There is considerable conversation on the meaning of human sexuality and marriage as well as specific work on reproductive technology. Among others, Charles

Curran and James Keenan have tackled with homage the development of Catholic moral teaching with a fresh look toward its future development. Lawler and Salzman's work on *The Sexual Person* gives due diligence to church teaching on these topics, while offering conclusions that seriously question past conclusions. Margaret Farley caused appropriate discomfort to Rome with *Just Love*. Within the last year, more women have joined the conversation. At a recent meeting of the Catholic Theological Society of America, Cristina Traina, Megan McCabe, and Elizabeth Antus presented papers on sexual justice. The session addressed rape culture, sexual pain, and unplanned pregnancy in poverty. Over fifty people attended—remarkable for the after-lunch slot—and conversation was spirited.

This brief romp through the current theological garden is not exhaustive. This article cannot examine the multiple works that have blossomed since the sun of Vatican II promoted verdant growth in Catholic thinking. Hopefully the references will add to the list.

Conclusion

Catholic sources for moral theology are multiple and evolving. A turn to the historical has changed radically their direction. Contextual and cultural realities continue to leave giant footprints, which disturb the gated and neatly rowed field of official Catholic teaching. With an historical understanding of natural law and the place of the community, with the contribution of science and ideas of forward-looking theologians, with the guidance of God's spirit, newness grows. Particularly in sexual issues and reproduction, there is an uptick in discussion. While official teaching moves slowly, the fertile field for change is ripe. Only the future will see the harvest.

Bibliography

Aquinas, Thomas. *Summa Theologiae*. Part II/1. Question 94. On the Natural Law. Article 2. https://www.newadvent.org/summa/2094.htm.

Cahill, Lisa Sowle, John Garvey, and T. Frank Kennedy, eds. *Sexuality and the U.S. Catholic Church: Crisis and Renewal*. New York: Crossroad Publishing Company, 2006.

Catechism of the Catholic Church. New York: Doubleday Image Book, 1995.

Christie, Dolores L. *Adequately Considered: An American Perspective on Louis Janssens' Personalist Morals*. Louvain: Peeters Press, 1990.

Christie, Dolores L. *Moral Choice: A Christian View of Ethics*. Minneapolis: Fortress Press, 2013.

Clifford, Richard J., and Roland E. Murphy. "Genesis." *The New Jerome Biblical Commentary*. Englewood Cliffs, NJ: Prentice-Hall, 1990.

Congregation for the Doctrine of the Faith. *Declaration on Procured Abortion.* The Vatican, 1974. http://www.vatican.va/roman_curia/congregations/cfaith/documents/rc_con_cfaith_doc_19741118_declaration-abortion_en.html.

Congregation for the Doctrine of the Faith. *Dignitatis personae: Instruction on Certain Bioethical Questions.* The Vatican, 2008. https://www.vatican.va/roman_curia/congregations/cfaith/documents/rc_con_cfaith_doc_20081208_dignitas-personae_en.html.

Congregation for the Doctrine of the Faith. *Donum vitae: Instruction on Respect for Human Life.* The Vatican, 1987. http://www.vatican.va/roman_curia/congregations/cfaith/documents/rc_con_cfaith_doc_19870222_respect-for-human-life_en.html.

Congregation for the Doctrine of the Faith. *Persona humana: Declaration on Certain Questions Concerning Sexual Ethics.* The Vatican, 1975. http://www.vatican.va/roman_curia/congregations/cfaith/documents/rc_con_cfaith_doc_19751229_persona-humana_en.html.

Coogan, Michael. *God and Sex: What the Bible Really Says.* New York: Hachette Book Group, 2010.

Curran, Charles E., ed. *Change in Official Catholic Moral Teachings: Readings in Moral Theology 13.* New York: Paulist Press, 2003.

Curran, Charles E. *The Development of Moral Theology: Five Strands.* Washington: Georgetown University Press, 2013.

Doherty, Dennis, ed. *Dimensions of Human Sexuality.* Garden City, NY: Doubleday and Company, 1979.

Farley, Margaret A. *Just Love: A Framework for Christian Sexual Ethics.* New York: Continuum, 2006.

Gaillardetz, Richard R. *Teaching Authority: A Theology of the Magisterium of the Church.* Collegeville: Liturgical Press, 1997.

Gallagher, John. "Marriage and Sexuality: Magisterial Teaching from 1918 to the Present." In *Change in Official Catholic Moral Teachings: Readings in Moral Theology 13*, edited by Charles E. Curran, 227–247. New York: Paulist Press, 2003.

Grisez, Germain. *Contraception and the Natural Law.* Milwaukee: Bruce Publishing Company, 1964.

Gula, Richard M. *Reason Informed by Faith: Foundations of Catholic Morality.* New York: Paulist Press, 1989.

International Theological Commission. *Sensus fidei in the Life of the Church.* The Vatican, 2014. http://www.vatican.va/roman_curia/congregations/cfaith/cti_documents/rc_cti_20140610_sensus-fidei_en.html.

Janssens, Louis. "Artificial Insemination: Ethical Considerations." *Louvain Studies* 8 (1980–1981): 3–29.

Janssens, Louis. "Rechten van de mens." *Tijdschrift voor Politiek* 2 (1952): 525.

Janssens, Louis. *Droits personnels et autorité.* Louvain: Nauwelaerts, 1954.

Janssens, Louis. *Personalisme en democratisering.* Brussels: Arbeiderspers, 1957; 1965.

John Paul II. *Familiaris consortio: The Fellowship of the Family.* The Vatican, 1982. http://w2.vatican.va/content/john-paul-ii/en/apost_exhortations/documents/hf_jp-ii_exh_19811122_familiaris-consortio.html.

John Paul II. *Centesimus annus: The Hundreth Year.* The Vatican, 1991. http://w2.vatican.va/content/john-paul-ii/en/encyclicals/documents/hf_jp-ii_enc_01051991_centesimus-annus.html.

John Paul II. *Evanglium vitae: On the Value and Inviolability of Human Life.* The Vatican, 1995. w2.vatican.va/.../hf_jp-ii_enc_25031995_evangelium-vitae.html.

John Paul II. *Veritatis splendor: The Splendor of Truth.* The Vatican, 1993. http://w2.vatican.va/content/john-paul-ii/en/encyclicals/documents/hf_jp-ii_enc_06081993_veritatis-splendor.html.

Kaiser, Robert Blair. *The Politics of Sex and Religion: A Case Study in the Development of Doctrine, 1962–1984.* Kansas City: Leaven, 1985.

Keenan, James F. *A History of Catholic Moral Theology in the Twentieth Century: From Confessing Sins to Liberating Conscience.* London: Continuum, 2010.

Kosnick, Anthony, et al. *Human Sexuality: New Directions in American Catholic Thought.* New York: Paulist Press, 1977.

Leo XIII. *Rerum novarum: On Capital and Labor.* The Vatican, 1891. http://w2.vatican.va/content/leo-xiii/en/encyclicals/documents/hf_l-xiii_enc_15051891_rerum-novarum.html.

Liebard, Odile M., ed. *Official Catholic Teachings: Love and Sexuality.* Wilmington, NC: McGrath Publishing Company, 1978.

Noonan, Jr., John T. *Contraception: A History of Its Treatment by the Catholic Theologians and Canonists.* Cambridge: Harvard University Press, 1967.

O'Rourke, Kevin, and Philip Boyle. *Medical Ethics: Sources of Catholic Teachings.* Second edition. Washington: Georgetown University Press, 1993.

Paul VI. *Dignitatis humanae: Declaration on Religions Freedom.* The Vatican, 1965. http://www.vatican.va/archive/hist_councils/ii_vatican_council/documents/vat-ii_decl_19651207_dignitatis-humanae_en.html.

Paul VI. *Humanae vitae: On the Regulation of Birth.* The Vatican, 1968. http://w2.vatican.va/content/paul-vi/en/encyclicals/documents/hf_p-vi_enc_25071968_humanae-vitae.html.

Pius XI. *Casti connubii*: On Christian Marriage. The Vatican, 1930. http://www.papalencyclicals.net/Pius11/P11CASTI.HTM.

Pontifical Biblical Commission. *The Bible and Morality. Biblical Roots of Christian Conduct.* The Vatican, 2008. http://www.vatican.va/roman_curia/congregations/cfaith/pcb_documents/rc_con_cfaith_doc_20080511_bibbia-e-morale_en.html.

Pontifical Biblical Commission. "The Interpretation of the Bible in the Church." *Origins.* January 6, 1994. https://www.vatican.va/roman_curia/congregations/cfaith/documents/rc_con_cfaith_doc_20081208_dignitas-personae_en.html.

Riddle, John M. "Population and Sex." *Contraception and Abortion from the Ancient World to the Renaissance.* Cambridge, MA: Harvard University Press, 1992.

Salzman, Todd A., and Michael G. Lawler. *The Sexual Person: Toward a Renewed Catholic Anthropology.* Washington: Georgetown University Press, 2008.

Selling, Joseph. "Magisterial Teaching on Marriage 1880–1986; Historical Constancy or Radical Development?" In *Change in Official Catholic Moral Teachings: Readings in Moral Theology 13*, edited by Charles E. Curran, 248–252. New York: Paulist Press, 2003.

Sullivan, Francis A. "Developments in Teaching Authority since Vatican II." *Theological Studies* 73 (2012): 570–589.

Sullivan, Francis A. *Magisterium: Teaching Authority in the Catholic Church.* Mahwah, NJ: Paulist Press, 1983.

U.S. Conference of Catholic Bishops. *Evaluation and Treatment of Infertility: Guidelines for Catholic Couples.* 2009. http://www.usccb.org/issues-and-action/marriage-and-family/natural-family-planning/resources/upload/Reproductive-Technology-Evaluation-Treatment-of-Infertility-Guidelines-for-Catholic-Couples.pdf.

U.S. Conference of Catholic Bishops. *Life-Giving Love in an Age of Technology.* Washington, DC: USCCB Publishing, 2009. http://www.usccb.org/upload/lifegiving-love-age-technology-2009.pdf.

CHAPTER 3

PROTESTANT SOURCES OF MORAL KNOWLEDGE

KAREN L. LEBACQZ

FROM the earliest beginnings of Protestant theology in the rebellion of Martin Luther against the Roman Catholic church to the most contemporary voices of liberation theology, Protestants strive to "do the will of God."[1] The great difficulty is how we are to know what that will is. A cursory glance reveals a cacophony of possibilities—from Scripture to bodily comfort. Historically, however, Protestant sources have been designated as being from one of four major categories: Scripture, tradition, reason, and experience—sometimes called the "Methodist quadrilateral."[2]

However, each category needs to be parsed and the distinction among them is somewhat arbitrary. Scripture gives us interpretations of people's experiences of God; hence, Scripture cannot be wholly separated from experience.[3] Religious ideas begin in a revelatory experience which is then shared, promulgated by a group, and only subsequently codified into a "canon" or Scripture. Thus, Scripture is "codified collective human experience."[4] Further, since received ideas are generally tested by what "feels right," experience may be the final touchstone. One could argue, however, that there is no Scripture without the tradition that carries it forward, making tradition or community primary. Hence, the sources are interwoven and their distinction is somewhat arbitrary.

Diversity within Protestantism presents a problem for identifying sources. "Protestants" include at least thirteen major denominational divisions,[5] and within each of these there may be multiple sub-traditions. The World Alliance of Reformed Churches, for example, consists of some 157 bodies representing the world-wide spread of the reformed tradition.[6] Thus, Chapman argues that there may be as much disagreement about sources *within* a denomination as *between* denominations.[7] Given this diversity, it is understandable that there is no single ethical method or agreement on sources of moral knowledge in Protestant circles.[8] Some Protestants will draw primarily on Scripture, some on experience; some will advocate general principles for conduct, while others will eschew principles, arguing that God's will is always concrete and particular.[9] Choices regarding moral sources may also depend on whether the theologian is addressing matters of *personal* ethics or of *social* ethics.[10]

Are denominational views better represented by group documents than by individual thinkers? While Ostnor and West prefer group documents, Chapman suggests that those may reflect views of the particular individuals in the group, not necessarily denominational views.[11] Moreover, group statements are often vague regarding sources of moral insight, and dialogue among individuals can illuminate denominational differences. For these reasons, this essay draws largely on individual Protestant writers.

From the beginning, Protestant scholars have been conversant with and influenced by both Roman Catholic moral theology and secular/humanist moral thinking. Ecumenical movements of the past decades and the loss of status of religious groups also means that most contemporary Protestants appeal not simply to those in their denomination but to a broad spectrum of Christians and non-Christians. Many simply say "Christians believe" or "Christian tradition teaches" and may not specifically identify as Protestant, much less acknowledging specific denominational traditions.[12]

In addition, thinkers are influenced by audience. In *Bioethics: A Primer for Christians*, Meilaender declares flatly: "I write as a Christian for other Christians."[13] By contrast, the editors of *Women's Consciousness, Women's Conscience: A Reader in Feminist Ethics* identify themselves as "white, middle-class Christian women" but they write for feminists who do not necessarily identify as Christian.[14] In the mid-1970s, Wogaman described a "crisis of confidence" in sources of moral authority.[15] While Heiene argues that Protestants continue to draw on Scripture and tradition,[16] Wogaman contends that "We can no longer believe . . . that such authorities as Scripture, church, and tradition are *necessarily* right and applicable to the decisions we face."[17] Distrust in traditional sources is reinforced by post-modernism, by feminist theologians who eschew ethical principles, and by liberation theologians who find Scripture and tradition oppressive. As both Veatch and Campbell note, in our current secular world, religious history and the moral insights drawn from it may not be compelling to many; hence, religious themes must often be translated into more secular categories.[18] Recognizing that the connection between religion and ethics has ceased to be self-evident for many people, Andolsen and her colleagues propose that religious norms must give way to feminist considerations.[19] The strength of sources of moral knowledge may therefore depend on the audience as well as the author of Protestant texts.

Further difficulties are encountered when dealing with "complex contemporary conundrums" related to science and technology.[20] Scripture and older traditions could not possibly address specifically many current medical technologies, so contemporary

Protestant moral theologians turn more to reason, science, and experience as sources of insight than to Scripture and tradition.

Finally, there are also differences between Protestant moral theology in the United States and in other parts of the world: with a tradition of pragmatism, American Protestants are often focused on action and decision-making rather than on analyses of theological roots and sources of moral knowledge.

Despite these difficulties, the four interlocking sources—Scripture, tradition, reason, and experience—remain to some extent mandatory for moral discernment in Protestant ethics. Each of these, however, is contested and needs further exploration.

SCRIPTURE

For most Protestants, Scripture is foundational. "Christians, of course, use the Bible," declare Bouma and colleagues in their review of medical practices.[21] "[T]he Bible has always been regarded as central for Christian morality and ethics," assert Birch and Rasmussen.[22] Luther's writings are peppered with references to Scripture, especially the writings of Paul.[23] For Calvin, too, the Scriptures are the supreme rule of faith and life, including church structures.[24] All Protestants share the assumption that the Bible is in some way a book that supplies distinctive content to the Christian moral life.[25] For Protestants, "Scripture" includes the Hebrew Scriptures commonly called the Old Testament and the Christian Scriptures known as the New Testament.

For some, the Bible gives content directly, by giving commandments such as the great commandment to "love the Lord your God with all your heart and mind, and your neighbor as yourself" (Matthew 22:35–40). For others, it does so indirectly by showing who God is and how God acts and hence, what it means to act in accord with God's purposes and will. For some, the Bible provides *images* of God—warrior, judge, or healer. For others, it provides *themes* or motifs—covenant, compassion, or hope.[26] Denominational documents often begin with general Biblically-based affirmations such as "We are not alone; we live in God's world"[27] or "Creation has its origin, existence, value, and destiny in God."[28] For some, the Bible is more a book of instruction in the development of Christian *character* than a rule book for action.[29] Despite these differences, for almost all Protestants, the Bible remains "the foundation sine qua non."[30] It is a central source of moral knowledge.

However, the ways in which the Bible is understood and used vary greatly. The Bible may be the "canon," but what this means is contested. For some, it alone is canon. From Luther, we get the motto "Sola Scriptura." Sola Scriptura can mean that there are no other sources of discernment beyond Scripture. Evangelical Protestants especially argue that Scripture is *all* that is needed for moral guidance.[31] Murray argues meticulously that Scripture is the *only* deposit of God's revelation; correctly interpreted, all parts of the Bible are cohesive.[32] This is a true "Sola Scriptura" approach in which

Scripture alone and complete is the "canon" for behavior. The Bible contains all normative content; no other sources are needed.

But Gushee, himself an evangelical, argues that evangelicals tend to use a small set of Biblical texts.[33] They have a "canon within the canon," as do most mainstream Protestants. Gushee argues further that Christians must engage with important data from science and human experience. Thus, not all evangelicals adhere to the claim that the Bible alone is sufficient as a source of moral knowledge. Some evangelicals join mainstream Protestants in utilizing a "canon plus" approach to moral knowledge. "Sola Scriptura" then means that Christians have a *distinctive* source in Scripture and that Scripture becomes the *final* reference to assess the wisdom of insights from tradition, reason, and experience. But Christian ethics is not synonymous with Biblical ethics.[34]

Whether "canon alone," "canon plus," or "canon within the canon," questions arise regarding criteria for the adequacy of interpretation and application of Scripture. For most Protestants, Biblical commands must be understood in their historical context, and differences between that context and ours may be morally relevant.[35] Waters, for example, begins his examination of reproductive ethics by noting the historical differences between Rachel's lamented childlessness and the contemporary situation of childless women.[36] "Historical perspectives, socio-economic data, scientific data, rational arguments, and an endless variety of other non-Biblical sources are authoritative in the making of particular moral judgments," suggest Birch and Rasmussen.[37] Mott goes further: it is not simply that non-Biblical sources help to make ethical decisions, but that "non-Biblical constructs aid the understanding of Scripture."[38] Hence, even the basic approach to Scripture requires use of reason, science, and experience.

This may be particularly true when confronted with contemporary problems for which there is no parallel in the Bible. Chapman and Verhey both note that Scripture is silent on most contemporary bioethical issues and is therefore subject to being ignored or misused.[39] The inadequacy of Scripture is also claimed by feminists and liberation theologians, who argue that Scripture was oppressive to women and others (e.g., slaves) and that Christians through the centuries have ignored the plight of oppressed people. Scripture therefore cannot serve as canon; there needs to be a "canon outside the canon" to guide moral discernment. For some, this will be experience, as discussed below.

Indeed, most Protestants would agree that there is no "uninterpreted" reading of Scripture.[40] "An ethic which is free from presuppositions has never existed; rather, the question is always *what* presuppositions the moral philosopher brings with him," declares Brunner.[41] Every Protestant brings to Scripture some presuppositions that affect the way Scripture is read and used.

Therefore, Gustafson argues that the use of Scripture first involves determining the ethical and theological principles that will bring coherence to the meaning of the texts.[42] Following Gustafson, Hauerwas notes that scholars reconstruct Biblical theology in accord with preconceived notions of what is central.[43] Meilaender, too, argues that most of our ethical decisions are based on background beliefs that are held at a pre-articulate level.[44]

Protestants thus select different basic values or central themes: Boesak and Cone argue that *liberation* is the key notion in Scripture,[45] while for Barth, Mott, and others, the key theme is God's *grace*. For Tillich, the "Protestant principle" is that no *earthly institution* has ultimate authority.[46] Jones makes *forgiveness* central.[47] Ramsey, Bouma, and Peters draw on *covenant*.[48] Bennett and Outka focus on *agape* (Christian love), which also looms large for Gustafson.[49] By contrast, Rauschenbusch argued for the *Kingdom of God* as the central concept.[50] If the heart of Protestant theology is justification by grace, received through faith (Ephesians 2:8), then *attitude* and *receptivity* may be key issues.[51] Thus, the Bible offers a range of possible foci that might guide behavior or develop Christian character, and it may be read differently, depending on whether one takes God's grace, God's love, God's covenant with humankind, the oppression of peoples, the vision of a coming kingdom, or something else as a central theme and concern.

Closely related to key values is finding in Scripture a basic *vision* that undergirds ethical discernment. Wheeler takes from Scripture and tradition several basic anthropological commitments: We are created, embodied, social, sinful, mortal, and redeemed.[52] These commitments guide her reflections on technology. Meilaender, too, derives his reflections on reproductive technologies from basic affirmations: We belong to God, sin distorts all our relationships, we are both embodied and free, and so on. Yoder cautions, however, that vision can get off track and needs to be returned to origins: "The Bible was always a liberation storybook; now we are ready to read it that way."[53]

Is Scripture a source of norms, rules, or principles for action? Referencing Genesis 9:6 and Exodus 20:13, Mitchell claims that "The Bible forbids the taking of innocent human life, no matter how young."[54] Here, a specific injunction is drawn from Scriptural references. Others also develop rules or principles, specific or general, from Scripture: in the "situation ethics" debate of the 1960s, Ramsey famously argued that Christian ethics needs rules and that those are explicit or implicit in Scripture.[55] But some prominent Protestants have argued forcefully that the Bible is *not* a book of moral rules for behavior.[56] Others argue for "middle axioms" to help apply basic Biblical insights to contemporary situations.[57]

Finally, as noted, the Bible may be seen more as a book of stories, poems, and visions that assist Christians in developing *character* rather than as a book of inspiration or moral knowledge oriented toward *action*. Gustafson and Hauerwas are prominent in this regard.

Given these possible approaches to Scripture, it is no surprise that different Protestants will emphasize different texts. Ramsey emphasizes Ephesians and the prologue to the Gospel of John; Bonhoeffer uses 1 Corinthians 13—Paul's discussion of love; West turns to the Magnificat but also notes the importance of the *silences* in Scripture—the things that are not addressed there.[58] Boesak believes that the Exodus is central because Jesus placed himself within the exodus tradition.[59]

One way to sort uses of Scripture is to see them in terms of the priority given to creation, Christology, or eschatology.[60] For Wogaman, creation is crucial because it specifies how God engages with the structures of this world.[61] Fedler also makes the creation stories of Genesis 1–3 central.[62] Thielicke, whose volume on sexual ethics influenced countless subsequent generations, also stressed Genesis as the foundation for a Christian view of sexuality and reproduction.[63] Yoder's pacifist ethics, by contrast, depends almost entirely on Jesus as the norm, urging a nonviolent orientation for Christians.[64] Ironically, Niebuhr, not a pacifist, also makes Jesus' ethic central.[65] Peters, a Lutheran, and Cole-Turner of the United Church of Christ (Reformed tradition) both argue that redemption is as important as creation.[66] Thus, different Protestants will emphasize different texts from Scripture as grounding for moral knowledge.

Tradition

Noting that the "authority" of Scripture is a political claim, Hauerwas declares that such authority derives from the existence of a community. Tradition is therefore crucial because it is the way a community remembers and reinterprets its past. Reinterpreting the past means that "traditions by their nature require change."[67]

However, just as there is no consensus among Protestants about proper use of Scripture, so Stout declares flatly: "There is no consensus among students of morality concerning the nature and significance of tradition in ethics."[68] Following Luther's rebellion against the Roman Catholic Church, Protestants have often seen tradition as too inconsistent and corruptible to be a good source of moral authority.[69]

Nonetheless, Protestants do make use of tradition as a source of moral insight, whether drawing on the written theologies of previous thinkers or simply on "the experience of churches during nearly two thousand years of history."[70] Some Protestants, notably Anabaptists and Mennonites, draw heavily on early church practices.[71] If community is crucial for Christian moral life, then the church is a necessary and decisive context for moral discernment.[72] Some would separate church as its own distinctive source of moral knowledge; others see it primarily as a bearer of tradition.[73] The church is important as the venue in which Scripture is read and the "Word of God" preached. Verhey, for instance, draws on the Apostles' Creed as a source of ethical wisdom.[74] The church, suggests Jones, helps us learn how to forgive.[75] Thus, while there may be no consensus on what is included in "tradition" or how it is to be used, clearly many Protestants would agree with Burtchaell that "we begin by being told, by listening to the tradition."[76] The church offers "theological companionship" to help us discern what our witness requires.[77] Protestantism itself began as a historical "renewal movement" and Rasmussen suggests that all such movements can be models for Christian decision-making and structure.[78]

In addition to the *teachings* of the church, *structures* and *practices* may be sources of moral discernment. Calvin's great work, the *Institutes of the Christian Religion*, gave considerable attention to the offices of the church and its polity.[79] Calvinists have tended to stress church discipline, believing that we meet God in the church, through its sacraments, preaching, and ministries.[80] In his classic *Social Teachings of the Christian Churches*, Troeltsch illuminated the ways in which the very structures of Protestant denominations and sects instill moral messages.[81] Churches teach not just by what they *say* but by what they *do* and how they are configured.

Practices within churches—worship, baptism, passing the peace, tithing, silence, testimony, prayer, communion, reading Scripture, and foot washing—provide sources of moral knowledge as well.[82] But West reminds us that church structures and liturgical practices can also be oppressive and need constant re-examination and revision.[83]

In ethics, later generations almost always refer to earlier ones. Calvin was in dialogue with the Fathers of the Roman Catholic Church and also with other Reformers.[84] Both he and Luther were influenced significantly by Augustine's theology.[85] Some contemporary authors draw specifically on statements from their own denominational tradition,[86] but with the strong ecumenical movement of the mid-twentieth century, most Protestants attend to a wide range of Christian views, including Roman Catholic theology.[87] Some utilize traditional African religions or the Asian tradition of "han," and so on. The range of sources of moral knowledge is expansive today. As Hefner puts it, "We are creatures of tradition, but it is a dynamic, living tradition—never static."[88]

This very expansiveness, however, raises questions regarding the criteria both for appropriation of one's own tradition and for inclusion of insights from other traditions. The clash may not be tradition versus Scripture, but faithful tradition versus irresponsible tradition.[89] With centuries of tradition oppressive to minority groups and women, liberation theologians are skeptical about the authority of tradition as a source of moral knowledge. As with Scripture, the question of correct interpretation and use of tradition is contested.

Reason

Reason can be a source of moral knowledge in several ways. Roman Catholic theology teaches that God created the world with an end or "telos" built into its structures.[90] This end is accessible to reason. Some Protestants pick up this "natural law" approach—e.g., Luther's "orders of creation"—and therefore give reason a strong place in moral discernment.[91] Both Luther and Calvin saw a place for reason to discern God's will through a law "written on our hearts" or in our "consciences."[92]

However, Protestants also assert that reason is distorted by sin. Calvin declares: "The soundness of reason in man is gravely wounded through sin."[93] For many Protestants, then, reason is fallible and not a certain guide to discerning right and wrong.[94] We thus need additional help: the Ten Commandments, the preaching of Scripture, the practices of churches, etc. The development of ethical *principles* or axioms can be seen as one expression of the use of reason in Protestant ethics. Ramsey's covenant fidelity would be one such principle.[95] Fletcher's principle of "love alone" would be another. Wogaman points to Bennett's development of "middle axioms" as an attempt to express the demands of the Gospels in terms that could be widely accessible.[96] Of course, some Protestants have argued strongly against principles: Bonhoeffer, sometimes considered the "father" of situation ethics, argues that general principles are inadequate to cope with everyday difficulties; ethical discourse must always be concrete and specific.[97] Brunner, Kierkegaard, and Barth also resist any effort to put "laws" into Christian ethics.

Another use of reason is in setting criteria for an adequate ethical approach. Arguing that we need a rational method of moral judgment, Wogaman proposes that any moral judgments must be tentative, faithful to central affirmations of Christian faith, and open to clarifying dialogue.[98] He suggests that we adopt an initial presupposition about the superiority of one course of action and then test it against contradictory evidence. Hence, reason, experience, and tradition work together. Grenholm also offers criteria for a "reasonable" ethical theory: universalizability, integration with scientific knowledge, consistency, agreement with human experience, and agreement with significant elements of Scripture and tradition.[99]

Thus, reason is a *sine qua non* for most Protestants, and some are noted for their reliance on reason. Calvin broke with humanism over the question of human sinfulness, but he was widely read in philosophy[100] and remained "respectful to well-conducted reasoning."[101] Jonathan Edwards attempted to formulate Christian theology in philosophical language not dependent on references to Scripture.[102] Brunner argued that Christians must give *reasons* for preferring monogamy.[103] Fletcher's *Situation Ethics* may be associated with the notion that "love is all you need," but he used reason as well as the collected wisdom of prior generations.[104] Bonhoeffer asserted that "possibilities and consequences must be carefully assessed."[105] Such assessment implies the use of reason. Indeed, Bonhoeffer thought the lack of "natural law" was a great loss to Protestant faith.[106]

Contemporary Protestants speaking to a broad audience, especially in fields such as bioethics, depend on cogency of argument.[107] Discussing gene therapy, for instance, Ramsey begins with careful definitions of terms and spends the bulk of his essay in reasoned critique of proposals for gene therapy.[108] Mott argues that social ethics requires that we bring in all that can be known about social and economic structures—hence, using modern social science. Property arrangements and land tenure systems in the Bible are quite different than Western property systems, and this means that Biblical injunctions cannot simply be applied to contemporary problems.[109] Thus, reason is crucial both in developing cogent argument and in distinguishing morally relevant differences. It is partly for these reasons that Swedish Lutheran Jackelen suggests that religion and science share much in their methods and processes.[110]

Scientific "expertise" has become important to moral discernment in Protestantism, and it is noteworthy that contemporary discussions of reproductive ethics (see below) often begin with reviews of scientific developments before turning to theological affirmations. Since science is always adding knowledge, this means that ethics can never be closed or finalized.[111]

Experience

While Scripture may be foundational and reason a "sine qua non" for most contemporary Protestants, some turn directly to human experience as the primary source of moral knowledge. Schleiermacher insisted that experience rather than reason is central to God-consciousness.[112] Soelle asserts that contemporary statements of religious claims "simply do not make sense unless they take into consideration the centrality of experience."[113] However, what is meant by experience and what experiences are taken as central differs dramatically among theologians.

"Conscience" or the "inner light" is invoked by some and is central for Protestants such as Quakers.[114] Certainly, for John Wesley, the movement of the spirit within the believer is a primary source of moral insight. He draws heavily on Scripture, but stresses the inward witness of the Spirit.[115] *Conscience* becomes a crucial source of moral knowledge. Luther also stressed that we hear Scripture moved by the Spirit.[116] To the extent that being Christian is primarily about transformation, inner experiences of transformation and calling will dominate. Mohrmann argues that the crux of a Biblically-informed ethics is not a list of rules or answers to dilemmas, but rather personal and social transformation.[117] Peters also argues for the centrality of transformation.[118] It is at least partly for this reason that he draws his ethics from eschatology—from the vision of a transformed society.

Sometimes the experiences stressed are those of everyday life or of crisis moments.

For Brunner, to obey God's will is to love your neighbor.[119] This requires response to the concrete needs of the neighbor. While these are known truly only in faith, through the Spirit, God's command reaches us "through the world around us."[120] To serve our neighbor, then, we must attend to circumstances—hence, biology and anthropology become sources for a Christian ethic.[121] The "theology of the cross" in Lutheran tradition emphasizes suffering as a source of revelation.[122] Illness can lead to ethical insight.[123] Compassionate ministry to the sick and dying can be another source of moral formation.[124] As the experience of illness or suffering can be a moral teacher, so can the experience of healing.[125]

While some may stress personal experience, for Soelle it is not individual suffering but "the sighing of the oppressed creation" that is central.[126] Similarly, Miguez Bonino reports that "Christians for Socialism" once required that all affirmations be tested against everyday experience.[127] Just as Luther turned to Scripture to correct what he saw as the abuses that had crept into church tradition, contemporary Protestants turn to experience to correct what they perceive as the abuses of tradition and of Scripture. Indeed, some liberation theologians have a distinct anti-tradition emphasis.[128]

If experience is the touchstone, then we must ask, *whose* experience and under what interpretation?[129] For Cone, theological truth must be grounded in the concrete experience of those who are humiliated and abused.[130] Bonhoeffer, too, stressed the centrality of the dispossessed, humiliated, and exploited.[131] For feminists, women's lived experience must be central.[132]

However, the feminist dictum "the personal is political" means that personal experience can never be separated from institutional structures or from the language and thought forms available for framing and expressing experience. Hence, Andolsen and colleagues argue that attention to experience then requires social analysis. So do liberation theologians such as Miguez Bonino, who uses Marxist methods of analysis, particularly an analysis of class and power. Thornton argues that the theology of the cross must be interpreted politically.[133] West argues that Christian social ethics must be interdisciplinary and draw on diverse disciplines such as African-American studies, women's studies, and Biblical studies.[134] Sources of moral knowledge thus include a wide range of social sciences.

If ordinary human experience serves as a source of moral knowledge, the possible sources expand exponentially. *Action* itself can be a source of moral knowledge.[135] Activist Martin Luther King Jr., formed his ethics from the crucible of the civil rights struggle in the United States.[136] West and Ross both stress learning from the lives of those who make constructive changes in our common moral life.[137] *Prayer* is a source of moral knowledge: "Intelligence, discernment, attentive observation of the given facts, all these now come into lively operation, all will be embraced and pervaded by prayer."[138] The *activity of the church, especially in the struggle against oppression*, can be a source of moral knowledge.[139] *Conversation* or *dialogue* is stressed by some.[140] *Community* is important not only as a source of tradition but also a source of accountability, conversation, and dialogue. *Worship* practices such as baptism and passing the peace shape attitudes and perceptions.[141] *Church leadership experiences* can be important.[142] Even *bodily experience* counts, not just in illness but in our instinctual responses to various situations: "Knowledge that we acquire through our bodily perceptions must not be discounted in ethics, for it is a crucial source of moral knowledge."[143]

Today, *social media* shapes perceptions, attitudes, and ethics.[144] *Music* is a shaping force, especially but not only in Black church tradition: Watching older women sing, Saliers reflects, "Over time, participation in the practice of lifting their voices to God had worked in subtle and complex ways to shape basic attitudes, affections, and ways of regarding themselves, their neighbors, and God."[145] Similarly, *novels* may not only shape perceptions in clandestine ways, but are even used explicitly by some Protestant ethicists.[146] Works of *art* such as Edwina Sandys' 1975 "Christa" shaped many feminist views of God and what it means to do God's will in the world. In some traditions, *silences* and *meditation* are crucial sources of insight.[147]

Thus, with an emphasis on human experiences, moral knowledge may come from many different quarters. The crucial question, then, may be whether experience trumps other sources or whether experience itself has to be tested by the light of reason, the weight of tradition, or the centrality of the Gospel message.[148]

Implications for Reproductive Ethics

From the beginning of the Protestant Reformation, reformers held that human sexuality has two goods or purposes—union and procreation—and that these are of equal importance. This has serious implications for reproductive ethics. Both Luther and Calvin believed that marriage and family are a vocation and that the greatest good of marriage is children, but both also valued the joy of conjugal sex apart from reproduction.[149] Thus, most Protestants accept contraception and planned parenting, and Brunner considered birth control a duty.[150] Protestants even countenance abortion under some circumstances.[151]

While Vaux suggests that artificial insemination and surrogate motherhood would also be accepted,[152] new technologies are raising challenges to traditional views and differences arise within Protestant circles. Methodist Ramsey threw down the gauntlet in 1970, arguing that just because we *can* do something does not mean that we *should* do it. Ramsey held that the two "goods" of sexuality should never be separated. Hence, artificial insemination using the husband's sperm would be acceptable, but artificial insemination using donor sperm would not, because it separates love-making from the generation of new life.[153] Lutheran Meilaender continues this line of thought. For him, using donated gametes from either man or a woman turns procreation into "reproduction," and this is contrary to the Christian understanding of children as a gift from God, created by love.[154]

In clear contrast to Meilaender is another Lutheran, Ted Peters. Peters begins with experience—with stories of children and childlessness. Taking both covenant and love as central themes, he argues that "God loves each of us regardless of our genetic makeup, and we should do likewise."[155] Because his ethics is based in eschatology—in God's promised future—the creation stories and human biology are not determinative. Peters therefore countenances surrogate motherhood and other modern technological interventions in childbearing, with the good of the child as the criterion.

Cole-Turner, representing the United Church of Christ from Reformed tradition, agrees with Peters that creation is not the important grounding for Christian ethics; rather, we must look to redemption. Theology must learn from science and traditional views of sin must be reinterpreted.[156] Adopting the United Church of Christ dictum, "God is still speaking," Cole-Turner suggests that God works through science; hence, new technologies can be embraced.

Also from Reformed tradition, Presbyterian Peterson-Iyer attempts to reconcile these divergent views while emphasizing a feminist perspective.[157] Like Cole-Turner, she begins with a review of the science and of liberal arguments made for "designer children" (specifically the argument of John Robertson's *Children of Choice*). It is not until the fourth chapter that Christian theology is introduced specifically. In dialogue with a number of contemporary figures—Gustafson, Hauerwas, Meilaender, Lebacqz, and others—Peterson-Iyer suggests that there are two primary paradigms operative. "Stewardship" has dominated in Christian history and is represented by Ramsey and Meilaender. In this paradigm, we accept limits to our powers in accord with God's intentions. By contrast, "co-creation"—adopted by Peters and Cole-Turner—stresses the creative power of humans and tends to support human intervention into reproductive processes. Peterson-Iyer walks a fine line between these paradigms, stressing the hopefulness that accompanies the co-creation approach and yet recognizing that nature may reflect God's will and set some limits to what we may ethically do. Like Peters, she offers as a basic principle the best interests of the child. To develop a picture of what it might mean for humans to flourish, she draws on philosopher Martha Nussbaum. As a feminist, Petersen-Iyer insists that any genetic technologies to be used must be safe for women. Drawing on these premises, she then uses reasoned argument to address specific cases: prevention of cystic fibrosis, memory enhancement, and sex pre-selection.

Peterson-Iyer's work illustrates many features of contemporary mainstream Protestant approaches to moral knowledge. She draws heavily on reason, science, and experience, somewhat lightly on Scripture and tradition; she remains in dialogue with Christian colleagues while addressing a wider audience; she finds some basic principles grounded in her faith; and she reasons carefully in applying those to specific cases. In a pluralistic world with challenges to tradition and Scripture, most mainstream Protestants will stress reason, experience, and science. They attempt to appeal to a broad audience and often translate Christian values and claims into more secular language.

Yet there remains a fundamental challenge to any Protestant ethics, laid down by Bonhoeffer. Christian ethics, he argued, must be a "critique of all ethics simply as ethics." For Bonhoeffer, Christians should know things only in God, and in the knowledge of God the knowledge of good and evil is overcome. Hence the very effort to know good and evil or right and wrong or to translate faith into secular categories or philosophical reasoning would already indicate alienation from the proper origins of moral discernment.[158] Brunner argued a similar point: since love is a response to the concrete needs of the neighbor, it is the end of all law and hence "of all ethics."[159] If ethics is taken to be encompassed by rules or philosophical categories, then Bonhoeffer and Brunner have a point: Protestant ethics must not lose its ultimate source in God. However, the review here suggests that Protestant ethics need not be equated with laws or rules, and that there is no single Protestant approach to moral knowledge. Perhaps it is best to join Brunner in saying that when it comes to marriage and procreation, "the Christian ethic must learn new ways."[160] That is what contemporary Protestants attempt to do, using Scripture, tradition, reason, and experience.

Notes

1. Karen Lebacqz, "Justice and Biotechnology: Protestant Views," in *The Routledge Companion to Religion and Science*, ed. James W. Haag et al. (New York: Routledge, 2012), 449. C.f. Paul Althaus, *The Ethics of Martin Luther*, trans. Robert C. Shultz (Philadelphia: Fortress Press, 1972), 12; Allan Aubrey Boesak, *Farewell to Innocence: A Socio-Ethical Study on Black Theology and Power* (Maryknoll, NY: Orbis Press, 1977), 142; Dietrich Bonhoeffer, *Ethics*, ed. Eberhard Bethge (New York: Macmillan, 1965), 142; James H. Smylie, "The Reformed Tradition," in *Caring and Curing: Health and Medicine in the Western Religious Traditions*, ed. Ronald L. Numbers and Darrel W. Amundsen (New York: MacMillan, 1986), 205; Kenneth L. Vaux, *Health and Medicine in the Reformed Tradition* (New York: Crossroad, 1984), 90; Collin W. Williams, *John Wesley's Theology Today* (Nashville: Abingdon Press, 1960), 196.
2. https://en.wikipedia.org/wiki/Wesleyan_Quadrilateral.
3. James M. Gustafson, *Can Ethics Be Christian?* (Chicago: University of Chicago Press, 1975), 161.
4. Rosemary Radford Ruether, *Sexism and God-Talk: Toward a Feminist Theology* (Boston: Beacon Press, 1983), 12.
5. Ron Hamel and Edwin R. Dubose, "Views of the Major Faith Traditions," in *Active Euthanasia, Religion, and the Public Debate*, ed. Ron Hamel and Edwin R. Dubose (Parkridge, IL: Parkridge Center, 1991).
6. Smylie, "The Reformed Tradition," 204.
7. Audrey R. Chapman, *Unprecedented Choices: Religious Ethics at the Frontiers of Genetic Science* (Minneapolis: Fortress Press, 1999), 245. See also John C. Bennett, *Christian Ethics and Social Policy* (NY: Scribner, 1946).
8. J. Philip Wogaman, *Christian Ethics: A Historical Introduction* (Louisville, KY: Westminster/John Knox Press, 1993), 267.
9. Karl Barth, *Ethics*, ed. Dietrich Braun; trans. Geoffrey W. Bromily (New York: Seabury Press, 1981), 350; Emil Brunner, *The Divine Imperative* (Philadelphia: Westminster Press, 1947), 59; Bonhoeffer, *Ethics*, 273.
10. Carl-Henric Grenholm, *Protestant Work Ethics: A Study of Work Ethical Theories in Contemporary Protestant Theology* (Uppsala, Sweden: Uppsala University, 1993); Reinhold Niebuhr, *Moral Man and Immoral Society: A Study in Ethics and Politics* (New York: Charles Scribner's Sons, 1932).
11. Lars Ostnor, "Stem Cells from Human Embryos for Research? The Theological Discussion within Christianity," in *Stem Cells, Human Embryos, and Ethics: Interdisciplinary*

Perspectives, ed. Lars Ostnor, 205–220 (Springer, 2008); Traci C. West, *Disruptive Christian Ethics: When Racism and Women's Lives Matter* (Louisville, KY: Westminster/John Knox, 2006); Chapman, *Unprecedented Choices*, 245.

12. See, for example, Robert M. Veatch, *The Foundations of Justice: Why the Retarded and the Rest of Us Have Claims to Equality* (New York: Oxford, 1986); Karen Peterson-Iyer, *Designer Children: Reconciling Genetic Technology, Feminism, and Christian Faith* (Cleveland: Pilgrim Press, 2004).
13. Gilbert Meilaender, *Bioethics: A Primer for Christians*, 2nd ed. (Grand Rapids, MI: Eerdmans, 2005), xi.
14. Barbara Andolsen et al., eds. *Women's Consciousness, Women's Conscience: A Reader in Feminist Ethics* (San Francisco: Harper and Row, 1985), xxiii.
15. J. Philip Wogaman, *A Christian Method of Moral Judgment* (Philadelphia: Westminster Press, 1976), 5.
16. Gunnar Heiene, "Theological Arguments in the Human Stem Cell Debate: A Critical Evaluation," in *Stem Cells, Human Embryos, and Ethics: Interdisciplinary Perspectives*, ed. Lars Ostnor, 226 (Springer, 2008).
17. Wogaman, *A Christian Method*, 152.
18. Veatch, *The Foundations of Justice*, 65; Courtney S. Campbell, "Religion and Moral Meaning in Bioethics," *Hastings Center Report* 20, no. 4 (July/August 1990): 5.
19. Andolsen et al., *Women's Consciousness*, xxi.
20. Chapman, *Unprecedented Choices*, 230.
21. Hessel Bouma III et al., *Christian Faith, Health, and Medical Practice* (Grand Rapids, MI: Eerdmans, 1989), 93.
22. Bruce C. Birch and Larry Rasmussen, *Bible and Ethics in the Christian Life* (Minneapolis: Augsburg, 1976), 11; cf. Allen Verhey, "The Bible and Bioethics: Some Problems and a Proposal," in *On Moral Medicine: Theological Perspectives in Medical Ethics*, 3rd ed., ed. M. Terese Lysaught and Joseph J. Kotva, Jr. (Grand Rapids, MI: Eerdmans, 2012), 100.
23. John Dillenberger, *Martin Luther: Selections from His Writings Edited and with an Introduction* (New York: Doubleday 1961), 86–87.
24. Smylie, "The Reformed Tradition," 205.
25. Birch and Rasmussen, *Bible and Ethics*, 22; cf. Richard J. Mouw, "Biblical Imperatives," in *From Christ to the World: Introductory Readings in Christian Ethics*, ed. Wayne G. Boulton, et al., 32 (Grand Rapids, MI: Eerdmans, 1994).
26. James M. Gustafson, "Ways of Using Scripture," in Boulton, *From Christ to the World*, 25ff.
27. Division of Mission in Canada, "A Brief to the Royal Commission on New Reproductive Technologies on behalf of the United Church of Canada," January 17, 1991: 1–24.
28. United Methodist Church Genetic Science Task Force, a background paper for the General Conference. Nashville, Tennessee: The United Methodist Publishing House, 1992.
29. Stanley Hauerwas, "The Moral Authority of Scripture," in Boulton, *From Christ to the World*; cf. Birch and Rasmussen, *Bible and Ethics*, 46–64.
30. Wogaman, *Christian Ethics*, 278.
31. David F. Wells, *No Place for Truth: Or Whatever Happened to Evangelical Theology?* (Grand Rapids, MI: Eerdmans, 1993).
32. John Murray, *Principles of Conduct: Aspects of Biblical Ethics* (Grand Rapids, MI: Eerdmans, 1957), 7–8.
33. David P. Gushee, "Reconciling Evangelical Christianity with Our Sexual Minorities: Reframing the Biblical Discussion," *Journal of the Society of Christian Ethics* 3, no. 2 (2015): 150.

34. Birch and Rasmussen, *Bible and Ethics*, 45.
35. Mouw, "Biblical Imperatives," 32; cf. Kyle D. Fedler, *Exploring Christian Ethics: Biblical Foundations for Morality* (Louisville, KY: Westminster/John Knox, 2006), 54.
36. Brent Waters, "A Theological Reflection on Reproductive Medicine," in *New Conversations: Medical Technology and Christian Decision-Making*, ed. Ronald Cole-Turner (Cleveland: United Church of Christ, 2002), 35–39.
37. Birch and Rasmussen, *Bible and Ethics*, 144.
38. Stephen Charles Mott, *Biblical Ethics and Social Change* (New York: Oxford, 1982), ix.
39. Chapman, *Unprecedented Choices*, 230; Verhey, "The Bible and Bioethics," 98–100.
40. Fedler, *Exploring Christian Ethics*, 53.
41. Brunner, *The Divine Imperative*, 87.
42. Gustafson, "Ways of Using Scripture," 21.
43. Hauerwas, "The Moral Authority of Scripture," 36.
44. Meilaender, *Bioethics*, 1.
45. Boesak, *Farewell to Innocence*, 9; James Cone, "Biblical Revelation and Social Existence," in Boulton, *From Christ to the World*, 58.
46. Wogaman, *Christian Ethics*, 226; cf. Reinhold Niebuhr, *An Interpretation of Christian Ethics* (New York: Seabury, 1979), 5.
47. L. Gregory Jones, "Forgiveness," in Bass, *Practicing Our Faith*.
48. Paul Ramsey, *The Patient as Person: Explorations in Medical Ethics* (New Haven, CT: Yale University, 1970), xi; Bouma et al., *Christian Faith, Health, and Medical Practice*, 83; Ted Peters, *For the Love of Children: Genetic Technology and the Future of the Family* (Louisville, KY: Westminster/John Knox, 1996), 3.
49. Bennett, *Christian Ethics and Social Policy*; Gene Outka, *Agape: An Ethical Analysis* (New Haven, CT: Yale University, 1972); Gustafson, *Can Ethics Be Christian*, 162.
50. Walter Rauschenbusch, *A Theology for the Social Gospel* (New York: Macmillan, 1917), 52.
51. Althaus, *The Ethics of Martin Luther*, 8; cf. Wogaman, *Christian Ethics*, 109.
52. Sondra Wheeler, "Power, Trust, and Reticence: Genetics and Christian Anthropology," in Cole-Turner, *New Conversations*, 21ff.
53. John Howard Yoder, "The Authority of Tradition," in Boulton, *From Christ to the World*, 95.
54. See the "Statement on Human Stem Cell Research" of the Ethics and Religious Liberty Commission of the Southern Baptist Convention, 2004 (www.erlc.com/statement)
55. Paul Ramsey, *Deeds and Rules in Christian Ethics* (New York: Charles Scribner's Sons, 1967).
56. Gustafson, *Can Ethics Be Christian*, 149; Barth, *Ethics*, 350.
57. Bennett, *Christian Ethics and Social Policy*, 76–77; Chapman, *Unprecedented Choices*, 66, 221, 235.
58. West, *Disruptive Christian Ethics*, 76, 93.
59. Boesak, *Farewell to Innocence*, 9.
60. Grenholm, *Protestant Work Ethics*, 216ff.
61. Wogaman, *A Christian Method*, 68.
62. Fedler, *Exploring Christian Ethics*, 81.
63. Helmut Thielicke, *Theological Ethics, Volume 3: Sex* (Grand Rapids, MI: Eerdmans, 1964), 3.
64. Wogaman, *A Christian Method*, 33.
65. Niebuhr, *An Interpretation*, 22.
66. Ted Peters, *The Stem Cell Debate* (Minneapolis: Fortress, 2007), 96; Peters, *For the Love of Children*, 25; Ronald Cole-Turner, *The New Genesis: Theology and the Genetic Revolution* (Louisville, KY: Westminster/John Knox, 1993).

67. Hauerwas, "The Moral Authority of Scripture," 34–40.
68. Jeffrey Stout, "Tradition in Ethics," in Boulton, *From Christ to the World*, 61.
69. For an excellent, concise summary of Protestant tradition, see Wogaman, *Christian Ethics*.
70. Bennett, *Christian Ethics and Social Policy*.
71. John D. Roth, "The Christian and Anabaptist Legacy in Healthcare," in Lysaught and Kotva, *On Moral Medicine*, 128; Willard M. Swartley, "The Bible and Christian Convictions," in Lysaught and Kotva, *On Moral Medicine*, 127.
72. Dietrich Bonhoeffer, *Life Together*, trans. John W. Doberstein (New York: Harper and Row, 1954); cf. Birch and Rasmussen, *Bible and Ethics*, 125f.
73. Birch and Rasmussen, *Bible and Ethics*, 127; David B. McCurdy, "End-of-Life Decisions and Medical Technologies: The Congregational Context," in Cole-Turner, *New Conversations*, 49–65.
74. Verhey, "The Bible and Bioethics," 103.
75. Jones, "Forgiveness," 138.
76. James Tunstead Burtchaell, C.S.C., "Community Experience as a Source of Christian Ethics," in Boulton, *From Christ to the World*, 66.
77. Waters, "A Theological Reflection," 46; cf. McCurdy, "End-of-Life Decisions," 9.
78. Larry Rasmussen, "Shaping Communities," in Bass, *Practicing Our Faith*, 128.
79. John Calvin, *Institutes of the Christian Religion*, ed. John T. McNeill; trans. Ford Lewis Battles (Philadelphia: Westminster, 1960 [1560]); cf. Francois Wendel, *Calvin: Origins and Development of His Religious Thought* (New York: Harper and Row, 1963), 111ff.
80. Smylie, "The Reformed Tradition," 205–209.
81. Ernst Troeltsch, *The Social Teachings of the Christian Churches*, trans. Olive Wyon (New York: MacMillan, 1931 [1911]); cf. Wogaman, *Christian Ethics*, 179.
82. Craig Dykstra and Dorothy C. Bass, "Time of Yearning, Practices of Faith," in Bass, *Practicing Our Faith*, 9; Stephanie Paulsell, "Honoring the Body," in Bass, *Practicing Our Faith*, 20; Shalon Daloz Parks, "Household Economics," in Bass, *Practicing Our Faith*, 56; Vaux, *Health and Medicine*, 93; West, *Disruptive Christian Ethics*, 113; Williams, *John Wesley's Theology*, 133–135; Thomas Hoyt, Jr., "Testimony," in Bass, *Practicing Our Faith*, 91.
83. West, *Disruptive Christian Ethics*, 125ff.
84. Wendel, *Calvin*, 122.
85. Williams, *John Wesley's Theology*, 52f; cf. Wogaman, *Christian Ethics*, 109.
86. See, for example, Olivia Masih White, "Stem Cell Research: Promise or Conflict?" in Cole-Turner, *New Conversations*, 74.
87. See, for example, Peters, *For the Love of Children*.
88. Philip Hefner, "Life in Religion-and-Science," *Theology and Science* 13, no. 1 (2015): 15; cf. Douglas Ottati, "What It Means to Stand in a Living Tradition," in Boulton, *From Christ to the World*, 82.
89. Yoder, "The Authority of Tradition," in Boulton, *From Christ to the World*, 94.
90. Gustafson, *Can Ethics Be Christian*, 150.
91. Grenholm, *Protestant Work Ethics*, 216ff.
92. Althaus, *The Ethics of Martin Luther*, 25; Wendel, *Calvin*, 193; Gustafson, *Can Ethics Be Christian*, 152.
93. Calvin, *Institutes*, 258.
94. Althaus, *The Ethics of Martin Luther*, 27.
95. Wogaman, *A Christian Method*, 24.

96. Ibid., 21. Chapman, *Unprecedented Choices*, 221, criticizes the lack of middle axioms in Protestant bioethics today.
97. Bonhoeffer, *Ethics*, 264ff.
98. Wogaman, *A Christian Method*, 36ff.
99. Grenholm, *Protestant Work Ethics*, 227ff.
100. Vaux, *Health and Medicine*, 112.
101. Wendel, *Calvin*, 35.
102. Jonathan Edwards, *The Nature of True Virtue* (Ann Arbor: University of Michigan, 1960). See the introduction by William Frankena. Descriptions of Edwards' philosophical approach to Christian ethics may also be found at www.jonathanedwards.com/text/JGEdwards.htm.
103. Brunner, *The Divine Imperative*, 342.
104. Wogaman, *A Christian Method*, 15.
105. Bonhoeffer, *Ethics*, 40.
106. Ibid., 143.
107. Gustafson, *Can Ethics Be Christian*, 163.
108. Paul Ramsey, "Genetic Therapy: A Theologian's Response," in *The New Genetics and the Future of Man*, ed. Michael P. Hamilton (Minneapolis: Eerdmans, 1972), 157–175.
109. Mott, *Biblical Ethics*, vii–ix.
110. Antje Jackelen, "Cosmology and Theology," in *The Routledge Companion to Religion and Science*, ed. James W. Haag et al. (New York: Routledge, 2012), 135–144.
111. Wogaman, *Christian Ethics*, 232.
112. Ibid., 166.
113. Dorothee Soelle, *Death by Bread Alone: Texts and Reflections on Religious Experience*, trans. David L. Scheidt (Philadelphia: Fortress Press, 1978), 33.
114. Vaux, *Health and Medicine*, 90; Wogaman, *Christian Ethics*, 139–141.
115. Williams, *John Wesley's Theology*, 33.
116. Althaus, *The Ethics of Martin Luther*, 32.
117. Margaret E. Mohrmann, *Medicine as Ministry* (Cleveland: Pilgrim Press, 1995).
118. Peters, *The Stem Cell Debate*, 95ff.
119. Brunner, *The Divine Imperative*, 59.
120. Ibid., 84, 118, and 125.
121. Ibid., 209.
122. Daniel R. Smith, "A Lutheran Theological Response to Climate Change," *Theology and Science* 13, no. 1 (2015): 68; cf. Sharon G. Thornton, *Broken Yet Beloved: A Pastoral Theology of the Cross* (St. Louis: Chalice Press, 2002).
123. Bradley Hanson, "School of Suffering," in Lysaught and Kotva, *On Moral Medicine*, 448; William Stringfellow, *A Second Birthday: A Personal Confrontation with Illness, Pain, and Death* (Eugene, OR: Wipf and Stock, 1970). However, Shelp and Sutherland argue that the Gospels provide little insight into the role of illness or suffering in God's creation. See Earl E. Shelp and Ronald H. Sutherland, "AIDS and the Church," in Lysaught and Kotva, *On Moral Medicine*, 453.
124. Amy Plantinga Pauw, "Dying Well," in Bass, *Practicing Our Faith*, 175.
125. John Koenig, "Healing," in Bass, *Practicing Our Faith*, 152.
126. Soelle, *Death by Bread Alone*, 128.
127. Jose Miguez Bonino, *Doing Theology in a Revolutionary Situation* (Philadelphia: Fortress Press, 1975), xxiii.

128. Ibid., 75ff.
129. Carol S. Robb, "A Framework for Feminist Ethics," in Boulton, *From Christ to the World*, 226.
130. James H. Cone, *A Black Theology of Liberation* (New York: J. B. Lippincott, 1970), 11.
131. Bonhoeffer, *Ethics*, 137.
132. Aana Vigen, "Listening to Women of Color with Breast Cancer: Theological and Ethical Insights for U.S. Healthcare; and 'Keeping It Real' While Staying Out of the 'Loony Bin': Social Ethics for Healthcare Systems," in Lysaught Lysaught and Kotva, *On Moral Medicine*, 165.
133. Thornton, *Broken Yet Beloved*, 17.
134. West, *Disruptive Christian Ethics*, xviii.
135. Miguez Bonino, *Doing Theology*, 88.
136. James M. Washington, ed., *A Testament of Hope: The Essential Writings and Speeches of Martin Luther King, Jr.* (San Francisco: HarperSanFrancisco, 1986).
137. West, *Disruptive Christian Ethics*, 141; Rosetta E. Ross, "Health Care and the Moral Imagination: Considering the Kind of Society We Want to Be," in Cole-Turner, *New Conversations*, 67.
138. Bonhoeffer, *Ethics*, 40.
139. Boesak, *A Farewell to Innocence*, 3, 11, 39.
140. Hefner, "Life in Religion-and-Science, 11; Vigen, "Listening to Women of Color," 165; West, *Disruptive Christian Ethics*, xv. The journal *Dialogue*, edited by Lutheran Ted Peters, also testifies to the importance of conversation and dialogue as sources of moral knowledge.
141. Paulsell, "Honoring the Body," in Bass, *Practicing Our Faith*.
142. West, *Disruptive Christian Ethics*.
143. Ibid., 42.
144. Gushee, "Reconciling Evangelical Christianity."
145. Don E. Saliers, "Singing Our Lives," in Bass, *Practicing Our Faith*, 185.
146. Katie G. Canon, *Black Womanist Ethics* (Atlanta: Scholars Press, 1988), 5; cf. West, *Disruptive Christian Ethics*.
147. Parks, "Household Economics," 56; cf. Soelle, *Death by Bread Alone*, 71–79.
148. Boesak, *A Farewell to Innocence*, 12.
149. See Althaus, *The Ethics of Martin Luther*, 83–96; Martin E. Marty, *Health and Medicine in the Lutheran Tradition* (New York: Crossroad, 1983), 127, 132; cf. Bonhoeffer, *Ethics*, 176; Smylie, "The Reformed Tradition," 211; Vaux, *Health and Medicine*, 94.
150. Brunner, *The Divine Imperative*, 369; see also Smylie, "The Reformed Tradition," 227.
151. Ibid., 227.
152. Vaux, *Health and Medicine*, 94.
153. Paul Ramsey, *Fabricated Man: The Ethics of Genetic Control* (New Haven, CT: Yale University, 1970), 36, 133.
154. Meilaender, *Bioethics*, 19.
155. Peters, *For the Love of Children*, 4, 34, 52.
156. Cole-Turner, *The New Genesis*, 89.
157. Petersen-Iyer, *Designer Children*.
158. Bonhoeffer, *Ethics*, 17.
159. Brunner, *The Divine Imperative*, 79.
160. Ibid., 372.

Bibliography

Althaus, Paul. *The Ethics of Martin Luther*. Translated by Robert C. Schultz. Philadelphia: Fortress, 1972.

Andolsen, Barbara Hilkert, Christine E. Gudorf, and Mary D. Pellauer, eds. *Women's Consciousness, Women's Conscience: A Reader in Feminist Ethics*. San Francisco: Harper and Row, 1985.

Barth, Karl. *Ethics*. Edited by Dietrich Braun; translated by Geoffrey W. Bromiley. New York: Seabury, 1981.

Bass, Dorothy C., "Keeping Sabbath." In *Practicing Our Faith*, edited by Dorothy C. Bass, 75–89. San Francisco: Jossey-Bass, 1997.

Bass, Dorothy C., ed. *Practicing Our Faith*. San Francisco: Jossey-Bass, 1997.

John C. Bennett. *Christian Ethics and Social Policy*. NY: Scribner, 1946.

Birch, Bruce C. and Larry L. Rasmussen. *Bible and Ethics in the Christian Life*. Minneapolis: Augsburg, 1976.

Boesak, Allan Aubrey. *Farewell to Innocence: A Socio-Ethical Study on Black Theology and Power*. Maryknoll, NY: Orbis, 1977.

Bonhoeffer, Dietrich. *Life Together*. Translated by John W. Doberstein. New York: Harper and Row, 1954.

Bonhoeffer, Dietrich. *Ethics*. Edited by Eberhard Bethge. New York: Macmillan, 1965.

Boulton, Wayne G., Thomas D. Kennedy, and Allen Verhey, eds. *From Christ to the World: Introductory Readings in Christian Ethics*. Grand Rapids, MI: Eerdmans, 1994.

Bouma, Hessel, III, Douglas Diekema, Edward Langerak, Theodore Rottman, and Allen Verhey. *Christian Faith, Health, and Medical Practice*. Grand Rapids, MI: Eerdmans, 1989.

Brunner, Emil. *The Divine Imperative*. Philadelphia: Westminster Press, 1947.

Burtchaell, James Tunstead, C.S.C. "Community Experience as a Source of Christian Ethics." In *From Christ to the World: Introductory Readings in Christian Ethics*, edited by Boulton et al., 64–79. Grand Rapids, MI: Eerdmans, 1994.

Calvin, John. *Institutes of the Christian Religion, Vols. I and II*. Edited by John T. McNeill; translated by Ford Lewis Battles. Philadelphia: Westminster, 1960 [1560].

Campbell, Courtney S. "Religion and Moral Meaning in Bioethics." *Hastings Center Report* 20, no. 4 (July/August 1990): 4–10.

Canon, Katie G. *Black Womanist Ethics*. Atlanta: Scholars Press, 1988.

Chapman, Audrey R. *Unprecedented Choices: Religious Ethics at the Frontiers of Genetic Science*. Minneapolis: Fortress, 1999.

Cole-Turner, Ronald, ed. *New Conversations: Medical Technology and Christian Decision-Making*. Cleveland: United Church of Christ, 2002.

Cole-Turner, Ronald. *The New Genesis: Theology and the Genetic Revolution*. Louisville: Westminster/John Knox, 1993.

Cone, James. "Biblical Revelation and Social Existence." In *From Christ to the World: Introductory Readings in Christian Ethics*, edited by Boulton et al., 58. Grand Rapids, MI: Eerdmans, 1994.

Cone, James H. *A Black Theology of Liberation*. New York: J. B. Lippincott, 1970.

Dillenberger, John. *Martin Luther: Selections from His Writings Edited and with an Introduction*. New York: Doubleday, 1961.

Division of Mission in Canada. "A Brief to the Royal Commission on New Reproductive Technologies on Behalf of The United Church of Canada," approved by the Executive of the Division of Mission, January 17, 1991: 1–24.

Dykstra, Craig, and Dorothy C. Bass. "Time of Yearning, Practices of Faith." In *Practicing Our Faith*, edited by Dorothy C. Bass, 1–12. San Francisco: Jossey-Bass, 1997.

Edwards, Jonathan. *The Nature of True Virtue*. Ann Arbor: University of Michigan, 1960 [1755].

Ethics and Religious Liberty Commission of the Southern Baptist Convention. "Statement on Human Stem Cell Research." 2004. www.erlc.com/statement on human stem cell research.

Fedler, Kyle D. *Exploring Christian Ethics: Biblical Foundations for Morality*. Louisville: Westminster/John Knox, 2006.

Grenholm, Carl-Henric. *Protestant Work Ethics: A Study of Work Ethical Theories in Contemporary Protestant Theology*. Uppsala, Sweden: Uppsala University, 1993.

Gushee, David P. "Reconciling Evangelical Christianity with Our Sexual Minorities: Reframing the Biblical Discussion." *Journal of the Society of Christian Ethics* 35, no. 2 (2015): 141–158.

Gustafson, James M. *Can Ethics Be Christian?* Chicago: University of Chicago Press, 1975.

Gustafson, James M. "Ways of Using Scripture." In *From Christ to the World: Introductory Readings in Christian Ethics*, edited by Boulton et al., 21–26. Grand Rapids, MI: Eerdmans, 1994.

Hamel, Ron, and Edwin R. Dubose. "Views of the Major Faith Traditions." In *Active Euthanasia, Religion, and the Public Debate*, edited by Ron Hamel and Edwin R. Dubose, 45–77. Parkridge, IL: Parkridge Center, 1991.

Hanson, Bradley. "School of Suffering." In Lysaught and Kotva, *On Moral Medicine*, 448–453.

Hauerwas, Stanley. *Character and the Christian Life: A Study in Theological Ethics*. San Antonio: Trinity University, 1975.

Hauerwas, Stanley (with Richard Bondi and David B. Burrell). *Truthfulness and Tragedy: Further Investigations in Christian Ethics*. Notre Dame: University of Notre Dame, 1977.

Hauerwas, Stanley. "The Moral Authority of Scripture." In Boulton et al., *From Christ to the World*, 33–50.

Hefner, Philip. "Life in Religion-and-Science," *Theology and Science* 13, no. 1 (2015): 8–24.

Heiene, Gunnar. "Theological Arguments in the Human Stem Cell Debate: A Critical Evaluation." In *Stem Cells, Human Embryos, and Ethics: Interdisciplinary Perspectives*, edited by Lars Ostnor, 221–235. Springer, 2008.

Hoyt, Thomas Jr. "Testimony." In Bass, *Practicing Our Faith*, 91–103.

Jackelen, Antje. "Cosmology and Theology." In *The Routledge Companion to Religion and Science*, edited by James W. Haag et al., 135–144. New York: Routledge, 2012.

Jones, L. Gregory. "Forgiveness." In Bass, *Practicing Our Faith*, 133–147.

Koenig, John. "Healing." In Bass, *Practicing Our Faith*, 149–162.

Lebacqz, Karen. "Justice and Biotechnology: Protestant Views." In *The Routledge Companion to Religion and Science*, edited by James W. Haag et al., 449–454. New York: Routledge, 2012.

Lysaught, M. Therese, and Joseph J. Kotva Jr., eds. (with Stephen E. Lammers and Allen Verhey). *On Moral Medicine: Theological Perspectives in Medical Ethics*. 3rd ed. Grand Rapids, MI: Eerdmans, 2012.

Marty, Martin E. *Health and Medicine in the Lutheran Tradition*. New York: Crossroad, 1983.

McCurdy, David B. "End-of-Life Decisions and Medical Technologies: The Congregational Context." In *New Conversations: Medical Technology and Christian Decision-Making*, edited by Ronald Cole-Turner, 49–65. Cleveland: United Church of Christ, 2002.

Meilaender, Gilbert. *Bioethics: A Primer for Christians*. 2nd ed. Grand Rapids, MI: Eerdmans, 2005.

Miguez Bonino, Jose. *Doing Theology in a Revolutionary Situation*. Philadelphia: Fortress Press, 1975.
Mohrmann, Margaret E. *Medicine as Ministry*. Cleveland: Pilgrim Press, 1995.
Mott, Stephen Charles. *Biblical Ethics and Social Change*. New York: Oxford, 1982.
Mouw, Richard J. "Biblical Imperatives." In Boulton et al., *From Christ to the World*, 31–33.
Murray, John. *Principles of Conduct: Aspects of Biblical Ethics*. Grand Rapids, MI: Eerdmans, 1957.
Niebuhr, Reinhold. *Moral Man and Immoral Society: A Study in Ethics and Politics*. New York: Charles Scribner's Sons, 1932.
Niebuhr, Reinhold. *An Interpretation of Christian Ethics*. New York: Seabury, 1979.
Ostnor, Lars. "Stem Cells from Human Embryos for Research? The Theological Discussion within Christianity." In *Stem Cells, Human Embryos, and Ethics: Interdisciplinary Perspectives*, edited by Lars Ostnor, 205–220. Springer, 2008.
Ottati, Douglas F. "What It Means to Stand in a Living Tradition." In Boulton et al., *From Christ to the World*, 79–87.
Outka, Gene. *Agape: An Ethical Analysis*. New Haven, CT: Yale University Press, 1972.
Parks, Sharon Daloz. "Household Economics." In Bass, *Practicing Our Faith*, 43–58.
Paulsell, Stephanie. "Honoring the Body." In Bass, *Practicing Our Faith*, 13–27.
Pauw, Amy Plantinga. "Dying Well." In Bass, *Practicing Our Faith*, 163–177.
Peters, Ted. *For the Love of Children: Genetic Technology and the Future of the Family*. Louisville: Westminster/John Knox Press, 1996.
Peters, Ted. *The Stem Cell Debate*. Minneapolis: Fortress Press, 2007.
Peterson-Iyer, Karen. *Designer Children: Reconciling Genetic Technology, Feminism, and Christian Faith*. Cleveland: Pilgrim Press, 2004.
Ramsey, Paul. *Deeds and Rules in Christian Ethics*. New York: Charles Scribner's Sons, 1967.
Ramsey, Paul. "Genetic Therapy: A Theologian's Response." In *The New Genetics and the Future of Man*, edited by Michael P. Hamilton, 157–175. Minneapolis: Eerdmans, 1972.
Ramsey, Paul. *Fabricated Man: The Ethics of Genetic Control*. New Haven, CT: Yale University Press, 1970.
Ramsey, Paul. *The Patient as Person: Explorations in Medical Ethics*. New Haven, CT: Yale University Press, 1970.
Rasmussen, Larry. "Shaping Communities." In Bass, *Practicing Our Faith*, 119–132.
Rauschenbusch, Walter. "Social Ideas in the New Testament." In Boulton et al., *From Christ to the World*, 27–31.
Rauschenbusch, Walter. *A Theology for the Social Gospel*. New York: Macmillan, 1917.
Robb, Carol S. "A Framework for Feminist Ethics." In Boulton et al., *From Christ to the World*, 223–229.
Ross, Rosetta E. "Health Care and the Moral Imagination: Considering the Kind of Society We Want to Be." In Cole-Turner, *New Conversations*, 67–72.
Roth, John D. "The Christian and Anabaptist Legacy in Healthcare." In Lysaught and Kotva, *On Moral Medicine*, 128–130.
Ruether, Rosemary Radford. *Sexism and God-Talk: Toward a Feminist Theology*. Boston: Beacon Press, 1983.
Saliers, Don E. "Singing Our Lives," In Bass, *Practicing Our Faith*, 179–193.
Shelp, Earl E., and Ronald H. Sutherland, "AIDS and the Church." In Lysaught and Kotva, *On Moral Medicine*, 453–461.
Smith, Daniel R. "A Lutheran Theological Response to Climate Change." *Theology and Science* 13, no. 1 (2015): 64–78.

Smylie, James H. "The Reformed Tradition" in *Caring and Curing: Health and Medicine in the Western Religious Traditions*, edited by Ronald L. Numbers and Darrel W. Amundsen, 204–239. New York: MacMillan, 1986.

Soelle, Dorothee. *Death by Bread Alone: Texts and Reflections on Religious Experience*. Translated by David L. Scheidt. Philadelphia: Fortress Press, 1978.

Stout, Jeffrey. "Tradition in Ethics." In Boulton et al., *From Christ to the World*, 61–62.

Stringfellow, William. *A Second Birthday: A Personal Confrontation with Illness, Pain, and Death*. Eugene, OR: Wipf and Stock, 1970.

Swartley, Willard M. "The Bible and Christian Convictions." In Lysaught and Kotva, *On Moral Medicine*, 126–128.

Thielicke, Helmut. *Theological Ethics, Volume 3: Sex*. Grand Rapids, MI: Eerdmans, 1964.

Thornton, Sharon G. *Broken Yet Beloved: A Pastoral Theology of the Cross*. St. Louis: Chalice Press, 2002.

Troeltsch, Ernst. *The Social Teachings of the Christian Churches*. Translated by Olive Wyon. New York: MacMillan, 1931 [1911].

United Methodist Church Genetic Science Task Force. Background paper for the General Conference. Nashville, Tennessee: The United Methodist Publishing House, 1992.

Vaux, Kenneth L. *Health and Medicine in the Reformed Tradition*. New York: Crossroad, 1984.

Veatch, Robert M. *The Foundations of Justice: Why the Retarded and the Rest of Us Have Claims to Equality*. New York: Oxford, 1986.

Verhey, Allen. "The Bible and Bioethics: Some Problems and a Proposal." In Lysaught and Kotva, *On Moral Medicine*, 97–113.

Vigen, Aana. "Listening to Women of Color with Breast Cancer: Theological and Ethical Insights for U.S. Healthcare; and 'Keeping It Real' While Staying Out of the 'Loony Bin': Social Ethics for Healthcare Systems." In Lysaught and Kotva, *On Moral Medicine*, 165–184.

Washington, James M., ed. *A Testament of Hope: The Essential Writings and Speeches of Martin Luther King, Jr*. San Francisco: HarperSanFrancisco, 1986.

Waters, Brent. "A Theological Reflection on Reproductive Medicine." In Cole-Turner, *New Conversations*, 35–47.

Wells, David F. *No Place for Truth: Or Whatever Happened to Evangelical Theology?* Grand Rapids, MI: Eerdmans, 1993.

Wendel, Francois. *Calvin: Origins and Development of His Religious Thought*. New York: Harper and Row, 1963.

West, Traci C. *Disruptive Christian Ethics: When Racism and Women's Lives Matter*. Louisville: Westminster/John Knox Press, 2006.

Wheeler, Sondra. "Power, Trust, and Reticence: Genetics and Christian Anthropology." In Cole-Turner, *New Conversations*, 21–34.

White, Olivia Masih. "Stem Cell Research: Promise or Conflict?" In Cole-Turner, *New Conversations*, 73–77.

Williams, Colin W. *John Wesley's Theology Today*. Nashville: Abingdon Press, 1960.

Wogaman, J. Philip. *Christian Ethics: A Historical Introduction*. Louisville: Westminster/John Knox Press, 1993.

Wogaman, J. Philip, *A Christian Method of Moral Judgment*. Philadelphia: Westminster Press, 1976.

Yoder, John Howard. "The Authority of Tradition." In *From Christ to the World: Introductory Readings in Christian Ethics*, edited by Wayne G. Boulton et al., 91–101. Grand Rapids, MI: Eerdmans, 1994.

CHAPTER 4

MUSLIM REPRODUCTIVE ETHICS

Sources and Methodology

ABDULAZIZ SACHEDINA

As scientists speak about the possibility of noncoital production of human embryos through somatic-cell nuclear transfer (SCNT or the "Dolly technique") or using the cells from in vitro human embryos that have lost their capacity to form a new individual, Muslim religious scholars, for the first time, are probing in detail the ethics of sexual and asexual procreation in the light of certain reproductive technologies that transgress the boundaries of normatively conceived sexual reproduction. The advent of new reproductive technologies made possible what is impossible in nature—except through some kind of divine intervention, such as the immaculate birth of Jesus reported in the Muslim holy book, the Qur'an. These new technologies also challenge respect for life and human dignity in radical ways, raising difficult ethical issues for all societies. Some of the ethical concerns are conveyed in a critical question in Muslim culture: What could happen to the heterologous child that was created from three or more genetic parents? The preservation of proper lineage in order for the child to be related to his/her biological parents is one of the fundamental purposes of the sacred law of Islam, the Shari'a. Accordingly, a child's homologous identity through a legitimate conjugal relationship between a man and a woman in marriage is so essential in Islam and Muslim culture that it is regarded as a child's inalienable right. Proper lineage in Muslim culture is critical in forging an appropriate relationship between parents and the child, and in claiming rights that accrue to the child in the Shari'a.

The sacred law of Islam, as a comprehensive religious-moral system, strives to integrate the private and public realms of human life to provide total guidance about the way human beings ought to live with one another and with themselves. Islam regards human institutions—whether cultural, religious, or political—as instruments of a single goal: fulfillment of the purposes of the Merciful and Compassionate God. Muslim ethics tries to make sense of human moral instincts, institutions, and traditions in order to provide a foundation of rules and principles that can govern a virtuous life. Its judgments are ethical in the sense that they seek to elaborate criteria for making basic moral distinctions such that reasonable people can agree on what is good and bad, praiseworthy and blameworthy, in human relationships and human institutions. This ethical philosophy encompasses the most important issues of human life: suffering, illness, and death; reproduction and abortion; law and justice; and so on. As God's creatures, humans' welfare and conduct ultimately fall under God's divine governance as mediated and interpreted by God's prophets.

Hence, under divine guidance, a child's lineage or genealogy signifies a reputed relationship with respect to father and mother, or with respect to fathers only. The term also suggests consanguinity based on blood relationship. In Islamic ethical-legal system lineage is understood as a genealogical relationship that emerges through biological reproduction relating to the union of male and female gametes in a sexual act between a man and woman in a marriage, thereby giving rise to the parent-child and brother-sister relationships. The term lineage (Arabic *nasab*) in the context of this paper is restricted to this homologous creation, which contains same genes located in the same places, without considering its legal ramifications. It is also important to underscore the distinction that is being made between natural and assisted reproduction in Muslim societies. As long as technologically assisted reproduction occurs within a marriage, the lineage of the child remains secure by relating the infant to his/her biological parents. However, if the gametes that are fertilized in IVF clinics cannot be related to a married couple, then the Shari'a denies lineage to the child, unless the identity of the donors is known. In that case, the child is related to the donor of the sperm.

The above, randomly cited Muslim judicial decisions regarding a child's lineage raise an important question for our readers: How do Muslims solve their ethical problems in biomedicine? Are there any distinctive theories or principles in Islamic ethics that Muslims apply in deriving moral judgments in bioethics? Is the revealed Law, the Shari'a, as an integral part of Islamic ethics, the only recognized source of prescriptive precedents in Islam? Can it serve as a paradigm for the moral experience of contemporary Muslims living in changing social and cultural contexts? Do human experience and/or intuitive reasoning have a legitimate role in Islamic moral reflection?

In this chapter I will examine the nature of Islamic ethical discourse in order to demonstrate that ethical judgments in Islam are an amalgam of the empirical—the relative cultural elements derived from the particular experience of Muslims living in a specific place and time—and the a priori—the timeless universal norms derived from the juridical sources composed by Muslim legal scholars.

The Islamic juridical tradition seeks to address and accommodate and reconcile the demands of justice and public good. In dealing with immediate questions about assisted reproduction technology (ART) Muslim jurists draw on legal doctrines and rules in addition to analogical reasoning based on some related paradigm cases. The practical judgments or legal opinions, known as *fata>wa>*, reflect the insights of a jurist who has been able to connect cases to an appropriate set of linguistic and rational principles and rules that can provide a basis for a valid conclusion of a given case.

The enunciation of underlying ethical principles and rules that govern practical ethical decisions is crucial for making any religious perspective an intellectually insightful voice in the contemporary debate about a morally defensible cross-cultural ethics of reproduction. All cultures share certain moral principles (beneficence, compassion, honesty, and so on), all require rules like truthfulness and confidentiality as essential elements in regulating a responsible physician-patient relationship, yet major global controversies persist on issues such as the right of a woman to terminate pregnancy or to receive a third-party donor semen to conceive a child against competing individual and community moral considerations. What kind of ethical resources do different traditions possess that might lead to a common ethical discourse about, and perhaps even a resolution of, global controversies in matters related to sex selection as a form of gender family planning in bioethics?[1]

The Question of Cultural Relativism in Ethical Values

Surrogate motherhood was not known to the classical Muslim jurists in the tenth century CE. With the provision of polygamy, the immediate solution to infertility was always a second wife, sometimes with the encouragement and approval of the first wife, and at other times with the disapproval or even divorce of the first wife. But the new possibility that the second wife now can gestate an embryo that carried the gametes of the husband and the first wife (who, because of the medical conditions, could not carry it to its full term) through IVF required precise determination about whether the procreation had occurred within the same family unit. The legal doctrine provided an important rule that required the jurists to avert probable harm before any consideration of benefit that accrued to the agent through such a medical intervention in modern times. Theoretically, ethical values seek cultural legitimacy by adapting themselves to prevailing economic and social-political circumstances. Accordingly, these values arise in a climate of cultural relativity. Since human reason depends on the data of experience to make correct ethical judgments, moral presuppositions interact with the specific social experiences to yield culturally conditioned moral justifications.[2] In fact, even objectivist ethical theories, which presuppose transcultural validity for moral standards, include a certain aspect of social or conventional relativism.[3] Similar arguments against the universalizability of a single bioethical theory in an inherently pluralistic ethical discourse are commonly heard in national and international biomedical ethics conferences.

In this chapter my purpose is not merely to search for Islamic equivalents of the primary principles of autonomy, nonmaleficence, beneficence (including utility), and justice, but also to make a strong case for a distinctly Islamic yet metaculturally communicable and principled deontological-teleological ethics[4] that could aid in the assessment of moral problems in Islamic biomedical ethics.

The process has already begun in Egypt and Iran, where religious scholars, medical professionals, and the government are searching for ontological foundations of Islamic law to enable them to reconcile Islamic teachings with the demands of modern clinical medicine and biomedical research. I mention Egypt and Iran only because these are the only Muslim countries where religious scholars, the ulema, are engaged in formulating national policies related to health care. In Iran one can even observe the relative independence enjoyed by the religious scholars from governmental interference in formulating their judicial decisions.

Let us keep in mind that in Islamic practice even when the source of normative life was believed to have been revealed by God in the Shari'a, the procuring of a judgment and its application was dependent upon reasons used in moral deliberation. This moral deliberation took into account particular human conditions. The prevailing custom, for instance, is the major source of legitimacy that relates a child to his/her biological parents. Under one circumstance, however, Islamic law has refused to grant a genealogical recognition to an offspring: when the child is conceived through an act of adultery, an illicit sexual relationship under Shari'a law. In more recent rulings, an exception is made when the act of penetration is regarded by man and the woman as inadvertent. In such a case, the lineage of the child is acknowledged as unblemished and he/she is related to the couple. In that way, the law has protected the child's lineage by relating him/her to biological parents even when the conception had occurred outside the legitimate sexual relation. To be sure, Islamic law developed its rulings within the pluralistic cultural and historical experience of Muslims living in the different parts of the Islamic world. It recognized the autonomy of other moral systems within its sphere of influence, without imposing its judgments on peoples with different cultural beliefs and practices. More importantly, it recognized the validity of differing interpretations of the same revealed system within the community, thereby giving rise to different schools of legal thought and practice in Islam. In the absence of an organized "church" or a theological body authorized to speak for the entire tradition or the community, Islam has remained inherently discursive and pluralistic in its methods of deliberation and justification of moral actions. Hence, on the basis of particular application of principles and rules to emerging ethical issues, like a woman's right to abortion following a rape or incest, it is possible to observe differing judicial opinions.

The Nature of Islamic Ethical Discourse

When one considers the normative sources for standards of conduct and character it becomes obvious that besides Scriptural sources, Muslim scholars have recognized the value of decisions derived from specific human conditions as an equally valid source for social ethics in Islam. Early on, the theologian-jurists conceded that the Scriptural sources could not easily cover every situation that might arise, especially when Muslim political rule required rules for urban life, commerce, and government in advanced countries. How exactly was human intellectual endeavor to be directed to discover the rationale (*'illa*), the philosophy and the purpose behind certain paradigm rulings (known as *al-as}l*, plural *us}u>l*) provided in God's commandments, in order to formulate principles for future decisions?

The question had important implications for the administrators of justice, who were faced with practical necessity of making justifiable, nonarbitrary legal rulings. There was a fear of reason in deriving the details of law. The fear was based on the presumption that if independent human reason could judge what is right and wrong, it could rule on what God could rightly prescribe for humans. However, it was admitted that although revealed law can be known through reason and aid human being in cultivating the moral life, human intelligence was not capable of discovering the reasons for a particular law, let alone demonstrate the truth of a particular assertion of the divine commandment. In fact, as these theologian-jurists asserted, the divine commandments to which one must adhere if one is to achieve a specific end prescribed in the revealed law are not objectively accessible to human beings through reason. Moreover, judgments of reason are deemed arbitrary since they often contradict each other and can simply reflect personal desire of the legal expert.

One problem, then, was resolving the substantive role of reason in understanding the implicit rationale of a paradigm case and elaborating the juridical-ethical dimension of revelation as it relates to the conduct of human affairs in public and private spheres. Another problem was situating credible religious authority empowered to provide validation to the ethical-legal reasoning associated with the philosophy behind legal rulings. On the one hand, Sunni Islam, following the lead of their early scholars, located that authority in the Qur'an and the Tradition. The Sunni scholars represented the predominant schools of Sunni theology, which held that questions of Islamic law could be resolved from the working out of an entire system based on a juridical elaboration of the Scriptural sources. On the other hand, following the line of thought maintained by the Shiite imams, Shiite Islam located that authority in the rightful successors to the Prophet. The Shiite imams maintained that there was an ongoing revelatory guidance available in the expository ability of human reason in comprehending the divine revelation. It is exemplified by the solutions offered by the Shiite religious leadership.

In general, Muslim theologian-jurists were interested in the extent of God's power and human freedom of will as it affected the search for a right prescription for human behavior. In view of the absence of the institutionalized religious body that could provide the necessary validation of the legal-moral decisions on all matters pertaining to human existence, it proved difficult to elucidate the Sacred Lawgiver's intent in juridical rulings that had direct relevance to the social life of the community. The intellectual activity related to Islamic juridical-ethical tradition can be summed up as the attempt to relate specific moral-legal rulings (*ah}ka@m*, singular *h{ukm*) to the divine purposes expressed in the form of norms and rules in the Qur'an and the Tradition, notwithstanding the tangle of ambiguities that impeded the task. Given the incomplete state of knowledge about the present circumstances and future contingencies, the jurists proceeded to make ethical judgments with a cautious attitude on the basis of what seemed "most likely" (*z}ann*) to be the case. Such ethical judgments were normally appended with a clear, pious statement that the ruling lacked certainty. Only God was knowledgeable about the true state of affairs.[5]

In due course, the jurists were able to identify two methods of understanding the justification behind a moral-legal decision. Sometimes the rationale was derived directly from the explicit statements of the Qur'an and the Tradition that set forth the purpose of legislation. At other times, human reason discovered the relationship between the ruling and the rationale. The jurists admitted and determined the substantive role of human reasoning in grounding the legitimacy of a legal or moral decision. Moreover, human reason's role depended upon the jurist's comprehension of the nature of ethical knowledge and the means by which humans can access information about good and evil. In other words, it depended upon the way the human act was defined in terms of human ethical discernment about good and evil and the relation of human act to God's will. Any advocacy of reason as a substantive rather than formal source for procuring moral-legal verdicts required authorization derived from sources like the Qur'an and the Tradition. It is possible to read the Qur'an as advancing a teleological view of human beings as endowed with the ability to use reason to discover God's will, especially when the revelation itself endorses reflection on the reasons for revealed laws as well sheer obedience to them. All the jurist-theologians, whether Sunni or Shiite, maintained that without the endorsement of revelation reason could not become an independent source of moral-legal decisions.

This precautious attitude toward reason has its roots in the belief that God's knowledge of the circumstances and of the consequences in any situation of ethical dilemma confronted by human existence is exhaustive and infallible. Whereas the Qur'an and the Tradition had provided the underlying justification for some moral-legal rulings when declaring them obligatory or prohibited, on a number of issues the rulings were expressed as divine commands that had to be obeyed even if the reasons behind them remained unfathomable to human reason. Thus, for instance, the effective cause for the duty of seeking medical treatment is to avoid grave and irremediable harm to oneself, whereas the reason for prohibition against taking human life is the sanctity of life as declared by the revelation. The commandments were simply part of God's prerogative as the Creator to demand unquestioning obedience to them. To act in a manner contrary to divine commands is to act both immorally and unlawfully. The major issue in legal thought, then, was defining the admissibility and the parameters of human reasoning as a substantive source for legal-moral decisions. Can reason discover the divine will in confronting emerging legal-ethical issues without being eclipsed by human self-interest?

The introduction of reproductive technologies in the Muslim world has introduced unprecedented possibilities for treating infertility and a host of other issues. Technologies such as in vitro fertilization, gamete intra-fallopian transfer (GIFT) and zygote intra-fallopian transfer (ZIFT) have provided women with the liberty to control reproduction and find solutions to infertility and unwanted pregnancies. Birth control technology raised ethical issues for a number of Muslim scholars, who, on the basis of the principle of rejection of harm, ruled that the use of such technology is forbidden. The option of terminating a pregnancy evoked debates about the rights of the fetus and responsibility of parents and medical practitioners in making such decisions.

In 1970s in vitro fertilization (IVF) to treat human infertility marked the beginning of the revolution in making possible what is impossible in nature. The technique of mixing the sperm and eggs in a petri dish was originally developed to get around the woman's damaged or absent fallopian tubes, which connect ovaries to the uterus. In 1978 the technique was successfully used to fertilize the eggs and implant the resultant product as a way to treat infertility. However, this procedure raised major ethical concern about a woman's egg being fertilized outside the body and then being injected in the fallopian tubes of the mother or surrogate mother. The Tradition had always traced the lineage of the child to the sexual union of a man and woman. In one case, however, the jurists had to rule on the legitimacy of a child who was conceived asexually by a woman who manually introduced into her uterus the sperm that she considered to be her husband's. An asexual pregnancy without penetration created a problem of attribution of the child to the man. When the man refused to recognize this child, who was conceived asexually, the jurists ascribed it to the mother as the Qur'an did (Q. 58:2), because they did not regard the pregnancy as adulterous. By analogy, then, although assisted reproductive technology has no precedent in the classical juridical formulations, its legitimization within a marriage is not difficult to infer.

The ethical debates among Muslim scholars were prompted by the potential of charge of illicitness of the artificial insemination with donor sperm (AID). While artificial insemination with husband's sperm (AIH) was more or less endorsed as permissible by majority of the Sunni and Shiite scholars, the traditions that prohibited depositing a stranger's sperm in a woman's vagina, in addition to the Qur'anic concern with the "guarding of the private parts" by abstaining from sexual relations outside a marriage, raised serious concerns about the morality of asexual in vitro reproductive procedures.

In deriving the new decisions about reproductive technology the jurists were engaged in providing fresh hermeneutics to the Qur'anic verses and the traditions that correlated the trustworthiness of the lineage of the child with the sexual modesty. According to the Qur'an, both man and woman were required to "guard their private parts" from illegitimate sexual relationship. The extrapolation of this prohibition to include or exclude assisted reproduction, whether AIH or AID, depended upon seeing the logical connection between sexual modesty and legitimate lineage of the offspring. The ruling to preserve the child's lineage, as the jurists were to argue, could not be guaranteed without restricting the access to the private parts only to the legitimate partners in a marriage. Hence, Fakhr al-Di>n al-Ra>zi> (d. 1209), the Sunni commentator, declares in no uncertain terms that all the references in the Qur'an to "guarding one's private parts" refer to abstaining from adultery, except one, in which, both men and women are required to refrain from looking at the private parts of one another (Q. 24:31–32).

Notwithstanding the unknowns in the traditional law, the benefits of IVF in treating infertility were obvious, as long as such fertilization was achieved within the legitimate boundaries of marriage. However, as was customary in Islamic juridical deliberations, little attention was paid to the moral and social implications of the procedure over the nature of the child's identity and relationship to the family, on the one hand, and the status of multiple human embryos that were produced in the petri dish, and then implanted to increase the possibility of pregnancy, on the other. In the case of multiple pregnancies doctors recommended abortion of some of the embryos to avoid endangering mother's health and improve the chances of survival for one. Besides two to three embryos that were injected for gestation, there were additional embryos that were frozen for use in further, future attempts. What is the status of these inseminated and frozen embryos? Could they be used later in further attempts at having a first child or for additional children? Who owns them if the couple later divorce or if one of them dies? Could they be simply discarded as "unwanted" embryos? Could they be used to derive stem cells for research and therapeutic purposes? According to recent developments in research ethics, currently all its ramifications are speculatively assessed in order to advance potential cures for many people with chronic, debilitating, fatal, degenerative disorders.

Undeniably, IVF had a limited goal of correcting a natural condition to allow a would-be-mother to carry a fertilized embryo to its full term of gestation. Keeping in mind the plurality in the Muslim legal opinions on new bioethical issues, in spite of the fact that there were some dissenting voices among both the Sunni and the Shiite scholars, a majority of them came to endorse the IVF technology with the stipulation that the procedure itself should not lead to any sinful act contrary to the rulings about the man-woman relationship in the Shari'a. Hence, even when some scholars had reservations about the procedures of producing gametes asexually, including the morally questionable act of masturbation to derive the sperm, IVF became a routine medical practice in the Muslim world to help women who could afford expensive reproductive technology to conceive. In addition, in order to avoid surgery, since doctors can now be guided by ultrasound to the ovaries to retrieve eggs vaginally, this somewhat invasive procedure raises questions about a third-party male physician (other than the woman's father, husband or brother) having access to the private parts of the woman. This is morally problematic from the Islamic code of modesty for women. There was no immediate solution to address this latter problem since there were not enough physicians, male or female, to perform the IVF procedures without invading the privacy that was protected by Islamic code of modesty.

In majority of the cases of infertility, if the family was well-to-do, the treatment was sought abroad, where such Islamic sensibilities about male-female relationships were altogether absent. Nevertheless, the issue, however academic in nature, was general enough to require a sensible and immediate solution in view of the shortage of women specialists in all areas of medicine. I have specified the problem as academic because for the generality of the people, if they could afford to see a physician for any ailment, it hardly mattered whether the patient was seen by a male or female doctor. Before the spread of modern mass education, infertility was a serious problem in the family and in the society at large. Married couples who could not have a child left no stone unturned to become parents, which included even financial hardship. Consequently, the legal hair-splitting that was part of the seminary culture and was meant for consumption among the traditional scholars of Islamic law rarely filtered down to the ordinary folks looking for practical solutions, except in the form of ruling that either permitted or forbade a procedure.

However, as pointed out earlier, IVF clinics were faced with serious questions like the frozen surplus embryos that were produced for the future implantation if the pregnancy did not occur the first time around. Juridical solutions were not hard to deduce when legal principles like public good (*mas}lah}a*) that promotes what is beneficial, and necessity (*d}aru>ra*) that overrules prohibition, could provide moral-legal justification for the use of surplus embryos as the source for derivation of stem cells for research. After all, as some prominent jurists were to point out, sanctity of life principle does not apply to the embryos that are outside the womb. Consequently, since stem cell research enhanced the possibility of discovering cures for incurable diseases, the principle of public good provided justification to use frozen embryos to isolate stem cells.

The future use of frozen embryos for posthumous transfer of intra-fallopian gamete to a widow was another problem that required meticulous understanding of the status of the frozen embryo to make sure whether it could be treated as a property that belonged to the legally married couple. If it were established that the frozen embryo is in the usual sense a property then it was subject to the laws governing ownership and transfer of property that belonged to the biological father and mother. However, is it really a property? There was no doubt that if the couple was alive, both had a right to determine the use of their embryos. What if one of them died? Then the complexity of the problem came to the fore as the jurists began to question the widow's right to use the frozen embryo, when legally, because of the death of her husband, the contract that wedded her to him became invalid. She was no more his wife, and hence, the newborn could not use his name as part of her/his identity.

The Principles and Rules in Islamic Juristic Ethics

Theological debates about ethical evaluation of human actions and of the nature of the human being as a moral agent were foundational in the development of Islamic jurisprudence. The consideration of ethical good and prevention of evil as self-evident to the sound mind made the legal doctrines adaptable to the contemporary legal problems and issues. The ultimate purpose of the legal deliberations entailed doing justice and preserving people's best interests on earth and in the Hereafter. How was that purpose to be fulfilled when all possible human contingencies in the future were not covered in the revelation, whether the Qur'an or the Tradition?

Here paradigm cases (preserved in the form of a *h}adi>th*-report) played a critical role as discoverers of divine purposes for human institutions. Contrary to commonsense expectations that the application of judicial decisions must be posterior to the prior elaboration of legal theory, Islamic jurisprudence actually antedated the genre of paradigm cases. Muslim scholars were able to appropriate these paradigm cases to resolve more immediate cases because these cases had the backing of the consensus built upon the practice of the community. The legal decisions preserved in the paradigm cases mark a transition point wherein the cumulative tradition, the Sunna, was utilized to document substantive law. As precedents for subsequent legal decisions, these cases indicated the underlying rationale (*'illa*) upon which depended the final judgment in those cases. Such cases became the sources for the development of juridical principles and rules. The novel issues were then settled through the evocation of these principles and rules.

At other times principles like justice and equity that were stated directly and in most general terms in the revelation were to be applied to concrete situations in the Muslim society to determine the level of culpability in cases of violation of justice. The intellectual responsibility of a Muslim legal expert included providing the definition of the nature of religiously prescribed justice and its determination in the given context of a particular case, whether it was distributive or corrective. Moreover, he had to determine whether the scale of violation necessitated financial or other forms of compensation recognized in the penal system. Undoubtedly, a major part of a Muslim jurist's training dealt with learning these principles and rules in the context of the Qur'an and the Tradition to offer new methods of approach to problem solving in the society. In the context of this chapter we need to determine the most important juridical doctrines and principles that have been evoked in the contemporary situation to provide the necessary solutions for novel issues in assisted reproductive technology.

ISLAMIC PRINCIPLES OF BIOETHICS

In our discussion about the ethical theories known among Muslims, human reason and its substantive role in deriving legal-ethical decisions, whether through the references to the relevant principles or prescriptive precedents, occupied a central place. Sunni Muslim ethicists assigned a minimal and, to a certain extent, formal role for reason to discover the correlation between divine command and human good. Here, precedents derived from the revelation, both the Qur'an and the Tradition, served as paradigmatic cases for casuistic decisions. Moreover, ethical reflection occurred within the Tradition as a process of discernment of principles that were embedded in propositional statements in the form of rulings (*fata>wa>*) as well as approved practice of the earlier jurists. The relationship between legal-ethical judgments and the principles in such cases is overshadowed by reference to revelation, however far-fetched it might appear. It is important to keep in mind that for Sunni Muslims, knowledge of rules of law and ethics is anchored in divine revelation and not in human intuitive reason (*'aql*). The process of deriving rules from the revelation is founded upon the interpretation of texts. In this sense, Islamic law is a body of positive rules by virtue of the formulations of jurists based on the revealed texts rather than the dictates of their own intuition. The exposition of law depended on text-oriented approach, although a great deal of positive law in the area of interpersonal relations was derived from individual discretion in employing intuitive reasoning.

The substantive role for reason was propounded by Muslim ethicists belonging to the Shiite school of thought who saw human reason capable of not only discovering the divine purposes for human society, but also establishing the correlation (*mula>zama*) between human moral judgment and divine commandments. They identified the major principles and rules ensuing from both revelation and rational sources that could be used to make fresh decisions in all areas of interpersonal relationship. In other words, these principles and rules became general action guides to determine the ethical valuation of an act and declare it as incumbent or necessary (*wa>jib*), prohibited (*h{ara>m*), permitted (*muba>h{*), recommended (*mustah{abb*), or reprehensible (*makru>h*) in the context of specific circumstances. But the process of ethical reflection did not necessarily involve unchanging norms from which other rules or judgments were deduced. Rather, it involved a dialectical progression between the insights and beliefs of the jurists and the paradigmatic cases in the revelation that embedded principles and rules for solving particular cases. Nevertheless, there were certain principles that transcended relative circumstances in history and tradition and which became the source for solving contemporary moral problems.

However, there was no unanimity among the representatives of four major Sunni legal schools of thought (Ma>liki>, H}anafi>, Sha>fi'i>, and H}anbali>) regarding the principles nor that these principles were derived from foundational, rationalistically established moral theories from which other principles and legal-moral judgments were deduced. Rather, scholars from different legal schools identified several principles, often but not always the same ones. Since the language of Shari'a is the language of obligation or duty, the primary principles (*qawa>'id us{u>l*) and rules (*qawa>'id fiqhi>*) in Islamic ethics are stated as obligations and their derivatives, respectively. Some jurists have identified principles to encompass both principles and rules and have indicated the primary and the subsidiary distinction in their application to particular cases.

Two such intellectual sources in Muslim jurisprudence were *istih{sa>n* (prioritization of two or more equally valid judgments through juristic practice) and *istis{la>h{* (promoting and securing benefits and preventing and removing harms in the public sphere). These represented independent juristic judgments of expedience or public utility. However, the legitimacy of employing these rationally derived principles depended upon their authentication extracted from the normative sources.

Thus, for instance, the duty to avoid literal enforcement of an existing law that might prove detrimental in certain situations has given rise to the principle of "juristic preference" (*istih{sa>n*).[6] This juridical method of prioritization of legal rulings, which takes into account the concrete circumstances of a case at hand, has played a significant role in providing the necessary adaptability to Islamic law to meet the changing needs of society. However, the methodology is founded upon an important principle derived from the directive of "circumventing of hardship," stated in the Qur'an in no uncertain terms: "God intends facility for you, and He does not want to put you in hardship" (2:185). This directive is further reinforced by the tradition that states, "The best of your law (*di>n*) is that which brings ease to the people." In other words, the principle of "juristic preference" allows formulating a decision that sidesteps an established precedent in order to uphold a higher obligation of implementing the ideals of fairness and justice without causing unnecessary hardship to the people involved. The obvious conclusion to be drawn from God's intention to provide help and remove hardship is that the essence of these principles is their adaptability in meeting the exigencies of every time and place on the basis of public interest. In the absence of any textual injunction in the Qur'an and the Tradition, the principle that "necessity overrides prohibition" furnishes an authoritative basis for deriving a fresh ruling.

The limited scope of this chapter in the context of technically assisted reproduction does not permit an exhaustive identification of all the principles that are applicable to juridical decisions in various fields of interpersonal relations in Islamic law. What seems to be most useful and feasible is to identify a number of fundamental Islamic principles that are in some direct and indirect ways discerned through the general principle of *mas{lah{a*, that is, "public good." This principle is evoked in providing solutions to a majority of novel issues in biomedical ethics, including the critical issue of justifying assisted reproduction in Muslim cultures. The rational obligation to weigh and balance an action's possible benefits against its costs and possible harms is central to social transactions in general and biomedical ethics in particular. As stated earlier, Islamic juridical studies are undertaken to understand the effective causes (*'ilal*, plural of *'illa*) that underlie some juridical decisions that deal with primary and fundamental moral obligations. The principles evoked in this chapter are not necessarily the same in priority or significance as those recognized, for instance, in Western bioethics, namely, respect for autonomy, nonmaleficence, beneficence (including utility), and justice. In comparison, Islamic principles overlap in important respects but differ in others. For instance, the two distinct obligations of beneficence and nonmaleficence in some Western systems are viewed as a single principle of nonmaleficence in Islam on the basis of the overlapping of the two obligations in the famous Tradition: "In Islam there shall be no harm inflicted or reciprocated" (*la> d{arar wa la> d{ira>r fi> al-isla>m*). This is the principle of "No harm, no harassment."[7] Moreover, the principle of "Protection against distress and constriction" (*'usr wa al-h{araj*) applies to social relations and transactions, which must be performed in good faith but are independent of religion. There are also a number of derivative rules that are an important part of the Islamic system but are underemphasized in secular bioethics. Thus, among the derivative obligations is the rule of consultation (*shu>ra>*), a feature of Islamic communitarian ethics, against the dominant principle of autonomy that is based on liberal individualism.

Moreover, although this chapter highlights the rulings compiled from four major Sunni legal schools and one Shiite school, I have attempted to identify only the most common principles or rules in biomedical jurisprudence without necessarily attributing them to one or the other school except when there has been fundamental disagreement on their inclusion in one or the other legal theory. These are the principles that have made possible the derivation of fresh rulings in bioethics by seeking to identify and balance probable outcomes in order to protect the society from harm.

In the last two decades jurists belonging to all the Muslim legal schools have met regularly under the auspices of ministry of health of their respective countries to formulate their decisions as a collective body. Some of these new rulings have been published under the auspices of *Majma' al-fiqhi> al-isla>mi>* (the Islamic Juridical Council). A close examination of the juridical decisions made in this council reveal the balancing of likely benefits and harms to society as a whole. In addition, these decisions indicate the search for proportionality (*tana>sub*) between individual and social interests of the community and the need, in certain cases, to allow collective interests to override individual interests and rights. The inherent tensions in such decisions are sometimes resolved by reference to a critical principle regarding the right of an individual to reject harm and harassment ("no harm, no harassment"), which constrains unlimited application of the principle of common good.

In terms of the principle's application, when a number of beneficial or corruptive aspects converge or when public good and corruption appear in the same instance, it gives rise to disagreement. For example, one of the issues in the Muslim world is assisted reproduction in sex selection. Sex selection is any practice, technique, or intervention intended to increase the likelihood of the conception, gestation, and birth of a child of one sex than the other. In the Muslim world, some parents prefer one sex above the other for cultural or financial reasons. Some jurists have argued in favor of sex selection, as long as no one, including the resulting child, is harmed. However, others have disputed the claim that it is possible for no harm to be done in sex selection. They point to violations of divine law, natural justice, and inherent dignity of human beings. More important, permitting sex selection for nonmedical reasons involves or leads to unacceptable discrimination on grounds of sex and disability, potential psychological damage to the resulting children, and an inability to prevent a slide down the slippery slope toward permitting designer babies. In such cases it becomes critical to assess the important criteria for the public good, or to lead the jurists to prioritize criteria that lead to public good or corruption, and provide the requisite ruling.[8]

In general, Sunni jurists were connected with the day-to-day workings of the government. Accordingly, they were required to provide solutions to every new problem that emerged in the society. In order to do this they devised methodological stratagems based on analogical reasoning (*al-qiya>s*), sound opinion (*al-ra'y*), efforts to promote the good of the people, selection of the most beneficial of several rulings (*istih}asa>n*), removal of obstruction to resolving a problem (*sadd al-dhara>y'i*), conventions and customs of the region (*'urf*), and, different forms of reasoning. Through these methodological tools they were, to a large extent, able to respond to the situations that arose in the medical practice. The Shiite jurists did not admit public good as a principle of problem resolution until more recently. Not until the Iranian revolution in 1978–79 did Shiite jurists take up the question of admitting public good as an important source for legal-ethical decision making. The direction followed by these jurists in Iran is not very different from the one followed by their Sunni counterparts throughout the political history of Sunni Islam. Shiite jurists, in contrast, were a minority and thus did not have to provide the practical guidance needed by the government or the people in everyday dealings. During the period of their imams there was little need for them to engage in intellectual approaches to ethical and legal matters.[9]

The Rule of "No Harm, No Harassment"

The rule of "No harm, no harassment" is regarded as one of the most fundamental rules for deducing rulings dealing with social ethics in Islam. Muslim jurists have discussed and debated the validity of this principle because it is regarded as one of the critical proofs in support of numerous decisions that were made in different periods of juridical development. What makes the rule authentic is its ascription to the Prophet himself. Jurists belonging to different legal schools are in agreement that the rule was set by no less a person than the founder of Islam. Hence, whether from the point of transmission or from the congruity in the sense conveyed by it, the jurists have endorsed its admission among the rules that are employed in making decisions that pertain to social and political life of the community. In fact, the Sha>fi'i-Sunni jurist al-Suyu>t}i> regards "No harm, no harassment" as one of the five major traditions that served as authoritative sources for the derivation of the rules on which depended the deduction of legal-ethical decisions in the Shari'a.[10] In addition, he affirms that the majority of juridical rubrics were founded on the principle of "No harm, no harassment," and that closely related to this principle are a number of other rules, among them this one: "Necessities make the forbidden permissible, as long as it does not lead to any detriment."[11] Some jurists include "No harm, no harassment" among the five major rules that shaped the new rulings in the area of interpersonal relations. These are as follows:

1. "Action depends upon intention." This rule is deduced from the tradition related by the Prophet: "Indeed, actions depend upon intentions."
2. "Hardship necessitates relief." This rule is inferred from the tradition that says: "No harm should be inflicted or reciprocated."
3. "One needs certainty." To continue an action requires linking the present situation with the past. This rule is rationally deduced on the basis of a juristic practice that links present doubtful condition to the previously held certain situation to resolve the case.
4. "Harm must be rejected." This rule is deduced on the basis of the need to promote benefit and institute it in order to remove causes of corruption or reduce their impact upon the possibility of having to choose the lesser of the two evils.
5. "Custom determines course of action." The rule acknowledges the need to take local custom into account when making relevant rulings.[12]

In the Shari'a, the definition of harm and harassment in negative sense depends upon custom (*al-'urf*), which determines its parameters. Custom also establishes whether harm to oneself or to another party has been done in a given situation. If custom does not construe a matter to be harmful, then it cannot be admitted as such by applying the rule itself, nor can it be considered as forbidden according to the Shari'a, even if the matter is lexically designated as "harmful." It is important to keep in mind that ultimately it is the Sacred Lawgiver who defines the parameters of harm. However, if custom regards as harmful something for which revelation offers no specific evidence against, the harm in that situation becomes more broadly defined as conditions that mediate injustice and violation of someone's rights. Moreover, harms differ as to who is causing the harm, as with self-harm and harm caused by another party. Hence, one's social status, culture, and the time in which one lives play a role in defining harm. Harm is relative to the person who experiences it. Therefore, what appears to be wrong prima facie and is regarded by one party as a harmful act may not be considered wrong or unjustified by another. Human experience, although subjective, attains considerable importance in the evaluation of the kind of harm that is to be rejected in the rule of "No harm, no harassment." The context in which the Prophet gave the rule clearly leaves the matter of harm to be determined by the situation. In the report that speaks about the harm caused by an inconsiderate neighbor who violated the privacy of his neighbor, it was a case of harmful invasion by one party of another's interest. To be sure, the rule of "No harm, no harassment" allows for the ruling that one must not become a cause for harm.[13]

The application of the ruling to reject harm has no bearing on the assessment of the actual situation when a person is going through setbacks to his interests. Nor does the Lawgiver's admission of harm in certain situations as a mediating causation for some rulings that require reparation or compensation. In the final analysis, it is the personal assessment of harm that functions as an important consideration in determining related obligations. Hence, for instance, when a person is sick, she determines whether she can keep the fast of Ramadan as required by the Shari'a in consideration of the harm that fasting can cause. Regardless of the criteria one applies to determine the level of harm, whether it is less or more, once custom establishes its existence, then the Shari'a endorses it as equally so, even when there might be a difference of opinion as to what forms of harm are more detrimental. In any case, when such a difference of opinion occurs, the law requires following the decision that leads to least harm and that causes the least damage to one's total well-being. Hence, in the case of terminally ill patient, if the decision to prolong life leads to more harm for the patient and his immediate family, then to keep him on life-saving equipment is regarded as causing further harm to the patient's and his family's well-being, and hence forbidden.

A number of subsidiary rules are related to the rule "No harm, no harassment," including the second rule, "Hardship necessitates relief," which becomes almost part of this rule. In addition, a number of traditions and verses of the Qur'an are cited to support its admission as a source of legal-ethical decision-making in order to seek benefits and avert sources of harm, or to choose the lesser of two plausible evils. In general, Muslim jurists mention subsidiary rules in various other contexts dealing with interpersonal relations to correlate the establishment of good in order to avert malevolence. Moreover, they provide guidelines that govern situations in which a person has to choose between two evils that appear to be equal, or a situation in which one of the two equal evils has preponderance because of the external or internal causes. It is important to keep in mind that although the jurists do not mention or allude to any traditions in support of the rule directly, in different contexts, when applying the five rules they assert that these are figured out on the basis of the four principal sources of Islamic jurisprudence: the Qur'an, the Tradition, consensus, and arguments based on reason.[14] Moreover, some jurists justify the rule "Hardship necessitates relief" on the basis of the same tradition that sets up the rule "No harm, no harassment," that is, "No harm shall be inflicted nor reciprocated."[15]

In sum, most jurists have accepted the rule of "No harm, no harassment" as being one of the principal sources of legal-ethical decision-making. Some others have regarded the rule being closely related to another rule that states, "No constriction, no distress," regardless of whether constriction or distress is caused by God or by human being. Many jurists base their decisions on the "No harm, no harassment" rule. They also mention the traditions that support the use of this principle in juristic method of deduction. "No harm, no harassment" is a well-established enduring principle, validated by long-standing traditions and the practice of scholars, who have viewed it as a valuable aid for promoting tolerance and averting social harm and hardship.

An obligation not to inflict harm (*nafy al-d}arar*) has been closely associated in Muslim ethics to an obligation to promote good (*istis}la>h}*). As a matter of fact, obligations of nonmaleficence and beneficence are treated under a single principle, *istis}la>h}* (promoting good). Obligations to promote good cannot be fulfilled without taking stringent measures not to harm others, including not killing them or treating them cruelly, obligations to take full account of proportionality in order to produce net balance of benefits over harms, and obligations to honor contractual agreements. Accordingly, Islamic bioethics regards the principle of "No harm, no harassment" as central to the Islamic conceptions of health care. It is for this reason that there is constant evaluation of the situation to prioritize obligations of preventing harm in order to make a final ethical decision. In cases of conflict between probable harm and probable benefit, each individual case of such a conflict requires careful weighing of the rule that states, "Preventing or removing harm has a priority over promoting good." To be sure, the principle of "No harm, no harassment" has as its source in both the revelation and reason. Reasonable people are capable of recognizing the sources of good life in the sacred texts and human intellection.

However, whether the obligation not to inflict harm can be regarded as one of the principles or rules of the bioethical system is contested by the Muslim jurists. To be sure, even the rationalist ethicists, that is, who regard human reason to be the sole judge in determining harm or benefit, have debated the centrality of this obligation in ethical deliberations in all fields of human interaction, including biomedical conditions. In almost 90 percent of cases confronting health care providers in the Muslim world, the issue of inflicting or reciprocating harm is at the heart of the ethical deliberations. In the rulings studied for the present work, the jurists almost unanimously provided reason based on the obligation not to inflict harm. For example, in the rulings against human cloning, most jurists refer to the infliction of harm on the well-being of an offspring who will be deprived of normal parentage, regarded as a necessary condition in the healthy upbringing of a child. Or in the rulings against population control through abortion, the references all point to the harm that could be done to the moral fabric of society through legalization of abortion.

As a subsidiary rule, "Preventing harm has a priority over promoting good" also provides the jurists with the principle of proportionality. This principle is a source for careful analysis of harm and benefit when, for example, a medical procedure prolongs the life of a terminally ill patient without advancing long-term cure. The principle also allows for reasoned choices about appropriate benefits in proportion to costs and risks for not only the patient but also his family. It is well known that in many complicated cases, decisions about most effective medical treatments are based on probable benefits and harms for the patients and their families. Islamic bioethics require that medical professionals and health care providers ascertain the implications of a given course of medical procedure for a patient's overall well-being by fully accounting for the probable harm or benefit. The principle of "No harm, no harassment" thus is critical in clinical settings where procedural decisions need to be made in consultation with all parties to a case and with a sense of humility in the presence of God: There is nothing for humans but to strive to do their best.

REPRODUCTIVE GENETICS

Introduction of genetic engineering and reproductive genetics marked another phase in infertility treatment, but with far-reaching implications for the fundamental Islamic value regarding reproduction within marital boundaries. Genetics not only made possible what is impossible in the order of nature as far as procreation is concerned; it radically challenged the basic assumption in biological sciences that reproduction required the presence of male and female to effect a new creation. Muslim scholars have as yet to assess the moral and genetic implications of the asexual production of embryos through somatic cell nuclear transfer (SCNT), which involves the introduction of nuclear material of somatic cell into an enucleated oocyte. The possibility of the experiments dealing with the creation of embryos from three or more genetic parents awaits meticulous estimation of religious-moral ramifications for future generations. It is ironic that some Muslim views correlating the good lineage to a legitimate sexual relationship between biological parents have utterly neglected to understand reproductive genetics to assess the consequences of artificial insemination with donor sperm.[16] Clarification of the lineage issue constituted a fundamental question in allowing assisted reproduction within a marriage. More critically, social-cultural as well as genetic consequences for sanctioning third-party donor sperm insemination could render the task of determining and protecting the child's identity and relation impossible. In retrospect, those scholars who opposed the AID, seem to have averted greater harm by insisting upon AIH. In other words, to protect the lineage of the child as conceived in the Muslim culture, the issue of donor's sperm or even donor's egg had to be ruled out in the context of IVF clinics. In general, on the basis of juristic practice in Islamic law, even when the asexually conceived child could be spared from carrying the stigma of being the fruit of an adulterous relationship and attributed to the mother only, it is difficult, if not impossible, to establish the child's legitimate lineage with certainty without information about the biological father. No Muslim scholar could endorse and justify the morality of such a procedure evoking the principle: "Necessity overrides prohibition" even if it provided the only solution to treat barrenness because in the long term it is the child who will suffer in the society. The oft-repeated religious guidance in the matter of infertility, as some religious and spiritual guides were to argue, was to trust in God's wisdom and submit to God's decree in the matter of infertility.

Reproductive genetics has far-reaching consequences for the future of humanity. It complicates the matter of human nature even further, rendering the traditional understanding of God-human and human-nature relationship irrelevant. Islamic normative sources had very little to offer in terms of guiding principles for determining the ethics of genetics. Although the Tradition has preserved an account of a form of eugenics that was practiced in the pre-Islamic tribal culture, since the practice did not resonate with Islamic morality it was forbidden. As we shall discuss below, the pre-Islamic practice actually speaks about the improvement of biological inheritance. Islam unreservedly prohibited the practice on the grounds that such an act involved an illegitimate sexual relationship and implicit discrimination against weaker individuals.

In modern medicine pre-selection eugenics has returned as a medical procedure of preimplantation genetic diagnosis (PGD), making it possible for the parents to choose an embryo on the basis of its desired and undesired physical traits and mental capacities. With its enormous therapeutic potential, the human embryo is gradually moving toward becoming a commodity, a product that could be ordered like any other product with specifications desired by the parents and the scientists. The nature of the parent-child relationship that was traditionally founded upon the parent's unconditional love for their offspring is being threatened. The ethical implications of PGD and its impact upon the parental decision about the future of a "defective" or "undesirable" embryo remain to be sorted out.

It is important to remind ourselves that there are hardly any public debates on the critical issues in biomedical ethics in Muslim countries, because of the absence of democratic governance. In general, Muslim public is kept in dark when decisions are filtered down from the top without holding public debates or hearings to determine whether any of these new reproductive technologies are beneficial or harmful to the well-being of the family and the child. More importantly, since most of the autocratic governments and their representatives in the public sector cannot be called upon to answer to the public when major health care blunders are committed, the public is left with no one to turn to except medical practitioners.

Undeniably, medical practice remains authoritarian in the Muslim world, where lack of a patient's right to question and hold a physician responsible for any detrimental procedure makes the attending physician the sole decision-maker, without accountability. On the other hand, since the religious seminaries know little about what is happening in the world of medical research and practice, ethical-legal deliberations generally lack deeper analysis of the complexity of the procedures reproductive technologies and genetics use to treat infertility. For instance, in the earlier rulings allowing the use of donor sperm or egg in IVF settings the serious harm this procedure could cause to the dignity of the child was overlooked. As detailed information about IVF procedures became gradually available to the jurists the rulings that once allowed the use of donor gametes for implantation were now reversed to forbid any tampering with the strict condition about the use of only a married couple's gametes and thus the preserving a child's lineage. It is important to note that even when the jurists knew that juridical method for deducing fresh decisions from the revealed texts had to depend upon conventional wisdom of the reasonable people (and not the other way round, as some had insisted), in the matter of reproductive technology, they sought to provide solutions by solely engaging in nonethical interpretations of the texts that made reference to sexual procreation or sexual modesty, whichever served their ultimate rulings about IVF procedures. Social interaction, as the Shariʻa visualized it, was time-bound and dependent upon realistic assessment of each case as it impacted upon the moral fabric of the society. Reproductive technology impinged upon social relations. Hence, just issuing a judicial decision about one or other forms of assisted reproduction was insufficient in assessing the potential damage it could do to the well-being of a woman or a child in Muslim cultural context. For instance, the revealed texts, especially traditions, forbade depositing a sperm that was not the husband's in the woman's vagina. It did not say anything about depositing an egg of another woman in the woman's vagina. Was it permissible? What were the implications of artificial insemination with a donor egg? Would the child be related to the donor of the egg or to the gestational surrogate mother?

In the classical formulations a possibility of depositing a woman's egg into another woman's body was inconceivable. There was no understanding of the genetic make-up of a gamete to assess the contribution of a woman's egg in relation to a man's sperm in the DNA of the child. Nevertheless, the silence over depositing an egg in the womb of a "stranger" (in this case, another probably unrelated woman), and its implication for the child's lineage, opened up hermeneutical opportunities, for some at least, to support it as a case of "substitute" or "surrogate motherhood." Based on the extrapolations from the verses that call upon Muslim women to "guard their private parts," it would not be impossible to rule out any gestational surrogacy, whether through commercial or altruistic surrogacy. According to this interpretation, implanting the zygote of a married couple in the womb of surrogate mother for gestation would constitute disregarding the command to guard the private parts. Gestational surrogacy then became another major issue in fertility possibilities that assisted reproduction offered to Muslim women.

In the light of the above discussion, the obvious concern among Muslims remains whether IVF procedures impinge upon the source of kinship: the mother's womb and the incontrovertible genetic fact about the semen being the source of the child's comprehensive medical as well as social history. The hesitation in endorsing IVF is based on a very important ethical principle: *al-'usr wa al-h}araj*—"Protection against distress and impairment": Did the technology cause distress and impair human relationships based on the sanctity of the family united by legitimate relationship between man and woman in marriage, and honor of the womb in birth? These criteria are at the center of the reproductive technology and genetics today. The critical questions are not confined to the moral and legal status of the fetus, which are important in themselves for different reasons; rather, the thrust of the debate is about woman-man relationship and its impact upon the child's right to have a decent life based on clearly documented genealogy that relates the newly born to her parents and others in the extended family. The rulings examined in this connection explicitly rule out the possibility of anyone beside the married couple as the guarantor of the child's immaculate genealogy. It is also in this light that artificial insemination with the sperm of a man other than her husband is construed by some as a form of adultery (*zina*) (although the act did not involve penetration), and the child born through such a process illegitimate (*walad al-h}ara>m* or *ibn al-zina>*).[17] As mentioned earlier, the Prophet's traditions declare most explicitly that placing the seed of another man (*ajnabi>*) in the womb of a married woman is a grievous sin that destroys the inviolability of a family.[18] However, majority of the rulings do not regard artificial insemination by means of donated egg and the husband's sperm implanted by non-coital procedure and carried through gestational surrogacy by the wife as adultery that affects the lineage of the child adversely.[19]

In addition to the textual sources that are usually marshaled as evidence against artificial insemination with donor sperm (AID), there are widespread cultural attitudes that refuse to address the problem of sterility connected with husband's sperm. Culturally, it is unthinkable for any Muslim man to consider donor sperm to treat infertility because of the stigma that such a revelation may carry for him and the child in the society. The identity of the father is important not only for cultural reasons; it is also critical for medical history of the child. More importantly, although the child's upbringing contributes to the overall development of the child's personality, the natural father's DNA has an undeniable impact upon the child's intelligence, general physical appearance, and susceptibility to specific medical conditions, including psychological tendencies. The genetic heritage makes it imperative that the identity of the child's natural father is known by the child.

The other reason for the need of clear identity of the natural father is the possibility of consanguineous marriage occurring between half-brother and half-sister. In recent years some Muslim physicians had sought a ruling on the basis of the possibility of using anonymous donor's sperm to avoid the adverse impact of this kind of assisted reproduction. But even the anonymity connected with the donor of the sperm, as some physicians were inclined to argue in support of donor insemination, could not relieve any party to the process of the responsibility, however remote, of the child mating with another of the the donor's biological offspring within another marriage in future. Such an endorsement might have led to incest between half-brothers and half-sisters through their common biological father. Regardless, whether such a marriage happens intentionally or unintentionally, with or without prior knowledge that there exists this biological relationship, the Shari'a considers such a marriage incestuous and a clear violation of the divinely instituted laws that govern legitimate conjugal relations.

To recapitulate, artificial insemination made gestational surrogacy possible to help those women who, for a number of known and unknown causes, might not be able to bear the child. The development of IVF, and later of the gamete or zygote intra-fallopian transfer to a woman other than the wife to carry the child to full-term gestation raised serious moral questions about the surrogate motherhood. Gestational surrogacy in particular appeared to be least problematic because this procedure is used (not always with much success as the statistics reveal[20]) when the wife can produce eggs of her own but has one or more fertility problems, including, for example, a malformed uterus or a medical condition that would either endanger her life or the life of the fetus. In addition, gestational surrogacy using the gametes of the parents appeared to fulfill, at least, the major requirement of the Shari'a, namely, the preservation of the lineage of the child. However, the use of another woman's womb as the fetus's incubator was culturally unacceptable because of the religious status of a mother's womb and the public perception about the involvement of a third party into the marital functions of sex and procreation. Moreover, the very term "rental womb," as some rulings indicate, was irreverent and scandalous.[21]

Consequently, in the context of technologically assisted reproduction, as we have discussed in this chapter, a mother's womb was of utmost importance for the preservation of the unblemished lineage of the child by carrying her husband's seed to the full term of gestation. It is not surprising to read a number of rulings, reaching a consensus among Muslim scholars, that emphasize the need to keep a woman's womb untainted from any doubtful procedure that might lead to defiling the child's lineage.

Notes

1. To speak about such a possibility in the highly politicized "theology" of international relations is not without problems. Like the development language for which modern Western society provides the model that all peoples in the world must follow, any suggestion of creating a metacultural language of bioethics runs the risk of being suspected as another

hegemonic ploy from the Western nations. However, there is a fundamental difference in the way development language is employed to connote Western scientific, technological, and social advancement, and a biomedical vocabulary that essentially captures universal ends of medicine as they relate to human conditions and human happiness and fulfillment across nations. It is not difficult to legitimize bioethical language cross-culturally if we keep in mind the cultural presuppositions of a given region in assessing the generalizability of moral principles and rules.

2. Contemporary moral discourse has been aptly described as "a minefield of incommensurable disagreements." Such disagreements are believed to be the result of secularization marked by a retreat of religion from the public arena. Privatization of religion has been regarded as a necessary condition for ethical pluralism. The essentially liberal vision of community founded on radical autonomy of the individual moral agent runs contrary to other-regarding communitarian values of shared ideas of justice and of public good. There is a sense that modern, secular, individualistic society is no longer a community founded on commonly held beliefs of social good and its relation to responsibilities and freedoms in a pluralistic society. See David Heyd, ed., *Toleration: An Elusive Virtue* (Princeton, NJ: Princeton University Press, 1996).

3. Ann Elizabeth Mayer, *Islam & Human Rights: Tradition and Politics* (Westview Press, 1991), in the chapter on "Comparisons of Rights Across Countries," has endeavored to analyze charges of cultural relativism against the Universal Declaration of Human Rights made by Muslim governments guilty of violating human rights of their peoples. However, in the process of arguing for the universal application of the UDHR document, she has paradoxically led to the relativization of the same by ignoring the historical context that actually produced the UDHR in the first place. See my review of her book in the *Journal of Church and State* no. , Fall 1992.

4. Deontological ethical norms determine the rightness (or wrongness) of actions without regard to the consequences of such actions. By contrast, teleological norms determine the rightness (or wrongness) of actions on the basis of the consequences of these actions. Deontological norms can further be subdivided into objectivist and subjectivist norms: objectivist because the ethical value is intrinsic to the action independently of anyone's decision or opinion; subjectivist because the action derives value in relation to the view of a judge who decides its rightness (or wrongness). See George Hourani, *Reason and Tradition in Islamic Ethics* (New York: Cambridge University Press, 1985), 17, introduces the latter distinction in deontological norms.

5. The usual practice among Muslim jurists is to end their judicial opinion (*fatwa>*) with a statement *alla>h 'a>lim*, that is "God knows best," indicating that the opinion was given on the basis of what seemed most likely to be the case (*zann*), rather than claiming that this was an absolute and unrebuttable (qat') opinion, which could be derived only from the revelatory sources like the Qur'an and the Traditions.

6. Mohammad Hashim Kamali, *Principles of Islamic Jurisprudence* (Cambridge: Islamic Texts Society, 1991), chapter 12.

7. Literally, the principle translates: "There shall be no harming, injuring, or hurting [of one person by another], in the first instance, nor in return, or requital, in Islam" (see Edward William Lane, *An Arabic-English Lexicon*, Part V, 1775). In this work I will refer to this principle as the principle or the rule of "no harm, no harassment."

8. *Al-Muwa>fiqa>t*, vol. 2, 9–10; But}i>, D{awa>bit} al-mas}lah}a, 219.

9. Since the establishment of the Shiite ideological state in Iran, the question of public good has become an important source of legal thinking and problem solving, similar to that

which has prevailed in the Sunni states from premodern days to the present. Under the leadership of Ayatollah Khomeini, Shiite jurisprudence has once again become research oriented. A number of conferences have been held since the revolution in 1978–79 to discuss the role of time and place in shaping rulings through independent reasoning. The proceedings have been published in several volumes under the title: *Naqsh-e zama>n va maka>n dar ijtiha>d*.

10. Suyu>t}i>, *Tanwi>r al-H{awa>lik: is'a>f al-mubatta' bi-rija>l al-Muwat}t}a'* (Beirut: al-Maktaba al-Thiqa>fi>ya, 1969), vol. 2, 122 and 218.
11. Suyu>t}i>, *al-Ashba>h wa al-naz}a>'ir fi> qawa>'id wa furu' fiqh al-Sha>fi'i>ya* (Mekkah: Maktabat Niza>r Mus}t}afa> al-Ba>z, 1990), p. 92.
12. Shahi>d Awwal, *al-Qawa>'id*, vol. 1, pp. 27–28.
13. There is a sustained discussion among jurists about the nature of harm that this tradition conveys. Undoubtedly, *d}arar* refers to general forms of harm that include setbacks to reputation, property, privacy, and setbacks to physical and psychological needs. See 'Ali> al-H{usayni> al-Si>sta>ni>, *Qa>'ida la> d}arar wa la> d}ira>r* (Qumm: Lithographie H{ami>d, 1414/1993), pp. 134–141.
14. Shahi>d Awwal, *al-Qawa'id*, vol. 1, p. 123.
15. Ibid.
16. In his earlier ruling, Aytollah Sayyid 'Ali> Khamenei had endorsed artificial insemination using the donor sperm or egg, which he repudiated later by actually withdrawing the collection of opinions in the area of bioethics. See his *Pizishki> dar a>'ina-yi ijtiha>d: Istifta>'a>t-ipizishki>* (Qumm: Intisha>ra>t-i Ans}a>riya>n, 1375/1996). See also M. S. Farid, "Ethical Issues in Sperm, Egg and Embryo Donation: Islamic Shia Perspectives," *HEC Forum* (2022). https://doi.org/10.1007/s10730-022-09498-4i.
17. Sind, *Fiqh al-T{ibb*, pp. 83–84, mentions a number of things that are negated for an illegitimate child: inheritance in particular from the father, the qualifications to administer justice, to lead prayers, and other such religiously ordained tasks.
18. Falak 'Urayb al-Ja'fari>, *Had}a>nat al-mar'a li-bayd}a mulh}aqa li-'imrat ukhra, H{ad}a>rat al-Isla>m*, vol. 19, no. 5–6: 42–43, where the author warns of the impending danger in abusing a woman's womb as a "rental" incubator. She cites several verses of the Qur'an and the traditions to support her contention that such a procedure is against God's religion.
19. Ru>ya> Kari>mi> Majd, "*Ijar-i rah}m: nuqt}a-yi pa>ya>n-i barvari>*," in *Zanan*, vol. 13, no. 87: 40–49, takes up the issue of artificial insemination as a solution to infertility in the Shi>'ite religious culture of Iran as it is practiced today. It is interesting to note that as a rule a surrogate mother must be a widow, and before the implantation of the gametes the husband is required to perform a temporary marriage with the candidate in accordance with the Shiite tradition, without seeing her. This allows the surrogate mother to be a "temporary" wife to the husband, resolving the problem related to the lineage. However, in her field research she found that surrogacy was given to a beautiful widow in the belief that the child would turn out to be as beautiful. And, sometimes, as she relates a real incident, if the husband finds out that the woman whom he has temporarily contracted to provide the rental womb for his child is beautiful, there is nothing to stop him from taking her as a second wife, and abandoning the first wife as "defective."
20. Center for Surrogate Parenting Newsletter (1993). The estimates vary, but the rate of success remains low.
21. Ja'fari>, *Had}a>nat al-mar'a*, ibid.

CHAPTER 5

THE ROLE OF AUTHORITY IN UNDERSTANDING RELIGIOUS ETHICS

DENA S. DAVIS

MANY readers who open this volume will be looking for answers to questions such as, "What does Judaism believe about contraception?" or "How does Islam approach abortion?" However, there is really no single entity corresponding to "Judaism" or "Islam," or any other religious tradition, when it comes to religious ethics. We might ask, "What do Jews believe about contraception?" or perhaps we might ask the empirical question, "How do Jews behave with respect to contraception?" We might ask how various Jewish organizations and leaders approach issues such as contraception, sexual orientation, etc., and find that different branches of Judaism have different answers, and even within those branches, different rabbis and scholars will have different answers. But what we need to know in order to make sense of any of these answers, is how a particular religious tradition handles the question of authority. For example, the words "Catholicism teaches" and "Islam teaches," while superficially parallel, actually refer to very different things, since Roman Catholic teaching, at least in some of its forms, claims to be authoritative and univocal, a claim with no parallel in Islam (or in Judaism or Protestant Christianity).

Each of the world's religious traditions must make moral decisions that are both responsive and responsible: responsive to new challenges, and responsible to the moral values that are grounded in the faith and life of its community. Each tradition has different understandings of the sources, vectors, and authority of its teachings. Much misunderstanding is caused by paying attention only to sacred texts and official pronouncements, and neglecting to investigate how those texts and pronouncements are vectored through established interpreters and the target community.

A simple way of constructing the inquiry is to ask four questions: (1) What are the sources of authority? (2) What is the method of interpreting those sources? (3) Who are the accepted interpreters? (4) How does the religious community receive those interpretations? Within the traditions, questions of authority are often the focus of the most serious debate. For conservative Protestants, for example, the question of biblical inerrancy is the primary dividing line between conservative and liberal denominations. In addition, the question of belief itself is often posed in an unclear fashion: the questions of what a religion teaches, what its members profess, and what its members practice can yield radically different answers. The question, "What is the Catholic stance on contraception?" could be taken to address what the church hierarchy teaches about the subject, what the church as a whole (including its lay members) believes, what the Church's political position is; or what members actually practice. Much depends on who is asking the question and for what purpose. The question of authority is especially salient for bioethics, because medical advances are constantly raising new questions. How does a tradition whose founding sources may go back thousands of years respond to issues such as stem cell research or withdrawal of a ventilator?

To add to the complexity, The question of authority is somewhat circular in almost any religious tradition because the question of who or what is authoritative is itself a matter for debate. For example, the primary theological distinction between two Quaker denominations is whether it is Scripture or the Inner Light that takes precedence.

What follows by necessity is a brief overview—not, it is to be hoped, veering toward caricature—of the Abrahamic traditions. The goal is to show how the locus of authority differs among various traditions: in other words, to explicate why the statements "Christianity teaches . . .," "Judaism teaches . . .," or "Islam teaches . . ." are not parallel in terms of the sources and vectors of authority or the expected responses of each faith's adherents.

Judaism

All three of the Abrahamic traditions (Judaism, Christianity, Islam) are grounded in an ultimate source of morality, that is, the Word of God as enunciated in Scriptures, or holy texts. However, the three traditions differ sharply as to what counts as "Scripture," how it is interpreted, and by whom.

The majority of religious Jews identify with one of three main branches of the tradition: Orthodox, Conservative, and Reform. The primary distinction among these branches is their relationship to *halakhah*, Jewish law. *Halakhah* is the compendium of Jewish jurisprudence that begins with the first five books of the Hebrew Bible (said to contain 613 precepts for behavior) and continues with rabbinic commentaries on the Bible, collected in the Mishnah and the Talmud. Among Orthodox Jews, *halakhah* is the unchanging will of God, not subject to historical development (but needing interpretation, nonetheless, to respond to new questions). Conservative Judaism takes *halakhah* as decisive but views it as a human rather than divine body of work; Conservative Jews are also more likely to use non-*halakhic* sources (such as science) as additional grounds for decision. Reform Judaism may use *halakhah* as one resource for understanding its history, values, and tradition, but does not consider it normative, relying instead on Enlightenment notions of personal autonomy, justice, and individual rights, grounded in divine warrant. Within these broad categories, rabbis, *poseks* (deciders or codifiers), and lay scholars, even when referring to the same texts, may disagree vigorously on practical topics such as when abortion is permissible. Although groups of Jews, especially among the Ultra-Orthodox, may follow a particular rabbi, there is no one overarching authority. Thus in *Contemporary Jewish Ethics*, Menachem M. Kellner observes: "One must not ask today, 'What is the Jewish position on such and such?' but rather, 'What is the Orthodox, Conservative, or Reform interpretation of the Jewish position on such and such?' Although many writers persist in presenting *the* Jewish position on various subjects, it very often ought more correctly to be characterized as *a* Jewish position."[1]

A further complication arises from Judaism's being both an ethnic and a religious category. In both Israel and America, perhaps half the people who check "Jewish" on a hospital admittance form or opinion survey observe few if any religious traditions and are usually referred to as "secular Jews." As Ronald M. Green points out in a 1999 essay, secular Jewish perspectives on bioethical issues may still be heavily influenced by the "bioethical sensibility" of Judaism (including, for example, respect for medicine and an activist approach to healing).[2]

CHRISTIANITY

The three largest categories within Christianity are the Eastern Orthodox Church, Roman Catholicism, and Protestantism in its many forms. In large part, the differences that led to these divergences were focused on issues of authority as well as on theology. The schism that led to separate Catholic and Anglican Churches was caused primarily by disagreement over the authority and jurisdiction of the Roman Pope.

All Christian authority is rooted in Christ and the Gospels. An important difference between Protestant and Roman Catholic Christianity is the former's emphasis on the accessibility of truth directly to the individual layperson, without the mediation of a priest. Although few Protestant sects dispensed entirely with ministers, the movement emphasized lay literacy and Bible reading in the vernacular, and it cannot be separated from Gutenberg's invention of the printing press in the mid-fifteenth century. In contrast, Roman Catholicism, at least until the Second Vatican Council (1962–65), located the power to proclaim and interpret God's word primarily in the bishops and priests, with the laity as relatively passive recipients. The discussion here focuses on Roman Catholicism because it is one of the most hierarchical and (ostensibly) univocal religious traditions, with a relatively clear set of official positions. Yet it is important to understand, first, how much room nonetheless remains for debate, and second, how unusual it is for a tradition to have such an official process that claims to discern the truth for all adherents. (The Church of Jesus Christ of Latter-day Saints [Mormons] is another example.)

James Gustafson points out that Catholicism is like Judaism in possessing a code of law (canon law): "Writings in moral theology are used not only to teach persons what principles ought to guide their conduct and what actions are judged morally illicit, they also provide the priest . . . with criteria by which he can enumerate and judge the seriousness of various sinful acts in order to assign the appropriate penance."[3] In Protestant church life this juridical role quickly withered (though one could certainly have witnessed it in the Massachusetts Bay Colony), rendering Protestant theological ethics more "pedagogical than juridical." Because one can hardly expect Scripture alone to answer directly such questions as the morality of organ transplants or sperm banks, all Christian denominations, as Margaret Farley explains in her 2006 book on Christian sexual ethics, have relied on some combination of Scripture, tradition, contemporary experience, and secular disciplines.

Catholic moral theology is pursued in the context of the teaching authority of the Church, which remains "a supreme court of appeals to adjudicate what is morally right and wrong."[4] In the second half of the twentieth century, after the liberalizing reforms of the Second Vatican Council, and in the beginning of the twenty-first century, during the conservative papacies of John Paul II and Benedict XVI, the outlines of Church authority have been very much contested. "Non-Catholics, as well as many Roman Catholics, often presume that the Catholic Church's teaching authority is clearer and simpler than it actually is either in principle or in practice."[5] Despite a certain amount of debate, however, the Catholic church makes a claim to monolithic institutional authority that is lacking in Protestantism; one consequence is a greater diversity in Protestant than in Catholic ethics.

A commonly misunderstood element of Roman Catholic teaching is the doctrine of infallibility, which states that the Pope is immune from error when speaking *ex cathedra* ("from the chair") on matters of faith and morals, with the intention of binding the Church. The bishops share in this infallibility when they define a dogma in union with the pope (e.g., at an ecumenical council). Defined only relatively recently, at the First Vatican Council (1868–70), infallibility appears to refer to a very few doctrines, specifically the Immaculate Conception and Assumption of Mary. Nonetheless, debate continues over the functional infallibility of other teachings, such as *Humanae vitae* (the 1968 encyclical on birth control) or Pope John Paul II's 1998 pronouncement (*Ad tuendam fidem* [*To Defend the Faith*]) that the ordination of women is a topic closed to discussion. Of great moment is the tension between the obligation of individual conscience and the obligation of obedience, a tension Charles Curran terms "faithful dissent."[6]

Islam

The Arabic term for Islamic law, *Shari'a*, literally means a path or way to a water hole in the desert. For the desert dwellers living in the time of the Prophet Muhammad, water and direction were essential to life. Shari'a is theoretically comprehensive, and Islam, meaning the way of submission to the will of God, is a complete way of life. Thus, as John Kelsay explains, there is no aspect of life that is not addressed in Shari'a.[7]

Shari'a rests on four sources. The Qur'an is the compilation of verses revealed orally to Muhammad through an angel, over a twenty-three-year period, and is believed by religious Muslims to be the verbatim word of God. In addition to the Qur'an, there are three supplemental sources of Islamic law. The most important is the Hadith ("narration"), the accounts of the sayings and doings of the Prophet that embody the Sunna, or normative prescriptions. Not all Hadith are considered canonic by all Islamic denominations and legal schools; furthermore, some Hadith are considered more authoritative than others. The degree to which a particular Hadith is accepted can depend on its coherence with the teachings of the Qur'an and also with the degree of reliability of its sources and "chain of transmission." The next source of law is *ijtihad*, analogical, case-oriented reasoning whose method closely parallels that of the Jewish and Roman Catholic casuistic traditions. *Ijtihad* comes from the root *jihad*, meaning to struggle (in this case, the religious scholar's struggle to implement God's law in human institutions). *Fiqh*, or Islamic jurisprudence, applies these resources to problems of the day, such as proper observance of ritual, medical issues, social legislation, and so on. Among Sunni Muslims, who comprise about 85 percent of Islam, there are four major schools of *fiqh*.

Finally, there is *ijma*, or consensus. According to Eric Winkel, consensus as the concept of the "informal agreement of the community" has an overriding authority, and yet "there is no consensus on the definition of consensus."[8] Consensus could include literally the whole community, or could apply only to the community of *ulama* (interpreters) or only to *ulama* of a certain age.

> The legal discourse of Islam may be conceived of as a more or less flexible superstructure erected over the Shari'a, which in turn may be defined as the set of injunctions emanating from the Qur'an and Sunnah. . . . Those who deal with this superstructure, and help it flex and bend to meet new circumstances, may be loosely defined as the *ulama*, those who have knowledge. This amorphous people, women and men, are recognized in their communities by their knowledge.[9]

Prominent religious leaders issue religious opinions in the form of a fatwa, but there is no one authority, even within the different branches of Islam. In that sense, Islam is much like Judaism, with adherents clustering around one or several leaders, who may issue differing fatwas on such bioethical issues as the permissibility of organ donation.

Reception

Bioethics is an applied field of study that can never lose its grip on real-world questions, responses, and behaviors. Thus it is important for bioethicists not to lose sight of the final source of religious authority: reception by the faith community. There are very few nations left in the modern world where religious authorities can dictate the attitudes and behavior of their community of adherents.

An interesting example in the United States is the reaction by a number of Roman Catholic organizations to a feature of the Affordable Care Act, signed into law by President Barack Obama in 2010. The healthcare law requires almost all employers to cover the cost of contraceptives as part of employee health insurance plans. Roman Catholic dioceses, schools, and other institutions protested that paying for their employees' contraceptives would force them to go against Church doctrine, which forbids artificial contraception. Public discussion of this issue in 2012 commonly cited a 2011 survey by the Guttmacher Institute that found that Catholic women were as likely as other American women to make use of artificial contraception.[10] What the official spokespersons say and what self-identified Catholics actually do are not necessarily the same thing. To use another example, formal Jewish teaching, which embraces the value of life, including at life's end, entails some of the most restrictive and vitalist teachings of any major religion. It leaves little room for withdrawal of life support, much less active assistance in hastening the dying process. And yet, in surveys of physicians cited by Ronald Green,[11] those who identified as Jewish were among the most open to accepting some form of physician-assisted death. Thus the way a faith community receives religious authority is mediated by numerous other factors, such as socioeconomic status, personal experiences, and the surrounding culture.

Notes

1. Menachem Marc Kellner, ed., *Contemporary Jewish Ethics* (New York: Sanhedrin Press, 1978), 15.
2. Ronald M. Green, 1999, "Religions' 'Bioethical Sensibility': A Research Agenda," in *Notes from a Narrow Ridge: Religion and Bioethics*, ed. Dena S. Davis and Laurie Zoloth, (Hagerstown, MD: University Publishing Group), 166.
3. James M. Gustafson, *Protestant and Roman Catholic Ethics: Prospects for Rapprochement* (Chicago: University of Chicago Press, 1978), 1–2.

4. Ibid., 5.
5. Ibid., 5.
6. Charles Curran, *Faithful Dissent* (Kansas City: Sheed and Ward, 1986).
7. John Kelsay, "Islam and Medical Ethics," in *Religious Methods and Resources in Bioethics*, ed. Paul F. Camenisch, 93–108. Dordrecht, Netherlands: Kluwer, 1994.
8. Eric Winkel, "A Muslim Perspective on Female Circumcision," *Women Health* 23, no. 1 (1995): 3.
9. Ibid.
10. Rachel K. Jones and Jeorg Drewerke, "Countering Conventional Wisdom: New Evidence on Religion and Contraceptive Use," The Guttmacher Institute. https://www.guttmacher.org/sites/default/files/pdfs/pubs/Religion-and-Contraceptive-Use.pdf.
11. Green, "Religions' 'Bioethical Sensibility.'"

Bibliography

Cahill, Lisa. "Can We Get Real About Sex?" *Commonweal* 117, no. 15 (1990): 497–503.
Curran, Charles. *Faithful Dissent*. Kansas City: Sheed and Ward, 1986.
Davis, Dena S. "Method in Jewish Bioethics." In *Religious Methods and Resources in Bioethics*, edited by Paul F. Camenisch, 109–126. Dordrecht, Netherlands: Kluwer, 1994.
Davis, Dena S. "It Ain't Necessarily So: Clinicians, Bioethics, and Religious Studies." In *Notes from a Narrow Ridge: Religion and Bioethics*, edited by Dena S. Davis and Laurie Zoloth, 9–19. Hagerstown, MD: University Publishing Group, 1999.
Farley, Margaret. *Just Love: A Framework for Christian Sexual Ethics*. New York: Continuum, 2006.
Green, Ronald M. "Religions' 'Bioethical Sensibility': A Research Agenda." In *Notes from a Narrow Ridge: Religion and Bioethics*, edited by Dena S. Davis and Laurie Zoloth, 165–182. Hagerstown, MD: University Publishing Group, 1999.
Gustafson, James M. *Protestant and Roman Catholic Ethics: Prospects for Rapprochement*. Chicago: University of Chicago Press, 1978.
Kellner, Menachem Marc, ed. *Contemporary Jewish Ethics*. New York: Sanhedrin Press, 1978.
Kelsay, John. "Islam and Medical Ethics." In *Religious Methods and Resources in Bioethics*, edited by Paul F. Camenisch, 93–108. Dordrecht, Netherlands: Kluwer, 1994.
McBrien, Richard P. *Catholicism*, vol. 2. Minneapolis: Winston Press, 1980.
Newman, Louis E. "Text and Tradition in Contemporary Jewish Ethics." In *Religious Methods and Resources in Bioethics*, edited by Paul F. Camenisch, 127–143. Dordrecht, Netherlands: Kluwer, 1994.
Winkel, Eric. "A Muslim Perspective on Female Circumcision." *Women & Health* 23, no. 1 (1995): 1–7.

CHAPTER 6

NATURAL LAW AND REPRODUCTIVE ETHICS

BETHANY KIERAN HAILE

BIOETHICS is a discipline that is explicitly practical. Rather than restrict its operations to theorists in the academy, bioethics naturally operates in the public square with the expressed purpose of influencing practice and policy. Yet, bioethics conversations in the public square are often subject to a number of intractable disputes. This is particularly evident in the field of reproductive ethics. Is the in vitro embryo a living person with human dignity, or a collection of cells that happen also to be human? Is research on the stem cells of these embryos a violation of fundamental human dignity or a demand under the principle of beneficence toward those who might benefit from such research? Is gestational surrogacy legitimate so long as it is pursued autonomously or does it violate a fundamental relationship between the biological mother and child? These questions admit no easy answers.

A few philosophers have proposed that natural law offers a significant contribution to bioethics as a means of forging consensus in a pluralistic environment marked by such intractable disputes.[1] Among bioethicists, only a minority work from an explicitly natural law perspective. This is due in part to a common assumption that natural law is a religious methodology, thus unsuited to a pluralistic public square. Indeed, the vast majority of natural law ethicists are religious, and more specifically, Roman Catholic, though there are a few key representatives of the natural law tradition outside of Catholicism. Defenders of natural law insist that the fact that most theorists tend to be religious is accidental, not essential to natural law reasoning, and that above all, it remains a philosophy, not a theology. John Keown asks, "Would the US Congress have been justified in dismissing Martin Luther King Jr.'s campaign for civil rights for African Americans, which invoked natural law, because he was a minister of the Christian religion?"[2]

Supporters are drawn to natural law because it claims to advance a form of moral reasoning that is grounded in the order of reality, and is, in this sense, objective and universal. Because of its foundation in an objective "nature" or, as in the case of the New Natural Law theory, in the objectivity of practical reason itself, the hope is that natural law can provide a sort of "moral Esperanto" or "lingua franca" for the pluralistic public square.[3] The vast majority of those embracing this argument, however, tend to advance very conservative positions in reproductive ethics that have failed precisely in forging the consensus they claim to offer. Even supporters of the natural law have been skeptical of its goal to provide a common moral framework for a universal ethic. Cardinal Joseph Ratzinger, Pope Benedict XVI, writes in his *Values in a Time of Upheaval*, a strident critique of modern relativism, that natural law has become a "blunt instrument" in secular society rather than a common language.[4]

Reproductive ethics provides a critical test of the natural law's ability to establish such common ground as this area of bioethics has been marked by the most intractability between camps. This essay will argue that natural law can indeed be an effective way to address the morality of reproductive issues in the public square, but that our expectations must be realistic. At its best, natural law reasoning can help foster some level of agreement between some opposing groups but will not lead to widespread consensus on the most pressing, and indeed most controversial, issues. The more particular the conclusions drawn on a point of contention, the more people of good will are likely to disagree, even when committing themselves to a natural law methodology. The virtue of prudence will need to guide the formulation of particular moral norms, and in liberal society, people committed to specific values (e.g., the inviolable dignity of the fetus from the moment of conception) will have to allow for compromise to account for the different ways "human nature" may be interpreted. This is not a failure of natural law. Indeed, most contemporary natural law ethicists do not expect the natural law to provide a universal and exhaustive ethic.[5]

In its examination of the potential of the natural law to function as a consensus-building theory in reproductive ethics, this essay will focus on two fundamental questions. The first concerns the technologies that result in the destruction of the embryo (e.g., therapeutic cloning, in vitro fertilization, pre-implantation genetic diagnosis) and the underlying question of the status of the embryo at its earliest stages. The second concerns technologies that separate sexual intercourse and reproduction. Though natural law is important as both a legal and political theory, the scope of this paper will be limited to natural law ethical theories, and particularly those in the Aristotelian-Thomistic tradition.

Origins

Natural law theory refers, most basically, to any perspective that grounds morality in nature, and specifically, human nature. Natural law has ancient roots. Though by no means the only ancient thinker embracing a natural law ethic, Aristotle is often credited as the founder of natural law theory.[6] The principal idea underlying Aristotle's ethical theory is the question of what is good for human beings. To answer this question, Aristotle asks what the function (*ergon*) of a human being is, and argues that this consists in the activity of reason in accordance with virtue.[7] The activity of reason here is key, because it is rationality that distinguishes human beings from other animals. Because human beings are made to be rational, using reason well is what the human good consists in. It is what will ultimately make humans happy. Natural law thinkers since Aristotle are indebted to his idea of "teleology," that is, beginning moral reflection with a prior question of "function" or "purpose" (*telos*).

Ancient foundations notwithstanding, it is Thomas Aquinas who is most identified with natural law theory. Aquinas is indebted to Aristotle's teleology, which he submits to a prior understanding of divine providence and eternal law. For Aquinas, "all things subject to Divine Providence are ruled and measured by the eternal law."[8] The eternal law works to move all things to their proper ends.[9] All things are subject to the eternal law, but rational creatures participate in a unique way in that God has endowed human beings with knowledge and freedom to both discover the eternal law and willingly participate in it. The natural law, then, is the rational creature's participation in the eternal law. The emphasis on Providence and God's eternal law does not preclude freedom, but it does "insist that underlying free acts (and every operation of intellect and will) there is some natural determination and necessity (I–II, 94.1 ad. 2)."[10]

Though Aquinas grounds natural law in the Christian God's governance over creation, Aquinas is not providing a distinctly Christian ethic. Aquinas insists that our knowledge of the natural law is not dependent on religion. Though the order of the universe has a divine source, we come to know this order from the ordinary application of reason to ordinary experience. In humans, practical reason functions to understand the natural order so as to direct human action.

Practical reason, like speculative reason, draws conclusion from self-evident premises. Practical reasoning is grounded in the recognition that all things act for the sake of an end, and this end has the nature of the good.[11] The first precept of practical reasoning flows from this: good is to be done, evil avoided. This first principle of practical reasoning is self-evident but without content. Content comes from the application of the first principle to natural inclinations: the inclination to survive, to reproduce, to enter society, to seek out knowledge. An action is good to the extent that it conforms with the ordained end of the inclination from which it proceeds. Thus, taking a drug for the purpose of harming the body is a violation of the natural law because it goes against the natural inclination the creature has for self-preservation. Masturbation (Aquinas calls it unisexual lust) is a violation of the natural law because it subverts the procreative end of the sexual inclination.

The natural law is often presented as a body of unchanging norms deposited into the natural order that the rational creature merely needs to discover (e.g., "Masturbation is a violation of the inclination of sexuality toward reproduction)." Contemporary theorists emphasize that for Aquinas, the natural law is primarily a *capacity* to make judgments about good and evil.[12] This is important in understanding the possibility of the natural law allowing the development of universal norms. For Aquinas, the natural law as a capacity is universal, given the universality of human nature and the universality of the first principle of practical reason. As a body of norms, however, natural law is not universal. Aquinas says explicitly in his treatment of natural law that practical reason is concerned with contingent matters and "consequently, although there is necessity in the general principles, the more we descend to matters of detail, the more frequently we encounter defects" (I–II 94.4). Furthermore, the specific normative content of the natural law is not universal because vice and custom can stand as obstacles to the effective operation of the practical intellect. Thus a culture may regard theft or lying as morally praiseworthy though it would be in violation of the natural law.

One of the most significant challenges to natural law comes from the natural sciences. It is certainly the case that many in liberal discussions no longer accept the thesis that there is a human nature concomitant with particular goods of human flourishing. The greatest challenge to natural law thinking was triggered, of course, by Charles Darwin's *On the Origin of Species* and the subsequent rise of the mechanistic understanding of the human person. Evolutionary theories have gained an increasing importance in the humanities, with some like E. O. Wilson and Richard Dawkins calling for ethics to be "biologicized."[13] Sociobiology, which has emerged from the work of Wilson and Dawkins, examines all human behavior in light of evolutionary science and genetics.

It is important to appreciate how great the challenge of science is to natural law reasoning. Genetic similarities between human beings and other mammals, particularly the higher apes, casts doubt on the uniqueness of human reason, that what characterizes the human person is, precisely, rationality. Genetic knowledge has also cast doubt on human freedom. Most importantly for natural law, evolutionary worldviews undermine the idea of natural things having a purpose or teleology, much less an objective moral order from which norms may be deduced. Undermining teleology undermines the very foundations of natural law.[14]

It is a mistake, however, to think that science has presented an airtight case against the veracity of natural law, and the reductionist methodology of sociobiology does not satisfy those who see human beings as biological but also capable of transcending biology. Nevertheless, natural law ethicists cannot, in light of the challenge presented by science, naively adopt an Aristotelian biology. Contemporary natural law ethicists must present theoretical positions in dialogue with the sciences and with an appreciation in particular for what science reveals about human nature. A more scientifically informed language of "teleology" is also critical, and particularly an appreciation of the role of biological or "pre-rational goods."[15] The reliance on an accurate science is especially important for reproductive ethics.

There has, however, been a tendency to overemphasize science, particularly biology, in natural law ethics, particularly in the first half of the twentieth century. Catholic natural law ethics during this time showed a tendency toward physicalism, that is, overemphasizing the body and its processes in the articulation of the human good. This was seen especially in the treatment of organ donation. Before the 1950s, most Catholic moralists argued—on the grounds of natural law—that living donations of organs were immoral because they involved direct harm to the body, and particularly to the body's anatomical integrity. Some criticized Catholic natural law for falling prey to the naturalistic fallacy, that is, deriving a moral "ought" from a biological "is."

One significant development to contemporary natural law theory, often called "New Natural Law Theory," departs significantly from the Thomistic tradition. The New Natural Law (NNL) was developed in part in an attempt to address the naturalistic fallacy in contemporary natural law scholarship and to present a natural law that could function in a pluralistic environment that did not have agreement on metaphysics and teleology. Rather than derive moral norms from the nature of the human person, the NNL turns to the first principle of practical reason (do good and avoid evil), which is itself underivable, and then derives a series of secondary principles from reason alone. Practical reason, which is oriented toward action, immediately grasps a number of basic goods that are constitutive to human flourishing. These goods include life and health, knowledge, friendship, aesthetic experience, play, religion, and practical reasonableness. These basic goods provide the underlying justification for human actions. All human actions are directed to one or more of these goods. This is the sort of pre-moral quality of the act. Morality plays a role in determining which goods, and which instantiation of goods, are pursued in a given action. The key moral norm is that one may never intentionally act in a way that is hostile to one of these basic goods. Thus, because life is a basic good, homicide, suicide, abortion, euthanasia, intentional killing in war, and capital punishment are forbidden.[16] The NNL has been particularly appealing to those wishing to employ natural law in reproductive ethics.

Many Protestants have traditionally resisted using natural law because of its association with Roman Catholic moral theology, and because of the emphasis that ethics should be based primarily on the command of the God.[17] Despite this, there has been some push from within Protestantism to embrace natural law, especially to address reproductive ethics. The Reformers Luther and Calvin did not reject natural law, and indeed, the Reformed tradition was fully committed to the natural law tradition inherited from Aquinas and the Scholastics.[18] Even among evangelicals, who have not shared in this inheritance, there has been a push to embrace the natural law in response to the perceived weakness of Protestant bioethical discourse due to lack of a moral framework to talk about foundational moral norms grounded in the very order of creation.[19]

Protestant natural law contributions to reproductive ethics tend to draw heavily on Aquinas but also, perhaps surprisingly, on the writings of Pope John Paul II.[20] The teachings of John Paul II in particular offer a language for Protestants to reconcile natural law language with the "ethics of Jesus" and to overcome the "false dichotomy" between "nature and freedom, law and grace."[21] Disagreements between the two camps arise when the magisterium of the Catholic Church pronounces authoritative interpretations in one of these two areas.[22]

Pope John Paul II's contribution to natural law is worth mentioning because it has had such an important influence on reproductive ethics. John Paul II's ethical theory combines Thomistic natural law with modern natural rights and a heavy emphasis on Scriptural exegesis. The pope insists on the need for religion and the wisdom of Scripture because modernity has dulled people's consciences such as to diminish their knowledge of the natural law. Religious faith becomes necessary, not because the natural law depends on it, but because the truth is so hard to discover in a world marred by sin. The pope insists, though, that the universal truths that the moral law is built on are possible to discover through reason and experience, pointing to the affirmation of human rights around the world as evidence that the natural law was intelligible. It is because of the natural law articulated as rights that we can condemn such atrocities as genocide and slavery regardless of culture or political structure.[23] The pope was particularly concerned about the way states may work to obscure the natural law through political power, a point which has particular bearing on reproductive ethics. States "must abide by the divine plan for responsible procreation."[24]

At the center of John Paul's natural law ethic is the dignity of the human person (hence, the pope is often said to have a "personalist" natural law ethic). Although "dignity" is a theological concept for him, the non-dualist nature of the human person is grounded very much in reason. Human persons, the pope insists, are both (and always) bodily *and* spiritual beings. The emphasis on the body underlies the pope's stance on the dignity of the embryo. In his encyclical *Evangelium vitae*, the pope writes that "even if the presence of a spiritual soul cannot be ascertained by empirical data," scientific studies on the human embryo "provide a valuable indication for discerning by the use of reason a personal presence at the first appearance of a human life: how could a human individual not be a human person?"[25] Because the human person is always embodied, and the beginning of the body exists immediately following conception, the embryo has the dignity of a human person at the earliest moments of its existence. It follows not only that abortion is immoral, but also any attack against the embryo including embryonic stem cell research. John Paul's approach on the status of the embryo and the obligation to treat it with dignity been narrowly influential in conservative Catholic as well as some Protestant circles, but has failed to garner the sort of consensus the pope seems to expect it should. It is to the nature of the embryo that we now turn.

Applying Natural Law to Reproductive Ethics: The Ontological Status of the Embryo

Concern for the human embryo, of course, overlaps with the abortion issue, but reproductive technologies bring different challenges to the status of the embryo and what may and may not be done to it. In abortion, the fundamental tension is between the dignity of the embryo or fetus in utero and the rights of the woman to reproductive liberty and privacy. In therapeutic cloning, as another example, the tension is between the alleged dignity of the cloned embryo and the possibility of easing suffering and curing disease that the research may allow. In the natural law tradition, the norms governing the treatment of the embryo depend first on the correct assessment of the nature of the embryo.

The Aristotelian-Thomistic tradition does not respond consistently to the question of the moral status of the embryo. According to Aristotelian ontology, the nature of a thing is determined by its "soul," which refers to the sort of principle of life that makes a thing what it is. In the Aristotelian tradition, a soul is not a kind of "addendum" to a body, but is rather inextricably connected to the body. As soon as there is a living organism, there is consequently also a soul as the "vivifying" principle underlying this organism's existence. Aquinas adopted Aristotle's biology and ontology, maintaining a theory of "delayed animation" (or delayed hominization) in which the human soul is not infused in an embryo immediately at conception but at some later time. The argument is not, to be clear, that the embryo is not alive, but rather that at its earliest stages it lacks a distinctly human soul.[26]

Aristotle holds that the embryos of humans are first animated by a vegetative soul, and then an animal soul, and even later a rational soul, when the embryo's biological matter is sufficiently organized to receive this soul.[27] Aquinas (and many other medieval philosophers) adopted Aristotle's notion of delayed animation, holding that the soul is the substantial form of a person but that in order to possess a human soul, there must be a sufficient level of biological organization.[28]

Contemporary embryology has challenged this view. Some hold that the fertilized egg (zygote), because it contains the entire genetic code that will direct the growth of the embryo over the course of its existence, does in fact constitute "adequate matter to discern the simultaneous existence of a human soul."[29] Various scholars conclude that if Aquinas's reasoning were interpreted in light of contemporary embryology, it would lead to the conclusion that the embryo is endowed with a rational soul as soon as it possesses its complete genetic code. Because it possesses a rational soul that is unique to persons, the embryo therefore *is* a person and must be treated as such. This, primarily, precludes its destruction.

Not all agree with this application of Aquinas' reasoning. Those who support the ongoing persuasiveness of delayed hominization argue that until the embryo is an "ontological individual" (approximately around the time of the development of the neural streak), it does indeed lack the biological complexity to be said to have a rational soul, or more generally, a human form.[30] As such, individuality is the precondition for the existence of the rational soul, which presumably happens after the possibility of "twinning" is over.[31] Though these arguments attract hearty theological and philosophical debate, they are less suited to the public square because of their reliance on metaphysical categories like "soul" and "human form."

An alternative way of framing this question is to ask whether the embryo is an *organism*. Organisms have coordinated and integrated functioning among all the parts in order to advance the good of the whole. They are, in other words, more than the sum of their parts. George and Tollefsen argue that acting as an organism is precisely what an embryo does from the moment of its existence, which can be seen in a variety of ways that the embryo acts: preventing more than one sperm from fertilizing the egg, moving down the fallopian tube, and implanting.[32] George and Tollefsen begin by arguing that the embryo is an individual human being from the earliest moments of its existence. In order to understand the "nature" of the human embryo, they rely heavily on embryological data to make the case that the embryo is endowed with the intrinsic capacity for self-development. In the tradition of the New Natural Law, they appeal to the intelligibility of basic moral goods (i.e., human life) without appealing directly to metaphysics or theology. Their basic argument is that, because the embryo is a human organism, it is also a human person, and thus deserves the full respect of persons.[33]

Another argument in favor of the personhood of the embryo draws from the ontology of Aristotle, and particularly the notion of *potentiality*. This argument is essentially that if something becomes an X, it was an X potentially. If something cannot become an X, it did not have the potentiality to become an X.[34] The human embryo has the potentiality to become an adult and because of this potentiality, a human embryo and a human adult are substantially the same. The embryo is an adult in potency. A human gamete or an embryo from another species cannot become a human adult. It does not have the same potency.

Drawing on genetics, some natural law ethicists equate potentiality with the genome of an organism. A human embryo has the potential to become a human adult because of the presence of a human genome. In other words, the presence of the genome makes the embryo a "self-directed organism," naturally endowed with all it needs to continue through the various stages of existence all the way up to adulthood. It is genetically unique and this genetic uniqueness, which is key to its identity, endures through all the future stages of life.[35]

It is important to note that the argument is *not* that an embryo is a potential person, but rather that it is a *human in potency*. Personhood can be conferred on a human embryo as a potential adult in the same way that personhood can be conferred on the human infant as a potential adult. Potency, thus, is the basis of ontology. The "genetic uniqueness" argument is widespread, even among those who do not rely on Aristotle's argument from potentiality. David Novak, who formulates a natural law ethic grounded in the Hebrew Bible, and particularly the Noahic law in Genesis 9:6, adopts a similar position. "Any entity, however and wherever it was conceived, that possesses its own unique DNA also possesses the human right to life."[36]

Arguments from potentiality and genetics are subject to a number of important objections that prevent them from leading to widespread consensus. Perhaps the most important pertains to "twinning," during which an embryo will split to become two identical embryos (and, in some circumstances can then fuse back together). The argument is that the embryo, because it can become two individuals, lacks the individuality necessary for full dignity in its totipotent stage. The President's Council on Bioethics' document on human cloning notes that the possibility of twinning "suggest[s] that the earliest-stage embryo is either not yet an individual or is a being that is not confined to becoming only one individual."[37] In response to the argument that the totipotent embryo lacks individuality, natural law ethicists respond with slightly different arguments based on the two different ways twinning may occur. In the first way, a blastomere may separate from an existing totipotent embryo to form a second embryo. Natural lawyers respond that an individual A can split to become A and B without undermining the individuality of A. A flatworm, for example, engages in such a process. So too, an embryo E can be an individual even if twinning occurs and E splits so that the individual E and a new individual F occur.[38] In the second way that twinning may occur, the embryo cleaves by fission into two separate individuals. Thus the individual E becomes two different embryos F and G.[39] Twinning by fission is considerably more difficult to justify if the original embryo E is an individual and endowed with dignity. Does embryo E "die" when fission occurs? Ought such an embryo be mourned? George insists that one does not mourn whom one does not know,[40] but the ontological difficulty remains that in the case of fission, the hypothetical individual E ceases to exist after fission, while two separate individuals do.

Another objection concerns the moral significance of the nature of pregnancy and implantation. An embryo is not completely an individually self-directed organism. The mother's body prepares for pregnancy and implantation well before conception, and from conception to implantation (and onward) directs the development of the embryo. The embryo, then, appears not so much an individual, but a "collective."[41] In other words, the directedness of the embryo toward development is external, not internal. Stretton notes that "the zygote's development until the four to eight cell stage is externally directed by the mother's RNA (inherited from the ovum), and so the zygote during this phase is not an organism.[42]

Yet another counterargument is that the potentiality of the embryo in vitro is different from the potentiality of the embryo in utero because the in vitro embryo has zero potential to become an adult human without some sort of external assistance, namely, the decision to implant it. R. Alta Charo notes that an embryo in vitro has an "intrinsic tendency" to continue to grow and divide for about one week, after which it requires the provision of an artificial culture medium: "If the provision of such medium is considered a form of external assistance akin to that at issue in passive potentiality, then the fertilized egg is a potential week-old embryo, not a potential baby.[43] Louis Guenin agrees the potentiality is based not only on intrinsic tendency but also "overall situation." Because an embryo cannot develop in vitro past a certain point, it lacks the same potentiality of an embryo formed by natural conception.[44]

George and Tollefson defend their position in light of the details of embryonic development by claiming that external factors do not act on the embryo in such a way as to fundamentally change or redirect the growth of the embryo. In other words, while implantation and external support from the mother's body are necessary for the embryo to actualize its potency, this external support does not influence the intrinsic and fundamental character of the embryo (which is identified mainly with its genome). All living things require external factors to actualize their potency, but the in vitro embryo is simply being denied those external necessities in an analogous way that an infant might be denied the probability of actualizing its potency by being starved. "A normal human teenager has the potentiality to become an adult but has zero probability of doing so if stranded on the moon without oxygen."[45] The points of disagreement between the two camps are fundamental and intractable: is the "overall situation" of the embryo in vitro part of its potentiality, or is location merely accidental? Is the embryo at its earliest stages self-directed or is it dependent on factors external to itself (maternal RNA, maternal hormones)?

Applying Natural Law to Reproductive Ethics: The Procreative Teleology of Sex

A second crucial question for the application of natural law to reproduction concerns the relevance of the connection between sexuality and reproduction. The tendency in the first half of the twentieth century among natural law advocates (usually Roman Catholic) was to answer this question in an overly reductionist manner, reducing sexuality merely to coitus. This follows from a literal reading of Aquinas, who evaluates the nature of human sexuality by comparing it with other mammals. Because the sexual organs in humans and other mammals are the same, the purpose of sexuality in both is the same. Thus the purpose of human sexuality is primarily procreation, and anything that intentionally violates this purpose (homosexuality, bestiality, masturbation, and most relevantly for the modern period, contraception) was a violation of natural law.[46]

Such an overly physical understanding of sexuality is no longer accepted, in either moral theology or moral philosophy. First, it does not follow that simply because something is biologically natural (i.e., heterosexual coitus) that it is therefore moral, nor that because something is biologically unnatural (i.e., homosexual coitus) that it is therefore immoral.[47] Furthermore, comparing sexuality with other mammals reveals not only similarities, but also important differences. Thus the second half of the twentieth century gave rise to more psychosocial views of human nature that emphasized the relevance of human psychology and will in the act of sexuality.[48]

The mid-twentieth century saw a development in Catholic natural law reasoning through the influence of personalism, which tended to view the person as a more substantial unity of body and soul, rather than merely a sum of biological process. This is seen in the 1968 landmark document for Catholic reproductive ethics *Humanae vitae* ("Of Human Life"), whereby Pope Paul VI invoked natural law to argue against the use of artificial forms of contraception. The encyclical relied on the traditional understanding of sexual intercourse having a natural end in reproduction. To intentionally block the given end in any particular act was to subvert the very purpose of human sexuality. However, the encyclical also revealed a richer understanding of the human person in arguing also for the unitive significance of sexuality, rather than merely the procreative. In *Humanae vitae*, a more personal view of human nature supplements rather than supplants biology.

The encyclical was ambitious, given the context of the sexual revolution in full swing, in that it was addressed not only to Catholics based on theological arguments particular to the faith, but rather to "all men of goodwill." Pope Paul VI wrote explicitly, "We believe that our contemporaries are particularly capable of seeing that this teaching is in harmony with human reason."[49] Given the loftiness of its expectations, that it could convince even a secular audience of the reasonableness of its arguments, its fallout was even more disappointing. *Humanae vitae* failed not only to convince its secular readers, but even the majority of Catholics. J. Budziszewski observes that the document "seems to lack the sense, which any discussion of natural law requires, of what must be done to make the self-evident evident, to make the intuitive available to intuition, to make what is plain in itself plain to us."[50] Vacek notes that "the objection is not so much that the Vatican position is not reasoned, but that it is not reasonable, not the sort of position a wise reasonable person would draw."[51]

The evaluation of reproductive technologies in Catholic magisterial teachings has flowed from the same understanding of sexuality present in *Humanae vitae*, namely that there is an "inseparable connection, established by God, which man on his own initiative may not break, between the unitive significance and the procreative significance which are both inherent to the marriage act."[52] As such, reproductive technologies have, more often than not, been condemned in magisterial documents as severing the process of reproduction from the human action of sexuality and its twofold orientation toward union and procreation. Of course, such reasoning precludes third-party interventions such as surrogacy or heterologous artificial insemination. But even "homologous" technologies are more often than not condemned. IVF, for example "dissociates" procreation from intercourse.[53]

The magisterial texts insist that technology may assist the naturally occurring process of intercourse but may not replace it.[54] Critics point out that the emphasis on biological sex, rather than the totality of the person and the relationship, manifests the same reductionism found in the early twentieth century treatments on natural law. A more holistic view of the person allows artificial reproductive technologies to potentially be seen within the larger context of a marriage, whereby conjugal love has *not*, despite the best intentions of the couple, resulted in procreation.[55]

Such a view is found in Leon Kass. In agreement with the starting point of *Humanae Vitae*, Leon Kass, who is not Catholic, faults the sexual revolution, spurred by the Pill, for allowing the widespread cultural assumption that sex need not be associated with procreation.[56] This denial of the "inherent procreative teleology of sexuality itself" is the basis for other dilemmas within reproductive ethics.[57] Unlike the Catholic magisterium, Kass employs a natural law reasoning that *does* make an important distinction between hetero- and homologous ARTs. Early in the development of IVF, Kass notes that there are no "intrinsic" moral reasons to reject the use of IVF within marriage, for the same reason that there are no good intrinsic reasons to oppose artificial insemination within marriage.[58] The natural connection between sex and reproduction is an important consideration for Kass, but ARTs may act to enhance this connection, not sever it. Within marriage, artificial insemination and IVF are even seen as a natural means of "fulfilling this aspect of their separate sexual natures and of their married life together."[59] Surrogacy, on the other hand, violates the basic natural duty to care for a child and introduces a third party into what should remain between two people. While adoption is necessary to provide for the needs of children without natural ties, producing a child specifically for adoption (through gamete donation and surrogacy) "deliberately deprives a child of his natural ties" and undermines the importance of lineage for self-identification.[60]

Kass' reliance on natural law reasoning about reproduction is seen also in his strident condemnation of human cloning. He argues that cloning is a total denial of human nature as "embodied, gendered, and engendering beings—and of the social relations built on this ground."[61] Our natural response to such a violation of nature is repugnance. Cloning reveals the inherent goodness of kinship, which flows necessarily from human nature and is not merely a cultural construct. Thus for Kass, cloning severs procreation from sexual love and intimacy, and not just from sex biologically considered.[62]

In recent years, New Natural Law theorists (Germain Grisez, John Finnis, Joseph Boyle, Gerard Bradley, Robert George, and Patrick Lee) have offered many contributions to reproductive ethics, including a critique of ARTs, based on the argument that marriage is a basic good (distinct from friendship). This is a controversial recent development in New Natural Law scholarship. Neither marriage nor procreation was part of Finnis's original list of basic goods.[63] Nevertheless, according to this argument, marriage is a community that forms a comprehensive unity, that is, a unity on all levels of the person, including biological, and a community that is fulfilled by procreating and rearing children together.[64] These two levels of community are intrinsically related: "the comprehensive (and therefore intrinsically sexual) relationship is fulfilled by, and is not merely incidental to, the procreating and rearing of children."[65]

The sexual union of a man and a woman constitutes a real, biological union (literally "one flesh"), making the couple a single agent in a single biological function, that is, procreation. Bradley, Lee, and George use a bodily system analogy to explain what is happening here. Just as the parts of the circulation system (heart, lungs, arteries) function together to perform a single biological function (circulating and oxygenating blood), so too do a man and a woman come together in coitus to form a single "reproductive system" with the purpose of producing a child. Thus procreation is the purpose of heterosexual marriage. Because the human being is personal and not just biological, the purpose of marriage is not only to reproduce but also to rear children together cooperatively. Though some marriages obviously do not result in procreation, Bradley, et al. insist that so long as it is an exclusive heterosexual union, it fulfills the basic good because it has the essential form that is open to begetting and rearing new life.[66]

The implications of this understanding of the basic good of marriage have important ramifications for reproductive ethics. Accordingly, the donation of gametes by third parties violates the basic good of marriage. Genetic parenthood "in and of itself constitutes an intimate personal relationship that gives rise to a special, personal obligation to love and (in most circumstances) raise one's genetic children."[67] While extreme circumstances may justify ending this relationship (i.e., via adoption), intentionally begetting offspring in order to forego this relationship is a violation of the basic obligation that flows from kin relationships—the commitment of the will to the good of that person.[68] Moschella's argument here overlaps with Kass's point that gamete donation undermines the importance of "natural ties." Even homologous ARTs are opposed, on the grounds that they instrumentalize the child. Grisez, for example, in his opposition to tubal ovum transfer with sperm (TOTS), argues that in using ARTs to produce a child, "a couple must be acting for their own fulfillment as parents, and since the child to be produced is, as such, extrinsic to that, it is inevitable that he or she initially be sought as an instrumental good, not loved for his or her own sake."[69]

Critics of the NNLT argue that the tendency toward traditionalism (and particularly a traditionalism that overlaps neatly with conservative religious views) is particularly glaring in the account of marriage and reproduction.[70] As such, an argument like Moschella's or Grisez's against heterologous ARTs has greater persuasive ability in the Church than in the public square.[71] Thobaben argues that natural law arguments about who should (or should not) be a parent generally fail in the public square, except in cases where the immediate safety of the child is in question.[72]

The Ongoing Relevance of Natural Law Contributions to Reproductive Ethics

On both the status of the embryo and the productive teleology of the sexual act, natural law thinkers have failed to garner the sort of consensus that makes natural law attractive in the first place. At first glance, it appears that natural law fails at its goal to provide the standards for a rational and universal moral discourse that appeals to all people of good will.

There are a variety of responses to the seeming failure of natural law. David Novak, a Jewish theologian and natural law theorist, argues that the rejection of natural law arguments concerning the dignity of the embryo, and the widespread acceptance of embryonic stem cell research, are evidence that society is moving further away from the basis of most of its moral norms, which is the natural law itself. This trajectory may eventually force adherents to the natural law to choose to no longer remain loyal to a political order with so little grounding in objective moral norms. Novak is optimistic, though, that natural law arguments will ultimately prevail, because of his faith in God and hope that God will enlighten his adversaries: "This hope is part of our belief that whereas reason can discover the justice that ought to be done, only faith leads us to hope that justice will be done, sooner or later."[73] This overlaps with certain critiques of natural law among Christian thinkers who point out the failure of natural law ethicists to fully account for the power of human sinfulness to mar human reason, and who insist that the fullness of moral knowledge cannot be achieved through the application of reason alone but depends on critical supplementation from revelation as well as a grounding in prayer and repentance: "By means of [prayer and repentance], an individual might break with the rationalization of misdirected choices that keep individuals locked into intractable controversy."[74]

Another possible explanation for the apparent failure of natural law to garner widespread consensus is found in the work of Alasdair MacIntyre. MacIntyre argues that it is futile to search for standards or rationality that are universally available regardless of a person's religious tradition. Practical rationality is "tradition-constituted and tradition-constitutive."[75] Rationality both emerges from a given history and is practiced within a given tradition. Because there are many traditions, so too are there many rationalities. The Enlightenment tradition presents a "tradition-less" rationality, but this tradition is no more normative than any other tradition of rationality. According to MacIntyre, we must accept that our most rational arguments cannot provide us with an objective "meta-rationality." Though there may indeed be universal truths in ethics, human rationality can only grasp these truths in a way that is bound up in one's own tradition, and conditioned by history.[76]

MacIntyre helps us understand why natural law approaches like that of the New Natural Law, which presents basic goods that ought to be compelling to all rational persons, end up *not* being compelling to all rational persons. Those who follow MacIntyre's understanding of rationality as a "tradition-guided inquiry" point to the necessity of understanding the critical importance of belief commitments in the operation of practical reasoning.[77] This does not mean that natural law relies on explicitly religious belief, but that any reflection on "human nature," "flourishing," and "goodness" requires reference to commitments that are grounded in some form of authority outside ourselves. Alasdair McGrath notes that "nature is already an interpreted category."[78] The authorities that help form and buttress our beliefs include religion, but also politics, medicine, and science. A "tradition" is a mode of communicating those various beliefs and their concomitant authorities. The various traditions we are part of (Roman Catholic, secular Jewish, materialist, utilitarian) form us in such substantial ways that we cannot strip our tradition away to enter the public square as a sort of rational "blank slate."

Arguments for and against the personhood of the embryo both rely, to some degree, on beliefs not only about the facts but also the relevance of the facts (i.e., the importance of potentiality or the importance of individuality). Thus, adopting either position cannot come from any "authority-neutral" pure reading of the facts of nature. So too with the procreative teleology of human sexuality. It is not so "immediately evident so as to determine one's intellect with the 'perfection of clear sight'" to say that sex is inherently procreative, or that it is not, or to say that sex is unitive and exclusive, or that it is not.[79] In the end, nature will be understood differently by different rational beings even when those rational beings are acting "rationally." Thus we should not expect that an appeal to "nature" and "reason" will allow us to transcend our particular belief commitments in order to arrive at some body of "meta-truths."

Does that mean natural law discussions are doomed to fail? Not at all, but we ought not to place undue expectations on what natural law can accomplish. It is not the nature of natural law, any more than any other moral theory, to guarantee widespread consensus on the most contentious moral issues. Thus for natural law conversations to succeed, they must no longer base the success of these conversations on the ability to make universally compelling arguments. That does not mean that there is no objective nature, but natural law theorists need to humbly recognize that as creatures grounded in both history and tradition, we have no "pure" access to that nature. Second, natural law theorists must be willing to acknowledge the belief commitments from which they proceed, whether those come from religion, politics, a post-Enlightenment anthropology, or any other tradition. We may rightfully argue for the superiority of our beliefs, but we may not ignore that they exist.

Natural law may not garner widespread consensus, but that does not mean that interlocutors from different traditions will not be able to come to any basic agreements. For example, the arguments of the natural lawyers concerning the dignity of the embryo certainly do not support widespread consensus that the embryo, and particularly the in vitro embryo, is a human person endowed with human dignity. The arguments do support, however, that the embryo is *something worthy of respect*, even it is not the same respect due to a human infant or a human adult. So what is the difference between dignity and respect? While natural law may not provide the basis for a universal ban on the destruction of human embryos, it may provide the basis for a universal norm against destroying embryos without a proportionate reason, or for the creation of embryos solely for destruction.[80] Charles Krauthammer adopted this position in his argument against cloning embryos for research as well in his opposition to the Castle-DeGette stem cell bill that allowed for the creation of new embryos designated specifically for research, namely that opposition to such practices reflects "the idea that, while a human embryo may not be a person, it is not nothing. Because if it is nothing, then everything is permitted. And if everything is permitted, then there are no fences, no safeguards, no bottom."[81]

Natural lawyers convinced of the inviolable status of the human embryo at all stages will, no doubt, be dissatisfied with this conclusion, but it is unclear that natural law alone can provide the grounds for any stronger consensus on the moral status of the in vitro embryo. We should not expect all reasonable people to submit to the obligation to protect human life at the very earliest stages, but natural law does give "reason for optimism that some substantial agreement in this area is yet achievable."[82]

NOTES

1. J. Daryl Charles, *Retrieving the Natural Law: A Return to Moral First Things* (Grand Rapids, MI: Eerdmans, 2008); Alfonso Gomez-Lobo and John Keown, *Bioethics and the Human Goods*, (Washington: Georgetown University Press, 2015); Patrick Tully, "From Pluralism to Consensus in Beginning-of-Life Debates: Does Contemporary Natural Law Theory Offer a Way Forward?" *Christian Bioethics* 22, no. 2 (2016): 143–168.
2. Gomez-Lobo and Keown, *Bioethics and the Human Goods*, xi.
3. Jeffrey Stout, *Ethics After Babel: The Languages of Morals and Their Discontents* (Princeton University Press, 2001), 5.
4. Joseph Ratzinger, *Values in a Time of Upheaval* (San Francisco: Ignatius Press, 2006), 38–39.
5. Jean Porter, *Natural and Divine Law: Reclaiming the Tradition for Christian Ethics* (Grand Rapids, MI, and Cambridge, UK: Eerdmans/Novalis, 1999); Jean Porter, *Nature as Reason: A Thomistic Theory of the Natural Law* (Grand Rapids, MI: Eerdmans, 2005); Russell Hittinger, *The First Grace: Rediscovering the Natural Law in a Post Christian World*, 2nd ed. (Intercollegiate Studies Institute, 2007).
6. Cicero too made important contributions to natural law theory. In his *De re publica* he claims that natural law provides universal moral principles that bind all human beings.
7. Aristotle, 1097b22–1098a20.
8. Thomas Aquinas, *Summa Theologica*, I–II: 91.2 (Thomas More Publishing, 1981); all citations from Aquinas refer to the *Summa Theologica*, book, question, and article.
9. Ibid., I–II: 93.1.
10. Clifford G. Kossel, S. J. "Natural Law and Human Law (Ia IIae, qq. 90–97)," in *The Ethics of Aquinas*, ed. Stephen J. Pope (Georgetown University Press, 2002).
11. Aquinas, *Summa Theologica*, I–II: 94.2.
12. Porter, *Natural and Divine Law*.
13. E. O. Wilson, *Sociobiology: The New Synthesis* (Harvard University Press, 1975), 562; Richard Dawkins, *The Selfish Gene* (New York: Oxford University Press, 1976).
14. Stephen J. Pope, "Reason and Natural Law," in *The Oxford Handbook of Theological Ethics*, ed. Gilbert Meilaender and William Werpehowski (Oxford University Press, 2007); Stephen J. Pope, *Human Evolution and Christian Ethics* (Cambridge University Press, 2011).
15. Pope, "Reason and Natural Law," 161; Porter, *Natural and Divine Law*.
16. John Finnis, *Natural Law and Natural Rights* (New York: Oxford University Press, 1980); Germain Grisez, *The Way of the Lord Jesus*, II: *Living a Christian Life* (Chicago: Franciscan

Herald Press, 1983); Robert P. George, *In Defence of Natural Law* (Oxford: Clarendon Press, 1999).
17. Karl Barth, *Church Dogmatics*, III/4 (Edinburgh: T. & T. Clark, 1961).
18. Stephen J. Grabill, *Rediscovering the Natural Law in Reformed Theology* (Grand Rapids, MI: Eerdmans, 2006).
19. Ibid.; Charles, *Retrieving the Natural Law*.
20. Michael J. Murray, "Protestants, Natural Law, and Reproductive Ethics," *John Paul II's Contribution to Catholic Bioethics* 84 (2004): 121–129.
21. Charles, *Retrieving the Natural Law*, 100.
22. Murray, "Protestants, Natural Law, and Reproductive Ethics," 128.
23. See Pope John Paul II, *Veritatis splendor*, #80.
24. Pope John Paul II, *The Gospel of Life: Evangelium Vitae: On the Value and Inviolability of Human Life* (Washington: United States Catholic Conference, 1995), #97.
25. Ibid., #60.
26. Father Juan R. Velez, "Immediate Animation: Thomistic Principles Applied to Norman Ford's Objections." *Ethics & Medicine* 21, no. 1 (2005): 11–28.
27. Aristotle, *On the Generation of Animals*, 735a35–736b16.
28. Joseph F. Donceel, S. J. "Immediate Animation and Delayed Hominization," *Theological Studies* 31 (1970): 76–105.
29. Velez, "Immediate Animation," 12; see also John Haldane and Patrick Lee, "Aquinas on Human Ensoulment, Abortion, and the Value of Life," *Philosophy* 78 (2003): 255–278.
30. Norman Ford, "The Human Embryo as Person in Catholic Teaching," National Catholic Bioethics Quarterly 1, no. (2001): 160.
31. John Mahoney, *Bioethics and Belief* (London: Sheed and Ward, 1984), 66–67.
32. Robert P. George and Christopher Tollefsen, *Embryo: A Defense of Human Life* (Doubleday, 2008).
33. Tully, "From Pluralism to Consensus."
34. Gomez-Lobo and Keown, *Bioethics and the Human Goods*.
35. George and Tollefsen, *Embryo*.
36. David Novak, *The Sanctity of Human Life* (Georgetown University Press, 2009), 81–82.
37. President's Council on Bioethics, *Human Cloning and Human Dignity: An Ethical Inquiry*. https://bioethicsarchive.georgetown.edu/pcbe/reports/cloningreport/, 136.
38. George and Tollefsen, *Embryo*; Gomez-Lobo and Keown, *Bioethics and the Human Goods*.
39. G. Damschen, A. Gomez-Lobo, and D. Schoenecker, "Sixteen Days? A Reply to B. Smith and B. Brogaard on the Beginning of Human Individuals," *Journal of Medicine and Philosophy* 21, no. 2 (2006): 165–175.
40. Gomez-Lobo and Keown, *Bioethics and the Human Goods*, 40.
41. William Saletan, "Little Children," *New York Times*, 2008.
42. Dean Stretton, "Critical Notice—*Defending Life: A Moral and Legal Case Against Abortion Choice*," *Journal of Medical Ethics* 34 (2008): 797, cited in Christopher Kaczor, *The Ethics of Abortion: Women's Rights, Human Life, and the Question of Justice* (New York: Routledge 2011), 141.
43. R. Alta Charo, "Every Cell Is Sacred: Logical Consequences of the Argument from Potential in the Age of Cloning," in *Cloning and the Future of Human Embryo Research*, ed. Paul Lauritzen (New York: Oxford University Press, 2001), 86.
44. L. Guenin, *The Morality of Embryo Use* (Cambridge: Cambridge University Press, 2008).

45. Gomez-Lobo and Keown, *Bioethics and the Human Goods*, 36; George and Tollefsen, *Embryo*.
46. Edward Collins Vacek, S. J., "Catholic Natural Law and Reproductive Ethics," *Journal of Medicine and Philosophy* 17, no. 3 (1992): 329–346.
47. Alan Soble, "The Fundamentals of the Philosophy of Sex," in *The Philosophy of Sex: Contemporary Readings*, ed. Alan Soble, p. xxix (Lanham, MD: Rowman & Littlefield Publishers, Inc., 2002).
48. Thomas Nagel, "Sexual Perversion," in *The Philosophy of Sex: Contemporary Readings*, ed. Alan Soble, 9–20. (Lanham, MD: Rowman & Littlefield Publishers, Inc., 2002).
49. Pope Paul VI, *Humana vitae*, #12.
50. Harold O. J. Brown and J. Budziszewski, "Contraception: A symposium," *First Things: A Monthly Journal of Religion & Public Life* 88 (1998): 17–29.
51. Vacek, "Catholic Natural Law and Reproductive Ethics," 341.
52. Pope Paul VI, *Humana vitae*, #12.
53. Vatican, *Donum Vitae* or "Instruction on Respect for Human Life in Its Origin and On the Dignity of Procreation," II.5, 1987. http://www.vatican.va/roman_curia/congregations/cfaith/documents/rc_con_cfaith_doc_19870222_respect-for-human-life_en.html.
54. See Vatican, *Donum vitae*, and Vatican, *Dignitas personae*, 2008. http://www.vatican.va/roman_curia/congregations/cfaith/documents/rc_con_cfaith_doc_20081208_dignitas-personae_en.html.
55. Vacek, "Catholic Natural Law and Reproductive Ethics," 341.
56. Leon Kass, *Life, Liberty and the Defense of Dignity: The Challenge for Bioethics* (Encounter Books, 2002), 143.
57. Leon Kass, "The Wisdom of Repugnance: Why We Should Ban Human Cloning," *New Republic* (June 2, 1997): 18.
58. Leon Kass, "Making Babies: The New Biology and the 'Old' Morality," *Public Interest* 26 (Winter 1972): 18–56. http://web.stanford.edu/~mvr2j/sfsu09/extra/Kass1.pdf
59. Leon Kass, "Making Babies Revisited," *Public Interest* 54 (1979): 44. http://www.nationalaffairs.com/doclib/20080528_197905403makingbabiesrevisitedleonrkass.pdf.
60. Leon Kass, *Towards a More Natural Science* (Simon and Schuster, 1985), 112; Kass, *Life, Liberty and the Defense of Dignity*, 98.
61. Kass, "The Wisdom of Repugnance," 20.
62. Ibid., 21.
63. Finnis, *Natural Law and Natural Rights*, 86–87; See Joshua D. Goldstein, "New Natural Law Theory and the Grounds of Marriage: Friendship and Self-Constitution," *Social Theory and Practice* 37, no. 3 (2011): 461–482.
64. Robert P. George and Gerard V. Bradley, "Marriage and the Liberal Imagination," *Georgetown Law Journal* 84 (1995): 301–320.
65. Gerard V. Bradley, Patrick Lee, and Robert George, "Marriage and Procreation: The Intrinsic Connection," *Public Discourse*, 2011. http://www.thepublicdiscourse.com/2011/03/2638/.
66. Bradley et al., "Marriage and Procreation."
67. Melissa Moschella, "The Wrongness of Third-Party Assisted Reproduction: A Natural Law Account," *Christian Bioethics: Non-Ecumenical Studies in Medical Morality* 22, no. 2 (2016): 105.
68. Ibid., 110.

69. Germain Grisez (1997), *The Way of the Lord Jesus, III: Difficult Moral Questions*. Question 52. http://www.twotlj.org/G-3-V-3.html.
70. Goldstein, "New Natural Law Theory," 463.
71. Heterologous refers to gametes that are not from the parental couple, e.g., donated sperm not from the husband.
72. James R. Thobaben, "Natural Law: A Good Idea That Does Not Work Very Well (At Least Not in the Current Society)," *Christian Bioethics* 22, no. 2 (2016): 228.
73. Novak, *The Sanctity of Human Life*, 72.
74. George Khushf, "What Hope for Reason? A Critique of New Natural Law Theory," *Christian Bioethics* 22, no. 3 (2016): 263.
75. Christopher Stephen Lutz, *Tradition in the Ethics of Alasdair MacIntyre; Relativism, Thomism, and Philosophy* (Lanham, MD: Lexington Books, 2009), 33.
76. Ibid., 37.
77. See Porter, *Nature as Reason*; Hittinger, *The First Grace*; William C. Mattison III, "The Changing Face of Natural Law: The Necessity of Belief for Natural Law Norm Specification," *Journal of the Society of Christian Ethics* 27, no. 1 (2007): 251–277.
78. Porter, *Nature as Reason*, 58; Alasdair McGrath, *A Scientific Theology, Vol I: Nature* (Edinburg: T&T Clark, 2001), 113.
79. Mattison, "The Changing Face of Natural Law," 264.
80. Saletan, "Little Children."
81. Charles Krauthammer, "A Secular Argument against Research Cloning," *New Republic* (March 22, 2002). http://www.freerepublic.com/focus/news/670891/posts.
82. Tully, "From Pluralism to Consensus," 163.

Bibliography

Aquinas, Thomas. *Summa Theologica*. Thomas More Publishing, 1981.
Aristotle. *Nicomachean Ethics*, trans. W. D. Ross, in *The Complete Works of Aristotle*, vol. 2, edited by Jonathan Barnes. Princeton University Press, 1984.
Aristotle. *On the Generation of Animals*, translated by A. Platt. In *The Complete Works of Aristotle*, vol. 2, edited by Jonathan Barnes. Princeton University Press, 1984.
Barth, Karl. *Church Dogmatics*, III/4. Edinburgh: T. & T. Clark, 1961.
Berkman, John, and William C. Mattison III, eds. *Searching for a Universal Ethic: Multidisciplinary, Ecumenical, and Interfaith Responses to the Catholic Natural Law Tradition*. Grand Rapids, MI: Eerdmans, 2014.
Bradley, Gerard V., Patrick Lee, and Robert George. "Marriage and Procreation: The Intrinsic Connection." *Public Discourse*. 2011. http://www.thepublicdiscourse.com/2011/03/2638/.
Brown, Harold O. J., and J. Budziszewski. "Contraception: A symposium." *First Things: A Monthly Journal of Religion & Public Life* 88 (1998): 17–29.
Brown, Brandon P., and Jason T. Eberl. "Ethical Considerations in Defense of Embryo Adoption." In *"The Ethics of Embryo Adoption and the Catholic Tradition*, edited by Sarah-Vaughan Brakman and Darlene Fozard Weaver, 103–118. New York: Springer, 2007.
Budziszewski, J. *Written on the Heart: The Case for Natural Law*. InterVarsity Press, 1997.
Charles, J. Daryl. *Retrieving the Natural Law: A Return to Moral First Things*. Eerdmans, 2008.

Charo, R. Alta. "Every Cell Is Sacred: Logical Consequences of the Argument from Potential in the Age of Cloning." In *Cloning and the Future of Human Embryo Research*, edited by Paul Lauritzen, 82–89. New York: Oxford University Press, 2001.

Cicero, Marcus Tullius. *De re publica: On the Commonwealth*, translated by George Holland Smith and Stanley Barney Smith. Indianapolis: Bobbs-Merrill, 1929.

Cromartie, Michael, ed. *A Preserving Grace: Protestants, Catholics and Natural Law*. Eerdmans, 1997.

Dawkins, Richard. *The Selfish Gene*. New York: Oxford University Press, 1976.

Damschen, G., A. Gomez-Lobo, and D. Schoenecker. "Sixteen Days? A Reply to B. Smith and B. Brogaard on the Beginning of Human Individuals." *Journal of Medicine and Philosophy* 21, no. 2 (2006): 165–175.

Donceel, Joseph F., S. J. "Immediate Animation and Delayed Hominization." *Theological Studies* 31 (1970): 76–105.

Finnis, John. "Marriage: A Basic and Exigent Good." *Monist* 91 (2008): 388–406.

Finnis, John. *Aquinas: Moral, Political, and Legal Theory*. Oxford: Oxford University Press, 1998.

Finnis, John. "Law, Morality, and 'Sexual Orientation.'" *Notre Dame Law Review* 69 (1994): 1049–1076, 1066.

Finnis, John. *Fundamentals of Ethics*. Washington: Georgetown University Press, 1983.

Finnis, John. *Natural Law and Natural Rights*. New York: Oxford University Press, 1980.

Ford, Norman. "The Human Embryo as Person in Catholic Teaching." *National Catholic Bioethics Quarterly* 1, no. 2 (2001): 155–161.

Ford, Norman. *When Did I Begin?* Cambridge University Press, 1988.

George, Robert P., ed. *Natural Law, Liberalism, and Morality*. New York: Oxford University Press, 1996.

George, Robert P. *In Defence of Natural Law*. Oxford: Clarendon Press, 1999.

George, Robert P., and Gerard V. Bradley. "Marriage and the Liberal Imagination." *Georgetown Law Journal* 84 (1995): 301–320.

George, Robert P., and Christopher Tollefsen. *Embryo: A Defense of Human Life*. Doubleday, 2008.

Goldstein, Joshua D. 2011 "New Natural Law Theory and the Grounds of Marriage: Friendship and Self-Constitution." *Social Theory and Practice* 37, no. 3 (2008): 461–482.

Gomez-Lobo, Alfonso, and John Keown. *Bioethics and the Human Goods*. Washington: Georgetown University Press, 2015.

Grabill, Stephen J. *Rediscovering the Natural Law in Reformed Theology*. Eerdmans, 2006.

Grisez, Germain. (1997) *The Way of the Lord Jesus, III: Difficult Moral Questions*. Question 52. http://www.twotlj.org/G-3-V-3.html.

Grisez, Germain. *The Way of the Lord Jesus, II: Living a Christian Life*. Chicago: Franciscan Herald Press, 1983.

Grisez, Germain. "Toward a Consistent Natural Law Ethics of Killing." *American Journal of Jurisprudence* 15 (1970): 64–96.

Grisez, Germain. "The First Principle of Practical Reason: A Commentary on the *Summa Theologiae*, 1–2, Question 94, Article 2." *American Journal of Jurisprudence* 10, no. 1 (1965): 168–201.

Grisez, Germain, Joseph Boyle, John Finnis, and William E. May. "Every Marital Act Ought to Be Open to New Life: Toward a Clearer Understanding." *Thomist* 52 (1988): 365–366.

Guenin L. *The Morality of Embryo Use*. Cambridge: Cambridge University Press, 2008.

Hall, Pamela. *Narrative and the Natural Law*. Notre Dame, IN: University of Notre Dame Press, 1994.

Haldane, John, and Patrick Lee. "Aquinas on Human Ensoulment, Abortion, and the Value of Life." *Philosophy* 78 (2003): 255–278.

Hittinger, Russell. *The First Grace: Rediscovering the Natural Law in a Post-Christian World.* Intercollegiate Studies Institute; 2nd ed. 2007.

Iltis, Ana S. "Moral Epistemology and Bioethics: Is the New Natural Law the Solution to Otherwise Intractable Disputes?" *Christian Bioethics* 22, no. 2 (2016): 169–185.

Kaczor, Christopher. *The Ethics of Abortion: Women's Rights, Human Life, and the Question of Justice.* New York: Routledge, 2011.

Kass, Leon. *Life, Liberty and the Defense of Dignity: The Challenge for Bioethics.* Encounter Books, 2002. 143–147, 153–157.

Kass, Leon. *Towards a More Natural Science.* Simon and Schuster, 1985.

Kass, Leon. "The Wisdom of Repugnance: Why We Should Ban Human Cloning." *New Republic* (June 2, 1997): 17–26.

Kass, Leon. "Making Babies Revisited." *Public Interest* 54 (1979): 32–60. https://www.nationalaffairs.com/public_interest/detail/making-babies-revisited.

Kass, Leon. "Making Babies: The New Biology and the 'Old' Morality." *Public Interest* 26 (Winter 1972): 18–56. http://web.stanford.edu/~mvr2j/sfsu09/extra/Kass1.pdf.

Khushf George. "What Hope for Reason? A Critique of New Natural Law Theory." In *Christian Bioethics* 22, no. 3 (2016): 238–264.

Kossel, Clifford G., S. J. "Natural Law and Human Law (Ia IIae, qq. 90–97)." In *The Ethics of Aquinas*, edited by Stephen J. Pope, 90–97. Georgetown University Press, 2002.

Krauthammer, Charles. "A Secular Argument against Research Cloning." *New Republic* 4554 (April 2002): 20–23. http://www.freerepublic.com/focus/news/670891/posts.

Lee, Patrick. *Abortion and Unborn Human Life.* Georgetown University Press, 2010.

Lee, Patrick. "The Human Body and Sexuality in the Teaching of Pope John Paul II." In *John Paul II's Contribution to Catholic Bioethics*, edited by Christopher Tollefsen, 107–120. Dordrecht, Netherlands: Springer, 2005.

Lee, Patrick. "Human Beings Are Animals." In *Natural Law and Moral Inquiry: Ethics, Metaphysics, and Politics in the Work of Germain Grisez*, edited by Robert George, 135–151. Georgetown University Press, 1998.

Lee, Patrick, and Robert P. George. *Conjugal Union.* New York: Cambridge University Press, 2014.

Lee, Patrick, and Robert P. George. *Body-Self Dualism in Contemporary Ethics and Politics.* New York: Cambridge University Press, 2008.

Lutz, Christopher Stephen. *Tradition in the Ethics of Alasdair MacIntyre: Relativism, Thomism, and Philosophy.* Lanham, MD: Lexington Books, 2009.

Mahoney, John. *Bioethics and Belief.* London: Sheed and Ward, 1984.

Mattison, William C., III. "The Changing Face of Natural Law: The Necessity of Belief for Natural Law Norm Specification." *Journal of the Society of Christian Ethics* 27, no. 1 (2007): 251–277.

McGrath, Alasdair. *A Scientific Theology, Vol I: Nature.* Edinburg: T&T Clark, 2001.

Murray, Michael J. "Protestants, Natural Law, and Reproductive Ethics." *John Paul II's Contribution to Catholic Bioethics* 84 (2004): 121–129.

Nagel, Thomas. "Sexual Perversion." In *The Philosophy of Sex: Contemporary Readings*, edited by Alan Soble, 9–20. Lanham, MD: Rowman & Littlefield Publishers, Inc., 2002.

Napier, Stephen, ed. *Persons, Moral Worth, and Embryos: A Critical Analysis of Pro-Choice Arguments.* Philadelphia, PA: National Catholic Bioethics Center, 2011.

Novak, David. *The Sanctity of Human Life.* Georgetown University Press, 2009.

Pope John Paul II. *The Gospel of Life: Evangelium Vitae: On the Value and Inviolability of Human Life*. Washington: United States Catholic Conference, 1995.

Pope John Paul II. *Veritatis splendor*. 1993. http://w2.vatican.va/content/john-paul-ii/en/encyclicals/documents/hf_jp-ii_enc_06081993_veritatis-splendor.html.

Pope John Paul II. "Address to the Academy of Sciences, no. 1." *L'Osservatore Romano*, English edition. Vatican City, The Holy See, November 24, 1986.

Pope Paul VI. *Humanae vitae*. Vatican City, The Holy See, 1968. http://w2.vatican.va/content/paul-vi/en/encyclicals/documents/hf_p-vi_enc_25071968_humanae-vitae.html.

Pope, Stephen J. *Human Evolution and Christian Ethics*. Cambridge University Press, 2011.

Pope, Stephen J. 2007 "Reason and Natural Law." In *The Oxford Handbook of Theological Ethics*, edited by Gilbert Meilaender and William Werpehowski, 148–167. Oxford University Press, 2011.

Porter, Jean. *Nature as Reason: A Thomistic Theory of the Natural Law*. Grand Rapids, MI: Eerdmans, 2005.

Porter, Jean. *Natural and Divine Law: Reclaiming the Tradition for Christian Ethics*. Grand Rapids, MI, and Cambridge, UK: Eerdmans/Novalis, 1999.

President's Council on Bioethics. *Human Cloning and Human Dignity: An Ethical Inquiry*. Washington, DC: The President's Council on Bioethics, 2002. https://bioethicsarchive.georgetown.edu/pcbe/reports/cloningreport/.

Ratzinger, Joseph. *Values in a Time of Upheaval*. San Francisco: Ignatius Press, 2006.

Saletan William. "Little Children," *New York Times*. 2008.

Soble, Alan. "The Fundamentals of the Philosophy of Sex." In *The Philosophy of Sex: Contemporary Readings*, edited by Alan Soble. Lanham, MD: Rowman & Littlefield Publishers, Inc., 2002.

Stout, Jeffrey. *Ethics After Babel: The Languages of Morals and Their Discontents*. Princeton University Press, 2001.

Stretton, Dean. "Critical Notice—*Defending Life: A Moral and Legal Case Against Abortion Choice*." *Journal of Medical Ethics* 34 (2008): 793–797.

Thobaben, James R. "Natural Law: A Good Idea That Does Not Work Very Well (At Least Not in the Current Society)." *Christian Bioethics* 22, no. 2 (2016): 213–237.

Tully, Patrick. "From Pluralism to Consensus in Beginning-of-Life Debates: Does Contemporary Natural Law Theory Offer a Way Forward?" *Christian Bioethics* 22, no. 2 (2016): 143–168.

Vatican. *Dignitas personae*. Rome: Congregation for the Doctrine of the Faith, 2008. http://www.vatican.va/roman_curia/congregations/cfaith/documents/rc_con_cfaith_doc_20081208_dignitas-personae_en.html.

Vatican. *Donum Vitae* or "Instruction on Respect for Human Life in Its Origin and On the Dignity of Procreation." Rome: Congregation for the Doctrine of the Faith, 1987. http://www.vatican.va/roman_curia/congregations/cfaith/documents/rc_con_cfaith_doc_19870222_respect-for-human-life_en.html

Vacek, Edward Collins, S. J. "Catholic Natural Law and Reproductive Ethics." *Journal of Medicine and Philosophy* 17, no. 3 (1992): 329–346.

Velez, Father Juan R. "Immediate Animation: Thomistic Principles Applied to Norman Ford's Objections." *Ethics & Medicine* 21, no. 1 (2005): 11–28.

Wilson, E. O. *Sociobiology: The New Synthesis*. Harvard University Press, 1975.

PART II

THE ETHICS OF BEING A PARENT

CHAPTER 7

BEYOND THE "FIRST COMMANDMENT"

Procreation and Parenting in Judaism

SETH GOREN

As one of the first directives given in the Torah, Judaism's "First Commandment" is to "be fruitful and multiply," imposing a binding and detailed obligation on traditional adherents to procreate. However, Jewish responses to and interpretations of this duty extend beyond simply bearing children. Instead, extensive resources offer guidance on parenting as individuals, and communal obligations to children, even those not one's own. When taken together, the effect of these sources is to urge even Jews who integrate little Jewish practice into their lives toward procreation and parenting, even if that pressure is not always reflected in higher Jewish birth rates.

Of particular note is the way in which Jewish tradition has responded to the basic principle of commanded procreation and parenting in new and creative ways. This was certainly the case in early times, but has become more pronounced as both options for procreation and parenting, as well as divisions in the Jewish community, have multiplied.

A further word about Jewish diversity: Judaism extends back at least three thousand years and around the globe. While it has had particularly influential centers of learning, it lacks centralized hierarchical structures that generate a single approach on any given topic. Thus, talking about "the Jewish tradition" as if it were a monolithic practice and perspective is misleading, and placing Judaism's multivocalic nature front and center is imperative to appreciating differences not just between, say, the fifth century BCE Middle East and today, but even between different communities and individuals in close geographic proximity in the same era. Indeed, it is this diversity that is the hallmark of Jewish approaches to procreation and parenting more than anything else. Consequently, this article presents a broad overview of Jewish perspectives on procreation and parenting, but is by no means exhaustive.

Procreation

Historically, Judaism has strongly embraced an obligation to procreate, with particular dictates on the scope and conditions of fulfilling that obligation. All Jewish religious movements continue to embrace the commandment to procreate, even if they interpret it differently. Indeed, in contemporary settings, even some secular Jewish voices place an emphasis on procreation, although the impact of these expectations is uneven.

General Obligation to Procreate

Of all 613 traditional Jewish commandments, the obligation to "be fruitful and multiply" is taken as the first one. It makes its initial appearance in Genesis 1:28 as God's initial set of instructions to the first human being, and is repeated to Noah twice in Genesis 9:1 and 9:7.[1]

Later, this first commandment takes on a particularly Jewish nature when it is imparted to Jacob in Genesis 35:11. When set against the backdrop of numerous divine promises to Abraham and Isaac to make their descendants "as numerous as the stars in the sky,"[2] the serious nature of this obligation, as well as its connection to the covenantal relationship with God, is clear.

Biblically, a failure to bear children is at times connected with punishment, with prayer and divine intervention sought as remedies, typically by women.[3] In 2 Samuel 6:20–23, David curses Michal with infertility for her criticism of his behavior, while in the opening of 1 Samuel, Hannah responds to infertility with prayer, even promising to surrender any offspring to serve Eli, the high priest.[4] Leah's ability to conceive, especially when contrasted with her sister Rachel's struggles, is divine compensation for her husband's preference for Rachel.[5] There are times where a couple's failure to conceive is stated or implied as flowing from male infertility,[6] but it is more common that a couple's failure to bear children is placed on the woman, often with significant degrees of scorn and derision[7].

At times in the patriarchal and matriarchal era, an individual's attempt to live up to this expectation comes up short, at least initially. Abraham and Sarah struggle to conceive together, leading Sarah to offer him her servant Hagar as an alternative.[8] Later, Rachel responds to her own apparent infertility with jealousy at her sister Leah's numerous children and by presenting her servant as a substitute for herself.[9] These two narratives differ in at least as much as Sarah fails to regard Hagar's son as her own (even seeing him as rival to her own son Isaac once he is born), while Rachel's presentation is accompanied by the hope that she "through her I too may have children."[10] Regardless, they present a social structure in which alternative methods for reproduction are seemingly approved.

Similarly, the Bible embraces levirate marriage as an obligatory method of family planning. As laid out in Deuteronomy 5, if a man dies without a living son, his surviving brother is obliged to take the widow as a wife, with the first son resulting from their relationship being proclaimed the deceased brother's child and heir. In the event that the brother seeks to avoid his responsibilities, as financial incentive might encourage him to do, the subsequent verses lay out a ceremony of "release" (*chalitzah*), in which the brother is ritually and publicly humiliated.[11] In this way, a deceased brother's family line continues, with his brother "procreating" on his behalf. While levirate marriage is exceedingly uncommon even among traditional Jews, Orthodox and Conservative Judaism continue to require the release ritual in situations where the circumstances apply.

In addition to the practical perspectives on procreation, numerous Jewish sources highlight the spiritual aspects and practical rewards of procreation. According to Tana Devei Eliyahu Zuta 14, a collection of midrashim redacted over a thousand years ago, the Israelites were redeemed from slavery in Egypt because they continued to procreate, and future redemption will also come with a willingness to procreate. Meanwhile, in the Babylonian Talmud, b.Nid.31a emphasizes that a human being is created in a tripartite partnership of a mother, a father, and God.

Through the ages, there have been extremely limited circumstances under which a man is delayed in or freed from his responsibility for procreating. Of particular note is when the individual is a religious scholar and fears the expenses and distractions of having children.[12] Each of these sources refers back to the specific example of Ben Azzai, who states his desire to focus solely on his studies and to leave procreation to others.[13]

In modern times, Jewish demographic considerations beyond religious obligations have loomed large in conversations about procreation as well. In noting the traditional Jewish view of children as a blessing, one Reform Jewish text remarks that they also serve as "an assurance of the continued existence of the Jewish people," and urges readers to factor in "the tragic decimation of our people during the Holocaust," "the threats of annihilation that have pursued the Jewish people throughout history," and "the problem of Jewish survival" when considering the number of children to have.[14] Echoing this, a Central Conference of American Rabbis responsum asserts that "[i]n light of the Holocaust and the current diminution of the world Jewish population, it is incumbent upon each of us to urge Jewish couples to have two or more children."[15] While these may not be new sentiments,[16] they reflect an emphasis on Jewish procreation across mainstream Jewish movements, one that is rooted in broader cultural and historical mores.

These exhortations to procreate have not yielded fruit with consistency. While birth rates in Orthodox communities tend to be high, in Israel and the United States, non-Orthodox Jewish birth rates are relatively low, especially when compared to other demographic groups in those countries.[17] Moreover, this ongoing approach to procreation and its continued hold even in the structures of liberal Judaism has, understandably, contributed to much discomfort and marginalization of Jews who struggle with infertility or choose not to become parents,[18] and has served as a basis for criticizing gay and lesbian Jews, both historically and in modern times.[19]

Specifics

While providing an overarching emphasis, the initial commandment to procreate leaves specific requirements unanswered, allowing subsequent Jewish texts to refine obligations with precision.

To provide structure for carrying out this obligation, the early rabbis devise the concept of *onah* or "season." The regulations governing *taharat mishpachah*, or "family purity," include the regularity with which a husband is obliged to have sexual intercourse with his wife,[20] with procreation being one of the reasons given. There are also corresponding times during this cycle when intercourse is prohibited, in particular during menstruation.[21]

In further assessing the obligation's scope, m.Yev.6:6 records two initial debates over to whom the commandment to procreate applies, and what satisfies the commandment's requirements:

> A person may not abstain from being fruitful and multiplying unless he has *banim* ["children," masculine plural]. The House of Shammai says two male children, while the House of Hillel says a male and a female, citing Genesis 5:2: "Male and female he created them." ... A man is commanded to be fruitful and multiply, but a woman is not. Rabbi Yochanan ben Baroka says it applies to both of them, citing Genesis 1:28: "And God blessed them, and he said to them, 'Be fruitful and multiply.'"

Although later commentaries try to explain excluding women from this obligation,[22] the text itself is silent as to why this is so. Regardless, this stance is accepted largely (though not entirely) without question until the modern era.[23]

Building on this mishnah, the Talmud records further differences of opinion as to how many children and of what gender one is obligated to have to satisfy the commandment of being fruitful and multiplying, with varying authorities positing that a man meets the requirements by having two sons and two daughters, a son and a daughter, or a son or a daughter.[24] The rabbis also debate whether having a child who ceases to be Jewish qualifies as fulfilling this obligation.

By the medieval period, these differences of opinion are resolved in favor of the House of Hillel, requiring a man to father at least both a son and a daughter. In his

Mishneh Torah, Maimonides endorses the House of Hillel's one boy/one girl requirement,[25] as does the Shulḥan Arukh, the preeminent Jewish legal code assembled in the sixteenth century. The latter also elucidates that if a man's children die, but leave the man a granddaughter and a grandson, the obligation is fulfilled.[26] However, if "the son is a eunuch, and the daughter is infertile," the man is obliged to continue his procreative efforts.[27]

Additional texts stretching back to the Talmudic period and earlier urge going further, beyond these minimal two-child requirements, to produce as many children as possible. In an extended discussion in b.Yev.62b, Rabbi Yehoshua instructs that "a man should marry a woman in his youth, and he should marry a woman in his old age; just as he has children in his youth, he should have children in his old age." In reaching this conclusion, he looks at the Ecclesiastes 11:6 exhortation to "sow your seed in the morning, and don't hold back your hand in the evening."[28] Others rely on the comment of Isaiah 45:18 that God did not create the earth as "a waste, but formed it for habitation [lashevet]," interpreting *shevet* as an indication that ongoing procreation is obligatory as a means of populating the earth. Bringing in teleological aspects, b.Yev.62b and b.Nid.13b concur that the messianic age will arrive when the available reservoir of souls is fully depleted, and having children beyond the bare minimum will bring that day closer.

Regardless of Rabbi Yehoshua's contemporaneous detractors, his position is subsequently codified in the Rambam's Mishneh Torah, if ambivalently. Speaking of a husband, Maimonides holds that, "even though a man has satisfied the commandment of procreation, he is still obligated by rabbinic interpretation not to refrain from procreation while he still has strength to do so, for each person who adds one soul to Israel, it is as if that person has built a world."[29] This stands in contrast to the texts of Mishneh Torah. Ishut 15:1 and 15:7, which appear to indicate that a man may forgo intercourse if he has already satisfied the basic procreative requirements.[30] The Shulḥan Aruch is silent on whether *shevet* extends beyond the House of Hillel's expectations. That said, EH 1:8 directs a man to have a wife capable of bearing additional children even if he has already fulfilled the basic commandment of having a daughter and a son, with the Mappah granting exceptions if doing so will lead to tensions between the man's children from a previous relationship and his new wife.

The Conservative movement's Committee on Jewish Law and Standards, which interprets *halachah* for the Conservative movement in North America, erases any distinction between men and women in terms of the obligation to procreate, noting that the commandment is given to both Adam and Eve. Similarly, while the committee maintains that a couple should seek to have at least two children, it specifically discards any overlaying requirements about the children's gender.[31] The Reform movement agrees with these stances, stating that "marriage without children is very distant from the Jewish ideal of marriage."[32]

Moshe Feinstein, a leading Orthodox authority, authorizes a couple to forgo further children beyond the minimal requirement if her pregnancy would be difficult or if doing so would cause her "great pain."³³ He holds that a husband need not have intercourse with his wife during each and every period of *onah*, but that *shevet* requires that they not give up on the possibility of having additional children entirely.

While not grounded in religious sources, even many secular Jewish perspectives take up the cause of Jewish procreation, some regarding low Jewish birth rates with alarm. Writing in *Tikkun*, a progressive Jewish publication, in 1985, feminist Anne Roiphe highlighted the dangers to Jewish continuity from "the relatively new dangers of low birth rate and divorcing, dissolving families, delayed marriage and single life choices."³⁴ The release of the 2013 Pew study on Jewish demographics in the United States unleashed a wave of secular Jewish press articles decrying low Jewish fertility rates, along with assimilation and intermarriage.³⁵

Consequences for Failing in the Commandment to Procreate

As the Jewish obligation to procreate is clear, traditional Jewish texts lay out rather extreme, if perhaps hyperbolic, consequences for failures to procreate. Two Talmudic rabbis alternately describe a man who does not procreate as "one who spills blood" and "one who lessens the divine image."³⁶ More practically, a man who was not a father was excluded from participation in certain aspects of Jewish life, including participating in the Sanhedrin.³⁷

If a couple did not have children in accordance with the commandment's directives, there were consequences for their marriage, with divorce being a possible or required outcome. Originally, man was required to divorce if, after ten years, the couple had not had a child.³⁸ Should the husband refuse to do so,³⁹ the court could compel him to issue a divorce decree. Similarly, if the infertility was attributable to the husband, a woman was permitted to ask a court to compel her husband to grant her a divorce.

Subsequent texts are substantially less harsh and decisive. In his commentary on EH 1:3, although he holds that a man who does not marry should not be "permitted to make a blessing or to engage in Torah" and "is not called a man," Moshe Isserles rejects any attempt to intervene in a couple's marriage and says that this has not been the traditional practice in "many generations."⁴⁰

Later sources offer alternate paths for those who are unable to bear children. Blending spiritual, theological, and earthly perspectives, Eliezer Papo contends in *Pele Yoetz*, his work on practical ethics, that attempting to procreate, however unsuccessfully, is the equivalent of having done so, with connected rewards. As a substitute for procreating, he advises a person without children to do the following:

> He should raise an orphan boy or girl or a child of poor parents in his home based on Torah and service such that it will bring upon him the promise that a person who raises

a child is considered as if he gave birth to them. He might also financially support for a wise scholar and provide whatever he might lack—this person will be considered his son, as is written in Psalms 77:16, "The sons of Jacob and Joseph, Selah."

This person should dedicate projects so that his name will be remembered. If he is a wise scholar, he should complete a book. A person who does these things earns a good name. Having one's name be remembered positively is better than sons and daughters.[41]

Contraception and Abortion

Against this relatively pro-procreation background, pre-modern Judaism's approach to contraception is decidedly mixed, even as early rabbis grappled with this question early on.[42] The primary basis for concern is found in Genesis 38, where Onan fails to fulfill his levirate obligation to his sister-in-law, and "spills his seed upon the ground." This episode gives rise to an entire line of rabbinic and subsequent thought that prohibits *hashchatat zera levatalah* or "wasting seed" and depositing semen anywhere other than the vagina.[43]

Nevertheless, the resistance to withdrawal before ejaculation is not total. In Tos. Niddah 2:4, Rabbi Meir grants explicit permission[44] to three categories of women to insert a *mokh*, an absorbent ball of cloth or wool into the vagina to prevent semen from reaching the uterus: a girl between the ages of eleven and twelve; a pregnant woman; and a nursing woman. In each of these cases, Rabbi Meir responds to concerns about the life or well-being of the woman, the fetus, or a nursing baby, and the passage concludes with the remainder of the rabbis disagreeing with him.[45] In a similar vein, in b.Yev.34b, Rabbi Eliezer permits withdrawal before ejaculation when a woman is nursing a child under two year of age, although this position evokes the strong objections of his peers based on the principles against "wasting seed."[46]

The Talmud also makes mention of a *sama de akarta*, or "sterilizing drug," on b.Tev.65b.[47] Similarly, Shabbat 110b *kos ikarin*, or "cup of roots," as a curative potion, but one that makes the imbiber sterile. The word *ikarin* makes an appearance in Tos. Yev.8:2, which allows a woman to partake of a drink that prevents pregnancy, but forbids a man to do the same.

The Rambam takes a strong stance against *hashchatat zera levatalah*,[48] phrasing the prohibition as barring a man from "threshing inside and winnowing outside."[49] It also agrees with the Tosefta's restrictions and permissions about sterilizing potions,[50] and the Shulḥan Arukh follows the Rambam on both of these positions.[51] That said, there are ongoing disputes that extend into the early modern period about when a *mokh* is permitted and even disagreements on how to interpret preceding rabbis' words.[52]

In the present day, the Conservative Jewish approach is relatively permissive with regard to contraception and allows a variety of methods and justifications to delay procreation and prevent conception, including the health of the couple's relationship.[53]

The Reform movement is quite similar, with both movements looking primarily to the end result of using contraception, and less at the particular method in question.[54]

There is far more difference of opinion in the Orthodox world, where modern scientific advances and the diversification of available types of birth control has contributed to a similar diversity of opinions on the permissibility of their use. Some Orthodox scholars approach certain types of contraception, such as a condom or diaphragm, as analogous to a *mokh*, with its concomitant restrictions. There is somewhat more leniency regarding spermicide, although not with consistency.[55] Moshe Feinstein initially permitted a couple's use of birth control pills after a man had fathered a boy and a girl,[56] but expressed concerns about adverse medical side effects and whether the pill's use was "like outsmarting G-d's will."[57] There is also serious disagreement as to what circumstances justify the use of contraception.[58]

The discussion of abortion in Jewish tradition is too lengthy and nuanced to consider here in detail, and we will consider it here only with relative brevity. Much of the discussion springs from Exodus 21:22–25, which addresses the accidental pushing of a pregnant woman when men are fighting. If "a miscarriage results, but no other damage ensues, the one responsible shall be fined." This consequence is far less severe than it would be in the case of an accidental death of a person, leading many to conclude that even Biblically, a fetus is not regarded as having full personhood.

There is more disagreement in subsequent discussions. b.San.57b backs a definition of murder that would include causing the death of a fetus, while b.Sanh.72b holds that a fetus is does not achieve personhood until the head or the majority of the body has emerged, and several sources state that until it reaches forty days, a fetus is "mere water."[59] Echoed elsewhere, with multiple Talmudic sources seeing the fetus as being a "limb of the mother."[60] One area of clarity: where a pregnancy endangers a mother's life, it must be terminated.[61]

The conflict continues to meander through the Middle Ages. The Rambam bolsters the case for abortion if a mother's life is as risk, considering the fetus like a "pursuer," which would justify murder even if it were a person.[62] The Maimonidean language is adopted wholesale in the Shulḥan Arukh.[63]

In a modern context, Orthodox authorities have been more reluctant to support the termination of a pregnancy,[64] while Conservative, Reform, and Reconstructionist authorities are generally far more permissive and have often been on the forefront of advocating for abortion rights.[65] The latter group tends to permit abortion not only for a sake of the mother's life but also as a response to fetal defects and threats to the mother's health.[66]

Assisted Reproduction

While scientific methods of assisted reproduction are relatively new, one can find creative responses to infertility even in Biblical narratives. As noted earlier, when Sarah and Rachel struggle to conceive children, they direct their husbands to their female servants in order to reproduce. In addition to prayer,[67] classical texts offer a variety of suggestions as to the sources of sterility and methods for increasing potency.[68] Some scholars also analogize assisted reproduction to traditional considerations of pregnancy without intercourse.[69]

In a more modern context, Jewish sources have often taken a positive approach to assisted reproduction, although there is great divergence depending on the method used and in which movement. The primary concerns about assisted reproduction exist among decisors and are twofold: (1) the prohibition on "wasting seed," as discussed above; and (2) potential uncertainty about the child's genetic parents (including egg and sperm donors), lineage, and resulting concerns about possible incest, however unintended.[70]

There is a particular divergence in an Orthodox setting. On the one hand, Moshe Feinstein grudgingly comes out in favor of permitting in vitro fertilization from a sperm donor.[71] Representative of the opposite view is Eliezer Yehudah Waldenberg, who refuses to apply a presumption of paternity in the father's favor and raises concerns about ejaculation, even for testing.[72] Moreover, in the event that the intended father's sperm is not used, there are ongoing differences over whether he has fulfilled the commandment of procreating,[73] and it is difficult to see how this commandment could be taken to apply to an anonymous donor.[74]

Taking a less rigorous approach, Conservative Judaism has supported in vitro fertilization, with a strong preference for using the intended father's sperm.[75] The movement has divided with regard to surrogacy as a means of assisted reproduction: one opinion holds that the possibility of allowing a couple to become parents outweighs any potential adverse consequence,[76] while a second elevates concerns about surrogacy, including reservations about exploitation of surrogates.[77] The Reform movement largely concurs with permissibility.[78]

Parenting

A significant number of Jewish sources, classical and contemporary, lay out requirements and provide instruction on an individual's obligations for one's own children and methods for taking parental responsibility for those who are not one's biological offspring. In addition, multiple texts point to collective obligations toward a community's children in ways that buttress parents' duties.[79]

Responsibilities and Guidance for One's Own Children

Most of the Genesis narratives are replete with examples of what most today would think of as exactly the *wrong* way to parent. Let us consider Abraham, the foremost of the Jewish patriarchs, as an example. To satisfy the complaints of Sarah, he sends one of his sons out into the wilderness, with only Divine Providence preventing his death.[80] Later, he willingly prepares Isaac for sacrifice and stops only when commanded to do so by angelic intervention.[81] If nothing else, the life-saving supernatural forces that protect Abraham's sons lend credence to the position that his actions were excellent demonstrations of bad parenting.

The other patriarchs are similar in their parental approaches. Isaac and Rebecca both demonstrate a clear preference for one son over the other, while Jacob's elevation of Joseph, combined with Joseph's ensuing acts of arrogance, pushes his brothers to the point that they sell him into bondage and fake his death.[82] All in all, the matriarchal and patriarchal drive to procreate is in evidence, but appropriate parenting appears to be in short supply.

In at least one narrative example, procreating itself is sufficient in and of itself, and raising a child one has borne does not figure into the presentation. In 1 Samuel 1, Hannah prays for a child and vows to "dedicate him to the LORD for all the days of his life."[83] When she conceives, and Samuel is born, she turns him over to serve under the priest Eli.[84]

Additional Biblical texts, including wisdom literature, supplement these narratives with commandments, aphorisms, and adages. Deuteronomy 4:9 and 6:7 lay out the expectation that parents instruct their children in Torah. Offering more direct, if violent advice, Proverbs 13:24 serves as a basis for the phrase, "Spare the rod, spoil the child,"[85] while 22:6 of the same book emphasizes early education with the maxim, "Teach a child a path, and they shall not depart from it."

There is no expectation that child rearing be easy. The concept of *tza'ar gidul banim*, "the pain of raising children," is seen as rooted in the divine curse Genesis 3:16 that Eve endure pain during childbirth.[86] The Talmud acknowledges later descendant's difficulties with their children.[87] However, men who experience, endure, and remember these are entitled to certain legal rights, like serving as witnesses.[88]

In the face of these challenges, a parent's obligation to children runs both deep and specific. The Babylonian Talmud demands that parents "teach them Torah, take a spouse for them, and teach them a craft. Some say, to teach them to swim as well."[89] A father is also obligated to provide his daughter with a dowry and appropriate clothing.[90]

As with procreative duties, parental responsibilities to children differ based on the parent's gender. As a rule, commandments to parents regarding care for and education of their children traditionally fall on fathers, but not mothers.[91] As an example, fathers must circumcise sons on their eighth day of life,[92] while firstborn sons, who would otherwise be given over to the priesthood, must be redeemed from priests.[93]

Under the Talmudic approach, fathers are also required to provide their children with food, along the lines of what they owe their wives, until the children reach the age of six.[94] Any father who fails to do so will be publicly humiliated, but if one has the means to pay, a court will compel him to do so.[95] This original obligation is rabbinically extended beyond the age of six,[96] a stance later codified in the Mishneh Torah and Shulḥan Arukh.[97] While a father may not renounce his obligations to his children, a mother may do so and turn her children over to their father.[98]

Traditionally, in the event that parents divorce, children remain with their mother until they reach the age of six. At that point, sons are put in the custody of their father, while daughters remain with their mother.[99] That said, numerous, although not all, rabbis and codes adopt an approach that places children according to what is determined to be their best interests.[100]

With regard to more specific parental responsibilities, one of the most significant is providing children with an education, which has its roots in Biblical text (see, e.g., Deuteronomy 11:19).[101] The Mishneh Torah requires a parent to hire a teacher for their child or to teach their child themselves.[102]

Some sources urge educational instruction to be individualized and geared toward that particular child. Relying on the instruction in Proverbs 22:6 to "train a child in the way the child should go," Sefer Hachasidim 208 directs instructors to allow child to find a path that matches that child's abilities and to focus the instruction in that sphere.

A person's parental responsibilities to descendants extends beyond one's children. Maimonides makes it clear that educational duties extend to teaching grandchildren as well, springing from Deuteronomy's direction to inform "your children and your children's children."[103]

Recent years have seen a proliferation of Jewish parenting resources. Many of these guides draw on Jewish traditions and texts for instilling Jewish values, even if few of these original traditions and texts speak exclusively to parenting. Perhaps more interesting is the diversity of audiences that these resources address; even a handful of decades ago, it is difficult to imagine books like *Jewish Lesbian Parenting* and *If I'm Jewish and You're Christian, What Are the Kids?: A Parenting Guide for Interfaith Families* finding much of a place in the Jewish parenting world. These speak to a recognition of a far more varied Jewish community and the adaptivity at least some segments of the community see in Jewish tradition.

Parenting through Adoption

Procreating biologically is only one of the possible ways to become a parent, and procreating in and of itself does not necessary mean that a person ultimately serves as that child's parent. Jewish tradition disentangles procreation and parenting, whether through narrative, legal structures, and communal and individual obligation.

There are numerous stories of those who take children to raise, even though those children are not their biological offspring, and secure an honored place in traditional literature. For all of his shortcomings in relationships with his biological children, Abraham takes his nephew Lot into his household and raises him until the tensions between their shepherds become problematic. After being given up by his parents to prevent his murder, Moses is fished out of the Nile, adopted, and raised by Pharaoh's daughter. In the Book of Esther, Mordechai is said to be Esther's uncle and offers her ongoing direction.

Midrashic sources echo the praise and primacy given the person who parents a child. In both Sanh. 19b and Meg. 13a, the Talmud asserts that "Scripture looks upon one who brings up an orphan as if he had begotten him." One midrashic source elevates the person who raises a child over the biological parent, stating "He who brings up a child is to be called its father, not he who gave birth."[104]

Legally, early rabbis created and developed the position of the *apotropos*, someone who essentially serves as the guardian of a child. While an *apotropos* does not substitute for a child's biological parents or negate their duties or relationship, this guardian may take on certain obligations with regard to the child, with the guardian entitled to the child's financial earnings.[105] These responsibilities are further fleshed out during the medieval period as encompassing providing an education, food, and clothing.[106]

The Shulḥan Arukh lays out extensive requirements for serving as an *apotropos*.[107] A woman traditionally was permitted to serve as an *apotropos*, so long as she was capable of carrying out the position's responsibilities.[108]

All this said, Jewish tradition separates the guardian's obligations to care for a child from the attribution of the guardian's legal and person status to the child. As an example, if a male guardian is a *kohen*, or member of the priestly caste, a male child in his care does not take on this status. Similarly, a non-Jewish child adopted by Jewish parents must undergo conversion before becoming a part of the Jewish community.

Again, traditional Judaism does not see an *apotropos* as an adopting parent per se, but allows certain tokens as recognition of the closeness of their relationship. A child may recite the mourner's kaddish in memory of an adopting parent, and is the natural choice to recite mourner's prayers in the event that no biological kin is available to do so.[109]

As with procreation, the modern streams of Judaism have diverged somewhat in responding to adoption. The extensive work *Sha'arei Uziel* examines guardianship from modern traditional perspective and lays out specific requirements, from the obligation to provide identical resources for biological and nonbiological children to a guardian's requisite qualifications. Even with a broader approach, it maintains many of the traditional approaches to guardianship.

In contrast, Reform Judaism recognizes adoption in alignment with secular law and regards adopted and biological children as identical for all purposes, dispensing with any traditional distinctions between the two.[110]

Communal Parenting Responsibilities

In Jewish tradition, it is not only the parents who have a role to play in raising children. Communal involvement is expected, especially in providing children with an education.

These responsibilities are best considered in the context of Jewish communal responsibilities as a whole. Texts repeatedly enjoin people to involve themselves in and connect with the community, with one text asserting that a person who fails to join with the community in times of difficulty will not experience communal joy (b.Ta'an.7b).

True, there are texts that distinguish among degrees of culpability, including the assertion in Deuteronomy that "parents shall not be put to death for children, nor children be put to death for parents: one shall be put to death only for one's own crime."[111] But what is more striking, from a current perspective, is declarations like, "Anyone who is able to influence the people of their home, and does not, is punished for the sins of the people of their home. Their city, are punished for the sins of their city. The whole world, are punished for the sins of the whole world."[112]

This sense of communal duty as it relates to a community's children is most explicitly stated in the repeated Biblical imprecations to tend to the needs of the orphan as one of many vulnerable individuals and as featured in the repeated Biblical phrase that also includes the widow and the "stranger."[113] This obligation is spelled out further in later sources, but has clear roots in Biblical texts.

The role of community in fulfilling, or failing to fulfill, commandments can be seen in the community's involvement in instructing and disciplining children. A precise example of the communal role in parenting is the set of commandments around the "stubborn and rebellious son," the text of which reads as follows:

> If a man has a wayward and defiant son, who does not heed his father or mother and does not obey them even after they discipline him, his father and mother shall take hold of him and bring him out to the elders of his town at the public place of his community. They shall say to the elders of his town, "This son of ours is disloyal and defiant; he does not heed us. He is a glutton and a drunkard." Thereupon the men of his town shall stone him to death. Thus you will sweep out evil from your midst: all Israel will hear and be afraid.[114]

Clearly parents have a role to play in carrying out this commandment, and multiple sources make clear that both the child's mother and the father must be involved in fulfilling its specifics.[115] That said, there clearly are communal dimensions to this act of child discipline: the parents' actions are undertaken in public, not in the private home; the parents' declaration of their son's wayward actions must be made to the town's elders; and the punishment is executed by the men of the town, not exclusively by the parents.[116]

While it is unclear how and if this directive was carried out in reality,[117] it makes clear the worldview that parenting is not something done in isolation, but rather a communal series of actions with general repercussions and entanglements.

Just as parents are not alone in disciplining their children, the parental responsibility for educating their children does not fall on them alone. There are repeated exhortations for communities to maintain a strong educational system. Some of these are more general: b.Ket.67b speaks of the communal obligations to fund education for orphans. Even after an orphan has come of age, the community's obligations continue. Additionally, there is a collective duty to support a male orphan in getting married, including renting a house and buying a bed and other household items.

In a similar vein, the Talmud records an extended discussion about the necessity of providing an education to everyone and throughout the land. Otherwise, the rabbis reasoned with concern, only those with living fathers who were obligated to educate would receive an education (b.Bava Batra 21a).

While there is a particular focus on those without parents, obligations are broader. The Mishneh Torah imposes a duty on "every Jewish scholar to teach all those who ask to be their students, even if they are not that person's own children."[118] To ensure a system of education, towns are required to maintain schools and teachers for their children, with a ban being placed on a town's residents if they fail to do so (Hilchot Talmud Torah 2:1).

Conclusion

The diversity of Jewish opinions makes it difficult to draw comprehensive and generalized conclusions about Jewish perspectives on procreation and parenting. If anything, the most consistent outcome of a survey like this is the tensions that exist among Jewish perspectives: a strong historical push toward procreation and a low modern fertility rate; strong support both for and against birth control and assisted reproduction; a reluctance to embrace adoption as it exists as an institution paired with directives to ensure that those without parental support receive care and education.

Notes

1. Jewish religious scholars have disputed whether this was in fact a commandment or a blessing. See Epstein, *Arukh HaShulḥan, Even Ha'ezer* 1:2.
2. See, e.g., Genesis 15:5, 22:17, 26:4; cf. Hebrews 11:12.
3. Indeed, some sources explain the patriarchs' and matriarchs' initial failure to conceive as an intentional catalyst to draw them into prayer and closer to God. Babylonian Talmud, Tractate Yevamot 64a; *Genesis Rabbah* 45:4.
4. *Pesiqta de-Rab Kahane* 22:2.
5. Genesis 29:31.
6. Genesis 20:17; Ruth 1:5–21.
7. See, e.g., 1 Samuel 1, *Genesis Rabbah* 73:5, *Pesiqta de-Rab Kahane* 42:5.
8. Genesis 16:2.
9. Genesis 30:1, 3.
10. Genesis 30:3.
11. Cf. Genesis 38:1.

12. Babylonian Talmud, Tractate Kiddushin.29b; Mishneh Torah, Hilchot Ishut, 15:2–3; Shulḥan Aruch, Even Ha'ezer 1:4
13. The other rabbis chastise Ben Azzai, asserting, "You interpret Jewish law beautifully, but do not carry out the law beautifully." Ben Azzai defends himself saying "What can I do? My soul desires Torah. The world will be sustained by others." In spite of this tension, the Mishneh Torah cites Ben Azzai positively and by name. Mishneh Torah, Hilchot Ishut 15:3.
14. Maslin, *Gates of Mizpah*, 11.
15. Jacob, "Jewish Marriage without Children." Cf. Abelson and Dorff, "Mitzvah Children" ("Although young people may marry reluctantly and late, the marriage at least represents a step in the direction of children").
16. See, e.g., Rawidowicz, "Israel: The Ever-Dying People."
17. Lugo, Cooperman, and Smith, "2013 Pew Research Center Survey of U.S. Jews: A Portrait of Jewish Americans"; Cooperman and Sahgal, "Israel's Religiously Divided Society."
18. For one response, see Gold, *And Hannah Wept: Infertility, Adoption, and the Jewish couple*.
19. See, e.g., Sefer HaḤinukh 209; Schulman, "Same-Sex Marriage and the Jews"; Geller, Fine, and Fine, "The Halakhah of Same-Sex Relations in a New Context"; cf. Rapoport, "Judaism & Homosexuality: An Alternate Rabbinic View" (criticizing the view that gay men should be pressed to marry women in order to fulfill the commandment to procreate).
20. Mishnah Ketubot 5:6. According to Rabbi Eliezer, the time frame varies depending on the husband's profession, ranging from every day for a man who has no regular work to every six months for sailors.
21. Leviticus 15:19–30, 18:19, 20:18. Although based in Biblical text, extensive rules governing menstruation and marital contact have developed over time. See, e.g., Babylonian Talmud, Tractate Niddah 66a; Mishneh Torah, Hilchot Issurei Biah; Shulḥan Arukh, Yoreh De'ah 183–200.
22. See, e.g., Ovadiah ben Avraham from Bartenura on Mishnah Yevamot 6:6. Based on the unpointed Biblical text of Genesis 1:28, he argues that, although the commandment to procreate is given in the plural, the directive to "master it" is directed solely at the man, and limits the scope of the original commandment to him alone.
23. As an outlying example, women's essential involvement in the procreative process pushes Nissim of Gerona in the fourteenth century to urge reconsideration of this stance. Ḥidushei id. HaRan on Babylonian Talmud, Tractate Kiddushin 41a.
24. Babylonian Talmud, Tractate Yevamot 62a.
25. Mishneh Torah, Hilchot Ishut 15:4.
26. Shulḥan Aruch, Even Ha'ezer 1:6.
27. Shulḥan Aruch, Even Ha'ezer 1:5. At least one rabbi allows the obligation of procreation to be satisfied through the adoption of a child, but this appears to be a minority, if not unique, opinion. Daniel Pollack, Moshe Bleich, Charles J. Reid, Mohammad H. Fadel, "Classical Religious Perspectives of Adoption Law," *Notre Dame Law Review* 79, no. 2 (2004): 697 n.18.
28. Other rabbis in the same Talmudic discussion disagree with Rabbi Yehoshua, in particular about his interpretation of this verse.
29. Mishneh Torah, Hilchot Ishut 15:16.
30. There is an attempt to harmonize these two positions in Birchei Yosef on Even Ha'ezer 1:1, which asserts that the attempt at procreation must be more concerted and regular before fulfilling the basic requirements than after.
31. Abelson and Dorff, "Mitzvah Children."
32. Jacob, "Jewish Marriage Without Children."

33. *Igrot Moshe*, Even Ha'ezer IV, 32.3.
34. "The Jewish Family: A Feminist Perspective," *Tikkun* 1, no. 2 (1985): 70.
35. See, e.g., Jack Wertheimer and Steven Cohen, "The Pew Survey Reanalyzed: More Bad News, but a Glimmer of Hope," *Mosaic* (November 2, 2014). Israeli law similarly maintains an open and supportive attitude toward a variety of methods of procreation. Kahn, *Reproducing Jews: A Cultural Account of Assisted Conception in Israel*, 15–17.
36. Babylonian Talmud, Tractate Yevamot 63b. This consequence is affirmatively cited in the Shulḥan Arukh, which adds that a person who fails to follow this commandment "causes the divine presence to depart from Israel." Even Ha'ezer 1:1.
37. Sanhedrin 36b.
38. Babylonian Talmud, Tractate Yevamot 65b; Mishneh Torah Hilchot Ishut 15:10; Shulḥan Arukh, Even Ha'ezer 1:10, 154:6. See also Tosefta Yevamot 8:5.
39. Traditional Judaism grants a wife leeway to accept or reject a divorce, but only a husband is permitted to initiate divorce proceedings.
40. Isserles, Mappah Even Ha'ezer 1.3 and 8; Even Ha'ezer 154.10.
41. Papo, *Pele Yoetz*, 308.
42. For two thorough looks at traditional Jewish views on contraception, see David Michael Feldman, *Birth Control in Jewish Law: Marital Relations, Contraception, and Abortion as Set Forth in the Classic Texts of Jewish Law* (Jason Aronson, 1998), and Ronit Irshai, *Fertility and Jewish Law: Feminist Perspectives on Orthodox Responsa Literature* (UPNE, 2012) (esp. 53–110).
43. Feldman, Birth Control in Jewish Law. In its most extreme form, this transgression is said to be "graver than any other in the Torah," Shulḥan Arukh, Even Ha'ezer 23:3, and the equivalent of murder, Babylonian Talmud, Tractate Niddah 13b. That said, while this prohibition developed over the centuries, there is some uncertainty as to whether this was, in fact, Er and Onan's sin, whether the prohibition is properly rooted here, and whether the prohibition is Biblical at all; Feldman, 144–165.
44. There is some later disagreement over whether this constitutes permission or obligation and even on the timing of the *mokh*'s use. Cf. Rabbeinu Tam and Rashi on this text.
45. This passage appears multiple times in the Talmud. See, e.g., Babylonian Talmud, Tractate Yevamot 12b.
46. Rashi concurs with Rabbi Eliezer. Rashi on Babylonian Talmud, Tractate Yevamot 34b.
47. Other appearances of this phrase in rabbinic literature indicate that it may have had additional health benefits.
48. Hilchot Issurei Biah 21:9.
49. Hilchot Issurei Biah, 21:18.
50. Hilchot Issurei Biah, 16:12.
51. Even Ha'ezer 5:12, 23:2, 5. One commentary on the Shulḥan Arukh says that the prohibition on men extends even to other medicinal uses, while the permission for women stands even if it is not for preventing pain in childbirth. Ashkenazi, Be'er Heiteiv on Even Ha'ezer 5:10 and 5:11.
52. Irshai, *Fertility and Jewish Law*, 62–74. This distinction between depositing semen outside the vagina and preventing conception when ejaculation has occurred inside the vagina is reinforced by several nineteenth century *halakhic* decisors. For a more extensive discussion of medieval stances, see Meyer and Henoch, "Contraception in Contemporary Orthodox Judaism," 9–26.
53. Berkowitz and Popovsky, "Contraception."

54. Lauterbach, "Birth Control."
55. Meyer and Messner, "Contraception in Contemporary Orthodox Judaism."
56. *Igrot Moshe* Even Ha'ezer 4:74:2.
57. Shulḥan Arukh, Even Ha'ezerSh 1:65, 2:17, 4:72. Of particular concern was vaginal bleeding, which could have implications for Jewish prohibitions on contact during menstruation.
58. Irshai, *Fertility and Jewish Law*, 77–84.
59. Babylonian Talmud, Tractate Yevamot 69b, Babylonian Talmud, Tractate Niddah 30a–b.
60. Babylonian Talmud, Tractate Gittin 23b, b.Hul.58a, b.Naz.51a.
61. Mishnah Ohalot 7:8.
62. Mishneh Torah, Hilchot Rotzeach uShemirat Nefesh 1:9.
63. Shulḥan Arukh, Ḥoshen Mispat 425:2.
64. See Irshai, *Fertility and Jewish Law*, 160–200, for a consideration of the diversity of Orthodox opinions.
65. See Lewis D. Solomon, "The Jewish Tradition, Sexuality and Procreation" (2002), 183–192.
66. Grossman, "Partial Birth Abortion and the Question of When Life Begins"; Feldman, "Abortion: The Jewish View"; "When is Abortion Permitted?"
67. *Pesiqta de-Rab Kahane* 22:2; *Song of Songs Rabbah* 1, 4:2.
68. Examples for potency enhancers are fish (Babylonian Talmud, Tractate Sotah 11b) and garlic (Babylonian Talmud, Tractate Bava Kama 82a). On the other hand, salt (Babylonian Talmud, Tractate Gittin 70a) and long lectures (Babylonian Talmud, Tractate Yevamot 64b) supposedly promote sterility.
69. Rosner 1970, 127–128. The source in question is Babylonian Talmud, Tractate Ḥagigah 14b–15a, which addresses a virgin who has become pregnant.
70. For further challenges, see Sinclair 89–94.
71. Feinstein, *Igrot Moshe, Even Ha'ezer* 1:71 and 4:32.5.
72. Waldenberg, "She'alot u 'Teshuvot Tzitz Eliezer" 7:48, ch. 1 (pp. 190–191), 15:45. Irshai also lays out the position of various rabbinical opponents to artificial insemination using a husband's sperm, *Fertility and Jewish Law*, 225–234.
73. Daniel B. Sinclair, "Assisted Reproduction in Jewish Law," *Fordham Urb. L.J.* 30 (2002): 73–74; Irshai, *Fertility and Jewish Law*, 247–248.
74. For additional investigations of Orthodox positions on assisted reproduction and artificial insemination, see Irshai, *Fertility and Jewish Law*, 225–268.
75. Dorff, "Artificial Insemination, Egg Donation, and Adoption," and Mackler, "In Vitro Fertilization."
76. Spitz, "On the Use of Birth Surrogates."
77. Mackler, "On the Use of Birth Surrogates."
78. Freehof, "Artificial Insemination."
79. As a counterpart to a parent's obligations to a child, Judaism outlines extensive duties of a child to a parent. These responsibilities will be less of a focus here.
80. While this is sometimes read as Abraham acting to protect Isaac, *Genesis Rabbah* 53, it seems an extreme response.
81. There are those who argue that, by attempting to sacrifice Isaac, Abraham failed the "test." Indeed, one of the parents' obligations to a child is relatively basic: not to sacrifice them to either God or another deity, Leviticus 20:1.
82. Cf. Babylonian Talmud, Tractate Shabbat 10b, emphasizing the importance of avoiding favoritism among children.
83. 1 Samuel 1:11.

84. 1 Samuel 2:11. Granted, Hannah, as a woman, may not have been seen retrospectively as subject to the same commandment to procreate as a man, and her husband had already fathered children with his other wife. Nevertheless, the story shows a clear distinction between procreation and parenting, especially given the mother's formative role in caring for children during their first six years, as discussed below.
85. Also, Proverbs 22:15, 23:14, 29:15. Rashi's commentary on the verse makes the clear connection between a failure to use physical discipline and a child's choice to engage in bad acts and poor behavior. Deuteronomy 8:5 likens G-d's discipline of the Israelites to that of a parent with children. Cf. *Ecclesiastes Rabbah* 13:4, in which Rabbi Eliezer posits that G-d's punishment of the Jewish people through their servitude among the nations of the world constitutes pre-atonement for sins to be committed. Also *cf.* Babylonian Talmud, Tractate Bava Batra 21a and Babylonian Talmud, Tractate, Mo'ed Katan17a, which take a critical approach to the corporal punishment of children.
86. Babylonian Talmud, Tractate Eruvin 100b. *Genesis Rabbah* 20:6 breaks it down further and locates the Biblical source of the curse in "children," with other words in the verse prescribing other sufferings.
87. See, e.g., Babylonian Talmud, Tractate Shabbat 89b.
88. Kesef Mishneh also says failure to experience *tza'ar gidul banim* is why eunuchs cannot sit on the Sanhedrin or provide testimony. Karo, Kesef Mishneh on Mishneh Torah Hilchot Eidut 16:6:5, Teshuvot HaRashba Part IV 192.
89. Babylonian Talmud, Tractate Kiddushin 29a.
90. Shulḥan Aruch, Even Ha'ezer 71.
91. Mishnah Kiddushin 1:7, Babylonian Talmud, Tractate Kiddushin 29a. *Exodus Rabbah* 28:2 imposes a requirement to education on mothers, but this extension appears to be a minority perspective.
92. Genesis 17:10–14.
93. Exodus 13:2,13.
94. Babylonian Talmud, Tractate Ketubbot 65b, 102b.
95. Later rabbinic authorities conclude that mothers are under no similar obligation. Mishneh Torah Hilchot Ishut 21:17–18, Shulḥan Aruch, Even Ha'ezer 82:6, 8.
96. Babylonian Talmud, Tractate Ketubbot 49b.
97. Mishneh Torah, Hilchot Ishut 12:14–15, 17, Shulḥan Aruch, Even Ha'ezer 82:7.
98. Shulḥan Aruch, Even Ha'ezer 82:8.
99. Shulḥan Aruch, Even Ha'ezer 82:7.
100. Even Ha'ezer 82:7. Teshuvot HaRashba Meyuchas LeHaRamban, no. 38; Teshuvot HaRadbaz, 1:123.
101. This obligation extends to grandchildren as well. Mishneh Torah, Hilchot Talmud Torah 1:2.
102. Mishneh Torah, Hilchot Talmud Torah 1:2–3.
103. Mishneh Torah, Hilchot Talmud Torah 1:2.
104. *Exodus Rabbah* 46:5.
105. b.Bava Metzia 12b.
106. See generally Mishneh Torah Hilchot Nachalot 11.
107. Shulḥan Aruch, Ḥoshen Mishpat 290.
108. Babylonian Talmud, Tractate Gittin 52a, Shulḥan Aruch, Ḥoshen Mishpat 290:2.
109. Shulḥan Aruch, Orakh Ḥayim 132:2.
110. "Kaddish for Adoptive and Biological Parents."

111. Deuteronomy 24:16. Cf. Jer. 31:29–30; Ez. 18:1–4.
112. Babylonian Talmud, Tractate Shabbat 54b.
113. See, e.g., Deuteronomy 16 v.11–14; 24 v.12–13.
114. Deuteronomy 21:18–21.
115. Mishnah Sanhedrin.8:4, Sifre 218, 219.
116. One commentary highlights the impact of a child of this kind on the entire community. Naftali Zvi Yehuda Berlin, Ha'amek Davar on Deuteronomy 21:21.
117. Rabbinic commentary whittles down the possibility of this commandment being carried out until it becomes all but impossible. Indeed, one source says that there has never been and never will be a stubborn and rebellious son. Babylonian Talmud, Tractate Sanhedrin 71a.
118. Mishneh Torah, Hilchot Talmud Torah 1:2.

Bibliography

Abelson, Kassel and Elliot Dorff. "Mitzvah Children." EH 1:5.2007. http://www.rabbinicalassembly.org/sites/default/files/assets/public/halakhah/teshuvot/20052010/mitzvah_children.pdf.
Ashkenazi, Yehudah ben Shimon. *Be'er Heiteiv*.
Babylonian Talmud.
Ben Aderet, Shlomo. *Teshuvot HaRashba*.
Ben Aderet, Shlomo. *Teshuvot HaRashba Meyuchas LeHaRamban*.
Ben Avraham, Ovadiah. *Bi'ur HaMishnah*.
Ben Maimon, Moshe. *Mishneh Torah*.
Ben Reuven, Nissim. "Chidushei HaRan."
Berkowitz, Miriam, and Mark Popovsky. "Contraception." EH 5:12.2010. http://www.rabbinicalassembly.org/sites/default/files/assets/public/halakhah/teshuvot/20052010/Contraception%20Berkowitz%20and%20Popovsky.pdf.
Berlin. *Ha'amek Davar*, 1880.
Cooperman, Alan, and Neha Sahgal, "Israel's Religiously Divided Society." In *Pew Forum*. 2016.
Dorff, Elliott. "Artificial Insemination, Egg Donation, and Adoption." EH 1:3.1994. http://www.rabbinicalassembly.org/sites/default/files/assets/public/halakhah/teshuvot/19912000/dorff_artificial.pdf.
Ecclesiastes Rabbah.
Epstein, Yechiel Michel. *Arukh HaShulḥan, 1884*.
Exodus Rabbah.
Feinstein, Moshe. *Igrot Moshe, 1967*.
Feldman, David M. "Abortion: The Jewish View." HM 425:2, 800–806. 1983a. http://www.rabbinicalassembly.org/sites/default/files/assets/public/halakhah/teshuvot/19861990/feldman_abortion.pdf.
Feldman, David Michael. *Birth Control in Jewish Law: Marital Relations, Contraception, and Abortion as Set Forth in the Classic Texts of Jewish Law*. Jason Aronson, 1998.
Freehof, Solomon B. "Artificial Insemination." In *American Reform Responsa: Collected Responsa of the Central Conference of American Rabbis, 1889–1983*, edited by Walter Jacob, 500. CCAR Press, 1983.

Geller, Myron S., Robert E. Fine, and David J. Fine. "The Halakhah of Same-Sex Relations in a New Context." EH 24. 2006f. https://www.rabbinicalassembly.org/sites/default/files/public/halakhah/teshuvot/20052010/geller_fine_fine_dissent.pdf.

Genesis Rabbah.

Gold, Michael. *And Hannah Wept: Infertility, Adoption, and the Jewish Couple.* Jewish Publication Society, 1988.

Grossman, Susan. "Partial Birth Abortion and the Question of When Life Begins." HM 425:2, 1–29. 2001b. http://www.rabbinicalassembly.org/sites/default/files/assets/public/halakhah/teshuvot/20052010/grossman_partial_birth.pdf.

Holtzman, Linda J. "Jewish Lesbian Parenting." *Families in the US: Kinship and Domestic Politics* (1998): 329–334.

Ibn Abi Zimra, David ben Solomon. *Teshuvot HaRadbaz.*

Irshai, Ronit. *Fertility and Jewish Law: Feminist Perspectives on Orthodox Responsa Literature.* UPNE, 2012.

Isserles, Moshe. *Mappah.*

Jacob, Walter, et al. "Jewish Marriage Without Children." In *American Reform Responsa: Collected Responsa of the Central Conference of American Rabbis, 1889–1983,* edited by Walter Jacob, 404–406. CCAR Press, 1983.

Kahn, Susan Martha. *Reproducing Jews: A Cultural Account of Assisted Conception in Israel.* Duke University Press, 2000.

Karo, Joseph. "Shulḥan Aruch."

Karo, Joseph. "Kesef Mishneh."

King, Andrea. *If I'm Jewish and You're Christian, What are the Kids?: A Parenting Guide for Interfaith Families.* URJ Books and Music, 1993.

Lauterbach, Jacob Z. "Birth Control." In *American Reform Responsa: Collected Responsa of the Central Conference of American Rabbis, 1889–1983,* edited by Walter Jacob, 486–499. CCAR Press, 1983.

Lugo, Luis, Alan Cooperman, and G. A. Smith. "Pew Research Center survey of US Jews: A portrait of Jewish Americans." In Pew Forum. 2013. Pew Research Center.

Mackler, Aaron L. "In Vitro Fertilization." EH 1:3. 1995. http://www.rabbinicalassembly.org/sites/default/files/assets/public/halakhah/teshuvot/19912000/mackler_ivf.pdf.

Mackler, Aaron L. "Surrogate Parenting." EH 1:3. 1997c. http://www.rabbinicalassembly.org/sites/default/files/assets/public/halakhah/teshuvot/19912000/mackler_surrogate.pdf.

Mackler, Aaron L. and Elie Spitz. "On the Use of Birth Surrogates" EH 1:3. 1997a. http://www.rabbinicalassembly.org/sites/default/files/assets/public/halakhah/teshuvot/19912000/macklerspitz_surrogates.pdf.

Maslin, Simeon J., ed. *Gates of Mitzvah: A Guide to the Jewish Life Cycle.* CCAR Press, 1979.

Meyer, Gedalia and Henoch Messner. "Contraception in Contemporary Orthodox Judaism." 2013. https://www.yumpu.com/en/document/read/11965688/contraception-in-contemporary-orthodox-judaism/2.

Mishnah.

Papo, Eliezer. *Pele Yoetz,* 1824.

Pesiqta de-Rab Kahane.

Plaut, W. Gunther, and Mark Washofsky. "Kaddish for Adoptive and Biological Parents," 5753.1. *Teshuvot for the Nineties: Reform Judaism's Answers to Today's Dilemmas.* CCAR Press, 1997.

Pollack, Daniel, Moshe Bleich, Charles J. Reid, and Mohammad Fadel. "Classical Religious Perspectives of Adoption Law." *Notre Dame Law Review* 79 (2004): 693–753.

Rapoport, Chaim. "Judaism & Homosexuality: An Alternate Rabbinic View." *Ḥakirah, The Flatbush Journal of Jewish Law and Thought* 13, no. 1 (2012): 29–46.

Rawidowicz, Simon. "Israel: The Ever-Dying People." In *Israel, the Ever-Dying People, And Other Essays*, edited by Simon Rawidowicz and Benjamin C. I. Ravid, 53–63. Fairleigh Dickinson University Press, 1986.

Roiphe, Anne. "The Jewish Family: A Feminist Perspective." *Tikkun* 1, no. 2 (1985): 70.

Rosenberg, Shelley Kapnek. *Adoption and the Jewish Family: Contemporary Perspectives*. Jewish Publication Society, 1998.

Rosner, Fred. "Artificial Insemination in Jewish Law." *Judaism* 19, no. 4 (1970): 452.

Schulman, Sam. "Same-Sex Marriage and the Jews." *Mosaic*, February 4, 2014. https://mosaicmagazine.com/essay/uncategorized/2014/02/same-sex-marriage-and-the-jews/

Sefer HaChinukh.

Sifre.

Sinclair, Daniel B. "Assisted Reproduction in Jewish Law." *Fordham Urb. L.J.* 30 (2002): 71.

Solomon, Lewis D. "The Jewish Tradition, Sexuality and Procreation." (2002).

Song of Songs Rabbah.

Spitz, Elie Kaplan. "On the Use of Birth Surrogates." EH l:3.529–550. 1997b. http://www.rabbinicalassembly.org/sites/default/files/assets/public/halakhah/teshuvot/19912000/spitz_surrogate.pdf.

Tosefta.

Uziel, Ben-Zion Meir Hai. *Sha'arei Uziel, 1946.*

Waldenberg, Eliezer Yehudah. "Sha'alot u 'Teshuvot Tzitz Eliezer." 1985.

Wertheimer, Jack, and Steven Cohen. "The Pew Survey Reanalyzed: More Bad News, but a Glimmer of Hope." *Mosaic*, Nov. 2, 2014. https://mosaicmagazine.com/essay/uncategorized/2014/11/the-pew-survey-reanalyzed/

"When is Abortion Permitted?" In *American Reform Responsa: Collected Responsa of the Central Conference of American Rabbis, 1889–1983*, edited by Walter Jacob, 23–27. CCAR Press, 1983.

CHAPTER 8

A LONG ROAD TO A CATHOLIC THEOLOGY OF PARENTHOOD

ANN SHEPARD FEELEY SWANER

THE theology and ethics of procreation and reproduction and parenthood has traditionally been firmly tied to the theology and ethics of marriage and sexuality in the Roman Catholic tradition. Conceptions of parenthood are related to conceptions of childhood and both are always considered in the context of "family." The focus on sexual ethics has tended to make parenthood something of an underdeveloped afterthought. This underdevelopment was perpetuated in the early Church by the preference for celibacy and the New Testament concern about the potential distractions of marriage (including children), in the medieval and scholastic Church by the legal understanding of marriage as a contract, and in the modern Church by the preoccupation with contraception and abortion. Since the papal encyclical *Casti canubii* in 1931 there has been some divergence between magisterial and theological teaching, especially as women's voices have been included in the theological thinking. In recent years theologians such as Lisa Sowle Cahill and Julie Hanlon Rubio have tried to place family ethics into a larger context of Christian social ethics rather than the more limited arena of sexual ethics. This chapter will trace the history of this topic in Scripture and Tradition, in modern magisterial and theological teaching, and identify some of the concerns and new directions in the discussions in the twenty-first century.

Marriage and Family in Scripture

The Scriptures say relatively little directly about marriage and even less about parenthood. But they do offer insights about human nature, human relationships, and human and divine love that undergird a specifically Christian understanding of marriage/family/parenthood.

The Scriptures emphasize that to be human is to be in relationship. Both the Hebrew Scriptures and the New Testament tell stories of intimate relationships between God and humanity as well as between humans. In the Hebrew Scriptures we have the stories of Jacob's love for Rachel, of Ruth's love for Naomi, of Hosea's marriage and the application of that story to God's love for Israel. The Wisdom literature frequently talks about relationships between men and women and the Song of Songs celebrates them. The New Testament tells of Jesus's relationships with his mother, his disciples, his friends, and his Abba.

On marriage specifically, the Hebrew Scriptures emphasize the goodness of sexuality and marriage as part of God's good creation "in the beginning." The first two chapters of the Book of Genesis contain two different creation stories. In the first story man and woman are created together in the image of God, are given dominion over the rest of creation, and are commissioned to be fruitful and multiply (Genesis 1: 27–28). The second account, actually written earlier, focuses on finding a suitable companion for Adam because "It is not good for the man to be alone (Genesis 2:18–25)." Both the Jewish and Christian traditions have taken from these complementary stories the lesson that sexual differentiation has the dual purposes of procreation and companionship. Children have been seen as a great blessing and barrenness as a curse.

The New Testament reaffirms what the Hebrew Scriptures taught about marriage. Jesus answers a question about marriage by referring back to Genesis (Mark 10:6–9; Matthew 19:4). Jesus's teaching is however stricter than Jewish teaching on divorce and adultery (Mark 10:2–12; Matthew 19:4–9). His firm condemnation of divorce and adultery suggests support for marriage but he relativizes the value of marriage in relation to the Kingdom of God and of celibacy for the sake of the Kingdom (Matthew 19:10–12; Luke 20:34–35). Both Jesus and Paul warn that the concerns of marriage and family can distract one from the work of the Kingdom (Matthew 19:11–12; 1 Corinthians 7:32–34). Paul's treatment of marriage is ambiguous. He affirms the value of both marriage and celibacy but warns against sexual immorality and says that in his opinion it is better not to marry (1 Corinthians 7:1–31).

Judith M. Gundry-Volf describes the New Testament teaching on children in the context of both Greco-Roman and Jewish culture.[1] She identifies five ways in which the significance of children is emphasized in Jesus's teaching and practice:

> He blesses the children brought to him and teaches that the reign of God belongs to them. He makes children models of entering the reign of God. He also makes children

models of greatness in the reign of God. He calls on his disciples to welcome little children as he does and turns the service of children into a sign of greatness in the reign of God. He gives the service of children ultimate significance as a way of receiving himself and by implication the One who sent him.[2]

The household codes affirm a hierarchical order in the household and require children to obey their parents and fathers to instruct and correct their children (Ephesians 6:1; Colossians 3:20). Yet Jesus undercuts the accepted norms of filial piety by repudiating his mother and brothers in favor of his disciples (Mark 3:31–35). This tension between the "natural" family and the Christian family has continued throughout the Tradition.[3]

Early Church

The cultural and religious atmosphere in which early church thinking about marriage and family developed was characterized by various forms of "dualism," including Gnosticism and Manicheanism. Gnosticism was marked by a radical dualism of body and spirit and a system of salvation that involved escaping the physical world to the realm of pure spirit by means of esoteric knowledge (*gnosis*). The Gnostics denied that the creator God was the ultimate God. Even for orthodox Christians at this time the relationship of the Hebrew Scriptures to the New Testament was problematic. This had consequences for the development of the theology of marriage because the New Testament texts without the balance of the Hebrew texts on the goodness of creation can lead to a negative view of marriage and procreation. The Gnostics' negative view of marriage ranged between two extremes: the ascetic Gnostics rejected marriage, sex, and procreation altogether; the antinomian Gnostics however reasoned that if the body is evil it doesn't matter what you do with it as long as you don't have children. Either way they were against procreation. The ascetical Gnostic teaching appealed to many Christians because of its apparent similarity to the New Testament stress on celibacy.

In this context the task of the Christian Fathers was to justify marriage, sex, and procreation in the face of both the dualist threats and the New Testament stress on celibacy and the demands of the Kingdom. In response to the ascetic Gnostics they had to explain the purpose of marriage and the value of procreation. To counter the antinomian Gnostics they had to specify what limits on sexuality bound the Christian. Their efforts eventually culminated in Augustine's formulation of the three "goods" of marriage which became the cornerstone of the Catholic theology of marriage and family.

Augustine's view of marriage was influenced both by his own sexual experience and by his association with the dualist Manicheans. During his years as a Manichean Augustine lived and had a child with a woman whom he did not marry. This experience convinced him that he needed to keep free from sexual intercourse and marriage. But against the Manicheans he needed to argue that marriage is good. Augustine distinguished between things that are good in themselves such as wisdom, health, and friendship, and things that are good for the sake of something else. Sexual intercourse and marriage are in the category of things that have to be justified by some external good or purpose. In *The Good of Marriage*, published in 400 CE, Augustine teaches that marriage is good on account of three things: offspring, fidelity, and sacrament. Offspring refers not only to procreation but to loving reception and religious education of children; but Augustine does not develop concretely what the reception and education of children entails. Fidelity means sexual exclusivity and the payment of the marital "debt" (sexual intercourse as described by Paul in 1 Corinthians 7: 3–5). Sacrament means "symbolic stability" or indissolubility.

After dispatching the Manicheans Augustine turned to the Pelagians, who denied the reality of original sin. Augustine argued against them that human reason is distorted as a result of original sin. Concupiscence is the "law of sin" in human beings. If Adam and Eve had not sinned the sexual organs would be completely under the control of the will and sexual intercourse would be possible without concupiscence. But that is not the fallen world we live in. So marriage is good but concupiscence is real and evil, and marriage and procreation are a mixture of good and evil.

Augustine's doctrine of original sin applied even to infants. He called infants "non-innocent"[4] because while infants are not physically capable of sinning and they have no language to understand sin or condemnation, their wills are still corrupt. As children grow and become more capable of acting on their distorted will it is the parents' duty to restrain and train them. But the parents' primary duty toward their children is to have them baptized without which their salvation would not be possible.

Meanwhile, in the East, John Chrysostom (c. 347–407) filled out the content of parental duties toward children with much more specificity than Augustine. Chrysostom lived during the time after Constantine when pagan society was in decline and Christianity was becoming the official religion of the Roman Empire. He was concerned that Christians were being compromised by their concern for material success, status, influence, and wealth. He was more concerned with the sin of greed than of lust. He taught that care of the poor was not to be left to the clergy but was the responsibility of all Christians. He was especially concerned about parents neglecting the spiritual and moral formation of their children. Chrysostom originated the description of the Christian family as "domestic church." He saw the relationship of parents and children reflecting the relationships of the Divine Persons of the Trinity and their households reflecting the church.

Chrysostom describes parents as artists creating their children in the image of God:

> To each of you fathers and mothers, I say, just as we see artists fashioning their paintings and statues with great precision, so we must care for these wondrous statues of ours. Painters when they have set the canvas on the easel paint on it day by day to accomplish their purpose. Sculptors, too, working in marble, proceed in a similar manner; they remove what is superfluous and add what is lacking. Even so must you proceed. Like the creators of statues so you give all your leisure to fashioning these wondrous statues for God.[5]

He is specific about the content of the character parents are to develop in their children:

> If a child learns a trade, or is highly educated for a lucrative profession, all is nothing compared to the art of detachment from riches; if you want to make your child rich, teach him this. He is truly rich who does not desire great possessions, or surrounds himself with wealth, but who requires nothing.... Don't worry about giving him an influential reputation, for worldly wisdom, but ponder deeply how you can teach him to think lightly of this life's passing glories, thus he will become truly renowned and glorious.... Don't strive to make him a clever orator, but teach him to love true wisdom. He will suffer if he lacks clever words, but if he lacks wisdom, all the rhetoric in the world can't help him. A pattern of life is what is needed, not empty speeches; character, not cleverness; deeds, not words. These things will secure the Kingdom and bestow God's blessings.[6]

He is also specific about how these virtues should be inculcated—by example, common worship and prayer, Bible study, instruction in the commandments, discipline, and religious education, including stories. He insists that parents have a responsibility for their children's salvation and that the parents' own salvation depends on how they raise their children. Vigen Guroian concludes that "Chrysostom raises parenthood to cardinal importance in the Christian religion as a moral and ecclesial calling, and he justifies doing so solidly on Trinitarian and Christological grounds."[7]

Not until the late twentieth century does anyone in the West fill out the content of Christian parenthood as thickly as does Chrysostom.

THE MIDDLE AGES

During the Middle Ages the understanding of marriage as one of the seven sacraments of the church was developed. Augustine's three "goods" were transformed by scholastic philosophy into "ends" of marriage. With the collapse of political stability in the West after the barbarian invasions, the church achieved more legal influence over marriage and so its approach became more juridical and focused on canon law. Marriage was understood as a "contract" and a "modified consent theory" was developed to define exactly when a marriage came into being.

Beginning in the tenth century the loss of power of civil authorities led to the church gaining increased jurisdiction over marriage and being called on to decide cases where the validity of a marriage was disputed. Because of this what had been primarily moral concerns in the patristic era became legal concerns. There were two views about the point at which a marriage comes into existence. In the Italian view sexual intercourse marked the beginning of marriage but the French courts held that the exchange of mutual consent created a valid marriage. These views were practically reconciled by Pope Alexander III's "modified consent theory" which held that consent is the only condition necessary for a valid marriage but that sexual consummation is necessary for a marriage to have the full significance of the indissoluble unity of Christ and the Church. The acceptance of the idea that consent makes the marriage favored the defining of marriage as a contract.

The scholastic theology of the seven sacraments was developed in the twelfth century when the various "sacred rites" were described in terms of the minister, the matter, the form, and the efficacy of each sacrament. Marriage did not fit easily into this structure so it was the last of the sacred signs to be recognized as a sacrament. The scholastics debated whether the minister of the sacrament was the priest or the couple themselves. They debated whether the sacramental sign was the exchange of consent, the blessing of the priest, or the sexual consummation. Eventually a consensus emerged that the couple were the ministers of the sacrament, that the sign was the exchange of consent and that the sacramental reality was the contract or bond which came into existence at the time of consent.

Thomas Aquinas distinguished three aspects of marriage: the natural institution, the social institution, and the sacrament. As a natural institution marriage was ordered to the good of nature and was governed by the natural law; as a social institution it was ordered to the good of society and was governed by the civil law; as a sacrament it was ordered to the good of the Church and was governed by divine law. In this distinction Aquinas turns Augustine's "goods" of marriage into "ends."

Aquinas added to Augustine's understanding of the child as affected by original sin an Aristotelian account of moral development. For Aquinas childhood is a necessary stage in the development of personhood. He accepted Augustine's teaching that an unbaptized child is not worthy of salvation because of original sin but, because he believed that a child that had committed no actual sins was not worthy of torment either, he posited the concept of "children's limbo," where unbaptized children are deprived of union with God but spared the pain of hell.[8]

Aquinas's treatment of parental responsibility is based on natural law. Parents naturally tend to take care of their own offspring and he is not concerned with describing exactly what form parenting should take because parents can rely on these natural tendencies.[9] So, again, the content of Christian parenting is not concretely filled out.

The Reformation to the Twentieth Century

The scholastic explanation of marriage was the basis for the Catholic theology of marriage and family until the twentieth century. The only significant modifications were the Council of Trent's imposition of a required form for marriage (to address the problem of clandestine marriage) and the nineteenth century identification of the contract and the sacrament.

The Protestant reformers denied the sacramentality and indissolubility of marriage which forced the Catholic Church at the Council of Trent to try to clarify its doctrine on marriage. It reiterated that marriage is a grace-giving sacrament and is indissoluble but there was not enough theological agreement to say much more than that. The Council issued a separate disciplinary decree establishing a form for marriage which required three witnesses including the parish priest. The Reformation and the Council of Trent thus reinforced the Church's legal focus on marriage.

The legal emphasis continued from Trent to the twentieth century as the Church struggled with increasingly secular states over the legal control of marriage. The concern for Church authority led Pope Leo XIII in 1880 to affirm the absolute inseparability of the contract and the sacrament of marriage:

> 23. Let no one, then, be deceived by the distinction which some civil jurists have so strongly insisted upon—the distinction, namely, by virtue of which they sever the matrimonial contract from the sacrament, with intent to hand over the contract to the power and will of the rulers of the State, while reserving questions concerning the sacrament to the Church. A distinction, or rather severance, of this kind cannot be approved; for certain it is that in Christian marriage the contract is inseparable from the sacrament, and that, for this reason, the contract cannot be true and legitimate without being a sacrament as well. For Christ our Lord added to marriage the dignity of a sacrament; but marriage is the contract itself, whenever that contract is lawfully concluded.[10]

Leo is emphatic about the identity of the contract and the sacrament but it is clear how dominant the Church-State controversy is in the development of this teaching.

This legal emphasis on marriage, the rights of the Church, and the rights of parents to educate their children, rather than the State, keeps attention away from the concrete content of distinctively Christian parenthood.

Casti connubii to Vatican II

The 1930 encyclical of Pius XI, *Casti connubii*, marks a shift in magisterial teaching on marriage. The major context of the discussion changes from the relationship of the Church and State in the jurisdiction over marriage to the morality of contraception. The encyclical was apparently occasioned by the Anglican Church's declaration in 1930 that married couples were free to follow their consciences on birth control. Pius XI's evaluation of modern thought is drastically negative: he sees (as from a "watchtower") the morality of his time as "new and utterly perverse" and sees the Catholic Church as the only protector left of human values.[11]

The source of the modern evils opposed to the nature of marriage is the denial of the divine institution of marriage and the remedy then is a return to the divine plan.

The Pope describes the divine plan for marriage in terms of Augustine's three goods. He describes the right and duty of parents to educate their children:

> 16. The blessing of offspring, however, is not completed by the mere begetting of them, but something else must be added, namely the proper education of the offspring. For the most wise God would have failed to make sufficient provision for children that had been born, and so for the whole human race, if He had not given to those to whom He had entrusted the power and right to beget them, the power also and the right to educate them. For no one can fail to see that children are incapable of providing wholly for themselves, even in matters pertaining to their natural life, and much less in those pertaining to the supernatural, but require for many years to be helped, instructed, and educated by others. Now it is certain that both by the law of nature and of God this right and duty of educating their offspring belongs in the first place to those who began the work of nature by giving them birth, and they are indeed forbidden to leave unfinished this work and so expose it to certain ruin. But in matrimony provision has been made in the best possible way for this education of children that is so necessary, for, since the parents are bound together by an indissoluble bond, the care and mutual help of each is always at hand.

But in regard to *fides* he goes much further than Augustine. For Augustine this was a "negative good," the exclusion of third parties. But Pius XI casts it more positively by rooting it in the mutual love of the spouses. The primary purpose of the expression of marital love is the mutual spiritual perfection of the spouses. The Pope suggests that this love that fosters the mutual spiritual perfection of the spouses is in one sense the primary purpose of Christian marriage:

> 24. This mutual molding of husband and wife, this determined effort to perfect each other, can in a very real sense, as the Roman Catechism teaches, be said to be the chief reason and purpose of matrimony, provided matrimony be looked at not in the restricted sense as instituted for the proper conception and education of the child, but more widely as the blending of life as a whole and the mutual interchange and sharing thereof.[12]

Pius XI devotes several paragraphs to the relationship of husband and wife and to the dangers inherent in the emancipation of women. He follows Leo XIII in asserting the equal "dignity" of women but sees movements for the emancipation of women as "debasing of the womanly character and the dignity of motherhood, and indeed the whole family" [75]. He provides a good summary of the magisterial teaching on the complementary natures of men and women, the proper subjection of women to their husbands, the romantic view of motherhood, and the suspicion of women as temptresses and distractions.

In discussing love, sex, and procreation, *Casti connubii* states that the "conjugal act is destined primarily by nature for the begetting of children" [54]. Pius XI also repeats the canonical language of primary and secondary ends: At the same time he says, as pointed out earlier, that in another sense, the chief reason and purpose of marriage is the love that leads to the spiritual perfection of the spouses. Pius XI does not try to reconcile these two viewpoints.

Despite its conservative intentions *Casti connubii* was seen as a revolutionary statement in recognizing for the first time in a magisterial document the importance of love in marriage. It invited, or at least seemed to allow, a new discussion of the meaning of Christian marriage.

Between *Casti connubii* and Vatican II the Catholic theology of marriage was influenced by the growing importance of personalist philosophy, developments in psychology and the social sciences concerning human sexuality, the increasing involvement of the laity, and developments in other theological areas such as Scripture studies and historical and sacramental theology.

Bernard Haring suggested that our understanding of marriage as a sacrament is a reflection of our understanding of personalism.[13] Personalism places more emphasis on conjugal love as constitutive of marriage:

> Marriage as an institution, the marriage legislation of Church and state, and the ethical norms for marriage must be tested according to this one great perspective: do they protect and foster the personalizing forces of marriage and the family; do they reveal discernment as to the true nature of conjugal love and the vocation of the spouses to convey the genuine experience of love to their children.[14]

The influence of personalism was evident in the theology of marriage in the late 1920s, especially in the work of Dietrich von Hildebrand,[15] Herbert Doms,[16] and Bernard Krempel.[17] The personalist discussion of marriage in this period was focused on the hierarchy of the ends of marriage. Pius XI had said that in one sense procreation is the primary end of marriage and in another sense the love of the spouses is primary. Attempts were made to reconcile these two "senses" and the canonical language of primary and secondary ends. Von Hildebrand distinguished between the primary *meaning* of marriage, which is conjugal love, and the primary *end* of marriage, which is procreation. Herbert Doms makes a similar distinction between the meaning and the end of marriage. Marriage, he says, *is* something in itself before it exists *for* something outside of itself. John Noonan described the impact of Doms's book:

> In his book he said eloquently what serious Catholic laymen were waiting to hear: not only marriage but marital intercourse, was a means of achieving holiness. The theory sketched by Von Hildebrand was given solidity and buttressed by scholarship.... *The Meaning and End of Marriage* was the most comprehensive attempt yet made to develop a theory of Catholic marriage different from that of Augustine. It did not succeed in wholly winning the professional moral theologians, but its influence on later Catholic writing on marriage was inescapable.[18]

Neither Von Hildebrand nor Doms denied that procreation was an essential end of marriage. Another personalist writer, Bernard Krempel, did reject procreation as an essential end. Marriage, he said, can have only one essential end and that end is the perpetual union of the lives of two persons of the opposite sex. Procreation is an effect or result of marriage rather than an end.

In 1944 a decree of the Holy Office rejected those modern views which "either deny that the primary end of marriage is the generation and education of children, or teach that the secondary ends are not essentially subordinate to the primary end, but they are equally principal and independent."[19] This decree mentioned no names and did not condemn personalist writings or emphases in general. And it did not end the discussion of the relationship of the ends of marriage.

Dietrich von Hildebrand was the first married layperson to contribute significantly to the discussion of marriage during this period. The preface to Herbert Doms's book suggests that its intended audience was not only priests and theologians but "the chief value of this book will be for the thoughtful layman who is determined to take his marriage seriously and to plumb all its depth and meaning."[20] John T. Noonan associates the increased role of the laity with the recovery of Catholic higher education and the growing acceptance of free speech in the Church.[21]

> Before the founding of magazines edited by Catholic laymen, but not under ecclesiastical control, there was no institutional forum designed to express the opinion of the laity on matters in the Church. In the United States the way was led by *Commonweal*, founded in 1924, followed by *Cross Currents*, *Jubilee*, *The Critic*, and *Ramparts*. These magazines were both symbols and outlets for an educated Catholic laity which was seriously concerned with the teaching of the Church.[22]

Pius XI and Pius XII strongly encouraged the participation of the laity in organized forms of "Catholic Action." Catholic Action was more organized in Europe than in the United States, where it was "made up of small informal groups loosely connected by their reading of Catholic lay periodicals like *Jubilee* or *Commonweal*."[23] In the area of marriage and family life however, the organized *Christian Family Movement* and *Cana Conference* were successful in the United States in the 1950s.

Pierre de Locht describes the renewal of marriage among the laity that took place between 1930 and 1960, mainly in Europe, under the impetus of Catholic Action:

> It is important to note that this burning desire to live a fully Christian life in the state of marriage came from the laity themselves, and that it arose out of renewed attention to the human reality of their day-to-day lives. Women as well as men dedicated themselves to this movement, operating on a level of equality as they had done in the youth organizations of their earlier school years. In the latter organizations women had not taken part as future wives and mothers but as equally dedicated partners in community life and its responsibilities. The renewed interest in marriage and marital life arose out of this context, and the latter gave it certain distinctive features and characteristics. One cannot overlook these facts if one wishes to truly grasp the dynamism and exigencies of the renewal.[24]

In the 1930s the first "family-circles" were formed, and in France the *Association du marriage Chretien* was founded. The orientations of these groups varied but they shared a basic concern "to harmonize the various and different components of the human reality that dominates their own lives; and in their view it was Christian marriage which would provide them with the best framework for doing just that and thereby achieving fulfillment."[25]

These groups provided a context for the elaboration and reinforcement of the personal values in the marriage relationship. Some of the concerns expressed in these groups included the need for marital communication, for a more positive evaluation of sexuality, for concrete solutions to the problem of birth control, and for a specifically marital spirituality that was not simply an offshoot of monastic spirituality. The existence of this organized family movement in Europe gave the married laity a means for organizing input for Vatican II.[26]

So from 1930 to 1960 the official teachers of the Church were preoccupied with the problem of the hierarchy of the ends of marriage and the morality of contraception while theologians and increasing numbers of lay people were developing an understanding of marriage which gave greater emphasis to personal values. These personalists paved the way for Vatican II which abandoned the terminology of a hierarchy of ends.

Vatican II

The Second Vatican Council put the traditional teaching on marriage into a new perspective by putting it into the schema on *The Church in the Modern World (Gaudium et spes)*. Marriage is treated as the first of several "problems of special urgency" in the world today. The decision to deal with marriage in the context of the modern world was a marked change in perspective from that of *Casti connubii*, which was understood as expressing "timeless" truth hostile to the questions raised by the modern world. The Council sets the context of the discussion of marriage as that of the dignity of the human person. It states that the problems of the present age are to be considered "in the light of the Gospel and of human experience" [Article 46].

Vatican II with its "return to the sources" recovers Chrysostom's description of the Christian family as "domestic church." The Council emphasizes the solidarity of the whole family in regard to salvation:

> With their parents leading the way by example and family prayer, children and indeed everyone gathered around the family hearth will find a readier path to human maturity, salvation and holiness. Graced with the dignity and office of fatherhood and motherhood, parents will energetically acquit themselves of a duty which devolves primarily on them, namely education and especially religious education.

As living members of the family, children contribute in their own way to making their parents holy. For they will respond to the kindness of their parents with sentiments of gratitude, with love and trust. They will stand by them as children should when hardships overtake their parents and old age brings its loneliness. Widowhood, accepted bravely as a continuation of the marriage vocation, should be esteemed by all. Families too will share their spiritual riches generously with other families. Thus the Christian family, which springs from marriage as a reflection of the loving covenant uniting Christ with the Church, and as a participation in that covenant, will manifest to all men Christ's living presence in the world, and the genuine nature of the Church. This the family will do by the mutual love of the spouses, by their generous fruitfulness, their solidarity and faithfulness, and by the loving way in which all members of the family assist one another. [48]

Humanae vitae

The Fathers at Vatican II were not allowed to talk about birth control because that matter had been given to a Pontifical Commission on Birth Control established by Pope John XXIII. In 1966, after the end of Vatican II, the majority on that commission recommended to Pope Paul VI that the teaching against all forms of "artificial" contraception be changed. But the Pope rejected that recommendation and on July 26, 1968, in the encyclical *Humanae vitae*, he reaffirmed the ban.

Humanae vitae was not intended as a fully developed theology of marriage or parenthood; it dealt with the limited question of "responsible parenthood." Pope Paul refers to the two "meanings" of the conjugal act, rather than its ends or purposes. He sees these two meanings, the unitive and the procreative, as inseparably connected. The condemnation of contraception in *Humanae vitae* is based on this inseparability of meanings, rather than on the priority of the "end" of procreation, as in *Casti connubii*.

John Paul II

Cardinal Karol Wojtyla, before he became Pope John Paul II, participated in Vatican II and was also a member of the papal birth control commission. He insisted that there was no inconsistency between *Gaudium et spes* and *Humanae vitae*. As John Paul II he continued the development of a phenomenological and personalist understanding of marriage and sexuality expressed as a "theology of the body." He sees relationships of total self-giving as central to human experience. A key component of the theology of the body is male/female complementarity and gender roles.

In 1980 an international synod of bishops met to discuss the Christian family in the modern world. A year later John Paul II issued "An Apostolic Exhortation on the Family" (*Familiaris consortio*). Like Vatican II, he emphasizes the need to read the "signs of the times." He cites the positive and negative aspects of the situation, the positive arising from the greater attention to personal values and the negative arising largely from the corruption of freedom [6].

In Part II he reflects on the divine plan for marriage. While Pius XI's understanding of God's plan was derived from Augustine's three goods, John Paul II's is based on the creation of mankind in the image of God, Who is love. God's plan is that the family is to be a communion of persons, an intimate communion of life and love. More specifically, the mission of the family includes four tasks: to form a community of persons, to serve life, to participate in the development of society, and to share in the life and mission of the Church [17]. The pope sees a "specific and original" role of the family in the mission of the church [50].

Since *Familiaris consortio* there has been a resurgence of the use of the domestic church metaphor. Lisa Cahill identifies two newer aspects of Catholic teaching about domestic church:

> First, it addresses economic inequities and holds Christian families responsible for just distribution of material and social wealth, not limited to almsgiving but demanding structural change.... Second, and on a truly novel note compared to Christian family teaching of centuries past, the domestic church is a sphere of relative gender equity.[27]

Benedict XVI continues the themes of John Paul II. In *Verbum Domini* He talks about God's plan for marriage and the importance of marriage, the modern threats to marriage, and the importance of parents' role in educating their children:

> 85. The Synod also felt the need to stress the relationship between the word of God, marriage and the Christian family. Indeed, "with the proclamation of the word of God, the Church reveals to Christian families their true identity, what it is and what it must be in accordance with the Lord's plan" [284]. Consequently, it must never be forgotten that *the word of God is at the very origin of marriage* (cf. Genesis 2:24) and that Jesus himself made marriage one of the institutions of his Kingdom (cf. Matthew 19:4–8), elevating to the dignity of a sacrament what was inscribed in human nature from the beginning. "In the celebration of the sacrament, a man and a woman speak a prophetic word of reciprocal self-giving, that of being "one flesh," a sign of the mystery of the union of Christ with the Church (cf. Ephesians 5:31–32)" [285]. Fidelity to God's word leads us to point out that nowadays this institution is in many ways under attack from the current mentality. In the face of widespread confusion in the sphere of affectivity, and the rise of ways of thinking which trivialize the human body and sexual differentiation, the word of God reaffirms the original goodness of the human being, created as man and woman and called to a love which is faithful, reciprocal and fruitful.
>
> The great mystery of marriage is the source of the essential *responsibility of parents towards their children*. Part of authentic parenthood is to pass on and bear witness to

the meaning of life in Christ: through their fidelity and the unity of family life, spouses are the first to proclaim God's word to their children. The ecclesial community must support and assist them in fostering family prayer, attentive hearing of the word of God, and knowledge of the Bible.[28]

Pope Francis calls for the Church to be a sign of mercy, hope, and forgiveness. He assembled two synods on marriage and the family one year apart. He summarized their findings in *Amoris laetitia*, a discursive set of reflections on love, marriage, family, education, spirituality, challenges, weakness, and pastoral care. He criticizes the extreme individualism that weakens family bonds. *Humanae vitae*'s ban on contraception is reaffirmed without discussion. He emphasizes the indissolubility of marriage but describes it as a gift rather than a yoke. For those whose marriages have broken down he offers "an invitation to mercy and the pastoral discernment of those situations that fall short of what the Lord demands of us." Critics suggest that Francis's highlighting of mercy and forgiveness undercuts doctrinal clarity but Francis counters with the startling statement that "not all discussions of doctrinal, moral or pastoral issues need to be settled by interventions of the magisterium. Unity of teaching and practice is certainly necessary in the Church, but this does not preclude various ways of interpreting some aspects of that teaching or drawing certain consequences from it" [3].

Magisterial teaching on marriage and family since Vatican II is characterized by a strong focus on gender complementarity, although the hierarchical ordering of husband over wife has been replaced (even though it had been held to be part of natural law) by the language of mutuality and partnership. It is also focused on sexual ethics because of the concern to uphold the condemnation of contraception and abortion; this focus on sexual ethics has tended to restrict the idea of responsible parenthood to issues surrounding conception and to downplay the idea that the specifically Christian aspects of parenthood have to do with spiritual education and social justice. The magisterium favors large families, consistently associating having more children with faith and generosity.

Adrian Thatcher writes about the neglect of children in Christian theology. He attributes this in part to the displacement of real families by the family of the church through the metaphorical and theological use of the vocabulary of childhood:

> The Gospel of John is more interested in the second birth, the birth "from above" (*anothen*) (John 3:3), than in the birth of actual children.... We are to call no-one on earth our father (unless he is our priest), for there is one Father in heaven. (Matthew 23:9) The church is our Mother, and we are made "children of God" through our baptism. OK, but has anyone noticed what is going on? There is a real danger that the appropriation of familial language in order to conceptualize the adult relation to God marginalizes earthly fathers, mothers, and children. This has been done by a patriarchal church run by men who have been removed from the joys and responsibilities of earthly parenting, and who in the main relegate women, children, and parenting to an

inferior status. The wholescale adoption of familial language by the church for theological purposes requires devices such as that of "the domestic church" to re-sacralise real families and restore them to their due spiritual dignity.[29]

Revisionist Theology since *Humanae vitae*

Michael Lawler and Todd Salzman explain the division in contemporary Catholic moral theology between traditionalists and revisionists:

> "Traditionalist" is the label assigned to moral theologians who support and defend absolute magisterial norms; "revisionist" is the label assigned to moral theologians who question and theologically challenge some absolute. These two schools differ in their approach to experience in the construction of their moral theology. Traditionalists argue that human experience is to be *judged* by moral norms derived from moral principles; revisionists argue that experience can help to *formulate* moral norms and principles. The traditionalist approach to experience is deductive, from guiding principles and norms to judged experience; the revisionist approach is inductive, from interpreted and evaluated experience to formulated norms and principles.[30]

Some of the concerns revisionists including Charles Curran, Margaret Farley, Todd Salzman, Michael Lawler, and Lisa Sowle Cahill have expressed about traditionalist and magisterial theology of marriage and sexuality are

- the role of experience and the social sciences as sources of Christian ethics;
- an overemphasis on sexuality in moral theology and in particular an overemphasis on sexual sin;
- a theological anthropology too focused on sexual complementarity and gendered parental roles;
- the limitation of "responsible parenthood" to procreative decisions;
- the overly idealized and romanticized norm of a "total gift of self" in every sexual act which does not conform to the actual experience of married people;
- the meaning of instant indissolubility and sacramentality at the moment the "I do's" are spoken and/or the marriage is sexually consummated.

These theologians are attempting to put marriage and family ethics into the broader context of social ethics rather than the more restrictive area of sexual ethics. Revisionist theology assumes that doctrine develops in history and that therefore particular human experience and insights from the social and historical sciences are necessary sources for Christian ethics.

Twenty-First Century

At the beginning of the twenty-first century scholars born after Vatican II, including Julie Hanlon Rubio, David Matzko McCarthy, Florence Caffrey Bourg, and Richard Gaillardetz, are trying to go beyond the division between the traditionalists and revisionists of the twentieth century. Lisa Cahill describes them as a "generation of scholars who write from a culture and for an audience pervaded by transience of relationships, trivialization of sex, and exploitation of just about every area of human meaning by market capitalism."[31] Cahill identifies six issues these scholars are concerned with: "romantic love; the social context of marriage; marriage as interpreted by faith, or as a sacrament; the function of specific evaluations of sexual behavior; gender equality; and social justice. There is complete and vehement unanimity that romantic love is a woefully inadequate basis for the Christian marriage commitment."[32]

As one example of how these theologians are filling out the content of Christian parenthood, Julie Hanlon Rubio, in *A Christian Theology of Marriage and Family*,[33] has two separate chapters on "Mothering in Christian Families" and "Fathering in Christian Families" following a chapter on "The Dual Vocation of Christian Parents." The dual vocation requires that both parents have a public role (work) as well as a household role. She encourages Christian mothers to ask themselves if they are fulfilling the public side of their vocation and Christian fathers to look to fuller participation in private life. In her later book, *Family Ethics*,[34] Rubio, like Lisa Cahill,[35] ties the duties of Christian parenthood directly to Christian social ethics and the demand for Christian families to be ethically responsive to contemporary social realities. Solidarity with the poor and commitment to social change are hallmarks of the new theology of the family. Rubio then describes distinctive practices that enable families to live out their faith in an often alien culture.

So, in the fourth century, in the East St. John Chrysostom developed a theology of the family as domestic church that was to inculcate Christian virtues in children to bring them into a Christian community that stood on the side of the poor and resisted the excesses of their age. But in the West it was not until married theologians with children started reflecting on Christian parenthood that this vision has been recovered and developed for the twenty-first century Church.

Conclusion

The teaching of Scripture on marriage and family is ambiguous: it is good but dangerous and distracting. The Patristic era ended with the formulation of Augustine's three goods of marriage. The medieval theologians made marriage a sacrament and a contract and turned Augustine's "goods" into "ends" but did not provide much content for the good/end of procreation and education. From the Council of Trent to the early twentieth century the Church was focused on legal jurisdiction over marriage and the rights of parents to educate their children. *Castii connubii* changes the subject to contraception. The twentieth century popes were all committed to defending the ban on contraception while trying to do it in more personalist language. But theologians, who are increasingly lay married persons, and the laity themselves have been trying to extract the theology of marriage and family from the narrow confines of sexual ethics and to understand it in a more personal, social context.

Notes

1. Judith M. Gundry-Volf, "The Least and the Greatest," in *The Child in Christian Thought*, edited by Marcia J. Bunge, 29–60 (Grand Rapids, MI: Eerdmans, 2001).
2. Ibid., 36.
3. The early third-century account of the Passion of Perpetua and Felicity illustrates the priority of the Christian commitment over family commitments in the early church. Both Perpetua and her companion Felicity are eager to leave their infants behind for the higher calling of Christian martyrdom. Perpetua's pagan father urges her to consider the welfare of her child but Perpetua sees her Christian duty as superseding her maternal duty.
4. Martha Ellen Stortz, "Where or When was Your Servant Innocent?" in Bunge 2001, 82.
5. John Chrysostom, "An Address on Vainglory and the Right Way for Parents to Bring Up Their Children," in *Christianity and Pagan Culture in the Later Roman Empire*, translated by Max L. W. Laistner (Ithaca, NY: Cornell University Press, 1951).
6. John Chrysostom, "An Address on Vainglory and the Right Way for Parents to Bring Up Their Children.".
7. Guroian, "The Ecclesial Family," 77.
8. Christina L. H. Traina, "A Person in the Making," in Bunge, *The Child in Christian Thought*, 114–115.
9. Ibid., 125.
10. Leo XIII, *Arcanum divinae sapientiae*, https://w2.vatican.va/content/leo-xiii/en/encyclicals/documents/hf_l-xiii_enc_10021880_arcanum.html.
11. Pius XI, *Casti connubii*, #3, https://w2.vatican.va/content/pius-xi/en/encyclicals/documents/hf_p-xi_enc_19301231_casti-connubii.html.
12. Ibid., #24.
13. Haring, *Morality Is for Persons*, 100.
14. Ibid., 100–101.
15. Dietrich von Hildebrand, *Marriage: The Mystery of Faithful Love* (1929); Dietrich von Hildebrand, *In Defense of Purity* (London: Sheed and Ward, 1931).
16. Herbert Doms, *The Meaning and the End of Marriage* (New York: Sheed and Ward, 1935).
17. Bernard Krempel, *Die Zweckfrage der Ehe in Neuer Beleuchtung (A New Perspective on the Ends of Marriage)*, 1941.
18. John T. Noonan, *Contraception* (Cambridge, MA: Harvard University Press, 1966), 496–497.
19. *Acta apostolicae sedis*, 36:103.

20. Doms, *The Meaning and the End of Marriage*, ix.
21. Noonan, *Contraception*, 488.
22. Ibid.
23. George Tavard, *The Church, the Layman, and the Modern World* (New York: MacMillan, 1959), 10.
24. Pierre DeLocht, "Conjugal Spirituality between 1930 and 1960," in *Sexuality in Contemporary Catholicism*, edited by Franz Bockle and Jacques-Marie Pohier (New York: Seabury, 1976), 43.
25. Ibid., 27.
26. Ibid., 34.
27. Lisa Sowle Cahill, *Family: A Christian Social Perspective* (Minneapolis: Fortress Press, 2000), 87.
28. Benedict XVI, *Verbum Domini*. https://w2.vatican.va/content/benedict-xvi/en/apost_exhortations/documents/hf_ben-xvi_exh_20100930_verbu.
29. Adrian Thatcher, "Theology and Children: Towards a Theology of Childhood," *Transformation* 23, no. 4 (October 2006): 195.
30. Michael G. Lawler and Todd A. Salzman, "Human Experience and Catholic Moral Theology," *Irish Theological Quarterly* 76, no. 1: 36. This is discussed at greater length in Todd A. Salzman and Michael G. Lawler, *The Sexual Person: Toward a Renewed Catholic Anthropology* (Washington, DC: Georgetown University, 2008).
31. Lisa Sowle Cahill, *Theological Studies* 64, no. 1 (March 2003): 2.
32. Ibid., 11.
33. Julie Hanlon Rubio, *A Christian Theology of Marriage and Family* (New York: Paulist Press, 2003).
34. Julio Hanlon Rubio, *Family Ethics: Practices for Christians* (Washington, DC: Georgetown University Press, 2010).
35. Lisa Sowle, Cahill, *Family: A Christian Social Perspective* (Minneapolis: Fortress Press, 2000).

Bibliography

Benedict XVI. *Verbum Domini*, Vatican. September 30, 2010. https://w2.vatican.va/content/benedict-xvi/en/apost_exhortations/documents/hf_ben-xvi_exh_20100930_verbu.
Bourg, Florence Bourg. *Where Two or Three Are Gathered: Christian Families as Domestic Churches*. Notre Dame, IN: Notre Dame Press, 2004.
Browning, Don S. *Equality and the Family: A Fundamental, Practical Theology of Children, Mothers, and Fathers in Modern Societies*. Grand Rapids, MI: Eerdmans, 2007.
Bunge, Marcia J., ed. *The Child in Christian Thought*. Grand Rapids, MI: Eerdmans, 2001.
Cahill, Lisa Sowle. *Family: A Christian Social Perspective*. Minneapolis: Fortress Press, 2000.
Cahill, Lisa Sowle. *Sex, Gender & Christian Ethics*. New York: Cambridge University Press, 1966.
Chrysostom, Saint John. "An Address on Vainglory and The Right Way for Parents to Bring Up Their Children." In *Christianity and Pagan Culture in the Later Roman Empire*, translated by Max L. W. Laistner. New York: Cornell University Press, 1951.
Curran, Charles. *The Development of Moral Theology: Five Strands*. Washington, DC: Georgetown University Press, 2013.

DeLocht, Pierre. "Conjugal Spirituality between 1930 and 1960." In *Sexuality in Contemporary Catholicism*, edited by Franz Bockle and Jacques-Marie Pohier, 22–36. New York: Seabury, 1976.

Doms, Herbert. *The Meaning and End of Marriage*. New York: Sheed and Ward, 1939.

Farley, Margaret A. *Just Love: A Framework for Christian Sexual Ethics*. New York: Continuum, 2010.

Francis I. *Amoris laetitia (On Love in the Family)*. Vatican. April 8, 2016. https://w2.vatican.va/content/dam/francesco/pdf/apost_exhortations/documents/papa-francesco_esortazione-ap_20160319_amoris-laetitia_en.pdf.

Gaillardetz, Richard R. *A Daring Promise: A Spirituality of Christian Marriage*. New York: Crossroad Publishing Company, 2002.

Gundry-Volf, Judith M. "The Least and the Greatest: Children in the New Testament." In Bunge, *The Child in Christian Thought*, edited by Marcia J., 29–60. Grand Rapids, MI: Eerdmans, 2001.

Guroian, Vigen. "The Ecclesial Family: John Chrysostom on Parenthood and Children." In *The Child in Christian Thought*, edited by Marcia J. Bunge, 61–77. Grand Rapids, MI: Eerdmans, 2001.

Haring, Bernard. *Morality Is for Persons*. New York: Farrar, Straus and Giroux, 1971.

John Paul II. *Familiaris consortio (On the Role of the Christian Family in the Modern World)*. Vatican. November 22, 1981. http://w2.vatican.va/content/john-paul-ii/en/apost_exhortations/documents/hf_jp-ii_exh_19811122_familiaris-consortio.

John Paul II. *Gratissimam sane (Letter to Families)*. Vatican. February 2, 1994. https://w2.vatican.va/content/john-paul-ii/en/letters/1994/documents/hf_jp-ii_let_02021994_families.html.

John Paul II. *Mulieris dignitatem (On the Dignity of Women)*. Vatican. August 15, 1988. https://w2.vatican.va/content/john-paul-ii/en/apost_letters/1988/documents/hf_jp-ii_apl_19880815_mulieris-dignitatem.html.

Krempel, Bernhardin. *Die Zweckfrage der ehe in neuer Beleuchtung*. Zurich and Koln: Verlagsanstalt Beniziger, 1941.

Lawler, Michael G., and William P. Roberts. *Christian Marriage and Family: Contemporary Theological and Pastoral Perspectives*. Collegeville, MN: Liturgical Press, 1996.

Lawler, Michael G. *Marriage and the Catholic Church: Disputed Questions*. Collegeville MN: Liturgical Press, 1989.

Leo XIII, *Arcanum divinae sapientiae (On Christian Marriage)*. Vatican. February 10, 1880. Accessed 3/2/2017. https://w2.vatican.va/content/leo-xiii/en/encyclicals/documents/hf_l-xiii_enc_10021880_arcanum.html.

Mackin, Theodore. *What Is Marriage?* New York: Paulist Press, 1982.

McCarthy, David Matzko. *The Good Life: Genuine Christianity for the Middle Class*. Grand Rapids, MI: Brazos Press, 2004.

McCarthy, David Matzko. *Sex and Love in the Home: A Theology of the Household*. 2nd edition. Eugene, OR: Wipf and Stock, 2004.

Miller-McLemore, Bonnie. *Let the Children Come: Reimagining Childhood from a Christian Perspective*. San Francisco: Jossey-Bass, 2003.

Noonan, John T. *Contraception*. Cambridge, MA: Harvard University Press, 1966.

Pius XI. *Casti connubii (On Christian Marriage)*. Vatican. December 31, 1930. https://w2.vatican.va/content/pius-xi/en/encyclicals/documents/hf_p-xi_enc_19301231_casti-connubii.html.

Pontifical Council for the Family. *Enchiridion on the Family: A Compendium of Church Teaching on Family and Life Issues from Vatican II to the Present*. Boston: Pauline Books and Media, 2000.

Rubio, Julie Hanlon. *A Christian Theology of Marriage and Family*. New York: Paulist Press, 2003.

Rubio, Julie Hanlon. *Family Ethics: Practices for Christians*. Washington, DC: Georgetown University Press, 2010.

Rubio, Julie Hanlon. "Family Ethics, Beyond Sex and Controversy." *Theological Studies* 74, no. 1 (March 1, 2013): 138–161.

Salzman, Todd A. and Michael G. Lawler. *Sexual Ethics: A Theological Introduction*. Washington, DC: Georgetown University Press, 2012.

Salzman, Todd A. and Michael G. Lawler. *The Sexual Person: Towards a Renewed Catholic Anthropology*. Washington, DC: Georgetown University Press, 2008.

Salzman, Todd A., Thomas M. Kelly, and John J. O'Keefe, eds. *Marriage in the Catholic Tradition: Scripture, Tradition, and Experience*. New York: Crossroad Publishing Company, 2004.

Stortz, Martha Ellen. "Where or When Was Your Servant Innocent?" In *The Child in Christian Thought*, edited by Marcia J. Bunge, 78–102. Grand Rapids, MI: Eerdmans, 2001.

Tavard, George. *The Church, the Layman, and the Modern World*. New York: MacMillan, 1959.

Thatcher, Adrian. "Theology and Children: Towards a Theology of Childhood," *Transformation* 23, no. 4 (October 2006): 194–199.

Traina, Christina L. H. "A Person in the Making: Thomas Aquinas on Children and Childhood." In *The Child in Christian Thought*, edited by Marcia J. Bunge, 103–133. Grand Rapids, MI: Eerdmans, 2001.

Von Hildebrand, Dietrich. *In Defense of Purity: An Analysis of the Catholic Ideals of Purity and Virginity*. London: Sheed and Ward, 1945. (First published in German in 1927.)

Von Hildebrand, Dietrich. *Marriage: The Mystery of Faithful Love*, translated by Dietrich Von Hildebrand, Emmanuel Chapman, and Daniel Sullivan. London: Longmans, Green, 1942. Originally published as *Die Ehe*. Munich: Verlag Ars Sacra, 1929.

CHAPTER 9

PROTESTANT PERSPECTIVES ON PROCREATION AND PARENTING

JOEL JAMES SHUMAN

The moral landscape of contemporary Protestantism is so broad and irregular as to make it practically impossible to account for the ways the various strands of Protestantism have instructed or failed to instruct their memberships with respect to practices of procreation and parenting. Today, many Protestant Christians unselfconsciously and in the name of compassionate love embrace nontraditional family arrangements and the full range of reproductive technologies, while others, whose understanding of Divine Providence approaches fatalism, are stricter than traditional Catholics in their rejection of all forms of contraception—including natural family planning. Both of these impulses are identifiably Protestant, for Protestantism was protean from the beginning, and has become progressively more so over its now five-hundred-year history.

This is not to say that the story of Protestantism is one of immediate and uninterrupted disintegration; the first Reformers had little interest in schism, and habits of belief shaped by centuries of creedal orthodoxy, combined with the fertile soil of regional political support, made so-called magisterial Protestantism—that is, churches with support from or connections to civil authorities—strong enough to make these new churches stable homes to thousands of European Christians.[1] One could argue, however, that certain of the very theological commitments that led the first Reformers to criticize and then break with Rome set in place a slow, steady movement toward today's exaggerated theological and moral pluralism. The Reformers' embrace of what came to be called the doctrine of *Sola Scriptura* set the tone in this regard; Brad S. Gregory may be exaggerating just a bit, but there is an element of truth in his claim that Protestantism was practically born to divide: "In Benjamin Kaplan's apt phrase, 'Protestantism itself was irrepressibly fissile.' Adamant claims that 'the Bible is the religion of Protestants' did not arrest the fissility—they caused it."[2] Just so, it is not simply the case that the pluralism of contemporary Protestantism proceeded from a progressive liberalization that included abandoning the authority of Scripture, but also that the first Reformers' reactions against the Catholicism of their day—particularly their rejection of ecclesial authority, their assertion of the immediacy of the individual believer's relationship to God, and their concomitant insistence that each believer was a potentially competent interpreter of the Biblical text—led to "an open-ended welter of competing and incompatible interpretations"[3] of Scripture. While this interpretive heterogeneity relates only indirectly to the subject of this chapter, it was and has been at the root of Protestant discord, and thereby helped create conditions under which it became increasingly difficult to identify concrete moral positions on matters like parenting and procreation as distinctly Protestant.

Even so, the Reformers' thinking—not just their reactions against Catholicism, but their particular theological commitments, practical concerns, and the sociopolitical conditions of the time—did contribute significantly to the emergence of new conceptions of family and parenting, many of which remain, at least vestigially, in the contemporary world. The Reformers' rejection of the clerically based ecclesial authority of Catholicism produced a social and moral space that was filled to a large extent by the Christian family.

The emergence and eventual establishment of Christianity in the Roman Empire had included a Christian sexual ethic that stood in stark contrast to that of pagan Rome, particularly in its limiting sexual activity to the marriage bed and its insistence upon "an openness in all sexual activity to the procreation, nurture, and education of children."[4] Yet although established Christianity had a high view of the goods of marriage, it came soon to value celibacy even more, and from early in the fourth century the church required clerical celibacy as part of the more rigorous half of a two-tiered ethic based in what came to be called the "counsels of evangelical perfection."[5]

Clerical celibacy was practiced and enforced unevenly in the years between its establishment and the Reformation. It was not uncommon in the late Middle Ages for priests in some regions of Europe to have less than secret concubines and for the practice to be tolerated by their bishops, which produced among the laity an undercurrent of suspicion and occasional open hostility toward the church and its clergy.[6] The Reformers were accordingly uniform in their critique of mandatory clerical celibacy, both the practice and its corruption, seeing them as signs of Rome's theological and moral bankruptcy. Their rejection of mandatory celibacy was one important part of their broader rejection of the two-tiered ethic of medieval Catholicism. This rejection was characteristic both of magisterial and radical Protestants, who "agreed that the distinction between commands and counsels was unacceptable in principle. . . . For them there was no heroic elite in the church; or, perhaps one should say, they regarded all Christians as called to join that heroic elite. There was one standard of sanctity, and one only, for all Christians."[7]

The Reformers' dismissal of mandatory celibacy meant that the pastors of the first Protestant churches were also husbands and fathers. Protestant preachers argued from the Biblical creation stories and the letters of Paul that women and men were created for relationships of mutual interdependence, and that marriage was the institution through and within which these relationships could be sustained. Marriage came to be seen not primarily as a grudging concession to the need to circumscribe disordered sexual desire, but rather as a positive means of cultivating and displaying Christian faithfulness. Along with the family it was anticipated to produce, marriage came to be understood as essential to the development of a healthy Christian society within which the household was both microcosm and building block.[8]

Belief in the Christian family as elemental to the construction of a Christian society was especially conspicuous among the magisterial Reformers—the Lutheran and Reformed, in particular—who believed that building a Christian society was part of the work of bringing about God's promised kingdom. In a significant sense, the Reformers were not so much architects as engineers, building both on early Christianity's incremental challenges to the patriarchal household rules and honor codes of pagan Greco-Roman culture and medieval Catholicism's emphasis on the centrality of mutual consent for defining marriage.[9] To these achievements, the Reformers—Luther in particular—added the notion of explicitly "public" marriage, which made the married couple accountable not only to the church, but also to the civil authorities, thereby making the "earthly kingdom" directly responsible for the Christian household.[10]

Within the emergent Protestant understanding of marriage and family, procreation and childrearing were for the most part simply assumed. Although *proles*—Augustine's name for the procreative good of marriage—was dislocated by the Reformers from its undisputed place of primacy, it remained an indispensable pillar of the familial society marriage brought into existence.[11] For Luther, procreation was simply a naturally given part of the marriage covenant, although his account of nature came not primarily from simply looking at the natural world, but rather from reading the creation myths in Genesis. He wrote in his treatise "The Estate of Marriage" that "just as God does not command anyone to be a man or a woman but creates them the way they have to be, so he does not command them to multiply but creates them so that they have to multiply."[12] Children were therefore assumed essential members of the Christian household, itself a society bound by mutual love.[13]

The ways and extent to which the Reformers' views on procreation and parenting affect the contemporary moral landscape cannot be adequately understood apart from the sequelae of another, slightly less explicitly theological development within early Protestantism. In 1620, the British jurist, statesman, and sometime philosopher Sir Francis Bacon published *The New Organon*, a wide-ranging call for the rejection of speculative philosophy and the inauguration of a new science devoted to serving the practical concerns of humanity. Philosophy to that point, Bacon claimed, had evidenced no ability to afford such service, which meant that it was largely mistaken, especially as it concerned the natural world. Were extant philosophies true, he declared, they would have borne "fruits," for "fruits and works are as it were sponsors and sureties for the truth of philosophies." Yet the philosophical systems descended from the most well known classical Greek philosophers had failed in this respect: "There can hardly after the lapse of so many years be adduced a single experiment which tends to relieve and benefit the condition of man."[14]

Bacon was a faithful churchman and very much a Protestant, especially in his rejection of medieval Catholic appropriations of Platonic and Aristotelian philosophy—as with many of the Reformers on the continent, Aristotle was to Bacon a *bête noire*. As such, he rejected speculative metaphysical intrusions into natural philosophy and called for a clear and complete separation between theology and the new science. To be fair, Bacon was not the first to go in this direction; as Neil Postman notes, the German Lutheran mathematician Johannes Kepler had, in developing his theory of planetary motion, rejected the long held teachings of the doctors of the Church, but understood himself in doing so simply to be making clear the proper boundaries between theology and science.[15] Bacon, however, went further, claiming theological sanction for his project, which was nothing less than the work of healing the physical effects of the fall:

> For man by the fall fell at the same time from his state of innocency and from his dominion over creation. Both of these losses however can even in this life be repaired; the former by religion and faith, the latter by arts and sciences. Or creation was not by the curse made altogether and forever a rebel, but in virtue of that charter "In the sweat of thy face shalt thou eat bread," it is now by various labors... at length and in some measure subdued to the supplying of man with bread, that is, to the uses of human life.[16]

According to Gerald McKenny, Bacon's vision demanded that nature—which includes the human body—be treated instrumentally, a demand that was made possible by his dividing theology and speculative philosophy from natural philosophy—the name given in Bacon's day to what would come to be called the natural sciences.[17] He sought to use the "arts and sciences" to control the natural world, "to make nature serve the business and conveniences of man."[18] Inheritors of Bacon's vision furthered his unmooring of technical control from theological commitment, giving rise to what McKenny calls the "Baconian project," a set of discursive practices "characterized by efforts to eliminate suffering and expand human choice and thereby overcome the human subjection to natural necessity or fate."[19] McKenny argues that this project's instantiation in modern medicine takes the form of a moral imperative that is increasingly unconstrained by seemingly arbitrary traditional restrictions, such that medicine is "therefore called upon to eliminate whatever anyone might consider a burden of finitude"[20]—something more often than not regarded today as consistent with Protestant thought and practice.

To this point I have identified two strands of Protestant thought: first, the emphasis by the early Reformers on the Christian family, which invariably included both parents and children as an essential element—both as microcosm and building block—in the creation of a Christian society; and second, the Baconian project's promise to deliver humankind, first from suffering and deprivation, and then later from the burdens of unhappy contingency. These strands converge in modern and contemporary Protestantism in at least two ways, which I'll attempt to account for first by way of an exemplary dispute between two notable twentieth century Protestant moralists, and then by way of a particular example.

Well before there was a discrete discipline called *bioethics*, two Protestant theologians were writing about medicine and ethics from the perspective of their respective understandings of Christian tradition—understandings based partly on their readings of Scripture.[21] The first party in this dispute was Joseph Fletcher (1905–1991), an Episcopal priest who worked for many years at the University of Virginia and who, although he eventually abandoned the Christian faith, seemed never completely to have shaken its influence. His interlocutor was Paul Ramsey (1913–1988), a Methodist who spent his career as a member of the faculty at Princeton. Each wrote a significant book published during the period when bioethics was just starting to take form: Fletcher's *Morals and Medicine* (1954) and Ramsey's *The Patient as Person* (1970). Both books were ostensibly about the need for medicine to treat patients as persons—as ones having a particular moral status and an agency that justifies their active participation in the clinical encounter. As Fletcher puts the matter, "Medical care is provided for persons," beings whom we treat in certain ways because we regard them as possessing dignity equal to our own.[22] And Ramsey echoes this assertion, saying "the doctor who attends *the case* has a reason to be attentive to the patient as person."[23] This superficial similarity, however, belies deep differences between the two, which may be most summarily characterized according to their differing views on the morality of technological control over the human body and its functioning—with procreation being an especially stark case in point.[24]

Ramsey's student Gilbert Meilaender suggests the differences between Fletcher and Ramsey run deep, characterizing them as a matter of contrary theological anthropologies, as incommensurable accounts of the human person that "have been at war with one another in the three decades or so that bioethics has been a burgeoning movement."[25] Ramsey's consideration of "human nature" in his *Basic Christian Ethics* (1950) rests within the mainstream of Christian orthodoxy; he asserts there that humans are human because they are created *imago Dei*, in the image of God. He goes on, however, to note that "there is a widespread opinion that the notion of *imago Dei* has been simply a peculiar religious manner or archaic way of saying what other interpretations of human nature manage to say more clearly, by speaking, for example, of the inherent dignity or worth of man on account of his freedom or reason."[26] This distortion has its origins in theological misconstruals of the *imago Dei* that either identifies human nature as resting on a particular human capacity, "something *within the substantial form* of human nature," or as some "inner capacity of mind, or soul, or will" that is "identified as the image of God *within* man."[27] Ramsey asserts that these ways of thinking have more to do with Greco-Roman or Cartesian philosophy than Christian theology, implying that insofar as theologians have gone in these directions, they have contributed to and participated in rendering theological accounts of the human uninteresting or irrelevant.

Yet the theological anthropology that identifies the *imago Dei* with particular human capacities represents only one account, and a fairly recent one, at that. A second view, which Ramsey calls "relational" and identifies with Saint Paul, Augustine, Kierkegaard, and Karl Barth, denies that anything "*within* the make-up of man, considered by himself apart from a present responsive relationship to God, has the form or power of being in the image of God."[28] In this view, the human "is a theological animal to the root of his essential being," who bears the image of God based on his "*position* before God, or rather, the image of God is reflected in man because of his position before him."[29] The human images God insofar as she images God's will for her as God's good creature; this involves the exercise of such human capacities as she may possess, but it is not these capacities that make her *imago Dei*.[30]

Fletcher's account of the person is nearly diametrically opposed to Ramsey's. In the first chapter of *Medicine and Morals*, he makes the generally uncontroversial claim that morality—the ascription of praise or blame to human actions—is necessarily predicated upon the assumption of freedom and understanding. Yet he asserts further that genuinely human actions are matters of *control*. "Just as helplessness is the bedsoil of fatalism, so control is the basis of freedom and responsibility, of moral action, of truly *human* behavior."[31] Control, freedom, and understanding—those things that make us genuinely human, by virtue of which we are *imago Dei*—he says, "are in us, not *out there*." "Physical nature," he says, "the body and all its members, our organs and their functions—all of these *things* are a part of 'what is over against us,' and if we live by the rule and conditions set in physiology or any other *it* we are not men, we are not *thou*."[32] Just so, Fletcher's account of the person seems to be thoroughly dualist; as he goes on the say, "the body is *it*," which is to say, an object. In explaining how person and body are related, he turns to an analogy that is not quite Cartesian: "Man the artist, the body the materials. A good artist loves and respects his materials, but *he* is the artist always."[33] This "artist"—the inward, non-corporeal, person—is the bearer of the divine image, "because it is precisely persons—and not souls or bodies or glands or human biology—that count with God and come first in ethics."[34]

Fletcher accordingly stands firmly within the camp that identifies the God-imaging person with a particular human capacity. Beginning around 1970, Fletcher claimed that there was a qualitative distinction between a mere human and a human *person*. He writes: "Defective fetuses, defective newborns, moribund patients—all of these are human lives. Some physicians would 'sacrifice' such human lives sometimes, others would not.... If there is any ground at all, ethically, as I would contend there is, for allowing or hastening the end of such lives, it must be on a qualitative ground, that such lives are subpersonal. What is critical is personal status, not merely human status."[35] This becomes for Fletcher a Rosetta stone—discovering or determining the criterion or criteria by which persons may be distinguished from mere humans.

Although it developed over time, Fletcher's position on the distinguishing characteristic tended from the beginning to focus on cognition. Early on, his views were very nearly mentalist; in 1954 he wrote that "To be a person, to have moral being, is to have the capacity for intelligent causal action. It means to be free of physiology!"[36] Then, in 1972 and 1975, he wrote two articles, both of which were published—the first in abbreviated form—in the *Hastings Center Report*.[37] In both he defended the distinction between the mere human animal and the human person as a matter of having certain capacities, all of which depend ultimately upon neocortical function, which he called "the cardinal or hominizing trait on which all other human traits hinge."[38] Without neocortical function, "the *person* is nonexistent. Such individuals are objects but not subjects."[39]

To be fair, Fletcher did not completely deny the bodily aspects of human existence.[40] Even so, the body-as-object and body-as-other language that permeates his work places him on a trajectory toward instrumentalizing the body in a way totally consistent with McKenny's description of the Baconian project. It is here that he most starkly contrasts with Ramsey, who was pointed in his rejection of dualism, writing in the preface to *The Patient as Person* that the human person possesses "a sacredness in bodily life. He is a person who within the ambience of the flesh claims our care. He is an embodied soul or an ensouled body."[41] From Ramsey's perspective, this account of the human was plainly Biblical. The Biblical authors, he said, "hold a very realistic view of the life of man who is altogether flesh (*sarx*). . . . No one who has been consciously formed by Biblical perspectives is likely to be beguiled by notions of the person whose origin is actually a Cartesian dualism of mind and body."[42] On this matter, Ramsey's student Meilaender echoes his teacher with great clarity, saying "To have a life is to be *terra animata*, a living body whose natural history has a natural trajectory. It is to be a someone who has a history, not a someone with certain capacities or characteristics."[43]

As one might expect, the vast differences in their respective theological anthropologies meant that Fletcher and Ramsey had radically divergent views on procreation and the use of procreative technologies. Fletcher was unsurprisingly enthusiastic, claiming in his 1972 *Hastings Center Report* article on humanhood that "A baby made artificially, by deliberate and careful contrivance, would be more *human* than one resulting from sexual roulette—the reproductive mode of the subhuman species."[44] For Fletcher, being human meant being able rationally to manipulate the circumstances of existence to achieve desired ends. Writing about medical genetics more than twenty years before the mapping of the human genome, he asserted: "To be men we must be in control. That is the first and last ethical word."[45] In this same vein he wrote a few years later of a "duty to the unborn," posing the rhetorical question, "If infectious diseases are in some cases serious enough to justify public or legal control of their transmission, why not genetic diseases too?"⁴⁶ To the extent we wish future generations to be healthy, "we have to learn as much as we can about controlling reproduction, to be free as much as possible from the dangers of blind, natural cause-and-effect."⁴⁷

Ramsey, while decidedly not a Luddite, was considerably more circumspect about the ways biotechnology might change procreation and parenting. He followed Karl Barth in asserting that parenthood is "a basic form of humanity,"⁴⁸ and claimed that from the perspective of Christian morality, the fundamental question attending all technologies affecting procreation was whether they might be used in the service of Christian "teaching concerning *the union between* the two goods of human sexuality," the so-called unitive and procreative goods.⁴⁹ Regardless of whether one of these goods is more significant than the other, he said, the "crucial question that remains is whether sexual intercourse as an act of love should ever be separated from sexual intercourse as a procreative act."⁵⁰ In principle, he argued, the two ends should remain united, and any ethics, whether Christian or not, that treated "procreation as an aspect of biological nature to be subjected merely to the requirements of *technical* control while saying that the unitive purpose is the free, human, personal end of the matter—pays disrespect to the nature of human parenthood."⁵¹

This is not to say that Ramsey believed procreation ought never to be subjected to technological intervention. He did not think contraception to be intrinsically morally wrong, and acknowledged there were perfectly good reasons a couple might not intend children at certain times over the course of their relationship. Further, he admitted that it would not necessarily disrupt the unity of the ends of a marriage "when a couple for grave, or for what in their case is to them sufficient, reason adopt a lifelong policy of planned *un*parenthood."⁵² Such reasons might include "voluntary eugenic decisions"; insofar as Christianity has always held that procreation entails a duty to future generations, a couple may be obliged for genetic reasons *not* to have children.⁵³

Importantly, however, Ramsey was skeptical about extending the uses of procreative technologies much beyond the realm of judicious prospective intervention to prevent the conception of children with serious congenital illnesses. In this regard his skepticism was driven not simply by his commitment to the integrity of the marriage covenant, but also by his concern to respect the givenness—the limits—of embodied life. Predictably, then, he was suspicious of or hostile toward then-nascent medically-assisted reproductive technologies. Writing years before the work of Drs. Edwards and Steptoe led to the 1978 birth of Louise Joy Brown, Ramsey claimed that "To put radically asunder what God joined together in parenthood when he made love procreative, to procreate from beyond the sphere of love (AID, for example, or making human life in a test-tube) . . . means a refusal of the image of God's creation in our own."⁵⁴

Ramsey believed that the acceptance of AID (artificial insemination with donor gametes) was a wedge issue, the beginning of a slippery slope down to a social milieu not unlike Huxley's *Brave New World*, where in vitro fertilization, preimplantation genetic diagnosis, surrogacy, and ectogenesis would be commonplace.[55] Such developments, he claimed, "will result with the destruction of parenthood as a basic form of humanity, and its recombination in various ways for extrinsic purposes."[56] He further averred that the transformation of procreation into manufacturing would be the result of parenting having become fully "*personalized*," abandoning the inherent givenness of embodiment in favor of the unconstrained freedom of disembodied reason.[57]

Whether a contemporary reader regards Ramsey as a prophet or an alarmist or a bit of both is probably a matter of personal, cultural, and theological perspectives. Many of the developments about which he was so concerned have come to pass. Our fashionable obsessions with the body notwithstanding, we seem less inclined than ever to receive the inherent limits of embodiment as gifts. If Ramsey's account of the human person as embodied is correct, we would do well to consider his particular take on the often reactionary screed against "playing God." He says: "Men ought not to play God before they learn how to be men, and after they have learned to be men they will not play God."[58]

We can get a broader sense of the way the aforementioned impulses endemic to Protestantism have played out—especially with respect to the ongoing medicalization and associated technologizing of procreation and parenting—by considering a particular cluster of examples. The Reformers' assertion that the (Protestant) Christian family was an essential element in the development of a healthy Christian society, along with the Baconian aspiration to use an emergent mastery of nature to alleviate suffering and generally improve the lot of humankind, undergo a disturbing mutation when they intersect with the medicalized procreation and bourgeois cultural expectations so conspicuous in twentieth and twenty-first-century North American consumer culture. As the Methodist theologian Amy Laura Hall has shown, contemporary American culture's commodification of children and concomitant obsession with "perfect" children are significantly Protestant in their origins.[59] Hall suggests a profound irony in the apparent fact that "the very Protestant tradition that should have emphasized a sense of divine gratuity, human contingency, sufficient abundance, and the radical giftedness of all life came in twentieth-century America instead to epitomize *justification by meticulously planned procreation*."[60]

That the technologies we have at our disposal shape the way we see, speak about, and live in the world is a well-rehearsed theme. As those technologies having to do with procreation provide seemingly ever-increasing control over when we have children and what kind of children we have, they cannot help but alter the way we understand what children are and what they are for.[61] Technological control over procreation does not simply expand reproductive choice so much as it replaces one limited range of choices with another as particular technologies and the implications of their use become socially normative.[62] Such "control" has contributed to the creation of what Hall calls a "national obligation to plan one's family for quality and quantity control" that "has become an assumption of twenty-first-century life."[63] Something about this assumption that typically goes unnoticed is its Protestant heritage and the explicitly theological language that was used in its formation.

When the World Council of Churches—about as close as Protestants come to an ecumenical council—convened in 1954 in Evanston, Illinois, it gathered under the theme "Christ, the Hope of the World." The Council's adjournment was followed by a national conference of the Methodist Church, which has as its theme "The Christian Family—the Hope of the World."[64] At first glance this theme could be taken as a relatively uncontroversial echoing of the Reformers' belief in the importance of the Christian household. Yet the keynote address, delivered by Bishop G. Bromley Oxnam, reinterprets the notion of the Christian family in a decidedly modern, technocratic way. The Christian family upon which the world depended was of a very particular sort, distinguished less by its devotion to Christ than by its sensible structure and conduct, especially as it pertained to procreation. "Christian parents," he claimed, "are morally obligated to plan for the coming of their children. The proper spacing of children is an expression of love and therefore a religious obligation."[65] Although unstated in the Bishop's address, it may be inferred that the planning he had in mind would employ the best available technology; further, given the global scope of the conference's theme, the aforementioned obligation and the technologies required to realize it would need to be exported to the benefit of other peoples.

These inferences were made explicit and writ large a few years later in a 1957 article in the Methodist publication *Together*. The article was written by Margaret Sanger, who was by then a well-known and widely accepted advocate of contraception and family planning. In "Too Many People," Sanger asserted that the world stood on the brink of realizing a threat even greater than nuclear war—overpopulation. "From the Orient to South America, from Eastern Europe to the U.S., soaring birth rates are posing future problems potentially more dangerous than the H-bomb."[66] Sanger's focus was on the problem presented by "have-not nations"; her solution was for her Methodist readers to advocate for the exportation of contraception, ostensibly as a way for these nations to move toward some facsimile of American common sense and middle-class prosperity.[67]

However minimal, Sanger's association with mainline Protestantism evokes another often unnoticed connection. In the first decades of the twentieth century, when her concern for the rights and welfare of women first led her to champion the widespread availability of contraception, Sanger also became part of the American eugenics movement. Although Sanger's writing was from early on steeped in eugenicist rhetoric—her 1922 book *The Pivot of Civilization* advocated both the coercive sterilization and the separation from respectable society of the "unfit"—her initial efforts to affiliate her birth control movement with prominent eugenics organizations like the American Eugenics Society were met with considerable resistance.[68] In spite of Sanger's clear embrace of eugenics and the broad overlap of her concerns with theirs, eugenicists resisted formal association with Sanger's movement for two reasons. The first of these was ideological; Sanger's broad concern for women's health led her to reject "constructive eugenics," the idea that "fit" (that is, prosperous northern European, and especially Anglo-Saxon) couples should have large families.[69] The second reason was practical, or at least tactical; Sanger's efforts offended the moral and religious sensibilities of many Americans, including, at least initially, some eugenicists.[70]

But those initial reservations about birth control based on moral and religious concerns were short-lived as Sanger continued to pursue connections with the eugenics movement, which had enjoyed the favor of many religious Americans, especially among Protestant progressives. As Christine Rosen notes, "During the first few decades of the twentieth century, eugenics flourished in the liberal Protestant, Catholic, and Jewish mainstream; clerics, rabbis, and lay leaders wrote books and articles about eugenics, joined eugenics organizations, and lobbied for eugenics legislation."[71] As enthusiasm for the social gospel waned after the first world war, Rosen says, many of its adherents found a new way to channel their often theologically inchoate passions for social reform—toward eugenics.[72]

Just so, whatever elements of eugenic thought might remain among contemporary Protestants are come by honestly. When the American Eugenics Society began actively recruiting progressive religious leaders in the early 1920s, it found Protestants especially receptive. The society even began sponsoring a eugenics sermon contest in 1926, quite obviously believing that the funds allocated for prizes would be well worth the mass distribution of eugenics propaganda.[73]

Save for a few devotees, American Protestant enthusiasm for the eugenics movement largely followed the enthusiasm of the general populace. As American eugenics found its way to Europe and was taken up into the service of Nazism and its ideology of genocidal hate, and as eugenic pseudo-science came under increasing scrutiny by developments in the natural sciences, the movement lost popularity and eventually fade into near-silence. Yet, claims Amy Laura Hall, strong traces of eugenic thinking remain among enthusiasts of the new genomics; "there are links," she says, "between current hopes for genius and past attempts to vaccinate the social body against the menace of poverty, disability, and deviance." These links, moreover, are manifest among today's Protestant church membership.[74] She cites as signs of this presence the increasing rate at which parents terminate pregnancies after having been presented evidence of fetal anomalies, the increased tendency among contemporary Americans to think and speak skeptically about black and brown families who seem indiscriminate in their breeding habits, and the cultural trajectory toward regarding all manner of reproductive decisions as belonging to individuals isolated from communal support. All she suggests, are part of the lineage of "the powerful rhetoric of eugenics."[75]

I conclude by calling attention to Protestant associations with eugenics and its genomic heritage as a way of returning to the particular Protestant impulse with which I began, namely its fissility—its tendency to divide—which has in later modernity taken the form of a trajectory toward individualism and the dissolution or abandonment of tradition.[76] Focusing on Protestant fissility, I would argue, offers a way of characterizing contemporary Protestantism that rises above difficulties presented by the inheritances bequeathed by the modernist-fundamentalist debates of the early twentieth century. Whether one's touchstone is Biblical inerrancy, or the a priori religious feeling of each person, makes little difference in a world where community-sustaining tradition is so remarkably absent. In such a world, as Gerald McKenny has noted, there are and probably can be no widely agreed upon reasons to constrain the development, implementation, and employment of technologies that give medical consumers what they want, which is not simply freedom from suffering and the expansion of control, but also "freedom from the need to care for others or the need to be cared for by them."[77] In this world, as Amy Laura Hall has pointed out and as McKenny explains, the kinds of bodily difference that demand care are destined to increased marginalization, even to the point of elimination. McKenny rightly asserts that certain Christian convictions can be developed to make for more faithfully Christian uses of modern medicine; he is also right to assert that these convictions may only be developed within particular communities of formation and discernment.[78] Whether contemporary Protestants of whatever political and theological bent can rediscover and sustain such communities remains for now an open question.[79]

Notes

1. Brad Gregory argues that this stability was due in large part to the fact that the theological positions of the so-called *magisterial* Reformers were backed and often even enforced by local political authorities. This is no doubt the case, but much of early Protestantism's stability seems also to have been a matter of creedal orthodoxy, which is to say habits of thought and life developed over the previous fifteen centuries. See Gregory's *The Unintended Reformation: How a Religious Revolution Secularized Society* (Cambridge, MA: Belknap, 2012), 92, as compared to David Steinmetz, "The Intellectual Appeal of the Reformation," *Theology Today* 57, no. 4 (January 2001): 459–472.
2. Gregory, *Unintended Reformation*, 92.
3. Ibid., 94.
4. David Steinmetz, "Marriage, Celibacy, and Ordination," in *Taking the Long View: Christian Theology in Historical Perspective* (New York: Oxford, 2011), 103–114, at 105.
5. Ibid., 106.
6. Ibid., 106–108.
7. Ibid., 109; cf. James Turner Johnson, "Marriage as Covenant in Early Protestant Thought," in *Covenant Marriage in Comparative Perspective*, ed. John Witte and Eliza Ellison, 128–129 (Grand Rapids, MI: Eerdmans, 2005).
8. Ibid., 110–111.
9. Don S. Browning, *Marriage and Modernization: How Globalization Threatens Marriage and What to Do About It* (Grand Rapids, MI: Eerdmans, 2003), 20–24.
10. Ibid., 94–95.
11. Johnson, "Marriage as Covenant," 128–129.
12. Quoted in Browning, 96, from *Luther's Works*, vol. 45, 18.
13. Browning, *Marriage and Modernization*, 116.

14. Francis Bacon, *The New Organon and Related Writings*, ed. Fulton H. Anderson (Upper Saddle River, NJ: Prentice Hall, 1960), 71.
15. Neil Postman, *Technopoly: The Surrender of Culture to Technology* (New York: Vintage, 1993), 30–32.
16. Bacon, *The New Organon*, 267–268.
17. Gerald McKenny, *To Relieve the Human Condition: Bioethics, the Body, and the Legacy of Bacon* (Albany: SUNY Press, 1997), 17.
18. Bacon, *The New Organon*, 180.
19. McKenny, *To Relieve the Human Condition*, 9.
20. Gerald McKenny, "Bioethics, the Body, and the Legacy of Bacon," in *On Moral Medicine: Theological Perspectives in Medical Ethics*, 3rd ed., ed. M. Therese Lysaught and Joseph Kotva (Grand Rapids, MI: Eerdmans, 2012), 398.
21. Allen Verhey, *Reading the Bible in the Strange World of Medicine* (Grand Rapids, MI: Eerdmans, 2003), 71–72.
22. Joseph Fletcher, *Morals and Medicine* (Princeton, NJ: Princeton University Press, 1954), 9.
23. Paul Ramsey, *The Patient as Person: Explorations in Medical Ethics* (New Haven, CT: Yale University Press, 1970), xi (italics original).
24. Verhey, *Reading the Bible*, 72–73.
25. Gilbert Meilaender, *Body, Soul, and Bioethics* (Notre Dame, IN: University of Notre Dame Press, 1995), 37–59, at 47.
26. Paul Ramsey, *Basic Christian Ethics* (Louisville, KY: Westminster/John Knox Press, 1993), 249.
27. Ibid., 250 (italics original).
28. Ibid., 254 (italics original).
29. Ibid., 255 (italics original).
30. Ibid., 257–259.
31. Fletcher, *Morals and Medicine*, 11 (italics original).
32. Ibid., 211 (italics original).
33. Ibid., 212–213 (italics original).
34. Ibid., 219.
35. Joseph Fletcher, *Humanhood: Essays in Biomedical Ethics* (Buffalo, NY: Prometheus Books, 1979), 11.
36. Fletcher, *Morals and Medicine*, 218.
37. The first article was published in the *Hastings Center Report* in November 1972, as "Indicators of Humanhood: A Tentative Profile on Man." Its full text was published as "Medicine and the Nature of Man," first in *The Teaching of Medical Ethics*, ed. R. M. Veatch, W. Gaylin, and C. Morgan (Hastings-on-Hudson, NY: Institute of Society, Ethics, and the Life Sciences, 1973), 47–58, and then in *Science, Medicine, and Man* I (1973): 93–102.
38. Joseph Fletcher, "Four Indicators of Humanhood—The Enquiry Matures," in *On Moral Medicine: Theological Perspectives in Medical Ethics*, 3rd ed., ed. M. Therese Lysaught and Joseph Kotva (Grand Rapids, MI: Eerdmans, 2012), 334–337. This article was originally published in the *Hastings Center Report* 4 (December 1975), 4–7. Stanley Hauerwas notes of Fletcher's criteria that Fletcher's "'profile' of man does not . . . provide operational criteria any doctor would recognize, but it is rather a statement of the working assumptions about the value of human life that are alive in our culture." Stanley Hauerwas, "The Retarded and the Criteria for the Human," in *Truthfulness and Tragedy: Further Investigations into Christian Ethics* (Notre Dame, IN: University of Notre Dame Press, 1977), 157–163, at 161.

39. Fletcher, "Indicators of Humanhood: A Tentative Profile on Man," 3.
40. On this, see, for example, *Morals and Medicine*, 211–212.
41. Ramsey, *The Patient as Person*, xiii.
42. Ibid., 187. See also Paul Ramsey, *Fabricated Man: The Ethics of Genetic Control* (New Haven, CT: Yale University Press, 1970), 31, 47–48.
43. Meilaender, *Body, Soul, and Bioethics*, 56–57.
44. Fletcher, "Indicators of Humanhood: A Tentative Profile on Man," 3.
45. Fletcher, *Humanhood*, 91.
46. Ibid., 106.
47. Ibid., 93.
48. Ramsey, *Fabricated Man*, 131.
49. Ibid., 32, italics original.
50. Ibid., 33.
51. Ibid., italics original.
52. Ibid., 34, italics original.
53. Ibid., 35.
54. Ibid., 39.
55. Ibid., 104–110.
56. Ibid., 109.
57. Ibid., 136, italics original.
58. Ibid., 138.
59. Amy Laura Hall, *Conceiving Parenthood: American Protestantism and the Spirit of Reproduction* (Grand Rapids, IN: Eerdmans, 2008).
60. Ibid., 10, italics original. Hal is speaking here of Methodism in particular, but similar things may also be said of other strands of mainline Protestantism.
61. Joel Shuman and Brian Volck, *Reclaiming the Body: Christians and the Faithful Use of Modern Medicine* (Grand Rapids, IN: Brazos, 2006), 79.
62. Here see Barbara Katz Rothman, "Prenatal Diagnosis," in *Bioethics and the Fetus: Medical, Moral, and Legal Issues*, ed. James Humber and Robert Almeder, (Totowa, NJ: Humana Press, 1991), 173–175.
63. Hall, *Conceiving Parenthood*, 15.
64. Ibid., 14. I am indebted to Professor Hall for her account of the conference and Bishop Oxnam's address.
65. Bishop G. Bromley Oxnam, "The Christian Family, the Hope of the World," in *Report: The Christian Home—The Hope of the World*, 3–6. Quoted in Hall, *Conceiving Parenthood*, 15.
66. Margaret Sanger, "Too Many People," *Together* (September 1957): 16. Quoted in Hall, *Conceiving Parenthood*, 16.
67. Hall, *Conceiving Parenthood*, 16.
68. Edwin Black, *War Against the Weak: Eugenics and America's Campaign to Create a Master Race* (New York: Four Walls Eight Windows, 2003), 127–135. Black quotes Sanger's eugenicist writing extensively, as well as the work of others published in *Birth Control Review*, the official publication of the American Birth Control League, which she founded.
69. Ibid., 131–133.
70. Christine Rosen, *Preaching Eugenics: Religious Leaders and the American Eugenics Movement* (New York: Oxford, 2004), 154 ff. Rosen notes (p. 154) that the eugenicists' initial aversion to Sanger's birth control movement was not simply a matter of moral trepidation, but also unfamiliarity. By the time Sanger founded the ABCL, "Eugenics had become more

mainstream; at a 1926 meeting in New Orleans, the Protestant Episcopal House of Bishops favored eugenic measures but thoroughly rejected birth control, for example."
71. Rosen, *Preaching Eugenics*, 4.
72. Ibid., 16–18.
73. Ibid., 111–128.
74. Hall, *Conceiving Parenthood*, 217.
75. Ibid., 217–218, at 218.
76. I follow Alasdair MacIntyre in his characterization of a living tradition as "an historically extended, socially embodied argument, and an argument precisely in part about the goods which constitute that tradition." Here see *After Virtue*, 2nd ed. (Notre Dame, IN: University of Notre Dame Press, 1984), 204–225, at 222.
77. McKenny, "Bioethics, the Body, and the Legacy of Bacon," 408.
78. Ibid., 406–408.
79. I am grateful to Dan Bell, Stanley Hauerwas, and Jim Wallace, among others, for their careful reading of earlier drafts of this chapter and their helpful suggestions for revision. Thanks as well are due to Ms. Jade Rombach, who prepared the bibliography.

Bibliography

Bacon, Francis. *The New Organon and Related Writings*. Edited by Fulton H. Anderson. Upper Saddle River, NJ: Prentice Hall, 1960.

Black, Edwin. *War against the Weak: Eugenics and America's Campaign to Create a Master Race*. New York: Four Walls Eight Windows, 2003.

Browning, Don S. *Marriage and Modernization: How Globalization Threatens Marriage and What to Do about It*. Grand Rapids: Eerdmans, 2003.

Fletcher, Joseph. "Four Indicators of Humanhood—The Enquiry Matures." In *On Moral Medicine: Theological Perspectives in Medical Ethics*, 3rd edition, edited by M. Therese Lysaught and Joseph Kotva, 334–337. Grand Rapids, IN: Eerdmans, 2012.

Fletcher, Joseph. *Humanhood: Essays in Biomedical Ethics*. Buffalo: Prometheus Books, 1979.

Fletcher, Joseph. "Indicators of Humanhood: A Tentative Profile on Man." *Hastings Center Report* 2, no. 5 (1972): 1–4.

Fletcher, Joseph. *Morals and Medicine*. Princeton, NJ: Princeton University Press, 1954.

Gregory, Brad. *The Unintended Reformation: How a Religious Revolution Secularized Society*. Cambridge, MA: Belknap, 2012.

Hall, Amy Laura. *Conceiving Parenthood: American Protestantism and the Spirit of Reproduction*. Grand Rapids, MI: Eerdmans, 2008.

Hauerwas, Stanley. "The Retarded and the Criteria for the Human." In *Truthfulness and Tragedy: Further Investigations into Christian Ethics*. Notre Dame, IN: University of Notre Dame Press, 1977.

Johnson, James Turner. "Marriage as Covenant in Early Protestant Thought." In *Covenant Marriage in Comparative Perspective*, edited by John Witte and Eliza Ellison, 124–152. Grand Rapids, MI: Eerdmans, 2005.

MacIntyre, Alasdair. *After Virtue*. 2nd edition. Notre Dame, IN: University of Notre Dame Press, 1984.

McKenny, Gerald. *To Relieve the Human Condition: Bioethics, the Body, and the Legacy of Bacon.* Albany, NY: SUNY Press, 1997.

McKenny, Gerald. "Bioethics, the Body, and the Legacy of Bacon." In *On Moral Medicine: Theological Perspectives in Medical Ethics*, 3rd edition, edited by M. Therese Lysaught and Joseph Kotva, 398–409. Grand Rapids, MI: Eerdmans, 2012.

Meilaender, Gilbert. *Body, Soul, and Bioethics.* Notre Dame, IN: University of Notre Dame Press, 1995.

Oxnam, Bishop G. Bromley. "The Christian Family, the Hope of the World." In *Report: The Christian Home—The Hope of the World*, 3–6. Nashville: Board of Education, 1954.

Postman, Neil. *Technopoly: The Surrender of Culture to Technology.* New York: Vintage, 1993.

Ramsey, Paul. *The Patient as Person: Explorations in Medical Ethics.* New Haven, CT: Yale University, 1970.

Ramsey, Paul. *Basic Christian Ethics.* Louisville, KY: Westminster/John Knox Press, 1993.

Ramsey, Paul. *Fabricated Man: The Ethics of Genetic Control.* New Haven, CT: Yale University Press, 1970.

Rosen, Christine. *Preaching Eugenics: Religious Leaders and the American Eugenics Movement.* New York: Four Walls Eight Windows, 2003.

Rothman, Barbara Katz. "Prenatal Diagnosis." In *Bioethics and the Fetus: Medical, Moral, and Legal Issues*, edited by James Humber and Robert Almeder, 171–186. Totowa, NJ: Humana Press, 1991.

Sanger, Margaret. "Too Many People." *Together.* (September 1957): 16–18.

Shuman, Joel, and Brian Volck. *Reclaiming the Body: Christians and the Faithful Use of Modern Medicine.* Grand Rapids, MI: Brazos, 2006.

Steinmetz, David. "Marriage, Celibacy, and Ordination." In *Taking the Long View: Christian Technology in Historical Perspective*, 103–114. New York: Oxford, 2011.

Steinmetz, David. "The Intellectual Appeal of the Reformation." *Theology Today* 57, no. 4 (2001): 459–472.

Verhey, Allen. *Reading the Bible in the Strange World of Medicine.* Grand Rapids, MI: Eerdmans, 2012.

CHAPTER 10

PARENTS AND CHILDREN IN THE QUR'AN AND PREMODERN ISLAMIC JURISPRUDENCE

JANAN DELGADO AND CELENE IBRAHIM

THIS chapter surveys parent-child relationships in Qur'anic ethics and issues related to child custody (ḥaḍāna) in premodern Islamic jurisprudence. We consider the balance in the Qur'an and Islamic jurisprudence between the rights and duties of parents and children. We highlight how ideas about gender inform rulings related to girls and boys as well as mothers and fathers. Religious rulings relating to procreation, childrearing, and family care are guidelines in processes of discernment wherein those involved can strive to faithfully apply Islamic ethical principles. Deducing religious law is the task of Muslim legal theorists and jurists who consult Qur'anic injunctions and the teachings of the Prophet Muhammad, or Hadith, to articulate rulings that protect the rights and responsibilities of parents and children, particularly in strained circumstances. The principles discerned by jurists are enforced, where possible, by legal authorities. Responsibility also falls on piety-seeking parents and children to abide by Islamic ethical imperatives and to mediate their affairs accordingly.

Given the close relationship between theology and law, we turn first to parent-child relationships as described in the Qur'an itself. Then we examine premodern Islamic approaches to child custody law, including the divisions of rights and responsibilities between mothers and fathers and the dilemmas potentially brought about by the dissolution of a couple's marriage. We draw upon the writings of premodern legal experts to show how children had significant rights over their parents. Child custody jurisprudence also brings into focus norms related to gender, as seen most clearly in the respective rights and responsibilities assigned to fathers versus mothers and the slightly differing expectations of sons and daughters.

THEOLOGICAL PERSPECTIVES ON PROCREATION

God does not beget offspring in Islamic theology, and the Qur'an never refers to God as "father" or as "mother"; moreover, human beings are never referred to as "children of God." In fact, verses refuting the idea that God has sons or daughters appear in numerous places in the Qur'an. One such verse emphasized divine unicity: "And say, 'Praise be to God, who has no child! He has no partner in sovereignty; nor has He any protector out of lowliness.' And proclaim his greatness" (Q 17:111).[1] Along these same lines, the Qur'an stresses that in contrast to God, things in God's creation procreate and have partners: "The Originator of the heavens and the earth, He has appointed for you mates from among yourselves, and has appointed mates also among the cattle. He multiplies you thereby; naught is like Him, yet He is the Hearer, the Seer" (Q 42:11). Many such verses celebrate the miraculous nature of procreation, human and otherwise, particularly as the creative power involved in reproduction reflects God's attributes of majesty: "God knows that which every female bears, how wombs diminish and how they increase. Everything with Him is according to a measure—Knower of the unseen and the seen, the Great, the Exalted" (Q 13:8–9). The natural life cycles, childbirth, children, and progeny are not only depicted in the Qur'an as signs of God's power, majesty, and knowledge but are also a means by which God tests the faithful in their awareness and devotion: "And God brought you forth from the bellies of your mothers, knowing naught. And He [God] endowed you with hearing, sight, and hearts, that perhaps you may give thanks" (Q 16:78).

However, human awareness—even in adulthood—is at the same time drastically limited, due in part to human's fundamental time-bounded nature compared to God's timeless, unbounded attributes.

In Qur'anic discourse, God has nurturing and caretaking roles vis-à-vis human beings and is the provider of material and immaterial blessings that serve as a sign of God's presence and care. As one such verse emphasizes: "And He it is who brought you into being from a single soul and [provided] a dwelling place and a repository. We [God] have expounded the signs for a people who understand" (Q 6:98). Related nurturing names for God include the Guardian (*al-Walī*), the Trustee (*al-Wakīl*), the One who Responds (*al-Mujīb*), the One who Averts Harm (*al-Māniʿ*), the watchful one (*al-Khabīr*), the Bestower *(al-Wahhāb)*, the Sustenance-giver (*al-Razzāq*), and related epithets. Even "Lord" (*Rabb*) can have nurturing connotations. These appellations, and others, are known as "God's most beautiful names" (*asmāʾ Allāh al-ḥusnā*). Other such appellations relate to God's disciplinary powers. God is the Hearer (*al-Samīʿ*), the Seer (*al-Baṣīr*), the Arbitrator (*al-Ḥākam*), and more. God is the disciplinarian, the one who takes into ultimate account those who avert justice or turn away from the divine decree. The Qur'an regularly describes how, ultimately, every individual bears a unique moral responsibility: "Your family relations and your children will not benefit you on the Day of Resurrection; He [God] will distinguish between you. And God sees whatsoever you do" (Q 60:3). The Qur'an is also clear that pregnancy and biological sex is the determination of God:

> To God belongs sovereignty over the heavens and the earth; He creates whatsoever He will, bestowing females upon whomsoever He will, and bestowing males upon whomsoever He will, or He couples males and females and causes whomsoever He will to be barren. Indeed, He is Knowing, Powerful. (Q 42:49–50)

The Qur'an also emphasizes that God has ordained the division of rights and responsibilities between human beings—in the present case parents and children, mothers and fathers or daughters and sons—no one should be wronged, and the balance of rights and responsibilities between parties reflects God's ultimate wisdom, justice, and decree.

From this vantage point, the Qur'anic discussions of the ethical and legal dimensions of parent-child relationships, and narratives depicting parents and children, are all in service of guiding human beings to inculcate virtuous action and accumulate credit for a day of recompense (*yawm al-dīn*), one of many Qur'anic descriptions of the impending moment of judgment and cosmic recreation. Parent-child relationships, as a feature of the human life cycle, is situated within this apocalyptic schema that ends in cosmic recreation of all existence, as described in one of many such verses as likened to the harvest seasons:

> O humankind! If you are in doubt concerning the resurrection, [remember that] We [God] created you from dust, then from a drop, then from a blood clot, then from a lump of flesh, formed and unformed, that We may make clear for you. And We cause what We will to remain in the wombs for a term appointed. Then We bring you forth as an infant, then that you may reach maturity. And some are taken in death, and some are consigned to the most abject life, so that after having known they may know nothing. And you see the earth desiccated, but when We send down water upon it, it stirs and swells and produces every delightful kind. (Q 22:5)

Such is the progression of human life, from helplessness in infancy to relative power in adulthood, back to helplessness in old age depicted in the Qur'an, and eventually to a moment of resurrection. Beyond creation and resurrection, the cyclical nature of human life is a trope in the Qur'an: "And whomsoever We [God] give long life, We cause to regress in creation. Do they not understand?" (Q 36:68). Another verse emphasizes how old age resembles the helplessness of infancy: "And among you are those who are brought back to the weakest of ages, such that they know nothing after having had knowledge" (Q 16:70, partial citation).

Given this cyclical nature of life, the period of childhood may be a set of years, but many of the rights and ethical duties of children toward parents extend over a lifetime, and relationships also extend beyond this earthly world. Indeed, the parent-child relationship remains beyond individuals' worldly existences: "Gardens of Eden that they will enter along with those who were righteous from among their fathers, their spouses, and their progeny; and angels will enter upon them from every gate" (Q 13:23). The Qur'an also suggests that some relationships that may have been troubled in worldly existence will dissipate: "We [God] will remove whatever rancor lies within their breasts—as siblings, upon couches, facing one another" (Q 15:46). Such theological concepts inform ethical action and impact religious jurisprudence.

Childhood and Parenting in the Qur'an

The Qur'an contains narratives of both righteous and unrighteous parents and offers much guidance regarding parenting, both by employing the medium of narrative to inculcate virtues and by providing clear ethical and legal directives. We will look first at ethical principles associated with parenting and narratives about parenting in the Qur'an before turning to comparisons between mothers and fathers and male and female children in the Qur'anic discourse.

Parents and Parenting in the Qur'an

At the most elementary level, the Qur'an has several frequently repeated imperatives directed toward parents. Prime among them is a condemnation of infanticide: "Slay not your children for fear of poverty. We [God] will provide for them and for you. Surely their slaying is a great wrongdoing" (Q 17:31). The Qur'an condemns infanticide in no uncertain terms,[2] and verses chastise cultural motives surrounding the practice of female infanticide in particular:

> And when one of them receives tidings of a female [child], his face darkens, and he is choked with anguish. He hides from the people because of the evil of the tidings her has

been given. Will he keep it in humiliation or bury it in the dust? Behold! Evil indeed is the judgment they make! (Q 16:58–59)

A rhetorically powerful rhymed surah in the Qur'an contains an equally chilling description of the testimony that an innocent slain female child will bear at the Day of Judgement as she bears witness against her oppressor:

> When the female infant buried alive is asked
> for what sin she was slain;
> when the pages are spread,
> and when Heaven is laid bare;
> when Hellfire is kindled,
> and when the garden is brought nigh,
> each soul will know what has been made ready. (Q 81:8–14)

With a similar emphasis on protecting vulnerable female children, the Qur'an expresses particular concern for the protection of orphan girls from being taken advantage of sexually (e.g., Q 4:3–4 and 4:127). Verses also outline prohibitions against incest with detailed directives to male family members specifically (Q 4:22–23). Many other verses urge parents to show concern and protect the material interests of vulnerable children, their own and others. For example, in a related passage dealing with the division of inheritance, the Qur'an urges parents to have empathy: "Let those who would dread if they left behind their own helpless progeny reverence God and speak justly." (Q 4:9). Immediately following this verse is a caution against consuming the wealth of bereft children (Q 4:10). Such topics are consistent with the broader focus of the Qur'an on urging the protection of vulnerable persons in society. In one instance, the Qur'an rhetorically asks:

> And what ails you that you fight not in the way of God, and for the weak and oppressed—men, women, and children—who cry out, "Our Lord! Bring us forth from this town whose people are oppressors, and appoint for us from You a proctor, and appoint for us from You a helper." (Q 4:75, see also Q 4:98)

This emphasis of the Qur'an on the protection of the socially vulnerable appears in tandem with verses that exhort individuals to develop virtue through character formation. For instance, several verses caution against patents having excess parental pride. Children can certainly be a source of joy, but bragging is a breach of etiquette, first and foremost with God. The Qur'an reinforces this lesson in a story of the fate of an arrogant man who bragged about his wealth and progeny to his pious companion, only to be chided and forewarned by the companion:

> When you entered your garden, why did you not say, "[This is] as God wills. There is no strength save in God." If you see that I am less than you in wealth and children, it may be that my Lord will give me something better than your garden, and unleash against

it a reckoning from the sky, so that it becomes a flattened plain. Or its water may sink deep so that you cannot seek after it. (Q 18:39–41)

Indeed, the garden in the parable was destroyed, and the man had "no party to help him apart from God; nor could he help himself" (Q 18:43). This episode occurs alongside several others involving parents and children in *Sūrat al-Kahf*, a section of the Qur'an that is traditionally recited every Friday as a weekly reminder of the temporal nature of blessings and the swift recompense of God.[3]

In this same context, the Qur'an stresses that children can be a blessing, but they are not a measure of a person's rank with God, even when they confer a worldly station to parents. On multiple accounts, the Qur'an stresses the point that parents should not be deluded by pride in material matters: "Wealth and children are the adornments of the life of this world, but that which endures—righteous deeds—are better in reward with thy Lord, and better [as a source of] hope" (Q 18:46). In other places, the Qur'an cautions against looking with envy at the children (or assets) of others since God's will is not apparent to the human beholder: "And let not their wealth or their children impress you. God desires but to punish them thereby in the life of this world, and that their souls should depart while they are disbelievers" (Q 9:55; see also Q 9:85 and 9:69).

Life is a test In Qur'anic theology, and the world is the testing grounds. Children are an aspect of that test: "And know that your property and your children are only a trial, and that God—with Him is a great reward" (Q 8:28; see also 2:155, 6:53, 6:165, 7:168). Children could prompt vanity on the part of the parent, which distracts from the central life purpose of worship: "O you who believe! Let neither your property nor your children divert you from the remembrance of God. Whosoever does so, it is they who are the losers" (Q 63:9). The Qur'an warns that dealings with immediate family can be a source of distraction, or worse, individuals in the nuclear family could be a source of direct malice: "Among your spouses and your children there is indeed an enemy to you; so be wary of them" (Q 64:14).

The desire to procreate without the ability to do so is another trial of faith in the Qur'an (e.g., Q 42:49–50). The "secret cry" (Q 19:2) of the prophet Zachariah (Zakariyyā) captures the sentiment of aspiring parents who may be approaching or past the typical childbearing age or who may otherwise have been unable to procreate:

> He [Zachariah] said, "My Lord! Verily my bones have grown feeble, and my head glistens with white hair. And in calling upon You, my Lord, I have never been wretched. Truly I fear my relatives after me, and my wife is barren. So grant me from Your Presence an heir who will inherit from me and inherit from the House of Jacob. And make him, my Lord, well-pleasing." (Q 19:4–6)

A dialogue between Zachariah and God ensues, the result of which is Zachariah and his wife receiving news of a righteous son, the prophet John (Yaḥyā, e.g., Q 3:39, 6:85, 19:7–15, and 21:90). Other surprise pregnancies of righteous children include the prophet Isaac (see Q 11:71–73, 15:53–56, and 51:28–30), Maryam, the "Chosen One"

(Q 3:42), and the prophet Jesus (ʿĪsā, e.g., Q 3:45 and 19:16–24).[4] These righteous children and parents stand in contrast to parents mentioned in the Qurʾan who pray for a healthy child and then are themselves ungrateful and unrighteous: "Then, when He [God] gave them a healthy child, they ascribed partners to Him regarding that which He had given them. Exalted is God about the partners they ascribe" (Q 7:190).

No Qurʾanic notion exists that a righteous person will beget a righteous person. Parents have moral and religious responsibilities to provide children with correct theological and moral guidance, but the outcome of that guidance follows the general Qurʾanic precept: "None will bear the burden of another" (e.g., Q 53:38). In Qurʾanic narratives, a parent being a pious exemplar does not guarantee that the individual's children or progeny will also be righteous. Several verses redefine the notion of kinship in cases where the immediate family is divided between righteous and unrighteous individuals. For instance, when the prophet Noah (Nūḥ) beckons his son to join him on the ark to avoid the floodwaters, his son "remained aloof" and refused to heed his father's calls: "And the waves came between them, and he [the son] was among the drowned" (Q 11:42–43). Noah proceeds to plead with God on behalf of his son, but without success:

> And Noah called out to his Lord and said, "O my Lord! Truly my son is from my family. Thy Promise is indeed true, and You are the most just of judges. He [God] said, "O Noah! Truly he is not from thy family; surely such conduct was not righteous. So, question Me not concerning that of which you have no knowledge; truly I exhort you, lest you be among the ignorant." (Q 11:45–46, see also Q 17:3)

A similar scenario of a prophet attempting to bargain with God over the fate of his progeny is the case of the prophet Abraham (Ibrāhīm), a figure who has importance in the ritual prayer, in pilgrimage rites, and in the sacred history of the establishment of Mecca. The Qurʾan narrates: "And [remember] when his Lord tried Abraham with [certain] words, and he fulfilled them. He [God] said, 'I am making you an imam for humankind.' He [Abraham] said, 'And of my progeny?' He [God] said, 'My covenant does not include the wrongdoers'" (Q 2:124). In another instance, Abraham is depicted praying to God for his children and descendants, saying: "And whoever follows me, he is of me. And whosoever disobeys me, surely You [God] are Forgiving, Merciful" (Q 14:30).

Qurʾanic narratives of Abraham's childhood revolve around his struggles and escapades as a monotheist in a society dominated by polytheistic worship and the veneration of idols, including a dramatic conflict with his father that eventually gets Abraham exiled. Abraham says to his father Āzar, "Do you take idols for gods? Truly I see you and your people in manifest error" (Q 6:74). The situation escalates, and Abraham destroys his father's idols in a bold display (Q 21:51–70). Abraham, a righteous child, deals with an incompetent and verbally abusive father.[5] This glaring example of ineffective parenting aside, many other Qurʾanic narratives focus on effective parents, including many fathers and mothers who are also prophets or otherwise exceptionally pious. Several moments in the Qur'an, including the words of Abraham to his own father, depict family members extending a spirit of forgiveness after experiencing wrongdoing. Abraham says to his father: "I will assuredly ask forgiveness for you, though I have no power to avail you aught from God" (Q 60:4). In contrast to his father, Abraham is depicted in numerous instances as a model parent. He is a figure grounded in monotheism whose tongue is consistently praising God and offering prayer (e.g., Q 14:35–41). Abraham is even mentioned in his roles as a grandparent (see Q 21:72–73 and 38:45–47)—even the life of his great-grandson, the prophet Joseph (Yūsuf), is mentioned at length in the Qur'an.

In Abraham's case, however, parenting is not an uncomplicated affair. The Qur'an details the imminent sacrifice of Abraham's beloved son. Abraham sees the command to sacrifice his son in a dream and approaches his son, asking, "O my son! I see while dreaming that I am to sacrifice you. Consider, what do you see?" The son replies, "O my father! Do as you are commanded. You will find me, God willing, among those who are patient" (Q 37:102). The consultation is notable, as is the son's resolution.[6]

On other occasions, parents wrestle with parenting under challenging circumstances. Abraham's grandson, the prophet Jacob (Yā'qūb), is faced with a series of parenting dilemmas that require "beautiful patience" (Q 12:18 and 12:83, see also Q 2:132–33 and 12:67). In another instance, the intentions of Lot (Lūṭ) concerning his daughters' hypothetical marriages as he navigates a drunken mob leave his intentions up for debate (see Q 11:78–79 and 15:71). The mother of the prophet Moses (Mūsā) must also make parenting decisions in trying circumstances (Q 28:4–7). In a climactic mother-daughter moment, she gives the following instructions to her reliable daughter: "And she said to his sister, 'Follow him.' So, she [the daughter] watched him from afar; yet they were unaware" (Q 28:11).

Abraham and his sons, Jacob and his sons, the mother of Moses and her daughter are among a host of parent-child relationships in the Qur'an. The prophet David (Dāwūd) confers with his son Solomon (Sulaymān), who also grows to be a prophet (see Q. 21:78–79, 27:15–16, and 27:19). A pious figure named Luqmān also gives sound guidance to his son (Q 31:13–20). The Qur'an depicts an endearing father-daughter moment when two sisters in Midian meet Moses at a watering hole, and one encourages her father to employ Moses: "O my father! Hire him. Surely the best you can hire is the strong, the trustworthy" (Q 28:26). Her father reads between the lines and says to Moses: "I desire to marry you to one of these two daughters of mine, on condition that you hire yourself to me for eight years" (Q 28:27). The Qur'an contains numerous parent-child dialogues, including several instances depicting sound and nurturing relationships.

In addition to the other prophets and holy figures in Qur'anic stories, the Prophet Muhammad also serves as a model father for Muslims. The Prophet Muhammad's love for and patience with children, including his own, is a repeated theme in the Hadith and biographical literature. The Prophet Muhammad had descendants, but unlike Abraham, Isaac, Jacob, David, and Zachariah in the Qur'an, he does not have an heir in prophecy. According to the Qur'an: "Muhammad is not the father of any man among you; although he is Messenger of God and the Seal of the prophets. And God is Knower of all things" (Q 33:40).

Motherhood and Fatherhood in the Qur'an

The Qur'an mentions concepts related to fatherhood and motherhood with striking frequency—and even near numeric equality. The root of the word *father* (*a-b-w*) and related concepts occur a total of 117 times (in three different words), and the root for "mother" (*'-m-m*) and related concepts occur a total of 119 times (in ten different words).[7] The Qur'an outlines some basic principles regarding the division of labor between parents, which become axiomatic in later discussions of child custody law:

> And let mothers nurse their children two full years for such as desire to complete the suckling. It falls on the father to provide for them and clothe them honorably. No soul is tasked beyond its capacity. Let no mother be harmed on account of her child, nor father on account of his child. And the like will fall upon the heir. If the couple desire to wean, by their mutual consent and consultation, there is no blame upon them. And if you wish to have your children wet-nursed, there is no blame upon you if you pay honorably that which you give. Revere God and know that God sees whatsoever you do. (Q 2:233)

In another verse, the Qur'an outlines what may be called the principle of equal opportunity regarding spiritual compensation: "I [God] will not let the work of any worker among you, male or female, be in vain; each of you is like the other" (Q 3:195). Another verse emphasized this point: "And whosoever performs righteous deeds, whether male or female, and is a believer, such will enter the garden [paradise], and they will not be wronged so much as the speck on a date stone" (Q 4:124; see also Q 16:97, 40:40, and 49:13). The Qur'an also contains multiple other verses honoring women who do the labor of birthing and suckling:

> And We [God] have enjoined man to be virtuous to his parents. His mother carried him in travail and bore him in travail, and his gestation and weaning are thirty months, such that when he reaches maturity and reaches forty years, he says, "My Lord inspire me to give thanks for Your blessing with which You have blessed me and have blessed my parents, and that I may work righteousness such that it pleases You; and make righteous for me my progeny. Truly I turn in repentance to You, and truly I am among those who submit."[8]

In addition, many positive connotations of mothers appear in Qur'anic metaphors. In describing itself, for instance, the Qur'an says: "Truly We have made it an Arabic Qur'an, that perhaps you may understand, and truly it is with Us [God] in the mother of the book, sublime indeed, wise" (Q 43:3–4, see also Q 3:7, 13:39). The blessed city of Mecca is the "Mother of Cities" (Q 42:7), and the Qur'anic word connoting community (*ummah*) also comes from the same root as the word mother. Much Qur'anic language is celebratory of the capacity of wombs, and the wives of the Prophet Muḥammad are given an exalted status as "Mothers of the Believers" (*ummahāt al-muʾminīn*, Q 33:6). The Qur'an depicts an incompetent father but contains no narratives featuring incompetent mothers.

Children, Childhood, and Siblings in the Qur'an

The Qur'an includes guidance for how to be a virtuous child, and Qur'anic narratives regularly feature young people with moral agency, including both righteous and unrighteous children. Righteous children in Qur'anic narratives display courage and obedience, collaborate with their parents on important matters, and are sources of wisdom. Many figures show kindness to parents (or kindness to the mother singularly in the case of Jesus), and children who pray for parents explicitly include Joseph, Solomon, Jesus, and Noah. The ethics of being a righteous child, in general, include being virtuous to parents and also extended kin (e.g., Q 17:23–24), remembering parents and relatives in bequests (e.g., Q 2:180), and being "steadfast maintainers of justice," even if it be against parents and kinsfolk (e.g., Q 4:135). The fostering of children is also a recurring theme in Qur'anic narratives.[9]

The idea of children features in Qur'anic metaphors, for instance, in phrases such as "Children of Adam" and "Children of Israel," which frequently occur in the Qur'an. Charity given without sincerity is compared to "weakly progeny" (e.g., Q 2:266), and the awareness of the Qur'an as revelation is made analogous to the recognition of a parent their child: "Those to whom We [God] gave the book [Scripture] recognize it as they recognize their own children. Those who have lost their souls, they do not believe" (Q 6:20).

Sibling relationships, both cooperative and dysfunctional, are also depicted in the Qur'an. The Qur'an does not include any narratives of unrighteous daughters or sisters, but it does include several cases of unrighteous brothers. In the first sibling relationship in Qur'anic sacred history, one of Adam's sons kills the other (Q 5:27–31). The theme of jealousy and fratricide again emerges when the brothers of Joseph (Yūsuf) dispose of him in order to get the attention of their father (Q 12:8). In this case, fratricide is narrowly averted by another brother who intervenes in favor of a slightly less extreme way of disposing of Joseph (Q 12:9–10). This story resolves with family harmony restored. The Qur'an depicts Joseph's endearment towards one brother when he reveals his secret identity: "He drew his brother close to himself and said, 'Truly I am your brother; so be not distressed on account of that which they used to do'" (Q 12:69). Joseph's saga ends with forgiveness and an affectionate reunion with his parents and brothers (Q 12:90–100).

Moses also has a mostly cooperative relationship with his brother Aaron (Hārūn) apart from a dramatic instance where Moses momentarily loses his temper:

> He cast down the tablets and seized his brother by the head, dragging him toward himself. He [Aaron] said, "Son of my mother! Truly the people deemed me weak, and they were about to kill me. So let not the enemies rejoice in my misfortune and place me not with the wrongdoing people." He said, "My Lord, forgive me and my brother and bring us into Your Mercy, for You are the most Merciful of the merciful." (Q 7:151)

Here and in another depiction of the same encounter, Aaron attempts to calm Moses by appealing to their womb connection: "O son of my mother! Seize not my beard or my head" (Q 20:94). In contrast to brotherly conflict, sisterly subterfuge is not a theme of any Qur'anic narrative. For instance, Moses' sister is heroically witty in her ability to get baby Moses returned to their mother after his episode in the river (Q 28:11–13).

Child Custody (Ḥaḍāna) in Premodern Jurisprudence

The subject of children's rights has a longstanding tradition in Muslim jurisprudence dating back to the lifetime of the Prophet Muhammad. For centuries onward, generations of scholars attempted to discern what constitutes the child's welfare and how it can be promoted and secured. They assumed that, barring exceptional circumstances and irregularities, within a marriage and the realm of the family, children's welfare and rights were secured by their parents. However, in the event of divorce or death of a parent, the care of the child could be assigned to alternative caretakers within a very large pool of potential guardians and custodians drawn from the child's relatives. In this section, we review select aspects of custody law and offer a glimpse into Muslim jurists' understanding of the child's welfare and rights. We rely primarily on the works of Muslim jurists of the Mālikī school of thought, one of the four extant schools in Sunni Islam whose eponym was the Medinan scholar Mālik b. Anas (d. 179/795).

Child Custody and the Child Ward

According to premodern Muslim jurisprudence, the lawful birth of a child produced several obligations upon her parents, in the first instance, and upon the child's extended relatives in cases where parents were absent or incapable of fulfilling the child's needs.[10] Three essential rights of the child included breastfeeding (riḍāʿa), custody or physical care (ḥaḍāna), and legal guardianship (wilāya). Jurists deemed that a child's natural first custodian was her mother, and a child's natural and first guardian was her father, although they did not appear overly concerned to fix this distribution of roles prior to the dissolution of a marriage. Most discussions of custody in the books of law deem the dissolution of marriage to be the starting point of *ḥaḍāna*. Few jurists explicitly stated that the period of custody began with the child's birth.[11]

Premodern jurists primarily identified a child entitled to *ḥaḍāna* by her physical vulnerability and dependency on her mother (or, in her absence or incapacity on other females). Hence, early jurists marked the end of *ḥaḍāna* at the moment the child was presumed capable of taking care of his own "feeding, drinking, dressing, standing, sitting, and sleeping," without assistance.[12] Mālikīs took this cue to end a boy's custody at puberty, but extended a girl's custody until marriage.[13] Despite differences regarding the end of the *ḥaḍāna* period, all jurists understood the child—boy or girl—as a vulnerable individual in need of physical assistance and care.[14]

Jurists from all Sunnī schools unanimously held that a mother was the most qualified to assume a child's custody, and they granted custody to her above anyone else. If the mother of the child had died or was found incapable of assuming custody (or in the event of her refusal), *ḥaḍāna* devolved primarily to several female cognates of the child and, secondarily, to the father and patrilineal females.[15] Women's prerogative to the right of *ḥaḍāna* was more substantial among Ḥanafī and Mālikī jurists than it was among Ḥanbalīs and Shāfiʿīs. In the Ḥanafī and Mālikī custodian order of precedence, the father and his male agnates ranked low after a long list of matrilineal and, secondarily, patrilineal female ascendants. In Shāfiʿī and Ḥanbalī jurisprudence, a father could acquire custody immediately after the mother and her female ascendants (i.e., before the paternal grandmother and his female ascendants).[16]

Though unanimous in privileging the mother as a custodian, Sunni schools of law differed on how they privileged the mother-child bond over other factors in irregular situations, such as when the mother was not a Muslim or was enslaved. Ḥanbalīs and Shāfiʿīs denied custody of a Muslim child to a non-Muslim mother.[17] Mālikīs, on the other hand, extended custody rights to non-Muslim mothers and made efforts to protect a non-Muslim mother's custody even if her conduct raised concerns.[18] ʿAbd al-Raḥmān b. al-Qāsim (d. 191/806) reports that Christian, Jewish, and Zoroastrian women are "like the Muslim woman" regarding their children. His interlocutor and fellow jurist Saḥnūn retorts: "She pours them alcohol!" "And she feeds them pork! Why did [Mālik] give them the rank of Muslim women?" Ibn al-Qāsim responds simply that the child was with his mother before her husband left her, and she could have fed them alcohol and pork then, had she so wished.[19] Nonetheless, if such concerns did exist, the mother should be "prevented from [feeding them such and such] *without taking the child from her*." Rather, it should be entrusted to Muslims, generally, that she not behave in such ways.[20] Similarly, and indicative of their insistence on granting custody rights to the child's mother, Mālikīs were unique in granting custody rights to mothers in bondage, with conditions. All other schools rendered freedom a precondition for acquiring this right.[21]

Concern over Unrelated Stepfathers

Despite the strong emphasis on a mother's right to *ḥaḍāna*, a mother's right to custody was potentially lost because of two main reasons: one, due to remarriage to a "foreign" male (i.e., a male who is not a close blood relative of the child), and second, due to the father's relocation to another locality. The first rule regarding a mother's loss of custody due to remarriage was shared across all Sunni schools. In the Ḥanbalī, Shāfiʿī and Ḥanafī schools, a mother's remarriage caused the immediate forfeiture of custody. In the Mālikī school, custody was only lost if the next custodian in line did not claim it within a year of a mother's remarriage to an unrelated male.[22] This principle of custody deferring a mother appears to be grounded in a well-known hadith cited in works of jurisprudence whereby a woman is said to have approached the Prophet Muhammad with the following custody dilemma:

> [She said] "Messenger of God, my womb is a vessel to this son of mine, my breasts, a water-skin for him, and my lap a guard for him, yet his father has divorced me, and wants to take him away from me." The Apostle of Allah, peace be upon him, said: "You have more right to him as long as you do not marry."[23]

As is often the case with hadith, this narration states the rule regarding a mother's remarriage but does not provide an explanation for it, nor does it mention any qualifications or exceptions to the rule. Determining these was the task of the jurist. In *Kitāb al-Kāfī*, Mālikī jurist Ibn ʿAbd al-Barr (d. 368/978) suggests that a married woman is "occupied with a husband."[24] This implies that a new husband's demands and needs upon a wife would compete with the child's need for attention, with adverse consequences to the latter.[25] A second reason was an assumed hostility between a stepfather and his step-children.[26] Mālikī jurists reasoned that such hostility would typically not originate from a relative to the child, and they allowed women who remarried an agnatic relative of the child to retain custody. At this point in the child's life, jurists imagined that sharing a home—and sharing their mother—with a stepfather was potentially equally harmful to both boys and girls. Concern that girls are more vulnerable to physical harm increased as girls near puberty. A father's remarriage to an unrelated woman would not cause him to lose custody, suggesting that jurists did not view an unrelated stepmother as a potential threat to the child's well-being.

A second potential cause for a mother's loss of custody was a father's travel with the intent of relocating. Jurists reasoned that a child—a boy or girl—had a right to physical care, legal guardianship, and lineage. Parents could easily accommodate these rights if they lived within reasonable proximity to the child; fathers provided legal guardianship and secured a child's lineage, and mothers provided physical care. If physical distance caused a conflict between a father's guardianship and a mother's custody, Mālikī jurists required that a father take the child with him to his new place of residence to safeguard her lineage.²⁷ Nonetheless, if a husband wished to relocate, a custodian had to be given the option to follow the child. If she agreed, custody continued to be hers in the new location.²⁸

In Mālikī law, the transfer of custody from a mother to a father caused by his relocation was not contingent on his wishes. The language used in the normative legal textbooks is one of obligation. This position is further corroborated by several Mālikī fatwas. For instance, in a fatwa that is recorded by Aḥmad b. Yaḥyā's al-Wansharīsī (d. 834/1430–1), the Andalusian mufti Abū ʿAbd Allah Muḥammad al-Ḥaffār (d. 811/1408) gives his legal opinion on the following situation: A woman died leaving behind a husband, her mother, and her two children. The maternal grandmother now exercised custody over the orphaned children per Mālikī law. The father's parallel guardianship duties initially faced no issues, but then he intended to relocate to get remarried. How, then, should he proceed? Should he leave the children with the maternal grandmother? Would he be exempted from his guardianship duty if the maternal grandmother refused to relocate with him? Al-Ḥaffār responded that if he wished to relocate, he had to take both the children *and* their maternal grandmother with him, if she agreed. If she refuses to join them, he would certainly not be exempt from his responsibility. Instead, she would lose custody of the child.²⁹

In this fatwa, the grandmother's wishes to relocate and the father's wishes to take his child are irrelevant if the jurists' understanding of the child's best interest is preservation lineage and legal guardianship. The questions in this fatwa indicate that this father and groom-to-be viewed the idea of taking his children from his first marriage as a "duty" he could be exempted from if the custodian conveniently refused to accompany them on the impending trip. Nevertheless, the mufti shows disinterest in this man's new marriage plans and reminds him of his duty towards his children from his first marriage. He then imposes upon the father the duty of including his ex-mother-in-law on his trip to his new bride, should the former agree to join them and thereby keep custody of her grandchildren. Thus, while the law did not curtail a man's agency to travel at his will, it also did not bend to exempt him from obligations that might be burdensome. The jurists prioritized the child's interests and rights as they understood them, even if this meant inconveniencing the child's female custodians and male guardians alike. Mālikī jurists also permitted a child's parents to reach consensual private agreements that departed from the established norms of custody in so far as these did not harm the child.

A Child's Right to Safety and Security

Premodern jurists repeatedly stressed that aptitude, suitability, safety, and security were preconditions for acquiring custody of the children. Relatives of the child who did not possess these qualities did not qualify as custodians, and in the jurists' eyes, the propensity to being an incompetent custodian cut across gender lines. Mālikī jurist ʿAbd al-Raḥmān Ibn al-Qāsim (d. 191/806) stated in explicit terms:

Nobody can take the child except that he/she can provide the child with *kifāya* (a state of suitability, competence, but also sufficiency), for perhaps a grandmother may be untrustworthy, or perhaps a father can be an incompetent shameless drunkard who exits his house and leaves his child behind.[30]

He adds on the authority of Mālik: "The child should not be harmed, and one should look for what is the best interest of the child and that which is safest to him."[31] Ibn 'Abd al-Barr echoes this sentiment and explains that the Mālikī list of custodians is contingent on these individuals' ability to take proper care of the child. Regarding the list he states:

> And this if and only each one of these [potential custodians] can be trusted with the child, and if the child is under a suitable, safe, and guarded state with [the custodian at hand]. If this is not the case for a given custodian, then she/he does not have a right over custody, but rather one should consider what is in the child's welfare.[32]

The Gendering of Ḥaḍāna Rules at Puberty

Mālikī legal works begin to register gender differences as the child approaches puberty when additional concerns about safety and security become a factor. When Saḥnūn asks Ibn al-Qāsim how long a girl stays under the custody of her mother, Ibn al-Qāsim responds:

> [It is] until she reaches marriageable age. If she reaches marriageable age and there is concern over her well-being, one must consider if the mother is in a safe place, guarded and fortified. If so, she has precedence over her absolutely until the girl marries.... But if the girl is not in a safe, guarded place ... the girl then joins the father or her guardians—if he is in a place that is conducive to her protection (*kafala*) and safety (*ḥirz*).[33]

A young man, in contrast, is said to be able to go "where he pleases"[34] upon reaching puberty, with no explicit mention of fear regarding his physical safety.

In the Ḥanafī school, fears regarding a girl's physical safety appear well before puberty. Although Ḥanafī doctrine had marked the end of a girl's custody under her mother upon reaching physical maturity, which is usually marked by menstruation, Muhammad al-Shaybānī (d. 187/803 or 189/805) is reported to have lowered the age from a girl's maturity to her development of sexual awareness (*ḥadd al-shahwa*). At this moment, a girl was to join her father and his male agnates, who were presumed to be more capable protectors of her safety and chastity.[35] This connection between the end of a girls' *ḥaḍāna* and her carnal awareness appears to register a fear about the girl's potential behavior that is not present in the early Mālikī doctrine, which instead suggests fears *for* the girls' safety *from* dangers in her physical environment.

The rules regarding the end of the ḥaḍāna period and the subsequent transition to male guardianship appears to mark the end of the undifferentiated boy or girl child (*walad*) and the beginning of the gendered young woman or man (*jāriyya* and *ghulām*). Out of all the four Sunni schools, only the Shāfiʿī school marks the end of the period of ḥaḍāna in the same way for boys and girls by allowing both to make their own choice. Other than the Shāfiʿīs, the Ḥanbalīs, Ḥanafīs, and Mālikīs developed different rules for the male and female youth. Ḥanbalīs extended the choice of guardian to the boy but not to the girl, deeming her best interests to lie with her male agnates. Ḥanafīs did not give the right to choose to a child of either sex, arguing that such a small child did not know what was best for him or her.[36] In contrast to Ḥanafīs and Ḥanbalīs, who believed that a post-pubescent girl's best interest lay with her father or male guardians, Mālikīs held that she was best placed with her mother until she was married. Regardless of the differences in these rules among—and sometimes within— schools, gendered considerations play a significant role as the child nears puberty.[37]

The relationship between legal rationales and rules is a complex phenomenon. For instance, in a recent study of the law of ḥaḍāna in the premodern period, Ahmed Fekry Ibrahim argued that a "proto-best-interests" discourse is discernable in the legal sources dealing with this topic. However, he cautioned that such notions would not have been the single factor in determining the custody law. Instead, "the final rules often resulted from a matrix of social practices, hermeneutic commitments, and methodological approaches that went beyond this bifurcation."[38] The same caution should apply when trying to determine the impact of gendered notions on the rules of ḥaḍāna.

Conclusion

From theological claims to didactic and ethical imperatives, parent-child relationships play a central role in defining human virtue in the Qur'an. We have mapped how the Qur'an depicts parent-child relations and have surveyed verses containing ethical imperatives related to parenting. We have also considered how premodern jurists defined custody, how they conceived of a child's interests and rights, and how they prioritized these interests and rights in the event of a parental conflict. We have highlighted occasions when the gender of the parent or the gender of the child impacted the law of custody—and occasions when it did not, noting that while there was relative uniformity in child's interests and rights at an early age, these rights became increasingly gendered as a child neared puberty. We also noted variations in the law of custody across schools of legal thought. In short, when formulating child custody law (ḥaḍāna), Muslim legal scholars aimed to balance the rights and duties of mothers, fathers, and children.

Notes

1. Verses that refute God having children include Q 2:116, 5:17, 5:116, 6:100, 9:30, 10:68, 16:57, 17:40, 18:4, and other verses. With minor stylistic adaptations, Qur'anic translations in this chapter are those of Seyyed Hossein Nasr et al., *The Study Quran: A New Translation and Commentary* (San Francisco: HarperOne, 2015).
2. For a detailed discussion of the themes surveyed here with a focus on mothers and girls, see Celene Ibrahim, *Women and Gender in the Qur'an* (New York: Oxford University Press); see especially chapter 2, "Procreation, Parenting, and Female Kin," 63–93. For condemnations of infanticide, see Q 6:137, 6:140, 6:151, 17:31, and 60:12. See also Chapters 18 and 24 in this volume.
3. For other verses involving a child in *Sūrat al-Kahf*, see Q 18:74–82.
4. See also Chapter 4 and 18 in this volume, on Islamic perspectives on reproductive technologies.
5. For other verses on Abraham's relationship with his father, see Q 9:114, 11:69–104, 19:42–9, 21:51–71, 37:85–99, 43:26–28, and 60:4.
6. The Qur'an does not mention the name of this son, thus sparking early Muslim debates as to the son's identity. The Qur'an mentions Abraham having been granted a son in Q 37:112, which could be interpreted as a divine reward for his passing the test of the sacrifice.
7. See entries in Elsaid M. Badawi and Muhammad Abdel Haleem, *Arabic-English Dictionary of Qur'anic Usage* (Leiden: E. J. Brill, 2008), 7 and 47 respectively.
8. Q 46:15. See also 31:14–15. In the Qur'an and subsequent Islamic law, suckling confers kinship status. See Avner Giladi, *Infants, Parents and Wet Nurses: Medieval Islamic Views on Breastfeeding and Their Social Implications* (Leiden: E. J. Brill, 1999).
9. See related chapters on adoption and fostering in this volume.
10. A child regarded as illegitimate could not claim filiation to his father in Sunni law and therefore had no legal claims upon his father. Filiation was traced to the mother only, and a mother and her family were responsible for fulfilling the child's rights and needs. Shiite jurists tended to hold that an illegitimate child had no claim to filiation to either father or mother; see N. J. Coulson, *Succession in the Muslim Family* (Cambridge, UK: Cambridge University Press, 1971), 22–23.
11. The Ḥanafī jurist al-Zaylaʿī (d. 1342), for instance, explicitly stated that a mother has the right to custody before and after the dissolution of a marriage; see Yvon Linant de Bellefonds, *Traité de Droit Musulman Comparé* (Paris: Mouton & Co, 1973), 157.
12. Muḥammad b. Saḥnūn b. Saʿīd, *al-Mudawwana al-kubrā* (Cairo AH 1324–5; reprint in six volumes: Beirut: Dar Sadir, 2005), 361. The *Mudawwana al-kubrā* of Muḥammad b. Saḥnūn b. Saʿīd (d. 240/854) consists of questions on a range of legal issues posed by Saḥnūn to ʿAbd al-Raḥmān b. al-Qāsim (d.191/806) regarding Mālik b. Anas (the eponym of the Mālikī school of law).
13. Ibid., 356.
14. Ḥanafīs ended *ḥaḍāna* for boys at seven years of age and at nine years of age for girls initially, and later to seven as well. Ḥanbalīs and Shāfiʿīs ended a mother's custody at similar ages (about seven years of age), yet they held that a young woman (for Shāfiʿī) and that a young man (for Ḥanbalī and Shāfiʿī) had a right to choose the parent they subsequently wished to join. See Ahmed Fekry Ibrahim, "The Best Interests of the Child in Pre-modern Islamic Juristic Discourse and Practice," *American Journal of Comparative Law* 63 (2017): 859–891.

15. For an analysis of the network of women who assume custody in the event of a mother's death or incapacity, see Janan Delgado, *The Ties that Bind: Child Custody in Andalusi Mālikism, Third/Ninth–Sixth/Twelfth Century* (PhD dissertation, Harvard University, 2022).
16. Ibrahim, "The Best Interests," 871; it was only among Shīʿī Jaʿfarīs, the dominant school of Shīʿī thought, that the father followed immediately after the mother in ḥaḍāna order of precedence; ibid., 871–872.
17. Ibid., 875.
18. For detailed discussions of Mālikī Muslim jurists' protection of non-Muslim women's right to custody, see Delgado, "The Ties that Bind."
19. Saḥnūn, *Mudawwana*, 359.
20. Ibid. About the rule of "dispatching overseers," Sherman Jackson asks: "A premodern counterpart to Child Protective Services?" see footnote 27, p. 34, in "Kramer versus Kramer in a Tenth/Sixteenth Century Egyptian Court: Post-Formative Jurisprudence between Exigency and Law," *Islamic Law and Society* 8, no. 1 (2001): 27–51.
21. Linant de Bellefonds, *Traité*, 162–163.
22. In the Ḥanbalī, Shāfiʿī and Ḥanafī schools, a mother's remarriage caused the immediate forfeiture of custody. See ibid., 168.
23. See *Sunan Abū Dāwūd*, book 12, no. 2269.
24. Yūsuf Ibn ʿAbd al-Barr, *Kitāb al-kāfī fī fiqh ahl al-Madina al-Mālikī* (Riyadh: Maktaba al-Riyadh al-Haditha, 1879), 626.
25. The reasoning is merely implied in this early text; it is mentioned explicitly several centuries later by the prominent Mālikī jurist Aḥmad al-Dardīr (d. 1201/1786), see Jackson, "Kramer," 36.
26. Ibid., 36; see also Ibrahim, "The Best Interest," 872.
27. Saḥnūn, *Mudawwana*, 358; Ibn ʿAbd al-Barr, *Kitāb al-Kāfī*, 625; and Sulaymān b. Khalaf al-Bājī, *Al-Muntaqā Sharḥ al-Muwaṭṭaʾ*, 2nd ed. (Cairo: Dār al-Kitāb al-Islāmī, n.d.), 18.
28. Ibn ʿAbd al-Barr, *Kitāb al-Kāfī*, 625.
29. al-Wansharīsī, *al-Miʿyār*, edited by M. Hajji, vol. 4 (Beirut: Dār al-Garb al-Islāmī, 1981), 48. The work *al-Miʿyār al-muʿrib wa-l-jāmiʿ al-mughrib ʿan fatāwā Ahl Ifrīqiyah wa-l-Andalus wa-l-Maghrib*, commonly known as *al-Miʿyār*, was collected by Aḥmad b. Yaḥyā al-Wansharīsī (b. 834/1430–1431) and contains approximately 6,000 legal opinions issued by Mālikī jurists from across the Iberian Peninsula and Africa.
30. Saḥnūn, *Mudawwana*, 357.
31. Ibid.
32. Ibn ʿAbd al-Barr, *Kitāb al-Kāfī*, 625.
33. Saḥnūn, *Mudawwana*, 356.
34. Ibid.
35. Ibrahim, "The Best Interest," 868–869.
36. Ibid., 868.
37. Saḥnūn's *Mudawwana* registers concerns over a father's access to his male child during his mother's custody for the purpose of teaching him a "craft." Jurists typically do not express similar concerns about girls, who would presumably learn needed skills from their mothers and other females at home. Still, this concern for transmitting a skill set does not affect the basic ḥaḍāna rulings. See Saḥnūn, *Mudawanna*, 356.
38. Ibrahim, "The Best Interest," 861.

Bibliography

'Abd al-Barr, Abū 'Umar Yūsuf b. 'Abdallāh b. Muhammad. *Kitāb al-kāfī fī fiqh ahl al-Madina al-Mālikī. (The Sufficient Book of Mālikī Jurisprudence of the People of Medina)*. Riyadh: Maktaba al-Riyadh al-Haditha, 1879.

Badawi, Elsaid M. and Muhammad Abdel Haleem. *Arabic-English Dictionary of Qur'anic Usage*. Leiden: E. J. Brill, 2008.

al-Bājī, Sulaymān b. Khalaf. *Al-Muntaqā Sharḥ al-Muwatta'*, 2nd edition. Cairo: Dār al-Kitāb al-Islāmī, n.d.

Coulson, N. J. *Succession in the Muslim Family*. Cambridge, UK: Cambridge University Press, 1971.

Giladi, Avner. *Infants, Parents and Wet Nurses: Medieval Islamic Views on Breastfeeding and Their Social Implications*. Islamic History and Civilization. Leiden: E. J. Brill, 1999.

Hallaq, Wael B. *An Introduction to Islamic Law*. New York: Cambridge University Press, 2009.

Ibrahim, Ahmed Fekry. "The Best Interest of the Child in Pre-modern Islamic Juristic Discourse and Practice." *American Journal of Comparative Law* 63, no. 4 (2015): 859–891.

Ibn Sa'īd, Muḥammad b. Saḥnūn. *al-Mudawwana al-kubrā*. Beirut: Dar Sadir, 2005.

Ibrahim, Celene. *Women and Gender in the Qur'an*. New York: Oxford University Press, 2020.

Jackson, Sherman. "Kramer versus Kramer in a Tenth/Sixteenth Century Egyptian Court: Post-Formative Jurisprudence between Exigency and Law." *Islamic Law and Society* 8, no. 1 (2001): 27–51.

Linant de Bellefonds, Yvon. *Traité de Droit Musulman Comparé*. Paris: Mouton & Co., 1973.

Nasr, Seyyed Hossein, Caner K. Dagli, Maria Massi Dakake, Joseph E. B. Lumbard, and Muhammad Rustom, eds. *The Study Quran: A New Translation and Commentary*. San Francisco: HarperOne, 2015.

O'Shaughnessy, Thomas J. "The Qur'ānic View of Youth and Old Age." In *The Qur'an: Style and Contents*, edited by Andrew Rippin, 177–195. Aldershot: Ashgate, 2001.

al-Sijistānī, Abū Dāwūd Sulaymān. *Sunan Abī Dāwūd: kitāb al- ṭalāq (The Sunnah of Abū Dāwūd: Book of Divorce)*, vol. 13, n.d.: https://sunnah.com/abudawud/13.

al-Wansharīsī, Aḥmad b. Yaḥyā. *al-Mi'yār al-mu'rib wa-l-jāmi' al-mughrib 'an fatāwā ahl Ifrīqīyah wa-l-Andalus wa-l-Maghrib (The Parsed Caliber and Extraordinary Collection of Fatwas of the People of Africa, Iberia, and Morocco)*, vol. 4. Edited by M. Hajji. Beirut: Dār al-Garb al-Islāmī, 1981.

CHAPTER 11

RELIGIOUS PERSPECTIVES ON GAY PARENTING

BRETT KRUTZSCH

THROUGHOUT the last decades of the twentieth century, Americans increasingly witnessed public debates about whether or not gays and lesbians can serve as suitable caretakers of children. When gay parenting was discussed within news media, Victoria Clarke (2001) found that opponents of same-sex parenting commonly justified their disapproval by citing religious beliefs. Clarke also discovered that whenever gay parenting was addressed in the media, journalists regularly solicited interviews from religious leaders to voice their opinions. One might question why religious authorities have been recurrently consulted whenever gay parenting has been a topic for public dialogue. But, as Janet Jakobsen and Ann Pellegrini (2004) have highlighted, when issues pertaining to (homo)sexuality have been debated in the American public sphere, religion has invariably been discussed as well. Gay parenting is no exception, and the current climate of religious voices publicly debating same-sex parenting has origins that became increasingly prominent in the late 1970s.

This chapter will explore public and internal religious perspectives on gay parenting from the late twentieth and early twenty-first centuries. In other words, the chapter will examine what religious traditions prescribe for their own members, as well as how religious groups have shaped public debates about gay parenting. Specifically, the chapter will present ideas, and the related scholarship, on gay parenting in evangelical and mainline Protestant Christianity, Roman Catholicism, and Judaism.

The chapter's focus begins in 1977 with Anita Bryant's "Save Our Children" campaign. While the "Save Our Children" movement was not limited to issues of gay parenting, the campaign created national dialogue about children in the presence of gays and lesbians. The movement's nationwide success made visible evangelical Protestant opposition to gay parenting, and it produced a long-lasting stereotype of gays as sexual predators of children that prospective gay and lesbian parents have tried to overcome. The triumph of Bryant's campaign also helped bring to the fore a Christian-motivated politics of "family values" that was grounded in conservative forms of Christianity that explicitly excluded gays and lesbians from what constitutes an American "family."

Not all religious groups are opposed to gay parenting, and the chapter will also address religious communities that support gay and lesbian childrearing. Among mainline Protestants, the greatest success for supporters of gay parenting has come to those who have argued that some people are "born gay." A few mainline Protestant denominations have declared that gays and lesbians should not be discriminated against because they were born gay and should, therefore, be allowed to raise children. Within Judaism, debates about gay parenting have largely focused on ensuring Jewish continuity and avoiding assimilation. By the early years of the twenty-first century, most Jewish movements supported same-sex parenting so gay Jews could contribute to building a Jewish future through childrearing.

The chapter concludes with a discussion of future directions in the study of religion and gay parenting. In particular, the final section focuses on adoption and how religious groups have lobbied to enact "religious freedom" laws to ensure that religiously affiliated adoption agencies will not be required to work with gay and lesbian couples. Following the 2015 *Obergefell v. Hodges* Supreme Court decision that made same-sex marriage a legal reality throughout the United States, gay parenting will likely become an increasingly contentious issue that will further expose the comingling of religion, law, and Christian moral assumptions about what constitutes a family in the United States.

Public Protestant Debates

Protestant concerns about gay parenting most visibly entered the American public sphere in 1977 when Anita Bryant, an evangelical Protestant and former popular singer and orange juice spokesperson, embarked on a campaign to repeal a Dade County, Florida, ordinance that provided antidiscrimination protections for lesbians and gay men. Although the ordinance was meant to prevent employment discrimination, Bryant focused on children and the ways she believed gays and lesbians preyed on youth. She famously declared that "homosexuals cannot reproduce—so they must recruit. And to freshen their ranks, they must recruit the youth of America" (Bryant 1977, 87). Since gays and lesbians, according to Bryant's logic, were unable to procreate, she insisted they recruited children who could be converted to homosexuality. Bryant's political movement to restrict the rights of gays and lesbians was, thus, framed as an effort to protect children. For Bryant and her many admirers, children in the care of, or even in the presence of, gays and lesbians were in a dangerous situation that necessitated state regulation. Bryant's rhetoric was successful, and the Dade County ordinance was overturned by a popular vote.

Bryant's political mobilizing in Florida attracted national attention, and she quickly became the emblem of the "Save Our Children" nation-wide campaign. To captive audiences across the country, Bryant proclaimed that she was fighting as a mother and as a (Protestant) Christian to overturn antidiscrimination laws that provided protections for gays and lesbians. Bryant showed up in cities and counties that had legal protections for gays and lesbians in order to convince Americans to nullify such ordinances. As Mark Jordan (2011) relates, throughout the country, "The slogan 'Save Our Children from Homosexuality!' appeared on bright posters and on the cover of a widely distributed pamphlet. Inside the pamphlet, there [was] a collage of newspaper clippings about child abuse and child pornography" (Jordan 2011, 143). Although the "Save Our Children" campaign and promotional materials did not specifically focus on gay parenting, the movement's rhetoric repeatedly emphasized that children were not safe with gays and lesbians, that gays and lesbians sexually abuse children, and that gays and lesbians will recruit children to homosexuality. The legacy of Bryant's campaign was long-lasting, and those gays and lesbians who have sought parenting rights in the United States have had to combat the habituated image of gays as preying on and sexually abusing children.

The success of the "Save Our Children" movement helped coalesce and bring into focus groups that were soon labeled the Religious Right. As Tina Fetner (2008), Gayle Rubin (2011), and Mark Jordan (2011) have illustrated, these predominantly white Protestant groups capitalized on the success of the "Save Our Children" campaign in order to bring conservative Christian ideals into the political spotlight. Antigay initiatives, along with opposing abortion and the Equal Rights Amendment, comprised the core of the Religious Right's agenda (Fetner 2008). Taking a cue from Bryant's success, these Protestant groups positioned their antigay platform within a framework of protecting children and the American "family." The Religious Right repeatedly reinscribed family to mean the heterosexual union of one wife to one husband and their potential to have children. Gay and lesbian adults, even if coupled or rearing children, were not part of this highly habituated configuration of "family" that, according to the Religious Right, needed protection. The Religious Right's influential lobby made child custody cases for lesbians and gay men particularly difficult. As Minnie Bruce Pratt (1984) and Gayle Rubin (2011) have discussed, lesbians and gay men were frequently cast as unfit parents in the eyes of the court because gays and lesbians were not regarded as suitable caretakers of children. The public and, in many cases, legal understanding of family was predicated on the Protestant Christian exaltation of marriage between one man and one woman as the ideal formula for rearing children.

Throughout the late twentieth and early twenty-first centuries American evangelical Protestants made their position on gay parenting clear not only through substantial political involvement, but also through the creation of multiple media outlets that recurrently denounced gays and lesbians as unfit parents. One of the largest evangelical Protestant media companies, Focus on the Family, began in 1977 at the same time Anita Bryant was making a national name for herself by condemning gays and lesbians. Focus on the Family started as a Protestant radio show but grew into a massive industry that produced books, magazines, tapes, pamphlets, and websites. Focus on the Family's materials largely target conservative Christians who want to uphold "Biblically based" Protestant views of marriage and childrearing where marriage necessitates not only the union of one man to one woman, but also adherence to a hierarchical relationship that places husbands in the dominant position over their wives and children (DeRogatis 2014). According to Ludger Viefhues-Bailey (2010), Focus materials primarily depict gay men as either hyper-sexual or as gender atypical and feminine. Lesbians, Viefhues-Bailey asserts, are commonly conflated with feminists, thereby representing women who do not adhere to the "rightful authority of male headship" within all Christian families (Viefhues-Bailey 2010, 111). Both gays and lesbians, but especially gay men, are depicted in Focus materials as sexual predators of children.[1] Despite the preponderance of data showing that heterosexually identified men are the most common sexual abusers of children, Focus on the Family has consistently proclaimed that gays are an omnipresent threat to children who should not be allowed to serve as parents (Rubin 2011).

The evangelical Protestant proscription against gay parenting is not simply a symptom of the Bible's condemnation of male same-sex sexual intercourse. Rather, the evangelical objection to gay parenting also reflects deeply held beliefs about gender complementarity that can only be achieved through heterosexual marital unions. Evangelical writer, Glenn Stanton, for example, argues that gay parenting will lead to a "Mister Potato Head Theory of gender differences (same core, just interchangeable parts)" (Stanton 2004). In other words, part of the opposition to gay parenting is that it undermines the presumed inherent differences between women and men, between mothers and fathers. Gay parents, from this perspective, are unable to provide children with a balanced view of genders that is imagined as both complementary and hierarchical. Additionally, Amy DeRogatis (2014) has documented in her study of evangelical Protestant sex manuals that the complementary presence of one man and one woman is the primary compulsory condition for evangelical marriage; procreation is not a necessary ingredient. Following, Viefhues-Bailey found that in much conservative Protestant discourse on sexuality, procreation is only emphasized as a significantly important component of marriage when gay relationships are discussed (Viefhues-Bailey 2010, 62–64). In other words, childless heterosexual evangelical couples are generally not condemned for being unable to have children. But the absence of children within gay relationships has been repeatedly used as evidence that homosexuality is a violation of God's plan for gender complementarity.

Mainline Protestant denominations have also engaged in debates about gay parenting throughout the late twentieth and early twenty-first centuries. As Heather White (2015) highlights, some mainline Protestant clergy were active in advocating for gay rights and the inclusion of lesbians and gay men in church communities from before the Stonewall riots of 1969. As gay marriage and gay parenting became a more commonplace occurrence throughout the United States in the early twenty-first century, many mainline denominations endured long, and in some cases, ongoing debates about whether or not to sanction gay relationships. Sociologist Dawne Moon found that "these debates were so volatile because they pointed to the socially contingent nature of things members thought of as essential, natural or divinely true" (Moon 2004, 3). In other words, mainline Protestant debates about gay parenting and marriage exposed deep divisions among Protestants about whether or not heterosexuality was the divine familial and sexual ideal for humanity. Moon also discovered in her ethnographic research that the most successful strategy for those who supported gay marriage and parenting within mainline Protestant communities occurred when Christians argued that some people are "born gay." As scholars such as Janet Jakobsen and Anne Pellegrini (2004) have demonstrated, "born gay" rhetoric has been a common attempt to reframe discussions of homosexuality from that of a sinful choice to that of an innate quality. Moon writes that "born gay" arguments have been successful within some liberal Protestant communities because they liken "being gay to being female or nonwhite, having characteristics that the church has traditionally devalued but which have, in a number of ways in mainline circles, been accepted as irrelevant to questions of moral or spiritual worth" (Moon 2004, 158). Thus, within mainline Protestant communities, the greatest success for advocates of gay parenting has been achieved through declarations that some people are "born gay," which denotes a valid aspect of God's plan for creation. In understanding sexuality as an innate orientation, a few mainline Protestant denominations, such as the Presbyterian Church (USA) and the United Church of Christ, have officially proclaimed that lesbians and gay men should not be punished for something they did not choose, and that they should be allowed to raise children within monogamous marital same-sex unions.[2]

Roman Catholic Perspectives

From an official perspective, the Roman Catholic Church is unambiguously opposed to gay parenting. Part of the Catholic Church's opposition to same-sex parenting stems from how the Church views marriage and sex. The Catholic Church has exalted marriage as a sacrament since the Middle Ages. Until then, the Church esteemed celibacy as the loftiest sexual ideal. When marriage became a sacrament, the Church held that procreation was the sole purpose of sex. For this reason, Roman Catholics have been forbidden from using contraception because it thwarts the purpose of sex and turns sex into an act of carnal pleasure. During Vatican II, the Church amended its position and declared that sex was allowed within marriage for both procreative and unitive purposes. That is, married couples could have sex even when no possibility of procreation existed because sex could also serve as a mechanism for making marriages stronger. However, the Vatican continued to forbid the use of contraception. Sex within marriage could not be simply unitive; it had to carry the possibility of procreation. Since same-sex sexual intercourse is not, theoretically, procreative, the Roman Catholic Church has not permitted same-sex couples to enter the sacrament of marriage, nor has the Church welcomed the possibility of gay parenting.

In addition to the Church's position on the primacy of procreative sex within marriage, the Roman Catholic Church has also opposed gay parenting because of the Church's insistence that heterosexual complementarity and gender role differences are a natural part of God's plan for creation. For instance, Mark Jordan (2005) asserts that, according to historical Catholic teachings, "women must be subordinate to men in domestic relationships and in church, and that men exercise their maleness precisely by dominating women" (Jordan 2005, 13). Familial relationships involving two mothers would, therefore, present a gender imbalance with two subordinates trying to rear a child without the presence of a dominant father. For this reason, Jordan contends that Catholic theological ideas about marriage and gender would necessitate a complete revision if the Church were to sanction same-sex unions and families. However, Victoria Clarke (2001) argues that Church officials do not typically rely on Catholic theology to substantiate their opposition to gay parenting. Instead, she found that Church leaders simply insist on the apparent obvious "naturalness of heterosexuality, and heterosexual conception and childrearing" without referring to Scripture or Tradition (Clarke 2001, 558–559). Along similar lines, the prominent Catholic organization, Catholic Answers, which is run by ordained and lay Catholics, cites Paul Cameron, an evangelical Protestant who was expelled from the American Psychological Association for distorting his findings on gays and lesbians, in order to justify the Catholic Church's opposition to gay parenting.[3] Rather than turn to Catholic teachings, the organization references a now-discredited Protestant researcher.[4] Nevertheless, through citations to Scripture, Catholic theology, and extra-Church research, the Roman Catholic Church has maintained that same-sex parenting transgresses the divine order and expectations for humanity.

Pope Francis, someone the national LGBTQ, the *Advocate*, named their "Person of the Year" in 2013 because of his perceived willingness to change the Vatican's opposition to homosexuality, has publicly denounced same-sex parenting as a violation of God's intent for creation.[5] He also affirmed that heterosexual parenting is necessary for healthy children. For example, in June 2015, to a crowd of 25,000 spectators in Rome, the Pontiff admonished that children need heterosexual parents and that gender differences are natural. He insisted that, "Children mature seeing their father and mother.... Their identity matures being confronted with the love their father and mother have, confronted with this difference" (quoted in Scammell 2015). Put differently, children are deprived if they are reared by a same-sex couple because they need to be exposed to the gender differences that inhere separately in men and women. For Pope Francis, only heterosexual couples are capable of good parenting. Children, from the Pontiff's perspective, will be at a disadvantage if raised by gay parents because same-sex parents cannot inculcate children with visible and tangible gender differences that the Pope understands as natural to the social order. Although some have exalted Pope Francis as a progressive pontiff more likely to move the Church in a pro-gay direction, his public rhetoric makes it clear that the Roman Catholic Church does not endorse gay parenting.

JEWISH APPROACHES

Among Judaism's major religious movements, the Reform, Reconstructionist, and Conservative movements all approve of gay parenting.[6] No Orthodox, Haredi, or Hasidic governing bodies have publicly sanctioned same-sex parenting. However, since 2010 more than one hundred Orthodox rabbis have publicly affirmed that the children of gay couples should be welcomed into synagogues even though same-sex wedding ceremonies remain proscribed.[7] Nevertheless, Judaism is not reducible to its religious movements. Many Jews in the United States and abroad classify themselves as secular Jews who do not desire a religious identification or justification to make decisions as Jews. In fact, for many Jews, Jewishness functions as an ethnicity that is passed from parents to children. The question, then, becomes not only what Jews believe about gay parenting, but also what Jews do to ensure that Jewishness is passed on to the children of gay and lesbian parents.

In examining Reform rabbinic statements that address gay parenting and marriage, the clearest theme that emerges from the literature is a concern that all Jews fulfill the *mitzvah* ("commandment") of procreation. Not only does this commandment come from the Biblical proclamation to "be fruitful and multiply," but also from the post-Holocaust Jewish communal concern with dwindling demographics and with assimilation to Christian culture. The anxiety over assimilation and a decline in the Jewish population has been widely shared by both secular and religiously affiliated Jews. For instance, Helene Meyers (2011) is one of many Jewish studies scholars who has illuminated the emphasis on reproduction in Jewish communities that has been exalted as the best way to ensure that Hitler will not have a posthumous victory. Meyers also notes that this fixation on producing Jewish children foreclosed many Jewish communities from welcoming gays and lesbians as parents for decades after the Holocaust because of how gays and lesbians were imagined as isolated and without the potential for creating their own families. As an example, the governing body of Reform rabbis declared in 1985 that rabbis could not perform same-sex wedding ceremonies because, "Judaism places great emphasis on family, children and the future, which is assured by a family" (CCAR Responsa 1985, 201). Raising children was, thus, seen as necessary for both Jewish continuity and for what constitutes a Jewish "family." The emphasis on children as a requisite for "family" is also made clear from an earlier Reform rabbinic declaration, in 1982, about whether or not children from a surrogate were considered

Jewish. In affirming that those children were Jews, the rabbinic governing body wrote that, "In a period when the number of Jewish children has declined rather rapidly, we should do everything possible to make children available to families who wish to raise them" (CCAR Responsa 1982, 159). The Jewishness, or lack thereof, of the surrogate became a minor issue when (heterosexual) Jewish parents promised to raise their children as Jews. By the end of the twentieth century though, the governing body of Reform rabbis shifted their perspective, allowed rabbis to officiate at same-sex unions, and welcomed gays and lesbians as a viable parenting group to help ensure a Jewish future.

The focus on children within Jewish communities has also contributed to debates about whether or not same-sex unions should be termed *kiddushin*, the Jewish legal term for marriage. Even after same-sex weddings were approved, the governing bodies of most Jewish movements did not regard gay partnerships as *kiddushin*. By initially refusing to refer to same-sex unions as *kiddushin*, liberal Jewish communities created a marital hierarchy where heterosexual unions were the most exalted possibility. While the Conservative movement still does not sanctify same-sex unions as *kiddushin*, in 2013 the governing body of Reform rabbis declared that same-sex partnerships could be considered *kiddushin* if they met three conditions.[8] The third condition was that same-sex couples must agree to raise their children, should they have any, as Jews. In other words, in order to receive the highest marital sanctification within Judaism, gay and lesbian couples must commit to raising their children as Jews.

The Reform movement, along with the Reconstructionist movement, had already made gay parenting a more achievable possibility prior to the 2013 *kiddushin* ruling by rejecting matrilineal descent as a necessary condition for Jewish identity. Historically, and still within Conservative and Orthodox Judaism, one became a Jew either by having a Jewish mother or by converting to Judaism. In recent decades, though, the Reconstructionist and Reform movements held that if either parent is Jewish, and if the child is raised as a Jew and considers herself Jewish, then the child is Jewish regardless of the mother's religious or ethnic affiliation. In turn, gay male couples within Reform and Reconstructionist Judaism have been able to adopt children and use surrogates without needing their children to go through a formal conversion process in order to be viewed as Jews.[9]

In addition to debates about Jewish identity, gay parenting also calls into question some Jewish rituals common for children. For example, Rebecca Alpert (1997) writes that the ritual of *brit milah*, the covenant of circumcision, is particularly fraught because it presupposes gender differences and it reaffirms that only boys carry on the ancient covenant between God and the Jewish people. Alpert writes that many lesbians, building off of earlier Jewish feminist critiques of circumcision, have abandoned the ritual, writing, "Those who choose this option do not want to make such a strong differentiation between male and female children's opportunity to identify as Jews; they therefore choose ceremonies for their sons that would be the same as for their daughters" (Alpert 1997, 94). While some gay and lesbian parents continue to circumcise, the rejection of the *brit milah* ritual by others reveals that including gay and lesbian parents within all facets of Judaism requires a reexamination of the historically pervasive patriarchal, heteronormative, and binary-gender-regulated aspects of the tradition.

Future Directions

Mark Jordan (2011) argues that as an increasing number of religious communities extend marital blessings to same-sex couples, gays and lesbians will more noticeably adhere to "well-established (and quite profitable) systems of stages" (Jordan 2011, 197). In other words, as marriage becomes a viable opportunity for more same-sex couples, gay men and lesbians will increasingly seek opportunities to further conform to dominant life scripts of coupled, domesticated childrearing. And, in many ways, Jordan's prediction has proven accurate. With same-sex marriage now legally recognized throughout the United States, religious groups that had actively lobbied against gay marriage have turned to adoption as a new battleground issue.

Even before same-sex marriage became a constitutional right throughout the United States, the Roman Catholic Church made adoption to gay couples a publicly contentious issue. For example, Church officials in Illinois made national news in 2011 after the state's bishops elected to close their adoption services, Catholic Charities, rather than comply with a state law that required them, as recipients of state money, to consider same-sex couples as potential adoptive parents. Prior to 2011, Illinois's Catholic leadership vigorously lobbied the state to prevent legalized same-sex marriage. But once same-sex marriage became a lawful reality in Illinois, the courts soon ruled that all adoption and foster-care agencies receiving tax money had to give equal consideration to prospective gay and lesbian parents. The Catholic Church chose to cease its adoption operations in Illinois rather than comply with the state's demand to consider same-sex couples as viable foster and adoptive parents. In so doing, the Illinois bishops followed a trend that had already begun in Massachusetts and Washington, DC, where Catholic adoption services in those areas also closed their doors rather than comply with laws that required them to consider potential gay and lesbian parents. In each of these jurisdictions, the courts ruled that the Church could not discriminate against prospective gay and lesbian parents and continue to receive tax dollars. The Catholic Church, however, argued that by forcing their adoption agencies to consider placing children with gay and lesbian couples, the government was infringing on their "religious freedom" that should be protected by the Constitution (Goodstein 2011).

Rhetoric of protecting antigay religious groups' "religious freedom" has become increasingly pervasive in the United States since the proliferation of state-sanctioned same-sex marriage. With gay marriage recognized in every state following the Supreme Court ruling in *Obergefell v. Hodges*, antigay religious groups, lobbyists, and politicians have made curtailing gay parenting a visible priority.[10] For example, even prior to the *Obergefell* decision, a bill was introduced into Congress in 2014 that was meant to protect adoption providers against an "anti-faith bias" (Stern 2014). Named the "Child Welfare Provider Inclusion Act," the bill's purpose was to invalidate state laws, such as the one in Illinois, which required adoption agencies to consider gay and lesbian couples. According to the Act, adoption and foster care agencies that had religious objections to homosexuality would not be required to work with gay and lesbian couples. The bill has not become a law at the federal level, but similar bills have been introduced into state legislatures. For example, in 2015 the Michigan and Florida state Houses passed religious exemption bills that specifically allowed adoption agencies to refuse gay and lesbian couples on religious grounds. In Michigan, the bill also quickly passed in the state Senate and was then signed into law by the governor. Consequently, in Michigan, religiously affiliated adoption agencies that refuse to work with gay and lesbian couples will continue to receive tax dollars.[11] Proponents of these bills have argued, as the Catholic Church did in Illinois, that requiring religiously affiliated adoption agencies to consider gay and lesbian parents forces them to cease their services and, in turn, no longer accommodate the needs of children who should be placed in loving homes (Stern 2014). Faced with the decision to close or to work with gays and lesbians, many have chosen to shut their doors. These religious freedom bills, therefore, are commonly presented as a way to protect the needs of deserving children who would be overlooked if religiously affiliated agencies ended their services.[12] Adoption is, thus, an important future area of investigation for scholars of religion, sexuality, and the law as various states enact antigay "religious freedom" laws and further codify Christian moral assumptions about what constitutes a family and acceptable parenting units.[13]

A final area for future consideration involves the ways in which religious perspectives on gay parenting reify coupled childrearing as the best familial formation. That is, religious perspectives on gay parenting, even those that are supportive, primarily promote, or presume, the idea that gay parenting involves a same-sex couple that lives together and that looks like a married heterosexual couple. But as Daniel Rivers (2013) highlights in his history of gay and lesbian parenting in the United States, many lesbian and gay parents have created diverse alternatives to the domestic couple model. Such possibilities include a lesbian having and raising a child with a gay male couple, three gay couples raising children collectively, a lesbian feminist community raising children together, or a three-person romantic household rearing a child. While one could predict that these forms of gay parenting will fade as same-sex marriage becomes the dominant model for adult gay romantic relationships, the possibility also exists that as adoption remains difficult for gays and lesbians, and as surrogacy remains financially impossible for many, lesbians and gay men will continue to pursue a variety of paths to become parents. Additionally, some gays and lesbians will reject coupled domestication as a necessary life script and precursor for establishing oneself as a viable parent. Therefore, by failing to acknowledge the many differing ways that gays and lesbians construct families, religious traditions that exclusively sanctify coupled parenting will not be able to adequately incorporate gay and lesbian parents, or their children, into their communities.

Notes

1. In his analysis of Focus on the Family literature, Viefhues-Bailey finds that "male homosexuals are talked about most frequently in Focus literature" (Ludger Viefhues-Bailey, *Between a Man and a Woman? Why Conservatives Oppose Same-Sex Marriage* [New York: Columbia University Press, 2010], 95) and that "women who love women are rarely a topic in Christian Right discourse" (Viefhues-Bailey, *Between a Man and a Woman?*, 110).
2. The Pew Research Center has collected data on various denominations' positions on sanctifying same-sex relationships. For a summary of that research, see David Masci, "Where Christian Churches, Other Religions Stand on Gay Marriage," *Pewresearch.org*, last modified March 18, 2015, http://www.pewresearch.org/fact-tank/2015/03/18/where-christian-churches-stand-on-gay-marriage/.
3. See "Gay Marriage," *Catholic.com*, http://www.catholic.com/documents/gay-marriage.
4. In addition to being expelled from the American Psychological Association, Cameron was also expelled from the American Sociological Association for misinterpreting and misrepresenting data on gay men, lesbians, and sexuality.
5. See Lucas Grindley, "Person of the Year 2013: Pope Francis," the *Advocate*, last modified December 16, 2013, http://www.advocate.com/year-review/2013/12/16/advocates-person-year-pope-francis.
6. The denominationalism of Judaism is most prevalent within the United States. Specifically, the Jewish movements that are explicitly approving of gay parenting include Reform, Reconstructionist, and Conservative Judaism. While these movements have a transnational presence, none have had the success that they have achieved in the United States.
7. A group of Orthodox rabbis created a document in 2010 that other rabbis have continued to sign as recently as February 2015. See "Statement of Principles on the Place of Jews with a Homosexual Orientation in our Community," last modified February 2015, http://statementofprinciplesnya.blogspot.com/.
8. For a full copy of this Reform Rabbinic decision, see "Same Sex Marriage as *Kiddushin*," *CCAR Responsa Committee*, https://ccarnet.org/responsa/same-sex-marriage-kiddushin/.
9. The question of who is a Jew, especially as it relates to Israel and its "right of return," is more complicated than explicated here. A child of a gay male couple adopted from a Christian mother would not be regarded as Jew within, for example, Orthodox communities, nor would the child be able to immigrate to Israel as a Jew unless the child had formally converted to Judaism.
10. Antigay religious groups that lobbied to prevent gay parenting have not only been operative in the United States. Stephen Hicks (2005) documents in his research that in the United Kingdom, "large and substantially funded organizations, such as the Christian Institute, have begun to commission research and mount well-organized campaigns" to demonstrate that children should not be reared by same-sex couples (Stephen Hicks, "Is Gay Parenting Bad for Kids? Responding to the 'Very Idea Difference' in Research on Lesbian and Gay Parents," *Sexualities* 8, no. 2 (2005): 155).

11. Kate Lambertz, "Michigan Governor Signs Controversial Religious Freedom Adoption Law," *Huffington Post*, June 11, 2015. http://www.huffingtonpost.com/2015/06/10/michigan-adoption-bill-lgbt-parents_n_7553952.html.
12. Jakobsen and Pellegrini (2004) note that antigay groups commonly couch their rhetoric in terms of defending or protecting children and families. As one example, they point out, "To its supporters, DOMA [the Defense of Marriage Act] was not about discrimination against same-sex couples, it was about defense—of 'the' American family" (Janet Jakobsen and Ann Pellegrini, *Love the Sin: Sexual Regulation and the Limits of Religious Tolerance* [Boston: Beacon Press, 2004], 63).
13. Marla Brettschneider has argued in "All Points Bulletin: Jewish Dykes Adopting Children" (in *Queer Jews*, edited by David Shneer and Caryn Aviv, 238–257 [New York: Routledge, 2002]) that Christian moral assumptions have been operative within the state regulation of adoption for decades in ways that not only disadvantage gays and lesbians, but also Jews. Brettschneider highlights that because most birth parents in the United States are Christian, state adoption services "evaluate just how important Christianity" will be to the child and prefer to protect "the interests of Christian children" by placing them with Christian parents. Thus, the religious exemption bills for adoption agencies, such as the 2015 bill in Michigan, carry the possibility of overt discrimination against not only gays and lesbians but also against religious minorities. For more on the complexities Jews and queer Jews in particular face in the Christian-dominated U.S. adoption market, see Marla Brettschneider, *The Family Flamboyant: Race Politics, Queer Families, and Jewish Lives* (Albany: SUNY Press, 2006).

Bibliography

Alpert, Rebecca. *Like Bread on the Seder Plate: Jewish Lesbians and the Transformation of Tradition.* New York: Columbia University Press, 1997.

Brettschneider, Marla. "All Points Bulletin: Jewish Dykes Adopting Children." In *Queer Jews*, edited by David Shneer and Caryn Aviv, 238–257. New York: Routledge, 2002.

Brettschneider, Marla. *The Family Flamboyant: Race Politics, Queer Families, and Jewish Lives.* Albany: SUNY Press, 2006.

Bryant, Anita. *The Anita Bryant Story: The Survival of Our Nation's Families and the Threat of Militant Homosexuality.* Ada, MI: Revell, 1977.

CCAR Responsa. "Surrogate Mother." *Central Conference of American Rabbis Responsa.* 1982. https://ccarnet.org/responsa/arr-505-507/.

CCAR Respona. "Homosexual Marriage." *Central Conference of American Rabbis Responsa.* 1985. https://ccarnet.org/responsa/carr-297-298/.

CCAR Responsa. "Same Sex Marriage as *Kiddushin*." *Central Conference of American Rabbis Responsa.* 2013. https://ccarnet.org/responsa/same-sex-marriage-kiddushin/.

Clarke, Victoria. "What About the Children? Arguments Against Lesbian and Gay Parenting." *Women's Studies International Forum* 24, no. 5 (2001): 555–570.

DeRogatis, Amy. *Saving Sex: Sexuality and Salvation in American Evangelicalsim.* New York: Oxford University Press, 2014.

Fetner, Tina. *How the Religious Right Shaped Lesbian and Gay Activism.* Minneapolis: University of Minnesota Press, 2008.

Goodstein, Laurie. "Bishops Say Rules on Gay Parents Limit Freedom of Religion." *New York Times*, December 28, 2011.

Hicks, Stephen. "Is Gay Parenting Bad for Kids? Responding to the 'Very Idea Difference' in Research on Lesbian and Gay Parents." *Sexualities* 8, no. 2 (2005): 153–168.

Jakobsen Janet, Janet and Pellegrini, Ann. *Love the Sin: Sexual Regulation and the Limits of Religious Tolerance*. Boston: Beacon Press2004..

Jordan, Mark. *Blessing Same-Sex Unions: The Perils of Queer Romance and the Confusions of Christian Marriage*. Chicago: University of Chicago Press, 2005.

Jordan, Mark. *Recruiting Young Love: How Christians Talk about Homosexuality*. Chicago: University of Chicago Press, 2011.

Lambertz, Kate. "Michigan Governor Signs Controversial Religious Freedom Adoption Law." *Huffington Post*. June 11, 2015. http://www.huffingtonpost.com/2015/06/10/michigan-adoption-bill-lgbt-parents_n_7553952.html.

Meyeres, Helene. *Identity Papers: Contemporary Narratives of American Jewishness*. Albany: SUNY Press, 2011.

Moon, Dawne. *God, Sex, and Politics: Homosexuality and Everyday Theologies*. Chicago: University of Chicago Press, 2004.

Pratt, Minnie Bruce. "Identity: Skin, Blood, Heart." In *Yours in Struggle: Three Feminist Perspectives on Anti-Semitism and Racism*, edited by Elly Bulkin, Minnie Bruce Pratt, and Barbara Smith. Long Haul Press, 1984.

Rivers, Daniel. *Radical Relations: Lesbian Mothers, Gay Fathers, and Their Children in the United States since World War II*. Chapel Hill: University of North Carolina Press, 2013.

Rubin, Gayle. *Deviations: A Gayle Rubin Reader*. Durham, NC: Duke University Press, 2011.

Scammell, Rosie. "Children Need Heterosexual Parents, Says Pope After Gay Pride March." *Religious News Service*. June 15, 2015. http://www.religionnews.com/2015/06/15/children-need-heterosexual-parents-says-pope-after-gay-pride-march/

Stanton, Glenn. *Marriage on Trial: The Case Against Same-Sex Marriage and Parenting*. InterVarsity Press, 2004.

Stern, Mark Joseph. "Some Conservatives Would Rather Keep Their Kids in Foster Care than Let Gays Adopt Them." *Slate.com* August 1, 2014. http://www.slate.com/blogs/outward/2014/08/01/conservatives_want_to_keep_gay_couples_from_adopting_or_fostering_kids.html.

Viefhues-Bailey, Ludger. *Between a Man and a Woman? Why Conservatives Oppose Same-Sex Marriage*. New York: Columbia University Press, 2010.

White, Heather. *Reforming Sodom: Protestants and the Rise of Gay Rights*. Chapel Hill: University of North Carolina Press, 2015.

CHAPTER 12

RELIGIOUS PERSPECTIVES ON POPULATION JUSTICE

DANIEL C. MAGUIRE

No species has ever been able to multiply without limit. There are two biological checks upon a rapid increase in numbers—a high mortality and a low fertility. Unlike other biological organisms [humans] can choose which of these checks shall be applied, but one of them must be.

—Harold F. Dorn. Biologist

For most of the history of our species, depopulation, not overpopulation was our main peril. We came into existence some 200,000 years ago and we picked a dreadful time to do it. We arrived during the two-and-a-half-million-year period of earth travail known as the Pleistocene. This was a time of recurrent glaciation and other horrors. Planet Earth was not at all hospitable to whatever life forms had managed to evolve. At one point, about 75,000 years ago, DNA analyses have revealed that the entire human population may have shrunk to some 15,000 fertile adults, huddled together on the high plateau of northern Ethiopia. This brought our species to the brink of extinction.[1] The earth almost did us in, before we acquired the ability to do that to ourselves.

The earth's problem is that it never got locked into a happy orbit. It has an eccentric orbital path around the sun. It staggers and wobbles and tilts and that accounts for its changing moods. Sometimes it is just reasonably close to the sun but sometimes it is too far away and so we vacillate between ice ages. Our current situation is described ominously as "interglacial." The next ice age is due in about 50,000 years. Some say sooner. Some say we have so overheated the planet that it will delay the inevitable icing but that overheating will have already caused enormous wreckage, so such thoughts are not consoling.

Enter, the Holocene

The good news for our species is that 10,000 years ago, Pleistocene horrors abated and humanity came in out of the cold into a gentle period of earth history known as the Holocene. By comparison, this was Paradise. Scratching out a living through hunting and gathering was the best we could do in the Pleistocene. Now, with the benign climate change, agriculture was born. A new phenomenon, "abundance," entered into human experience.

This was surely a blessing, but a mixed one. Along with good supplies of food, came increased fertility. Overcrowding was not an insoluble problem as long as there was land to move to. But we did discover early on that too many people in too little space is toxic. Some 4,000 years ago the ancient Babylonians spoke of this problem. On an ancient stone tablet, they carved out a kind of history of humankind. They claimed that the gods made humans to do scut work that was unworthy of the divinities. Then a problem arose. Humans overreproduced and the gods had to develop a population policy. They sent plagues to reduce the population and they made it a religious obligation to exercise fertility management. As Joel Cohen says, this "is perhaps the earliest extant account of human overpopulation and the earliest interpretation of catastrophe as a response to overpopulation."[2] The Babylonians saw that too many people chasing too few resources is a public policy problem.

Jack Miles argues that the Genesis story also addressed this issue. After creating humans and telling them to increase and multiply and take "dominion" over life, the creator soon saw that "the unchecked multiplication of humans" posed a problem.[3] As Miles puts it: "In Genesis 12 and the remaining chapters of the Book of Genesis, we see the deity ... in an ongoing struggle with humankind over control of human fertility."[4] Having promised the gift of lavish fertility to Abraham, the divinity came quickly to realize that some strings had to be attached to this promise. "God is demanding that Abram concede, symbolically, that his fertility is not his own to exercise without divine let or hindrance."[5] In less symbolic language, the ancient writers were saying that population policy is a necessity, given the exuberant fertility of the species and the finitude of resources.

Confucian teacher Hans Fei (297–233 BCE) called for controlling the growth of the population in order to strike a balance "between the people's needs and the natural resources."[6] It was simple common sense, he said. "For every family having at least five sons, each son will have another five, before the grandfather dies there will be twenty-five offspring." The result? "The society will end up in turmoil."

In the fourth century BCE when world population was less than 200 million, both Plato and Aristotle recommended control of birth rates by the state. Aristotle said in his *Politics* that the number of children generated should not exceed the provisions of the community. If too many people were generated, he recommended moving off to form new colonies where resources could be found. The Christian saint Thomas Aquinas agreed with Aristotle. Johannes Messner summarizes Thomas' position: he says that Aquinas offered these two main solutions: "First, the limiting by law of the size of the family; secondly the founding of colonies, or as we should say today, emigration."[7] Messner, a Catholic scholar, comments: "It is, therefore, not without surprise that one finds St. Thomas (in *II Pol., lects. 8, 17*) suggesting the restriction of procreation after a certain number of children."[8] It rises from Thomas' commonsensical recognition that there cannot be, as Messner put it, "an infinite growth of the population."

Aquinas, however, did not go along with all of Aristotle's suggestions. When Aristotle suggests homosexuality as a fertility control strategy, Aquinas demurs and would not give blessing to a practice he found "turpid." He was clear, however, that if more than a certain number of citizens were generated, the resultant stress would breed "thievery, sedition, and chaos." He saw that population policy is an issue of social and distributive justice and as such it is a matter of public policy and political concern. This is more obvious today than in Thomas's time, when our population has soared to over seven billion people with more than 200,000 more ore coming every day and over 75 million more each year. Much of that increase is in the poorest parts of the world and it is happening at a time when all of the arable land on the planet is already in use, when the oceans are suffering pollution and are swelling with glacier melt threatening coastal regions and islands, limiting habitable land.

After saying the state must limit births, Aquinas adroitly sidestepped the question of how this state-imposed limitation of births would be achieved. Still he was clear that population policy raises justice issues and is state business. It would be a stretch to read Thomas as siding with the Chinese experiment in allowing only "one child per family." Today we know that there are many other ways the state can promote population management. Mandatory education on sex and reproduction, education for women, delaying the average age at marriage, making contraceptive means freely available, legalizing abortion as a necessary backup to birth limitation methods. Our foreign aid programs can also include fertility management provisions for contraception and abortion. We can also confront the damaging teaching coming from some influential world religions in the area of reproductive ethics.

What Is the Earth's Carrying Capacity?

The grim fact is that we are now at a point where overpopulation is in some way related to every single problem on this ecologically stressed planet. Estimates vary widely on how many people the planet can support, ranging from 4 billion to 16 billion.[9] To survive at those upper levels, however, would require that people be content to live on a level of nutrition comparable to prisoners at Auschwitz and settle for the comfort level of Artic Inuit and Calahari bushmen.[10] Obviously people do not display a tolerance for such a deprived life. We hunger for affluence and the burgeoning appetites that are its natural sequel.

A formula might capture this: H + A + A + A = A. **Hyperfertility + Affluence + Appetite for more consumption = Apocalypse**. According to that formula any population over 4 billion would create demands for resources that this planet could not meet. Going beyond that number (as we have done) is a form of greed and a formula for systemic injustice. Justice is classically defined as *suum cuique*, giving to each their due. It is the first moral barrier and defense against greed and overaccumulation.[11] Overpopulation kills the possibility of doing justice to people and to the earth itself, and to its future inhabitants.

Justice requires that we limit our numbers to stop the anthropogenic wreckage of land, sea, and air that is now accruing apocalyptic momentum. This puts humankind into a Cassandra moment. Cassandra was cursed with knowing the future without being able to convince anyone. Data on damage done and damage foreseeable is copiously available but is meriting only flaccid response and ineffectual policy gestures. Even belated efforts at the United Nations to address the incipient catastrophe are hamstrung by a lack of plausible enforcement mechanism, as was demonstrated in the United Nations Paris Conference in 2015.

Doing Population Justice in the Anthropocene

Step one in doing justice is to face the facts. Science is making it clear today: the Holocene holiday is ending. The time when the earth's ability to heal trumped our ability to destroy has ended. Some place that moment symbolically in 1945 when we first unleashed the atomic bomb. People-power taking malignant forms has initiated this new epoch in the history of the planet. Paul Crutzen, a Dutch chemist and Nobel Prize winner, coined the word *Anthropocene* to describe this new epoch. People (*anthropoi*) power is controlling the destiny of the planet in a way that never happened before. No one species ever achieved this dubious distinction of being able to threaten not only its own existence but the existence of most of the rest of life. One of Crutzen's scientific colleagues, looking at the work of ecological science, commented: "The work is going well, but it looks like it might be the end of the world." [12] Sadly ... tragically ... that gallows humor is not hyperbolic.

Life on this capricious earth has faced five "great extinctions," when as much as 90 to 95 percent of species were extinguished. As Elizabeth Kolbert argues in her Pulitzer

Prize-winning book, *The Sixth Extinction*, we have ominously entered a largely anthropogenic sixth great extinction.

During the sweet spot known as the Holocene, humanity, behaving like *nouveaux riches*, developed a fatal naivete regarding the planet's limits. Hamlet gave this flaw a religious basis. "There is a divinity that shapes our ends rough hew them how we will." Muck up the worlds as we might, the deity, like an indulgent parent, will clean up the messes we make and tuck us into our beds of juvenile contentment. As our technical expertise grew, this religious overconfidence was buttressed by a faith in our boundless technical ingenuity: there is always a technical fix for whatever ills beset us. Enveloped by this strategic naivete and buoyed by an overdeveloped capacity for *denial*, we are ill prepared to respond appropriately as this surging crisis unfolds.

REQUIEM FOR OUR DELUSIONS

We can only look at the sun for a brief moment. We shy with similar instinctive alacrity from uncomfortable facts. Only kooks and mad men claim the sky is falling and "the end is nigh!" But serious science which is neither kooky nor mad is sounding that same message of gloom and doom. Clive Hamilton of the Australian National University, who has also taught at the University of Cambridge and Yale University, writes in his ominously entitled book *Requiem for a Species:*

> The reluctant conclusion of the most eminent climate scientists is that the world is on a path to a very unpleasant future and it is too late to stop it. Behind the facade of scientific detachment, the climate scientists themselves now evince a mood of barely suppressed panic. No one is willing to say publicly what the climate science is telling us: that we can no longer prevent global warming that will this century bring about a radically transformed world that is much more hostile to the survival and flourishing of life.[13]

Mark Serreze, director of the US National Snow and Ice Data center has said that "Arctic ice is in its death spiral." NASA climate scientist Jay Zwally said, "The Arctic is often cited as the canary in the coal mine for climate warming. Now, as a sign of climate warming, the canary has died."[14] To switch metaphors, Arctic soil emerging from under ice is a time bomb. "If the carbon contained in just the top 50 cm (19.60) inches of soil were to be released, "it would exceed all the carbon humans have emitted since the industrial revolution began 250 years ago."[15]

These scientists are not writing only about future calamities. The calamities have begun. MIT physicist Alan Lightman writes, "Due to irreversible erosion, California has been losing its coastline at the rate of eight inches per year."[16] Notice: he describes the erosion as "irreversible." One billion people in Asia depend on the waters from the Himalayan glaciers, and global warming is a threat to this essential life support.

Catastrophe could not be made of starker stuff. Already one quarter of the world's rivers do not reach the ocean.[17] At the United Nations Conference in Paris the goal was to keep global warming at no more than 2 degrees Celsius. The assembled nations could not agree, however, to make the reforms needed for this mandatory. But even if they had, the goal is not good enough. Some 120,000 years ago we had that 2 degrees Celsius warming and "the global sea level was 4–8 meters (13–26 feet) higher than today."[18] So even if the Paris goals were reached, coastal cities around the planet would be inundated and island nations would disappear.

Indeed, the International Energy Agency meeting in Morocco in November 2016 to review the Paris accords concluded that the plans were inadequate and the likelihood is that there will be a rise of 2.7 Celsius by 2100. Small wonder the protests of island nations is at panic level.[19]

The most hopeful book from the science world is certainly that of Johan Rockstrom and Mattias Klum: *Big World, Small Planet: Abundance within Planetary Boundaries*. They believe we have the ingenuity to preserve good living for centuries and even to be able to feed as many as 9 billion people. They cite examples of great promise in countries like Germany and Sweden and elsewhere; they show how the greening process that will add some longevity to this earth can be financially profitable. Greed and fear could be greened, and an effort greater than that marshaled and mustered for our world wars could converge on this crucial planetary rescue mission. "Could" is the key word.

For all those wonderful things to happen, this hope-filled book stipulates a formidable condition. The entire planet would have to go fossil-fuel-free in twenty-five to thirty years.[20] That, of course, has a zero chance of happening since all mechanized nations would have to totally retool and there is no reasonable hope that they will do that, especially now that oil is cheaper and more abundant due to discoveries under the melting polar ice.

Overpopulation Is a Worldwide Justice Issue

Because of individualistic biases, much reproductive ethics has focused on individuals and families. Personal issues regarding reproduction have their importance but on this planet at this time, population must be seen in both religion and in ethics as issues primarily of social and distributive justice. Lester R. Brown of the Worldwatch Institute says that overpopulation can exacerbate "nearly all the other environmental and social problems."[21]

We are faced with what demographers call "population momentum," the amount of growth that will occur if our fertile youth only reproduce themselves. Half the world's residents are under twenty-five: we have one billion adolescents. We have on earth today more fertile people than there were people in 1960. Because we do not know their future reproductive behavior, predictions vary on whether the planet in this century will peak at 9, 10, or 11 billion people.[22] Predictions of overall gradual leveling of fertility are comforting but not for people in places like Ethiopia, Pakistan, and Nigeria, whose numbers may triple in the next fifty years. Half the children today in Ethiopia are already undernourished.

These are the paramount issues of social and distributive justice today. Social justice requires that individuals contribute to the needs of the common good; distributive justice requires that governments and other distributive powers in society distribute goods and burdens in an equitable way. Individuals contribute to the common good regarding reproduction by limiting their fertility in view of social needs. Government as the prime agent of distributive justice must use its power to promote and provide the means necessary for reasonable fertility management, particularly for those who need aid most, the poor.

Unmet need for contraceptive aid among the poor of the world is the premier challenge for distributive justice in international ethics today. Nafis Sadik, former head of the United Nation Fund for Population activities, estimated that "half of all pregnancies may be unwanted."[23]

Of course it is simplistic to think that the problem of population excess can be solved by simply throwing condoms at it, as necessary as such means truly are. Poverty, illiteracy, and sexism have to be addressed. The justice issue here is multi-factorial. The United Nations Population and Development Conference in Cairo in 1994 saw that the economic and educational empowerment of women is the key to fertility limitation. In the remarkable state of Kerala in India, the literacy rate for women is 86.3 percent and they have reached fertility rates as low as 1.8 percent.[24] Empowerment of women, it seems, is the best "contraceptive."

Religion: Problem or Part of Solution?

Because of their unique authority and influence, religions have a great responsibility to help make this happen. Sociologist and demographer Anrudh Jain laments that "religion and population growth are rarely discussed together." He sees this as a serious error since "religion has had a powerful role in many countries' population programs." Religion, he recognizes, also has "a profound effect on individuals' sexual and reproductive behavior, which is one of the major determinants of population growth."[25] Here is a social scientist calling on religion to pull its oar. Demography expert Jose

Barzelatto writes that in demography "the debate has moved from numbers to values, and thus religions have an even more important role to play in this significant process of social change."[26]

In her study of reproductive policy in the United States, Jean Reith Schroedel writes: "The contemporary pro-life movement is predominantly a religious movement. Most of the early activists were Catholic, and the Catholic Church occasionally helped establish local pro-life groups, the strongest of which developed in heavily urban and Catholic states."[27] In Latin America where the influence of the Catholic hierarchy is considerable, the injustice of denying reproductive rights is clear. In a study entitled "Abortion as a Public Health Problem in Colombia," sociologist Lucero Zamudio writes: "According to the World Health Organization, Latin America is the region with the highest rate of unsafe abortions, approximately 41 abortions per 1,000 women. This is almost three times higher than the world average (15 per 1,000) and five times higher than the rate for industrialized nations."[28] This proves saliently that, at the public policy level, reproductive injustice is tendentially murderous.

Reproductive Justice and World Religions

The need to regulate births is a human right and necessity for families and for the common good. Negative religious influences can create what could be called a crisis of undemanded need, meaning that people convinced by false religious teaching do not feel free in conscience to ask for and use proper contraception.

Primum non nocere . . .

Since religion, for good or for ill, is a significant player in population justice issues, it is good to start with medicine's fundamental axiom: *primum non nocere*; the first duty for religion is to do no harm. Face the fact: the contraceptive and abortion taboos propagated by religions have done serious harm and hampered population policy work internationally.

Small wonder that religions generated in a world where longevity was rarely possible would have a strong natalist thrust. Peter Brown notes that Christianity was born "in a society that was more helplessly exposed to death then is even the most afflicted underdeveloped country in the modern world." When the Roman Empire was at its height in the second century CE, the average life expectancy was less than twenty-five years. "Death," he says, "fell savagely on the young." Only four out of every hundred men and fewer women lived beyond the age of fifty. It was as the Christian John Chrysostom said a world "grazed thin by death." Roman emperors made it a matter of law to reproduce abundantly. Emperor Augustus penalized bachelors and rewarded families for producing children. The average age of Roman brides was fourteen. "For the population of the Roman Empire to remain even stationary, it appears that each woman would have had to produce an average of five children."[29] The pressure on women to reproduce was enormous. Maximal fertility was a necessity for a society to survive. Religions developed in such conditions would understandably privilege fertility.

Religious Good Sense

The religious story is not all negative. Religionists have actually done a lot of good practical ethics on issues of reproductive justice. The pity is that this is not well known by policy-makers. There are neglected positive resources within the religions for realistic and just population policies. These include religious support for contraception and for abortion as a necessary backup. Abortion as a backup will continue to be necessary as long as people and contraceptives are imperfect.

Looking primarily at the Abrahamic religion, Judaism, Christianity, and Islam, here is a primer on some of their best insights.

Judaism

Judaism is very open to family planning, including contraception as well as abortion. In the Mishnah, written in the early Talmudic period (200 BCE) it says that birth prevention, using a variety of methods, is permitted after two children.[30] However, Orthodox Jewish theologian Laurie Zoloth writes, "Abortion appears as an option for Jewish women from the earliest sources in the Bible and Mishnaic commentary."[31] Indeed, if the woman's physical or mental health is at issue, abortion is not only permitted, it is mandated.

Jewish traditions are at pains to address the moral status of the fetus, saying that in the first forty days of pregnancy the *conceptum* is considered "like water" (Babylonian Talmud: Tractate Yebamoth Folio 69a). The fetus is not considered to have full personal status. Even in the last trimester, the fetus has a lesser moral status than a born person. As with Aristotle, this idea of "delayed ensoulment," or delayed personhood, is found in Judaism as it is in most religions.[32] The moral standing of the fetus grows with its physical size.

Christianity: Catholic and Protestant

Influenced by Stoic views on the rational purpose of sexuality, an anti-contraceptive tradition was absorbed into Christianity. John T. Noonan traces it out in his magisterial work *Contraception: A History of Its Treatment by the Catholic Theologians and Canonists*.[33] There is little vestige of that taboo in contemporary Protestantism though it lingers in conservative portions of the Protestant and Catholic churches. It is influential still in Latin American countries due to its defense by some members of the hierarchy, and in the United States it surfaced in resistance to contraceptive coverage in President Obama's Affordable Care Act.

Still, even in Catholicism's more rigorous period, childless marriages were permitted and the "rhythm method of family planning" was permitted. As Catholic ethicist Christine Gudorf writes, "When Pius XII approved the rhythm method in this 1954 address to midwives, he approved both contraceptive intent and results."[34]

In early Christianity there was no fervid preoccupation with abortion such as is found in some Christians today. Major discussion of abortion did not develop until the Middle Ages. Delayed ensoulment was the prevailing teaching through most of Christian history following upon the leadership of theological giants such as Augustine and Thomas Aquinas. Only when the fetus was "formed" could God infuse a spiritual soul and only at that point did the fetus attain to the moral status of a person. Given the limits of medieval physiology there was uncertainty as to when the fetus was sufficiently "formed" to be able to receive a spiritual soul. Estimates varied from forty to eighty days into the pregnancy. Today, as Catholic philosophers Daniel Dombrowski and Robert Deltete write, "the fetus becomes morally considerable between twenty-four and thirty-two weeks when sentiency and then the cerebral cortex start to function."[35] Understandably with the development of scientific physiology, the understanding of when a fetus is "formed" changed and that is reflected in the position of Professors Dombrowski and Deltete.

An influential Catholic theologian, Jesuit Thomas Sanchez (1550–1610), was the premier authority on sexual and reproductive ethics in his day. He got down to cases and found multiple reasons justifying early abortions: abortion was permissible if the pregnancy was a threat to the life of the pregnant woman; if a girl might be killed for having had extramarital sex; if a girl was engaged to one man but pregnant of another. It was mistakenly thought that intercourse early in a pregnancy could kill the embryo. Sanchez said such coitus in early pregnancy was still moral since the embryo was at that point "unformed matter" and it would not be "such a great loss" if it were dislodged.[36] This is just an application of Thomas Aquinas' teaching on the nature of ethics: "Human actions are moral or immoral according to the circumstances."[37]

Pope Francis, a moderate reformer, has not challenged the hierarchical ban on abortion but he has urged Catholics to restrain their overstress on abortion and to direct their moral energies more to the basic problems of environmental destruction, militarism, and the coexistence of extreme poverty and obscene levels of wealth.

Islam

In Islam, as in other religions, there is strong stress on the protection of the fetus but also permission for abortions. Those in Islam who oppose abortion turn to texts such as "Kill not your children, on a plea of want, we provide sustenance for you and for them" (Q 6:151). Scholars point out that the text was mainly targeting and condemning the murder of born children, especially girls.[38] Still it has been used by those who would argue that "God" will provide even if we reproduce imprudently. This kind of simplistic piety is not the prevalent view in Islam.

In Islam there is a prioritization of the quality of life rather than a large quantity of children. For that reason children should not be as the steps of a stairway. Contraception is not forbidden. Islam does not have a pope who would attempt to enforce unanimity on such moral issues. Legal positions range from total prohibition of abortion to unqualified permission for abortion up to 120 days into the pregnancy. However, even after 120 days exceptions are allowed for serious reasons such as the woman's health.

Sa'diyya Shaikh writes that there is "broad-based legal permissibility of contraception" in Islam. "Muslim physicians in the medieval period conducted in-depth investigations into the medical dimension of birth control, which were unparalleled in European medicine until the nineteenth century."[39]

AL-Azl, the term for coitus interruptus, is permitted by many authorities in Islam.[40]

Beyond *Al-Azl*, "it is permissible to use the modern devices which are designed to prevent pregnancy temporarily for a certain period, such as contraceptive pills, the IUD, or a similar device that would not adversely affect the couple's fertility." Indeed it is said that such devices are actually better than *Al-Azl* because with their use "sexual intercourse is conducted in a natural manner," which is less disturbing to the couple.[41]

Legal Implication for Religious Freedom

In none of the world religions is there one single attitude toward contraception or abortion. Instead there are authentic moral traditions supporting both the pro and the con positions. For a government to take sides in these long-standing debates within the world's religions would constitute an attack on religious freedom. The world's religions are pluralistic on these moral issues. Adherents of these religions can take either position and find support for it in their religion. Government has no right to strip those on one side of the eternal debate of their religiously grounded legal rights. To do so would be fascistic.

In a democratic pluralist society, when issues are respectably debated, issues such as the permissibility of contraception, on which there are good reasons and good authorities on both sides of the debate, a democratic government should not outlaw one side of the debate. There are two tests that mark a moral issue as "respectably debated" and therefore one that should not be outlawed: (1) good and plausible reasons that have strong public approval and support from respected authorities, i.e., experts on these issues; and (2) approval by mainstream humanitarian institutions, such as mainstream professional organizations, the United Nations, churches, and other religious bodies. Moral issues that meet these tests, even if other people and other authorities strongly disapprove, should not be outlawed. The effort to do so will fail since such a legal effort would lack the consensual base needed for any viable law.[42]

The American experiment with Prohibition, the banning of alcoholic beverages, was a failure that illustrates the principle of respectable debate. There were good and plausible reasons for the use of alcohol supported by good authorities and also by mainstream humanitarian institutions such as the Catholic Church, which requires the use of alcohol in its central eucharistic liturgy. The law did except the use of wine in the liturgy, but overall there was no consensual base on which to build the prohibition and so Prohibition failed.

The issues of contraception and abortion also fall within the ambit of respectable debate. Humanitarian institutions including the world's religions have strong support for these options. If government tries to impose the conservative restrictive view it would be trampling on the consciences of religious people who have solid support for their views in their religious moral traditions. That would violate both religious freedom and democratic principles.

Duties of Judges and Legislators

Saints Thomas Aquinas and Augustine both held that Catholic legislators could vote to legalize prostitution if they foresaw greater evils coming from banning it. Augustine said, and Aquinas agreed, that if this outlet for aberrant sexual energy were closed, greater evils could ensue. Thus, they said, the good legislator should imitate God who permits some evils lest worse evils result.[43] Today a Catholic legislator who thinks all abortions are evil could still vote to sustain its legality since banning legal abortion leads to illegal abortions with a high loss of life, especially for poor women. Past history proves this.

When the religious traditions are properly understood, they contain firm support for a sound theory of reproductive justice and population management.

NOTES

1. Johan Rockstrom and Mattias Klum, *Big World, Small Planet* (New Haven, CT: Yale University Press, 2015), 31.
2. Joel E. Cohen, *How Many People Can the Earth Support?* (New York: W. W. Norton & Company, 1995), 6.
3. Jack Miles, *God: A Biography* (New York: Alfred A. Knopf, 1995), 47.
4. Ibid.
5. Ibid., 53.
6. Geling Shang, "Excess, Lack and Harmony," in *Sacred Rights: The Case for Contraception and Abortion in World Religions*, edited by Daniel C. Maguire, 230 (Oxford, UK: Oxford University Press, 2003).
7. Johannes Messner, *Social Ethics: Natural Law in the Western World* (St. Louis: B. Herder Book Co, 1965), 704.
8. Ibid., 705.
9. Cohen, *How Many People Can the Earth Support?*, 368.
10. Ibid., 359.
11. See "Theories of Justice" in *Ethics: A Complete Method for Moral Choice*, edited by Daniel C. Maguire, pp. 51–61 (Minneapolis, MN: Fortress Press, 2010).
12. Elizabeth Kolbert, *The Sixth Extinction: An Unnatural History* (New York: Picador: Henry Holt and Company, 2015), 107.
13. Clive Hamilton, *Requiem for a Species: Why We Resist the Truth About Climate Change* (Washington DC: Earthscan 2010), x–xi.
14. Ibid., 3–4.
15. Rockstrom and Klum, *Big World Small Planet*, 79.
16. Alan Lightman, *The Accidental Universe: The World You Thought You Knew* (New York: Pantheon Books, 2013), 30.
17. Rockstrom and Klum, *Big World Small Planet*, 78.
18. Ibid., 88.
19. "Climate Goal Called Too Weak to Meet Goals," *New York Times*, November 17, 2016, A12.
20. Rockstrom and Klum, *Big World Small Planet*, 26.
21. Maguire, *Sacred Rights*, 7.
22. Ibid.
23. Maguire, *Sacred Rights*, 15.
24. Ibid.
25. Anrudh Jain, Religion, "State and Population Growth," in *Sacred Rights: The Case for Contraception and Abortion in World Religions* (Ch. 11), edited by Daniel C. Maguire, 237–254 (NY: Oxford University Press, 2003).
26. Jose Barzellatto and Elizabeth Dawson, "Reproduction and Sexuality in a Changing World: Reaching Consensus," in *Sacred Rights: The Case for Contraception and Abortion in World Religions* (Ch. 12), edited by Daniel C. Maguire, 255–271 (NY: Oxford University Press, 2003). (Also, in the text, please add Elozabeth Dawson's name where the text says "Demography expert Jose Barzellato," make that "Demography experts Jose Barzellatto and Elizabeth Dawson.")
27. Jean Reith Schroedel, *Is the Fetus a Person?: A Comparison of Policies Across the Fifty States* (Ithaca, NY: Cornell University Press, 2000), 39.

28. In *Meeting of Parliamentarians from Latin America and the Caribbean on Induced Abortion* (Bogata, Colombia: Centro De Investigaciones Sobre Dinamica Social 1998), 27.
29. Peter Brown, *The Body and Society: Men, Women, and Sexual Renunciation in Early Christianity* (New York: Columbia University Press, 1988), 6.
30. Laurie Zoloth, in Maguire, *Sacred Rights*, 31–32.
31. Ibid.
32. See Daniel C. Maguire, *Sacred Choices: The Right to Contraception and Abortion in Ten World Religions* (Minneapolis: Fortress Press, 2001).
33. John T. Noonan Jr., *Contraception* (Cambridge, MA: Harvard University Press, 1986).
34. Christine Gudorf, in Maguire, *Sacred Rights*, 66.
35. Daniel A. Dombrowski and Robert Deltete, *A Brief Liberal, Catholic Defense of Abortion* (Urbana: University of Illinois Press, 2000), 56.
36. See John T. Noonan Jr., ed., *The Morality of Abortion: Legal and Historical Perspectives* (Cambridge, MA: Harvard University Press, 1970), 28–29.
37. Thomas Aquinas, *Summa Theologiae* III, q. 18, a. 3.
38. See Fazhur Rahman, "The Status of Women in Islam: A Modernist Interpretation," in *Separate Worlds: Studies of Purdah in South Asia*, edited by Hannan Papanek and Gail Minault (New Delhi: South Asia Boo, 1982), 89–90.
39. Sa'diyya Shaikh, "Family Planning, Contraception, and Abortion in Islam: Undertaking Khilafah," in *Sacred Rights: The Case for Contraception and Abortion in World Religions*, edited by Daniel Maguire (NY: Oxford University Press, 2003), 105–128.
40. D. Atighetchi, The position of Islamic tradition on contraception. *Med Law* 13, nos. 7–8 (1994): 717–725. PMID: 7731352.
41. Ibid., 54.
42. See Daniel C. Maguire, *Ethics: A Complete Method for Moral Choice* (Minneapolis: Fortress Press, 2009), 232–233..
43. Thomas Aquinas, *Summa Theologiae*, II, q. 10, a. 11.

PART III
DIFFERENT WAYS OF MAKING FAMILIES

CHAPTER 13

ADOPTION, PERSONAL STATUS, AND JEWISH LAW

MICHAEL J. BROYDE

Judaism did not recognize the Roman institution of adoption since the Roman concept is directed toward substituting a legal fiction for a biological fact and thus creating the illusion of a natural relationship between the foster parents and the adopted son. Judaism stated its case in no uncertain terms: . . . the natural relationship must not be altered. Any intervention on the part of some legal authority would amount to interference with the omniscience and original plan of the Maker. The childless mother and father must reconcile themselves with the fact of natural barrenness and sterility. Yet they may attain the full covenantal experience of parenthood, exercise the fundamental right to have a child and be united within a community of I-thou-he. There is no need to withhold from the adopted child information concerning his or her natural parents. The new form of parenthood does not conflict with the biological relation. It manifests itself in a new dimension which may be separated from the natural one.

—Rabbi Joseph B. Soloveitchik[1]

THERE are two basic models of adoption found in legal systems. One framework has a full legal category of adoption, by which children become—as a matter of law—as if they were born to the adoptive parents and the original biological relationship is severed. The other construct has no legal category of adoption at all and denies that children become as a matter of law as if they were born to the adoptive parents, but instead views such situations as a form of raising the children of another, or long-term foster care. Jewish law (like Islamic law[2] and the ancient common law[3]) does not have a category of full adoption,[4] but merely of long-term foster care.[5] Modern American law[6]—like the Code of Hammurabi,[7] Roman law,[8] and the Napoleonic code[9]—has a policy of full legal adoptions. The differences between these two approaches are quite dramatic. This article will focus on Jewish law, and will allow the reader to see how Jewish law—with no legal category of adoption—addresses situations where children need a new home.

Why Is There No Adoption in Jewish Law?

Jewish law (*halakha*) did not and does not have a court system with juridical authority to change people's most basic family law status. When disputes arise in family matters, they are treated as factual disputes under the law—but basic status issues cannot be changed by the legal system or judicial decree. Mother and father (and, by extension, brothers and sisters), once determined at birth, remain parents (and blood relatives), and cannot have that status removed. Indeed, the inability of the court system to change personal status is a general theme of all of Jewish family law.

Four examples—from dramatically different areas and eras of Jewish family law, but all sharing the underlying model of family law as governing issues of status—make this clear within Jewish law. The first example is from the most basic area of family law, namely marriage and divorce. As the Talmud explains, marriage and divorce are essentially private acts—or contracts—which do not require a court system, permission from a judge, or a license from government.[10] Courts cannot create marriages or end them. Annulments or divorce are essentially beyond the reach of Jewish law or a Jewish court.[11] A Jewish court can, in exceptional situations, order a husband to give a Jewish divorce, and a wife to accept one (and it even use physical force in a small set of cases[12]), but it cannot grant the writ of divorce itself. Marriage and divorce are private status issues and fundamentally beyond the reach of the Jewish court systems.[13]

A second example is in the modern Jewish law discussion of artificial insemination.[14] Although there is a wide-ranging debate within Jewish law about the propriety of such conduct, no one proposes that a husband who consents to the artificial insemination of his wife with sperm other than his own is the legal father of the resulting baby as a matter of Jewish law, as he is not such as a matter of biological fact.[15] A similar discussion takes place in the area of surrogate motherhood and cloning.[16] Jewish legal scholars were forced to come to grips with some of the religious challenges in vitro poses, which other traditions are now finding out on their own as well.[17] Biological fatherhood and motherhood are status issues in Jewish law and beyond judicial reordering.

Yet another example is the discussion of child custody, which will be elaborated in Part IV of this article. Although there is a wide-ranging and intense dispute among various Jewish law decisors of the medieval era as to whether Jewish law can ever take custody of children away from fit parents and give the children to more fit "strangers," such as grandparents, it is always made clear in the discussion that the basic issue is of "mere" custody, and not who is the parent. Fundamental notions of parenthood are immutable.[18]

A further example is sex change surgery. According to Jewish law, the removal of sexual organs is prohibited; hence, sex reassignment surgery is prohibited according to Biblical law for men,[19] and it is disputable whether the removal of sexual organs is a Biblical or rabbinic prohibition for women.[20] What is the status of a person who actually has such an operation? Jewish law is clear that a person who has a sex change operation does not, in fact change his or her gender according to Jewish law. Gender, too, is immutable. The earliest discussion concerning the sexual status of a transsexual is found in the twelfth-century commentary of Rabbi Abraham Ibn Ezra,[21] where he, quoting eleventh-century authority Rabbenu Hananel, states that intercourse between a man and another man, in whom the sexual organs of a woman have been fashioned, constitutes a violation of the Biblical prohibition of homosexuality, despite the presence of apparently female sexual organs. Thus, Ibn Ezra rules that sexual status cannot be changed surgically, for if this person were now legally a woman, no violations of the sodomy laws could occur. This view is, indeed, the view accepted by Jewish law authorities.[22] Primary sexual status cannot be changed.[23] For all religious traditions—Judaism included—it remains an easy answer to reach, but enormously complicated to put into practice.[24] Indeed, the contrary view—which has gained some currency in contemporary Jewish law—has been to reformulate the problem away from questions of gender status to question about presence or absence of particular sexual organs, in order to move away from the status issue, which is functionally uncontested.[25]

Thus, understanding how Jewish law has consistently viewed its own judicial and legal power in the area of family law allows adoption to be placed in context. Jewish law views status issues such as parenthood as matters of natural law, which can be adjudicated by a Jewish law court when in dispute,[26] but cannot be changed once established.[27]

The Theoretical Basis for Parental Custody: The Predicate to Adoption

The initial question in all adoption determinations is frequently unstated: by what "right" do natural parents have custody of their children?[28] Two very different theories, one called "parental rights" and one called "best interest of the child," exist in Jewish law. These two theories are somewhat in tension, but they lead to similar results in many cases, as the best interests of the child will often coincide with granting parents rights. By what right parents have custody of their children is simply another way of considering when they should not.

There is a basic dispute within Jewish law as to why and through what legal claim parents have custody of their children. Indeed, this dispute is crucial to understanding why Jewish law accepts that a "fit" parent is entitled to child custody—even if it can be shown that others can raise the child in a better manner.[29] It also sets parameters for when adoption is proper.

Rabbi Asher ben Yehiel (R. Asher),[30] in the course of discussing the obligation to support one's natural children, advances what appears to be a naturalist theory of parental rights. R. Asher asserts two basic rules. First, there is an obligation (for a man)[31] to support one's children, and this obligation is, at least as a matter of theory, unrelated to one's custodial relationship (or lack thereof) with the child, with one's wife, or with any other party.[32] A man who has children is Biblically obligated to support them. Following logically from this rule, R. Asher further states[33] that, *as a matter of law*, the parents are always entitled to custody against all others.[34] Of course, R. Asher would agree that in circumstances in which the father or mother are factually incapable of raising the children—are legally unfit as parents—they would not remain the custodial parents.[35] However, R. Asher appears to adopt the theory that the father and mother are the presumptive custodial parents of their children based on their obligations and rights as natural parents, subject to the limitation that even natural parents cannot have custody of their children if they are factually unfit to raise them.[36] While this understanding of the parents' rights is not quite the same as a property right, it is far more a right (and duty) related to possession than a rule about the "best interest" of the child. The position of R. Asher seems to have a substantial foundation in the works of a number of authorities.[37]

There is a second theory of parental custody in Jewish law, the approach of Rabbi Solomon ben Aderet (Aderet).[38] Aderet indicates[39] that Jewish law always accepts—as a matter of law—that child custody matters be determined according to the "best interest of the child." Thus, Aderet rules that in a case where the father is deceased, the mother does not have an indisputable legal claim to custody of the children. Equitable factors which make up a determination of the best interest of the child, are the *sole* determinant of custody. This *responsum* is generally read as a theory for all child custody determinations.[40] Aderet maintains that all child custody determinations involve a single legal standard: *the best interest of the child*, regardless of the specific facts involved, and this is the standard to be used to place children in the custody of non-parents as well.[41] According to this approach, the "rules" that one encounters in the field of child custody are not really "rules of law" at all, but rather the presumptive assessment by the Talmudic Sages as to what generally is in the best interest of children.[42] Jewish law presumes that parents are the most fit guardians of the children.

An enormous theoretical difference exists between R. Asher and Aderet. According to R. Asher, parents[43] have an intrinsic right to raise their progeny, unless unfit. In order to remove children from parental custody, it must be shown that these parents are unfit for that role and that some alternative arrangement to raise these children consistent with the parents' wishes and lifestyle, either through the use of relatives as agents or in some other manner,[44] cannot be arranged.[45] According to Aderet, the law allows the permanent transfer of custodial rights (quasi-adoption) in any situation where it can be shown that the children are not being raised in their best interests and that another would raise them in a manner more in line with those interests.[46]

This legal dispute is not merely theoretical: the particular *responsa* of Rabbis Asher and Aderet, elaborating on these principles, present vastly differing rulings as a result. Aderet rules that when the father is deceased, typically *it is in the best interest of the child to be placed in quasi-adoption with male relatives of the father rather than with the mother*; R. Asher rules that as a matter of Jewish law, *custody is always to be granted to a parent (unless he or she is unfit); quasi-adoption is a last resort.* To Aderet, the legal rule provides the answer; to Asher, equitable principles relating to best interest do.

These two competing approaches provide the relevant framework to analyze many of the theoretical disputes present in prototypical cases of child custody disputes that often form the predicate to quasi-adoption in the Jewish tradition. According to one theory, children are only taken from their parents in cases of categorical unfitness; according to the other approach, quasi-adoption is *always* proper in the "best interests of the child."

Jewish Law and Adoption

Although the institution of adoption, through its widespread use in Roman law,[47] was well known in Talmudic times, the redactors of Jewish law willfully refused to recognize such an institution within Jewish law. Rather, they created an institution which they called "A Person Who Raises Another's Child,"[48] which is quasi-adoption. Unlike either Roman law or current *civil* adoption law, this institution does not change the legal parents of the person whose custody has changed.[49] One who raises another's child is an agent of the natural parent; and like any agency rule in Jewish law,[50] if the agent fails to accomplish the task delegated, the obligation reverts to the principal. Thus, the Biblical obligations, duties, and prohibitions of parenthood still apply between the natural parents and the child whose custody they no longer have.[51]

This is not to diminish the value of this form of quasi-adoption. The same Talmudic statement that denies adoption posits that such conduct is meritorious, and thus encouraged. Rabbi Samuel Eliezer Edels,[52] in his commentary on this passage in the Talmud, notes that the value and importance of raising others' children is not limited to orphans, but applies also in situations where the children's parents are alive but cannot take care of the children.[53] However, those who raise the child of another are still obligated in the duty of procreation, and do not fulfill their obligation through adoption. The rationale for this is clear: while raising the child of another is meritorious conduct, this is not an act of procreation, and these are not the natural children of the person caring for them and cannot take the place of one's obligation to procreate.[54]

In modern times, the erudite reflections of noted Talmudist and philosopher Rabbi Joseph B. Soloveitchik sum up the Jewish law view. He states:

> Judaism saw the teacher as the creator through love and commitment of the personality of the pupil. Both become *personae* because an I-Thou community is formed. That is why Judaism called disciples "sons" and masters "fathers." . . . Our Talmudic sages stated, "Whoever teaches his friend's son Torah acquires him as a natural child" (Sanhedrin 19b). . . . Judaism did not recognize the Roman institution of adoption since the Roman concept is directed toward substituting a legal fiction for a biological fact and thus creating the illusion of a natural relationship between the foster parents and the adopted son. Judaism stated its case in no uncertain terms: what the Creator granted one and the other should not be interfered with; the natural relationship must not be altered. Any intervention on the part of some legal authority would amount to interference with the omniscience and original plan of the Maker. The childless mother and father must reconcile themselves with the fact of natural barrenness and sterility. Yet they may attain the full covenantal experience of parenthood, exercise the fundamental right to have a child and be united within a community of I-thou-he. There is no need to withhold from the adopted child information concerning his or her natural parents. The new form of parenthood does not conflict with the biological relation. It manifests itself in a new dimension which may be separated from the natural one. In order to become Abraham, one does not necessarily have to live through the stage of Abram. The irrevocable in human existence is not the natural but the spiritual child; the threefold community is based upon existential, not biological, unity. The existence of I and thou can be inseparably bound with a third existence even though the latter is, biologically speaking, a stranger to them.[55]

Rabbi Soloveitchik's view—fully reflective of the Jewish legal tradition—is that the process of quasi-adoption is special, sacred, a manifestation of holiness, and covenantal. It is such precisely because it is one of choice, like a student-teacher relationship,[56] and thus different from—and not to be confused with—natural parenthood, which lacks these basic covenantal components. Biological relationships are less covenantal in nature—because of the absence of choice—than relationships of selection (such as husband and wife, student and teacher, or as Rabbi Soloveitchik highlights, adoptee and adoptor) precisely because the central characteristic of covenant is selection and choice.

Contrasting the view of Jewish law with American law is deeply illuminating of both systems. Between 1860 and the end of World War II, all states passed adoption and child welfare acts that closely scrutinized requests for adoption. Their basic theme and thrust was that "[a]doption laws were designed to imitate nature."[57] They were intended to put children in an environment where one could not determine that they had been adopted; even the children themselves many times did not know. The law reflected this, and severed all parental rights and duties with an adopted child's natural parents and reestablished them in total with the adoptive parents, as per the Roman model of adoption law. Significant change in adoption practice has occurred in the last thirty years, the most important regarding the ability or propriety of a state to seal its adoption records—an issue which goes to the very heart of the current American approach to adoption. If adoption records cannot or should not be sealed, then it is beyond the state's power to create an adoption system which effectively mimics the creation of a new parental unit, since the children will become aware of the fact that they have biological parents separate from their adoptive parents. Historically, almost all states sealed adoption records and provided virtually no access. The original birth records were sealed, and if, by coincidence, the adopted child was to meet and marry a natural sibling, the state would permit such a marriage since the adopted child would have no legal relationship with his or her natural family. The "right to know" controversy has resulted in a number of states granting adoptees (upon attaining their majority) access to all the information collected. Once children have a right to know who their natural parents are, the adoption law must reflect the dichotomous relationship between one's natural parents and one's adoptive parents;[58] These tensions have not yet been resolved in American law. Most states still ascribe to adoption law the ability to totally recreate maternal and paternal relationships notwithstanding the knowledge of one's biological parents. Along with their ability to completely recreate parental relationships, states also maintain the ability to legally destroy any such relationships. It is well within the power of the state to not only create new parental rights and duties, but also to remove the rights of a parent towards a child and the duties of a parent to a child as well.

Quasi-Adoption as Granting Some Parental Rights

Even as the Jewish tradition does not have an institution of real adoption, certain nonbiblical aspects of parenthood established by the rabbis of the Talmudic era have been connected to custody rather than parenthood, and thus have been granted to adoptive parents. For example, in Talmudic times it was decreed that the possessions, earnings, and findings of a minor child belong to his or her father.[59] Although the wording of the Talmud refers only to *father*, it is clear from later discussions that this law applies to anyone who supports the child, i.e., adoptive parents.[60] The reason for the rabbinic decree is that it was equitable that one who supports a child should receive the income of that child.[61] Therefore, a financially independent minor does not transfer his or her earnings to his or her parents.[62] Similarly, the earnings of an adopted child go to his or her adoptive parents since the rationale for the decree applies equally well to biological and adopted children.[63] A similar line of reasoning allows adoptive parents to perform the redemption of the firstborn ritual (*pidyon haben*, in Hebrew) described in Numbers 18:1 for their adopted son if he is a firstborn (to his natural parents).[64]

However, one who raises another's child does not assume the Biblical prohibitions or obligations associated with having a child of one's own. For example, regardless of who is currently raising the child, it is never permitted for a natural parent to marry his or her child; on the other hand, the assumption of custody cannot raise to a Biblical level the prohibition of incest between a parent and the adopted child.[65] Indeed, the Talmud explicitly discusses whether or not adopted children raised in the same home may marry each other, and concludes that such marriages are permitted.[66] One medieval authority, Rabbi Judah of Regensberg,[67] decreed that such marriages not be performed,[68] but this decree has not been generally accepted,[69] and in situations where there is a known, open[70] adoption, such marriages are permitted.[71]

Other examples of adoptive parents being treated as natural parents can be found in the areas of ritual law. For example, while the rabbis prohibited two unrelated unmarried people of the opposite sex from rooming together alone (in Hebrew, the laws of *yihud*),[72] it is widely held that these rules do not apply in the adoption scenario. Although some commentators disagree,[73] many maintain that it is permissible for an adopted child to room and live with his adopted family[74] notwithstanding the *prima facie* violations of the prohibition of isolation.[75] As one authority has noted, without this lenient rule, the institution of raising another's child would disappear.[76] The same is said for the general prohibition of people unrelated to each other engaging in kissing or hugging, which these same authorities permit in situations where the relationship between the adoptive parents and the child is functionally similar to a natural relationship.[77] The basic argument is simple: One's children are exempt from the general prohibitions of physical interactions with the opposite sex, as no erotic intent is generally present. The same is true for quasi-adopted children.

Another example of a change in Jewish ritual law due to the quasi-adoption of a child appears in the obligation of mourning. Adopted children are no longer obligated to, for instance, recite the mourner's prayer (*kaddish*) upon the death of their natural parents—instead, there is an incumbent obligation to mourn upon the death of their adoptive parents.[78] This is so because the institution of mourning as we know it is totally rabbinic in nature, and seems to be a proper reflection of the sadness one feels when one who raised a person passes on.[79] Numerous other examples exist of rabbinic institutions that are not strictly applied in the context of raising another's child, since Jewish law would like to encourage this activity.[80]

Notwithstanding the high praise Jewish law showers on a person who raises another's child,[81] it is critical to recognize that the institution of "adoption" in Jewish law is radically different from the adoption law of American jurisdictions. In Jewish law adoption operates on an agency theory. The natural parents are always the parents; the adoptive parents never are—they are merely agents of the birth parents (or the rabbinical courts). While a number of incidental areas of parental rights are associated with custody and not natural parenthood, they are the exception and not the law. In the main, Jewish law focuses entirely on natural relationships to establish parental rights and duties. Jewish adoption looks much more like long-term foster care than like classic American adoption.

Open versus Closed Adoption

Secretive adoptions have always taken place in every society and every culture,[82] and there is a case history of such in the Jewish legal tradition as well.[83] Given the Jewish law view that adoption is really a misnomer, and that quasi-adoption or long-term foster care are better terms, the Jewish tradition favors "open" rather than "closed" adoptions: children always need to know that their current caretakers are not their parents. This point is first addressed directly by Rabbi Moses Sofer,[84] who notes that many different aspects of Jewish law are predicated on an awareness of who one's progeny are, and when people are raising other children in their home, they bear a duty to not hide that fact.[85] Similar views are expressed by many different authorities of the last century.

Rabbi Moses Feinstein, one of the leading decisors in America of the last century, notes in his *responsa*[86] that it is obvious that Jewish law mandates that the identity of the natural parents be shared with an adopted child, when the identity is known. Rabbi Feinstein posits that without this knowledge, such a child will never be certain of whom his or her natural siblings are and might[87] enter into an illicit marriage with a natural sibling. Indeed, a contemporary of Rabbi Feinstein, Rabbi Joseph Eliyahu Henkin, carries this view to its logical conclusion and posits that adoptive children should not call their parents by the term *mother* and *father* (since they are not, and using such titles would be deceptive) but should instead use the diminutive *aunt* and *uncle*, which more commonly denote in our society a respectful (but not biological) relationship.[88] Similar such views are posited by many other rabbinic decisors who have written on adoption, including Rabbi Gedalya Felder and Rabbi Mair Steinberg in their contemporary classic works, both of whom concur that adoptions in the Jewish tradition ought to be open adoptions.

Jewish law authorities generally posit that eight distinctly different pieces of information need to be provided:

1. Is the mother Jewish?
2. Is the mother eligible to marry in the Jewish community?
3. Is the mother single or married?
4. Who is the father, and is he eligible to marry in the Jewish community?
5. Is the child eligible to marry in the Jewish community?
6. Is the child a *kohein*, Levite, or Israelite?

7. Does the mother or father have other children (potential siblings) placed for adoption?
8. Is this child Jewish? May she marry a *kohein*?[89]

The purpose of these eight questions is to give a child a sense of who is the child's natural parents and to not allow the adoptive parents to pretend that they are the natural parents. Most authorities posit that closed adoptions are absolutely forbidden,[90] although Rabbi Feinstein is prepared to contemplate the possibility that if the identity of the biological parents cannot be determined, and yet one can ascertain that the children are Jewish, there may be no formal obligation to tell adopted children that they are adopted, although such is merely a good idea.[91] Rabbi Soloveitchick echoes this formulation when he states, "There is no need to withhold from the adopted child information concerning his or her natural parents."[92]

In those societies where secular law does not permit open adoption, Jewish law posits that the relevant information needs to be kept in some form of a communal central registrar that people have to check before they get married. Such registries were—and still are—kept in many communities in the United Kingdom, where for many years adoptions were closed.[93]

Conversion of Minor Children in the Course of Adoption

The ease with which adoption of Gentile children takes place within the community that adheres to Jewish law remains somewhat uncertain, and is fundamentally a question related to conversion law and not directly adoption. The crucial question is what are the proper standards for converting minors? Not surprisingly, that matter is in dispute.

In general, conversion to Judaism requires some form of acceptance of the commandments, (*kabbalat hamitzvot*), and without such acceptance, the conversion is widely considered void. **The conversion of a minor child is inherently different, since there clearly can be no obligation that the minor child accept mitzvot as he or she is without any legal ability to accept anything;** rather, his conversion is done with the consent of the rabbinical court. But, when ought a rabbinical court provide its consent?

No less than four views can be found on when a rabbinical court ought to consent.

- The first view is the view of Rabbis Kook and Elyashiv[94] that a bet din ought not to convert a child to Judaism unless it is nearly certain that the child will grow up to be religious. The consent of the rabbinical court is a substitute in this view

for the consent of the child, and no person would consent unless they expect to be observant in fact.
- The second school of thought is that of Rabbi Chaim Ozer Grodzinsky,[95] who advises not to perform such conversions unless the child will grow up to be religious, but recognizes that there will be situations where such a conversion can be validly done, even if the children will not grow up observant, as such a conversion is sometimes in the best interest of the child.
- The third view is the initial view of Rabbi Moshe Feinstein, which permits conversions when the child will attend an Orthodox school since in such a case it is likely that the child will be religious.[96] Rabbi Ovadiah Yosef indicates agreement with this view of Rabbi Moshe Feinstein.[97]
- The final view is the concluding view of Rabbi Feinstein, which is that it is always better for a person who is not obligated in mitzvot to be Jewish and thus the conversion of all minor children is possible.[98] Rabbi Joseph B. Soloveitchik adopted a view that reaches the same conclusion as the most liberal view of Rabbi Feinstein, albeit with a completely different mechanism (*kibosh*).[99]

At first blush, Rabbi Feinstein's final view is difficult to understand, but I think that the explanation is as follows. Rabbi Feinstein avers that every person is better off being Jewish if they can, but since conversion to Judaism generally requires acceptance of mitzvot, most people, even if they wanted to be Jewish, are not prepared to accept mitzvot in fact, and thus cannot convert. Indeed, the sinning associated with violating Jewish law makes conversion a bad idea (as a matter of Jewish law) for people who do not generally obey Jewish law. Minors, however, only benefit from being Jewish at the time of their conversion, since they cannot sin (as they are minors), whereas the theological benefits of Judaism accrue to them immediately even as they are not obligated in mitzvot. Thus, conversion is always of benefit to a minor at the time of conversion.

Obviously, the underpinning of Rabbi Feinstein's view is that the rabbinical court need only determine whether the conversion is of benefit to this child at this very moment without pondering into the uncertain future, a view which seems to be consistent with the general parameters of the rules of examining when something if of benefit to another.[100]

Conclusion

The Jewish tradition has no legal institution called "adoption," even as it recognized that there would be cases where people other than natural parents would care for children. Indeed, Jewish law denied itself the legal authority to authorize the transfer of parental status from the natural parents to the "adoptive" ones. This is consistent with the general rules of status in Jewish family law, where personal status and private acts are beyond the jurisdiction of the legal system. The refusal of Jewish law to create the new legal fiction of an adoptive family stands in stark contrast to Roman and modern American law, both of which recognize the rights of the court system to recast parenthood to fit into the custodial arrangement. The divergence between these law codes on a policy level in fact reflects a fundamental difference between the American and Jewish legal systems in terms of the scope and reach of the law. Jewish law articulates the fundamental inability of a governing body to destroy essential parental relationships created at birth. American jurisprudence grants itself that power; the law can artificially create parental relationships in the best interest of the child. Jewish jurisprudence denies itself that power; families once naturally created cannot ever be destroyed. However, as Rabbi Soloveitchik observes, the relationship between children and their nonbiological custodial parents is one of greater moral, philosophical, and religious significance than a natural parental relationship, as the former is predicated on voluntary choice, which is the hallmark of all sacred covenantal relationships.

Notes

1. Rabbi Joseph B. Soloveitchik, *Family Redeemed: Essays on Family Relationships*, edited by David Shatz and Joel Wolowelsky, 60–61 (New York: Meorot Harav Foundation, 2002).
2. See Kulsoom K. Ijaz, "Shifting Paradigms: Promoting an American Adoption Campaign for Afghan Children," *Syracuse Journal of International Law and Commerce* 42 (Fall 2014): 233. For an excellent article on the situation in Israel through a Jewish lens, see Mark Goldfeder, "The Adoption of Children in Judaism and in Israel: A Conceptual and Practical Review," *Cardozo Journal of International and Comparative Law* 22 (2014): 321.
3. C. M. A. McLauliff, "The First English Adoption Law and Its American Precursors," *Seton Hall Law Review* 16 (1986): 659–660. It was not until the late 1920s that adoption became possible in England without a special act of Parliament.
4. Indeed, as noted by Rabbi Ben Tzion Uziel, 2 *Sha'arei Uziel* 185(7), the Hebrew term for adoption ("*imut*") (derived from Psalm 80:16) connotes the grafting of a branch onto a tree and is a misnomer in Jewish law. The classical term used in Jewish law ought to be *benai amunim*, which means "the children of people who raise them."
5. For a side-by-side comparison from the Jewish, Catholic, and Muslim perspectives, *see* Daniel Pollack, Moshe Bleich, Charles J. Reid, Jr., and Mohammad H. Fadel, "Classical Religious Perspectives of Adoption Law," *Notre Dame Law Review* 79 (February 2004): 693.
6. See Arielle Bardzell and Nicholas Bernard, "Adoption and Foster Care," *Georgetown Journal of Gender and the Law* 16 (2015): 3.
7. *The Code of Hammurabi, King of Babylon: About 2250 B.C.*, ed. Robert Francis Harper (Chicago: University of Chicago Press, 1904), §185–186.
8. See John Francis Brosnan, "The Law of Adoption," *Columbia Law Review* 22 (1922): 332–342; Leo Albert Huard, "The Law of Adoption: Ancient and Modern," *Vanderbilt Law Review* 9 (1956): 743–763 (summarizing various ancient adoption laws).
9. See Leo Albert Huard, "Law of Adoption: Ancient and Modern," *Vanderbilt Law Review* 9 (1955–1956).

10. For a discussion of this, see Michael Broyde, *Marriage, Divorce and the Abandoned Wife in Jewish Law: A Conceptual Approach to the Agunah Problems in America* (Hoboken, NJ: KTAV, 2001).
11. The Talmud recounts six cases of annulment, three of which were pre-consummation, and thus suspect, and three of which involved duress in the creation of the marriage, thus causing the marriage to be naturally void.
12. See Shulchan Aruch Even Haezer 154 in many places.
13. This stands in sharp contrast to American law.
14. For a discussion of artificial reproduction in the Jewish and Israeli law context, see Avishalom Westreich, "Changing Motherhood Paradigms: Jewish Law, Civil Law, and Society," *Hastings Women's Law Journal* 28 (Winter 2017): 97 . See also Karin Carmit Yefet, "Feminism and Hyper-masculinity in Israel: A Case Study in Deconstructing Legal Fatherhood," *Yale Journal of Law and Feminism* 27 (2015): 47 .
15. Four lines of argument have been advanced by different scholars of the years. See Moses Feinstein, *Iggrot Moshe*, 1 Even Ha-Ezer 10, 71; 2 Even Ha-Ezer 11; 3 Even Ha-Ezer 11; J. Teitelbaum, 2 *Divrei Yoel* 110, 140; E. Waldenberg, "Test Tube Infertilization," *Sefer Asya* 5 (1986): 84–92 and 9 *Tzitz Eliezer* 51:4; Jacob Breish, 3 *Helkat Yakov* 45–48. Each of these, however, is consistent with the basic model of Jewish law: fatherhood, once established, is unchangeable.
16. See Michael Broyde, "Cloning People: A Jewish View," *Connecticut Law Review* 30 (1998): 2503–2535 and "The Establishment of Maternity and Paternity in Jewish and American Law," *National Jewish Law Review* 3 (1988): 117–152.
17. Tyler L. Smith, "Kosher Babies: How Israel's Approach to IVF Can Guide the United States in Fighting Separation of Church and State Abuses," *Indiana International & Comparative Law Review* 26 (2016): 292 .
18. See Eliav Shochatman, "The Essence of the Principles Used in Child Custody in Jewish Law," *Shenaton LeMishpat HaIvri* 5, no. 5738 (1977): 285 (Hebrew), and Ronald Warburg, "Child Custody: A Comparative Analysis," *Israel Law Review* 14 (1978): 480–503.
19. See Leviticus 22:24 and Babylonian Talmud, *Shabbat* 110b.
20. Compare Tosaphot, commenting on Babylonian Talmud, *Shabbat* 110b, s.v. *v'Hatanya* (rabbinic violation) with Maimonides, *Mishneh Torah, Sefer Kedusha, Hilkhot Isurei Biah* 16:11 (Biblical prohibition).
21. Ibn Ezra (1089–1164) of Toledo, Spain, was a well-known Biblical commentator; see his commentary on Leviticus 18:22.
22. A contrary view is taken by Rabbi Eliezer Waldenberg, 10 *Tzitz Eliezer* 25:26, 6, but his view is widely disagreed with. See, e.g., F. Rosner and M. Tendler, *Practical Medical Halacha* (New York: Rephael Society, Medical-Dental Section of the Association of Orthodox Jewish Scientists, 1980), 44. When discussing transsexual surgery, it is important to note that the law concerning children born with ambiguous sex status is different from that of sex reassignment surgery in an adult. See Rosner and Tendler at pp. 43–45; Moshe Steinberg, "Change of Sex in Pseudo-hermaphroditism," *Assia* 1 (1976): 142–153.
23. In contrast, American law does allow for gender change.
24. See Shawn Markus Crincoli, "Religious Sex Status and the Implications for Transgender and Gender-Nonconforming People," *FIU Law Review* 11, 137 (Fall 2015) (discussing specific examples of issues within a Jewish and Catholic setting).
25. Of course, this formulation is not without a logical Jewish law foundation, exactly because it concedes that while status is immutable, physical reality can change. This is well explained

in the work by Rabbi Edan Ben-Ephraim (who argues strongly for the phenotype approach) in his 2004 monograph on transsexuality, *Sefer Dor Tahepuchot* ("The Generation of Perversions"), p. 112ff. Ben-Ephraim cites rabbinic opinions in support of phenotype, including a letter appended by Rabbi Asher Weiss. Ben-Ephraim also infers support for phenotypic gender assignment from R. Hayyim Greinman (*Sefer Hidushim u-Beurim.* Kiddushin EH 44, p. 104.3, s.v. *ve-hineh*), R. Shaul Breisch (*Sheilat Shaul*, EH 9.1–2), and R. Yehoshua Neuwirth (oral communication cited in *Nishmat Avraham*, expanded second edition, YD 262.11, p. 326). But see R. Neuwirth's objection to Waldenberg's reasoning on intersex assignment to female (*Nishmat Avraham* EH 44.2, p. 268). See also R. Meir Amsel, "On Sex Change Surgery [Heb.]," *Ha-Maor* 25, no. 2 (Kislev-Tevet 5733 1972): 14–21, who views surgery as a total change in gender, though he also adumbrates the opposing view. R. Klein elaborates on a position against genotype in *Mishneh Halakhot*, 16:47. See also Hillel Gray, "Not Judging by Appearances: The Role of Genotype in Jewish Law on Intersex Conditions," *Shofar: An Interdisciplinary Journal of Jewish Studies* 30, no. 4 (2012): 126–148.

26. Such as uncertain paternity; see *Shulhan Arukh, Even Ha-Ezer* 3:8.
27. This is not the model with which Jewish law views monetary matters, where a Jewish law court has the right of eminent domain to transfer property (thus providing a basis for regulating all financial matters), or ritual law, where decisors of Jewish law are allowed to add observances or suspend them.
28. The Jewish law answer to this question has changed over time. See Yehiel S. Kaplan, "Child Custody in Jewish Law: From Authority of the Father to the Best Interest of the Child," *Journal of Law and Religion* 24 (2008–2009): 89.
29. This article will not address the extremely important question of *how* Jewish law determines parental fitness; for an excellent discussion of that topic, see Rabbi Gedalya Felder, 2 *Nahalat Tzvi* 282–287 (2nd ed.).
30. Known by the Hebrew acronym "Rosh," R. Asher (1250–1327) was a late (perhaps the last) Tosaphist who emigrated from Franco-Germany to Barcelona, then Toledo, Spain.
31. R. Asher might claim that the Talmudic rule which transferred custody of children (of certain ages) from the husband to the wife did so based on a rabbinic decree, and that this rabbinic decree gave the custodial mother the same rights (but not duties) as a custodial father; for a clear explication of this, see Rabbi Shemuel Alkalai, *Mishpatai Shemuel*, 90.
32. Rabbi Asher ben Yehiel, *Responsa of R. Asher (Rosh)* 17:7; see also Rabbi Judah ben Samuel Rosannes, *Mishnah Lemelekh, Hilkhot Ishut* 21:17.
33. *Responsa of R. Asher*, 82:2.
34. In any circumstance in which the marriage has ended and the mother is incapable of raising the children, the father is entitled to custody of his children, even if one were to agree that the children would be "better off" being raised by grandparents. Much of this basic dispute can be found in American law as well. See *Painter v. Bannister*, 140 N.W. 2d 152 (Iowa 1966).
35. This could reasonably be derived from the Babylonian Talmud, *Ketubot* 102b, which mandates terminating custodial rights in the face of life-threatening misconduct by a guardian.
36. In cases of divorce, in situations where the Talmudic rabbis assigned custody to the mother rather than the father, that custody is based on a rabbinically ordered transfer of rights, and the mother gets custody, even if the children are best served by another. For a longer discussion of this issue, see *responsa* of Rabbi Yehezkail Landau, *Nodah BeYehudah, Even Ha-Ezer* 2:89, and Rabbi Yitzhak Weiss, *Minhat Yitzhak* 7:113.

37. See, e.g., Rabbenu Yeruham ben Meshullam, *Toldot Adam veHava* 197a in the name of the *Geonim*, Rabbi Yitzhak deMolena, *Kiryat Sefer* 44:557 in the name of the *Geonim*, and Rabbi Yosef Gaon, *Ginzei Kedem* 3:62, where the theory of custodial parenthood seems to be based on an agency theory derived from the father's rights. R.
38. Known by the Hebrew acronym "Rashba," Rabbi Aderet (1235–1310) of Barcelona, Spain, was an eminent and prolific decisor.
39. *Responsa of Rashba Traditionally Assigned to Nahmanides*, 38. Throughout this chapter, the theory developed in the *responsa* is referred to as Rashba's, as most latter Jewish law authorities indicate that Rashba wrote these *responsa* and not Nahmanides; see Rabbi David Halevy, *Turei Zahav, Yoreh Deah* 228:50, and Rabbi Hayyim Hezkeyahu Medina, *Sedai Hemed, Klalai Haposkim* 10:9 (typically found in volume nine of that work).
40. For example, see *Otzar HaGaonim, Ketubot* 434, where this rule is applied even when the father is alive.
41. Perhaps this allows one to claim that this rule—custody is granted in the best interest of the child—is the rationale why, according to Rashba, Jewish law would not allow one to remove children from the home of their parents to be raised in the house of another who is better capable of raising the children unless the natural parents are unfit. See Sylvan Schaeffer, "Child Custody: Halacha and the Secular Approach," *Journal of Halacha and Contemporary Society* 6 (1983): 36–39.
42. See Warburg, "Child Custody," 496–498, and Shochatman, "Principles Used in Child Custody," 308–309.
43. It is this author's opinion that later authorities disagree as to the legal basis of the mother's claim. Most authorities indicate that the mother's claim to custody of the daughter is based on a transfer of rights from the father to the mother based on a specific rabbinic decree found in the Talmud. On the other hand, many other authorities understand the mother's claim to custody of boys under six to be much less clear as a matter of law and are inclined to view that claim based on an agency theory of some type, with the father's rights supreme should they conflict with the mother's.
44. For example, sending a child to a boarding school of the parent's choosing; see, e.g., 4 *P.D.R. (Piskai Din Rabbani)* 66 (1959), where the rabbinical court appears to sanction granting custody to the father, who wishes to send his child to a particular educational institution (a boarding school) which will directly supervise the child's day-to-day life.
45. It is possible that there is a third theory also. Rabbenu Nissim (Hebrew acronym "RaN," commenting on Babylonian Talmud *Ketubot* 65b), seems to accept a contractual framework for custodial arrangements. R. Nissim appears to understand that it is intrinsic in the marital contract (*ketubah*) that just as one is obligated to support one's wife, so too one is obligated to support one's children. This position does not explain why one supports children out of wedlock (as Jewish law certainly requires; see *Shulhan Arukh, Even Ha-Ezer* 82:1–7) or what principles control child custody determinations once the marriage terminates. *Mishnah LeMelekh, Hilkhot Ishut* 12:14 notes that R. Nissim's theory was not designed to be followed in practice.
46. As a matter of practice, this would not happen frequently. Indeed, this author has found no *responsa* which actually permit the removal of children from the custody of parents who are married to each other.
47. Frederick Parker Walton, *Historical Introduction to the Roman Law*, 4th ed. (Edinburgh: W. Green & Son, 1920), 72.

48. See Babylonian Talmud, *Sanhedrin* 19b. This is viewed as a righteous deed; see *Exodus Rabbah*, ch. 4.
49. Although it is true that there are four instances in the Bible in which adopted parents are called actual parents; see 1 Chronicles 4:18, Ruth 4:14, Psalm 77:16, 2 Samuel 21:8. These are assumed to be in a nonlegal context. See Babylonian Talmud, *Sanhedrin* 9b.
50. Israel Herbert Levinthal, *The Jewish Law of Agency, with Special Reference to the Roman and Common Law* (New York: [printed at the Conat Press, Philadelphia], 1923), 58–73.
51. J. Caro, *Shulhan Arukh, Even Ha-Ezer* 15:11.
52. Known by the Hebrew acronym "Maharsha," R. Edels (1555–1631) wrote his famous analytical commentary on the Talmud while an active communal leader of Eastern Europe (in what is now Poland). Interestingly, he adopted the surname Edels in tribute to his mother-in-law Edel, who covered all the expenses of his Yeshiva in Posen for some twenty years.
53. *Commentary of Maharsha*, Babylonian Talmud, *Sanhedrin* 19b.
54. *Shulhan Arukh, Even Ha-Ezer* 1:3–6. A contrary view is taken by Rabbi Shlomo Kluger in his commentary on *Shulhan Arukh, Even Ha-Ezer* 1:1. He posits that adoption is a form of procreation, since without the adult's actions these children would die. His opinion has been widely discredited.
55. Soloveitchik, *Family Redeemed*, 60–61.
56. Rabbi Soloveitchik quotes as a proof-text Maimonides, who states:

> This obligation [of teaching Torah] is to be fulfilled not only towards one's son and grandson. A duty rests on every scholar in Israel to teach all disciples, even if they are not his children, as it is said, "and you shall teach them to your children" (Deuteronomy 6:7). The oral tradition teaches: "Your children" includes your disciples, for disciples are called children as it is said: "And the sons of the prophets came forth" (II Kings 2:3).
>
> *Hilkhot Talmud Torah* [The Laws of Torah Study] 1:2.

57. Sanford N. Katz, "Re-writing the Adoption Story," *Family Advocacy* 5 (1982): 9–10.
58. See, e.g., Carol Amadio and Stewart Deutsch, "Open Adoption: Allowing Adopted Children to 'Stay in Touch' with Blood Relatives," *Journal of Family Law* 22 (1983): 59 .
59. Babylonian Talmud, *Baba Metzia* 12b.
60. J. Caro, *Shulhan Arukh, Hoshen Mishpat* 370, 2.
61. J. Falk, *Meirat Einaim*, commenting on ibid.
62. J. Caro, *Shulhan Arukh, Yoreh Deah* 370, 2.
63. Ibid.; Z. Mendal, *Be'er Haytaiv*, §4, on J. Caro, *Shulhan Arukh, Yoreh Deah* 370:2.
64. David Tzvi Hoffman, *Melamed Lehoil, Yoreh Deah* 97–98.
65. By inference the same can be said of adoptive siblings; see Hoffman, *Melamed Lehoil, Yoreh Deah* 15, 11 ("It is permitted to marry one's adopted sister").
66. Babylonian Talmud, *Sotah* 43b.
67. Also known as Rabbi Judah HaHasid (the Pious). He was a renowned ethicist and scholar of the Rhineland Jewish community (1150–1217).
68. Judah of Regesberg, *Sefer Ha'Hasidim*, Comm. 29. See also Babylonian Talmud, *Sotah* 43b.
69. See Moses Sofer, *Responsa* 2 *Yoreh Deah* 125.
70. See the next section.
71. See *Minhat Yitzhak* 4:49. Although legally permitted, few such marriages are actually performed; however, there was a time when such was exactly the motive of people who raised children other than their own in their household.

72. J. Caro, *Shulhan Arukh, Even Ha-Ezer* 22:2. According to one commentator, this rabbinic prohibition even included the rooming together of a married woman with a man not her husband. See Maimonides, *Mishneh Torah, Sefer Kedushah, Hilkhot Isurai Biah* 22:2.
73. M. M. Shneerson, *Zikhron Akedat Yitzhak* 4:33–37. For a complete list of those authorities agreeing with this position, see Aryeh Berzon, "Contemporary Issues in the Laws of Yichud," *Journal of Halacha and Contemporary Society* 13 (1986): 108.
74. This, for example, occurs when a couple adopts a boy, and the boy's adoptive father later dies, leaving the adopted child living alone with a woman not his natural mother.
75. See E. Waldenberg, 6 *Tzitz Eliezer* 40:21; C. D. Halevi, *Aseh Lekha Rav* 194–201. Rabbi Joseph B. Soloveitchik has also been quoted as permitting this. See Melech Schacter, "Various Aspects of Adoption," *Journal of Halacha and Contemporary Society* 4 (1982): 96. Rabbi Feinstein has also commented on this issue; see M. Feinstein, *Iggrot Moshe* 4 *Even Ha-Ezer* 64:2.
76. E. Waldenberg, 6 *Tzitz Eliezer* 226–228.
77. This matter is conceptually easier in this writer's opinion, as nonsexual touching is arguably permitted anyway in Jewish law, and the essential characteristic of this touching is that it is nonsexual. For more on this topic, see Babylonian Talmud *Kiddushin* 81b, and Rashi, Tosaphot, Ritva, and Yam Shel Shlomo *ad locum*; *Shulhan Arukh, Even Ha-Ezer* 21, 4–7; Gr"a, *Even Ha-Ezer* 21:19; *Pit'hai Teshuva, Even Ha-Ezer* 21:3 and *Iggrot Moshe*, 2 *Even Ha-Ezer* 14. For an article on this topic in English, see Rabbi Yehuda Herzl Henkin, "The Significant Role of Habituation in Halakha," *Tradition: A Journal of Orthodox Jewish Thought* 34, no. 3 (2000): 40.
78. M. Sofer, *Responsa*, 1 *Orah Hayyim* 174. Rabbi Sofer also notes the praise Jewish law lavishes upon one who raises another's child.
79. This issue is in dispute. Compare J. Caro, *Shulhan Arukh, Yoreh Deah* 398:1 with M. Isserles, commenting on J. Caro, *Shulhan Arukh, Yoreh Deah* 399:13.
80. See generally J. Caro, *Shulhan Arukh, Orah Hayyim* 139:3. See also A. Auli, *Magen Avraham*, commenting on Caro's *Shulhan Arukh, Orah Hayyim* 139:3, and M. Feinstein, *Iggrot Moshe*, 1 *Yoreh Deah* 161. For a summary of various laws of adoption, see Schacter, "Various Aspects of Adoption."
81. See Babylonian Talmud, *Sanhedrin* 19b.
82. See for example, Lucy S. McGough and Annette Peltier Falahahwazi, "Secrets and Lies: A Model Statute for Cooperative Adoption," *Louisiana Law Review* 60 (1999): 13.
83. See Rabbi Hayyim Bachrach, *Havot Yair* 92–93. These *responsa*, from just before the dawn of the eighteenth century, recount the story of a couple who (it was claimed) switched children with their maid after one of their own children died. Needless to say, many difficulties and questions arose from these actions. The solution advocated by one of the rabbis in this *responsa* is second-guessed by Rabbi Moses Sofer in *Teshuvot Hatam Sofer*, 2 *Even Ha-Ezer* 125.
84. In *Teshuvot Hatam Sofer*, 2 *Even Ha-Ezer* 125. Rabbi Sofer (1762–1839) lived in Hungary.
85. There is a dispute as to whether adopted children inherit from their adoptive parents; see *Lekutai Mair* 18:2. However, all agree that such children do not inherit by operation of the intestacy rules of Jewish law. Those who argue that such children inherit, do so based on the presumptive will of the parents. For more on this, see Rabbi Moshe Findling, "Adoption of Children," *Noam* 4 (1961): 65–93 (Hebrew).
86. *Iggrot Moshe*, 1 *Yoreh Deah* 162.
87. See *Beit Shmuel, Even Ha-Ezer* 13:1, who notes that this is a rabbinic fear and not grounded in Torah Law.

88. See Y. E. Henkin, *Kol Kitvai Hagaon Rav Yosef Eliahayu Henkin* 2:98 (1989). This letter is undated, but appears to be from the 1950s.
89. See Rabbi Gedalya Felder, *Nahalat Tzvi* 35–40 (2nd ed.), and Rabbi Mair Steinberg, *Lekutai Mair*, 19–23. The correctness of the final question is discussed in my "May the Daughter of a Gentile Man and a Jewish Woman Marry a Kohein," *Journal of Halacha and Contemporary Society* 52 (2009): 97–126.
90. *Minhat Yitzhak* 4:49. See also Rabbi Menashe Klein, *Mishnah Halakha* 4:49.
91. Moses Feinstein, *Iggrot Moshe, Yoreh Deah* 161–162. See also *Yam Shel Shlomo, Ketubot* 1:35; but see Moshe Sternbuch, *Teshuvot veHanhagot* 2, 678.
92. Soloveitchik, *Family Redeemed*, 61.
93. Meyer Steinberg, *Responsum on Problems of Adoption in Jewish Law*, edited and translated by Maurice Rose (London: Office of the Chief Rabbi, 1969), 11–12. Although the issues of accidental brother/sister incest seem rare, such cases clearly do arise. Consider, for example, Bob Herbert, "A Family Tale," *New York Times*, December 31, 2001, sec. A, p. 11, which notes:

    In 1979 Mr. Klahr met and began dating a woman named Micka Zeman. "One time her mother said to me, 'Gary, are you adopted?' I was dumbfounded. I said, 'No, I'm not.' She asked me that question because she knew her daughter was adopted and there were other kids around, but she didn't know which families had gotten them." Ms. Zeman was Mr. Klahr's sister. They dated for about six months. "My relationship with my sister is the kind of thing that could have you jumping out the window," said Mr. Klahr. "But we didn't know. Thank God we didn't get married."

    The reverse of this situation is discussed in *Israel v. Allen*, 195 Colo. 263; 577 P.2d 762; (Supreme Court of Colorado, 1978), which permitted adopted siblings to marry each other.
94. Rabbi Kook, *Da'at Kohen, Milah veGerut* 147–148 and Rabbi Shalom Yosef Elyashiv, *Kovetz Teshuvot YD* 2:55.
95. *Achiezer* 3:28.
96. See *Igrot Moshe YD* 1:158 and *EH* 4:26(3).
97. See *Yabia Omer EH* 2:3 and 2:4.
98. See *Igrot Moshe EH* 4:26(3) and see also *Igrot Moshe YD* 1:158.
99. See Rabbi Joseph B. Soloveitchik, "Community, Covenant and Commitment" at pages 21–22. (For an alternative explanation of Rabbi Soloveitchik's view, see Rabbi Tzi [Hershel] Schachter, *Nefesh Harav*, 245, in which Rabbi Soloveitchik's view is understood to be similar to the first view of *Igrot Moshe*.
100. *zachin le-adam shelo be-fanav*. For more on this issue, see "Zachin Le'adam shelo be-fanav," *Encylopedia Talmudit* 12:135–197. This issue is worthy of further analysis. It might well be that which view of the propriety of conversions to Judaism for minors who will not be religious one adopts depends on whether one thinks that such children can, in fact, reject the choice of Judaism made for them as children when they become adults. For more on this, see *Shulchan Aruch Yoreh Deah* 268:7 and commentaries ad locum.

CHAPTER 14

ISLAMIC PERSPECTIVES ON ADOPTION

FAISAL KUTTY

THROUGHOUT history, adoption has held a contentious and ambiguous role in the social imagination of many cultures. It goes without saying that adoption is a complex social, legal, and economic phenomenon that has existed in one form or another in most societies since ancient history. Some may believe that religion plays a minor role in adoption, but the reality is that "religion in family law generally and in adoption law particularly reveals a complex nexus of societal, familial, and individual interests."[1] Indeed, religion has been used to both advance and restrict adoption and similar child care arrangements. Some religions have encouraged adoptions while others have initially been interpreted to restrict it, and other religions continue to restrict or advocate alternative arrangements.[2]

There is the perception among both many Muslims and some non-Muslims that adoption per se is prohibited by the dictates of Islam.[3] However, adoption in Islam and Western adoption practices, international law with respect to children's rights, and Islamic dictates are more complex than this.

In order to understand adoption in the Islamic context it is important to have an appreciation of the nuances of Islamic law. This chapter will therefore begin with a brief background on Islamic law, its sources, principles, and methodology for development and evolution in Part I. The major focus of this chapter is Part II, which sets out a description of adoption and alternatives under classical Islamic law as understood and accepted by the orthodox Sunni[4] community. Part III will explore and highlight a few areas of tension and convergence with modern Western conceptions of adoption and child welfare. Part IV will briefly canvas some reinterpretation attempts and some potential areas of reform that scholars, jurists, and activists are contemplating.

At the outset, two *caveats* are in order. First, any endeavor that attempts to provide an overview of complex systems and institutions often runs the risk of oversimplification. Clearly, it is an impossible task to articulate a comprehensive discussion of the systems, institutions, and principles in a short chapter. Indeed, such a task can easily take up volumes. Therefore the chapter does not claim to provide an exhaustive study, but rather a basic or even cursory survey of some of the central issues and themes surrounding "adoptions" from within the Islamic tradition. Such a survey will hopefully contribute to a better understanding of the classical Islamic views on adoptions, provide some insights into some of the existing tensions and points of convergence, and mention some aspects of reformation and reinterpretation brought forth by scholars of today.

Second, we need to settle on an acceptable definition of adoption for the purposes of this chapter. This again necessitates simplification and will result in lack of nuance. Adoption can have the following definitions:

1) The legal creation of a parent-child relationship, with all the responsibilities and privileges thereof, between children and adults who are not their biological parents with the concomitant permanent severing of all connections and relationships with the biological parents;[5]
2) The legal creation of an artificial family relationship analogous to that of parents and child between a child and adults who are not the biological parents while not severing or negating the child's biological connection;[6]
3) Arranging for the care of children in homes with adults who are not their biological parents.[7]

Though far from exhaustive, these definitions provide a window into the spectrum of what could technically fall under the purview of adoptions (or variation thereof) in various cultures and societies. For the purposes of our discussion, we will use the first definition as the prevalent Western understanding. However, we would be lax, if we did not point out that there is nevertheless a growing push and indeed some significant movement on the ground in terms of seeing adoption moving closer to definition number two from above.[8] The third definition is far too broad for most observers to accept as satisfying the criteria to make up an adoption as opposed to guardianship or fostering, though it clearly is one of the objectives of adoption. It should also be noted that at least on the surface the last definition appears the closest to the pre-modern or classical[9] Sunni Islamic alternative proffered as adoption, *kafala*.[10]

Part I—Islamic Law

The first issue that must be addressed in dealing with the concept of adoption/guardianship under Islamic law is to define the term *Islamic law* itself. Islamic law, or legal derivatives known as *fiqh*, is often conflated and confused with the Shariʻa.[11] The Shariʻa is literally translated as the "path to the drinking fountain." The Shariʻa encompasses the legal, political, social, economic moral and spiritual worldview that practicing Muslims are supposed to be bound by. According to the prevalent Islamic view, all human legislation must conform to the divine will as discerned from the primary sources of the Shariʻa, the Qur'an and Sunna and understanding of *al dhawq al shar'i*, or intuitive knowledge of the purposes of the law.[12] God created human beings with the potential to ascertain the divine imperatives through rational thought and keeping in mind the higher objectives of the Shariʻa (*maqasid al sharīʻah*). The six *maqasid al sharīʻah* are preservation of life, property, family, religion, honor and *al aql* (reason or rational knowledge).[13]

The Qur'an is believed by Muslims to be the last revelation sent to mankind. The Qur'an is not a legal treatise, but rather lays down certain guidelines and general principles for an ideal civilized society. The Sunna[14] is the term used to refer to the normative behavior, decisions, actions, and tacit approvals and disapprovals of the Prophet. The Sunna was heard, witnessed, memorized, recorded, and transmitted from generation to generation.[15] They were compiled into collections of traditions, known as *ahadith*.[16] The traditions have the practical effect of elaborating upon and interpreting the principles laid down in the Qur'an. Along with the primary sources of Qur'an and Sunna, secondary sources of Islamic law such as *ijmaʻ* (community consensus), *qiyas* (analogical reasoning), *ijtihad* (independent reasoning or intellectual effort) and *urf* (custom) are expanded to create a body of law.[17] That said, Muslims believe that unlike revelation, humanity's understanding of revelation is fallible, therefore Islamic scholars do not feel that there is any contradiction between reason and revelation; reason is there to correct man's erroneous understanding of the *data revelata*.[18]

Naturally, there evolved much scholarship in this area after the death of the Prophet and numerous schools of jurisprudence in the loose sense of the word *schools* developed, of which five survived with significant following. The five dominant schools of jurisprudence are named after the respective founders: the Hanafi School (Abu Hanifah, d.767), the Maliki School (Malik ibn Anas, d.795), the Shafi'i School (al-Shafi'i, d.820), and the Hanbali School (Ahmad bin Hanbal d.855) and the Ja`fari School (Ja`far ibn Muhammad al-Sādiq, d.765). Of these, the first four are of the Sunni tradition and the fifth from the Shi'a tradition. The focus of this chapter is on the Sunni tradition.[19]

Classical Islamic legal rules developed over hundreds of years under jurists who propounded *fiqh* (derivative Islamic rules) using the primary sources of the Qur'an and Sunna and the secondary sources of *qiyas*, *ijmaʻ*, and *ijtihad*. This was done relying on the principles and consistent with the agreed upon methodology (even if the details may vary). In exercising *qiyas* and *ijmaʻ*, jurists engaged in *ijtihad* in crafting new rules and making sense of the Qur'an and Sunna in different social, economic, political and legal contexts.[20] This resulted in a great deal of diversity in what was considered to fall within the purview of *fiqh* oftentimes referred to as Islamic law.

Part II—Adoption in Pre-Modern or Classical Islamic Law

Adoption Per se

Notwithstanding diversity and legal pluralism, it appears that when it came to adoption, there was consensus among classical Sunni jurists that adoption as conventionally understood today (and practiced in pre-Islamic Arabia) is prohibited or *haram*. There are exceptions, with some classifying it *mubah* or an "act towards which religion is indifferent."[21] The prohibition is traced to the Qur'an and Prophetic traditions. As Mohamed Fadel notes, the primary sources negate the idea that someone other than the biological parents can be a parent.[22] He points out that the Qur'an 58:2 states "[t]heir mothers are only those who have given birth to them,"[23] and with respect to the father the Qur'an 33:4–5 states:

> God did not make those whom you call your sons your sons [in reality]. That is no more than an expression from your mouths and God speaks the truth and He guides to the [correct] way. Attribute them to their fathers: That is more just in the eyes of God, but if you know not the names of their fathers, then they are your brothers in faith and your dependents.[24]

Pre-Islamic Arab society practiced a form of adoption similar to the common Western practice, which was known as *tabanni*.[25] Pursuant to this practice the biological child of one was made the child of the adoptive parent(s) and the child stood in the same footing with the other children of the adoptive parent(s).[26] When referred to by classical jurists, *tabbani* is defined as an act whereby one person takes another as a son (*ittakhadhahu ibnam waladan*).[27]

For explication of the above-mentioned verse, pre-modern scholars relied on the experience of the Prophet, which is reflected as the Sunna. The traditions teach that the Prophet Muhammad adopted a freed slave by the name of Zayd b. Haritha prior to the advent of Islam.[28] Zayd reportedly chose to stay with the Prophet rather than returning to his father who had come to claim him after Zayd was freed. Zayd accepted the Prophet's offer to "adopt" (*tabanna*) him. As was customary at the time, a declaration of the adoption was publicized and Zayd b. Haritha became known as Zayd b. Muhammad.

Zayd was married to Zaynab b. Jahsh, the Prophet's cousin, but later divorced her. Subsequently the Prophet married her.[29] Pre-Islamic custom considered it taboo for a man to marry the divorced wife of his adopted son due to the fictive relationship of descent created upon public announcement of an adoption. Moreover the Qur'an also prohibited a man from marrying a woman divorced by his son.[30] Naturally, the Prophet came under heavy attack from both those who thought this was against prevalent custom and those who thought this violated the Qur'anic prohibition on marrying a son's divorcee. Both classical/pre-modern and contemporary jurists are in agreement that Qur'an 33:4–5 and 33:37–40 were revealed to defend the Prophet and to clarify the Islamic position vis-à-vis marriage to an adopted son's divorced wife. Qur'an 33:4–5 asserted that a child's pedigree must be traced back to the biological father,[31] while Qur'an 33:37–40 stated:

> Behold! Thou didst say to one who had received the grace of Allah and thy favour: "Retain thou (in wedlock) thy wife, and fear Allah." But thou didst hide in thy heart that which Allah was about to make manifest: thou didst fear the people, but it is more fitting that thou shouldst fear Allah. Then when Zaid had dissolved (his marriage) with her, with the necessary (formality), We joined her in marriage to thee: in order that (in future) there may be no difficulty to the Believers in (the matter of) marriage with the wives of their adopted sons, when the latter have dissolved with the necessary (formality) (their marriage) with them. And Allah's command must be fulfilled.[32]
>
> Muhammad is not the father of any of your men, but (he is) the Messenger of Allah, and the Seal of the Prophets: and Allah has full knowledge of all things.

Zayd's adoption was quickly rescinded and his name returned to his former name upon the revelation of these verses. This incident and the resulting verses made it Islamically permissible for a man to marry the divorced wife of his adopted son contrary to prevailing custom in Arabia. The Qur'an also negated the creation of any fictive relationship of lineage. Scholars have also interpreted the verses to postulate that consanguinity is not deemed or achieved through adoption. It appears that pre-modern jurists accepted the view that the interplay of the incident and the verses prohibited adoption and therefore did not fully explore any alternative readings or explore the situational context (*azbab ul nuzul*) in any depth.

Reviewing the classical *fiqh* and the work of more recent scholars examining classical writings suggests a number of reasons why *tabbani* may have been prohibited. These range from pragmatic explanations to those entailing broader social and ethical considerations.

Some orientalists suggest that *tabbani* may have been prohibited because it was simply the effect—intended or unintended—of allowing the Prophet to fulfill his desire to marry Zaynab b. Jahsh, the divorcee of Zayd b. Haritha. This polemical position is quickly dismissed when you consider a holistic reading of Qur'an 33:37, which makes it clear that the Prophet was opposed to Zayd divorcing his wife and in fact hesitated in marrying her even after her divorce for fear of what people might think given the taboo.[33] The verse makes it clear that God ordered him to marry Zaynab and cautioned him to fear God and not people.[34] Though it may be argued that this was merely a self-serving objection on his part, believers would obviously find it difficult to accept the legitimacy of this position because it questions the very motives of the Prophet. Moreover, there would have been no need to extend the adoption prohibition to the entire Muslim community if the purpose of the verse was to allow the Prophet an exception. Indeed, there are instances of exemptions being made for the Prophet and even his wives that are not applicable to other Muslims.[35] In other words the verse could have been more specific to defend the Prophet only if it was meant to be a self-serving verse to facilitate or approve of the Prophet's selfish motive as alleged by some orientalists.

There are also those who argue that one of the objectives of prohibiting *tabbani* was to clarify the degrees of consanguinity. *Tabbani* was seen as contrary to the Qur'an's emphasis on maintaining authenticity in lineage, consanguinity and upholding truth and acknowledging reality.[36]

Others have argued that the prohibition was meant to "contain and in certain cases to root out social evils."[37] Adoption abuses ranged from the Arab practice of accumulation, to inheriting from adopted children, to perpetuating gender discrimination.[38] Accumulation essentially involved the adoption of sons—and only sons—to expand the clan to add to the clan's prestige through numbers and to add extra hands for tribal warfare and work.[39] This also allowed for children to be adopted with the intention of usurping their property.[40] Secondly, given that *tabbani* enabled adults, even those with known fathers, to be adopted, jurists saw at least two other possible issues. It arose from the fact that if a child could adopt a new father and thus circumvent his filial duties, then his biological father would not be able to rely on the child in his old age as is expected in collectivist societies. Conversely, the possibility of such adoptions would also give biological fathers less incentive to care for their children when they were young. Arguably adoption was not in the best interest of either the biological parents or the children in such situations. Lastly, another form of abuse was the perpetuation and aggravation of gender discrimination because only sons were adopted.[41] Therefore it could be argued that *tabbani* was also objected to due to Islam's broader ethical vision to address gender inequality over time.

Yet another argument revolves around the idea of the significance of lineage and family identity. As M. S. Sait notes, "the Qur'an not only confers the basic rights of name, identity and paternity but reiterates a broad framework for the physical, material, emotional and spiritual rights of the child."[42] According to many scholars, the practice of *tabbani* entailed a complete "erasure of natal identity."[43] This of course is totally contrary to the clear teachings of the Qur'an and Sunna, which ensures that a child has the right to know his or her biological parents' identity and lineage.

The practice of *Tabanni* may have had negative effects but it also would have alleviated some of the pressure with respect to caring for orphans and foundlings. The existence or nonexistence of adoption laws in most Muslim countries is directly attributable to the purported "prohibition" of this practice in classical iterations of Islamic law. To make it even more confusing, different Muslim countries apply different iterations of classic Islamic law. That said, there are laws, rules, and procedures in many of these nations and within classical *fiqh* which provide alternatives or similar practices for the care of orphans and foundlings. These practices included *raadah* (establishment of milk bonds through suckling), *kafala* (fostering or sponsorship), and *istilhaq* or *al-iqrar bi-l-nasab* (acknowledgment of paternity both true and fraudulent). Each of these were employed to work around the prohibition of *tabanni*.

Radaah (suckling): In pre-Islamic Arabia there was a practice whereby natural parents would hire outside mothers to nurse their children up to a certain period of time.[44] In fact, it was a popular custom for city dwelling Arabs to send their children to be taken care of and be suckled in the free and healthy surroundings of the desert.[45] Indeed, the Prophet himself was only suckled by his mother Amina for seven days and then sent off to Thuwaibah[46] before ending up with his long-term wet nurse Halimah whom he would later say he considered like his mother.[47] Halimah suckled the Prophet for two years and he lived with her in the desert for another two years. The practice was approved by the Qur'an and therefore it was not opposed by Islamic jurists.[48] *Radaah* (suckling) is literally translated as "sucking breast and drinking its milk." There are strict technical conditions to make this legally effective,[49] but it essentially requires that a child be breastfed. Classical *fiqh* established that once a baby is breastfed by any woman then a biological link is established. This biological link makes them *mahram* (prohibited in marriage) to each other.[50] This is based on the Qur'an 4:23 which states:

> Prohibited to you [for marriage] are your mothers, your daughters, your sisters, your father's sisters, your mother's sisters, your brother's daughters, your sister's daughters, your [milk] mothers who nursed you, your sisters through nursing, your wives' mothers, and your step-daughters under your guardianship [born] of your wives unto whom you have gone in.[51]

This Qur'anic dictate was reinforced by several *ahadith* of the Prophet reported in all of the leading collections of Hadith.[52] These primary and secondary sources support the notion that other than the birth mother, any lactating woman can be the milk-mother of a child and give that child the same birthrights as her own. It is agreed upon by a majority of the classical jurists that five nursing sessions will establish marriage prohibition.[53] There are differences between the schools when less than five sessions are involved.[54] There are some additional technical requirements and conditions which are detailed in the *fiqh* of the various schools.[55] Once this milk-bond is established then according to a majority of classical jurists the foster mother has rights to the child that are identical to those of any birth mother.

Being a milk-mother means that the suckled child will be a child to the wet nurse's husband, a sibling to her children, and a relative to all extended family members.[56] This is seen as the quick fix when it comes to Islamic adoptions and the consanguinity issue, because a child who is breastfed stands in equal footing to biological children on the issue of consanguinity.[57] However all of the other issues with respect to adoptions remain. As Azizah Mohd notes:

> It is worth mentioning that, even though breastfeeding will establish blood relationship between foster family and foster children, it does not establish any maintenance and inheritance right upon the foster children. Similarly, the foster family will legally owe no duty to maintain the foster children and have no right to inherit their property.[58]

The *raadah* option is of limited utility in that obviously it can only be used with very young children amenable to breastfeeding and it also assumes that the mother is in a position to carry out breastfeeding[59] (although there is some evidence to suggest that breast milk can be induced medically).[60] In addition to these practical considerations, as noted above, even though *raadah* solves the consanguinity issue, it does not automatically solve the other objections and hurdles raised in the context of adoption as we know it, inheritance and lineage addressed in greater detail below.[61]

Istilhaq or *al-iqrar bi-l-nasab* (*Acknowledgment of Paternity*)

Another practice that existed in pre-Islamic Arabia to deal with orphans and abandoned children (*lakits*) was that of acknowledgment of paternity.[62] The rules with respect to such admissions were known as *istilhaq* or *al-iqrar bi-l-nasab*.[63] Though distinct from adoption some classical jurists and even some contemporary scholars confuse the two because in some cases it resulted in the effective "adoption" of a child.[64] The relationship established by *istilhaq* was identical to the parent-child relationship with some differences from *tabbani* depending on whether it was genuine acknowledgment or a functional/fictive one.[65] The jurists also highlighted two significant differences between the practice of *tabbani* and *istilhaq*. They noted that when a person adopts another he declares that he is adopting someone, while "when a person acknowledges paternity of another, he declares him to be his begotten son." The second distinction was the fact that while there appears to be no evidence of adopted daughters, there appears to have been no gender discrimination when it came to acknowledgment of paternity. Another point to note is that similar to the practice of the pre-Islamic adoption, acknowledgment of paternity was not restricted to children. In other words, in some cases adults were acknowledged by other adults as being begotten.

Jurists from the Hanafi, Shafi, Hanbali, and Maliki schools did formulate a number of conditions that generally had to be met. Laudau-Tasseron documents that the most important of these were:

a) that the acknowledged person have no known father (*majul al-nasab*);
b) that there be no obvious reason to disbelieve the statement (*an yulad mithluhu li-mithlihi*) so, for example, a person cannot acknowledge as his son another person who is older than himself; and
c) that a father may not acknowledge as his offspring the fruit of illicit relationships (*walad al-zina*).

Notwithstanding the conditions, some early jurists reportedly allowed the acknowledgment of children born out of wedlock in situations where the mother was unmarried or a slave. In fact, the Hanafis even allow marriage between the mother and the father of the illegitimate child while other jurisprudential schools precluded it to punish pre-marital relationships and adultery. Under most, if not all, pre-modern schools of Islamic jurisprudence any child born out of wedlock is considered an illegitimate child.

The requirement that the acknowledged person have no known father ensured that such acknowledgment only occurred in situations where there was no dispute. When there was a dispute, classical jurists relied on the Prophet's ruling that *al-walad li-l firash* "the child belongs to the bed [where it was born]" (the *firash* principle). Even this principle was not unanimously followed. In fact, there are at least two documented instances when Umar settled disputed paternity without resorting to the *firash* principle. Umar is reported to have ruled that persons born to slave-girls in illicit relationships during the pre-Islamic period may be acknowledged by their biological fathers and may be given their patronyms. In another instance:

> Two tribes, Ju'fiyy ad Uqayl, claimed the notable Rabi'a b. Asim as a member. The dispute arose from the report that Rabi'a's mother was divorced from her Ju'fiyy husband, Hubayra, while pregnant. She gave birth while already married to the next husband, the Uqayli Asim. . . . Umar decreed that Rabi'a was the son of the first, Hubayra, even though he was born on the bed of the second.[66]

Umar's deviation from the prevalent practice was reinforced by some later jurists who pushed the door open a little more to make *istilhaq* a legal device to add someone to a family. For instance, the Hanbali jurist allowed *istilhaq* of *lakits* (foundlings) even based on fiction:

> If someone acknowledges a foundling to be his own, it should be accepted, because it is an acknowledgment of a child whose origin is not known (*majhul al nasab*), and who is acknowledged by someone who could indeed have been his father; no harm is done, nobody objects, no obvious fact refutes it. . . . it is for the welfare of the child who needs care, shelter and pedigree.

Shafi scholar Abu Ishaq al-Marwazi is also reported to have spoken approvingly of an old childless man who acknowledged his step-son as his own, with the full knowledge that this was a fiction.[67]

It appears from the classical sources that most jurists took measures to prevent blatant lies when it came to acknowledging paternity, but absent any clear and convincing refutation, it was assumed that such acknowledgments were made in good faith and accepted, in many cases on the basis of public interest or best interest of the child.[68] In fact, the Hanbali and Hanafi schools legitimated such acknowledgments of foundlings without requiring any proof:[69]

> [I]f a person acknowledges that [the foundling] is his child, paternity is established, whether the claimant is a Muslim or a non-Muslim, man or woman, and whether the foundling is dead or alive.

This option appears to only exist for men, though ostensibly a women may assert paternity only by acknowledging that the child belongs to her husband. Moreover, some jurists even go as far as to assert that paternity of a foundling can be established by the admission of the rescuer or a third party.[70] The Hanafi position appears to be openly grounded in public policy considerations of the public interest and the best interest of the child.[71] As Mohamed Fadel points out, Al Kasani[72] argued:

> Policy justifies [accepting an admission of paternity in this context] because [it] is a report regarding something that may be true and it is obligatory to accept reports that may be true, if only to give [the speaker] the benefit of doubt, unless accepting the report's truth harms a third party. Here, however, accepting the report and establishing a relationship of paternity is beneficial to both: [It is beneficial for] the foundling by providing him with the dignity of paternity, education and protection from death and injury as well as other benefits. [It is beneficial for] the putative parent by providing him with a child who can assist him in satisfying his religious and secular needs.

This contrasted with the Malikis and Shafis, who had a more restrictive approach.[73] The Malikis required proof while the Shafis appeared to follow the Hanbalis and Hanafis when it came to foundlings but rejected such admissions in situations where the child was illegitimate.[74]

A good summary of the majority position is the one offered by Ibn Hajar al-Asqalani who suggested that

> he knows traditions condemning the disavowal of children on the one hand, and false genealogical claims on the other, but that he never saw a tradition condemning acknowledgment of paternity even when it is known to be based on fiction.[75]

Classical works appear to suggest that both fictive or fraudulent and genuine acknowledgment of paternity were used to incorporate someone new into a family. It can be assumed that someone adopted into a family through genuine acknowledgment in this way would enjoy all the same rights and privileges and be in the same position as one's biological children. The discussions on this topic did leave much unsaid about the nature of the relationship when the acknowledgment was not proven but accepted based on public policy and best interest of the child considerations.[76]

Kafala

Whenever the question of adoptions and Islam arises, the discussion invariably shifts to the concept of *kafala*. *Kafala*, literally means "sponsorship" and comes from the root word meaning "to feed."[77] It is most accurately translated to mean "legal fostering" or "foster parenting."[78] Algerian family law defines the concept thusly: "*Kafala*, or legal fostering, is the promise to undertake without payment the upkeep, education and protection of a minor, in the same way as a father would do for his son."[79] Adoption scholar Jamila Bargach defines it as "primarily a gift of care and not a substitute for lineal descent."[80] With *kafala* comes the responsibility of upbringing the adopted child as your own.[81] It tries to achieve a balance between raising the child as your own all the while ensuring the adopted child's identity is not absorbed into the identity of the adoptive family.[82] Negation of the biological identity would be considered *haram* or forbidden, of course.[83]

The practice of *kafala* also developed out of the particular care and concern for the maintenance and upbringing of orphans and foundlings inherent in Islamic teachings.[84] *Kafala* is touted by many Muslims as the closest form to adoption in Islamic law that best resembles adoption as it is practiced in the West. However there are a few key differences between *kafala* (as well as the other Islamic alternatives to varying degrees) and Western adoption. These are again: 1) identification and protection of bloodlines and lineage, 2) inheritance, and 3) possibility of marriage partners.[85] The differences and similarities between these Islamic child care arrangement and Western adoption practices will be explored further in the next section.

Part III—Tensions and Points of Convergence between Islamic and Modern Western Conceptions of Adoption and Child Welfare

There are obviously both points of convergence and differences between the two conceptions of adoption (used in the loose sense of the word here). This section starts with the similarities and then proceeds to highlight the differences.

It has been convincingly argued by many scholars that the primary sources, secondary sources, and the *maqasid al sharī'ah* all support the notion that human welfare is the *sine qua non* of the Shari'a.[86] This notion of human welfare of course by definition includes child welfare. Passages used to narrow down to emphasize child welfare and care of orphans for instance were ones like in Sura Nissa verse 127:

> And concerning the children who are weak and oppressed: that you stand firm for justice to orphans. There is no good deed which you do; but God is well acquainted therewith.[87]

Another verse which provides a general command to do good to all humans and specifically enumerates orphans and the needy is Sura 4, verse 36:

> Serve God, and join not any partners with Him; and do good— to parents, kinsfolk, orphans, those in need, neighbors who are near, neighbors who are strangers, the

companion by your side, the wayfarer (ye meet), and what your right hands possess: For God loveth not the arrogant, the vainglorious;—[88]

There are additional verses that deal with the treatment of orphans and potentially abandoned children in the context of property and inheritance. Though they did not explicitly provide comprehensive guidance as to how to treat such children, perhaps this allowed for greater variation in interpretation and allowed cultural, familial, time, and contextual readings into the text.

These included the following verses:[89]

> To orphans restore their property (When they reach their age), nor substitute (your) worthless things for (their) good ones; and devour not their substance (by mixing it up) with your own. For this is indeed a great sin. . . . Make trial of orphans until they reach the age of marriage; if then ye find sound judgment in them, release their property to them; but consume it not wastefully, nor in haste against their growing up. If the guardian is well-off, Let him claim no remuneration, but if he is poor, let him have for himself what is just and reasonable. When ye release their property to them, take witnesses in their presence: But all-sufficient is Allah in taking account. Those who unjustly eat up the property of orphans, eat up a Fire into their own bodies: They will soon be enduring a Blazing Fire!

From the above verses it is quite evident that the Qur'an prioritized the caring of orphans and potentially needy children. A close and holistic reading of this last verse may also allow one to infer that it is directed toward those who have taken in an orphan. Given the emphasis on taking care of children evident from the Qur'an, the Sunna and the works of leading jurists, this is not far-fetched, though this is not the traditional reading by classical jurists, who appeared to focus on remarriage situations.[90]

The Sunna reinforced the Qur'an's directive to care for God's creation. In fact the Prophet taught that "the best of mankind is the one who does good to others."[91] In another tradition the Prophet is reported to have held up his index and middle fingers and joined them together and "I and the one who looks after an orphan will be like these two (referring to his fingers) in Paradise."[92] The Prophet also taught that child abandonment was a sin while taking custody of foundlings was an important act of piety.[93] It is generally accepted by Muslim jurists that the nature of these obligations is one of charity and taking care of God's creation.

As we noted above, there is significant support for the position that welfare of children and considerations of their best interest is at the core of Islamic jurisprudence when it comes to orphans and foundlings.[94] This of course is a point of convergence with the Western conception of adoption. It is beyond the scope of this chapter to go into the evolution and history of adoption in the West but there is a body of scholarship arguing that the underlying objective of present day legislation in this area is to protect the welfare of the child by looking out for the child's best interests.[95] Indeed, according to some scholars, in the American context, for instance, this shift came in 1851 with the *Act to Provide for the Adoption of Children* commonly known as the Massachusetts Adoption Act.[96] The Massachusetts legislature, in what became known as the first modern adoption law in the United States, introduced, for the first time, the concept of the "best interests of the child," requiring judges of Massachusetts state courts to determine whether the adoptive parents had the resources to educate and support the child, and whether the adoptive parents were in other ways suitable to parent.[97] Thus, the "best interests of the child" has a long history in the American adoption context.

Despite this point of convergence, there are certain key differences between adoptions in the West and the classical Islamic law perspective on adoption. The first relates to lineage and identity. The Western form of adoption, similar to *tabanni*, involves making another's child one's own and treating him in the same way one would treat a biological child in terms of family relationship, guardianship, custody rights, maintenance, inheritance, lineage and so on. Indeed, an essential characteristic of historical Western adoptions is that the adopted child is cut off from all ties with his biological parents (although there is a movement toward "open adoption"). Another significant difference between the classical Islamic law approach to adoption and Western adoptions relates to inheritance. Namely, by severing an adopted child's ties with his biological parents and replacing them with fictive ties to the adoptive parents, Western adoptions replace a child's right to inherit from his biological parents with the right to inherit from adoptive parents.[98] The third point of tension revolves around the issue of *mahramiya* or consanguinity. The prevalent Western idea of adoption in creating the fictive relationship put up a barrier for marriage by deeming the adopted child as a biological equal. In other words, in the Western context, the deemed blood lines precluded adopted children from marrying the adoptive parents' biological children, and of course the parents themselves in the event of divorce or death. The taboo extended to the same circle that would apply to those connected by biology. The classical jurists interpreted the Qur'an and Sunna on this matter and opposed these restrictions as being based on a falsification of reality based on the deemed fictive relationship established.

Reformation

Despite complexity and changeability in Islamic jurisprudence—and despite the fact that classical jurists struggled to find ways to look after foundlings and orphans—not much scholarship evolved on the issue of adoption. Jurists from each of the four leading Sunni schools did not go deeply into questioning the reasoning behind the Qur'an's prohibition of adoption as practiced by pre-Islamic Arabs, *tabbani*. The assumptions underlying the position and the justifications advanced to uphold the classical jurists' ban on adoption survived into the modern era pretty much unchallenged.

This did not mean that Muslims were prevented from caring for abandoned children and orphans. On the contrary, pre-modern jurists were conscious that closing down an avenue of permanent child care (*tabbani*) made it difficult to fulfill the mandatory religious obligations to take care of orphans and abandoned children. This essentially forced them to bless and encourage other means of caring for children such as *radaah*, acknowledgment of paternity, and *kafala*. These alternative long-term child-care arrangements were possible due to the special significance attached to child welfare in Islam.

However, there have been some movements toward reforming and reinterpreting adoption within Islam using interpretations that are consistent with the spirit of Islam and present realities.[99] Islamic reformists assert that the context specific and evolutionary nature of the Shari'a, Islam's emphasis on child welfare, the *maqasid al Shari'a*, the dynamism inherent in the sources and principles of Islamic jurisprudence, and the significance of human agency in the formulation of or "discovery" of *fiqh* provide much leeway in reforming Islamic legal rulings on adoption. Indeed, even the diversity, pluralism, and flexibility evident in the works of premodern jurists on the issues of *radaah*, acknowledgment of paternity, care of foundlings, and *kafala* offer much room for hope in the context of reforming or reinterpreting adoption law and practice in Muslim jurisdictions.

Such a reinterpretation, they argue, would also be consistent with the long-established Islamic traditions *tajdid* (renewal) and *islah* (reform), which reflect "a continuing tradition of revitalization of Islamic faith and practice within the historic communities of Muslims."[100] These concepts imply, among other things, a return to the authentic sources of Islamic law, the Qur'an and the Sunna, for guidance in present practice; "the assertion of the right of independent analysis (*ijtihad*) of the Qur'an and the Sunna in this application," rather than reliance on and application of the opinions of past jurists (*taqlid*); and finally, a reassertion of the "authenticity and uniqueness" of the Qur'anic message, a universal experience applicable to all times and places.[101]

Through these methods, renewers (*mujaddidun*) and reformers (*muslihun*) revisit the sources anew in light of present circumstances and reinterpret the universal and timeless Islamic ideals in light of present realities and prevailing ideas.[102] Through *tajdid*, scholars embark on a "renewal of the reading, understanding, and consequently, the implementations of texts in light of the various historic cultural contexts in which Muslim communities or societies exist," while *islah* accordingly encourages "reforming the human, spiritual, social, or political context" in light of these readings.[103]

Such reform attempts are already evident in the *fatawa* (legal rulings) being issued in Western contexts.[104] For example, a significant development in the field of adoption and Islam has come from a group of female scholars, activists, and thinkers. In an effort to push the discussion in the area of adoption, the Muslim Women's Shura Council published a groundbreaking study in 2011.[105] The report concluded as follows:

After examining Islamic texts and history alongside social science research and the international consensus on children's rights, the Council finds that adoption can be acceptable under Islamic law and its principal objectives, as long as important ethical guidelines are followed. This statement consults the Qur'an, the example of the Prophet Muhammad (Sunna), the objectives and principles of Islamic law (maqasid al-Sharī'ah), Islamic Jurisprudence (*fiqh*), and social science data. The Shura Council finds that, instead of banning adoption, Islamic sources have brought various ethical restrictions to the process, condemning dissimulation and foregrounding compassion, transparency, and justice. These restrictions closely resemble what is known today as the practice of open adoption. Therefore, when all efforts to place orphaned children with their extended family have been exhausted, open, legal, ethical adoptions can be a preferable Islamically-grounded alternative to institutional care and other unstable arrangements.[106]

The study represents a form of *ijtihad* (independent reasoning) and brought about some much-needed attention to this issue and may contribute toward shaping a future consensus (*ijma'*) on the question of Islamic adoptions.[107]

In conclusion, Islam plays a major role in determining the issue of adoption in the Muslim world and has had a history of prohibiting and limiting it. However, with a strong emphasis on taking care of the young, Muslims have and will continue to try to find alternatives to care for orphans and foundlings that are more in line with the Islamic spirit of child welfare.

Notes

1. Daniel Pollack et al., "Classical Religious Perspectives on Adoption Law," *Notre Dame Law Review* 79, no. 2 (2004): 733.
2. Ameenul Hasan Rizvi, "Islamic Law and the Indian Adoption Bill," *Islamic & Comparative Law Quarterly* 2, no. 2 (1982): 118.
3. Most Muslims will say that it is *haram* (prohibited) to adopt but then will automatically say that Islam imposes an obligation to care for orphans and abandoned children. See Mohammad Yasir, "Is Adoption Haram or Halal in Islam? Islamic Adoption Method," *Halal Adviser*, https://halaladviser.com/is-adoption-haram-or-halal/; See also "Adoption of Children from Countries in which Islamic Shari's Law is Observed," https://travel.state.gov/content/travel/en/Intercountry-Adoption/Adoption-Process/how-to-adopt/adoption-of-children-from-countries-sharia-law.html#:~:text=Generally%2C%20howe ver%2C%20Islamic%20family%20law,live%20in%20the%20United%20States; Shanifa Nasser, "How Canada barred adoptions from Muslim countries- and used Shariah law to do it," *CBC*, https://www.cbc.ca/news/canada/adoptions-kafalah-pakistan-canada-ban-muslim-1.4855852. Attorney Yusra Gomaa documents the reaction from the mainstream Muslim community quite accurately in her article "The Case for Adoption in Islam," available at http://www.patheos.com/blogs/altmuslim/2013/05/the-case-for-adoption-in-islam/. Recently the Canadian government banned adoption from Pakistan, citing Islamic law. Immigration Canada spokesman Glenn Johnson said: "Pakistan applies the Islamic

system of *kafala*, or guardianship, which neither terminates the birth parent-child relationship nor grants full parental rights to the new guardian. This means that there are further legal incompatibilities in accepting Canadian applications for adoption." See Nicholas Keung, "Canada's Ban on Pakistani Adoptions Baffles Parents, Clerics," *Toronto Star*, August 5, 2013. http://www.thestar.com/news/canada/2013/08/05/canadas_ban_on_pakistani_adoptions_baffles_parents_clerics.html. See also the Citizenship and Immigration Canada notice, available at https://www.canada.ca/en/immigration-refugees-citizenship/news/notices/adoptions-pakistan.html, which states: "The provinces and territories will no longer accept applications for adoption placements from Pakistan, effective July 2, 2013. The Government of Canada, in support of this decision, will no longer process related immigration applications as of the same date. Pakistani law allows for guardianship of children, but does not recognize our concept of adoption. Proceeding with further such placements would violate Canada's obligations under The Hague Convention on Protection of Children and Co-operation in Respect of Intercountry Adoption. Prospective parents whose cases were in progress should be contacted by the Mission in Islamabad regarding the status of their application. Other related inquiries should be directed to the responsible adoption agency and/or provincial/territorial Central Adoption Authority."
4. Those claiming to be Muslims fall into the following categories: Sunnis, Shiites and Ahmadiyyas. The largest percentage of Muslims fall into the Sunni group. See https://www.cia.gov/the-world-factbook/field/religions/
5. Ashley Dawn Harvel, *The Myth of the Unknown Child: Creating a New Face for Adoption in America* (PhD dissertation University of Southern California: ProQuest, 2006), 11.
6. This would be more akin to the Islamic conception of adoption. This is also advocated to varying degrees by proponents of open adoption. See generally Arthur D. Sorosky, Annette Baran, and Reuben Pannor, *The Adoption Triangle: The Effects of the Sealed Record on Adoptees, Birth Parents, and Adoptive Parents* (Garden City, NY: Anchor Press, 1978).
7. Pollack et al., "Classical Religious Perspectives," 733.
8. For an illustrative timeline on open adoptions see http://www.adoptionhelp.org/open-adoption/timeline. Also see Marisa Gerber, "Reuben Pannor Dies at 90; Trailblazer for Open Adoptions," *Los Angeles Times* (January 1, 2013), http://articles.latimes.com/2013/jan/01/local/la-me-reuben-pannor-20130101.
9. I will interchangeably use pre-modern and classical, in line with its use by different scholars.
10. Discussed in further detail and with additional nuance further in the chapter.
11. As Noah Feldman points out: "Shari'a, properly understood, is not just a set of legal rules. To believing Muslims, it is something deeper and higher, infused with moral and metaphysical purpose. At its core, the Shari'a represents the idea that all human beings—and all human governments—are subject to justice under the law.

    In fact, Shari'a is not the word traditionally used in Arabic to refer to the processes of Islamic legal reasoning or the rulings produced through it: that word is *fiqh*, meaning something like Islamic jurisprudence. The word Shari'a connotes a connection to the divine, a set of unchanging beliefs and principles that order life in accordance with God's will. See Noah Feldman, "Why Shariah?," *New York Times Magazine*, March 16, 2008, at 46.
12. A. Hasan, *The Early Development of Islamic Jurisprudence* (Islamabad: Islamic Research Institute, 1970): 34.
13. See Robert Crane, "Maqasid al Shari'ah: A Strategy to Rehabilitate Religion in America," https://waqfacademy.org/wp-content/uploads/2013/03/Dr.-Robert-D.-Crane-RDC.-Date.-Maqasid-al-Shari%C3%86ah.-Place.-Pub.pdf; see also Muhammad Khalid Masud,

"Itkhtilaf al-Fuqaha: Diversity in Fiqh as a Social Construction," in *Wanted: Equality and Justice in the Muslim Family*, edited by Z. Anwar, pp. 65–93 (Musawah); Some scholars refer to them as five maqasids while others consider it six and Tariq Ramadan extends this into fifty-four; see Brad Amburn, "Who's Afraid of Tariq Ramadan?" *Foreign Policy*, https://foreignpolicy.com/2009/10/26/whos-afraid-of-tariq-ramadan/. The Shari'a identifies three factors that must be kept in mind in pursuing the *maqasid al sharī'ah* or objectives of the law. These include: educating the individual (*tahdhid al fard*) to inspire faith and instill the qualities of trustworthiness and righteousness; to establish justice (*adl*), which is one of the major themes of the Qur'an; and consideration of public interest (*maslaha*). There are at least fifty-three instances where the Qur'an commands *adl* or justice, for instance. See Kamali W. Chan et al., *The Great Asian Religions: An Anthology* (New York: MacMillan Publishing Co., 1969) at 309: "Islam puts its trust in reason, the supreme faculty of knowledge with which man is endowed, as the only method possible for ever deciding the issue"; and I. Khaldun, Muqaddimah, III: 481.

14. The majority of theologians accept the Sunna as the second main source of Shari'a but one group of scholars, mainly the Mu'tazilah theologians, did not accept this. For a discussion and refutation of their position see S. M. Darsh, *Islamic Essays* (London: Islamic Cultural Centre, 1979) at 79.
15. M. Cherif Bassiouni and Gamal M. Badr, "The Shari'ah: Sources, Interpretation, and Rule Making," *UCLA Journal of Islamic and Near Eastern Law* 1: 135: 141.
16. Ismail Faruqi and Lamya Faruqi, *The Cultural Atlas of Islam* (New York: MacMillan Publishing Co., 1986), 114.
17. Bassiouni and Badr, "The Shari'ah: Sources, Interpretation, and Rule Making," 135.
18. Faruqi and Faruqi, *The Cultural Atlas of Islam*, 265.
19. The two main branches of Islam are the Sunni and Shiite branches. The schism occurred after the arbitration between Ali Ben Abu Taleb and Muawiyat Ben Sufiane for the Caliphate. The Shiites insisted that the Caliphate had to remain in the family of the Prophet (represented by his cousin Ali) while the Sunni tradition did not insist on this. It is also worth pointing out at this stage that there are differences between the Sunni and Shiite traditions in what significance and emphasis they attach to each of the sources and even as to which Hadith are authentic and not.
20. See Part II below.
21. K. M. Sharma, "What's in a Name: Law, Religion, and Islamic Names," *Denver Journal of International Law and Policy* 26 (1998): 151, at 176.
22. Pollack et al., "Classical Religious Perspectives," 733.
23. Qur'an 58:2 states: "If any men among you divorce their wives by Zihar (calling them mothers), they cannot be their mothers: None can be their mothers except those who gave them birth. And in fact they use words (both) iniquitous and false: but truly Allah is one that blots out (sins), and forgives (again and again)."
24. Qur'an 33:4–5. Abdullah Yusuf Ali, a translator and commentator on the Qur'an, notes with respect to this verse: "Adoption in the technical sense is not allowed in Muslim Law." Abdullah Yusuf Ali (trans.), *The Holy Qur'ān* (USA: Muslim Students' Association of the United States and Canada, 1975), 1103, note 3671.
25. Two or three sources support this but also Landou challenges this. See Ella Landau-Tasseron, "Adoption, Acknowledgement of Paternity and False Genealogical Claims in Arabian and Islamic Societies," *Bulletin of the School of Oriental and African Studies, University of London* 66, no. 2 (2003): 169; See also Nadjma Yassari, "Adding by Choice: Adoption

and Functional Equivalents in Islamic and Middle Eastern Law," *The American Journal of Comparative Law* 63, no. 4 (2015): 927.

26. Azizah Mohd, "Protection of Children through Foster Care under Islamic Law: Sustaining Foster Children Protection through Breastfeeding," *Journal of Applied Sciences Research* 7, no. 13 (2011): 2231. Again Landou disagrees about the same rights. ...
27. Landau-Tasseron, "Adoption, Acknowledgement of Paternity," at 169..
28. Muhammad B. Ahmad al-Qurtubi, "Al-Jami Li-Ahmkam Al-Qur'ān," 118–119, Dar wa-Matabi al-Shab (1967).
29. There is some disagreement about the reasons for the divorce, with some scholars stating that she was divorced for the sole reason that the Prophet could marry her. See for instance Ella Landau-Tasseron, "Adoption, Acknowledgment of Paternity." Others disagree or are silent on it. See, for instance, Mohammad H. Fadel, "Two Women, One Man: Knowledge, Power and Gender in Medieval Sunni Legal Thought," *International Journal of Middle East Studies* 29 (1997): 185–204. A plain reading of Qur'an 33:37 suggests that the Prophet was against Zayd divorcing her but was later ordered to marry her after Zayd divorced her. Ordered by whom?
30. Qur'an 4:23 states: "Prohibited to you (For marriage) are:- Your mothers, daughters, sisters; father's sisters, Mother's sisters; brother's daughters, sister's daughters; foster-mothers (Who gave you suck), foster-sisters; your wives' mothers; your step-daughters under your guardianship, born of your wives to whom ye have gone in,- no prohibition if ye have not gone in;- (Those who have been) wives of your sons proceeding from your loins; and two sisters in wedlock at one and the same time, except for what is past; for Allah is Oft-forgiving, Most Merciful."
31. Qur'an 33:4–5.
32. Qur'an 33:37–40.
33. The verse makes it clear that the Prophet asked Zayd to stay married to her and hesitated to marry Zaynab for fear of what people may think. Qur'an 33:37–40
34. Qur'an 33:37.
35. For instance what is deemed by some as the *niqab* verse is interpreted by some scholars as only applicable to the Prophet's wives.
36. Shaheen Sardar Ali, "Rights of the Child under Islamic Law and Laws of Pakistan: A Thematic Overview," *Journal of Islamic State Practice in International Law* 2, no. 1 (2006): 2.
37. Ibid., 8.
38. Ibid., 2.
39. Ibid., 2.
40. Ingrid Mattson, "Adoption and Fostering," in *Encyclopedia of Women & Islamic Cultures: Family, Law, and Politics*, edited by Suad Joseph and Afsaneh Najmabadi (Brill, 2005), 1. Part of the reasoning appears to have been to prevent the possibility of retirement planning by an adoptive parent contrary to the best interest of the adoptee. Since adding a male member to the family and clan was seen as a source of wealth and prestige, this benefited the adoptive father. Moreover, the adoptive father can also inherit from the adoptee, who could have been a grown adult with known parents from whom he could inherit. In other words, adoptive parents could adopt to secure their financial future by adopting other adults. Amira Sonbol, "Adoption in Islamic Society: A Historical Survey," in *Children in the Muslim Middle East*, edited by Elizabeth Warnock Fernea, 45–67 (Austin: University of Texas Press, 1996), 46. Also see Ella Landau-Tasseron, who found no cases of adopted females, in her article, "Adoption, Acknowledgement of Paternity, 173.

41. Sardar Ali. This may be seen as a bit of a stretch but a holistic reading of the Qur'an and Sunna and its social agenda of attacking pre-Islamic gender discrimination practices does give this some credence.
42. M. S. Sait, "Islamic Perspectives on the Rights of the Child," in *Revisiting Children's Rights*, edited by D. Fottrell (Kluwer Law International, 2002), 31–50.
43. See for instance Jamila Bargach, *Orphans of Islam: Family, Abandonment, and Secret Adoption in Morocco* (Rowman & Littlefield, 2002), 27. This is of course akin to the closed adoption practices in the West.
44. Mohd, "Protection of Children," 2232.
45. Ibid.
46. The concubine of his uncle Abu Lahab. Ibid.
47. Ibid.
48. Qur'an 2:233 states: "Mothers may breastfeed their children two complete years for whoever wishes to complete the nursing [period]. . . . And if you wish to have your children nursed by a substitute, there is no blame upon you as long as you give payment according to what is acceptable. And fear Allah and know that Allah is seeing of what you do." Also Qur'an 65:6 which states in the context of disagreement and the mother refusing to breastfeed: "But if you are in discord, then there may breastfeed for the father another woman."
49. Mohd, "Protection of Children," 2230.
50. Mattson, "Adoption and Fostering," at 2–3.
51. Qur'an 4:23
52. "What is unlawful by reason of consanguinity is unlawful by reason of fosterage." See Sahih Bukhari, Sahih Muslim, Sunan Ibn Majah, Sunan At-Tirmidhi and An-Nasaie. See also Mohd, "Protection of Children," 2230.
53. Mohd, "Protection of Children," 2230.
54. Ibid.
55. For a detailed discussion of the rules in classical *fiqh*, see ibid.
56. "Adoptive Breastfeeding." http://babymaghrib.wordpress.com/in-islam/breastfeeding-in-islam/.
57. See also "How Muslim Families Use Breastfeeding to Make Adopted Babies Their Own," *Green Prophet*, http://www.greenprophet.com/2013/04/breastfeeding-islam-adoption/.
58. Mohd, "Protection of Children," 2232.
59. Though some women are using modern science to induce lactation even when they have never been pregnant. See "What You Need to Know About Adoption," *Pakistan Adoption*, http://www.pakistanadoption.com/adoptionfacts.htmndalso; "How Muslim Families Use Breastfeeding."
60. Elizabeth Hormann, *Breastfeeding an Adopted Baby and Relactation* (La Leche League International, 2007).
61. To better understand how suckling would create blood relations making it easier to treat the adopted child as one's own please read "How Muslim Families Use Breastfeeding."
62. Landau-Tasseron, "Adoption, Acknowledgement of Paternity," 169-192. See also M. S. Sujimon, "Istilhaq and Its Role in Islamic Law," *Arab Law Quarterly* 18, no. 2 (2003): 117–143. See also Pollack et al. "Classical Religious Perspectives," 735.
63. Landau refers to it as *istilhaq* (though she acknowledges it may be known as *iddia* or sometime even *iqrar i tiraf*). Fadel refers to it as *aliqrar bi-l-nasab*. M. S. Sujimon also refers to it as *istilhaq*.
64. See for instance Landau-Tasseron, "Adoption, Acknowledgement of Paternity," 169–192.

65. Some scholars, such as Ibn Manzur, are of the view that an acknowledged child assumes the patronym of the acknowledging one but only inherits if the acknowledgment is based on genuine paternity as opposed to one based on fiction. See discussion later in this chapter.
66. Landau-Tasseron, "Adoption, Acknowledgement of Paternity," 169–192. This was subsequently overruled by Ali.
67. Ibid.
68. Pollack et al., "Classical Religious Perspectives," 749.
69. Ibid., 748.
70. Ibid., 749.
71. Al-Sarakshi, p. 154 argued that such an acknowledgment benefits the child. Ibid. at 154.
72. Pollack et al., "Classical Religious Perspectives," 748, see note 348.
73. Ibid., 748.
74. Ibid., 748.
75. Ibid., 748.
76. There is sparse discussion on whether fraudulent or fictive acknowledgments resulted in less inheritance or brought about the same treatment in terms of consanguinity.
77. Imad-ad-Dean Ahmad, "The Islamic View of Adoption and Caring for Homeless Children," in *Adoption Fact Book III* (Washington: National Council for Adoption, 1999).
78. Ibid.
79. International Reference Centre for the Rights of Children Deprived of their Family (ISS/IRC), "Specific Case: Kafalah," Fact Sheet No. 51, (Geneva: ISS, 2007).
80. Bargach, *Orphans of Islam*, 27.
81. ISS/IRC, "Specific Case: Kafalah."
82. Muslim Women's Shura Council and American Society of Muslim Advancement, "Adoption and the Care of Orphan Children: Islam and the Best Interests of the Child," 7.
83. Ibid.
84. Ahmad, "The Islamic View of Adoption."
85. Ibid. See also Rizvi, "Islamic Law," 118.
86. Interview with Sabith Khan, "5 Myths About Sharia Law," https://www.mic.com/articles/55727/5-myths-about-sharia-law.. The legal philosophers of Islam, such as Ghazālī, Shāṭibī, and Shāh Walīullāh explained that the aim of Shari'a is to promote human welfare.
87. Qur'an 4:127.
88. Qur'an 4:36.
89. Qur'an 4:2–10.
90. Traditionally it is interpreted to deal with situations where children have a mother but no father and also to deal with situations where a man marries a woman who has a child prior to the marriage. In both these cases the child would be treated as an orphan according to classical jurists. See for instance Laura M. Thomason, "On the Steps of the Mosque: The Legal Rights of Non-Marital Children in Egypt," *Hastings Women's Law Journal* 19, no. 121 (2008): 140.
91. Dr. Muhammad Hamidullah, *Introduction to Islam* (Lahore: Sh. Muhammad Ashraf, 1974), paras. 111, 225, 227.
92. Ṣaīḥ al-Bukhārī: 5659.
93. Pollack et al., "Classical Religious Perspective of Adoption Law," 737.
94. Ibid., 748.
95. See for instance the discussion here about the State's *parens patriae* powers regarding children. C. Guthrie and J. L. Grossman, "Parental Rights vs. Best Interests of the Child: A False

Dichotomy in the Context of Adoption," *Duke Journal of Gender Law and Policy* 2, no. 63 (1995).
96. "An Act to provide for the Adoption of Children," Acts and Resolves passed by the General Court of Massachusetts, Chapter 324 (1851). Can be accessed at http://darkwing.uoregon.edu/~adoption/archive/MassACA.htm See M. Kahan, "'Put Up' on Platforms: A History of Twentieth Century Adoption Policy in the United States," *Journal of Sociology and Social Welfare* 33, no. 3 (2006): 55.
97. C. Guthrie and J. L. Grossman, "Adoption in the Progressive Era: Preserving, Creating, and Re-Creating Families," *American Journal of Legal History* 43, no. 3 (1999): 238.
98. Adoption rights to biological parents may be moot in most cases involving orphans and foundlings, of course.
99. See Ziba Mir-Hosseini, "The Construction of Gender in Islamic Legal Thought and Strategies for Reform," *Hawwa: Journal of Women in the Middle East and the Islamic World* 1 (2003): 1.
100. John O. Voll, "Renewal and Reform in Islamic History: *Tajdid* and *Islah*," in *Voices of Resurgent Islam*, edited by John L. Esposito (New York: Oxford University Press, 1983), 32.
101. Ibid., 35.
102. Tariq Ramadan, *Radical Reform: Islamic Ethics and Liberation* (New York: Oxford University Press, 2009), 12–13.
103. Ibid., 13.
104. There have been a proliferation of dozens, if not hundreds, of websites in Europe and North America that cater to Western Muslims by issuing rulings that are more relevant to the social, political, and economic realities they find themselves in. These rulings are not issued by judicial bodies but by clerics who provide their religious opinions.
105. Muslim Women's Shura Council and American Society of Muslim Advancement, *Adoption and the Care of Orphan Children: Islam and the Best Interests of the Child*, 7. http://www.wisemuslimwomen.org/images/activism/Adoption_(August_2011)_Final.pdf
106. Ibid.
107. For more information on reformation in the adoption field please read, Faisal Kutty, "Where There's a Will There's a Way: The Case for Islamic Adoption Reform Consonant with Changing Western Laws and the *Maqasid Al Shariah*."

Bibliography

Al-Qurtubi, Muhammad B. Ahmad. "Al-Jami Li-Ahmkam Al-Qur'ān." (1967): 118–119.
Bassiouni, M. Cherif, and Badr, Gamal M. "The Shari'ah: Sources, Interpretation, and Rule Making." *UCLA J. Islamic & Near E. L.* 1, 135 (2001).
Fadel, Mohammad. "Two Women, One Man: Knowledge, Power and Gender in Medieval Sunni Legal Thought." *International Journal of Middle East Studies* 29 (1997): 185–204.
Faruqi, Ismail, and Faruqi, Lamya. *The Cultural Atlas of Islam* (New York: MacMillan Publishing Co., 1986).
Harvel, Ashley Dawn. *The Myth of the Unknown Child: Creating a New Face for Adoption in America*. (PhD dissertation, University of Southern California: ProQuest, 2006).
Hormann, Elizabeth. "Breastfeeding an Adopted Baby and Relactation," *La Leche League International*, https://llli.org/breastfeeding-info/adoption/.

Landau-Tasseron, Ella. "Adoption, Acknowledgement of Paternity and False Genealogical Claims in Arabian and Islamic Societies." *Bulletin of the School of Oriental and African Studies* 66, no. 2 (2003): 169.

Mohd, Azizah. "Protection of Children through Foster Care under Islamic Law: Sustaining Foster Children Protection Through Breastfeeding." *Journal of Applied Sciences Research* 7, no. 13 (2011): 2230.

Pollack, Daniel et al., "Classical Religious Perspectives on Adoption Law." *Notre Dame L Rev* 79, no. 2 (2004): 733.

Ramadan, Tariq. *Radical Reform: Islamic Ethics and Liberation*. New York: Oxford University Press, 2009.

Rizvi, Ameenul Hasan. "Islamic Law and the Indian Adoption Bill." *Islamic & Comparative Law Quarterly* 2, no. 2 (1982): 118.

Sardar Ali, Shaheen. "Rights of the Child under Islamic Law and Laws of Pakistan: A Thematic Overview." *Journal of Islamic State Practice in International Law* 2, no. 1 (2006): 2.

Sait, M. S. "Islamic Perspectives on the Rights of the Child." In *Revisiting Children's Rights*, edited by D. Fottrell, pp. 31–50, 2002 (Kluwer Law International).

CHAPTER 15

ADOPTING EMBRYOS

JOHN BERKMAN

PERIODICALLY, cultural traditions are confronted by what seem like intractable bioethical issues. One such issue in contemporary America is abortion; in contemporary Japan it is organ donation from brain-dead patients. The Roman Catholic moral tradition also periodically confronts such issues internally. In the 1980s and 1990s, disagreement over (tube) feeding patients in a persistent vegetative state (PVS) included dueling statements from groups of US bishops, before something approaching a definitive resolution for Catholicism came in 2003 with a statement from Pope John Paul II.

The morality of a woman's choice to adopt an embryo (EA) is another seemingly intractable moral issue for Catholic ethicists. It has been debated for over twenty-five years with no Vatican intervention to resolve it. This issue seems even less liable to resolution than that of feeding PVS patients. Whereas disagreement on the PVS issue broadly follows the orthodox versus revisionist (or "conservative" versus "liberal") divide, the morality of embryo adoption is debated almost exclusively by Catholic moralists that the Vatican sees as "reliable."

Originally, the moral question that was posed was about gestating an "abandoned" or "spare" embryo, because of the specific context that sparked the initial debate. At that time, many Catholic ethicists ignored the question of the morality of gestating an abandoned embryo, considering it of marginal interest. However, the issue was soon recognized to be genuinely new, not subject to any existing Catholic moral principle or clearly recognizable categorization. In a 2006 speech, John Allen—one of the most astute analysts of the Vatican—recognized that a resolution of the issue of embryo adoption would require a development of Catholic doctrine. Allen was not surprised that the Vatican was not intervening on the issue. He expected it would avoid doing so until it perceived a consensus amongst the Catholic moralists it trusted.[1] As of 2020, there is no evidence that consensus is developing on the issue, either among theologians or at the Vatican.

Analyzing the morality of embryo adoption has proven irresistible for many Catholic ethicists because it involves a truly novel moral question, requiring a moral discovery process. This process of moral reasoning, typically referred to as casuistry, is analogous to a judge's process of discernment in legal cases with no clear precedent. It is a matter of classification—discerning which of different possible paradigms are most appropriate to understanding the case at hand.

While the debate over embryo adoption has been carried on almost exclusively by Catholic ethicists, the anecdotal evidence as to who actually adopts most embryos points to evangelical Protestants.[2] Furthermore, the number of embryo adoptions in the US was until recently very low. From 1998 until about 2014, there were between 1,000 and 1,500 embryo adoptions resulting in live births, on average less than one hundred per year.[3] However, by 2016 the number of embryo adoptions (donor transfers of embryos) in the US was 1,940, and the numbers have increased since then.[4]

If, until recently, few embryos were actually adopted, and it was primarily evangelical Protestants who are adopting them, why was it that between 1997 and 2007 Catholic ethicists debated the issue so extensively? I suggest two possible reasons. First, as a novel and unresolved moral question, it is an open debate to which Catholic moralists are keen to contribute. This is presumably in part because these Catholic ethicists wish to serve their fellow Catholics and all those sympathetic to Catholic moral reasoning in thinking and acting appropriately on this question.

Second, for some Catholic moralists embryo adoption is more than a moral issue, having become freighted with broader symbolic significance. This point requires some explanation and another example. A generation ago, in the decades following Vatican II (1962–1965), Catholics departed from their Church's teaching on contraception on an unprecedented scale. As a result, for some Catholic ethicists the question of contraception was never *merely* about contraception. Larger concerns and agendas were at play, whether spoken or unspoken. Because this Church teaching had been abandoned in a seemingly unprecedented manner, the contraception issue implied questions about church authority, i.e., "Can you depart from this particular teaching and remain a good Catholic?" and more generally, "Who qualifies as a good Catholic?" In other words, sometimes a particular moral question comes to symbolize or stand in for other broader concerns that are more difficult to address or even to articulate.

The analogy being drawn is in no way meant to lead the reader to see any direct relationship between the issues of contraception and embryo adoption. Rather, the point is that the embryo adoption debate, like the contraception debate, has come to symbolize, or is a way to crystalize, larger and more amorphous concerns that typically conservative Catholic ethicists have about their moral tradition, and its role both within the Church and as a witness to contemporary culture.

With regard to the embryo adoption debate, there is undoubtedly a fear of the "domino" effect. On the one side, will allowing embryo adoption ultimately undermine traditional Catholic teachings on marriage, sexuality, family, and/or gender roles? On the other side, is the effort to prohibit embryo adoption an attempt to illegitimately transform a particular form of Catholic piety into a moral norm—in so doing undermining a key part of the Gospel's social imperative to care for the "least of these?" If these kinds of concerns (or something like them) hover in the background for some of the Catholic moralists engaged in the embryo adoption debate, whether consciously or unconsciously, then it is not surprising that the question of embryo adoption continues to provoke what would otherwise seem to be an inordinate level of continuous debate.

Origin of Issue

The issue first came to widespread attention in the mid-1990s. A provision in a British law (the 1990 *Human Fertilisation and Embryology Act*) required the destruction of "unclaimed" cryopreserved embryos after five years. Beginning in August of 1996, this resulted in the destruction of thousands of embryos in British fertility clinics.[5] When this was publicized, it struck a chord of dismay in the Catholic world, particularly in Italy.[6] Many Catholic women offered to gestate these embryos.[7] These offers touched off a debate among Catholic ethicists: Was it morally acceptable for a woman to gestate embryos of whom she was not the genetic mother? Was it acceptable for single women to do so? Perhaps for orders of nuns? As a result of this particular context, the initial debate that ensued focused almost entirely on whether rescuing these "spare" or "abandoned" embryos was morally acceptable, or whether it constituted surrogacy, a practice prohibited by Church teaching. As the debate developed, some argued that such a "rescue" was only acceptable if the woman intended to adopt the child. Once it was generally agreed that embryo adoption was not a form of surrogacy as "surrogacy" was understood in Church teaching, some raised more abstract objections based on Catholic sexual ethics.[8]

In 2001, embryo adoption was thrown headlong into the US political arena. President George W. Bush prohibited the use of federal funding for research involving the destruction of cryopreserved embryos. At that time, some government ethicists were arguing that while embryos should not be deliberately created merely for destructive research purposes, if there were "spare" embryos—those left over from IVF treatment and no longer wanted—it would be morally acceptable to use such embryos for research, since they would be destroyed regardless. When President Bush weighed in on the issue, banning government funding, he displayed his moral rationale in an unusual way. Sharing the stage with Bush were seventeen children. Bush said that so-called "spare" embryos should not be destroyed for research purposes, but should be gestated, and referred to the seventeen children on the stage as examples of the alternative.

Shortly after banning federal funding of destructive embryo experimentation, President Bush announced a Department of Health and Human Services (HHS) initiative that would promote awareness of the option of embryo adoption. The mission of the HHS initiative was to "educate Americans about the existence of frozen embryos . . . available for donation/adoption." Between 2002 and 2015, the HHS provided $24 million in grants to agencies to publicize and promote embryo adoption—$11 million under the Bush administration and over $13 million under the Obama administration. These grants have continued to the present.

Historical—Medical Background

As of 2020, it is estimated that there are upward of one million cryopreserved embryos in the United States alone. How did this come about? Louise Brown, the first "test tube" baby produced by IVF (in vitro fertilization) and ET (embryo transfer), was born in Great Britain in 1978. In 1981, the physicians who had developed the techniques that led to Louise Brown's birth announced a method by which IVF embryos could be frozen for later transfer to the womb (ET). The first live birth of a child from a previously frozen embryo occurred in Australia in 1984. In the United States, the first "embryo adoption" baby was born in 1998.

Early on, IVF was relatively unregulated. Since the techniques were new, their success rate was relatively low. The IVF-ET protocol typically involved the production of more embryos than could be safely implanted at any one time. The production of excess embryos allowed for, among other things, eugenic screening to determine the healthiest or otherwise most desirable embryos. Besides the desire to maximize the return on a significant investment of time and money, it also generated the notion of "designer babies."

Once the technique for cryopreserving embryos was established, even more extra embryos were typically created, and these extra embryos would be frozen for future possible use, if the woman did not become pregnant from the first set of embryos that were transferred to her womb. The cryopreservation of extra embryos reduced the future burden on the woman if more than one cycle of IVF-ET was required to achieve pregnancy and successful gestation to birth. The burden was lessened in the sense that the woman would not need to repeat the process of hyper-stimulation to retrieve ova from the woman, as this process was (and is) lengthy, unpleasant, and not without health risks. Thus, if a second cycle of ET was needed or desired, using the cryopreserved embryos would be advantageous—less invasive and would save time and expense.

In the early years of IVF-ET, the rate of live birth from ET varied tremendously, with clinics reporting success rates between 2 and 37 percent. With the US having no regulatory oversight of IVF at the time, some clinics would try to maximize their "live birth" rates by implanting a large number of embryos, thus the strange spike in multiple births at that time—with women at times becoming pregnant with four to six embryos.[9]

According to the HFEA, the UK's independent fertility regulator, in 2015 the number of babies born through IVF and other fertility treatments passed 250,000. The rate of live births from IVF-ET went from around 14 percent in 1991 to 26.5 percent in 2014.[10] In 2014 in the United States, the rate of live births from IVF-ET or ET of frozen embryos was 33.7 percent.[11]

Furthermore, there are some studies that claim a medical advantage to implanting "frozen" versus "fresh" embryos. Fresh embryos are typically implanted in a woman from whom ova have just been harvested. This harvesting involves hyperstimulating the woman's ovaries, with a side-effect of temporarily reducing the woman's uterine lining. This in turn decreases the likelihood of the implantation of embryos that are transferred at that time. Therefore, all other things being equal, previously cryopreserved embryos—which can be transferred when the uterine lining is thicker—have a greater likelihood of implantation after ET. The 2014 CDC report would seem to show evidence that this is increasingly practiced, as in that year 17 percent of IVF cycles started were expressly for the purpose of banking all the embryos created.[12] In 1996, when the debate over abandoned embryos began, the number of cryopreserved embryos in the US was estimated to be about 100,000. By 2016 that number had increased tenfold, to about 1,000,000.[13]

THE INITIAL SCHOLARLY DEBATE

The first scholarly article on embryo adoption appeared in 1995, shortly after the publicity over the UK's law requiring the destruction of cryopreserved embryos. Between 1997 and 2007 the debate raged, with a variety of viewpoints articulated and developed. These articles were overwhelmingly written by Catholic ethicists. The scholarly discussion reached its zenith with two edited volumes of essays on the topic in 2006 and 2007.[14] Since then, the last fifteen years have seen a steady stream of new articles, a few of them refining and/or nuancing already staked-out positions, and/or critiquing opposing viewpoints. However, no further substantive development has occurred.

One part of the debate within the Catholic tradition was on whether there was defined Catholic teaching on the subject. It very quickly became apparent that that the question was truly novel in a number of ways and would require a development of Catholic doctrine in order to resolve the question.[15] Although the question has been debated by Catholic theologians for twenty years (or perhaps because it has continued to be hotly debated for twenty years), the Magisterium of the Catholic Church apparently has seen fit *not* to resolve the question. The Church's relative silence on the issue is itself evidence that the Catholic Church considers the issue of embryo adoption both as genuinely novel and one upon which "orthodox" moral theologians are deeply divided. It is generally thought that the Catholic Church is not likely to make any definitive pronouncements on the issue until it sees some unanimity on the issue among the theologians from whom it takes advice.

At various points in this chapter, the reader will find the various interlocutors referring to embryos as children or babies, or presuming that embryo adoption, if morally acceptable, will take place in the context of traditional marriage. The author, in reproducing these and other assumptions without comment, does not expect that all readers will share the underlying views presumed by some of the arguments. However, as in any moral debate, some assumptions are shared by almost all interlocutors in the debate, and the logic of arguments from all sides of the debate at times presume, for example, the humanity and/or personhood of the human embryo.[16] Readers who do not share these views are invited to consider this chapter an opportunity to come to understand the internal logic of the moral views of this group of ethicists.

RESPONSES

In the scholarly literature there are four paradigmatic moral descriptions regarding the kind of act chosen by the woman who chooses to gestate an abandoned or relinquished embryo.[17] One is that it is analogous to a *rescue* of a human being in a life-threatening or demeaning situation. A second is that it is analogous to an *adoption*. A third is that it is analogous to *surrogacy*. A fourth is that it is analogous to *procreative infidelity*. The rescue and adoption descriptions have been proposed throughout the debate. The surrogacy description was initially advanced, but soon given up. As the surrogacy description waned, the procreative infidelity viewpoint arose, and sophisticated variations of it have been continuously advanced. While these four viewpoints are distinct, they are not all mutually exclusive, for example, those who advocate the rescue description consider it morally good for a woman to adopt the embryo she gestates.

These alternative ways of describing a woman's decision to gestate a relinquished embryo are integral to its moral evaluation, as, for example, one's description of a military rebel alternatively as a "terrorist" or a "freedom fighter" also shapes and/or reflects one's moral evaluation of that rebel. Because moral description is so important, Tonti-Filippini proposed *heterologous embryo transfer* (HET), which he considered a more neutral characterization.[18]

However, as Brakman and Weaver note in their introduction, there is no neutral or even relatively neutral way to describe what is going on.[19] While the description "heterologous embryo transfer" may seem more neutral because it is so abstract, it obscures the agency of the woman receiving the embryo, and the fact that she is entering into a relationship with that embryo. In fact, the description HET ignores agency altogether, without which no moral evaluation can proceed. In contrast, *embryo adoption* is the most common and accessible characterization of what is going on. Thus, I follow them in characterizing the issue at hand as embryo adoption.

Advocates of "embryo rescue" are not opposed to embryo adoption, but argue that the "adoption" characterization leads to overly restrictive moral conclusions about gestating embryos. Those who take the "surrogacy" or "procreative infidelity" viewpoint, and who consider embryo adoption intrinsically wrong, typically do not deny that the woman's motivation to transfer the embryo to her womb and gestate it may well be adoption, but add that whatever the woman's motivation, the intention in having the embryo transferred is in itself intrinsically wrong. Thus, to call the practice *embryo adoption* does not per se rule out the possibility of making a further allowance for non-adoptive rescues, nor does it preclude the view that embryo adoption may be (intrinsically) morally wrong. It also allows for the possibility that while embryo adoption may not be intrinsically wrong, there might still be a variety of other moral objections which, while not ruling out embryo rescue or embryo adoption in principle, may rule it out in many, most, or all practical situations. At this point, I turn to the four main analogical notions that are proposed. In summarizing them, I will evaluate the strengths and weaknesses of each analogy.

Embryo Rescue

As discussed above, the initial moral analysis regarding embryo adoption arose in the context of the imminent demise of large numbers of abandoned embryos in the UK. In such a context, it is not surprising that the earliest moral analysis of women offering to gestate these embryos would focus on the benefits derived by the embryos who would be rescued from their situation. When the analysis focuses squarely (and more or less uniquely) on the benefits for the embryo, it is natural to think in terms of rescue and the heroism of those women who choose to get involved.

Indeed, the earliest analyses characterized it as an instance of moral heroism, as a choice to "rescue" an embryo. This was the initial characterization of both opponents and proponents of women gestating these abandoned embryos.[20] In characterizing the choice of a woman to gestate an abandoned embryo as a rescue, proponents draw analogies between the woman's action and that of quintessential rescuers (firefighters, police officers, lifeguards, child welfare officers, etc.). Typical was language such as "rescuing this person in distress," and trying "to save the baby's life."[21]

How apt is the analogy? While rescuers save lives or at least deliver others from danger, not all lifesaving or deliverance is typically considered a rescue. It is with good reason that Grisez cites firefighters and lifeguards as paradigms of rescuers. When one thinks of firefighters and lifeguards, what characterizes a rescue is that a) it is done in an emergency situation (often at significant risk to the rescuer), and b) the rescuer has a transitory (if any) relationship with the one being rescued. While sometimes people speak of "rescuing" someone from a boring or criminal life, or a parent "rescuing" a child, such ways of speaking invoke hyperbole, and clearly stretch the notion of *rescue* beyond the uses in which the term properly and happily resides.[22] Would one not speak of adoptive parents "rescuing" a child from a life in foster care? The paradigmatic features of a rescue are its heroic and altruistic character.[23]

In order to evaluate the adequacy of "rescue" as the appropriate moral characterization of the action, we must evaluate its limits. What does the rescue characterization downplay or ignore? It minimizes the significance of *the relationship between the woman and the embryo*. As noted above, "rescue" focuses on the actions of a heroic individual. Neither the firefighter nor the lifeguard enters into a significant "relationship" with you when they save your life, any more than does the surgeon who performs an emergency life-saving appendectomy on you. Nor do search party members who rescue you in the Alps or Himalayas.

When pressed to characterize the nature of the relationship, rescue advocates analogize it to that of a foster parent. We are left with questions of the aptness of the analogy between a rescuer and a foster parent. Are foster parents what we think of when we think of those who rescue? Do rescuers become foster parents of those they rescue? What is central to the rescue viewpoint is that it is acceptable for the gestational relationship to be intentionally transitory. Unlike the adoption viewpoint, as we shall see, the rescue viewpoint entails that the choice to gestate the child is not necessarily a choice to become the child's mother in the moral sense, with any of the resultant obligations of parenthood.[24]

Embryo Adoption

Not long after the initial analysis of embryo rescue was proposed, Helen Watt challenged it, arguing that to adequately characterize the woman's choice morally, the nature of the relationship entered was primary. Claiming that a woman, once pregnant, is always already a mother, she defended the centrality of adoption for the discussion, arguing that that was the best analogy in terms of characterizing the nature of a gestational relationship into which a woman might be justified in entering. Watt maintained that "it is ... wrong to *plan in advance* of conception (or, if one is not the genetic mother, in advance of gestation) to bear a child who will be brought up by others."[25]

Watt advanced this norm as a reply to the objection that for a woman to rescue an embryo would be surrogacy. In concluding that adoption was the appropriate characterization of what a woman would be engaged in if she chose to gestate an embryo with the intention of adopting the embryo, Watt was arguing that the gestational relationship had both an inherent and a specific kind of *moral* significance. In choosing to gestate an embryo, a woman necessarily initiates a parental relationship with the embryo that she ought to be acknowledging. In initiating a parental relationship, the woman takes on the moral responsibilities associated with parenthood.

Here we see the fundamental difference between the advocates of the rescue view and of the adoption view. The former do not see in the gestational relationship a necessarily parental relationship, whereas the latter see pregnancy as always parental. According to the former, the choice to gestate an embryo with the intention to relinquish the child at birth is simply part of the nature of a rescue; for the latter, to make such a choice is to fail to understand one of the fundamental moral requirements of parenthood.

That there would be disagreement on this point is not surprising. After all, up until this point, Catholic ethicists had not had to seriously think through the moral significance of the gestational relationship independently from the "lineal" (i.e., genetic/biological) relationship. Although Catholic ethicists had previously addressed the issue of surrogacy, it had been rejected without the need to seriously consider the independent moral significance of the gestational relationship. When the question of embryo adoption arose, for the first time there was a plausible moral scenario in which gestational and lineal motherhood could be separated.

As is evident, while rescue and adoption advocates differ on the moral significance of the gestational relationship, they agree that it can be morally acceptable to separate the gestational relationship from the lineal relationship. In other words, both viewpoints consider it morally acceptable for a woman to initiate a relationship (whether it is foster parenting or adopting) at the point of gestation, as well as at conception.[26] However, as we shall see in the next section, it is this viewpoint—shared by rescue and adoption advocates alike—that is at the heart of one of the main objections of those who see embryo adoption as intrinsically morally wrong.

As we asked regarding "rescue," we can also ask what the "adoption" characterization of the act downplays or ignores. First, while either a woman or a man (or a couple) can post-natally adopt, only a woman (or a couple) can adopt an embryo.[27] Second, depending on a variety of factors, the likelihood of the adopted embryo surviving to birth can vary tremendously. In post-natal adoptions, no such uncertainty exists.[28] Third, embryo adoption is in certain respects rather more than post-natal adoption. Advocates of embryo adoption generally argue for the moral significance of the gestational relationship. Is there perhaps something about the nature of the gestational relationship that is inimical to its characterization as "adoptive"? What exactly, in moral terms, should be made of the mother-child relationship in utero? There is typically (though by no means universally) a strong *psychological* bond, evident to pregnant women and those with newborns. This bond is also recounted by many birth mothers who give up their children for adoption, as well as by surrogate mothers, some of whom refuse to give up the children they have gestated.[29] However, can one compare this bond (which varies tremendously) with the bond between parents and the children they adopt post-natally (which also varies tremendously) in a way that can justify any significant moral conclusion?[30]

Surrogacy

When the moral debate regarding embryo adoption began, some theologians characterized it as surrogacy. Reference was made to *Donum vitae*'s characterization and rejection of surrogacy.[31] *Donum vitae* uses the standard definition of surrogacy, a surrogate mother being one who gestates a child under contract to relinquish the child at birth. Early in the debate, some argued embryo rescue or adoption constituted surrogacy in this ordinary sense[32] but that claim was soon abandoned.[33] No participant in the debate currently claims that embryo rescue necessarily constitutes surrogacy as it is defined by *Donum vitae*.

Some argued that embryo rescue and/or embryo adoption were analogous to surrogacy, and that the meaning of surrogacy should be extended to include embryo rescue and/or embryo adoption. To understand what would be involved in extending the notion of surrogacy to include embryo rescue or adoption, it is helpful to carefully distinguish various possible meanings of surrogacy. The question then becomes whether the attempted extension(s) of the notion of surrogacy discussed below are convincing.

At least four distinct understandings of surrogacy appear in the debate. Surrogacy most typically refers to the "selling" of babies, a contractual arrangement with emphasis on the *gainful* nature of the transaction. Surrogacy also typically refers to a specific agreement by a gestational mother to relinquish the baby, prior to and as a condition of gestating the embryo. When the gestational mother acts as a surrogate out of a desire to help others have a child, it is usually referred to as *altruistic* surrogacy. These two types of situations constitute what *Donum vitae* means by surrogacy. For these two understandings of surrogacy, the focus is on the relationship between those commissioning the baby and the woman gestating the baby.

Some involved in the debate attempt to apply the notion of surrogacy to the nature of the relationship between the gestational mother and the baby. According to this third view, which I call *transitory* surrogacy, what makes a gestational mother a surrogate is her decision to gestate the embryo with no specific intent to enter into a permanent relationship with the embryo, that is, with no plans to adopt the child.[34] A transitory surrogate may be choosing to rescue an embryo, or perhaps choosing to gestate the embryo because she enjoys the experience or state of pregnancy. Finally, a fourth view, which I call *disintegrative* surrogacy, is the view that any decision by a woman to gestate—and thus become pregnant with—an embryo of whom she is not the genetic mother becomes a disintegrative surrogate in her very choosing to formally separate genetic from gestational motherhood.[35]

It was relatively quickly established that embryo adoption constituted neither *gainful* nor *altruistic* nor *transitory* surrogacy. However, embryo rescue, while neither gainful nor altruistic surrogacy, does constitute *transitory* surrogacy. Of course, if one takes the *disintegrative* view of surrogacy, then embryo adoption, or for that matter any choice to transfer a heterologous embryo into a woman, would by definition constitute surrogacy. Almost all the Catholic ethicists inherently opposed to embryo adoption have declined or ceased to use the language of surrogacy, recognizing that their argument does not fit any ordinary-language use of "surrogacy," stretching that notion too far to work analogically.

Procreative Infidelity

We saw in the previous two sections that those who take the embryo adoption or the surrogacy viewpoint focus on the *relationship* between the *woman and the embryo*. In contrast, others argue that the primary focus must be the *relationship* between the *woman and her husband*.[36] Those who focus on the spousal relationship typically argue that pregnancy must be the fruit of a conjugal act. Becoming pregnant in any other way constitutes adultery, or at least some form of infidelity. Advocates of this view have coined the term *procreative integrity*, drawing an analogy to sexual integrity (i.e., the virtue of chastity).[37]

The adultery objection is a rhetorical stretch, since adultery refers to having sexual relations with a partner other than one's spouse. Early in the debate some ethicists attempted to sexualize the physician's act in transferring the embryo to the woman's uterus, speaking of the physician's act of "impregnating" the woman.[38] Leaving aside sexist assumptions that the physician would be male, this claim reveals more about equivocal uses of "impregnate" than about sexual sin.

However, claims that embryo adoption is a "procreative infidelity," drawing an analogy to "sexual infidelity" is a serious one. The most developed and sophisticated versions of the argument are by Geach and Watt. Although they both use the term *reproductive integrity*, I use the phrase *procreative infidelity* to make evident what they consider morally *wrong* about embryo adoption.[39]

To analyze the objections, I consider the paradigmatic case where a married couple formally adopt a frozen embryo, with the wife then gestating their adopted child by means of ET.[40] According to Geach, in the act of ET the woman engages in a defective "conjugal" act, which is a marital infidelity.[41] Her argument is as follows. "Conjugal" acts (i.e., acts of sexual intercourse between spouses) must be open to conceiving a child (the procreative good), and the conception of children must be the result of the "one flesh union" of spouses (the unitive good).[42] Since ET has a *procreative* good, but no *unitive* good, Geach asserts that ET is a defective conjugal act. However, Geach notes that "an act that does not contain both [unitive and procreative] meanings is not a marriage act."[43] If it is not a marriage act, it cannot be a defective marriage act. Since ET after embryo adoption has neither the unitive nor the procreative meanings of the marriage act, how can it be considered anything like, much less a failed imitation of a marriage act? Geach argues that embryo adoption can be considered an imitative or defective marriage act because embryo adoption "share[s] with the marriage act a description which is specific to it." Making this argument is the overall burden of Geach's essay.[44]

Watt approaches "procreative infidelity" differently, beginning with what she considers the two morally acceptable means to becoming a mother: via conjugal acts, and post-natal adoption. Conjugal acts are the "natural" means, whereas adoption is the "conventional" means.[45] The nature of conjugal acts is that they do not allow a woman to become pregnant and thus a mother by fiat, but only according to the contingencies of her (and/or her spouse's) fertility.[46] In contrast, the nature of an act of adoption is that the woman does becomes a mother by fiat, through a direct choice and commitment by the spouses. Since adopting has nothing per se to do with the conjugal acts, it in no way contravenes the morally appropriate respect for such acts.

What Watt rejects are acts that seek to overcome the contingency of the couple's fertility, allowing the couple to become "natural" parents by "conventional" means, by fiat.[47] According to Watt, the choice of embryo adoption is this kind of choice, whereby the woman becomes a mother by direct choice, becoming a mother once an embryo is transferred to her body. becomes pregnant through requires a manipulation of a woman's natural fertility by transferring an embryo to her body. Like Geach, Watt concludes that procreative infidelity is morally wrong in a way analogous to sexual infidelity.

Where Watt diverges from Geach is her claim that her approach to sexual ethics generally, and views on embryo adoption specifically, derives from concerns for the good of children. Watt claims that the long-term good of children is best safeguarded when they are conceived by conjugal acts, that is, acts of a couple who are expressing a life-long commitment to each other and to their potential children.[48] She argues that what is hugely important for the welfare of children is that their parents are in a reasonably well-functioning marital relationship, both for their actual security and their sense of security, that they know that they have a mother and father both committed to them and to each other. For only in such a context can children begin their lives with a sense that they are completely accepted and cared for.

Watt's emphasis on the good of children is laudatory, and one consonant with the emphases of the historic Christian tradition. While one might quibble with details of her child welfare analysis, her approach finds extremely wide support in the social science literature, particularly her claim that her focus is to give a social rather than a psychological analysis.[49]

However, what is confounding is the relevance of her concern for child welfare to embryo adoption. Does Watt have any evidence that children who are adopted as embryos by a committed married couple are less unconditionally loved or socially provided for than children born naturally or who are post-natally adopted? While there is no evidence, one can reasonably imagine that in empirical terms, the social situation of children adopted as embryos is more likely to be ideal in terms of child welfare than either the general population of children born "naturally" or adopted "post-natally."

Beyond this, there is a fundamental problem with both Geach's and Watt's argument. Geach's starting point is with what is normative for marital sexual ("conjugal") acts—that they have indissoluble unitive and procreative meanings. While the telos or orientation of conjugal acts is, as Geach puts it, the "one flesh union" and the "begetting" of children, with embryo adoption there is neither one flesh union nor begetting of a child. With embryo adoption the spouses become parents conventionally, like post-natal adoption.

Similarly, Watt's explicit objection to embryo adoption is that "if it truly is the case that a woman becomes a mother in becoming pregnant," then those who accept embryo adoption "need to explain why another 'technical' way of becoming a mother —embryo adoption—is not also a harmful supplanting of a deeply significant interpersonal act as a way of entering on parenthood" (Watt 2016, 114). Watt here forgets her basic distinction between the two ways of becoming a mother. When a woman becomes a mother via a conjugal act, Watt is correct that a woman becomes a mother in becoming pregnant. However, when a woman becomes a mother via adoption, she becomes a mother by shared choice and commitment. So with embryo adoption, she is a mother prior to being impregnated via ET, and does not become a mother by "technical" means any more than one who adopts post-natally. Thus embryo adoption does not supplant conjugal acts because, as Watt herself tells us, adoption has nothing to do with the conception of children.

Embryo Adoption Acceptable in Principle, but Still Morally Wrong?

A few Catholic moralists who have no intrinsic objection to embryo adoption (e.g., as surrogacy or procreative infidelity) consider it problematic nonetheless.[50] One concern is that EA involves inappropriate cooperation with the IVF industry. Another is that EA can be a source of scandal (in the Catholic tradition, scandal means to lead another person into sin by leading them to think that something sinful is not sinful). The main fear seems to be that a Catholic adopting an embryo might lead other Catholics to think that IVF itself is thus morally acceptable. Some of these ethicists even argue that those who adopt an embryo might encourage others to create even more embryos (unlikely in that there are already upward of a million embryos already in storage).

However, with regard to embryo adoption the objection of "scandal" is inherently weak, since it relies on baseless predictions about the future (can one reasonably predict the influence of a Catholic adopting an embryo on other Catholics without experience of such influence?) If such objections are to be taken seriously, rather than as a kind of moral fear-mongering, there is a strong burden of proof to establish "scandal." And even if scandal were caused, that would not make in itself an otherwise morally acceptable action wrong.

As for the possibility of embryo adoption involving "cooperation with the wrongdoing of others," such a possibility is not unique to embryo adoption. Similar moral problems can be involved in "traditional" adoptions. Although adoption in general is a great social good to be encouraged, discernment is also needed there. For example, with some international adoptions, is one cooperating with oppressive actions of governments? Can one be sure that the child has been freely relinquished by its parent(s)? With some private domestic adoptions, could the large fees involved invite questions about whether this is an adoption or the purchase of a commodity? Is the move to more "open" adoptions a good thing? Despite the many moral questions that can arise in some contexts of traditional adoption, no one doubts the inherent goodness of adoption when wisely conducted, both for the children and parents involved and for the common good of a society.

So too with embryo adoption. If it is indeed appropriate and good, it will still continually require wise moral judgments as to the proper contexts, regulations, and circumstances in which it is appropriate for it to occur.[51] In the right circumstances, and with the right safeguards in place, the above objections are more a vague fear of the unknown than serious moral objections.

Further Moral Considerations with Regard to Embryo Adoption

The response that has caught the imagination, both of those who choose to gestate embryos and those who write about the issue, is that adoption is the most appropriate paradigm, that adopting and parenting the embryo best captures the appropriate moral response to the plight of the orphaned embryo. When one takes this paradigm seriously, one is confronted by a number of additional issues; not the least of these is that many well-meaning persons have naive and/or one-sided views about what is involved in adopting either a pre-natal or post-natal child. It is also common for people to make unfounded generalizations about the intentions or character of prospective adoptive parents. Thus are warranted some concluding comments on the complexity of intentions in those adopting or relinquishing embryos, and also about more general theological attitudes to adoption and parenthood that have emerged in the context of this debate.

When one begins to read literature on adoption, one quickly discovers that on the one hand, some commentators idealize the prospective adoptive parents, waxing lyrical as to how such prospective parents will be acting sacrificially and displaying unparalleled charity. On the other hand, other commentators are inordinately suspicious of those adopting children, sometimes accusing adoptive parents of "shopping" for a child, engaging in an egotistical quest to accessorize their lives with a child. One can find similarly extreme viewpoints by commentators when discussing those parents who choose to relinquish their excess embryos for adoption. Some are unduly praised for "their compassionate gift of life to others," while others are harshly criticized for "abandoning their children."

With regard both to prospective adoptive parents and those considering relinquishing their embryos for adoption, in the vast majority of cases the truth lies somewhere in the middle. While embryo adoption has an aspect of charity in many cases, that neither is nor should be the primary motivation for adoption. Why is that? Any prospective adoptive parent who understands their relationship to their child as one of pure charity is either self-deceived and will find himself or herself in a problematic relationship to the child over the long term.[52] More significantly, adoptive children should be received by Christians as all children should be received. That is, as gifts from God. That is the fundamental norm for Christian parenthood. But developing a theology of parenthood belongs elsewhere.

In concluding, I return to the larger cultural questions with which I began. How does this issue function for what is largely a subculture of Catholic Christians in which the issue so resonates, despite the fact that evidently, very few Catholics adopt embryos? For a significant part of the Catholic community living in cultures of the West where media and technology typically divorce sexuality and procreation, arguments such as those by Geach and Watt are highly evocative, and with good reason. The idealism and stringency of their sexual and procreative ethic will be (and should be) highly appealing to those Catholics and other Christians wishing to live an unambiguously countercultural Christian sexual ethic, which is arguably the only possible alternative when one perceives oneself to be minority steeped in a sexually permissive society.

In a quest for an unambiguous alternative, the question of embryo adoption has seemingly become a kind of litmus test for procreative purity. However, as I have argued above, the arguments against it do not hold up. Furthermore, some of those who argue against embryo adoption bring forth a deeply troubling and anti-Christian conviction, one that is often implicit, but at times breaks out into the open. Some opponents of embryo adoption show a disdain for adoption more generally, going to far as to claim that adoptive parents are not "really" parents at all. A number of other ethicists have noted this common if not pervasive attitude among "principled" opponents of embryo adoption.[53]

In their quest for a "natural" sexual and procreative ethic, some seem to have forgotten the demands of the Christian gospel. From its earliest beginnings, one of Christianity's most distinctive practices was the adoption of infants who were abandoned by pagan parents. In the Roman empire adoption was rare, restricted to favored sons of the leading nobility to facilitate the distribution of wealth and power. In choosing to adopt abandoned and often disabled infants, the early Christians acted in a radically countercultural way, introducing this extraordinary practice to the wider culture. It is rather ironic that today, with contemporary culture having embraced the practice of adoption via Christian witness, some Catholic thinkers should be sufficiently theologically illiterate as to denigrate the practice of adoption.

Those who argue in this way unwittingly adopt a pagan rather than a Christian preoccupation with blood lines. In Christian tradition "natural" means of conception and birth are ultimately inferior to "conventional" birth, birth in the Spirit. The rejection of the priority of bloodlines is also highly evident in Catholic Christianity's advocacy of celibacy, which is arguably unparalleled in any other major religious tradition.

Christians more than anyone should recognize the priority of being "born again," becoming adopted children of a heavenly Father. One cannot help but wonder how those Christian theorists who implicitly (or even explicitly) claim that adoptive parents are not "real" parents could possibly believe that they have a "real" heavenly Father. For Christianity, the normative category for spiritual birth and life is adoption. As a moral practice, it is arguably superior to natural procreation, in its potential to imitate God's love. Arguments against embryo adoption which implicitly question or denigrate the Christian practice of adoption should be viewed with great suspicion.

Notes

1. Allen's lecture, entitled "Pope Benedict and Moral Theology," was presented at the Society of Christian Ethics in Phoenix, Arizona, on January 5, 2006. See Allen, "Ethical Issues facing Benedict XVI," *National Catholic Reporter* 5, 19 (January 13, 2006), http://nationalcatholicreporter.org/word/word011306.htm
2. See e.g., C. Lester, "Embryo 'Adoption' is Growing, But It Is Getting Tangled in the Abortion Debate," *New York Times*, February 17, 2019, https://www.nytimes.com/2019/02/17/health/embryo-adoption-donated-snowflake.html. When one reads the "personal stories" from various embryo adoption websites, one realizes that both those who donate to and adopt from these agencies almost universally explain their decision-making process and journey through embryo adoption in explicitly religious terms, that in donating their embryos or adopting embryos, they are e.g., obeying God's will for these embryonic children, that they pray regarding their decisions, some donors have written into the contract that the babies must be baptized, and so on. See, e.g., https://embryoadoption.org/personal-stories/#eds.
3. In contrast, in the United States in 2014 alone there were over 57,000 in vitro fertilization (IVF) babies delivered.
4. Lester, "Embryo 'Adoption' is Growing."
5. Beginning on August 1, 1996, in compliance with the 1990 law, fertility clinics in Great Britain moved to destroy over 3,000 frozen embryos, thawing and then incinerating them. See Tom Utley, "Time Runs Out for 3,000 Embryos as Last Appeals Fail," *Daily Telegraph* (London), August 1, 1996. For details on the law, see *The Human Fertilisation and Embryology Act 1990*, ch. 37.
6. In *L'Osservatore Romano*, a Vatican periodical known for promulgating quasi-official Vatican viewpoints, Mauricio Faggioni proposed that as a last resort, these embryos could

be transferred to another woman if they could not be transferred to the genetic mother. More than three hundred Italian women offered to participate in such adoptions and an Italian clinic offered to accept all the embryos for future adoption. The Catholic hierarchy in the UK did not take the same stance. The UK's leading bishop, Basil Cardinal Hume— while proclaiming the destruction of these embryos revealed, as with abortion, the UK's moral bankruptcy—he did not sanction embryo adoption. Instead, Hume concluded that the embryos should be "disposed of with dignity."

7. Catholic World News wire service reported that "Mario Ciampi of the Center for Help to Life said his office had heard from one hundred women in the central Italian town of Massa Carrara and more requests were coming in from all over Italy." CWN Wire Service, "More Than 100 Italian Women Offer to Adopt Frozen Embryos," July 26, 1996.
8. While the early debates focused on rescuing abandoned embryos, the overwhelming number of embryos currently adopted involve the active participation of donors who relinquish rather than abandon their embryos.
9. As recently as 2007 there was the case of Nadya Suleyman delivering octuplets after having twelve embryos implanted in her. As of 2009, the rate of twins born through IVF was between 16 and 33 percent, whereas the rate of natural twins is about 1 percent. Sarah Richards, "In Defence of Twins," *Slate*, August 15, 2011.
10. http://www.hfea.gov.uk/10536.html.
11. Historically, US data is less reliable than that of the UK. US fertility clinics were traditionally not required to report their data to the CDC, and while about 90 percent of fertility clinics currently report their data to the CDC, there is suspicion about the accuracy of the data supplied by some clinics, since the commercial success of the clinics is so highly dependent on their success rates.
12. Centers for Disease Control and Prevention, American Society for Reproductive Medicine, Society for Assisted Reproductive Technology, *2014 Assisted Reproductive Technology National Summary Report* (Atlanta, GA: US Dept of Health and Human Services, 2016), 3–5. 2014 CDC Summary Report. Some of these 35,000+ banking cycles were to freeze retrieved eggs rather than embryos.
13. References from National Embryo Donation Center, 2015 *New York Times* article and 2013 *Telegraph* article.
14. T. Berg and E. Furton, eds., *Human Embryo Adoption: Biotechnology, Marriage, and the Right to Life* (Philadelphia: National Catholic Bioethics Centre, 2006); S.-V. Brakman and D. F. Weaver, eds., *The Ethics of Embryo Adoption and the Catholic Tradition* (New York: Springer, 2007).
15. The two most authoritative documents produced by the Roman Catholic Church relevant to the question of embryo adoption are *Donum vitae* (1987), and *Dignitatis personae* (2009).
16. Many of the participants in the embryo adoption debate do in fact make arguments about the moral status of the human embryo, and whether, e.g., non-married women should adopt embryos. However, those and other related questions, while inherently interesting and important, are beyond the scope of this chapter.
17. Early and/or key advocates of the various positions, including the year of their first publication on the subject. *Embryo Rescue*: G. Surtees, "Adoption of a Frozen Embryo," *Homiletic and Pastoral Review* 96 (1996): 7–16; G. Grisez, "Should a Woman Try to Bear Her Dead Sister's Embryo?" in *The Way of the Lord Jesus, Vol. 3: Difficult Moral Questions* (Quincy, IL: Franciscan Herald Press, 1997); W. E. May, *Catholic Bioethics and the Gift of Human Life*

(Huntington, IN: Our Sunday Visitor, 2000); E. C. Brugger, "In Defense of Heterologous Embryo Transfer," *National Catholic Bioethics Quarterly* 5, no. 1 (2005): 95–112; P. Ryan, "Our Moral Obligation to the Abandoned Embryo," in Berg and Furton, *Human Embryo Adoption*, 297–326; T. Williams, "The Least of My Brethren: The Ethics of Heterologous Embryo Transfer," *Human Life Review* 31 (2005): 87–98. *Embryo Adoption*: H. Watt, "Are There Any Circumstances in Which It Would Be Morally Admirable for a Woman to Seek to Have an Orphan Embryo Implanted in Her Womb (2)?" in *Issues for a Catholic Bioethic*, edited by Luke Gormally, 347–352 (London: Linacre Centre, 1999); J. R. Berkman, "Adopting Embryos in America," *Scottish Journal of Theology* 55, no. 4 (2002b): 438–460; M. J. Iozzio, "It Is Time to Support Embryo Adoption," *National Catholic Bioethics Quarterly* 2, no. 4 (2002): 585–593; M. Barahona et al. "The Moral Licitness of Adopting Frozen Embryos, with Answers to Objections," in *Human Embryo Adoption: Biotechnology, Marriage, and the Right to Life*, edited by T. Berg and E. Furton (Philadelphia: National Catholic Bioethics Centre), 273–296; D. F. Weaver, "Embryo Adoption Theologically Considered: Bodies, Adoption, and the Common Good," in Brakman and Weaver, *The Ethics of Embryo Adoption*, 141–160; S.-V. Brakman, "Real Mothers and Good Stewards: The Ethics of Embryo Adoption," in Brakman and Weaver, *The Ethics of Embryo Adoption*, 119–138; B. Brown and J. Eberl, "Ethical Considerations in Defense of Embryo Adoption" in Brakman and Weaver (2007), 103–118; C. Tollefsen, "Could Human Embryo Adoption be Intrinsically Immoral?" in Brakman and Weaver, *The Ethics of Embryo Adoption*, 85–102. *Surrogacy*: W. Smith, "Rescue the Frozen?" *Homiletic and Pastoral Review* 96 (1995): 8–9; M. Geach, "Are There Any Circumstances in Which It Would Be Morally Admirable for a Woman to Seek to Have an Orphan Embryo Implanted in Her Womb?" in *Issues for a Catholic Bioethic*, edited by Luke Gormally, 341–346 (London: Linacre Centre, 1999); N. Tonti-Filippini, "The Embryo Rescue Debate: Impregnating Women, Ectogenesis, and Restoration from Suspended Animation," *National Catholic Bioethics Quarterly* 3, no. 1 (2003): 111–137; S. A. Long, "An Argument for the Embryonic Intactness of Marriage," *Thomist* 70 (2006): 267–288. *Procreative Infidelity*: Geach, "Are there Any Circumstances?," 341–346; N. Austriaco, "On the Catholic Vision of Conjugal Love and the Morality of Embryo Transfer," in Berg and Furton (2006), 115–134; H. Watt, "Becoming Pregnant or Becoming a Mother?," in Berg and Furton (2006), 55–67; F. de Rosa, "On Rescuing Frozen Embryos," *Linacre Quarterly* 69, no. 3 (2002): 228–260; C. Althaus, "Can One 'Rescue' a Human Embryo? The Moral Object of the Acting Woman," *National Catholic Bioethics Quarterly* 5, no. 1 (2005): 113–141; C. Oleson (2005), "The Nuptial Womb: On the Moral Significance of Being 'With Child,'" in Berg and Furton, *Human Embryo Adoption*, 165–196.

18. Tonti-Filippini, "The Embryo Rescue Debate"; W. Stempsey, "Heterologous Embryo Transfer: Metaphor and Morality," in Brakman and Weaver, *The Ethics of Embryo Adoption*, 25–42.
19. Brakman and Weaver, *The Ethics of Embryo Adoption*.
20. Smith, "Rescue the Frozen?"; Grisez, "Should a Woman Try."
21. Grisez, "Should a Woman Try," 241–242.
22. J. R. Berkman, "Gestating the Embryos of Others: Surrogacy? Adoption? Rescue?" *National Catholic Bioethics Quarterly* 3, no. 2 (2003a): 309–329.
23. It is true that "rescue" is sometimes used in other analogous ways. For example, a rescue may retrospectively be seen as constituting the beginning of a relationship, as in "she rescued him from a life of alcoholism," or "he rescued her from an abusive family." However, the standard persona of the rescuer is one who suddenly arrives on the scene, performs his/

her heroic rescue and then walks or rides off into the sunset, with the person being rescued often not even getting an opportunity to express thanks. Grisez's choice of firefighters, police officers, and lifeguards as examples of rescuers shows that he shares this assumption.
24. M. Moschella, "Gestation Does Not Necessarily Imply Parenthood: Implications for the Morality of Embryo Adoption and Embryo Rescue," *American Catholic Philosophical Quarterly* 92, no. 1 (2018): 21–48.
25. Watt, "Are There Any Circumstances," 347.
26. Another way of characterizing the difference is as follows: both the rescue and adoption views recognize that with abandoned frozen embryos the normative link between the three elements of motherhood (i.e., genetic, gestational, and social aspects) has already been severed; and both agree that it can be legitimate for a woman to choose to become a gestational mother even if one is not the genetic mother of a child; they differ in that rescue advocates argue a woman can choose to become a gestational mother fully intending NOT to be the social mother of the child, whereas adoption advocates argue that one should never intend to separate the gestational and the social aspects of motherhood.
27. Of course, this is also true with regard to the rescue characterization.
28. I am ambivalent regarding the moral relevance of this point.
29. For more on this, including reflection on surrogate mothers who win custody of the children they gestate in legal proceedings, see H. Watt, *The Ethics of Pregnancy, Abortion, and Childbirth: Exploring Moral Issues in Childbearing* (London: Routledge, 2016).
30. Elsewhere I discuss medical studies which a biological "bond" which occurs in gestation. The mother and fetus exchange cells, which remain in the body of the other permanently. This is true whether or not the gestational mother is also the lineal mother. On this basis, some argue that this biological relationship has a moral character, which is alternatively used to argue either for or against embryo adoption (Berkman, "Gestating the Embryos of Others," 309–329).
31. Congregation for the Doctrine of the Faith (CDF), "Instruction on Respect for Human Life in Its Origin and on the Dignity of Procreation," February 22, 1987; *Acta Apostolicae Sedis* 80 (1988): 70–102. In the first decade of the debate over embryo adoption, *Donum vitae* was universally regarded by Catholic moral theologians as the most authoritative Catholic Church teaching on the moral questions most relevant to that of embryo adoption.
32. Smith, "Rescue the Frozen?"; Geach, "Are There Any Circumstances?"
33. J. R. Berkman, "The Morality of Adopting Frozen Embryos in Light of *Donum vitae*," *Studia Moralia* 40, no. 1 (2002a): 1–27; Berkman "Gestating the Embryos of Others," 2003; and Stempsey, "Heterologous Embryo Transfer."
34. William May argues that morally speaking, there is no intrinsic relationship between the roles of the gestational and social mother because in a variety of situations a woman can choose to give up her child for adoption without being involved in any moral wrongdoing. He cites examples of a young, unwed mother who gives up her child for adoption and a woman who gives up for adoption a child she has conceived by rape (May, *Catholic Bioethics*, 106–108).
35. On this view, even if the relationship between the genetic mother and the embryo is definitively broken (e.g., the genetic mother has died), it is surrogacy to become the gestational mother of an embryo of whom one is not also the genetic mother.
36. Tonti-Filippini, "The Embryo Rescue Debate." Arguments that liken embryo adoption to "adultery" or "procreative infidelity" ignore the fact that there are cases all around the world where single persons rightly post-natally adopt children in need. Since it can be

appropriate for a single woman to (post-natally) adopt a child, do advocates of this viewpoint object to single women adopting embryos? For arguments based on "procreative infidelity" are limited to spouses. This is ironic, since the original context of "rescuing" abandoned embryos would have involved unmarried women.

37. NB: Geach and Watt speak of "violating *reproductive* integrity." I substitute "procreative" for "reproductive" because in the Catholic perspective that Geach and Watt both follow, it is clearly the superior and authoritative term, as reflected by its overwhelming dominance in authoritative Church teaching. For example, *Donum vitae* uses "procreation" and its variants sixty-nine times, but "reproduction" only once, putting the term in scare quotes as a debased substitute for procreation (CDF, "Instruction on Respect for Human Life"). Similarly, *Dignitas personae* speaks of "reproduction" only when referring to cloning, consistently using "procreation" to refer to the beginning of human life (CDF, *Instruction Dignitas personae on Certain Bioethical Questions*, Vatican website, September 8, 2008, https://www.vatican.va/roman_curia/congregations/cfaith/documents/rc_con_cfaith_doc_20081208_dignitas-personae_en.html).

    The only reason I can fathom as for using the anti-theological term "reproductive" is that it obfuscates the clear distinction between "conception" and "gestation" that in all other contexts Geach and Watt morally affirm.

38. Geach, "Are There Any Circumstances?"; Tonti-Filippini, "The Embryo Rescue Debate."
39. For my reason for using "procreation" instead of Geach's choice of "reproduction," see endnote 37.
40. I use "adopted child" rather than adopted embryo because Geach speaks of the wife who is newly impregnated as being "with child."
41. Geach, "Rescuing Frozen Embryos," 217–230.
42. The view that the *unitive* and *procreative* goods of conjugal acts must be respected in each conjugal act is standard Catholic sexual teaching. See e.g., CDF, "Instruction on Respect for Human Life," 70–102.
43. M. Geach, "Motherhood, IVF, and Sexual Ethics," in *Fertility and Gender: Issues in Reproductive and Sexual Ethics*, edited by Helen Watt, 169–183 (Oxford: Anscombe Bioethics Centre, 2011), 169.
44. Ibid., 177.
45. Watt says that since adoption has nothing to do per se with her fertility, it does not contravene the necessary respect for conjugal acts and the natural limits of her fertility.
46. H. Watt, "Becoming Pregnant or Becoming a Mother?" in Berg and Furton, *Human Embryo Adoption*, 60. Watt's argument for restricting "natural" means of becoming a mother to conjugal acts is that these acts "express the marital relationship in which the child is best nurtured." She goes on to make the stronger claim that for the good of the child, lineal and gestational (what Watt together calls "biological") motherhood should be initiated in conjugal acts which come to their natural fulfillment in pregnancy and birth.
47. Ibid., 61.
48. Watt puts it as follows: "Embryo adoption also fails to respect the crucial social role of pregnancy in "placing" a child in the world in terms of the child's origin." Personal communication.
49. Watt, *The Ethics of Pregnancy, Abortion, and Childbirth*.
50. Stempsey, "Heterologous Embryo Transfer," 25–42; J. Grabowski and C. Gross, "*Dignitas personae* and the Adoption of Frozen Embryos," *National Catholic Bioethics Quarterly* 10,

no. 2 (2010): 307–328; G. Meilaender, *Not by Nature but by Grace: Forming Families through Adoption* (South Bend, IN: University of Notre Dame Press, 2016).
51. J. R. Berkman and K. Carey, "Ethical and Religious Directives for a Catholic Embryo Adoption Agency: A Thought Experiment," in Brakman and Weaver, *The Ethics of Embryo Adoption*, 251–274.
52. For an extended discussion of parental motivation in those who adopt and those who relinquish embryos, see Berkman and Carey, "Ethical and Religious Directives," 266–269.
53. Berkman, "Virtuous Parenting and Orphaned Embryos," 13–36; Tollefsen, "Could Human Embryo Adoption Be Immoral?"

Bibliography

Althaus, C. "Can One 'Rescue' a Human Embryo? The Moral Object of the Acting Woman." *National Catholic Bioethics Quarterly* 5, no. 1 (2005): 113–141.
Austriaco, N. "On the Catholic Vision of Conjugal Love and the Morality of Embryo Transfer." In Berg and Furton 2006, 115–134.
Bankowski, B. J., Lyerly, A. D., Faden, R. R., and Wallach, E. E. "The Social Implications of Embryo Cryopreservation." *Fertility and Sterility* 84 (2005): 823–832.
Berg, T., and Furton E., eds. *Human Embryo Adoption: Biotechnology, Marriage, and the Right to Life* (Philadelphia: National Catholic Bioethics Centre, 2006).
Berkman, J. R. "The Morality of Adopting Frozen Embryos in Light of *Donum vitae*." *Studia Moralia* 40 no. 1 (2002a): 1–27.
Berkman, J. R. "Adopting Embryos in America." *Scottish Journal of Theology* 55, no. 4 (2002b): 438–460.
Berkman, J. R. "Gestating the Embryos of Others: Surrogacy? Adoption? Rescue?" *National Catholic Bioethics Quarterly* 3, no. 2 (2003a): 309–329.
Berkman, J. R. "Response to Tonti-Filippini on 'Gestating the Embryos of Others.'" *National Catholic Bioethics Quarterly* 3, no. 4 (2003b): 660–664.
Berkman, J. R. "Virtuous Parenting and Orphaned Embryos." In Berg and Furton 2006, 13–36.
Berkman, J. R., May, W., and Tonti-Filippini, N. "The Embryo Rescue Debate." *National Catholic Bioethics Quarterly* 4, no. 1 (2004): 9–14.
Berkman, J. R. and Carey, K. "Ethical and Religious Directives for a Catholic Embryo Adoption Agency: A Thought Experiment." In Brakman and Weaver 2007, 251–274.
Boswell, J. *The Kindness of Strangers: The Abandonment of Children in Western Europe from Late Antiquity to the Renaissance*. New York: Pantheon Books, 1988.
Brakman, S.-V. "Real Mothers and Good Stewards: The Ethics of Embryo Adoption." In Brakman and Weaver 2007, 119–138.
Brakman, S.-V. and Weaver, D. F., eds. *The Ethics of Embryo Adoption and the Catholic Tradition* (New York: Springer, 2007).
Brown, B., and J. Eberl. "Ethical Considerations in Defense of Embryo Adoption." In Brakman and Weaver 2007, 103–118.
Brugger, E. C. "In Defense of Heterologous Embryo Transfer." *National Catholic Bioethics Quarterly* 5, no. 1 (2005): 95–112.

Congregation for the Doctrine of the Faith (CDF). "Instruction on Respect for Human Life in Its Origin and on the Dignity of Procreation," February 22, 1987: *Acta Apostolicae Sedis* 80 (1988): 70–102.

Congregation for the Doctrine of the Faith (CDF). *Instruction* Dignitas personae *on Certain Bioethical Questions.* Vatican website. September 8, 2008. https://www.vatican.va/roman_curia/congregations/cfaith/documents/rc_con_cfaith_doc_20081208_dignitas-personae_en.html.

de Rosa, F. "On Rescuing Frozen Embryos." *Linacre Quarterly* 69, no. 3 (2002): 228–260.

Furton, E. "Embryo Adoption Reconsidered." *National Catholic Bioethics Quarterly* 10, no. 2 (2010): 329–345.

Geach, M. "Are There Any Circumstances in Which It Would Be Morally Admirable for a Woman to Seek to Have an Orphan Embryo Implanted in Her Womb? (1)." In *Issues for a Catholic Bioethic*, edited by Luke Gormally, 341–346 (London: Linacre Centre, 1999).

Geach, M. "Rescuing Frozen Embryos." In Edward Furton (ed.), *What Is Man, O Lord? The Human Person in a Biotech Age*, 217–230 (Boston: National Catholic Bioethics Center, 2002).

Geach, M. "The Female Act of Allowing an Intromission of Impregnating Kind." In Berg and Furton 2006, 251–271.

Geach, M. "Motherhood, IVF, and Sexual Ethics." In *Fertility and Gender: Issues in Reproductive and Sexual Ethics*, edited by Helen Watt, 169–183 (Oxford: Anscombe Bioethics Centre, 2011).

Grabowski, J. and Gross, C. "*Dignitas personae* and the Adoption of Frozen Embryos." *National Catholic Bioethics Quarterly* 10, no. 2 (2010): 307–328.

Grisez, G. "Should a Woman Try to Bear Her Dead Sister's Embryo?" In *The Way of the Lord Jesus, Vol. 3: Difficult Moral Questions* (Quincy, IL: Franciscan Herald Press, 1997).

Hoffman, D. I., et al. "Cryopreserved Embryos in the United States and Their Availability for Research." *Fertility and Sterility* 79 (2003): 1063–1069.

Iozzio, M. J. "It Is Time to Support Embryo Adoption." *National Catholic Bioethics Quarterly* 2, no. 4 (2002): 585–593.

Krivak, J. A. *Heterologous Embryo Transfer as an Act of Adoption: A Moral Analysis Based on a Catholic Theology of Adoption.* PhD diss., Fordham University, 2015.

Lester, C. "Embryo 'Adoption' is Growing, But It Is Getting Tangled in the Abortion Debate." *New York Times*. February 17, 2019, https://www.nytimes.com/2019/02/17/health/embryo-adoption-donated-snowflake.html

Long, S. A. "An Argument for the Embryonic Intactness of Marriage." *Thomist* 70 (2006): 267–288.

May, W. E. *Catholic Bioethics and the Gift of Human Life* (Huntington, IN: Our Sunday Visitor, 2000).

May, W. E. "On 'Rescuing' Frozen Embryos: Why the Decision to Do So Is Moral." *National Catholic Bioethics Quarterly*, 5, no. 1 (2005): 51–57.

May, W. E. "The Object of the Acting Woman in Embryo Rescue." In Berg and Furton 2006, 135–163.

Meilaender, G. *Not by Nature but by Grace: Forming Families through Adoption* (South Bend, IN: University of Notre Dame Press, 2016).

Montgomery, L. M. *Anne of Green Gables.* (Boston: L. C. Page, 1908).

Moschella, M. "Gestation Does Not Necessarily Imply Parenthood: Implications for the Morality of Embryo Adoption and Embryo Rescue." *American Catholic Philosophical Quarterly* 92, no. 1 (2018): 21–48.

Oleson, C. (2005), "The Nuptial Womb: On the Moral Significance of Being 'With Child.'" In Berg and Furton 2006, 165–196.

Onder, R. "Practical and Moral Caveats on Heterologous Embryo Transfer." *National Catholic Bioethics Quarterly* 5, no. 1 (2005): 75–94.

Pinches, C. *Theology and Action* (Grand Rapids, MI: Eerdmans, 2002)

Poza, R. "The Frozen Children: The Rise—and Complications—of Embryo Adoption in the U.S." *Pacific Standard*, May 5, 2014.

Rex, E. "IVF, Embryo Transfer, and Embryo Adoption: A Response to Repenshek and Delaquil," *National Catholic Bioethics Quarterly* 14, no. 2 (2014): 227–234.

Ryan, P. "Our Moral Obligation to the Abandoned Embryo." In Berg and Furton 2006, 297–326.

Smith, W. "Rescue the Frozen?" *Homiletic and Pastoral Review* 96 (1995): 8–9.

Stanmeyer, J. "An Embryo Adoptive Father's Perspective." In Brakman and Weaver 2007, 231–236.

Stanmeyer, S. "An Embryo Adoptive Mother's Perspective." In Brakman and Weaver 2007, 237–251.

Stempsey, W. "Heterologous Embryo Transfer: Metaphor and Morality." In Brakman and Weaver, 25–42.

Surtees, G. "Adoption of a Frozen Embryo." *Homiletic and Pastoral Review* 96 (1996): 7–16.

Tollefsen C. "Could Human Embryo Adoption be Intrinsically Immoral?" In Brakman and Weaver 2007, 85–102.

Tollefsen C. "Divine, Human, and Embryo Adoption." *National Catholic Bioethics Quarterly* 10, no. 1 (2010): 75–85.

Tonti-Filippini, N. "The Embryo Rescue Debate: Impregnating Women, Ectogenesis, and Restoration from Suspended Animation." *National Catholic Bioethics Quarterly* 3, no. 1 (2003): 111–137.

Watt, H. "Are There Any Circumstances in Which It Would Be Morally Admirable for a Woman to Seek to Have an Orphan Embryo Implanted in Her Womb (2)?" In *Issues for a Catholic Bioethic*, edited by Luke Gormally 1999, 347–352 (London: Linacre Centre).

Watt, H. "A Brief Defense of Frozen Embryo Adoption." *National Catholic Bioethics Quarterly* 1, no. 2 (2001): 151–154.

Watt, H. "Becoming Pregnant or Becoming a Mother?" In Berg and Furton 2006, 55–67.

Watt, H. *The Ethics of Pregnancy, Abortion, and Childbirth: Exploring Moral Issues in Childbearing* (London: Routledge, 2016).

Weaver, D. F. "Embryo Adoption Theologically Considered: Bodies, Adoption, and the Common Good." In Brakman and Weaver 2007, 141–160.

Williams, T. "The Least of My Brethren: The Ethics of Heterologous Embryo Transfer." *Human Life Review* 31 (2005): 87–98.

CHAPTER 16

BIBLICAL CONTEXTS FOR ADOPTION AND SURROGACY

DAVID M. SMOLIN

This chapter will analyze Biblical materials relevant to adoption and surrogacy.[1] As to adoption, the chapter will concentrate on the Biblical treatment of "adoption" and "orphan," and associated Biblical narratives and teachings. While contemporary methods of assisted reproductive technology of course did not exist in Biblical times, nonetheless narratives in Genesis are commonly cited as precursors of surrogacy. Hence, the chapter will analyze these purported "surrogacy" narratives.

The chapter cautions against reading contemporary assumptions and practices related to adoption and surrogacy into the ancient Scriptural texts. Whether the Scriptures are viewed simply as historically influential precedents, or as religiously authoritative, reading our presuppositions and practices into the texts inappropriately supplies contemporary practices with a false patina of legitimacy.

BIBLICAL CONTEXTS FOR ADOPTION

Adoption in the Christian Scriptures

Old Testament (Hebrew Bible)
The Absence of Adoption from the Law of Moses

There is no law of adoption in the Law of Moses.[2] Both the term and the practice are missing from the more than six hundred laws of the Torah. Later Jewish interpretations of the Torah, such as the Talmud, verify this absence, and agree that Jewish law lacks any law or practice of adoption. Instead, within Jewish law (outside of the Bible) there is provision for a role known as caring for another's child. While such role is praised, it does not involve a change in the legal identity of the child. The child's name, identity, and family history are not altered by this form of care. However praised, this quasi-adoptive role in traditional Jewish law is more akin to foster care or guardianship than to formal adoption.[3]

The reasons for this absence are clear. The Law of Moses is created for a patriarchal, patrilineal, and tribally organized society in which biological lineage through the father and male line are paramount. Children belong not only to their father, but also to a lineage going back ultimately to one of the twelve tribes and hence one of the sons of Israel (Jacob).[4] Within this family system, it would be virtually unthinkable to take a child of dead parents and legally remove the child from their father's lineage. Such would be to blot the father and family from Israel, in a society where continuation of the patriarchal, inter-generation family line is a paramount goal of the family system.[5] Thus, within such a system one would assume that when infants or children lose their father or parents through death or otherwise, it would be the responsibility of the relatives to raise the child while preserving the child's original identity.[6]

One situation where a child is reassigned fathers by the law is that of levirate marriage, whose object is to preserve the family line of a man who dies without an heir. In such a situation, the brother and widow are obligated to marry and assign the first son legally to the (deceased) brother and husband.[7] Of course in such an instance the child would be raised in the household of the biological father and mother, and so such an instance is certainly not comparable to contemporary forms of adoption. Indeed, this custom underscores the importance of the patriarchal family line within Israel.

It is noteworthy that there is no provision in the Law of Moses for adopting the children of foreigners, whether of those abandoned by foreigners or the children of those conquered by Israel. By contrast, the law makes specific provision for marrying foreign women conquered by Israel and bringing them into Israel.[8] Thus, Biblical and Jewish law generally rejects the fundamental legal concept of adoption, the legal change in the child's identity. This rejection occurred despite interactions with other cultures in which this legal concept did exist and was practiced, and thus was a self-conscious distinction between the law of the people of God and that of the "nations." Interestingly, this rejection of the fundamental concept of adoption is similar to what would later occur in Islam.[9] Ultimately, both Judaism and Islam provide a category for raising someone else's child in one's household, without changing the legal identity of the child and without removing them, in identity, name, and law, from their original family.[10]

Purported Instances of Adoption in the Old Testament

Moses The few examples of adoption or adoption-like practices in the Hebrew Bible underscore the lack of adoption in the Mosaic and Jewish law. The most prominent of these is the adoption of Moses.[11] While some modern Christians include Moses in their discussions of Biblical foundations for adoption,[12] the story more naturally supports a negative perspective on adoption. The story begins with Pharaoh ordering the Hebrew midwives to kill all of the Israelite male children.[13] Pharaoh's purpose was in modern terms genocidal, as he wanted either to destroy entirely, or destroy partially, the Hebrew people, and it is considered genocide to intentionally destroy a people "in whole or in part" through "killing members of the group."[14] The male line was attacked presumably because the continuation of the patriarchal Hebrew people depended on the continuity of the male line, rendering it unnecessary to kill the daughters of the Hebrews. However, the Hebrew midwives "feared God" and did not obey the command to murder the male infants, subsequently lying to Pharaoh to cover up their disobedience.[15] Subsequently Pharaoh directly orders that the Hebrew sons be "cast into the river."[16]

Moses is born into the tribe of Levi in the midst of this genocidal infanticide. Moses's mother hides him as long as possible, and then finally places him into an ark or basket, placing it in the reeds by the riverbank. Moses's sister watched to see what would occur. It is in this context that the "adoptive parent," Pharaoh's daughter, discovered Moses. Knowing this was a Hebrew child, and presumably knowing the decree of Pharaoh, she had "compassion" on him, intervening to save the child's life. Pharaoh's daughter hired Moses's mother to nurse him, with Moses initially cared for by his own mother within his mother's household.[17] (It is unclear from the text whether Pharaoh's daughter realizes what anyone would suspect, that the Hebrew girl who approaches her is a relative of the child and the nurse the girl locates is the child's mother.) Given the common custom of nursing for several years, and the textual statement that Moses was taken to Pharaoh's daughter after he had grown, it is apparent that Moses was raised for at least several years within the family of his birth. Pharaoh's daughter thus effectively shielded Moses from Pharaoh's decree of death even as he remained initially with his own mother. Thus, only when Moses was older did his mother bring him to Pharaoh's daughter, and then "he became her son."[18]

Whether one thinks of Pharaoh's daughter as a woman moved by compassion to save a child's life, or as a woman exploiting the vulnerability of those whom her father had condemned to death, the portrayal certainly does not refer to any kind of adoption that one would want to systematize into a law or practice. Giving mothers a choice of their children being murdered by an oppressive, genocidal decree, or adopted, is hardly an ethical practice. Moreover, Pharaoh's daughter was not necessarily acting contrary to the ultimate purpose of her father, the Pharaoh, for his main goal was to reduce the number of Hebrew children. If the adoption had been successful in making Moses permanently into an Egyptian, there would indeed have been one less Hebrew male child to carry on the lineage of the Hebrew people. Taking and forcibly adopting the children of another's people can be, like the murder of a people's children, an effective means of eliminating or reducing that people: literally a form of genocide under contemporary international law.[19]

However, the adoption, as an *adoption*, failed. As a man, Moses identified completely with the people of His birth, the Hebrew people. Thus, when he saw an Egyptian beating a Hebrew, "one of his brethren," he killed the Egyptian; when this becomes known, Moses flees from Pharaoh to preserve his own life.[20] The commentary of the New Testament on Moses's choice to reject his adoptive family and people and return to the people of his birth is clear:

> By faith Moses, when he was come to years, refused to be called the son of Pharaoh's daughter; choosing rather to suffer affliction with the people of God, than to enjoy the pleasures of sin for a season; esteeming the reproach of Christ greater riches than the treasures in Egypt: for he had respect unto the recompense of the reward. By faith he forsook Egypt, not fearing the wrath of the king: for he endured, as seeing him who is invisible.[21]

Moses not only returns to his people in general; he also returns to his specific family. Thus, Moses' sister Miriam and brother Aaron are by his side as he leads Israel.[22] Moses is one of the most important figures in the Hebrew Bible and, from a Jewish or Christian point of view, one of the most consequential people in history. While Pharaoh's daughter saved his life, as a commentary on adoption the message is clear: Moses's critical role in the history of his people, and the history of the world, hinges on him rejecting his adoptive identity and returning to the people and family of his birth. The extra-Biblical Jewish traditions praising Pharaoh's daughter underscore this conclusion, for they add narratives in which she ultimately rejects her own people, goes with Moses and the Israelites as a part of the Exodus, and ultimately becomes a part of the lineage of Israel through marriage and bearing children. These traditions identify Moses's adoptive mother with "Bithiah the daughter of Pharaoh," who married Mered of the tribe of Judah in 1 Chronicles 4:18.[23] From this perspective the adoption worked in reverse, with the adoptive mother becoming absorbed into the original family and people of the child. Yet, even in this reverse adoption, she remains in the Biblical text "the daughter of Pharaoh," for even absorption into the people of God does not eliminate her lineage. Indeed, her name, "Bithiah," means daughter of the Lord (YHWH), so the Biblical text calls her, literally, "daughter of the Lord, daughter of Pharaoh": even God does not deny her biological lineage in making her a daughter of God.[24]

It is difficult not to see in the story of Moses not only a dramatic story of a man caught between two identities, but also a Jewish rejection of the central concept of adoption, that a legal procedure could change the fundamental identity of a human being. Adoption turns out to be a pagan, foreign custom, whose fundamental premise is proven false in the story of Moses, a man who accepted his birth identity even if it meant choosing the identity of a slave people over the identity of a royal prince of a great and powerful people and dynasty.

Esther One of the most famous of the purported "adoptions" in the Hebrew Bible concerns Esther, the Jewish woman who, married to the Persian king, intercedes with the king for the survival of her people.[25] The text indicates that Esther was taken as a daughter by Mordecai, her cousin, after the death of her parents.[26] It is unclear under the text whether this was a formal legal adoption under Persian law, or an informal extended family arrangement of the kind one would expect within Hebrew extended families. The word *adoption* is not used in the Hebrew text, nor in the Septuagint (LXX), but the Latin term for adoption is used in the Vulgate; hence English translations based on the Hebrew text don't contain the word *adoption*, while Roman Catholic translations based on the Vulgate do use the term *adoption*.[27] The Biblical text emphasizes the family relationship between Mordecai and Abihail, Esther's father, calling Esther "the daughter of Abihail the uncle of Mordecai, who had taken her for his daughter."[28] The Vulgate is similar but instead considers Abihail and Mordecai brothers. Thus, Mordecai was either the first cousin or the uncle of Esther.[29] Thus, the text stresses not only Esther's relationship to both her original family and to Mordecai, who raised her, but also the relationship of either uncle/nephew or brothers, between Esther's father Abihail and Mordecai. It would seem that Mordecai taking Esther as a daughter in no way denigrated Abihail as a father, but in fact instead fulfilled a kind of family responsibility of a nephew to his uncle, or as a brother, within the strong clan bonds of Israelite extended family life. This interpretation is underscored by the message Mordecai sends to Esther when she at first does not want to heed his urgent request to go to the king and beg for the lives of the Jews: "Think not ... that thou shalt escape in the king's house, more than all the Jews. For if thou altogether holdest thy peace at this time, then shall ... deliverance arise to the Jews from another place; but thou and *thy father's house* shall be destroyed."[30] Hence, Mordecai appealed to Esther's desire to preserve the survival of her biological father's lineage, for the reference is clearly to her biological father, rather than to Mordecai. Overall, while Mordecai's relationship with Esther is praiseworthy, and although Esther is a daughter to Mordecai, Esther is still also accounted as the daughter of Abihail, her biological father.[31] Thus, Esther is a precedent for some form of extended family "adoption" or "care," in which the child's original name and identity are preserved, rather than for a law and practice that systematically allows strangers to adopt and change the identity of the children of others.

Other Purported Adoptions in the Old Testament Another event sometimes cited as an Old Testament adoption occurs when Jacob declares that two of Joseph's sons, Ephraim and Manasseh, would count as Jacob's children.[32] Thus, the grandfather declared two of his grandchildren as his sons.[33] Whatever the significance of this event, it is not adoption as we would understand it. The event occurred shortly before Jacob's death, as virtually a deathbed pronouncement, and thus had absolutely nothing to do with the rearing or custody of children.[34] The change of status of Ephraim and Manasseh from grandchildren of Jacob to children of Jacob is significant within the emerging "twelve tribes" structure of "Israel,"[35] but did not truly constitute the kind of change of people, family, and identity normally associated with adoption. At most, it is precedent, like Esther, for a kind of extended family adoption; in this case grandparent adoption, although its special circumstance as a virtual deathbed declaration makes it very unlike Mordecai's raising of Esther.

Incredibly, some cite Abraham's purported "adoption" of Eliezer as a precedent for adoption.[36] There is a tradition that Eliezer was the unnamed servant who ruled over Abraham's entire household, whom Abraham later entrusted with finding a wife for his son Isaac.[37] Regardless of their relationship, all that occurs in the text is that Abram complains to God that because he is childless, Eliezer will be his heir. This hardly seems to constitute an adoption, as it appears simply to be a case of one childless man designating another man as his heir, a matter more akin to designating a beneficiary in a will than adoption. No term for adoption is used, either in the Masoretic Hebrew text or typical English translations.[38] Ironically, if this is an adoption, it is one that is directly overruled by the voice of God; according to the text, God tells Abram that Eliezer shall not be his heir, but instead that one from Abram's own body shall be his heir.[39]

Adoption in the New Testament

First, it is important to clarify that Joseph did not "adopt" Jesus, according to either Biblical or modern understandings of adoption. Joseph became the legal father of Jesus directly through marrying the pregnant Mary without any legal form of adoption.[40] No legal form or procedure of adoption would have been either necessary or possible, as there is no need to adopt a child who at birth is ascribed to you, and the Jews still lacked any law or practice of adoption.[41] While it is true that Joseph provided Jesus with a legal identity and patrilineal identity within Israel, conceptualizing this as an "adoption" in the modern sense does severe damage to the Biblical meaning of their relationship. If Joseph had "adopted" Jesus in the modern sense this would have required the repudiation of God's fatherhood of Jesus, for God would be the "birth" father who upon the adoption would cease to be Jesus' father. Joseph, who was informed in a dream prior to the marriage that Jesus was the child of the Holy Spirit,[42] surely did not intend this kind of displacement. Jesus Himself makes it clear, even in His childhood, that He answered ultimately to God His father, explaining His disappearance to Joseph and Mary by explaining that He had to "be about My Father's business": indeed, Jesus admonishes Joseph and Mary that they should have known this already.[43] Since the Father-Son relationship between God the Father and Jesus is one of the primary themes of the New Testament and a basic tenet of Christianity,[44] it would be a distortion of the Biblical texts to envision Joseph's act as an adoption in the modern sense. As in the stories of the Old Testament, it is the original parent, in this case God, who is far more important than the so-called "adoptive" parent.

It is true that Joseph was a nonbiological "father" who took on the legal, social, and relational role of a father for a child not genetically related to him. Even if this were to be analogized to an adoption, it would be precedent, at most, for stepparent adoption, which is an entirely different matter than infant relinquishment adoption. Joseph, after all, supported the "birth mother" Mary in being able to raise and mother her own child, rather than removing Jesus from Mary. As we will see later in our examination of the Biblical treatment of "widows" and the "fatherless," what Joseph did in helping an otherwise "single mother" to keep and raise her own child was consistent with the ministries of Jesus and Elijah in assisting single women and their children in staying together.[45] Honoring the "birth" mother—honoring the motherhood of Mary—is exactly contrary to modern forms of full adoption which involve a full severance of birth parent rights. If Joseph had acted in a way typical of modern infant adoptions, Mary would have lost Jesus at birth.

Looking beyond the question of Jesus and Joseph, it is important that the four gospels as a whole never use any Greek or other language term for "adoption."[46] Indeed, this absence of any reference to adoption is found in every part of the Bible except three of the letters of Paul. Hence, the ascribed writings of John, Peter, Jude, and James, as well as the authors of the gospels and Acts (Matthew, Mark, Luke, and John) similarly fail to use either the language or concept of adoption.[47]

The argument for a Biblical doctrine of adoption thus depends on five purported references to adoption in three Pauline letters: Romans 8:15, 8:23, 9:4; Galatians 4:5; Ephesians 1:5.[48] These references thus bear close analysis and scrutiny.

The first difficulty is linguistic. The Greek word often translated as adoption, *huiothesia*, consists of two parts: *huios* meaning son and *thesia*, from the verb *tithemi*, which means "to set, put, or place." The word literally means something like to put in the place of a son.[49] This has created the question of whether "adoption" or "sonship" is the better translation.[50] This translation issue raises the question of whether the Apostle Paul was referring to a legal practice of adoption as a metaphor.[51] It is possible that Paul was merely referring to the status of being a son (sonship), without intending to refer to adoption as a means to that status. If so, then in fact there are essentially no New Testament references to adoption, for these five uses of the term *huiothesia* are the only possible instances of the word *adoption* occurring in the New Testament.

For purposes of discussion I will assume that Paul is in fact referencing some kind of "adoption."[52] However, it is important to keep in mind that even if Paul is referencing adoption, he is also directly referencing coming into the place or status of a son. Thus, even if adoption is the means for attaining the status of a son, that status (sonship) remains central to understanding Paul's meaning.[53] In addition, it is possible that "sonship" would be a better translation for at least one of the five uses of *huiothesia*.

Four of the passages in question relate to the relationship of the Christian (Jew or Gentile) to God in Christ, that allow the Christian to call upon God as Father.[54] The fifth passage, Romans 9:4, refers to the Israelites, to whom pertains "the adoption, and the glory, and the covenants, and the giving of the law, and the service of God, and the promises; Whose are the fathers, and of whom as concerning the flesh Christ came."[55] Whether translated "the adoption" or "the sonship" Romans 9:4 describes the relationship Israel had with God the Father before the birth of Jesus, as the rest of the items in the list (apart from sonship or adoption) refer to an event or status established in the Old Testament.

To the degree that the human law or practice of "adoption" is being referenced by Paul, it is clearly a metaphor meant to help convey to the reader something about their actual or potential relationship to God. As a metaphor, it is important to understand to what Paul is referencing when he uses the term "adoption," and what Paul intends to convey to the reader about their relationship to God through use of that metaphor.[56]

The most commonly accepted viewpoint is that Paul is invoking the Roman law and practice of adoption as his allusion or referent.[57] This viewpoint is based on the prominence of the practice of adoption among the Romans, especially Roman emperors and nobility; the fact that Paul is a Roman citizen; and the use of the term in letters to three communities living under Roman law.[58] Indeed, three of the five references occur in Paul's letter to the church at Rome![59] In addition, a reference to Greek law, custom or practice of adoption is possible.[60] Considering the absence of a law or practice of adoption among Jews, and in the rest of the Bible, the evidence is very strong that the referent of Paul's adoption metaphor is not Jewish. This explains why such a reference to adoption is found only in Paul, for Paul is self-consciously the Apostle to the Gentiles.[61] If Paul is invoking adoption as a metaphor, it is to explain to Gentiles their actual or potential relationship to God in Christ.

Paul's invocation of the Israelites as having the *huiothesia* is potentially problematic in terms of a translation of "adoption." It would be entirely unproblematic for Paul to say that the Israelites had the "sonship," the status or position of sons of God, as the sonship of Israel is a central theme of the Hebrew Bible.[62] Viewing Israel's status of sonship as being accomplished through "adoption" would, however, be unique to this single reference, and in Jewish terms would be a virtually meaningless statement, given the lack of a law or concept of adoption in Judaism. At most, then, in Romans 9:4 Paul is using a Greco-Roman concept as a metaphor to explain to Gentile Christians the history of God's relationship to Israel. The purpose of this metaphor would presumably be to stress that it is not merely Gentile Christians who are adopted by God, but rather all who are sons of God: Jew and Gentile alike, including historical old covenant Israel. Thus, Paul would be avoiding the inference that Israel is the "natural" son of God while Gentile Christians are the unnatural, adopted sons of God. Such a theme would be consistent with one of Paul's major themes, which is the equality of Jew and Gentile in Christ, a point essential to Paul's rejection of circumcision and the Mosaic ceremonial law for Gentile Christians.[63] If that is the point, however, we must recognize that Paul is willing to mix his metaphors and to some degree his message on this point, for in Romans chapter 11 Paul characterizes Israel as the "natural" branches of an olive tree, with the Gentiles contrasted as a "wild" olive tree whose branches are "grafted" into the good olive tree.[64] According to this metaphor of an original "natural" olive tree and wild branches "grafted" in to the tree, the Gentiles are in fact not "natural" parts of the tree but added through the human artifice of grafting.[65] Some of the natural branches (some of the Jews) were broken off by God due to unbelief.⁶⁶ However, Paul warns the Gentile Christians: "If you were cut out of the olive tree which is wild by nature, and were grafted contrary to nature into a cultivated olive tree, how much more will these, who are natural branches, be grafted into their own olive tree?"⁶⁷

Paul, then, is probably using the Roman and/or Greek law and practice of adoption as a metaphor to help Gentiles understand their relationship to God, as well as to understand the equality of all, Jew or Gentile, male or female, slave or free, in Christ. An examination of the Roman law and practice of adoption underscores how apt this metaphor or comparison would have been for Paul's purposes, and also helps us identify Paul's meaning.⁶⁸

Roman adoption law had its context within the broader principles of Roman family law where the virtually absolute power of the father was central. Thus, the *pater familias* (father of the family) possessed the power known as the *patria potestas* (fatherly power). The father had virtually absolute and sole authority over his children, including the right to have them "exposed" or killed in infancy, or sold into slavery. The wife and mother of the children, by contrast, had no legal authority over the children, however much she may have exercised extensive moral and emotional authority. The father's authority over his children normally continued until the father's death, irrespective of the age and marital status of the children.⁶⁹ (Fathers sometimes passed their authority over their daughters to the husband at marriage, but in practice this form of marriage by the time of Jesus had become unpopular, with married daughters normally remaining under the *potestas* of her father.⁷⁰ Married sons were under the *potestas* of their fathers until the father's death regardless of their marital status.⁷¹) Indeed, fathers commonly played a central role not only in their children contracting marriages, but also in the divorces of their children.⁷²

The Roman family particularly focused on the continuation of the male line and family name, and the inheritance and transmission of property—especially real property—from generation to generation. The continuation of the family line and name generally required a legitimate son born of a marriage. Marriage and procreation were thus duties.⁷³ The continuation of the family line also involved the maintenance of the family cult, which included sacrifice to ancestors. Honoring ancestors and the family name through the display of images of ancestors in the home and public processions was also a normal practice of great families. Fitting funerals and commemorations were also important. A great stress was laid upon the honor of the family and family name. The lack of a suitable heir was thus potentially a great crisis for a significant family, endangering the fundamental purposes of the Roman family.⁷⁴

This problem of a suitable heir was the animating purpose of Roman adoption law. Thus, adoption played a particularly prominent role in upper class families.⁷⁵ Significantly, adoption also was a common means of choosing the most appropriate successor for an emperor, and hence a number of Roman emperors adopted or were adopted.⁷⁶ Adoption was thus an accepted solution to the problem of a man lacking a living son who could be his heir.⁷⁷ Although subject to criticism, adoption could also occur even if there was already a living son or heir, for example because the father did not view his natural son as having the qualities necessary to carry out the responsibilities involved in being his heir.[78]

Given this purpose, adoption in ancient Rome was usually the adoption of an adult male. Adults were chosen because their character and suitability to play the critical role of heir of a great family, or even emperor, could be ascertained, and because of their readiness to assume their responsibilities. Males were chosen because of the limitations placed in Roman law and custom upon the roles of women. There were two forms of adoption, *adoptio* and *adrogatio*, depending on whether the adoptee was still under the authority of a living father. If so, the transaction was from father to father (*adoptio*); if not, the adult essentially placed himself under the *potestas* of the adoptive father (*adrogatio*). Adoption was always by a male, and the wife of the adoptive father did not join in the adoption. Legally, the adoptee attained a new name and identity, even having all of his debts cancelled, since the prior legal personality ceased to exist.[79] Nonetheless, commonly a form of the adoptee's original family/clan name was adapted and retained as a part of his new name (in the form of a cognomen), indicating some continuity with his original identity. Practically, adopted persons commonly continued their personal relationships with their original family, and even were expected to fulfill some filial duties to their original families. Indeed, since adoption was in legal form often a family to family transaction, it could be a means of creating alliances between families, similar to the role of marriage in creating alliances between families. In addition, adoption quite frequently occurred within extended families, with an uncle or great-uncle, for example, adopting a nephew.[80]

Thus, the Roman law and practice of adoption served as an excellent metaphor for Paul in conveying to Roman Gentiles their status and inheritance as sons of God. When Paul's audience heard his references to adoption, they would have had in their minds young adult males who became emperors, or who otherwise moved upward in Roman society, through adoption. Paul's reference to adoption in a Roman context implicitly invites a comparison between the Roman view of the emperor as "Lord," and the Christian insistence that God is Lord of Lords and King of Kings and His Son, Jesus Christ, is Lord. The clear message is that the inheritance the Christian receives from adoption by God would be even greater than the inheritance received by those who are adopted by Roman emperors. In a society obsessed with honor, Paul is communicating that there is no higher honor than being a Christian, which makes one a co-heir with the Lord Jesus Christ, Heir of God the Father.[81]

The historical record of adoptions in the imperial line proximate to the time of Jesus and Paul makes it very probable that Paul was invoking not only the Roman law of adoption in general, but the use of adoption by emperors in particular. Thus, the first true emperor of the Roman Empire, Octavius, known later as Augustus, was adopted by his great-uncle, Julius Caesar, posthumously through Julius Caesar's will in 44 BCE. Augustus Caesar is the emperor who in Luke 2:1 issues the decree at the time of Jesus's birth that the Roman world be registered. "Caesar" was in fact the adopted name of Octavius given him by his great-uncle and adoptive father, Julius Caesar; over time the name "Caesar," coupled with the title Augustus he was given, became virtual titles for the position of emperor. Octavius (Augustus) eventually adopted his stepson, Tiberius, a Claudian, who was also married to his daughter, making Tiberius emperor. From that time forward the famous Julio-Claudian dynasty of emperors were related through a complex and interlocking combination of blood, marriage, and adoption. A primary role of adoption within this dynasty was to pick, amongst the various candidates within this interconnected set of families, the next emperor. Thus, the emperor Tiberius was both the great-uncle and adoptive grandfather of the next emperor, Gaius Caligula (and is sometimes listed as his adoptive father as well). Gaius Caligula's uncle Claudius became emperor after Caligula was assassinated. The next emperor, the notorious Nero, the infamous persecutor of the Christians, was the grandnephew of both Caesar Augustus and of the emperor Claudius; when Claudius married Nero's mother he became the stepson of Claudius as well, and he later (after adoption) married Claudius's daughter, Claudia Octavia. Nero also became emperor through adoption when his great-uncle and stepfather, the emperor Claudius, adopted him; in the end, then, Emperor Claudius had been the great-uncle, stepfather, father-in-law, and adoptive father of Nero. Amongst these interlocking relationships, it was the adoption that made Nero the designated heir and next emperor (after his mother and possibly Nero himself murdered Claudius).[82] These sets of adoptions within the line of Roman emperors occurred in the period immediately before Paul wrote the books of Romans, Galatians, and Ephesians, and hence would have been prominent in the minds of both Paul and his readers.[83]

The claims of divinity by and on behalf of the Roman emperors, and the accompanying imperial cult, underscored Paul's implicit meaning. In Roman experience and culture one could become not merely an emperor, but ultimately a god, by being adopted by the prior emperor and god.[84] By contrast, Paul made the claim to these primarily Gentile Christians living under Roman rule that they had been brought into the family life of the true God, and His Son and Heir, Jesus Christ, and thus could be made co-heirs with the true Son of God through a kind of divine adoption.[85]

The fact that in Roman adoption the adoptee did not receive his full inheritance at the time of the adoption, but only later at the death of the adoptive father, similarly served Paul's rhetorical point that the Christian's inheritance, while in existence now, would only be received in full at some later time. Thus, the Roman law of adoption and inheritance helps Paul convey the "already, not yet" aspect of the Christian's inheritance from God in Christ. Just as the adopted children of the emperors and nobility of Rome did not receive their full inheritance until the death of their adoptive fathers, the adopted sons of God would not receive their full inheritance until some future time.[86]

While the Roman referent is most persuasive, it should be noted that adoption under Greek law and custom, while different in some respects, shared a fundamental continuity with Roman adoption in being focused principally around adoption of adult males for the purpose of providing a family with continuity and an heir. Thus, although the clearest and most likely reference point is Roman adoption, much of the same analysis would be found in analyzing Greek adoption as a possible referent of Paul's adoption metaphor.[87]

For purposes of this chapter, a fundamental point is that neither Roman nor Greek adoption was focused on the adoption of child orphans. Adoption generally had nothing to do with providing for the weak, the poor, dependents, or children. Adoption took young adult males who generally had families and a position in society, and gave them a social promotion to a higher position in society through provision of a new legal identity; in exchange, the adopted adult fulfilled the responsibilities and duties of a son and heir of a great family, whether that meant leading the empire or managing an upper-class noble household. While it was theoretically possible to adopt a young child, such was rarely done, since such a child was unprepared to lead the empire or family and his capacities to do so in the future were still unknown.[88]

Indeed, adoption in the Greco-Roman context was not even about providing a family for an adult "orphan." The men "adopted" by the Roman emperors generally were already related to those emperors through combinations of blood and marriage (their own and that of their mothers) in addition to their adoptions. The distinctive purpose of adoption within this web of family relationships was to make them heirs, not to provide them with a family. Thus, even though one of the two forms of adoption concerned a man without a living father, this occurred primarily because by the time many men reached an appropriate age to be adopted—preferably in the prime of their adulthood—their fathers were already dead. Of course the other form of adoption involved a transfer of parental authority from one father to another, and hence involved adults who still had a living father. Whether their fathers were alive or dead, the men chosen for adoption were picked because of their competency and strength—as established adults—to lead a family, clan, or empire. Adoptees were not viewed as either children or as orphans, but as adult candidates for honor, wealth, greatness, and power.

It should be noted, in addition, that adoption was certainly not shameful or a secret in the ancient Roman context. To the contrary, in the ancient Greco-Roman world where honor and shame were such important social and emotional markers, adoption would have been highly publicized and indeed was one of the greatest honors one could attain.[89] Moreover, despite the fact that adoption marked a new legal identity, it did not in any way require the adoptee to cut himself off socially from their original family members. Of course since only fathers adopted—there being no legal form of maternal adoption—adoption did not imply or require a break with one's original mother. (In some prominent cases, of course, the mother was married to the adoptive father.) Despite the change in legal identity, adoptive sons were understood to still have duties to their original fathers.[90] Thus, adoption in the ancient world did not bear the marks of secrecy and shame, and the complete cutting of relationship and ties to all members of the original family, that have so often marked the modern history of adoption.

If we want to understand the Pauline doctrine of divine adoption, we must see adoption through the lens intended by Paul and understood by his original audience. Indeed, if we substitute our modern conception of adoption as primarily a means to provide a family to a helpless and vulnerable orphan child, we will completely miss what Paul is saying. Similarly, if we substitute our modern concept of adoption as involving a "pretense" that it is "as if" one was born to the adoptive family, thus necessitating secrecy and the complete cutting of ties, we will also miss the point. Instead, to understand Paul we must understand adoption as a very public means of attaining honor, elevation, inheritance, and greatness through the choice of a divine or noble father to bestow the title of son and heir on a particular individual. Paul's message of divine adoption was about the high honor of being co-heirs with Jesus, the Heir and Son of God, through the divine selection of each Christian as an adopted son of God: an honor and an inheritance that exceeded even that of the great Roman emperors.

The Absence of Adoptions in the New Testament

The New Testament does not record any instances or practice of adoption, nor any calls for Christians to adopt orphan children. Despite clear New Testament admonishments to assist the poor and widows,[91] and despite a clear New Testament record of the early church in fact engaging in organized efforts to assist the poor and widows,[92] there is no parallel New Testament record of anyone being urged to adopt an orphan, or of anyone doing so. Instead, as will be seen below, the references in the Old and New Testament to assisting the orphan and the fatherless were taken in a direction unrelated to that of adoption.

In the midst of this silence, some strain to find such an adoption in, for example, Jesus' famous statement from the cross: "Woman, behold your son!" indicating a new relationship between the apostle John and Mary.[93] The Roman Catholic Church interprets this text as a symbolic giving of Mary to the entire church as mother of the church.[94] Whether or not that spiritual interpretation is accepted, there is a more literal meaning. As Jesus prepares to die, one of his final acts is to fulfill his earthly responsibilities as a son by providing his widowed mother with an adult male to take care of her. In the patriarchal world of the ancient world, Mary the widow needed an adult male to provide for and protect her. John is to be a son to her, in the sense in which an adult son is charged to provide for his widowed mother.

This tendency to miss the widow in the Biblical language about widows and orphans, and the fatherless, is typical of some distorted modern interpretations. Hence, we must now pass to an examination of the terms "orphan" and the "fatherless" in the Scriptures. As we will see, the Christian Scriptures do command care for the widow and the orphan, and for the fatherless, but in Biblical contexts this has nothing to do with adoption.

Orphans and the Fatherless in the Bible

Old Testament

Traditional English translations of the Old Testament (such as the King James Version) have few or no uses of the English word *orphan*, but instead use the term *fatherless*.[95] Some modern translators prefer the word *orphan* for these uses. The underlying Hebrew word, *Yatom*, is used forty-two times in the Old Testament.[96] It can be translated either *fatherless* or *orphan*.[97] The word *fatherless* generally appears as a suitable translation because the Hebrew word clearly refers to a child whose father is dead or absent even when the mother is still alive and caring for the child.[98] Thus, if we are to use the word *orphan* for these Hebrew Bible usages, we must be aware of the misconception that can result, for in English we do not always consider a child living with their mother to be an "orphan."

In the Hebrew Bible, the term *fatherless* or *orphan* is very closely associated with the term *almanah*, meaning widow.[99] Thus, the two terms appear together frequently in the law (Exodus 22:22, 22:24; Deuteronomy 10:18, 14:29, 16:11, 16:14, 24:17, 24:19, 24:20, 26:12, 26:13, 27:19), in Psalms (Psalms 68:5, 94:6, 109:9, 146:9), in prophetical books (Isaiah 1:23, 9:17, Jeremiah 7:6, 22:3, 49:11; Malachi 3:5), as well appearing together in Job 24:3 and Lamentations 5:3. Thus, the fatherless or orphans and widows are in many respects a unit.

Generally, these passages assert God's protection of the widow and fatherless (i.e., Deuteronomy 10:18, Psalm 68:5), or a legal or ethical imperative not to exploit but instead to assist or provide for, the widow and fatherless (i.e., Deuteronomy. 24:17, 19, 20). In a few passages, the couplet of widow and orphan relate to a curse or punishment (i.e., Psalm 109:9, Exodus 22:24). Exodus 22:22–24 makes abundantly clear that widows and orphans are not merely two separate categories of needy or vulnerable persons, but are the natural unit created by the death or absence of a husband and father:

> You shall not afflict any widow or fatherless child. If you afflict them in any way, and they cry [out] at all to Me, I will surely hear their cry; and My wrath will become hot, and I will kill you with the sword; your wives shall be widows and your children fatherless.[100]

Thus, while the terms *widow* and *orphan/fatherless* often appear together in passages including other vulnerable persons—particularly the poor or strangers—it is important to understand them as a unit belonging together, rather than being merely separate categories. Of course it is possible to have a childless widow or a fatherless child also lacking a mother; normally, however, widows and the fatherless/orphan comprise a vulnerable family unit.

The reason for this vulnerability is not difficult to discover. Within the patriarchal world of the Hebrew Bible, and of the ancient world generally, the woman's lack of a husband and the child's lack of a father both rendered them potentially bereft of protection and provision. The absence of the father and husband not only created grief and loss, but also very practically could create risks of starvation and exploitation. The lack of a male protector could thus be literally fatal. Within that context, God asserts his role as the protector and provider of this vulnerable family unit, and demands that His people imitate Him by protecting and providing for the widow and fatherless.[101]

The Hebrew Bible is specific about the kinds of intervention that are required for widows and the fatherless. Beyond abstaining from exploiting the desperation, need, and powerlessness of the widow and fatherless (i.e., Deuteronomy 24:17), these interventions focus primarily on economic provision, with the Mosaic law being specific as to the sources of assistance, which include leaving provision in the fields at harvest for gleaning, and the tithe set aside every third year and stored (i.e., Deuteronomy 14:29; 24:19–21; 26:12–13). Thus, within the Mosaic Law and Israelite society, assistance to these vulnerable family units was not left to the mere discretionary charity of the people, but was a mandatory duty within the law and was to be systematically carried out from specified sources.

Another strategy within Israelite society was remarriage for the widow. The book of Ruth presents such a solution as a kind of redemptive event. Ruth presents the intertwined problems of vulnerable widows and a family line within Israel lacking a male heir. The crisis is resolved by the figure of the kinsman-redeemer (*go'el*), the close relative who will, through marriage and the conception of a child, both provide for the widows and save the family from extinction.[102] In the Ruth narrative, set during the era of the Judges, Elimelech, a man from Bethlehem in Judah, his wife Naomi, and two sons, move from Judah to Moab during a famine. While in Moab, the husband dies, after which the two sons marry Moabite women, and then also die.[103] Naomi is thus left with two former Moabite daughters-in-law and no grandchildren. The famous decision of one of the two widowed daughters-in-law, Ruth, to identify with her mother-in-law, sets the stage for the rest of the story. Ruth famously tells Naomi that "your people shall be my people, [and] your God, my God," and insists on accompanying Naomi back to Bethlehem.[104] This vulnerable family unit of two widows initially survives through gleaning from the fields of a man named Boaz, just as was envisioned in the Mosaic Law.[105] Ultimately, however, Boaz, who is a close relative of Naomi, chooses to redeem Elimelech's land and name and, acting as a close relative kinsman-redeemer, marry Ruth.[106] The son (Obed) who is born to Boaz and Ruth is then, in a situation analogous to levirate marriage, accounted to Elimelech and Naomi, so that their family line within Judah may be continued.[107] The redemptive implications of this story are highlighted by the fact that Obed is named at the end of the story as the grandfather of King David.[108] From a Christian perspective the redemptive significance is further heightened by the inclusion of Boaz and Ruth as the parents of Obed within the genealogy of Jesus presented in Matthew,[109] and Boaz as the father of Obed in the genealogy of Jesus in Luke.[110]

Interestingly, both the New Testament genealogies, as well as the genealogy at the end of Ruth, follow the literal biological genealogy in accounting Obed the son of Boaz, rather than accounting as Obed's father the apparent beneficiaries of the symbolic levirate system (Elimelech, the deceased husband of Naomi, and/or Mahlon the deceased husband of Ruth).[111] The only one of the three books to include a mother in the genealogy, Matthew, names Ruth as the mother, despite the symbolic laying of Obed on Naomi's breast and statement by the women that a son has been born to Naomi.[112] Hence, despite the legal significance of continuing the family lines of these deceased men, there is an insistence in the Old and New Testament genealogies in presenting the actual biological lineage. Another interpretation would be that both the literal biological parents, and those accounted as being parents for certain legal purposes, are acknowledged in different ways as the parents of Obed.

The book of Ruth makes abundantly clear that the central hope of a widow within Israel was to be found either through her own remarriage, or through her children or grandchildren. If a widow did not herself remarry, but had a son, she could look forward to that son growing up and providing for her. Her son would become her male provider and protector. If a widow had a daughter, she could look to the man who would marry her daughter (or ex-daughter-in-law in the case of Ruth) as the one who would provide for her. For the widow, her child represented not only her future physical survival, but also the hope of the continuation of her family line, which was of course an overriding purpose of family life, and even of life itself, within Israel.[113]

From this perspective, one of the most essential interventions one could do for a widow was to protect and preserve her relationship to, and the life of, her child. The Hebrew Bible illustrates this principle through a set of stories about Elijah and Elisha.[114] In the first of these, after Elijah has prophetically enunciated God's decree of a drought, God sends him to a widow in Zarephath, who will provide for Elijah. When they meet, the widow tells Elijah that she was about to prepare a last meal from their scant provisions for herself and her son, "that we may eat of it, and die."[115] Elijah assures her that the bin of flour and jar of oil will not run out; a miracle that enables Elijah, the widow, and her fatherless son to survive.[116] A crisis ensues, however, when the son becomes sick and dies. Elijah cries out to God, stretches himself out on the child three times, and ultimately the child is revived and restored to his mother. By this miracle the widow is persuaded that Elijah is truly a "man of God."[117]

Within this story we see God's provision for this widow and orphan, through the miraculous provision of food amidst a drought. We also are able to see that the loss of the child precipitates a crisis of faith, as the widow doubts Elijah's good intentions: "What have I to do with you, O man of God? Have you come to me to bring my sin to remembrance, and to kill my son?"[118] We see here a model of intervention for widows and orphans, as Elijah is able to restore the child to his mother. While the means of restoration (a resurrection from the dead) is miraculous in this instance, the ethical point is that the widow needs her son, and hence acting to restore a child to his widowed mother is the appropriate intervention.

Elijah's successor, Elisha, performs a similar miracle. In this context, a widow comes to Elisha in crisis, telling him: "Your servant my husband is dead, and you know that your servant feared the Lord. And the creditor is coming to take my two sons to be his slaves."[119] In this instance, the widow is faced with the twin disasters of destitution and the loss of her children. Elisha responds by instructing the widow to gather a large number of jars from her neighbors; by a miracle, all of the jars become filled with oil. Elisha then instructs the widow to sell the oil and pay off the debt, using the rest to support herself and her sons. Here, Elisha provides economically for the widow and orphans of this household, while preventing the separation of the widow from her fatherless children.[120]

Given that Elijah and Elisha are, in New Testament terms, forerunners and types of Jesus, and that in the New Testament Jesus raises a widow's son from the dead,[121] the ethical message of these texts is clear. God is the provider for widows and orphans in two senses: economic provision, and preventing the separation of the widow from her child (the so-called "orphan"). God restores children to their widowed mothers, rather than removing them from widows. Not surprisingly, this ethical message is consonant with the Mosaic Law and the Prophets.

Against this clear record from the Law, Prophets, Psalms, and narrative texts, regarding the intertwined needs of widows and orphans for provision and one another, there is not a single Biblical text on assisting orphans through removing them from their widowed mothers and placing them with other families. Indeed, there are no positive instances of stranger adoption in the entire Hebrew Bible. The one clear instance of care provided to a child with a dead mother and father—Esther—involves Mordecai, her cousin or uncle, taking her into his household and raising her as a daughter, while simultaneously still accounting Esther to be the daughter of her original father, Abihail. Esther thus cannot be considered a Biblical precedent for instances of stranger adoption where the child's name, identity, and lineage are altered, at the expense of any acknowledgment of the original parentage, as typically occurs in modern full severance adoption of "orphans."[122]

New Testament

The primary text in the New Testament on orphans is the much quoted text from James: "Pure religion and undefiled before God and the Father is this, To visit the fatherless and widows in their affliction, and to keep himself unspotted from the world."[123]

The Greek word used here, *orphanos*, can be variously translated *fatherless*, *orphan*, or *bereft*.[124] It is used only twice in the New Testament.[125] In the context of James, a book often viewed as written within a primarily Jewish-Christian context,[126] the clear reference of the phrase "fatherless and widows" is to the unit of "widow and fatherless/orphan" so prominent in the Hebrew Bible.[127] Hence, the analysis made above, in regard to widows and orphans in the Hebrew Bible, is fully applicable to this New Testament usage. James is referring to the unit of orphan and widow, rather than to two separate unrelated categories of persons needing assistance. James presumably intended to incorporate into the New Testament the Old Testament presumption that widows and orphans normally were to be protected and assisted as a family unit. To assist orphans and widows thus would have included protecting their relationship with one another and seeking to keep them together. This of course does not rule out assisting widows with no children, or assisting children lacking both a father and mother, but nonetheless presupposes that typically widows and orphans comprise a family unit who are assisted together.

This interpretation of James is borne out by the organized focus of the early church on assisting widows, as reflected in both the book of Acts and 1 Timothy, one of the Pastoral Epistles.[128] Thus, according to the book of Acts, in the period immediately after the beginnings of the church on the day of Pentecost, there arose a complaint that the widows of the Greek Jews were being neglected by the Hebrew Jews "in the daily distribution" of assistance.[129] This indicates that organized widow assistance was in existence at the very outset of the church. This dispute over widow assistance apparently threatened to undermine the unity of the early church along cultural/ethnic lines. The church's response to this dispute was to appoint a group of men to oversee such widow assistance, which is commonly cited as the origin of the deaconate in the church.[130] The fact that widows are mentioned, but not orphans, is consistent with the interpretation that ordinarily "orphans" would have been assisted through provision to their widowed mothers.

The same organized focus on assistance to widows is found in 1 Timothy 5. The details of this passage present many difficult interpretative issues, which are beyond the scope of this chapter.[131] The point at present is that the epistle addresses in detail the question of which "widows" should be supported by the church.[132] The passage also evidences some of the strategies for the support of widows found in the Hebrew Bible. Thus, despite some ambivalence in this passage and also in 1 Corinthians 7 regarding remarriage,[133] 1 Timothy 5:14 advises that the younger widows remarry.[134] Similarly, Paul states that widows with children or grandchildren should be supported by their own families. Paul thus regards adult children as under an ethical imperative to support their widowed mothers and grandmothers, stating that those who do not provide for their own have "denied the faith" and are "worse than an unbeliever."[135] Thus, just as in the Hebrew Bible, remarriage and the assistance of adult children and other household or family members are prime strategies for the support of widows. The church is to provide for widows only when these family-based strategies are not available.

Widows are a motif throughout the New Testament, with widows generally seen quite favorably. Thus, Anna the aged widow and prophetess who greets the baby Jesus in the Temple, is a model of piety.[136] Similarly, Jesus publicly praises the generosity and faith of the poor widow's gift of "two mites" at the Temple.[137] Jesus incorporates the figure of the persistent widow seeking justice in the parable of the unjust judge,[138] while condemning the religious hypocrisy of the scribes who "devour widow's houses and for a pretense make long prayers."[139] In the book of Acts, the widows testify to the assistance provided to them by the dead disciple Tabitha/Dorcas; in response, Peter raises the disciple from the dead and presents her to the "saints and widows," thus recapitulating the miracles of Elijah, Elisha, and Jesus in restoring the life of someone dear to widows.[140] It is a commentary on the church that in this case it is a fellow church member, rather than a son, who is resurrected and then presented to widows; the implication is that this Dorcas has been, in a New Testament church setting, fulfilling the role of a son to many widows.

Compared to the repeated and elaborated New Testament treatment of widows, and their assistance, the theme of assistance to the fatherless or orphan is quite minimal. There are essentially no relevant texts, other than the famous James text just discussed. The only other uses of the Greek words that can be translated *orphan* or *fatherless* appear in two texts about Jesus and His relationship to Christians: Jesus's promise in the last supper discourse to not leave His disciples bereft, or as orphans (John 14:18), and a description of the great priest Melchizedek (Hebrews 7:3, *apator*). The contrast with the theme of widows is striking. It is obvious from the New Testament that support of widows was a practical problem that the church confronted on a daily basis. If the same was true of "orphans," it left virtually no trace in the New Testament, unless one assumes that the vast majority of orphans were a part of a widow-orphan unit that were cared for through provision to their widowed mothers.

Presumably, the reasons for the lack of an "orphan" problem in the New Testament church was due first to the initial Jewish setting of the New Testament church. Judaism had, in contrast to the ancient pagan Greco-Roman world, a pro-life ethic that generally protected the lives of Jewish infants. Jews regarded children as a blessing, took seriously the Genesis commandment to be fruitful and multiply,[141] and with some notorious exceptions generally did not participate in the pagan practices of infanticide or exposure of their infants.[142] Jews were also religiously and culturally focused on the intergenerational continuation of their family groups as a primary goal.[143] As a comparatively small and vulnerable minority in the larger Gentile world, the Jews were not likely to consider children as expendable, but rather would have been motivated to enlarge the population of their people. Hence, in instances where both parents died, other relatives, as in Mordecai's care of the orphan Esther, would have stepped in to raise the child while safeguarding the name and lineage of the dead parents.[144] These practices presumably continued into the New Testament era. Indeed, Jesus' striking and positive teachings on children and childhood would have added even more to the high valuation placed on children in Judaism.[145] In this context, Jews, including Jewish-Christians, presumably did not experience the same proliferation of abandoned and relinquished babies as existed in the wider Greco-Roman world, where the practice of exposure was accepted and widespread.[146] By contrast, widowhood would have been quite common due to the high death rates and modest longevity of people in the ancient world.[147] Under these circumstances, the death of one parent prior to the child attaining adulthood would have been a commonplace. Where the survivor was the wife—the widow—the difficult economic and social position of a lone woman in a patriarchal society would have created an immediate issue, whenever the woman either had no children, or only had minor or young children. Hence, it is easy to see why the issues of widows generally eclipsed and subsumed the issue of orphans in a Biblical context.

As the New Testament church increasingly became Gentile rather than Jewish through the increasing success of the mission to the Gentiles, the collision with the very different pagan ethics on matters related to sex, reproduction, abortion, infanticide, and the exposure of infants would become increasingly prominent. There are clear echoes of this collision in the Pauline epistles, particularly in regard to sexual matters,[148] but little trace of the collision on issues such as infanticide and exposure. Apparently the initial effort was directed primarily at teaching an ethic that would, if followed, direct sexual activity within the context of Christian marriage, thereby providing for the love and care of the children. Teaching a Christian sexual and marital ethic within the Gentile church presumably was the initial frontline against the entire package of pagan practices of abortion, infanticide, and exposure. Presumably the traditional impetus for the poor in the ancient world to abandon children simply because they could not afford to raise them was met with a church community which, even at the very outset of the church in Acts, directed assistance to the poor within the community.[149] Hence, the programs of assistance within the church also would have been the initial and frontline responses to transforming the ethic of the Gentile converts. So far as it appears from the New Testament, remedying the infanticide, abandonment, and the exposure of infants in the wider Gentile world outside of the church was not a project of the church during the New Testament era. The tiny size of the church during the New Testament era, its various crises of survival, unity, and persecution, and its position of political vulnerability and powerlessness, presumably mediated against any organized efforts to assist the comparatively vast numbers of infants victimized by the pagan practices of infanticide and exposure. Those efforts would have to await another day.

Conclusion: Why It Matters

One response to the analysis of Scriptural texts presented above would be to ask if it makes much practical difference. Even if the Scriptures do not directly advocate or address adoption of nonrelated orphan children, couldn't such a practice still be a faithful application of the general Scriptural principles of concern for such children? Even if the early church was too small to address the care of abandoned children in the wider non-Christian world, does that mean that the church, as it grows, should not do so? Surely abandoned and institutionalized children still need families? Surely the church should widen its scope of concern once it attains the size and means to do so?

These questions are another way of asking about the harms of reading contemporary practices of adoption into the Scriptures. Do these misreadings lead to harmful practices, or do they just constitute mistaken Scriptural justifications for what are otherwise laudable actions?

A full answer to these questions is beyond the scope of this article. However, the outlines of an answer can be summarized as follows.

The View of Horizontal Adoption as an Absolute, Redemptive Good Makes the Adoption Movement Uncritical, Incapable of Self-Correction, and Resistant to Accountability

Reading the contemporary practice of adoption into the Bible tends to support an uncritical, naive view of adoption that views it as an absolute, even redemptive, good. Viewed correctly, however, adoption is a relative good. Every adoption involves a profound loss for the child and the child's original family. Sometimes the good done by adoption outweighs the loss; sometimes it does not. Understanding adoption as a relative good reminds us that it can be done ethically or unethically, and thus can constitute, depending on the manner in which it is done, either a good or an evil.[150] Being aware of adoption as a relative, rather than absolute, good, allows one to accept the extensive evidence that adoption has often been practiced in deeply exploitative and unethical ways.[151] Being aware of this history reminds us that there are often other interests involved in adoption besides a pure humanitarian or spiritual impulse, such as the desire of intermediaries for monetary compensation,[152] and the desire of the infertile for children.[153] There is nothing wrong with the desire of the infertile for children, and seeking payment for services is a legitimate motivation; such impulses, however, are necessarily subject to ethical and legal limits, particularly when the means of satisfying them is to obtain someone else's children.[154]

Exploitation of the Poor and the Widow

Modern adoption advocates have sometimes focused so exclusively on "orphans" and the absolute good of adoption as to miss the unfortunate role of adoption in sometimes exploiting the families of those "orphans," and hence of the "orphans" themselves. Adoption practice in seeking to assist orphans, exploits widows and the poor. Presenting the full scope of this exploitation of the poor, and the widow, in adoption practices, is beyond the scope of this chapter. As has been extensively documented elsewhere, such exploitative practices go far beyond occasional abuses. Corrupt practices that systematically exploit the poor have been commonplace in the modern adoption era, becoming the bases of child laundering and child trafficking practices in a number of sending nations in the inter-country adoption system, including Cambodia, China, Ethiopia, Guatemala, India, Nepal, Samoa, Uganda, and Vietnam.[155] In addition, modern intercountry adoption systems routinely accept poverty as an appropriate justification for intercountry adoption. The intercountry adoption system routinely is willing to spend $20,000 to $40,000 on an intercountry adoption, while not being willing to spend even a few hundred dollars on the preservation of the original family. Intercountry adoption systems that offer family preservation assistance to avoid relinquishment due to poverty have been, in developing nations, the exception rather than the rule.[156] Hence, a naive reading of modern adoption practice into Scriptural texts can lead to legitimating exploitative practices, while a fuller understanding of those texts provides helpful warnings against modern forms of exploitation.

Demeaning and Minimizing the Significance of the Natural Family and the Ties of Adoptees to Their Original Families

The core legal concept of modern "full" adoption is the complete severing of ties between the child and their family of origin, and then the full transfer of the child into the adoptive family. This concept of adoption involves a complete change in the legal identity of the child, and has often included closed records and secrecy in order to support that complete severance of ties and change of legal identity. However, this concept of adoption, as a practice involving infants and children, arose relatively recently, as can be illustrated by a summary of its development in the law of the United States.

The adoption law of the United States does not come from that of any historical system, as United States law is rooted in English common law, and English common law lacked adoption as a legal practice or system. Adoption law in the United States is thus rooted in positive, statutory law, which began around 1851 and developed its characteristic form over approximately the next hundred and thirty years. For our purposes, what is most significant is the full adoption, closed records system that has become the normative, although not universal, model of adoption in the United States. The closed record system was developed in the period from 1930 to 1980, primarily in relationship to the perceived problems of the unmarried mother and her child. Under the law prior to 1972, non-marital children were legally fatherless, and faced legal and social disadvantages as "illegitimate" children—what British law had called "bastards." Unwed mothers also faced significant social stigmas and disadvantages. In response, adoption law developed a secret, closed records system, purportedly to protect the adopted child and original mother from social stigma, and also apparently to prevent original family members from contacting the child or adoptive family. This system involves the creation of official "birth" certificates showing the adoptive parents as the "birth" parents of the child, and the sealing of the original birth certificate. Initially, records were closed to outsiders but remained open to the parties; later, records were closed to everyone but the adult adoptee. The closing of records to adult adoptees was in many states a separate and last stage that did not occur until after 1960. Thus, the adoptee, even as an adult, in most states in the United States was and is not permitted to access the records containing the identity of his or her original parents. The original family is not allowed access to information that would disclose the adoptive identity of their child. The severing of the relationship between the adoptee and the natural family thus goes beyond a formal legal transfer, to an attempt to practically and permanently prevent any contact between them, and to prevent the adoptee from ever knowing their original lineage and identity. The law used the device of a legal fiction, in which it is "as if" the child had been born to the adoptive parents: which means that it is "as if" the child had never been born to the natural mother and father. Hence, adoption became a secret event that could potentially be hidden: particularly where the adoptee looks enough like his or her adoptive parents to "pass" as their child.[157] Even when (as is commonly the case today) the fact of adoption was openly acknowledged, the facts regarding the child's original identity remained hidden. Thus, American law developed an adoption system in which the adoptee's ties to their original family are normatively defined as completely insignificant, as the child and his or her "birth" mother and father are considered legal strangers to one another. The security and legitimacy of the adoptive relationship are built, legally and psychologically, upon the complete denial of any relationship between the adoptee and their original family. In such a system and viewpoint, it becomes impossible to honor and acknowledge both adoptive and biological relationships.[158]

Reading this kind of full adoption system into the Bible naturalizes, normalizes, and legitimates what is actually a quite contemporary and arguably unnatural and inhumane set of practices. Indeed, the above analysis suggests that this modern practice of adoption is not only absent from the Biblical texts, but also contrary to the Biblical emphases on the importance of lineage and family ties.

Surrogacy and the Bible

A 1994 study of surrogacy published by the American Bar Association (ABA) and authored by attorney Julia J. Tate is titled *Surrogacy: What Progress since Hagar, Bilhah, and Zilpah!*[159] The use of the exclamation mark, rather than a question mark, suggests the author's viewpoint that great progress has been made.[160] The stories of Hagar, Bilhah, and Zilpah, and their roles in reproductive practices commonly cited as ancient or Biblical forms of surrogacy, are, of course, drawn from the Scriptural book of Genesis.[161] Unfortunately, much legal scholarship provides erroneous or misleading portraits of these ancient practices. For example, Tate's study says:

> In Biblical times, three little-known women, Hagar, Bilhah, and Zilpah, all served as involuntary surrogates, bearing a total of four [sic] sons, after their mistresses, Sarai, Rachel, and Leah, had given them over to their husbands, Abram and Jacob. No doubt these involuntary surrogates had very different experiences than those of today's surrogates. They had no choice about the matter, being slaves. They certainly were not paid the equivalent of today's $10,000.00 fee! Their sons were taken from them and their mistresses named them. No court intervened on their behalves when their mistresses' husbands raped them or when their children were taken from them.[162]

This ABA published study follows a strategy of distancing: by denigrating the ancient practices of surrogacy as particularly brutal, the author means to establish a contrast that will establish the ethical legitimacy of contemporary surrogacy practices. As we shall see, however, in significant ways the practice of surrogacy in Genesis was more humane, particularly in the context of their time, than the comparative practices today.[163] This is particularly true when one considers the developments—since Tate's study—of large-scale commercial international surrogacy.[164]

First, Tate is simply wrong when she assumes that "their sons were taken from them."[165] The Hagar Genesis narrative make it clear that Hagar is the primary mother raising Ishmael. After Sarah gives birth to Isaac, Sarah demands that Abraham cast out Hagar and Ishmael together as mother and son.[166] The story of God's repeated provision and intervention for Hagar and her son Ishmael is a significant part of the Genesis narrative.[167] Indeed, the Genesis narrative has an angel of the Lord promising Hagar that God would greatly multiply Hagar's descendants.[168] This is a promise that in the narrative is clearly to be fulfilled through Hagar's status as Ishmael's mother—a status that no one in the narratives denies.[169] Thus, in the Genesis narrative, God considers Hagar to be Ishmael's mother.[170] Of course, in Islamic tradition Hagar (Hajar) is especially revered as a matriarchal figure who, through Ishmael, is a progenitor of the Prophet Mohammed and a devout and brave woman.[171] Indeed, Muslims remember Hagar's travails, bravery, faith, and special role as the mother of Ishmael as a part of the hajj, or pilgrimage, to Mecca.[172]

While Hagar is a particularly significant figure in Genesis and in Islamic tradition, the acknowledgment of her as the mother of her child would have been typical in this kind of arrangement.[173] At a time when there was no substitute for nursing, one would assume that surrogates nursed and cared for their children. As maidservants of the intended mothers, surrogate mothers likely helped raise even their mistresses' natural children, and nursed and raised the children the surrogates themselves carried and birthed.[174] The assignment of the children to the intended mothers was symbolic, while practically speaking the children were raised primarily by the surrogate mothers.[175]

The Genesis narratives involving Bilhah and Zilpah, the maidservants of Rachel and Leah, are the other major examples of so-called surrogate motherhood in Genesis.[176] Again, Tate's characterization of the arrangements as ones in which the children are simply taken from the surrogate mothers is erroneous.[177] Thus, in the Genesis genealogies, the sons of Jacob (Israel) who comprise the roots of the twelve tribes of Israel are grouped according to the four mothers (Rachel, Leah, Bilhah, and Zilpah) who bore sons to Jacob, with the four sons born to Bilhah and Zilpah assigned as their sons, rather than their mistresses Rachel and Leah.[178] Hence, Genesis reads: "The sons of Bilhah, Rachel's handmaid; Dan, and Naphtali: and the sons of Zilpah, Leah's handmaid; Gad, and Asher."[179] The very structure of the twelve tribes of Israel, which comprise the family roots and structure of the nation of Israel in the Hebrew Bible,[180] are based on acknowledging the motherhood of Bilhah and Zilpah.

Tate accuses Abraham, the father of the faith for Jews, Muslims, and Christians alike, as well as Jacob, the namesake (when he is renamed Israel)[181] of the Jewish nation, as rapists of the surrogates.[182] She clearly misunderstands the nature of the relationship between the fathers and the so-called surrogates (the Bible never uses this term). The Genesis narrative states that Sarah gave Hagar to Abraham to be his wife.[183] The arrangement, in which a first wife gives her husband her maidservant as a wife for the sake of providing children and heirs, would have substantially raised the status and position of the maidservant—particularly if she succeeded in bearing children.[184] These wives were sometimes called concubines because they were secondary wives, lesser in position than the first wife, but wives nonetheless.[185] To their mistresses they remained servants or slaves, but in relationship to their husbands they were wives and in relationship to their children they were mothers.[186] The surrogates, as we call them, were not women to be used and then discarded, but rather were wives and mothers to whom other family members owed continuing and significant duties.[187]

Tate's accusation that the women were involuntary surrogates who were raped misses the point. While it is true that the text does not record whether or not the women's consent was gained, since this was consent to a form of marriage, this would have been typical in this cultural context.[188] In a world in which marriage was generally arranged by parents—and for servants or slaves by their masters—the consent of the spouses was secondary and perhaps assumed or viewed as gratuitous.[189] For example, the Genesis text never tells us if Abraham's son Isaac ever "consents" to the marriage his father (and father's servant) arranges for him. Isaac's bride Rebekah is brought home to him without him ever having met her.[190] Rebekah appears to be given somewhat of a choice, although she must make her decision before ever meeting her groom.[191] Jacob contracts with Laban, Rachel's father, to marry Rachel in exchange for seven years of labor, but the text never indicates whether Rachel herself (presumably a child at the time) was consulted prior to the agreement.[192] Thus, Hagar, Bilhah, and Zilpah, as servants and slaves, were involved in an arranged marriage where their consent was assumed or secondary.[193] In this respect, they were no different from innumerable women—and also men—in the ancient world, both free and slave, who could really only avoid an arranged marriage by running away. However, in this particular instance, the marriages, as grotesque as they may be by some modern sensibilities, would have been seen as a profound and permanent benefit to these women and, culturally speaking, completely different from a rape.[194] While it is possible to view them as rapes according to some modern sensibilities, such a view would condemn most marital sexual acts in the ancient world as rapes. Taking the ideological position that in a patriarchal society, or a society with arranged marriages—whether in the past or present—marriage is always rape[195] hardly helps us evaluate the situation of Hagar, Bilhah, and Zilpah within its cultural context.

Tate perhaps believes that Hagar, Bilhah, and Zilpah were raped and impregnated against their will with the children then taken from them, presumably because she views surrogacy through the lens of modern practice, where the primary goal is to use and then discard the surrogate while taking the child from her.[196] The customs of the Genesis narratives, however, were different.[197] God intervenes to help Hagar and Ishmael, when Abraham (at Sarah's instigation) abandons them in the desert, and Abraham drives Hagar and Ishmael away after God promises to care for them.[198] The men and women who use surrogates in the Bible become obligated and connected to the surrogates in a way that is virtually unthinkable today.

Professor Field's insight that surrogate wife is a better label for surrogacy in some ways fits the Biblical narrative, except that the Genesis surrogates were real, albeit secondary, wives rather than merely surrogate wives.[199] In a polygamous context, this custom of elevating the wife's maid to secondary wife created a need to balance the primacy and status of the first rank wife (or wives in the instance of Rachel and Leah) against the need to provide status and protection to the secondary wife who was bearing children and heirs for the husband and father of the family.[200]

The "realness" of the marital status of the surrogates is made clear when Reuben, the firstborn son of Jacob with his wife Leah, had sexual relations with Bilhah, Rachel's maidservant and the mother of Dan and Naphtali.[201] In today's terminology, we would say that Reuben is having sex with a surrogate his father used in the procreation of two of his half-brothers. In the terminology of Genesis, however, Reuben is having sex with his father's concubine (secondary wife), although of course Bilhah is not Reuben's mother. Since Reuben is old enough to have intercourse with Bilhah, the event is occurring many years after the births of the children Bilhah bore for Jacob.[202] Yet, the Biblical narrative clearly considers Bilhah to be the secondary wife and concubine of Jacob, such that Reuben's act constitutes a kind of incest, which permanently mars Reuben's reputation and strips him of the benefits of his status as firstborn.[203]

Interestingly, the kind of slavery involved in these narratives, while repugnant in a post-abolitionist world, was in certain ways less brutal than the kinds of slavery that existed in the United States and other places in more recent history. For example, the presumed or probable children of President Thomas Jefferson and his slave Sally Hemings[204]—and any other children conceived by a master with his slave at that time—would have been born slaves. This policy of slavery passing through the mother seems to have been based on the racist perspective that black persons—including those of mixed race—were presumed to be, and best suited to be, slaves, and hence viewed as property (like livestock) rather than persons. Therefore, the child's racial identity as even partially black doomed the child to the status of presumed enslavement (absent emancipation by the master), even if he or she was the master's child.[205] By contrast, Ishmael initially was presumed to be an heir of Abraham and was sent away precisely because he was a competitive threat to the status and inheritance of Sarah's son, Isaac.[206] The sons of Bilhah and Zilpah—the slaves and maidservants of Rachel and Leah—are considered descendants of Jacob, along with the children Jacob had with the sister-wives Rachel and Leah.[207] The very twelve-tribe structure of the nation of Israel is predicated on the children of the maidservants being descendants of their father.[208] Presumably, the practice of slavery in the patriarchal narratives is not built upon any kind of viewpoint of racial superiority, and hence the practice is cabined by an understanding of the common humanity of master and slave. Slavery was an inhumane practice of the time and culture of the patriarchs, but ironically it was less brutal and inhumane than the kinds of slavery that predominated the modern world thousands of years later.

The Scriptural and religious contexts of the patriarchal narratives raise particular religious questions for billions of people worldwide of either Jewish, Christian, or Islamic faith who look to Abraham as a preeminent founder of their faith.[209] While detailed analysis of such religious questions is beyond the scope of this chapter, it seems appropriate to at least acknowledge the issues, given the large proportion of humankind involved. The problem is this: Scriptural narratives and religious tradition describe customs and practices of extreme patriarchy, slavery, concubinage, and the use of maidservants as secondary wives to provide children for a family.[210] Do Scriptural *descriptions* of the very founders of the faith being engaged in such practices make them *normative* for religious believers today? It may be surprising to nonreligious people to understand that for many—and perhaps most—religious believers, the answer is a clear "no." For many religious believers of the large monotheistic faiths, Abraham is a father of the faith because of his "faith," trust, belief, and obedience in relationship to God, but nonetheless is simply a man of his time in many aspects of his family life and cultural practice.[211] Calling Abraham a rapist is jarring for religious believers but considering all aspects of his lifestyle normative for today would be equally jarring.

There are several lessons that could be drawn from examining the narratives and traditions concerning Hagar, Bilhah, and Zilpah. First, the passage of time does not automatically bring progress. Some practices later in time are more brutal and degrading to human dignity than some practices earlier in time. Dr. Martin Luther King Jr. may have been correct when he famously said that the "moral arc of the universe is long, but it bends toward justice,"[212] but in the interim, sometimes things get worse instead of better. Of course this is undeniable in certain ways:[213] the genocides, wars, and brutality of the twentieth century represented a change for the worse, as new technologies and capacities for war and killing were unleashed upon the world.[214] Advances in technology can be used for better or worse.[215] The mere passage of time and technological advancements do not inevitably bring progress in ethics and human rights and indeed may bring new threats to human dignity and new ethical dilemmas.

A related point is that each society has groups that are particularly vulnerable and thus each society is responsible to self-consciously protect those vulnerable groups against exploitation in a manner that realistically takes account of the inequalities of that society. While the extreme patriarchy, slavery, and concubinage depicted in Genesis and common in that cultural milieu were brutal and inhumane in many respects, the narratives of Hagar, Bilhah, and Zilpah reveal that the customs and morals of the time worked to some degree within those negative contexts to ameliorate some of the harms.[216]

In our times and diverse cultural contexts, we need to be realistic regarding who is most vulnerable to exploitation and vigilantly protect them without pretending that we have created societies in which no one is vulnerable. Equality before the law is a guiding ideal and legal principle in our time[217] but should not be used as a pretense to ignore the very real inequalities in our societies and the accompanying vulnerability of certain segments of society. Otherwise the ideal of equality will ironically facilitate exploitation and the expansion of inequality.

The more powerful actors in contemporary surrogacy, including the intermediaries, the industry, and the prospective parents, commonly seek a legal structure in that they are provided legal rights to enforce their societal advantages of wealth, power, and position to the detriment of the rights of the more vulnerable parties. Certainly we cannot pretend that an infant can protect itself, nor that a poor woman of low status and little education in a developing nation can negotiate on fair and equal terms with a powerful transnational industry. In the context of contemporary surrogacy, this means protecting the child and surrogate mother as the most vulnerable parties, particularly in the context of a contemporary commercial surrogacy industry of international scope and significance. Preventing the sale and commodification of children and the exploitation of surrogate mothers should be primary considerations as societies determine how to regulate, or whether to prohibit, the present large-scale practice of commercial surrogacy. To the degree that surrogacy is permitted, the Biblical record could also suggest protection of the identity rights of children as an important value. If the ancient Biblical narratives could indicate concern and protection for the more vulnerable parties to the surrogacy-like practices of the past, perhaps our contemporary societies, claiming to be protective of human rights, can seek to do so within our own societal contexts.

Notes

1. This chapter's section on adoption is adapted from David Smolin, "Of Orphans and Adoption, Parents and the Poor, Exploitation and Rescue: A Scriptural and Theological Critique of the Evangelical Christian Adoption and Orphan Care Movement," *Regent Journal of International Law* 8 (2012): 269. This chapter's section on surrogacy is adapted from David Smolin, "Surrogacy as the Sale of Children: Applying Lessons Learned from Adoption to the Regulation of the Surrogacy Industry's Global Marketing of Children," *Pepperdine Law Review* 43 (2016): 265, 289–299.
2. See Genesis, Exodus, Leviticus, Numbers, Deuteronomy; Francis Lyall, "Roman Law in the Writings of Paul: Adoption," *Journal of Biblical Literature* 88 (1969): 458, 459; Daniel Pollack et al., "Classical Religious Perspectives of Adoption Law," *Notre Dame Law Review* 79 (2004): 693, 696 (stating that "adoption as a formal legal institution does not exist in Jewish law"); Michael J. Broyde, "Adoption, Personal Status, and Jewish Law," in *The Morality of Adoption* ed. Timothy P. Packson (Eerdmans, Grand Rapids, MI, 2005), 128–147.
3. Pollack et al., "Classical Religious Perspectives," 696; Broyde, "Adoption, Personal Status, and Jewish Law," 129.
4. See Genesis 46, 48–49; Exodus 1:1–7; Leviticus 1–4; Joshua 7:14, 15–24.

5. See Deuteronomy 25:6 (stating that levirate marriage was instituted so that a dead brother's "name will not be blotted out of Israel"); Robert L. Hubbard Jr., "The Goel in Ancient Israel: Theological Reflections on an Israelite Institution," *Bulletin for Biblical Research* 1 (1991): 3, 15; Lyall, "Roman Law in the Writings of Paul," 459–460.
6. See Esther; see later in this chapter notes 54–60 and accompanying text.
7. See Genesis 38:8; Deuteronomy 25:5–10; Lyall, "Roman Law in the Writings of Paul," 459–461. Cf. Leviticus 18:16 (stating that a man shall not have sexual relations with his sister-in-law).
8. See Deuteronomy 21:10–14.
9. See Pollack et al., "Classical Religious Perspectives," 732–752; Broyde, "Adoption, Personal Status, and Jewish Law," 129. See also *Convention on the Rights of the Child*, Art. 20(3), November 20, 1989, 1577 U.N.T.S. 3 (recognizing that Islam has a separate doctrine apart from adoption, *kafalah*, to provide for children separated from their parents).
10. See Pollack et al., "Classical Religious Perspectives," 696–711, 732–52; Broyde, "Adoption, Personal Status, and Jewish Law."
11. See Exodus 2.
12. See, e.g., Tony Merida and Rick Morton, *Orphanology: Awakening to Gospel Centered Adoption and Orphan Care* (2011), 70. Moore instead tries to distinguish the adoption of Moses. See Russell D. Moore, *Adopted for Life: The Priority of Adoption for Christian Families & Churches* (2009); *Resolution No. 2 On Adoption and Orphan Care*, S. Baptist Convention (June 2009).
13. See Exodus 1:15–16.
14. See *Convention on the Prevention and Punishment of the Crime of Genocide*, Art. 2, December 9, 1948, 78 U.N.T.S. 277 [hereinafter *Genocide Convention*].
15. See Exodus 1:17–20.
16. Exodus 1:22.
17. See Exodus 2:1–10.
18. Ibid.
19. See *Genocide Convention* (genocide includes "forcibly transferring children of the group to another group.").
20. Exodus 2:11–15.
21. Hebrews 11:24–27 (KJV).
22. See, e.g., Exodus 4:14–16; 7:1–2 (God appoints Aaron, identified by God as Moses's brother, as Moses's spokesman); Exodus 15:20–22 (Miriam); Numbers 20 (death of Miriam and Aaron); Micah 6:4 (prophetical book recounts redemption of Israel from Egypt, stating "I sent before thee Moses, Aaron, and Miriam").
23. See 1 Chronicles 4:18.
24. See 1 Chronicles 4:18 (*Bithiah bat pharaoh* in the Hebrew text).
25. See generally the book of Esther.
26. See Esther 2:7. The Protestant English versions, following the Hebrew, say that Esther was Mordecai's uncle's daughter—hence Mordecai and Esther were cousins. They are apparently uncle and niece in the Vulgate.
27. Cf. Esther 2:7, in: *Hebrew Bible* (Hebrew Publ. Co.), http://www.mechon-mamre.org/p/pt/pt3301.htm; Esther (Douay-Rheims Version with Vulgate, http://www.latinvulgate.com/verse.aspx?t=0&b=19; Esther (English Septuagint), http://ecmarsh.com/lxx/Esther/index.htm; Esther (Greek Septuagint); Esther (Greek, Vulgate, and English texts), www.newadvent.org.

28. Esther 2:15.
29. See Esther 2:7, 2:15 in the Hebrew Bible; see note 27.
30. Esther 4:13–14 (KJV) (emphasis added).
31. See Esther 2:15, 9:29.
32. See Genesis 48; Merida and Morton, *Orphanology*, 70 (citing Jacob's adoption of Ephraim and Manasseh to show that "God is pro-adoption").
33. See Genesis 48:5.
34. See Genesis 48–49.
35. See, e.g., Genesis 49:28.
36. See Genesis 15:2–3.
37. See Genesis 24.
38. See Genesis 15; Masoretic text available at http://www.mechon-mamre.org/p/pt/pto115.htm.
39. See Genesis 15:4.
40. See, e.g., Matthew 1:16 (genealogy of Jesus through Joseph, the "husband of Mary, of whom was born Jesus").
41. See notes 2–3 in this chapter, and accompanying text.
42. See Matthew 1:20–21.
43. See Luke 2:49 (KJV).
44. See Philip Schaff, *Creeds of Christendom*; see, e.g., Apostle's Creed; Nicene Creed.
45. See later in this chapter notes 146–153 and accompanying text.
46. See Trevor J. Burke, *Adopted into God's Family: Exploring a Pauline Metaphor*, ed. D. A. Carson (IVP Academic, Downer's Grove, IL, 2006), 21–22; see also Dan Cruver et al., *Reclaiming Adoption: Missional Living Through the Rediscovery of Abba Father*, ed. Dan Cruver (Create Space Independent Publishing Platform in Scotts Valley, CA, 2011), 12.
47. See Burke, *Adopted into God's Family*, 21–22.
48. See ibid., 22. The text will assume for purposes of discussion that these letters traditionally ascribed to Paul were primarily authored by Paul, which is a common scholarly viewpoint for Romans and Galatians but not for Ephesians. See Andreas J. Kostenberger, L. Scott Kellum, and Charles L. Quarles, *The Cradle, the Cross and the Crown* (2009), 580.
49. Ibid., 21–22.
50. See, e.g., Douglas J. Moo et al., *Romans, Galatians*, ed. Clinton E. Arnold (2007), (at Romans 8:15).
51. See Burke, *Adopted into God's Family*, 32–45.
52. See generally Moo et al., *Romans, Galatians*.
53. See, e.g., Moo et al., *Romans, Galatians*; see also Burke, *Adopted into God's Family*, 71.
54. See Ephesians 1:5; Galatians 4:5; Romans 8:15, 8:23.
55. Romans 9:4 (KJV).
56. See generally Burke, *Adopted into God's Family*.
57. See, e.g., Burke, *Adopted into God's Family*, 46–71; Lyall, "Roman Law in the Writings of Paul," 458–466.
58. See, e.g., Burke, *Adopted into God's Family*, 60–71.
59. See Romans 8:15, 8:23, 9:4.
60. See Burke, *Adopted into God's Family*, 58–60.
61. See, e.g., Romans 11:13; Acts 9:15; Acts 15; Galatians 1 and 2; Ephesians 3:1–13.
62. See Burke, *Adopted into God's Family*, 71.
63. See, e.g., Ephesians 3:1–13; Galatians; Romans 3:28–30.

64. See Romans 11:16–24.
65. Ibid.
66. See Romans 11:19–21.
67. Romans 11:24 (NKJV).
68. See Burke, *Adopted into God's Family*, 60–70.
69. See, e.g., Burke, *Adopted into God's Family*, 63–64; Suzanne Dixon, *The Roman Family* (Johns Hopkins University Press, Baltimore, MD, 1992), 40–41; Geoffrey S. Nathan, *The Family in Late Antiquity* (Routledge, NY, NY, 2000), 24–28.
70. See Nathan, *The Family in Late Antiquity*, 16–17.
71. See Dixon, *The Roman Family*, 40–41.
72. See, e.g., Dixon, *The Roman Family*, 40–47; Susan Treggiari, "Divorce Roman Style: How Easy and Frequent Was It?," in *Marriage, Divorce, and Children in Ancient Rome*, ed. Beryl Rawson (Oxford University Press, NY, NY, 1991), 34.
73. See Nathan, *The Family in Late Antiquity*, 1–28.
74. See Burke, *Adopted into God's Family*, 66; Nathan, *The Family in Late Antiquity*, 26–27; Beryl Rawson, "The Roman Family," in *The Family in Ancient Rome, New Perspectives* (1986), 12.
75. See, e.g., Burke, *Adopted into God's Family*, 60–70; Dixon, *The Roman Family*, 108–113; Nathan, *The Family in Late Antiquity*, 25; Rawson, "The Roman Family," 12; Mireille Corbier, "Divorce and Adoption in Roman Familial Strategies," in *Marriage, Divorce, and Children in Ancient Rome*, ed. Beryl Rawson (1991), 41, 63–78.
76. See Burke, *Adopted into God's Family*, 62–63; Pliny the Younger, *Pliny: Letters and Panegyricus*, vol. II, translated by Betty Radice (Harvard University Press, 1969), 333–349; Rawson, "The Roman Family," 12; Tacitus, *The Annals*, Book I, chs. 2–3, translated by John Jackson, (Harvard University Press, 1962); Tacitus, *The Annals*, Book XII, chs. 25–26, translated by John Jackson (Harvard University Press, 1962); Tacitus, *The Histories*, Book I, chs. 15–21, translated by Clifford H. Moore (Harvard University Press, 1962).
77. See Dixon, *The Roman Family*, 108–113; Rawson, "The Roman Family," 12.
78. See *Brill's New Pauly: Encyclopaedia of the Ancient World* (2002), 146–152; Corbier, "Divorce and Adoption," 66.
79. See, e.g., *Brill's New Pauly*, 146–152; Burke, *Adopted into God's Family*, 60–70; Dixon, *The Roman Family*, 108–113; Rawson, "The Roman Family," 12; Corbier, "Divorce and Adoption," 63–78.
80. See, e.g., *Brill's New Pauly*, 146–152; Burke, *Adopted into God's Family*, 60–70; Dixon, *The Roman Family*, 108–13. Corbier, "Divorce and Adoption," 63–78.
81. See, e.g., Romans 8:15–23.
82. See, e.g., *Brill's New Pauly*, 146–152; Burke, *Adopted into God's Family*, 62; Rawson, "The Roman Family," 12; Corbier, "Divorce and Adoption," 63–78.
83. See notes 48, 76, and 78.
84. See, e.g., Moyer V. Hubbard, *Christianity in the Greco-Roman World* (2010), 127–131.
85. For contrasting views on the significance of the Imperial Cult as background to the early church and the writings of Paul, cf. *Paul and Empire: Religion and Power in Roman Imperial Society*, ed. Richard A. Horsley (1997); and Seyoon Kim, *Christ and Caesar: The Gospel and the Roman Empire in the Writings of Paul and Luke* (2008).
86. See, e.g., Romans 8; Galatians 4:1–7.
87. See *Brill's New Pauly*, 146–152; Burke, *Adopted into God's Family*, 58–60.

88. Ibid.
89. See, e.g., *Brill's New Pauly*, 146–152; Burke, *Adopted into God's Family*, 65–66; Pliny, *Pliny: Letters and Panegyricus*.
90. See Dixon, *The Roman Family*, 112.
91. See, e.g., James 1:27; James 2:15–16; Luke 12:33; Luke 14:12–14; Luke 18:22.
92. See, e.g., Acts 2:44–45; Acts 4:34–37; Acts 6:1–6; Acts 11:28–30; Romans 15:26; 1 Timothy 5:1–16.
93. See, e.g., Moore, *Adopted for Life*, 33 (citing John 19:26–27).
94. See *Catechism of the Catholic Church*, paragraphs 964–970.
95. See, e.g., James Strong, *The New Strong's Exhaustive Concordance of the Bible* (1990); The Bible (KJV); *Strong's H3490—yathowm*, Blue Letter Bible, http://www.blueletterbible.org/lang/lexicon/lexicon.cfm?Strongs=H3490&t=KJV [hereinafter Strong's *yathowm*] (translating *yathowm* to "an orphan, fatherless").
96. See Harold V. Bennett, *Injustice Made Legal* (2002), 48; Strong's *yathowm*.
97. See Strong's *yathowm*.
98. See, e.g., Bennett, *Injustice Made Legal*, 48–56.
99. See ibid., 24–56; Strong's H490—*almanah*, Blue Letter Bible, http://www.blueletterbible.org/lang/lexicon/lexicon.cfm?Strongs=H490&t=KJV (translating *almanah* to *widow*).
100. Exodus 22:22–24 (NKJV).
101. See, e.g., Bennett, *Injustice Made Legal*, 23–56; Hubbard, "The Go'el in Ancient Israel," 15.
102. See Robert L. Hubbard Jr., *The Book of Ruth* (1988); see generally Hubbard, "The Go'el in Ancient Israel."
103. See Ruth 1:1–5.
104. See Ruth 1:16–18.
105. See Deuteronomy 24:19–21; Ruth 2.
106. See Ruth 4:1–12.
107. See Ruth 4:10 (Boaz marries Ruth "to perpetuate the name of the dead"); Ruth 4:16–17 (Naomi nurses Ruth's baby and neighbor women declare that a son has been born to her).
108. Ruth 4:22.
109. See Matthew 1:5–6.
110. See Luke 3:31–32.
111. See Matthew 1:5–6; Luke 3:31–32; Ruth 4:21.
112. Compare Matthew 1:5–6, with Ruth 4:15–17.
113. See Hubbard, *Christianity in the Greco-Roman World*, 127–131.
114. See 1 Kings 17; 2 Kings 4:1–7; see also 2 Kings 4:8–37.
115. 1 Kings 17:12 (NKJV).
116. See 1 Kings 17:13–16.
117. 1 Kings 17:17–24 (NKJV).
118. 1 Kings 17:18 (NKJV).
119. 2 Kings 4:1 (NKJV).
120. See 2 Kings 4:1–7.
121. See, e.g., Matthew 11:13–14, 17:1–13; Luke 7:11–17, 9:28–36; Bruce Waltke, "Meditating on Scripture," *Tabletalk*, September 1, 2009, http://www.ligonier.org/learn/articles/meditating-scripture/.
122. See in this chapter notes 25–31 and accompanying text.
123. James 1:27 (KJV).

124. See Strong's G3737—*orphanos*, Blue Letter Bible, http://www.blueletterbible.org/lang/lexi con/lexicon.cfm?Strongs=G3737&t=KJV (translating *orphanos* to *bereft* (of a father, of parents) or "orphaned").
125. Beyond James 1:27, the other usage is from John 14:18: Jesus, as a part of the Last Supper discourse, assures the apostles that he will not leave them *orphanos*, which is variously translated in the NKJV as *orphans* or *comfortless* in the KJV.
126. See Donald Guthrie, *New Testament Introduction*, 4th ed. (1990), 722–759.
127. See in this chapter notes 96–118 and accompanying text.
128. See Acts 6:1–6; 1 Timothy 5:3–16.
129. Acts 6:1.
130. See Acts 6:1–6.
131. See 1 Timothy 5:1–16. The difficulties include whether the passage concerns something like an "order" of older widows in some kind of church office or ministry, interpreting the details of the requisites for receiving support, and the ambivalence concerning remarriage of widows. For varying views, see, e.g., Gordon D. Fee, *1 and 2 Timothy, Titus 1:14–26*, ed. W. Ward Gasque (1988); Donald Guthrie, *The Pastoral Epistles: An Introduction and Commentary* (1990), 112–117; Benjamin Fiore, *The Pastoral Epistles* (2007), 100–109.
132. See ibid.
133. See, e.g., 1 Timothy 5:11–14 (the very section urging that younger widows remarry itself seems to be critical of the act). See also 1 Corinthians 7:8–9, 7:39–40; 1 Timothy 5:9 (KJV) (requirement of having been "the wife of one man").
134. 1 Timothy 5:14.
135. 1 Timothy 5:8; see also 1 Timothy 5:4, 5:16.
136. See Luke 2:36–38.
137. See Luke 21:1–4.
138. See Luke 18:1–8.
139. Luke 20:47 (NKJV).
140. Acts 9:36–42 (KJV).
141. See Genesis 1:28; see, e.g., Psalms 127:3–5. See also Marianne Meye Thompson, "Children in the Gospel of John," in *The Child in the Bible*, ed. Marcia J. Bunge (2008), 195, for a discussion on ancient Jewish and early Christian pro-life viewpoints opposing abortion and infanticide.
142. See generally Ezekiel 20:25–26; Jeremiah 7:31, 32:35; Leviticus 18:21, 20:1–5; (selections from the Hebrew Bible that are commonly interpreted to indicate that some Israelites participated in infanticide/child sacrifice, and also that it was forbidden).
143. See in this chapter notes 4 and 35 and accompanying text.
144. See in this chapter notes 4–6, and 25–31, and accompanying text.
145. See, e.g., Matthew 18:1–6, 10–14, 19:13–16.
146. See, e.g., W. V. Harris, "Child-Exposure in the Roman Empire," *Journal of Roman Studies* (1994): 1.
147. See, e.g., George T. Montague, *First and Second Timothy, Titus*, ed. Peter S. Williamson and Mary Healy (2008), 108 (estimating that 40 percent of the women in the ancient world between ages forty and fifty were widows).
148. See, e.g., Ephesians 4:17–5:20; Galatians 5:13–25.
149. See, e.g., Acts 4:34–35, 6:1–6.
150. For a fuller explanation of adoption as a relative good, see David M. Smolin, "Intercountry Adoption as Child Trafficking," *Valparaiso University Law Review* 39 (2004): 281, 283–286, http://works.bepress.com/david_smolin/.

151. See David M. Smolin, "Child Laundering as Exploitation: Applying Anti-Trafficking Norms to Intercountry Adoption Under the Coming Hague Regime," *Vermont Law Review* 32 (2007): 1; ISS, *Responding to Illegal Adoptions*, ed. C. Baglietto, N. Cantwell, and M. Dambach (2016).
152. See *Hague Convention on Protection of Children and Co-operation in Respect of Intercountry Adoption*, 32 I.L.M. 1134 (1993), Art. 8, 32 (addressing financial aspects of intercountry adoption); Smolin, "Intercountry Adoption as Child Trafficking" (addressing line between licit and illicit roles of money in relationship to intercountry and domestic adoption).
153. See "Infertility FAQ's," *Centers for Disease Control and Prevention* (June 28, 2011), http://www.cdc.gov/reproductivehealth/infertility/ (discussing the incidence and causes of infertility in the United States).
154. See in this chapter note 152.
155. See in this chapter note 151.
156. See generally David M. Smolin, "Intercountry Adoption and Poverty: A Human Rights Analysis," *Capital University Law Review* 36 (2007): 413.
157. See, e.g., *Stanley v. Illinois*, 405 U.S. 645 (1972); E. Wayne Carp, *Family Matters: Secrecy and Disclosure in the History of Adoption* (1998); Barbara Melosh, "Adoption Stories," in *Adoption in America*, ed. E. Wayne Carp (2002), 218; Elizabeth J. Samuels, "The Idea of Adoption: An Inquiry into the History of Adult Adoptee Access to Birth Records," *Rutgers Law Review* 53 (2001): 367; Elizabeth J. Samuels, "The Strange History of Adult Adoptee Access to Original Birth Records," *Adoption Quarterly* 5 (2001): 63.
158. See Samuels, "The Idea of Adoption"; Samuels, "The Strange History of Adoption"; Smolin, "Child Laundering as Exploitation," 4–10.
159. See in this chapter note 1; see Julia Tate, *Surrogacy: What Progress Since Hagar, Bilhah, and Zilpah!* (1994).
160. See ibid., 1 ("No doubt these involuntary surrogates had very different experiences than those of today's surrogates").
161. See Genesis 16:1–16, 17:17–26, 21:8–21, 29:24, 29, 30:1–13; Naomi Steinberg, *Kinship and Marriage in Genesis: A Household Economic Perspective* (1993), 35–86, 115–134.
162. Tate, *Surrogacy*, 1.
163. Cf. Usha Rengachary Smerdon, "Crossing Bodies, Crossing Borders: International Surrogacy Between the United States and India," *Cumberland Law Review* 39 (2008): 15, 16–17 (contrasting the Genesis narrative of Hagar and Sarah with contemporary commercial surrogacy).
164. See ibid., 22.
165. Tate, *Surrogacy*, 1.
166. See Genesis 21:10.
167. See ibid., 16:1–16, 17:17–26, 21:8–21.
168. See ibid., 16:10.
169. See ibid., 16:1–16, 17:17–26, 21:8–21.
170. See ibid., 16:7–14.
171. Robert Crotty, "Hagar/Hajar, Muslim Women and Islam: Reflections on the Historical and Theological Ramifications of the Story of Ishmael's Mother," in *Women in Islam: Reflections on Historical and Contemporary Research*, ed. Terence Lovat (2012), 165 and 182.
172. See ibid., 165, 182. See generally Phyllis Trible and Letty M. Russell, *Hagar, Sarah, and Their Children: Jewish, Christian, and Muslim Perspectives* (2006); "Hajj: Pilgrimage to Mecca," *World Religions*.

173. See Steinberg, *Kinship and Marriage in Genesis*, 35–86, 115–134.
174. See Barbara Katz Rothman, "Motherhood: Beyond Patriarchy," *Nova Law Review* 13 (1989): 481, 485.
175. See Steinberg, *Kinship and Marriage in Genesis*, 62; Rothman, "Motherhood," 485.
176. See Genesis 29:24, 29, 30:1–13.
177. See Tate, *Surrogacy*, 1.
178. See Genesis 35:23–26.
179. Ibid.
180. See, e.g., Genesis 49:1–28; Joshua 13–22.
181. See Genesis 32:28.
182. See Tate, *Surrogacy*, 1.
183. See Genesis 16:3. At this point in the text, Sarah is still named "Sarai" and Abraham is still named "Abram." Ibid.
184. See Genesis 16:4–5; Hennie J. Marsman, *Women in Ugarit and Israel: Their Social and Religious Position in the Context of the Ancient Near East* (2003), 105, 143–144, 451–452; Steinberg, *Kinship and Marriage in Genesis*, 61–65.
185. See Marsman, *Women in Ugarit and Israel*, 485; Steinberg, *Kinship and Marriage in Genesis*, 79.
186. See Marsman, *Women in Ugarit and Israel*, 485; Steinberg, *Kinship and Marriage in Genesis*, 65.
187. See Marsman, *Women in Ugarit and Israel*, 485.
188. See ibid., 452–453.
189. See, e.g., ibid., 450–451, 472; Victor H. Matthews, *Manners & Customs in the Bible: An Illustrated Guide to Daily Life in Bible Times*, 3rd edition (2006), 36.
190. See Genesis 24:1–66.
191. Ibid.
192. See Genesis 29:15–20.
193. See Genesis 16:3, 30:4, 30:9.
194. See Marsman, *Women in Ugarit and Israel*, 143–144.
195. See, e.g., Rebecca Whisnant, "Feminist Perspectives on Rape," *Stanford Encyclopedia of Philosophy*, http://plato.stanford.edu/entries/feminism-rape/.
196. See Tate, *Surrogacy*, 1.
197. See Genesis 16:3, 30:4, 30:9.
198. See Genesis 16:1–16, 17:17–26, 21:8–21.
199. See Genesis 16:3; Marsman, *Women in Ugarit and Israel*, 143–144, 437–454; Steinberg, *Kinship and Marriage in Genesis*, 61–65.
200. See Genesis 16:1–16, 17:17–26, 21:8–21; Marsman, *Women in Ugarit and Israel*, 143–144, 437–154; Steinberg, *Kinship and Marriage in Genesis*, 61–65.
201. See Genesis 35:22.
202. See Genesis 29:32, 35:22.
203. Genesis 35:22, 49:4; Leviticus 18:8; 1 Chronicles 5:1; Marsman, *Women in Ugarit and Israel*, 379 and n. 44; Steinberg, *Kinship and Marriage in Genesis*, 112–114, 121–122.
204. See Report of the Research Committee on Thomas Jefferson and Sally Hemings, Thomas Jefferson Foundation (January 2000), http://www.monticello.org/site/plantation-and-slavery/report-research-committee-thomas-jefferson-and-sally-hemings; "Thomas Jefferson and Sally Hemings: A Brief Account," Thomas Jefferson Foundation, http://www.monticello.org/site/plantation-and-slavery/thomas-jefferson-and-sally-hemings-brief-account.

205. See, e.g., Paul Finkelman, "Slavery in the United States: Persons or Property?," in *The Legal Understanding of Slavery: From the Historical to the Contemporary*, ed. Jean Allain (2012), 105-134. See generally *Dred Scott v. Sandford*, 60 U.S. 393 (1856); Herbert G. Gutman, *The Black Family in Slavery and Freedom: 1750-1925* (1976); Thomas D. Morris, *Southern Slavery and the Law: 1619-1860* (1996); "Review of Mark Tushnet, *The American Law of Slavery, 1810-1860: Considerations of Humanity and Interest*," American Bar Foundation Journal 7 (1982): 274.
206. See Genesis 16:1-16, 17:17-26, 21:8-21; Marsman, *Women in Ugarit and Israel*, 451-452; Steinberg, *Kinship and Marriage in Genesis*, 61-81.
207. See Genesis 35:23-26.
208. See Genesis 35:23-26, 49:1-28; Derek Kidner, *Genesis: An Introduction and Commentary* (1967), 126 (noting that sons born of Bilhah and Zilpah "were to count in Jacob's family as full members and heads of tribes").
209. See "The Global Religious Landscape," Pew Research Center (December 18, 2012) "The Global Religious Landscape: A Report on the Size and Distribution of the World's Major Religious Groups as of 2010," Pew Research Center (December 2012), http://www.pewforum.org/files/2014/01/global-religion-full.pdf.
210. See in this chapter notes 159-210 and accompanying text.
211. See, e.g., Hebrews 12:8-19 (praising the faith of Abraham).
212. See "The Arc of the Moral Universe Is Long But It Bends Towards Justice," *Quote Investigator*, http://quoteinvestigator.com/2012/11/15/arc-of-universe/ (indicating that King was himself quoting or paraphrasing a statement originating in the nineteenth century from Theodore Parker).
213. See Mark Levene, "Why Is the Twentieth Century the Century of Genocide?," *Journal of World History* 11 (2000): 305 (noting an estimated 187 million people killed in political violence in the twentieth century).
214. See generally ibid.
215. See ibid., 305-308.
216. See Marsman, *Women in Ugarit and Israel*, 143-144.
217. See *African Charter on Human and Peoples' Rights*, Art. 2-3, October 21, 1986, 21 I.L.M. 59; *American Convention on Human Rights*, Art. 1, November 21, 1969, 1144 U.N.T.S. 143; *International Covenant on Civil and Political Rights*, Pmbl., December 16, 1966, 999 U.N.T.S. 171; *European Convention for the Protection of Human Rights and Fundamental Freedoms*, Art. 14 (November 4, 1950), 213 U.N.T.S. 221; G. A. Res. 2200A (XXI), *International Covenant on Economic, Social and Cultural Rights*, Pmbl., Arts. 2-3 (December 19, 1966); G.A. Res. 217 (III) A, *Universal Declaration of Human Rights* (December 10, 1948), Pmbl., Arts. 1-2, 6-7.

CHAPTER 17

JEWISH PERSPECTIVES ON GAMETE USE, DONATION, AND SURROGACY

ELLIOT N. DORFF

BEFORE delving into the complex legal, moral, and psychological issues involved in gamete use, donation, and surrogacy,[1] it is important to state that Jewish law does not require the use of any of them. The command to procreate in Genesis 1:28, like all other commandments, applies only to those people who can fulfill them on their own accord, so couples who cannot have children through their own sexual intercourse are no longer bound by the duty to procreate. Moreover, because the financial and psychological tolls of using donor gametes or a surrogate mother are considerable, couples considering these procedures are well advised to learn about their pitfalls and to make plans to cope with their psychological strains in advance. Couples are also reminded that adoption is a very honored activity in Judaism, with the Talmud asserting that people who bring up an orphan boy or girl and ultimately enable that child to marry are to be considered as if they gave birth to that child, and they fulfill the verse in Psalms, "Happy are they that act justly, who do right at all times" (Psalms 106:3).[2] Finally, although this article will focus on Jewish perspectives on third-party pregnancies, readers should note that these pregnancies have led to many court cases in civil law, with varying results according to the specific circumstances and the particular state's law.

I shall treat the use of donor sperm first, then the additional concerns raised by using donor eggs, and then the issues surrounding providing such services through surrogacy and gamete donation. Limits of space will confine this discussion to a description of the issues and some responses to them across the Jewish denominational spectrum;

for fuller treatments of these topics in each of the Jewish movements, see, for example, the books listed in this endnote.[3]

ARTIFICIAL INSEMINATION WITH A DONOR'S SPERM: CONCERNS BASED ON JEWISH LAW

1. *Adultery and Illegitimacy.* In cases where it is a married woman who is being inseminated with the sperm of a man other than her husband, some rabbis construe donor insemination (hereinafter DI) as adultery. Rabbi Eliezer Waldenberg, for example, takes this position.[4]

Adultery, however, is repugnant primarily because it violates the trust between husband and wife that must be the foundation of their relationship. On a more technical level, the Talmud, Maimonides, Rabbi David Halevi (the "Taz"), and the majority of recent authorities maintain that the legal category of adultery is incurred only when there is sexual penetration.[5] That is clearly not the case when insemination takes place artificially.

2. *Unintentional incest in the next generation.* If the sperm donor is anonymous, the person produced by artificial insemination might happen to marry one of the children of the donor and his wife. Because the two children share a father, they would each be marrying their biological half-brother or half-sister. Consanguinity of the couple raises the odds of genetic defects and diseases. This concern is all the more worrisome because sperm banks are largely unregulated by state law, and many use the same donors for numerous inseminations.[6]

Nevertheless, the practice of most sperm banks and the preference of most sperm donors and recipients are that the parties involved remain unknown to each other, largely for the psychological reasons described below. Such confidentiality is permissible from the point of view of Jewish law *if* the sperm bank keeps thorough records on all its donors and recipients and conscientiously updates them as necessary. Furthermore, as much as possible of the donor's medical history must be revealed to the child in order to prevent possible genetic diseases in that child's own offspring.

3. *The identity of the father.* The identity of the father is potentially an issue in four matters: the child's Jewish identity, priestly status, and inheritance rights, and the father's duty to procreate.

Because Jewish law determines a person's Jewish identity according to the bearing mother,[7] a Jewish woman's offspring are automatically Jewish, no matter the source of the sperm.

Priestly status is determined by genetics, for it is, according to the Torah, "the seed of Aaron" who are to perform the priestly duties.[8] Therefore, if the donor is known to be, respectively, a *kohen*, *levi*, or *yisrael*, the son born using his sperm has that status as well. If the donor's priestly status is not known, which is usually the case, the child is treated as a *yisrael*, like that of over 90 percent of Jewish men. This would apply to daughters as well in the modern liberal movements that ascribe that status to women.[9]

Matters of inheritance are governed in the Americas and in Europe by civil law, not Jewish law. In Israel, the matter is more complicated, but for the 80 percent of non-Orthodox Jews there and for some Orthodox Jews as well, inheritance in Israel is also determined by civil law.

What Jewish law does determine, though, is whether a Jewish man fulfills the commandment to be fruitful and multiply if he consents to have his wife impregnated with another man's sperm, if his own sperm is artificially implanted in his wife's uterus, or if he himself is a sperm donor. By and large, rabbis who have ruled on these matters thus far have maintained that the father for purposes of this commandment is the man who provides the sperm. That would make a man who impregnates his wife through artificial insemination (AIH = artificial insemination by the husband) the father of his child in Jewish law, and it would also make a sperm donor the father of any children born through the use of his sperm for purposes of fulfilling the command to procreate, while it would deny the status of fatherhood to men who consent to have their wives impregnated with donor sperm. These last two results are clearly alarming for donors and disappointing for social fathers.

The first point to mention in evaluating these rulings is that donor insemination stretches our understanding of fatherhood. We normally assume that the same man who sired a child will be the one who raises him or her. When that does not happen, the legal category of fatherhood and the concept underlying it must be applied to circumstances not contemplated when the concept and the law were first formulated, so we should not be surprised if the traditional concept of fatherhood does not fit exactly right, no matter how we classify the new forms of procreation.

In our case, several factors would lead us to call the sperm donor the father for purposes of the commandment of propagation, the most important of which is that the child inherits the biological father's DNA, not the social father's. Modern research has made us increasingly aware of the impact of our genes on who we are as people, not only biologically, but in a number of character traits as well.

On the other hand, there are other factors that would lead us to classify the social father as the one who fulfills the command to propagate. According to the Biblical law of levirate marriage, when a man dies childless, it is the duty of his brother to have conjugal relations with the deceased man's widow so that a child might be born bearing the parentage of the deceased brother. That precedent would argue that the sperm donor is not always the father.[10] Moreover, one classical Rabbinic source ascribes fatherhood to the man who raises a child, not to the one whose sperm gave him birth.[11] Furthermore, according to Jewish law a Gentile who renounces the idolatrous status of a given idol thereby converts it into a mere statue.[12] Similarly, it could be argued that the donor's explicit intention to have someone else raise the child amounts to a renunciation of his status of fatherhood and a transfer of it to the social father. Yet another precedent that argues in this direction is that of Jacob, who adopts Joseph's sons, Ephraim and Menashe, as his own. Their descendants thus become two of the twelve tribes of Israel, along with the descendants of the rest of Jacob's sons.[13]

Aside from these arguments based on facets of Jewish law and other classical Jewish texts, a number of contemporary realities would argue in this direction. The social father, after all, invests a lifetime of energy, love, and substance in the child, while in most cases the donor never even meets the child. Jewish law generally awards privileges only to those who bear concomitant responsibilities, and that would certainly suggest in this case that the man who raises the child, rather than the man who merely ejaculates, should merit the status of fulfilling the commandment of propagation. Such a ruling would also accord with the intentions and the actions of both men involved.

Whichever man is deemed the father, then, some aspects of the decision will seem counterintuitive, for in some ways the sperm donor is clearly the father, and in some ways the social father is. Moreover, identifying exclusively one or the other as the father hides important aspects of the child's being. To be true to the identity of the child and to the roles that both men play in the child's life, then, the fatherhood of both men involved must be recognized for the distinctive ways in which they are the child's father.

Thus while the social father is not the father in the technical sense of being the biological parent and therefore does not fulfill through DI the specific commandment to procreate, he is the "real" father in some of the most significant ways for the child. Therefore, the social father's name should be invoked when the child is being identified by his or her Hebrew name, son or daughter of the names of the father (and mother), as, for example, when called to the Torah or in a marriage document.[14] Similarly, children of donor insemination should consider themselves obligated to fulfill the Torah's commands to honor one's parents (Exodus 20:12; Deuteronomy 5:16) and to respect them (Leviticus 19:3) as applied to the social parents. Conversely, the social parents should consider themselves responsible to fulfill the duties that the Torah and the Jewish tradition impose upon parents vis-à-vis their children.[15]

Artificial Insemination with a Donor's Sperm: Moral Concerns

1. *Licentiousness.* Because the strictly legal concerns discussed above can be resolved, most rabbis who have objected to donor insemination have done so on moral grounds. In my own view, positive law and morality are one undifferentiated web, where each can and should influence the other. That is especially true in a religious legal system

like the Jewish one, where a fundamental assumption is that the law must express the will of a moral—indeed, a benevolent—God. Thus the moral concerns raised by donor insemination are not, for me, "merely" moral, but fully legal.[16]

It is especially interesting to note, though, that Orthodox rabbis, who usually shun moral arguments in their legal decisions, have invoked them to deny the legitimacy of donor insemination. So, for example, Rabbi Immanuel Jakobovits voices these moral concerns in strong language:

> If Jewish law nevertheless opposes AID [artificial insemination by a donor] without reservation as utterly evil, it is mainly for moral reasons, not because of the intrinsic illegality of the act itself. The principal motives for the revulsion against the practice is the fear of the abuses to which its legalization would lead, however great the benefits may be in individual cases. By reducing human generation to stud-farming methods, AID severs the link between the procreation of children and marriage, indispensable to the maintenance of the family as the most basic and sacred unit of human society. It would enable women to satisfy their craving for children without the necessity to have homes or husbands. It would pave the way to a disastrous increase of promiscuity, as a wife, guilty of adultery, could always claim that a pregnancy which her husband did not, or was unable to, cause was brought about by AID, when in fact she had adulterous relations with another man. Altogether, the generation of children would become arbitrary and mechanical, robbed of those mystic and intimately human qualities which make man a partner with God in the creative propagation of the race.[17]

I take a much more positive attitude toward donor insemination. After all, people who want to be licentious will find many ways to do so without artificial insemination. Indeed, donor insemination is so onerous a mode of illicit sex—if it be that at all—that it is downright implausible that people would go to the trouble and expense of using it for such purposes.

Furthermore, the couple is, by hypothesis, using DI when they have no other way to achieve a precious goal in Jewish law and thought, the bearing of children. Even if the social father does not technically fulfill the obligation to procreate through DI, we should applaud the couple's willingness to use DI for three reasons: the Jewish tradition has always valued children; in their efforts to have children, couples who use DI will undergo hardships that other couples need not endure, as described below, and they consequently need every encouragement they can get; and, finally, having and raising Jewish children is a demographic imperative for the Jewish community in our time, as described below.

2. *The Impact on the Marriage and on the Parent-Child Relationship.* In a philosophically penetrating article probing the nature of parenthood, Paul Lauritzen, a man whose own wife was artificially inseminated with donor sperm, argues that children can have confidence that their social fathers can be trusted to care for them and not abandon them at least as much as biological fathers can be.[18] The moral issues involved in DI, then, are secrecy and the genetic asymmetry donor insemination creates in the relationship between each of the parents and the child. He argues strongly that

children born through DI should be told about that as early as the child can understand such matters in order to preserve the needed trust that the child has for his or her parents.

He also wisely suggests that the couple undergo counseling so that the social father is assured that his wife appreciates him as a manly man, despite his inability to procreate, and that she sees him fully as the father of their child.

The same point applies to grandparents and other members of the family. As Mahlstedt and Greenfeld point out,

> The social attitudes which concern infertile couples most are *not* those of the church or the law, but those of their families. . . . It is their support that most effectively enables confidence, conviction, and courage to emerge in the couple's experience with donor conception. Couples who receive family love and support reflect less ambivalence about their choice, more comfort in sharing their means of conception with others, and more confidence in their abilities to cope with negative social attitudes.[19]

3. *Racism and Eugenics.* Even if the identity of the sperm donor is kept secret, couples considering DI often want to make sure that he is like them so that the child will resemble them.

If the couple's rationale for preferring a child who looks like them is indeed because they value one race over another, that is, by definition, racist. Such an attitude is both theologically and legally problematic for a Jew to have. Theologically, the Bible proclaims that God created all people, with no race inherently more worthy than any other. Legally, membership in a particular race is neither a necessary nor a sufficient condition for being Jewish: the plethora of races among Israel's Jews and increasingly among Jews in other countries amply attests that membership in any one race is not necessary for being Jewish, and, conversely, the fact that there are many non-Jews of all races shows that membership in any given race is not a sufficient condition for being Jewish either.

Couples, though, generally prefer a child who looks like them for other reasons that are not inherently racist. Specifically, if the child resembles them, it may be easier for the parents and child to bond with each other. Moreover, it will minimize the awareness of family, friends, and others that the child became the couple's through any process other than their own sexual intercourse. To desire these things is understandable; after all, for all of us, part of the lure of having children is that they represent one of the ways for us to gain eternity; children are a piece of us that remains after we die. Moreover, the child stands to benefit from his or her likeness to the social parents, for parents and family often find it easier to bond with children who look like them. This is clearly not necessary, as many families who are adopting children of other races are discovering, and it is certainly permissible to use sperm or eggs from someone of a race different from one's own; but choosing sperm or eggs from someone of the same race is not necessarily racist and objectionable on those grounds.

DI is sometimes used, however, for eugenic purposes. From a Jewish perspective, it would be permissible to screen out, as sperm banks usually do, donors with genetic disorders or other diseases like HIV, syphilis, hepatitis, gonorrhea, and chlamydia, for those characteristics of the donor are likely to affect the physical health of the child; but it would not be permissible to choose only those donors with outstanding mental or physical traits. That would no longer be using medicine to assist God in maintaining creation, but would rather be playing God in an attempt radically to change it. Contemporary Jewish ethicists have provided a variety of Jewish grounds for permitting genetic testing, choice, and intervention for therapeutic reasons, but not for eugenic ones.[20]

4. *Compassion for the couple.* Underlying any moral assessment of any of the artificial reproductive techniques, including the use of donor gametes, must be compassion for the infertile couple who desperately want to have children. As the Biblical stories of the Patriarchs and Matriarchs graphically demonstrate, infertility often causes severe tensions in the couple's relationship. Moreover, because of the extraordinary efforts these techniques require to produce children, couples who use them are likely to be devoted parents, and so society as a whole will benefit from children being raised by such parents.

5. *Demographic Concerns.* In addition to these moral issues that affect couples of all faiths involved in donor insemination, there are specific Jewish issues in judging its morality, especially the demographic crisis in which Jews now find themselves. Jews lost a third of their numbers during the Holocaust, so that today they represent about 0.2 percent of the world's population. (In contrast, 31 percent are Christian and 23 percent are Muslim.[21]) Moreover, Jews are not reproducing themselves; instead of the 2.1 or 2.2 reproductive rate required for replacement, the rate among American Jews is 1.9.[22] Furthermore, as many as half of Jews who are marrying have chosen a spouse of another faith, and only 20 percent of the children of such couples will be raised as Jews.[23] So this demographic context would argue strongly in favor of Jews using any artificial reproductive technique they need, including the use of donor gametes, so that both the Jewish people and Judaism can survive.

Using Donated Eggs

1. *Health risks.* In cases where a woman cannot produce eggs but can carry a fetus, she may have eggs of a donor woman fertilized in a petri dish with either the sperm of her (that is, the infertile woman's) husband or of a sperm donor, and then the zygote is implanted in her uterus for gestation. This is in vitro fertilization (IVF). Moreover, even if a woman over age forty can produce eggs, the success rate of IVF in such women is so dismal that doctors generally recommend the use of a younger woman's eggs instead.

One can understand the benefits of the use of donor eggs. Unlike adoption, the woman will go through pregnancy, an experience many women want to have. Moreover, in most cases, the husband's sperm is used, and so the child will bear the genetic imprint of at least one of his or her parents—the same advantage that leads couples to use DI when necessary.

One critical factor that makes egg donation less acceptable than donor insemination, though, is that some studies suggest that the process makes the donor more susceptible to contracting ovarian, breast, or uterine cancer. The evidence of such a link is not clear, though, and, in any case, the risks to the egg donor are not so great as to require a ban on the procedure entirely out of concern for her life or health.[24] Still, they are significant enough to say that a Jewish couple may ask a woman to undertake those risks only when the couple has seriously considered all other options for having children, including adoption, and when the donor is assured by her physician that she can donate eggs safely.

2. *Moral and psychological issues in egg donation.* For the infertile couple, most of the moral and psychological issues in egg donation are the same as those in donor insemination. The openness in communication required of all parties involved in donor insemination must therefore characterize cases of the use of donor eggs as well. The same demographic crisis and the same compassion for the infertile couple that should affect the moral evaluation of donor insemination should likewise make the use of donor eggs morally acceptable and even laudable when the couple cannot have a child in any other way.

From the perspective of Jewish law, in egg donation as in artificial insemination, contact of the genital organs and intent to have an adulterous relationship are both missing, and so the prohibition against adultery does not apply. Furthermore, because the use of donor eggs costs much more than donor sperm, it is even less plausibly construed as a form of licentiousness.

What about sibling donors? First, may a fertile brother donate sperm for the impregnation of his infertile brother's wife? That would have the advantage of carrying on the husband's family genes and the likelihood of producing a child who resembles the husband as much as any biological child of his would. Nevertheless, such donations are generally inadvisable, for although they are not technically incest, they *feel* very close to it and raise all kinds of boundary problems for the brothers and the child later on ("Is Uncle Barry really only my uncle, or is he my substitute father when I want him to be?").[25] Moreover, sperm donations from others are easy to procure and inexpensive.

An egg donation from a fertile sister to an infertile one involves the same boundary issues for both the sisters and the child. Because donated eggs are relatively scarce and expensive, though, and because the lack of genital contact means that legally there is no taint of incest, a fertile sister may donate eggs to her infertile sibling, but only after appropriate counseling and careful consideration of how the sisters will handle these boundary questions as the child grows.

3. The identity of the mother. As noted earlier, Jewish law defines children of a Jewish woman as Jewish.[26] If different women supply the ovum and bear the child, however, which one transfers Jewish identity to the child?

One could argue in both directions. Because Jewish law, for purposes of redemption of the firstborn son, defines that child as the one who "opens the womb,"[27] it seems that the bearing woman should be defined as the child's mother for purposes of transferring Jewish identity. On the other hand, one might argue that there should be a parallelism between the identity of the father and that of the mother, and because Jewish law defines the man who provides the sperm as the father, the woman who provides the egg should likewise be seen as the mother.

Because the case can be argued both ways and for other reasons as well, the Conservative Movement's Committee on Jewish Law and Standards has determined that it is the Torah's phrase, *peter reḥem* ("opening the womb") that should be determinative.[28] Opinions in the other movements vary.[29]

4. The obligation to procreate. Couples who choose *not* to use egg donation as a means of overcoming their infertility need not feel guilty in doing so. Even though the Mishnah rules that a man who cannot procreate with his wife after trying for ten years must divorce her and marry another in an attempt to make it possible for him to fulfill that commandment,[30] by the late Middle Ages, that rule had fallen into disuse.[31] Even though the Rabbis knew full well that both men and women are necessary for procreation, for exegetical reasons, and probably to avoid imposing the danger of pregnancy on the woman, especially before the advent of safe Caesarian sections, they ruled that only men were responsible to fulfill that commandment.[32] As a result of these precedents, as stated at the beginning of this chapter, couples who cannot procreate through their own sexual intercourse are exempt from the commandment; they may use donor sperm or eggs or other artificial reproductive techniques in an effort to have a child, but they need not do so.

Surrogacy

When the wife cannot become pregnant in the first place or cannot retain a pregnancy for any of a number of known or unknown causes, the couple may try to find another woman to bear their child. The Bible tells stories of several surrogate mothers—Hagar for Sarah and Abraham, Bilhah for Rachel and Jacob; and Zilpah for Leah and Jacob.[33] In all of those cases, the man had sexual intercourse with his wife's handmaid to create a child that would be credited to his wife. In the nineteenth century artificial insemination became possible,[34] and so surrogacy could happen without sexual intercourse. These forms of surrogacy are called "traditional" surrogacy because they were the first to be used, or "ovum" surrogacy because the surrogate mother's egg is used in the process of producing the child. Ovum surrogacy has been used by gay men as well as heterosexual couples to have children.

With the advent of IVF in 1978, "gestational surrogacy" became possible, where the surrogate does not provide an ovum but gestates the fetus created using someone else's ovum. This is used primarily by heterosexual couples who have viable gametes but where the woman cannot carry the fetus to term.

The major argument in favor of surrogacy, of course, is that it enables infertile couples to have children with the gametes of at least one of them. Not only is surrogacy thus a response to the pain of infertility for the couples involved, straight or gay, but it also is a way for that couple to fulfill an important Jewish value and hope.

Those arguing against surrogacy have raised several objections. Some, like Orthodox Rabbi Immanuel Jakobovits, find it inherently demeaning: "To use another woman as an incubator . . . for a fee . . . [is a] revolting degradation of maternity and an affront to human dignity."[35] In like manner, Conservative Rabbi Daniel Gordis holds that surrogacy is degrading because it involves a "commodification" of the surrogate woman's body—that is, a transformation of the woman's reproductive abilities into a commodity that can be traded on the market. Further degradation comes from the limits imposed on the surrogate, which can include limits on a woman's sexual activity after insemination, the drugs and foods she may consume, and her option of abortion.

Gordis also worries about the social effects of surrogacy. Surrogacy will, in his view, accentuate the social and economic differences between the relatively rich couple and lawyer as against the relatively poor surrogate mother. Moreover, the costs of surrogacy mean that only the rich will be able to pass down their genes in this way, and that is effectively saying that the rich are more entitled to reproduce than the poor. Indeed, if surrogacy were legitimized, Gordis fears, women on welfare might have to explain why they would *not* be willing to earn money as surrogates, another aspect of the inherent slavery involved. Because that burden could only be imposed on women, it would serve further to degrade women vis-à-vis men in our society, in this case women on welfare versus men on welfare.[36]

Reform Rabbi Marc Gellman expresses yet another moral concern. Although surrogacy may not technically be adultery, introducing a third party to the couple's reproductive process may *feel* dangerously close to that and may ultimately undermine the couple's relationship altogether. Furthermore, in ovum surrogacy using the husband's sperm, the wife is being asked to raise a child who is genetically her husband's but not hers—and one carried by another woman to boot.[37]

In a landmark responsum adopted by the Conservative Movement's Committee on Jewish Law and Standards, however, Rabbi Elie Spitz responds to all of these concerns and permits surrogacy. It is indeed true that only the rich will be able to afford such a procedure, and one certainly must create social safeguards to ensure that the poor will have access to essential services and will not foment a revolution for lack of them; but few children are born through surrogacy in comparison to sexual intercourse, and thus surrogacy is not an essential service or perceived as one.

The concern about the degradation of the woman, an issue raised by both Rabbis Jakobovits and Gordis, has been substantially ameliorated during the brief history of surrogacy. Rabbi Spitz reports that at least eight doctoral dissertations and other professional studies probing surrogacy have indicated that surrogate mothers are not generally black and poor; instead,

> the typical surrogate mother was twenty-eight years old, married with children, employed full-time, and had thirteen years of education. Her husband was supportive of her decision to serve as a surrogate. Most were Caucasian, middle-range in income bracket, in good health, and had positive experiences in past pregnancies. While money was a factor in choosing to become a surrogate, it rated consistently lower than the desire to help another couple.[38]

Because in the United States the surrogate mother is generally not poor, Rabbi Gordis' worries about women on welfare being forced to serve in this capacity in this country have proven to be unfounded. That issue, though, does arise in other countries where surrogacy is not carefully regulated, such as in many in South America.[39]

Moreover, these studies should allay the fear that it is inherently disgraceful. The money involved certainly makes surrogacy less than totally altruistic, but to deny the altruism of surrogate mothers simply because it is not pure is to misunderstand the complex nature of human motivation in general and the conscious desires of these women in particular. Their predominant motivation to help infertile couples makes their act not morally degrading, but, quite the contrary, morally praiseworthy. (The same arguments apply to the overwhelming numbers of sperm or ovum donors.)

The concern that the surrogate mothers might virtually be slaves has largely been allayed by developments in American civil law. According to William Handel, an attorney with special expertise in surrogacy, the items often contained in a surrogacy agreement include: (1) complete freedom of choice for the surrogate to withdraw from the agreement prior to conception; (2) a guarantee of the surrogate's right over her body during pregnancy, including the right to abortion and to operations to protect her health; (3) a commitment on the part of the intended parents to accept the newborn, regardless of the child's condition; and (4) payment for the surrogate of all medical costs, psychological counseling, attorney fees, and living expenses in addition to her fee. As in any contract, there are some responsibilities that she must also assume—namely, not to abuse her body in a way which would likely cause damage to the fetus (e.g., by taking drugs), and to turn over the child to the intended parents once born.[40] These provisions in modern surrogacy agreements of both parties' rights and duties make the contract clearly one between free agents.

In Rabbi Spitz's view, then, and in my own, surrogacy should be permitted to enable infertile couples have the children they so desperately seek.

SINGLE PARENTHOOD

Most single parents become so through divorce or the death of their spouse. Donor insemination, though, makes it possible for single women or lesbian couples who want a child to be artificially inseminated for that purpose (and, in some cases, use the egg of another woman), and surrogacy makes it possible for single men, whether straight or gay, to become fathers that way. In addition, of course, single men or women, whether straight or gay, might adopt children.

Jewish law clearly assumes that it is best for children to have parents of both genders, for it describes differing roles for mothers and fathers.[41] Current research indicates that children, on average, do indeed do worse with one parent rather than with two, but only when that single parent is isolated as the only caregiver for the child. If the parent has sufficient funds to hire help, or if, in poor as well as rich families, there is a strong network of support from family and friends, children do no worse, on average, than they do with two parents. If only one adult is raising one or more children, or if both parents are of the same gender, their children should be regularly in contact with role models of the opposite gender through family ties or programs like Jewish Big Brothers and Jewish Big Sisters, for although each person is unique, men and women as groups do contribute differently to their children's upbringing. That is, men and women as groups are equal, but not the same.[42] In making these comparisons between two-parent and one-parent families, one must remember that the criteria for measuring adjustment and well-being are themselves sometimes at issue and that many contemporary families with two parents are themselves dysfunctional. Still, one-parent families are usually at a disadvantage in comparison to two-parent ones, and so it is not surprising that two Conservative rabbis—Rabbi David Golinkin and Rabbi Susan Grossman—have written opposing rabbinic rulings on the permissibility of using artificial reproductive techniques to create one-parent families.[43]

DONATING ONE'S SPERM OR EGGS

1. *Donating sperm.* As noted earlier, in Jewish law donor insemination constitutes procreation by the donor. This introduces an appropriate note of seriousness to sperm donation. It is not, and should not be construed as, simply another job for a college or medical student to earn some spare change. The (typically) young man involved should recognize that he is making it possible for a couple to have a child, with all the positive implications of that for the couple and, if Jews are the recipients, for the Jewish people. He should approach this whole process duly appreciative of the awesomeness

of the human ability to procreate and of his role in helping an infertile couple make that happen.

He should also understand that, like it or not, he will have an important biological relationship to the offspring. He may want to keep his identity confidential so as not to incur any risk of personal or legal problems with the couple or with the child later on. Because the child will inherit the donor's genes, however, he should supply the child with as much information about his physical and personal characteristics as possible without compromising the confidentiality of his identity.

The donor should also be concerned about his own future children not unwittingly marrying a genetic relative. This too argues for sharing information with the child born through artificial insemination so that the child as well as the donor are both guarding against such an occurrence.

The donor's present or future spouse and children are affected by his decision to donate. They should definitely be informed of the donation if it happened in the past, and if a married man is considering a sperm donation, he owes it to his wife to gain her consent. This duty of disclosure stems from a marital form of "truth in advertising." Part of the essence of marriage is that it functions as the sole context of one's procreative activities. That expectation, in fact, is built into the very construct and meaning of marriage. If that has not been true, as in the case of a previous marriage or of a sperm or egg donation, or if that is not going to be true because of a planned sperm or egg donation now, the spouse has a right to know that this common assumption of marriage will be, or has been, breached in these specific ways so that the bonds of marriage can be assumed and maintained with full honesty, understanding, and trust.

None of these difficulties should make sperm donation forbidden; the great good of enabling an infertile couple to have a child outweighs them all. Similarly, any objections to the masturbation through which the sperm will be procured are also set aside, for the intent to produce a child removes any stigma of "wasting the seed."

2. *Donating eggs.* The same concerns apply to egg donation, but that procedure incurs the additional risks involved in procuring the eggs. As indicated above, there is some evidence that hyperovulation involves increased risk for ovarian, cervical, or uterine cancer. Jewish law does not permit one to endanger oneself unduly: "[The strictures against] endangering oneself are more stringent than [those against violating] a prohibition," says the Talmud.[44] In line with this, a Jewish woman who chooses to donate her eggs should do so only once or twice, and then only if she is assured by physicians after due examination that she personally can donate her eggs without much danger to her own life or health. Enabling an infertile couple to have children is a great good, but in Jewish law preserving one's own life and health clearly takes precedence over that.

Egg donors face some of the same issues of confidentiality as do sperm donors. Because, though, an egg donor, like a sperm donor, contributes substantially to the child's genetic structure, she too should reveal as much as possible of her medical history and personal characteristics for the good of the child.

The Blessings of Children

It is appropriate to close this discussion noting the great value the Jewish tradition puts on children, the point of using these methods in the first place. Children are, after all, not only the way parents develop in their own experiences and sensitivities[45] and gain a measure of eternity; they are also the way the Jewish tradition continues from one generation to the next. Thus God's blessings of all the Patriarchs and Matriarchs includes children,[46] children figure prominently in the Torah's of life's chief goods,[47] and the Psalmist's blessing is "May you live to see your children's children."[48] Through all the complications and concerns discussed above about using or donating sperm and ova or serving as a surrogate mother, then, one must recognize that the children born through these methods are a great blessing for the specific people involved, the Jewish People as a whole, and the Jewish tradition.

In all of the following notes,

M = Mishnah, edited c. 200 CE
T = Tosefta, c. 200 CE
B = Babylonian Talmud, edited c. 500 CE
MT = Maimonides' *Mishneh Torah,* completed in 1177 CE
SA = Joseph Karo's *Shulḥan Arukh,* completed in 1563 CE with glosses later added by Moses Isserles to indicate where northern European Jewish practice differed from the Mediterranean practices that Karo recorded

Notes

1. This chapter deals with the Jewish aspects of third-party reproduction. For a brief treatment of the issues in medicine generally and in American law, see the following fact sheet of the American Society of Reproductive Medicine: https://www.reproductivefacts.org/news-and-publications/fact-sheets-and-infographics/avoiding-conflict-in-third-party-reproduction/?_t_id=xYc4KJ8pyp2Jem6aaROFSQ==&_t_uuid=f5IN-yJwR6uvm5wyBDtyvQ&_t_q=Fact_Sheets_and_Info_Booklets/Avoiding_conflict_in_third-party_reproduction_FINAL&_t_tags=siteid:db69d13f-2074-446c-b7f0-d15628807d0c,language:en&_t_hit.id=ASRM_Models_Pages_ContentPage/_d04bd6ae-312c-46b8-b5c2-d8e96d76bb2f_en&_t_hit.pos=1
2. As if giving birth: B, *Megillah* 13a. Doing right at all times: B, *Ketubbot* 50a. See also *Exodus Rabbah,* chapter 4; SA, *Orah Hayyim* 139:3; *Magen Avraham* on SA, *Orah Hayyim* 156; Moshe Feinstein, *Iggrot Moshe* on *Yoreh De'ah* 161.
3. Conservative: Elliot N. Dorff, *Matters of Life and Death: A Jewish Approach to Modern Medical Ethics* (Philadelphia: Jewish Publication Society, 1998), chapter 4. Orthodox: Avraham Steinberg, *Encyclopedia of Jewish Medical Ethics* (New York: Feldheim, 2003), 3 volumes,

1: 58–68, 2: 571–586. Reconstructionist: David Teutsch, *A Guide to Jewish Practice* (Wycnote, PA: Reconstructionist Rabbinical College Press, 2011), 3 volumes, 1: 495–497. Reform: Mark Washofsky, *Jewish Living: A Guide to Contemporary Reform Practice* (Union of American Hebrew Congregations Press, 2000), 233–239.

4. *Tzitz Eliezer* IX, 51, chapter 5, sec. 1, 251. See also Rabbi Joel Teitelbaum (1954) and the discussion of this in Grazi and Wolowelsky (1992), 157–158. R. V. Grazi and J. B. Wolowelsky, "Donor Gametes for Assisted Reproduction in Contemporary Jewish Law and Ethics," *Assisted Reproduction Reviews* 2, no. 3 (Aug 1992): 154–160. PMID: 11659759.

5. B, *Shevu'ot* 18a; cf. M, *Yevamot* 6:1 (53b), B, *Yevamot* 54a, and B, *Horayot* 4a. MT, *Laws of Forbidden Intercourse* 1:10–11. For more recent rabbis who take this position, see Dorff, *Matters of Life and Death*, 348–349, note 9.

6. The *New York Times* recently reported a case in which a sperm donor had 150 biological children: see Jacqueline Mroz, "One Sperm Donor, 150 Offspring," September 5, 2011, http://www.nytimes.com/2011/09/06/health/06donor.html?_r=1&ref=health. According to that article, the American Society of Reproductive Medicine recommends restricting births from one donor to twenty-five in a population of 800,000.

7. M, *Kiddushin* 3:12; B, *Kiddushin* 68b); MT, *Laws of Forbidden Intercourse (Issurei Bi'ah)* 15:3–4; S.A. *Even Ha-Ezer* 4:5.

8. See, for example, Leviticus 21:17, 21; 22:3, 4; etc. Although it is clearly true that the word *seed* (*zera*) often is, in both Hebrew and English, a synonym for children, the rules of priestly status were not interpreted in that metaphoric way. See M, *Middot* 5:4; M, *Kiddushin* 4:5; *Laws of Entering the Temple* 9:1.

9. See, for example, Joel Roth, "The Status of Daughters of *Kohanim* and *Leviyim* for Aliyot," https://www.rabbinicalassembly.org/sites/default/files/assets/public/halakhah/teshuvot/19861990/roth_daughtersaliyot.pdf (1989) and Mayer Rabinowitz, "Women, Raise Your Hands," https://www.rabbinicalassembly.org/sites/default/files/assets/public/halakhah/teshuvot/19912000/rabinowitz_women.pdf (1994).

10. Deuteronomy 25:5–10. This law may refer only to inheritance rights, but the language of Deuteronomy seems to indicate a stronger relationship, for the levir is to have a child with his sister-in-law, whom he takes "as his wife," but "The first son that she bears shall be accounted to the dead brother, that his name may not be blotted out in Israel" (Deuteronomy 25:6).

11. *Exodus Rabbah* 46:5.

12. M, *Avodah Zarah* 4:4–7; T, *Avodah Zarah* 6:2; B, *Avodah Zarah* 43a, 52a–55a; MT, *Laws of Idolatry* 8:9–12; SA, *Yoreh De'ah* 146:1–12.

13. Genesis 48:5–6.

14. Avram Reisner, "On the Conversion of Adopted and Patrilineal Children" (1988), http://www.rabbinicalassembly.org/sites/default/files/assets/public/halakhah/teshuvot/19861990/reisner_conversion.pdf; Elliot N. Dorff, "Artificial Insemination, Egg Donation, and Adoption" (1994), http://www.rabbinicalassembly.org/sites/default/files/assets/public/halakhah/teshuvot/19912000/dorff_artificial.pdf, 483, or Dorff, *Matters of Life and Death*, 79.

15. For a description of filial and parental obligations, as defined by Jewish tradition, see Elliot N. Dorff, *Love Your Neighbor and Yourself: A Jewish Approach to Modern Personal Ethics* (Philadelphia: Jewish Publication Society, 2003), chapter 4. The Talmud and later Jewish law codes require that children honor and respect their stepfather and stepmother (B,

Ketubbot 103a; SA, *Yoreh De'ah* 240:21, 21), and the same would clearly apply to the social parents of DI children.
16. See Elliot N. Dorff, *For the Love of God and People: A Philosophy of Jewish Law* (Philadelphia: Jewish Publication Society, 2007), esp. chapters 2 and 6.
17. Immanuel Jakobovits, *Jewish Medical Ethics* (New York: Bloch, 1959, 1972), 248–249.
18. Paul Lauritzen, "Pursuing Parenthood: Reflections on Donor Insemination," *Second Opinion* (July 1991): 65–66.
19. Patricia P. Mahlstedt and Dorothy A. Greenfeld, "Assisted Reproductive Technology with Donor Gametes: The Need for Patient Preparation," *Fertility and Sterility* 52, no. 6 (December 1989): 913.
20. See Elliot N. Dorff and Laurie Zoloth, eds., *Jews and Genes: The Genetic Future in Contemporary Jewish Thought* (Philadelphia: Jewish Publication Society, 2015), Part 4.
21. Pew Research Center, "The Future of World Religions: Population Growth Projections 2010–2050," April 2, 2015, http://www.pewforum.org/2015/04/02/religious-projections-2010-2050/
22. Pew Research Forum, *A Portrait of Jewish Americans* (2013), http://www.pewforum.org/2013/10/01/chapter-2-intermarriage-and-other-demographics/#fertility, showing a reproductive rate of 4.1 among the Orthodox, 1.8 among Conservative Jews, 1:7 among Reform Jews, and 1.4 of Jews with no denominational affiliation, producing an overall rate among American Jews of 1.9.
23. Ibid.
24. Helen Pearson, "Health Effects of Egg Donation May Take Decades to Emerge," *Nature* 442 (August 10, 2006): 607–608, http://www.nature.com/nature/journal/v442/n7103/full/442607a.html?foxtrotcallback=true.
25. A brother's sperm was, of course, used in levirate marriages (Deuteronomy 25:5–10), but there the husband had died, and so there is no threat of the complications inherent in the blurring of roles between the brothers. Indeed, in that case it would actually be in the child's best interest if the uncle acted as a substitute father.
26. See note 8 above.
27. Exodus 13:2, 12, 15; 34:19; Numbers 3:12; 18:15.
28. Aaron L. Mackler, "In Vitro Fertilization," 1995, https://www.rabbinicalassembly.org/sites/default/files/assets/public/halakhah/teshuvot/19912000/mackler_ivf.pdf and "Maternal Identity and the Religious Status of Children Born to a Surrogate Mother," 1997, https://www.rabbinicalassembly.org/sites/default/files/assets/public/halakhah/teshuvot/19912000/mackler_maternal.pdf.
29. For the range of opinions on this among the Orthodox, see J. David Bleich, "In Vitro Fertilization: Maternal Identity and Conversion," *Contemporary Halakhic Problems*, vol. 4 (New York: Ktav and Yeshiva University Press, 1995), 237–272. The representative Reconstructionist and Reform rabbis cited in note 4 above do not address this issue, perhaps because they accept patrilineal descent and/or raising the child as a Jew as sufficient to designate the child as Jewish, and so the identity of the mother does not matter for this purpose.
30. M, *Yevamot* 6:6.
31. SA, *Even Ha-Ezer* 1:3, gloss.
32. M, *Yevamot* 6:6; MT, *Laws of Marriage* 15:2. SA, *Even Ha-Ezer* 1:1, 13.
33. Hagar and Sarah: Genesis 16:1–6. Bilhah for Rachel: Genesis 30:1–8. Zilpah for Leah: Genesis 30:9–13.

34. The first recorded case occurred in 1884 in Philadelphia; it was reported twenty-five years later in *The Medical World*, 163–164. See *Fertility and Sterility*, 16 (April 1909): 130–134.
35. Jakobovits, *Jewish Medical Ethics*, 264–265.
36. Daniel H. Gordis, *"Give Me Progeny": Jewish Ethics and the Economics of Surrogate Motherhood* (Los Angeles: University of Judaism, 1988).
37. Marc Gellman, "The Ethics of Surrogate Motherhood," *Sh'ma* 17, no. 334 (May 15, 1987): 105–107.
38. Elie Kaplan Spitz, "On the Use of Birth Surrogates," 1997, https://www.rabbinicalassembly.org/sites/default/files/assets/public/halakhah/teshuvot/19912000/spitz_surrogate.pdf. For the list of studies about the identity of surrogates, see 532, notes 16–18.
39. G. Torres, A., Shapiro, and T. K. Mackey, "A Review of Surrogate Motherhood Regulation in South American Countries: Pointing to a Need for an International Legal Framework," *BMC Pregnancy Childbirth* 19 (2019), 46. https://doi.org/10.1186/s12884-019-2182-1.
40. Reported in Spitz, ibid., 531–532.
41. So, for example, in the case of divorce, children below the age of six must be placed in the custody of their mother, for they are mainly in need of the physical care and attention that mothers typically give children at that age. Above six years of age, boys must be with their father so that he can carry out his obligation to teach his male children Torah and a trade, while girls must be with their mother so that she can instruct them in the ways of modesty; see B, *Ketubbot* 102b–103a; MT, *Laws of Marriage (Ishut)* 21:17; SA, *Even Haezer* 82:7.
42. See, for example, Deborah Tannen, *You Just Don't Understand: Women and Men in Conversation* (New York: Ballantine Books, 1990); John Gray, *Men Are from Mars, Women Are from Venus* (New York: HarperCollins, 1992); Carol Gilligan, *In a Different Voice: Psychological Theory and Women's Development* (Cambridge, MA: Harvard University Press, 1993).
43. David Golinkin, "Artificial Insemination for a Single Woman," vol. 3, 1989 http://www.responsafortoday.com/eng_index.html. Susan Grossman, "Choosing Parenthood: IVF, ART, and the Single Parent," a ruling that permits donating and using gametes to create single-parent families, is currently being discussed by the Committee on Jewish Law and Standards and once approved will appear on the Rabbinical Assembly website in the section on Jewish Law.
44. B, *Hullin* 10a. See B, *Berakhot* 32b; B, *Shabbat* 32a; B, *Bava Kamma* 15b, 80a, 91b; MT, *Laws of Murder and the Guarding of Life* 11:4–5; SA, *Orah Hayyim* 173:2; *Yoreh De'ah* 116:5, gloss.
45. The Rabbis recognize this in decreeing that only a man with children may serve as a judge on a capital case, for only a parent can understand the deep value of life of both the culprit and, in a murder case, the victim. See T, *Sanhedrin* 7:3; B, *Sanhedrin* 36b; MT, *Laws of Courts (Sanhedrin)* 2:3.
46. God's blessings of the Patriarchs and Matriarchs promise numerous children: Genesis 15:5; 17:4–21; 18:18; 22:15–18; 26:4–5; 28:13–15; 32:13.
47. Leviticus 26:9; Deuteronomy 7:13–14; 28: 4 and 11.
48. Psalm 128:6.

CHAPTER 18

ISLAMIC PERSPECTIVES ON GAMETE DONATION AND SURROGACY

AYMAN SHABANA

Modern assisted reproductive technology (ART) has revolutionized human reproduction not only by solving intractable fertility problems barring natural conception but also by maximizing control over the reproductive process. With artificial insemination, in vitro fertilization (IVF), and gamete donation, adoption no longer seems to be the only option available to couples suffering from traditional infertility problems. But, despite the ease and convenience that they brought about, assisted reproductive technologies raise several ethical, legal, and social concerns. Most of these concerns revolve around the (re)conceptualization of family structure and relationships in the wake of these technologies. One of the fundamental questions surrounding the use of ART is the perception of infertility and the extent to which it should be considered a medical condition that requires medical intervention. While some argue that infertility is a disease, others argue that such perception of infertility sustains and confirms traditional gender stereotypes and biases against women.

The introduction of assisted reproductive technology was initially met with a great deal of concern, reservation, and even outright condemnation. In particular, from a conservative religious perspective, the creation of an embryo outside the body was perceived as a challenge to God's order and also to human civilization.[1] Over the years, however, public perception of ARTs has significantly changed. According to recent estimates IVF is responsible for the birth of more than 50,000 babies annually in the United States. Worldwide, it is estimated that more than 3 million babies have been born with the help of IVF or some other means of ART.[2] Despite this popularity, however, the ethical questions that ART raised when it was developed remain open and they even inspire additional questions with the steady emergence and implementation of new techniques. Within the Islamic context, these techniques raise important concerns on the continued association between marriage and parentage, involvement of a third party in the procreative process, and permissibility of surrogacy as well as definitions of paternity and maternity in different surrogacy arrangements. This chapter examines Muslim deliberations on these questions, with a particular focus on gamete donation and surrogacy, and explores emerging areas of agreement and disagreement in Islamic ethico-legal discourses.

ISLAMIC VIEW OF FAMILY STRUCTURE AND CONCERN OVER LINEAGE

The various applications of ART have given rise to a host of concerns such as the moral status of the embryo, cryopreservation of (pre)embryos, post-marital or postmortem conception, manipulation of oocytes in vitro, the treatment of surplus embryos, and the commodification of the human reproductive function. However, the most important concern that Islamic normative discourses on ART often highlight is preservation of one's lineage (*nasab*). Islamic conceptualization of lineage is rooted in a number of passages in the two Scriptural sources, the Qur'an and the Sunna of the Prophet. For example, the Qur'an (33:5) indicates that children should be attributed to their fathers. This indication supports the Islamic patrilineal system of kinship but it is also used to support the abrogation of the pre-Islamic practice of adoption. In general, Muslims are encouraged to care for orphans but without giving them the family name as if they were from one's bloodline. Similarly, in a famous tradition, the Prophet is reported to have indicated that the child should be attached to the (spousal) bed. Accordingly, one's lineage is defined in terms of a licit sexual relationship between one's parents in the form of marriage (*nikāḥ*). Within the Islamic ethical-legal tradition, this definition of lineage serves as the foundation of the entire family structure, and it determines many legal and ethical duties and entitlements. Preservation of lineage is considered one of the five essential values that the Islamic ethical-legal system aims to ensure, along with preservation of religion, intellect, life, and property. For example, lineage determines one's prohibited degrees within the family whom one cannot marry, mainly on the basis of consanguinity but also on the basis of affinity or breastfeeding. Similarly, one's lineage determines eligibility for important entitlements such as shares of inheritance in addition to other financial rights and obligations within the family. Preservation of lineage, including its certainty and authenticity, is emphasized as one of the goals of marriage, which is considered the only legitimate framework for procreation.

Children born out of wedlock are considered illegitimate and cannot be attached to their biological fathers.

This formulation of lineage creates an impediment for any type of third-party involvement in the procreative process, and may explain the general attitude of most Muslim religious authorities against both gamete donation and surrogacy arrangements. This is particularly the case among Sunni religious scholars, who are almost unanimous in their opposition to any form of third-party involvement in the reproductive process. By contrast, some Shiite scholars argue for the permissibility of both gamete donation and surrogacy arrangements. The main distinction between these two views can be traced to the conceptualization of the act of gamete donation and the extent to which it would be analogous to adultery. While the Sunni view compares gamete donation to the prohibited act of adultery in terms of the resulting consequences, the Shiite view limits the definition of adultery to actual physical contact between unmarried couples. In practice, however, anthropologists emphasize the difficulty of drawing sharp distinctions along sectarian lines, particularly in social and cultural contexts where high premiums are placed on the value of childbearing and reproduction.[3]

Muslim Responses to ART

Islamic normative discourses on the various applications of ART provide an important illustration of how Muslim scholars respond to the challenges of modern scientific and technological advances. By separating reproduction from the intimate act of coitus, ART has transformed the human reproductive function and turned it into a purely technical process, subject to greater levels of control and manipulation. Such transformation forces Muslim scholars to revisit important legal-ethical presuppositions and tests the boundaries of the classical definition of both legitimacy and illegitimacy. This becomes evident in the multi-dimensional ethical-legal deliberations over ART in general and over gamete donation and surrogacy in particular. Apart from their various ethical, legal, and social implications, both gamete donation and surrogacy also raise the issue of commercialization of the human reproductive function and the extent to which it can be subject to contractual transactions. Moreover, these normative deliberations reveal different levels of ethical-legal analysis, especially in light of the view that proscribes both gamete donation and surrogacy. Even the scholars who denounce both gamete donation and surrogacy often proceed to explore their implications as well as appropriate ethical-legal means to address their consequences. This attitude is premised on the view of Shar'ia as an eternally valid system, which is capable of responding to the emerging needs of Muslims both at the individual and collective levels. This view of Shar'ia enables the possibility to both condemn practices which are deemed in conflict with Islamic moral-legal principles, and to address their implications if they were undertaken in the real world, despite their ethical-legal reprehensibility.

Muslim discourses on ART can be traced to the late 1970s and early 1980s, shortly after the successful birth of the first test-tube baby (Louise Brown) in the United Kingdom on January 25, 1978. This scientific breakthrough marked the beginning of a new phase in human reproduction. It stirred heated debates on the propriety of the procedure and its potential moral ramifications. Muslim responses came mainly in the form of fatwas both by individual scholars and, more importantly, by scholarly institutions. Prior to this landmark, however, individual scholars responded to questions associated with earlier experiments on artificial insemination in humans after successful trials on plants and animals. For example, in his response to a question on the permissibility of artificial insemination, the late rector of al-Azhar University in Cairo Maḥmūd Shaltūt (d.1963) emphasized the distinctive features of human reproduction, as governed by important religious and moral norms through the institution of marriage. Accordingly, artificial insemination can be undertaken within the framework of an existing marriage and the sperm used to fertilize a woman's ovum must come only from her husband. Using sperm belonging to a man other than a woman's husband would bring the procedure close to adultery in light of the similar consequences in both cases. These early discussions invoked pre-modern discussions in the legal corpus on the permissibility of depositing semen in a woman's uterus without intercourse, mainly due to inability on the part of the husband to complete the sexual process naturally. The main point that the classical jurists discussed is the source of the sperm and whether it came from the husband or from someone else.[4]

Starting from the early 1980s a number of institutional fatwas were issued by important national and transnational entities to address the rapidly evolving applications of ART. Discussions over gamete donation and surrogacy have always been connected to this larger discourse on ART, including earlier responses to artificial insemination. One of the earliest institutional fatwas on gamete donation was issued by the late rector of al-Azhar Jād al-Ḥaqq ʿAlī Jād al-Ḥaqq (d.1996) in 1980 in response to a number of questions concerning the various applications of ART in the wake of IVF.[5] With regard to gamete donation, Jād al-Ḥaq, invoking classical juristic discussions on the consequences of manual insertion of sperm (without intercourse), emphasized the prohibition of fertilizing a woman's ovum with semen belonging to someone other than her husband. The fatwa also bans sperm banking on the grounds that this would result in the mixing of genealogies (ikhtilāṭ al-ansāb). The only exception made is the case of IVF in which the gametes of married couples are used provided that necessary precautions are taken to avoid technical errors leading to replacement or confusion of gametes. Although the fatwa does not address the question of surrogacy, it discusses the possibility of placing the fertilized ovum in the uterus of an animal for a certain period of time before it can be transferred to the wife's uterus. Jād al-Ḥaqq denounces this scenario, noting that this would amount to unauthorized interference in the natural course of divine creation. This fatwa by Jād al-Ḥaqq is considered one of the important sources on ART issues and it has often been reiterated in subsequent individual as well as institutional fatwas, including later fatwas by several al-Azhar-affiliated institutions such as the International Islamic Center for Population Studies and Research (1992, 1997) and the Islamic Research Council (2001).[6]

Another important institutional statement was issued by the Kuwait-based Islamic Organization for Medical Sciences (IOMS) in the form of a set of recommendations at the conclusion of a specialized meeting on the theme of reproduction in Islam in 1983. The statement approves IVF only in case the procedure is undertaken to assist married couples to overcome infertility problems and as long as necessary measures are taken to ensure that the gametes used belong to the designated married couples. The statement proscribes any type of third-party involvement in the reproductive process outside the framework of marriage, whether in the form of gamete donation (ovum, sperm, or embryo) or surrogacy arrangement. Some participants did not approve of IVF at all by highlighting the difficulty of avoiding technical errors that may result in the confusion of gametes. They also argued that the procedure would likely entail significant violations of certain moral norms, particularly those pertaining to inter-gender interaction within the clinical setting, which may involve uncovering and touching of private parts during the process.[7] The importance of this meeting is not only due to the set of recommendations that it proposed in its concluding statement, but in the joint and interdisciplinary deliberations that it facilitated between medical experts on the one hand and Muslim religious scholars on the other. It was within these deliberations that some important questions were raised, which have largely shaped Islamic discourses on ART issues both by IOMS during subsequent meetings and also by other entities. These questions include religious conceptualization of both gamete donation and surrogacy, including possible comparison with adultery; guidelines that should govern IVF procedures; boundaries of third-party involvement (if any); implications and consequences of religiously-questionable practices; and definition of maternity in the wake of surrogacy arrangements.

One of the important reasons behind the religious reprehensibility of both gamete donation and surrogacy has been their association with adultery. While some scholars compare the involvement of a third-party through ART applications to adultery,[8] other scholars, although condemning any type of third-party involvement, insist that the latter cannot be equated with adultery. Accordingly, punishment for these procedures, if undertaken, should be in the form of discretionary penalty rather than the stipulated punishment for adultery. According to this view a significant distinction should be made between adultery and gamete donation/surrogacy. One of the main objections underlying the prohibition of adultery, when it results in pregnancy, is falsification of the baby's lineage, since any child that a married woman gives birth to is automatically attributed to her husband, rather than to the biological father. In the case of planned gamete donation/surrogacy, on the other hand, the identities of the parties involved are known and therefore the risk of misattributed lineage is ruled out.[9]

From another dimension, third-party involvement automatically raises the issue of the legal status of all the parties involved as well as their roles in the (re)definition of parenthood in general, especially the relationship between the genetic donor and the gestational mother/surrogate. Regardless of the religious status of either gamete donation or surrogacy, one of the important questions in the Islamic discourses on ART applications since this initial IOMS meeting has been the (re)definition of motherhood and the extent to which it should be decided on genetic or gestational grounds. During this meeting a distinction could be observed between medical experts, on the one hand, who argued for the definition of maternity mainly on genetic grounds in light of scientific explanations concerning the formation of the embryo and jurists and religious scholars, on the other, who emphasized the gestational and childbirth dimensions in light of Qur'ānic passages that seem to define maternity accordingly. This divide between the medical experts and the religious scholars was not absolute. While some medical experts emphasized the role of the gestational mother as well as other types of environmental factors in the constitution of embryos,[10] some religious scholars integrated scientific explanations in their arguments. Still others argued against a sharp distinction between the genetic and gestational aspects of maternity. According to this latter view, maternity constitutes a comprehensive process that starts with impregnation and does not end with breastfeeding and weaning.[11] The proceedings and conclusions of this IOMS meeting were also reiterated in a later IOMS meeting that was held in 2006 on the general theme of genetics and human reproduction.[12] For example, in this later meeting, some participants problematized the usual distinction between genetic and gestational factors, which tends to favor the former over the latter in the evaluation of maternity claims. By contrast, they argued that the role of the gestational mother is no less important for the constitution and well-being of the embryo. It should be noted, however, that this argument is made not to privilege gestational over genetic grounds but rather as part of a larger argument against surrogacy in general, by highlighting its various negative implications.[13]

One of the important strategies for the accommodation of the genetic and gestational dimensions of maternity since the initial IOMS meeting has been the comparison of the gestational mother/surrogate to the breastfeeding mother in classical Islamic law. According to this view, a child should be attached to the genetic parents, while the gestational mother should be treated like a milk mother on the grounds that both gestational and milk mothers provide necessary nourishment for the baby. This view, however, was criticized by those who argued against the separation of genetic and gestational aspects of maternity.[14] The comparison between the gestational mother and the milk mother is sometimes also used by those who argue for the permissibility of gestational surrogacy by way of analogy to the permissibility of contracting a milk mother to breastfeed a baby in return for a fee. Yet, this comparison is also criticized on the grounds that a milk mother is needed for an already existing baby, while a gestational mother would be contracted for a baby that does not exist at the time of the contract. According to this argument, existing needs cannot be compared to nonexisting ones.[15]

The joint scientific-juristic deliberations that the IOMS facilitated were echoed and sustained by other transnational institutions, most notably by the Islamic Fiqh Council (IFC) of the Muslim World League and the International Islamic Fiqh Academy (IIFA) of the Organization of Islamic Conference. Both institutions issued several statements on ART procedures involving gamete donation and surrogacy arrangements. One of the most influential statements was issued by IFC in the form of a resolution on the issue of artificial insemination and IVF during its seventh session in 1984. The resolution discusses two main types of artificial insemination: internal (injection of semen in the uterus) and external (IVF). In total, the resolution addresses seven scenarios: two through internal insemination and five through external insemination. The main distinction between the two types of internal insemination is the source of the injected semen. In the first scenario the semen used in the procedure belongs to the husband of the woman, while in the second scenario the semen comes from a third party. The first scenario is considered legitimate as long as the procedure is undertaken within an existing marriage and necessary precautions are taken to ensure the authenticity of the gametes. By contrast, the second scenario is considered illegitimate. The third scenario involves extraction of an ovum from a married woman and its fertilization by her husband's semen in vitro. The resulting embryo is then planted in the woman's uterus until the end of the pregnancy term. Similar to the first scenario, this scenario is considered legitimate as long as the procedure is undertaken within an existing marriage and necessary measures are taken to ensure the authenticity of the gametes used. The fourth scenario involves a married couple in addition to an egg donor and the fifth scenario involves an egg donor, who also serves as a gestational mother. The sixth scenario involves a married couple in addition to a gestational surrogate. These three scenarios are considered illegitimate due to the existence of a third party. The last scenario is similar to the sixth scenario with the exception that the gestational surrogate is a co-wife, married to the same man. This last scenario is considered legitimate as long as it is done on a voluntary basis, and in this case the voluntary surrogate is compared to the milk mother. This resolution, however, was revised in the following session of IFC in 1985 to withdraw the legitimacy of the seventh scenario on the grounds that it may lead to confusion of lineages in case the second wife becomes pregnant with a second baby during the same pregnancy cycle. Accordingly, only two scenarios were considered legitimate, while the remaining five scenarios were considered illegitimate due to the involvement of a third party.[16] Following the deliberations that the IFC facilitated along with the resultant resolutions, the IIFA also investigated both gamete donation and surrogacy within the framework of artificial insemination and IVF. Eventually, it issued a resolution during its third session in 1986, which reiterated and confirmed the revised resolution of IFC. Accordingly, only two scenarios were considered legitimate, while the remaining five were considered illegitimate on the grounds that they violate the sanctity of the marital relationship.[17]

In general, the statements and resolutions that these transnational institutions issued on gamete donation and surrogacy arrangements were informed by a number of reservations that were reiterated during successive cycles of deliberations. These reservations can be categorized into three main types: legal, psychological, and social. As noted above, the legal reservations revolved around two main issues: association with adultery, and concern over authenticity of the baby's lineage. Other legal concerns were also raised concerning issues such as: individual privacy and permissibility of uncovering as well as touching of private parts; moral status of the embryo, including proper ways of dealing with surplus embryos during the IVF procedure, cryopreservation of gametes and permissibility of postmortem or postmarital use of stored gametes, genetic counseling, sex selection, selective abortion, and transplantation of sexual organs. The psychological reservations revolve around the potential negative impact of artificial insemination and surrogacy arrangements on family relationships. For example, critics point out the extent to which these procedures would reshape the procreative process independently of the intimate relationship within marriage. In turn, this reconstructed image of reproduction would affect the emotional connection between married couples and also between parents and their offspring. One example that critics often highlight is the impact of surrogacy on the reconstruction of parenthood in general and maternity in particular. In general, the relationship between the gestational surrogate and the resulting baby is often underestimated and even compromised in favor of the genetic mother. If surrogacy contracts can settle disputes over maternity claims at the formal legal level, psychological ramifications on adversely affected parties can hardly be removed or ruled out. The social reservations revolve around potential repercussions on the family as the main foundation of the social order. Both gamete donation and surrogacy raise concerns over their potential use for eugenic purposes, by targeting individuals who possess desirable genes and excluding others who possess deficient ones. These procedures also raise concerns over social justice and proper allocation of scarce medical resources to benefit socially privileged groups. Moreover, IVF is a costly procedure and often requires repeated cycles of trial and error. Similarly, surrogacy raises concerns over medical and nonmedical cases that justify resort to assisted reproductive technology. In other words, to what extent can a woman resort to surrogacy to avoid pregnancy and childbirth for professional or cosmetic reasons? And, from a social justice perspective, to what extent can remuneration place undue influence on gestational surrogates, especially in cases of extreme need or poverty? Finally, critics often point out the consequences of surrogacy on the social status of a gestational surrogate, whether she is married or not. If married, surrogacy is likely to have an impact on the surrogate's relationship with her husband as well as his legally protected rights.

Controversy over Gamete Donation and Surrogacy Arrangements

The foregoing discussion reflecting the collective fatwas and resolutions of several transnational institutions give the impression that gamete donation and surrogacy arrangements are totally banned. This general impression, however, does not rule out dissenting views concerning the permissibility of at least some forms of surrogacy, especially in case both the egg donor and the surrogate are married to the same man, which were expressed or implied during the deliberations undertaken within these institutions themselves.[18] As noted above, the 1984 resolution of the IFC allowed this latter scenario before it was revised in the subsequent session to ban all types of surrogacy arrangements. This exceptional scenario, however, continued to inspire further discussions and even more daring opinions, mostly in the form of individual fatwas. This, in turn, translates into three main attitudes concerning surrogacy: conditional permissibility of gestational surrogacy, impermissibility of all types of surrogacy arrangements, and permissibility of surrogacy only in case the gestational surrogate is married to the husband of the egg donor.[19]

Supporters of the first attitude draw on the similarity between gestation and breastfeeding, which is supported by textual references in the foundational sources combining them. Both processes provide necessary nourishment for the baby, without affecting basic genetic traits or features. If Shar'ia allows the possibility to hire a milk mother, the same rule can be extended to gestation as well. On the other hand, critics note that this analogy cannot be sustained on the grounds that unlike gestational surrogacy, breastfeeding is pursued for the satisfaction of a dire need for an already existing child. Moreover, breastfeeding does not create any uncertainty concerning the lineage of the child while surrogacy, by contrast, creates competing parental claims. Some supporters make an argument in favor of gestational surrogacy on the basis of necessity, arguing that modern scientific means should be utilized to achieve the need of infertile couples for children. This argument, however, is criticized on the grounds that necessities are evaluated on the basis of existing, rather than projected or conjectural, considerations. In other words, necessity should be invoked in order to meet an urgent need for an existing situation, as is the case with preserving the life of an existing child. From this perspective, use of questionable means in order to facilitate the birth of a child does not qualify as a case of justified necessity. Moreover, pursuit of modern scientific methods can be categorized as a form of utility (*maṣlaḥah*) only when their benefits outweigh their harms. From this perspective, gestational surrogacy is considered problematic due to its likelihood to cause disputes, confuse lineages, and commodify the human reproductive function.

Supporters of the second attitude, banning all types of surrogacy arrangements, highlight these negative consequences of surrogacy by pointing out the extent to which it undermines the meaning of motherhood and compromises the social status of the surrogate, regardless of whether she is single or married.[20] With regard to the lineage of the child born through gestational surrogacy, the scholars are divided along the same lines. Supporters of gestational surrogacy (including those limiting gestational surrogacy to the situation involving a co-wife) hold that the child should be attached to the donating couple and the gestational surrogate should be treated like a milk mother. Opponents to surrogacy arrangements hold that, if it is undertaken, the child should be attributed to the gestational surrogate and her husband on the grounds that motherhood is defined on the basis of gestation and childbirth.[21]

In addition to this general disagreement on the permissibility of gestational surrogacy, especially in the case of a volunteering co-wife, the past few decades witnessed a growing controversy over the permissibility of gamete donation. The main dissenting views, arguing for the permissibility of gamete donation, were expressed in the form of fatwas by some prominent Shiite scholars, especially on the basis of temporary (*mut'ah*) marriage.[22] These dissenting views are often traced to a famous fatwa that the current supreme leader of Iran Ayatollah Ali Hussein Khamene'i issued in the late 1990s.[23] From this perspective, gamete donation and surrogacy do not amount to adultery because they do not involve physical contact between unmarried couples. Shiite scholars, however, are not monolithic and a great deal of diversity exists within the Shiite' context concerning different types and scenarios of gamete donation and surrogacy arrangements. For example, some Shiite scholars make a distinction between artificial insemination by donor sperm, which is generally seen as impermissible, and fertilization of the ovum by donor sperm in the lab (IVF) and implantation of the resulting embryo in the woman's uterus, which is considered permissible by many Shiite scholars as long as no physical contact is made between unrelated gamete donors.[24] This distinction, in turn, involves another distinction between traditional surrogacy, in which the surrogate contributes the ovum, and gestational surrogacy, in which the surrogate only hosts the embryo of a married couple. While the former is not approved by most Shiite scholars, the latter is considered permissible. These distinctions translate into prohibition of placing a man's semen (but not an embryo) in a womb that is prohibited for this man.[25] Shiite scholars also disagree on the definition of maternity on the basis of genetic or gestational grounds. In line with the majority of Sunni scholars, some Shiite scholars hold that maternity is defined primarily in gestational terms on the basis of the Scriptural references that seem to support this connection. By contrast, the majority of Shiite scholars, following the technical possibilities of gamete donation and surrogacy, hold that maternity should be defined on the basis of genetic grounds in light of the role of gametes in the formation of embryos. Some scholars recognize both the egg donor and the gestational surrogate as equal partners in maternity. Finally, while some scholars argue against gamete donation in the form of sperm or egg, they approve embryo donation as long as the embryo consists only of the gametes of a married couple. Embryo donation is made legally possible in Iran under the 2003 Law on Embryo Donation to Infertile Spouses. As the title indicates, the law limits embryo donation to married couples. Technically, the law does not prohibit embryo donation among relatives (e.g., siblings), which has also been approved by some Shiite scholars such as Ayatollah Sadeqi.[26]

These accommodating fatwas within the Shiite context are said to have caused a revolution in the practice of ART, as demonstrated by anthropological fieldwork in countries such as Iran and Lebanon.[27] In contrast to the predominantly Sunni attitude, proscribing any form of third-party intervention, this divergent attitude by some Shiite scholars, allowing gamete or embryo donation as well as surrogacy arrangements, is best explained by placing it within the normative Shiite tradition, which is based on the fundamental doctrine of the imamate. According to this doctrine, divine guidance is maintained through an uninterrupted chain of leaders from the descendants of the Prophet through his daughter Fāṭimah and her husband and the Prophet's cousin ʿAlī ibn Abī Ṭālib. In the absence of the rightful imam and with the development of the notion of "sources of imitation," lay shiʿīs are obligated to follow the opinions of particular jurists, who are capable of undertaking independent legal reasoning.[28] The Shiite tradition, therefore, gives more room for individual juristic opinions and, in comparison with the Sunni tradition, has made the development of a unanimous attitude less feasible.

Notwithstanding these accommodating opinions, both gamete donation and surrogacy arrangements remain religiously and also culturally problematic even within the Shiite context.[29] In addition to the main religious concern over the certainty of lineage that these procedures involve, they also raise concerns over the possibility of incestuous relationships, which may result inadvertently from anonymous gamete donation. Moreover, gamete donation may also raise significant cultural concerns in light of the social stigma associated with the role of genetic factors in determining bodily features as well as the meaning of relatedness.[30]

Legislating Gamete Donation and Surrogacy

In most Muslim majority countries legislation does not address gamete donation or surrogacy arrangements directly. Implicitly, however, since family status issues are regulated in light of Sharʿia, both gamete donation and surrogacy arrangements are considered reprehensible in light of the reservations discussed above concerning lineage, consanguinity, and commodification of the human body and its reproductive functions. Therefore, a gamete donation or surrogacy contract is generally considered invalid on the grounds that the human body or bodily functions cannot be subjected to contractual or commercial transactions.[31] In the absence of binding legislation to regulate various applications of assisted reproductive technology, the cumulative body of Islamic normative pronouncements remains the main resource for moral decision-making concerning these applications. In particular, the collective fatwas, statements, and resolutions issued by prominent national and transnational institutions play a significant role in inspiring individual fatwas, formulating practice guidelines in clinical settings, and also in developing formal policies and draft laws. For example, in 2001 the Egyptian parliament discussed a draft law to ban and criminalize any form of commercial surrogacy. The ban included publicizing surrogacy with penalties for both intending mothers and surrogates in the form of a prison term of up to five years. The physician facilitating the process is also penalized with a prison term of up to three years in addition to withdrawal of license for a minimum of ten years and confiscation of medical equipment used in insemination, transfer, and plantation of gametes for a minimum of one year from the date of the incident. The draft law cited the IOMS and IFC resolutions indicating the impermissibility of all types of surrogacy arrangements. The proposed law, according to its author, was meant to prevent the exploitation of the financial needs of poor women and to protect established social norms and religious values.[32] In 2010, the Health Committee in the Egyptian Parliament approved a draft law to regulate artificial insemination and IVF. Reiterating the rationale of the 2001 proposal, the draft law also banned surrogacy arrangements to protect poor women against any form of exploitation in return for financial rewards. The draft law required certain conditions for undertaking artificial insemination and IVF. They include the existence of a medical report, indicating the necessity of the procedure (only for married couples and during an existing marital relationship). The physician performing the procedure must obtain a written consent from the couple. And, finally, the resulting child would be recognized as a legitimate child. On the other hand, the draft law banned any form of gamete donation, indicating that, if undertaken, the resulting child would be illegitimate. The proposed law restricted implementation of assisted reproduction only to licensed hospitals and health centers. Finally, it indicated that violations would result in significant financial as well as prison penalties.[33]

In the past few years, with increasing demands for adequate laws on reproductive health and assisted reproductive technology, some countries sought to fill legislative gaps in these critical areas. For example, in 2008 the United Arab Emirates issued a federal law to regulate ART practice within the country, which includes indications of permissible methods and scenarios. In general, the law echoes the guidelines and recommendations issued by the major transnational institutions discussed above, particularly the ban on any form of third-party involvement including the case of the co-wife.[34] As noted above, Iran is the only Muslim-majority country with legislation allowing embryo donation, which has been facilitated by the fact that it is a predominantly Shiite country. This legislation, however, does not include gamete donation or surrogacy.[35]

Conclusion

Assisted reproductive technologies have introduced considerable challenges to the inherited Islamic ethical-legal structure. Most of these challenges revolve around the relationship between reproduction and marriage and also the definition of relationships within the nuclear family. Muslim responses to questions pertaining to assisted reproduction come mainly in the form of fatwas (considered yet non-binding opinions) by religious scholars as well as institutions. With few exceptions, legislation in most Muslim-majority countries does not regulate the various applications of assisted reproductive technologies. The normative Islamic literature that has been generated over the past few decades reveals a wide range of opinions concerning these applications. In general, researchers often underscore a distinction between Sunni and Shiite perspectives. While most Sunni scholars uphold the traditional connection between marriage and reproduction, most Shiite scholars show greater flexibility on the nature of this connection and also the extent to which it should be maintained either at all or through the temporary *mut'ah* marriage. These perspectives translate into different attitudes on issues such as gamete donation and surrogacy, which are condemned by most Sunni scholars while being allowed by most Shiite scholars. Finally, as much as these Sunni-Shiite disagreements can be attributed to the differing attitudes on the connection between marriage and reproduction, they can also shed light on the nature of the normative decision-making process within each of these communities. While Sunnī scholars place greater emphasis on juristic consensus, Shiite scholars enjoy greater discretion, especially in the case of jurists who are acknowledged as sources of emulation for their followers.

Acknowledgment Statement

This publication was made possible by NPRP grant #NPRP8-1478-6-053 from the Qatar National Research Fund (a member of Qatar Foundation). The statements made herein are solely the responsibility of the author.

Notes

1. Vincent Barry, *Bioethics in a Cultural Context* (Boston: Wadsworth, 2012), 206.
2. Ibid. According to the Centers for Disease Control and Prevention, about 1.6 percent of all babies born in the United States are conceived through ART. In 2015, 72,913 live infants were born out of a total of 231,936 ART cycles, which were performed at 646 registered clinics in the United States. See https://www.cdc.gov/art/artdata/index.html.

3. See, for example, Marcia Inhorn, "Globalization and Gametes: Reproductive 'Tourism,' Islamic Bioethics, and Middle Eastern Modernity," *Anthropology and Medicine* 18, no. 1 (2011): 97.
4. Maḥmūd Shaltūt, *al-Fatāwá: Dirāsah li-Mushkilāt al-Muslim al-Muʿāṣir fī Ḥayātih al-Yawmiyyah al-ʿAmmah*, 19th edition (Cairo: Dār al-=Shurūq, 2009), 279–282. Other scholars also such as Muḥammad Abū Abū Zahrah (d.1974) reiterated the same points; see Muḥammad ʿUthmān Shubayr, ed., *Fatāwá al-Shaykh Muḥammad Abū Zahrah* (Damascus: Dār al-Qalam, 2010), 826–831. See also Ayman Shabana, "Foundations of the Consensus against Surrogacy Arrangements in Islamic Law," *Islamic Law and Society* 22 (2015): 92–93
5. *al-Fatāwá al-Islāmiyyah min Dār al-Iftāʾ al-Miṣriyyah*, 20 vols. (Cairo: al-Majlis al-Aʿlá li al-Shuʾūn al-Islāmiyyah, 1993), vol. 9: 3213–3228.
6. Shabana, "Foundations of the Consensus against Surrogacy Arrangements in Islamic Law," 93. For an English summary of this *fatwa*, see Marcia Inhorn, *The New Arab Man: Emergent Masculinities, Technologies, and Islam in the Middle East* (Princeton, NJ: Princeton University Press, 2012), 325–329.
7. Aḥmad Rajāʾī al-Jindī, ed., *al-Injāb fī Ḍawʾ al-Islām* (Kuwait: al-Munaẓẓamah al-Islāmiyyah li al-ʿUlūm al-Ṭibbiyyah, 1983), 350.
8. Ibid., 226.
9. Ibid., 219.
10. Ibid., 232.
11. Ibid., 220.
12. Aḥmad Rajāʾī al-Jindī, ed., *al-Nadwah al-ʿAlamiyyah ḥawla al-Wirāthah wa al-Takāthur al-Basharī wa Inʿikāsātuhā: Ruʾyat al-Adyān al-Samāwiyyah wa wijhat Naẓar al-ʿAlmāniyyah*, 2 vols. (Kuwait: al-Munaẓẓamah al-Islāmiyyah li al-ʿUlūm al-Ṭibbiyyah, 2008).
13. Ibid., vol. 2, 490.
14. al-Jindī, ed., *al-Injāb fī Ḍawʾ al-Islām*, 219–220.
15. al-Jindī, *al-Nadwah al-ʿAlamiyyah*, vol. 2, 484.
16. *Qarārāt al-Majmaʿ al-Fiqhī al-Islāmī bi-Makkah al-Mukarramah* (Mecca: al-Majmʿ al-Fiqhī al-Islāmī, 2004), 148–154.
17. *Majallat Majmaʿ al-Fiqh al-Islāmī* 3, no. 1 (1987): 515–516.
18. al-Jindī, *al-Injāb fī Ḍawʾ al-Islām*, 219–230
19. ʿAṭā ʿAbd al-ʿĀṭī al-Sunbāṭī, *Bunūk al-Nuṭaf wa al-Ajinnah, Dirāsah Muqāranah bayna al-Fiqh al-Islāmī wa al-Qānūn al-Waḍʿī* (Cairo: Dār al-Nahḍah al-ʿArabiyyah, 2001), 258.
20. Ibid., 259–267.
21. Ibid., 271.
22. Farouk Mahmoud, "Controversies in Islamic Evaluation of Assisted Reproductive Technologies," in *Islam and Assisted Reproductive Technologies*, edited by Marcia Inhorn and Soraya Tremayne (New York: Berghahn Books, 2012), 81.
23. For an English summary of this *fatwa*, see Inhorn, *The New Arab Man*, 329–331. Similar opinions are also expressed by other Shiite scholars. For example, the prominent Iraqi cleric Sayyid ʿAlī al-Sistānī notes that fertilization of a woman's egg by semen from someone other than her husband would be impermissible. If this scenario occurred, however, the child should be attached to the genetic father. Accordingly, all rules pertaining to lineage would also be applicable. See ʿAlī al-Hussaynī al-Sistānī, *Minhāj al-Ṣāliḥīn*, 3 vols. (Beirut: Dār al-Muʾarrikh al-ʿArabī, 2008), vol. 1, 459–460 and Muhammad Riḍā

al-Sistānī, *Wasāʾil al-Injāb al-Ṣināʿiyyah, Dirāsah Fiqhiyyah* (Beirut: Dār al-Muʾarrikh al-ʿArabī, 2012), 414.
24. Shiite scholars show more lenience toward sperm donation when it goes into the formation of an embryo. Therefore, embryo donation is generally seen as less problematic than gamete donation. See Farouk Mahmoud, "Controversies in Islamic Evaluation of Assisted Reproductive Technologies," 81–82.
25. Shirin Garmaroudi Naef, "Gestational Surrogacy in Iran: Uterine Kinship in Shia Thought and Practice," in *Islam and Assisted Reproductive Technologies*, 164–166.
26. Ibid., 169–170.
27. See Mohammad Jalal Abbasi-Shavazi, Marcia Inhorn, Hajiieh Bibi Razeghi-Nasrabad, and Ghasem Toloo, "The 'Iranian ART Revolution': Infertility, Assisted Reproductive Technology, and Third-Party Donation in the Islamic Republic of Iran," *Journal of Middle East Women's Studies* 4 (2008): 4; and Morgan Clarke, *Islam and New Kinship: Reproductive Technology and the Shariah in Lebanon* (New York: Berghahn Books, 2009).
28. Marcia Inhorn and Soraya Tremayne, eds., *Islam and Assisted Reproductive Technologies* (New York: Berghahn Books, 2012), 8.
29. Abdulaziz Sachedina, *Islamic Biomedical Ethics: Principles and Applications* (Oxford, UK: Oxford University Press, 2009), 111.
30. Sachedina, *Islamic Biomedical Ethics*, 119; see also Soraya Tremayne, "The 'Down Side' of Gamete Donation: Challenging 'Happy Family' Rhetoric in Iran," in *Islam and Assisted Reproductive Technologies*, 130–156.
31. Faraj Muḥammad Muḥammad Sālim, *Wasāʾil al-Ikhṣāb al-Ṭibbī al-Musāʿid wa Ḍawābiṭuh* (Alexandria: Maktabat al-Wafāʾ al-Qānūniyyah, 2012), 836.
32. "Mashrūʿ Qanūn amām al-barlamān al-Miṣrī li-Ḥaẓr wa Tajrīm Ījār al-Arḥām," *al-Sharq al-Awsaṭ*, July 1, 2001, http://archive.aawsat.com/details.asp?section=31&issueno=8251&article=45401&feature=#.WVTqWU2we72.
33. "Taqnīn al-Talqīḥ al-Ṣināʿī wa Aṭfāl al-Anābīb," *al-Ahrām al-Yawmī*, March 1, 2010, https://www.masress.com/ahram/9658.
34. *Qawānīn Ṭibiyyah* (Abū Dhabi: Maʿhad al-Tadrīb wa al-Dirāsāt al-Qaḍāʾiyyah, 2010), 15.
35. Leila Afshar and Alireza Bagheri, "Embryo Donation in Iran: An Ethical Review," *Developing World Bioethics* 13 (2013): 122. With regard to surrogacy, a draft law has been prepared but it has not yet been approved by the parliament. In the meantime, actual practice is regulated according to religious decrees; see K. Aramesh, "Iran's Experience with Surrogate Motherhood: An Islamic View and Ethical Concerns," *Journal of Medical Ethics* 35 (2009): 321.

Bibliography

Abbasi-Shavazi, Mohammad Jalal, Marcia Inhorn, Hajiieh Bibi Razeghi-Nasrabad, and Ghasem Toloo. "The 'Iranian ART Revolution': Infertility, Assisted Reproductive Technology, and Third-Party Donation in the Islamic Republic of Iran." *Journal of Middle East Women's Studies* 4 (2008): 1–28.
Afshar, Leila, and Alireza Bagheri. "Embryo Donation in Iran: An Ethical Review." *Developing World Bioethics* 13 (2013): 119–124.
Aramesh, K. "Iran's Experience with Surrogate Motherhood: An Islamic View and Ethical Concerns." *Journal of Medical Ethics* 35 (2009): 320–322.

Barry, Vincent. *Bioethics in a Cultural Context*. Boston: Wadsworth, 2012.
Clarke, Morgan. *Islam and New Kinship: Reproductive Technology and the Shariah in Lebanon.* New York: Berghahn Books, 2009.
al-Fatāwá al-Islāmiyyah min Dār al-Iftā' al-Miṣriyyah, 20 vols. Cairo: al-Majlis al-Aʻlá li al-Shuʼūn al-Islāmiyyah, 1993.
Inhorn, Marcia. "Globalization and Gametes: Reproductive 'Tourism,' Islamic Bioethics, and Middle Eastern Modernity." *Anthropology and Medicine* 18, no. 1 (2011): 87–103.
Inhorn, Marcia. *The New Arab Man: Emergent Masculinities, Technologies, and Islam in the Middle East*. Princeton, NJ: Princeton University Press, 2012.
al-Jindī, Aḥmad Rajāʼī, ed. *al-Injāb fī Ḍawʼ al-Islām*. Kuwait: al-Munaẓẓamah al-Islāmiyyah li al-ʻUlūm al-Ṭibbiyyah, 1983.
al-Jindī, Aḥmad Rajāʼī, ed. *al-Nadwah al-ʻAlamiyyah ḥawla al-Wirāthah wa al-Takāthur al-Basharī wa Inʻikāsātuhā: Ruʼyat al-Adyān al-Samāwiyyah wa wijhat Naẓar al-ʻAlmāniyyah*, 2 vols. Kuwait: al-Munaẓẓamah al-Islāmiyyah li al-ʻUlūm al-Ṭibbiyyah, 2008.
Mahmoud, Farouk. "Controversies in Islamic Evaluation of Assisted Reproductive Technologies." In *Islam and Assisted Reproductive Technologies*, edited by Marcia Inhorn and Soraya Tremayne, 70–97. New York: Berghahn Books, 2012.
Majallat Majmaʻ al-Fiqh al-Islāmī, vol. 3, no. 1 (1987): 515–516.
"Mashrūʻ Qanūn amām al-barlamān al-Miṣrī li-Ḥaẓr wa Tajrīm Ījār al-Arḥām." *al-Sharq al-Awsaṭ*, July 1, 2001. http://archive.aawsat.com/details.asp?section=31&issueno=8251&article=45401&feature=#.WVTqWU2we72
Naef, Shirin Garmaroudi. "Gestational Surrogacy in Iran: Uterine Kinship in Shia Thought and Practice." In *Islam and Assisted Reproductive Technologies*, edited by Marcia Inhorn and Soraya Tremayne, 157–193. New York: Berghahn Books, 2012.
Qarārāt al-Majmaʻ al-Fiqhī al-Islāmī bi-Makkah al-Mukarramah. Mecca: al-Majmʻ al-Fiqhī al-Islāmī, 2004.
Qawānīn Ṭibiyyah. Abū Dhabi: Maʻhad al-Tadrīb wa al-Dirāsāt al-Qaḍāʼiyyah, 2010.
Sachedina, Abdulaziz. *Islamic Biomedical Ethics: Principles and Applications*. Oxford, UK: Oxford University Press, 2009.
Sālim, Faraj Muḥammad Muḥammad. *Wasāʼil al-Ikhṣāb al-Ṭibbī al-Musāʻid wa Ḍawābiṭuh*. Alexandria: Maktabat al-Wafāʼ al-Qānūniyyah, 2012.
Shabana, Ayman. "Foundations of the Consensus against Surrogacy Arrangements in Islamic Law." *Islamic Law and Society* 22 (2015): 82–113.
Shaltūt, Maḥmūd. *al-Fatāwá: Dirāsah li-Mushkilāt al-Muslim al-Muʻāṣir fī Ḥayātih al-Yawmiyyah al-ʻAmmah*, 19th edition. Cairo: Dār al-=Shurūq, 2009.
Shubayr, Muḥammad ʻUthmān, ed. *Fatāwá al-Shaykh Muḥammad Abū Zahrah*. Damascus: Dār al-Qalam, 2010.
al-Sistānī, ʻAlī al-Hussaynī. *Minhāj al-Ṣāliḥīn*, 3 vols. Beirut: Dār al-Muʼarrikh al-ʻArabī, 2008.
al-Sistānī, Muḥammad Riḍā. *Wasāʼil al-Injāb al-Ṣināʻiyyah, Dirāsah Fiqhiyyah*. Beirut: Dār al-Muʼarrikh al-ʻArabī, 2012.
al-Sunbāṭī, ʻAṭā ʻAbd al-ʻĀṭī. *Bunūk al-Nuṭaf wa al-Ajinnah, Dirāsah Muqāranah bayna al-Fiqh al-Islāmī wa al-Qānūn al-Waḍʻī*. Cairo: Dār al-Nahḍah al-ʻArabiyyah, 2001.
"Taqnīn al-Talqīḥ al-Ṣināʻī wa Aṭfāl al-Anābīb," *al-Ahrām al-Yawmī*, March 1, 2010. https://www.masress.com/ahram/9658
Tremayne, Soraya. "The 'Down Side' of Gamete Donation: Challenging 'Happy Family' Rhetoric in Iran." In *Islam and Assisted Reproductive Technologies*, edited by Marcia Inhorn and Soraya Tremayne, 130–156. New York: Berghahn Books, 2012.

PART IV

CONTRACEPTION AND ABORTION

PART IV

CONTRACEPTION AND ABORTION

CHAPTER 19

CATHOLIC TEACHING ON CONTRACEPTION

An Unsettled Business?

ALINE H. KALBIAN

IN spring of 1965, the United States Supreme Court ruled that the legal basis of the convictions of Estelle Griswold, executive director of the Planned Parenthood League of Connecticut and C. Lee Buxton, medical director of a Planned Parenthood Clinic in New Haven, Connecticut, were unconstitutional. As described by Justice Douglas in his opinion, Griswold and Buxton had been arrested in 1961 for giving "information, instruction, and medical advice to *married persons* as to the means of preventing conception."[1] In the nineteenth century, the Comstock Act had deemed contraception to be an "obscenity" in the United States and thus made the dissemination of birth control through the mail or across state lines a federal offense. According to the case, Griswold and Buxton had violated Connecticut statues that criminalized any action that assisted or abetted the use of a "drug, medical article or instrument" that was intended to prevent conception. They appealed their convictions all the way to the Supreme Court, claiming that the Connecticut statutes violated the Fourteenth Amendment of the US Constitution. The justices voted 7–2 in favor of the appellants, and as a result invalidated any US laws that made the use or encouragement of contraceptives to married couples a criminal act. The majority argued that the 14th Amendment created guarantees to "certain zones of privacy," and that the marital relationship, while not mentioned explicitly in the Constitution, was one such zone.[2] *Griswold v. Connecticut*'s protection of married couples' rights to contraception was followed seven years later by *Eisenstadt v. Baird*, which afforded the same right to unmarried persons.³ The Eisenstadt case challenged a Massachusetts law that made it a felony to "give away a drug, medicine, instrument, or article for the prevention of conception except in the case of (1) a registered physician administering or prescribing it for a married person or (2) an active registered pharmacist furnishing it to a married person presenting a registered physician's prescription."⁴ Together these two cases essentially settled the legal (and to some extent the moral) debates about the permissibility of contraception in the United States.⁵

By the 1960s, most major Christian denominations were moving in a similar direction by acknowledging that "family planning" was a responsible activity that did not in any way affect the morality of sexual intercourse. Most famously, the Anglican Church accepted the use of artificial contraception, tentatively at first in 1930, and then more definitely at the 1958 Lambeth Conference.⁶ The Anglicans, along with other Protestant Christian denominations, did not draw a sharp distinction between natural and artificial ways to limit births. Indeed many saw the development of new technologies of birth control as progress towards a more humane world, citing concerns about economic deprivation, and child and maternal health.⁷ In sharp contrast, the Catholic Church, which had consistently expressed its opposition to the use of contraception, especially in the late nineteenth and early twentieth centuries, continued to oppose to the use of artificial contraception. The Church had approved the moral permissibility of the "rhythm method" in the 1950s,⁸ but by the 1960s attention was shifting to the newly available birth control pill, thus raising the question of whether there was a morally relevant distinction between "natural" and "artificial" means of birth control. The term *natural* referred to avoiding conception by limiting sexual intercourse to infertile periods in a woman's cycle. The term *artificial* referred to actions that interfered with a sexual act—either through barrier methods or anovulants such as the birth control pill.

The Church engaged in a relatively public discussion of its views at about the same time that *Griswold* was passed, spurred by the availability of the birth control pill and rising anxiety about rapid population growth globally. Many perceived this public discussion as a sign that the Catholic Church might change its stance and allow married couples to use "artificial" contraception in certain cases. However, in 1968, Pope Paul VI issued an encyclical letter proclaiming that any use of "artificial" contraception constituted a deeply immoral act and was forbidden by Church teaching. The Catholic Church, at least in its official teaching capacity, asserted an absolute prohibition of "artificial" means of contraception at roughly the same time that United States society was reaching a general consensus that the use of contraception was not a morally troublesome act. Officially, the Catholic Church opted out of this consensus by holding strongly to its anti-contraceptive view. In less official ways, however, many avowed Catholics ignored their church's teaching and chose to use contraceptives. This dissonance has led to a fracture in the community of Catholics, especially in the United States and Europe. In the years since 1968, the Church's official position has not changed. By remaining adamant in its refusal to accept any use of artificial contraception, the Catholic Church complicates the seemingly smooth cultural narrative that normalized contraceptive use by giving people complete access to a range of ways for preventing pregnancy.

What seems to interest people the most about the Catholic view is the matter of when, and if, the Church will change its teaching. With each new pope, there is renewed interest in whether or not the Vatican will finally join the broad Christian consensus on this issue. Rather than speculating on the future of Catholic teaching in this essay, I look back to try to understand why the Catholic position remains unchanged. I suggest the following possible explanation: it has remained unchanged because the issue of the human relationship to nature, which remains at the center of official Catholic discourse about contraception, reinforces a strong and unhelpful distinction between artificial and natural means. Put differently, the rhetoric of artificial versus natural, which is presumably grounded in a set of ideas about where humans stand in relation to nature, keeps the position against contraceptives deeply entrenched.

Theologians and scholars of religion tend to characterize the Catholic opposition to contraception in a number of ways—either as a return to a pre–Vatican II natural law methodology; as a rejection of modernity; or as an expression of Catholic patriarchy and misogyny. These descriptions, while certainly accurate, keep the focus on social and cultural phenomena and are a distraction, I believe, from Catholic beliefs about theological and metaphysical matters such as how to interpret God's creative activity in the world or how to understand the human relationship to nature. Framing the Catholic opposition as a theological one about creation, dominion, and nature is an important supplement to the cultural/social accounts because it can better explain the intransigence of the Catholic teaching. To be clear, Catholic teaching about contraception is not always explicitly framed purely in terms of a worry about dominion; nevertheless, theological concern about human dominion over nature, especially via technological means, is integral to the discourse about contraception, especially in the distinction between natural and artificial that the Church upholds.

I begin my explanation of the grounds of the Catholic argument against certain means of contraception by focusing on questions about what it means to talk about official teaching. I then turn to the content of the teaching in central Catholic documents with a view on portrayals of creation, nature, and dominion. I conclude by identifying the practical implications of my analysis.

Grounding the Catholic View

What Makes the Official Teaching Official?

Attempting to identify the Roman Catholic perspective on anything is both easy and complicated. It is easy insofar as one can usually find public written documents that state the Church's official perspective: The Catholic Church is a hierarchical structure governed by an ecclesial authority that issues statements on a number of issues relating to doctrine and morality. Thus, the Church's official position is easy to identify and is almost always stated in clear and definitive terms. The complications arise in two regards. First, these statements are usually issued in the form of densely argued documents that draw on a variety of sources and use a range of argumentative strategies to support their positions. Thus, while the statements express definitive positions, it is possible to discern internal conflicts both in terms of reasoning and of the sources that the Church privileges. Second, not all who identify as part of the Roman Catholic community agree with the official view. It would be a mistake to argue that these dissenting positions fall outside of the Roman Catholic perspective, since many utilize central Catholic insights and sources. Indeed, the so-called dissenters often perceive of themselves as expressing a more authentically Catholic view.

Numerous surveys (most recently in 2014 in the lead-up to the Synod on Marriage) confirm that the majority of practicing Catholics worldwide do not support the Church's teaching on contraception, and one can suppose that they choose to follow their conscience.[9] Moreover, Pope Francis has recently challenged the question of authority in his post-synodal Apostolic Exhortation *Amoris letitia* where he embraces a range of position and encourages an approach for the church that is less dogmatic and more pastoral. He suggests that "not all discussions of doctrinal, moral or pastoral issues need to be settled by interventions of the magisterium. Unity of teaching and practice is certainly necessary in the Church, but this does not preclude various ways of interpreting some aspects of that teaching or drawing certain consequences from it. Each country or region, moreover, can seek solutions better suited to its culture and sensitive to its traditions and local needs."[10] By delegating teaching responsibility to the local level, the Pope challenges the traditional hierarchical model.

Yet, this is a model with a history. The Vatican's authority was strengthened in the period between the first and second Vatican Councils (1870–1962), and pronouncements issued by the pope were viewed as more binding and authoritative than they had been in the past. Many historical and cultural circumstances led to the creation of a more powerful papacy in the nineteenth century, and that power continued to be on full display, especially in the early twentieth century, when the Catholic Church was struggling with its response to modern ideas and developments. On the issue of contraception, the popes of the early twentieth century pronounced that it was immoral, and these pronouncements represented the Catholic position on the issue and left little if any room for dissent.

Vatican II ushered in a new ecclesiological model—one that emphasized collegiality over hierarchy. Todd Salzman and Michael Lawler label this model the "church as communion" versus the older "church as institution" model. Relying on Yves Congar's analysis of Catholic ecclesiology, they assert that the communion model was in fact the prominent one in the West during the first thousand years of the Church's history. It was only in the period between the Reformation and Vatican II that the hierarchical model of the church as institution prevailed. In the period around the Second Vatican Council, many Catholics (especially in Europe and the United States) embraced the communal model and responded by questioning the ultimate authority of magisterial statements. For them, the appropriate response to the church was not blind obedience, but rather thoughtful deliberation and dialogue directed towards consensus.[11] This conflict between a model of hierarchical authority and one of consensus is perhaps best typified by the deep strife that the debates about artificial contraception have caused in the Catholic Church.

Pope John XXIII illustrated this sharp divide between an authoritative church and a church of consensus in 1963 when he convened the Papal Commission on Family Planning and Population. What was most remarkable about this move was that instead of issuing a definitive ruling, he called together a wide range of lay and ecclesial experts on population, family, and sexual ethics. By opening up a conversation about the morality of contraception, he embraced the model of church as communion. That the conversation included more than clerics as participants was a significant development in how the church reasoned about matters. The story of this commission has been recounted in various contexts.[12] It is often told as a tale of how the Catholic Church missed the opportunity to truly embody the idea of church as communion, because in spite of the openness of many of the commission's conversations, in the end, the pope (at this point, Pope Paul VI) ignored its recommendations. The commission urged the pope to evaluate the moral act of contraception using a framework that grasped human actions holistically as deeply embedded in a set of contexts and circumstances that affected the meaning of the action. Pope Paul VI explicitly rejected their proposed framework in *Humanae vitae* (HV), and exerted his authority by saying that "The conclusions at which the commission arrived could not, nevertheless, be considered by us as definitive, nor dispense us from a personal examination of this serious question" (6). His primary reason for rejecting their recommendations is that the commission "departed from the moral teaching on marriage proposed with constant firmness by the teaching authority of the Church" (6).

In addition to asserting papal authority, the encyclical *Humanae vitae* outlined in some detail the contours of the Church's position on contraception. A close look at the thicket of arguments and assertions, especially as they pertain to the divide between artificial and natural, is the focus of the next section of the essay. Here I advance the argument by showing the centrality of the concern about dominion to this issue for the church. This reading of HV does not reject readings that identify the natural law methodology or gender bias as the driving forces of the document.[13] Rather, it adds another interpretive layer—one that enables us to understand and apply the Catholic teaching more clearly.

The Heart of the Catholic View: *Humanae vitae*

Catholic popes issue encyclical letters to teach, affirm, and elaborate on the doctrine of the Church. They are promulgated to bishops, clerics, the faithful and "all men of goodwill" to address a pressing theological or moral issue that needs clarification in light of new changes or developments. The encyclical is the most authoritative of a pope's utterances. In the mid-1960s, the Catholic faithful were expecting a pronouncement from Pope VI on the matter of contraception. There was a general sense among the Catholic laity that the church's position on contraception was being reconsidered in light of a wider range of available contraception. This sense was reinforced by the common knowledge that the previous pope, John XXIII, had convened a commission to address the matter of population and family planning. This commission, which was retained by Pope Paul VI when he ascended to the see, had met several times in the mid-1960s and had consulted with a wide range of specialists including lay Catholics. In 1965, the Commission issued its final report, a report that only represented a minority of the Commission members. Many in the Church were angered by this apparent "silencing" of Catholic voices, and were hoping that the Pope would speak and render a different conclusion. The official pronouncement came in 1968 in the form of *Humanae vitae*.

The document, a surprisingly short one for a papal encyclical, begins by acknowledging that Catholics may be confused about what to think about contraception in light of a number of developments. The purpose of the letter is to restate the Church's "coherent teaching concerning both the nature of marriage and the correct use of conjugal rights and the duties of husband and wife" (4). Paul VI acknowledges changes in society. He notes rapid demographic growth, changing place of women in society, and "stupendous progress" in the "domination and rational organization of the forces of nature" (2). He identifies how this domination of humans over nature has insidious effects on the human person: "It tends to extend ... to his own total being: to the body, to physical life, to social life and even to the laws which regulate the transmission of life"(2). It is the interventions into the process of transmission of life that the letter addresses, namely: Is it morally legitimate to use "a materially sterilizing intervention" to control birth? The response is an unequivocal no:

> The Church, calling men back to the observance of the norms of the natural law, as interpreted by its constant doctrine, teaches that each and every marriage act (*quilibet matrimonii usus*) must remain open to the transmission of life. (11)

Remaining open to the transmission of life means that there can be no deliberate interruption of the process of fertilization that can result from an act of sexual intercourse (marriage act), thus ruling out artificial interventions such as barrier methods, the birth control pill, and so on.

In this encyclical, the Pope expresses concerns about dominion using argumentative moves that are not explicitly about dominion. Paul VI does not rely heavily on Scriptural passages to support the Catholic view about contraception. There are only a handful of these in *Humanae vitae*, and when they do appear it is not as evidence or proof of a commandment from God, but rather to support a particular worldview and understanding of marriage. As we shall see, later popes turn to a more Scripturally grounded argument against contraception, focusing especially on the first few verses of Genesis.[14]

Rather than relying on Scripture, the pope bases the Catholic opposition to birth control on natural law and reason. He asserts the point about natural law, but makes little effort to argue for it in a careful and nuanced way. For example, early in the document, Pope Paul VI describes the magisterium's teachings on marriage as "founded on the natural law" and as "illuminated and enriched by divine revelation" (para. 4). The precise meaning of the natural law comes through to varying degrees in the document. For example, natural law appears to be the human intellectual capacity to know the natural purpose of the body and its functions. He writes that the "human intellect discovers in the power of giving life biological laws which are part of the human person" (para. 10). Put differently, this knowledge of the purpose of bodily functions is knowledge of God's objective moral order. The norms of the natural law are derived through human reason (with the assistance of Church) reflecting on what God intended for human bodies. In the context of marriage, this means that every act of sexual intercourse "must remain open to the transmission of life" (par. 11).

Natural law reasoning in the Catholic tradition moves along two different trajectories, both of which can be seen in the encyclical. One trajectory—the one mentioned above in connection with the principle of totality—is based on an understanding of nature as revelatory of God's order and wisdom. On this view, humans can "read" moral norms from physical phenomena such as the human body's purposes and functions. Natural law can also be tracked in another direction—one also mentioned in paragraph 10 of the document—as capturing human intellectual capacity. In other words, natural law is a way to talk about human reason. In paragraph 12, Paul VI writes, "We believe that the men of our day are particularly capable of seizing the deeply reasonable and human character of this fundamental principle." This capacity to grasp reasonable principles is the very working out of the natural law. The emphasis on reason rather than on the body captures an important tension in Catholic teaching about sexuality. While the Church understands human sexuality as a social phenomenon, it wants to protect it from cultural whims and trends. Thus, there is a need to assert the static and immutable nature of sexual purpose, which necessarily requires static and unchanging moral norms. In some sense, this is quite a different argument than worrying about control over nature. It is not human dominion over nature that is a worry, but rather cultural relativism.[15]

It might be that the emphasis on nature and the natural suggests a strong distinction between natural and artificial—a view reinforced by the Church's championing of "natural family planning" (NFP) as a morally viable alternative to "artificial contraception."[16] This distinction can be quite misleading, however, since the encyclical's concern with artificial contraception is not its artificiality per se, but rather its deliberate attempt to subjugate the natural purpose and end of the sexual act: in other words, to interfere with and to dominate nature. NFP is natural because it works with the rhythms of nature and the body. In the words of the encyclical, NFP respects "the laws of the generative process," and through it "the married couple makes legitimate use of a natural disposition" (para. 16). By doing so a person accepts that he is "not to be the arbiter of the sources of human life, but rather the minister of the design established by the creator" (para. 13). Artificial contraceptives aim to control and dominate nature; suggesting the belief that God's ordered world can be brought under human control.

To understand this more clearly we need to unpack what the term *artificial* means. We usually understand artificial things or artificial people to be fake, not real—to be imitations of something real. There are however, different intentions behind the artificial: to improve on the natural by creating the artificial, as in the case of fake eyelashes or artificial sweetener; to replace the natural when it is no longer functional as in the case of an artificial limb, or dentures; or to deceive someone into believing that what is artificial is in fact real. All three of these intentions are concerns for official Catholic teaching about artificial contraception. In contrast to NFP, artificial means seek to replace or improve upon the natural rhythms of the human body. Moreover, some Catholics, such as John Paul II, claim that sexual intercourse when using artificial contraceptives is "fake" or "intrinsically dishonest" since it fails to enact an authentic act of self-giving.[17] Whereas, when done for just motives, abstaining from sexual intercourse during fertile periods of a woman's cycle is "proof of a truly integral and honest love" (para. 16).

In addition to the language of nature and the natural law, human dominion over nature is also evident in the appeal to the "principle of totality" which claims that each human organism is ordered and designed according to its biological functions. This design is what determines the nature of the organism. Although humans do have some limited dominion over their bodies, God has set "unsurmountable limits ... which no man, whether a private individual or one invested with authority, may licitly surpass." Thus the moral norms that pertain to the body are determined by asking whether or not they violate God's design. Totality refers to the unhindered "natural" functioning of an organism. Some Catholic critics of HV argue that this principle reduces the person to their body by basing moral norms on whether or not they maintain or violate bodily integrity. Supporters of more freedom to use birth control invoked totality in a different way. For them the whole ought to refer to "the ensemble of conjugal life, rather than to its single acts" (para. 3). Pope Paul VI clearly rejects this position.

Alongside the intrinsic concerns about nature and human biological processes, the Pope also identifies potential negative consequences that could result from an embrace of contraception. This is surprising insofar as the Church usually avoids a consequentialist framework for supporting absolute norms. In other words, certain things are wrong not because they bring about bad consequences, but because humans have a duty to some larger (and in some cases transcendent) moral order. Pope Paul VI identifies a number of consequences. Three appear to be the most significant. First, human weakness is such that increased access to artificial contraception will increase marital infidelity, and decrease morality more broadly. Second, the pope expresses concern that uses of contraception will ultimately lead to a devaluing of women. They will come to be viewed as "instruments of selfish enjoyment." Third, if artificial contraception gets into the hands of wrong sorts of rulers, they will abuse their power and intervene into the sacred realm of the family by imposing family planning measures (para. 17).

One final and relevant component of the encyclical is a short paragraph that does not often get the same scrutiny as other parts of the document. This is the paragraph that allows for the use of a contraceptive pill for health-related purposes. It is a paragraph with significant practical implications, but it also offers some insight into how the Church understands the matter of human dominion over nature. This apparent exception is defended along the following lines: "The Church, on the contrary, does not at all consider illicit the use of those therapeutic means truly necessary to cure diseases of the organism, even if an impediment to procreation, which may be foreseen, should result therefrom, provided such impediment is not, for whatever motive directly willed" (para. 15). This paragraph draws on a tradition of Catholic moral theology that acknowledges that culpability in moral actions can be affected by whether or not one directly wills an action. Described either as part of the principle of double effect or as the distinction between direct and indirect willing, this idea allows Paul VI to accept that the birth control pill is not per se evil; by allowing that it might be used in morally licit (or at least morally neutral ways), paragraph 15 could open up the possibility of exceptions to the very firm Catholic opposition to contraception. Indeed, Catholic moral theologians who support a change in Catholic teaching often stress this type of argument. This paragraph also affirms that humans do have dominion over nature insofar as they are permitted, and perhaps even obligated to cure a disease that strikes the organism. Thus, even if preventing conception is a foreseen but unintended consequence of medical intervention, the necessity of such an intervention into the "natural" processes of the organism is warranted.

The Catholic View after *Humanae Vitae*

Theologians and bishops throughout the world responded to the greatly anticipated teaching of *Humanae vitae*. These responses were not generally framed in terms of the human relationship to nature; however, it is possible to interpret them as such. Perhaps the most remarkable statement (and the only one I shall discuss in the context of this essay) issued by Catholic theologians in the immediate aftermath of the encyclical was the one issued on July 30, 1968, by a group of American Catholic theologians.

They identify places where they find the teaching to be inadequate and assert that the encyclical does not represent infallible teaching. Thus, in their role as theologians they have the "special responsibility of evaluating and interpreting pronouncements of the magisterium in light of the total theological data operative in each question or statement. They go so far as to urge Catholics to rely on their individual consciences to decide whether or not to use artificial contraception.[18]

Most central for my argument, however, is their general claim about the inadequacy of the natural law concept the pope uses in HV. For these theologians, the term "natural law" functions as a placeholder for human dominion over nature. They identify the inadequacy as a failure to attend to "the multiple forms of natural law." Later, they state their concern more directly when they accuse the encyclical of overemphasizing "the biological aspects of conjugal relations as ethically normative" (para. 136). They are referring here to the way Pope Paul VI derives ethical norms from perceived biological realities. The following passage from HV best exemplifies that point: "Indeed, it is by its intimate structure, the conjugal act, while most closely uniting husband and wife, capacitates them for the generation of new lives, according to laws inscribed in the very being of man and woman" (para. 12). These laws that are inscribed into the very being of man and woman entail a particular type of structure which unites the couple (presumably at an emotional level), but it is also fundamentally biological insofar as it leads to the creation of a new life. In the church's view, when reasonable humans observe this biological structure, they can reach no other conclusion but that the unity brought about by the sexual act is only legitimate if the biological purpose is preserved. The use of contraceptive methods thwarts this purpose and is thus an example of inappropriate human dominion over nature.

Not all theologians and clerics dissented from the papal promulgation. One of its most prominent champions was John Paul II, who as both theologian and pope sought to deepen and extend the Catholic opposition to contraception, a teaching that he referred to as "always old yet always new."[19] He did so in ways that draw on the importance of the worry about human dominion and nature. In various of his writings, he tethers the argument to different sets of orienting points; for example, the dignity of the human person and the full, reciprocal self-giving that constitutes the marital relationship and the sexual act. Nevertheless, he too draws on the language of dominion over nature to argue against the use of artificial contraception. He begins by positing the important theological belief that when humans transmit "the gift of human life," they do so in an act of ultimate cooperation with God, the creator.[20] Contemporary culture has lost track of this truth and has embraced a very different mentality. It is one that is driven by the promise of technological and scientific progress whereby "man is continually expanding in his dominion over nature." He acknowledges that this progress can be driven by good intentions such as the betterment of humanity, but it can also lead to a kind of despair and hopelessness. An absolute belief in the promise of technology also leads humans to place spiritual dimensions as secondary to the material, mostly because they are "imprisoned in a consumer mentality."[21] Those who are more advantaged hoard technology greedily, and end up imposing contraception (or sterilization or abortion) on others against their wills.

His bottom line Is that this expansion of dominion over nature leads to the "absence in people's hearts of God," which in turn leads to an anti-life mentality. The pursuit of technology, on this view, is like an insatiable hunger. Dominion over nature does not give humans more security; indeed, it has the opposite effect. It leads to insecurity, fear, and panic. When speaking of technology in the context of human sexuality, the tone is one of caution. In other contexts, however, he embraces technology more readily. For example, in *Laborem exercens* (LE), his encyclical letter on the meaning of work, he writes, "technology is undoubtedly man's ally" and it is "a historical confirmation of man's dominion over nature."[22] He builds his definition of work around the Genesis passage "Be fruitful and multiply, and fill the earth and subdue it." He emphasizes that this passage can only be understood in the context of the earlier Genesis passage indicating that God created "man" in his image "male and female." He writes, "Man is the image of God partly through the mandate received from his creator to subdue, to dominate, the earth. In carrying out this mandate, man, every human being, reflects the very action of the creator of the universe."[23] This claim is interesting insofar as it draws a close connection between the biological reality of gender identity and dominion. Moreover, work and family are naturally connected on his view. Work enables man to found and support a family. Work is also connected to the Genesis passages mentioned above in significant ways. God places the material resources of the earth at man's disposal and it is through work that man can transform these resources (make them bear fruit): "He takes over all these things by making them his workbench. He takes them over through work and for work."[24] All human work presupposes the gifts of creation.

The more interesting and unique part of his argument about contraception, however, is the way he articulates a pronounced difference between artificial contraception and natural family planning. He appeals to the abuse of human dominion to make his case. Those who use artificial contraception act as "'arbiters' of the divine plan" and abuse their dominion over their bodies; whereas those who limit family size by "recourse to periods of infertility" act as "'ministers' of God's plan." He explains the difference in more explicit terms when he describes natural family planning as a practice that is attuned to the natural rhythms of the female cycle. Working with the cycle is, in John Paul's view, a way to respect and value the body, and to practice self-control. It also ensures that sexuality is not viewed as an object. Acceptance of the natural cycle of the woman's body also expresses an acceptance of other interpersonal features: "dialogue, reciprocal respect, shared responsibility."[25] In other places, John Paul elaborates on the distinction between natural and artificial contraception in slightly different ways. Writing in the early 1960s as Karol Wojtyla, he takes up the question of whether or not there is a difference between the natural and the artificial methods of birth control. He asks, "Why should the natural method be morally superior to the artificial methods, since the purpose is the same in each case—to eliminate the possibility of procreation from sexual intercourse?"[26] He proceeds to argue that the natural method is superior because it "seeks to regulate conception by taking advantage of circumstances in which conception cannot occur for biological reasons." By contrast, artificial methods "destroy the naturalness of sexual intercourse" because infertility is "imposed in defiance of nature."[27] This stark contrast between the artificial and the natural is deeply connected to his ideas about the human relationship to the natural. Indeed, he states quite clearly, "there is a close connection between the biology and the morality of reproduction in conjugal life."[28] This connection exists because in the act of sexual intercourse, humans "enter[s] so deeply into the natural order"—they immerse themselves in its "elemental processes." The danger of this immersion is that humans can forget their personhood. They forget that although they are biological beings who are a part of nature, they are decision-making creatures who use reason to exercise love and responsibility.[29]

John Paul II's most eloquent and impassioned defense of the "natural" is seen in his encyclical letter *Evangelium vitae*. He diagnoses the root cause of the ills of modern culture as a turning away from God and a rejection of the transcendent. Without God as reference point, all else loses meaning—"everything else becomes profoundly distorted."[30] Modernity has reduced nature and the body to objects of manipulation without due attention to their transcendent dimension. He writes, "This is the direction in which a certain technical and scientific way of thinking, prevalent in present-day culture, appears to be leading when it rejects the very idea that there is a truth of creation which must be acknowledged or a plan of God for life which must be respected."[31] This is relevant to the Church's position about contraception because here we see how central procreation is to this divine plan. More importantly, though, is the connection the pope draws between rejecting the divine plan and embracing materialism, which devolves into "efficiency, functionality and usefulness."[32]

Later in the encyclical, the pope once again invokes the Genesis 1:28 passage where God grants dominion over nature to humans. He emphasizes that the dominion is not absolute; God placed limitations on humans. As John Paul II describes it, "When it comes to the natural world, we are subject not only to biological laws but also to moral ones, which cannot be violated with impunity."[33] We see echoed here the same worry expressed by Paul VI in *Humanae vitae*—that humans often fail to recognize the precise nature of their dominion. It is a dominion that is about responsibility rather than control. In EV, dominion is the foundation of love and respect for human dignity.

Thus far I have described the Catholic position against contraception and argued that the hermeneutical key for understanding this position is human dominion over nature. I did so by narrating *Humanae vitae*'s argument as primarily one that emerges out of deep anxieties about the human relationship to nature, and then by showing how two types of responses—one dissenting, and one supportive—show similar anxieties. I also attempted to argue that the lens of human dominion over nature highlights the theological implications of the Catholic view. It brings to the fore the epistemological overconfidence in human capacity. In what remains, I demonstrate how this hermeneutical key can be helpful both in terms of understanding the Catholic view and thinking about how to engage with it in practical contexts related to health care delivery and public health policy.

Practical Considerations

The primary focus of the Catholic Church's writings about contraception has been its use in the context of marriage as a way to manage family size. As we have seen, the Church accepts the principle of family planning, but rejects the use of so-called artificial means for achieving that end. In recent years, the question of contraceptive devices as a means of protection in medical or "medicalized" circumstances has emerged, and while it doesn't necessarily challenge the logic of the Catholic argument against contraception, it both raises questions about the argument based on dominion, and highlights some of its limitations.

Human medical interventions are driven by a belief that humans can and may exercise some dominion over nature. Illness and disease can be overcome by human ingenuity. In other words, nature is not a force that humans can never tamper with. Humans are able, and indeed encouraged, to manipulate nature to advance their own and their community's good. A central issue with contraception is that it is an intervention that is medicalized in a very particular kind of way. Most uses of contraception are not medically indicated—that is they are not necessary for the physical health and well-being of the person using them. Of course, a broad understanding of health that includes mental health could certainly encompass these concerns. As stated in the discussion of HV, Pope Paul VI did allow for the use of contraceptives that would regulate women's menstrual cycles for medical purposes, not as a way to prohibit conception.

It appears, then, that looking at cases where contraception has direct and obvious medical benefits affords us a way to apply insights about nature and dominion. The most prominent examples include using barrier methods to prevent the spread of sexually transmitted diseases. The Catholic Church's response to the HIV/AIDS epidemic and the recent outbreak of the Zika virus highlight this issue.

The most recent evidence of the continuing contestation of Catholic views about contraception involved the response of Pope Francis to directives from the World Health Organization that were warning couples to avoid conceiving for a set period of time to ensure that newborns would not suffer from the damaging effects of the Zika virus. In 2015, reports from Brazil indicated that the Zika virus was causing microcephaly in the fetuses of pregnant women infected with Zika. In this context, where the threat to humans is coming directly from the natural world via a mosquito, public health experts were urging couples to deliberately prevent conception as a way to protect potential fetuses from debilitating deformities. Moreover, it was discovered that in addition to transmission through the *Aedes* genus of the mosquito, sexual transmission was also possible. Thus, the use of condoms was being urged both to prevent the spread of Zika and to prevent pregnancies in women who might have been exposed to the virus.

Pope Francis made headlines when he was asked to comment on whether abortion could be considered a "lesser evil" when used to protect an unborn child from the dangers of Zika. The pope responded that abortion is never a "lesser evil"—it is always an "absolute evil" that allows for no exception. He contrasted abortion with contraception and suggested that there was a precedent in Catholic moral theology to support the view that the use of contraception to prevent pregnancy is not an "absolute evil" but a "lesser evil." He referred to an alleged case in the 1960s when moralists debated whether nuns who were under the threat of rape in the Belgian Congo might be allowed to use contraception to avoid pregnancy. In his brief comments, Pope Francis suggested that Pope Paul VI had sanctioned a particular use of this "lesser evil."[34] There has not been any further elaboration of the Church's teaching on this matter since Francis's 2016 mid-air comments.

In a similar way, Pope Benedict XVI had also signaled what appeared to be some acceptance of the use of condoms as a way to prevent the transmission of HIV/AIDS. In this case, Benedict invoked theological language about sin and portrayed the use of condoms as a lesser of two evils in this very particular circumstance.[35] Here again, as with the case of Pope Francis, the initial sense that a shift in teaching might be occurring was quickly overridden by the Vatican's assurances that the teaching was immutable and unchanging.

Conclusion

What are scholars to make of this apparent tension between the Catholic idea that moral laws are immutable and the recent messages of greater receptivity to particular circumstances uttered by popes? What I have tried to argue in this paper is that the teaching about contraception remains unchanged because of its reliance on particular attitudes about human control over nature that end up overemphasizing a divide between the natural and the artificial. That control is especially evident in the Catholic teaching about gender as a biological concept and about gender roles as existing in complementary relationship. Hence, a change on contraception requires a rethinking of Catholic views about gender and sexuality more generally. The Catholic leadership teaches that male and female exist in a relationship of complementarity—a relationship where each party is equal, but with each gender having specific roles and attributes that are embedded in biological and natural realities. The Church views complementarity as part of the natural, created order, and thus any attempt to subvert gender roles is an instance of human manipulation of nature. On this view, gender complementarity is subverted any time men and women stray from their assigned roles. Complementarity also applies to the sexual act. Any sexual act that occurs outside of a marriage between a man and woman "contradicts the nature of both man and woman and of their most intimate relationship, and therefore . . . contradict(s) also the plan of God and His will."[36] Translated to the context of contraception, this means that when men and women choose to plan or avoid a pregnancy by using artificial means, they interfere with biology and exert an improper dominance over nature.

The Catholic worry about artificial contraception is a worry about the limits of human dominion over nature. Humans must respect the natural order because to do so is to remain faithful to God's design. In the context of gender and sexuality, this view rejects common assumptions about the easy interplay between the natural and the cultural. It is for this reason that teaching authorities of the Church resist loosening the prohibition on artificial contraception. From their perspective, the stakes are much too high.

Notes

1. *Griswold v. Connecticut*, 381 U.S. 479 (1965).
2. Ibid.
3. *Eisenstadt v. Baird*, 405 U.S. 438 (1972).
4. Ibid.
5. The legal foundation of these decisions was brought into question by the June 2022 Supreme Court decision, *Dobbs v. Jackson Women's Health Organization*. That decision overruled *Roe v. Wade* and *Planned Parenthood of Southeastern Pa. v. Casey*, the decisions that had guaranteed women's rights to abortion for almost fifty years. The opinion of the court on *Dobbs* clearly linked it to *Griswold* and *Eisenstadt*. As Justices Breyer, Sotomayor, and Kagan write in their dissent, "The right *Roe* and *Casey* recognized does not stand alone. To the contrary, the Court has linked it for decades to other settled freedoms involving bodily integrity, familial relationships, and procreation. Most obviously, the right to terminate a pregnancy arose straight out of the right to purchase and use contraception." (*Dobbs v. Jackson Women's Health Organization*, 4).
6. John Noonan, *Contraception: A History of Its Treatment by the Catholic Theologians and Canonists* (Cambridge, MA: Harvard University Press, 1965), 490.
7. See Mark Jordan's discussion of this in *The Ethics of Sex* (Oxford: Blackwell, 2002), 138–142.
8. Pius XII.
9. Jordan sees this as a sign of how little power the churches actually have over the sexual activities of their followers (Jordan, *The Ethics of Sex*, 139).
10. Pope Francis, *Amoris Letitia*.
11. Lawler and Salzman, "Following Faithfully: The Catholic Way to Choose the Good," *America* 212, no. 3 (February 2, 2015).
12. Kaiser, McClory, Kalbian, and others.
13. See Miller and Kalbian for examples of an emphasis on gender.
14. See especially John Paul II's *Theology of the Body*.

15. *Veritatis splendor* makes this point.
16. *Natural family planning* is a term that describes periodic abstinence to avoid pregnancy (Salzman and Lawler, *The Sexual Person*, 69).
17. See *Theology of the Body* for a detailed discussion of this idea. Also, see par. 13, *Humanae vitae*.
18. "Statement by Catholic Theologians Washington, D.C., July 30, 1968," in *Readings in Moral Theology, No. 8: Dialogue About Catholic Sexual Teaching*, ed. Charles E. Curran and Richard A. McCormick, S.J. (New York: Paulist Press, 1993), 135–137.
19. John Paul II, *Familiaris consortio*, 29.
20. John Paul II, *Familiaris consortio*, 28; *Evangelium vitae*, 43.
21. John Paul II, *Familiaris consortio*, 30.
22. John Paul II, *Laborem exercens*, 5.
23. Ibid., 4.
24. Ibid., 12.
25. John Paul II, *Familiaris consortio*, 32.
26. Wojtyla, *Love and Responsibility*, 240.
27. Ibid., 241.
28. Ibid., 235.
29. Ibid., 236.
30. John Paul II, *Evangelium vitae*, 22.
31. Ibid.
32. Ibid., 23.
33. Ibid., 42.
34. Pope Francis, "In-Flight Press Conference of His Holiness Pope Francis from Mexico to Rome," Wednesday, 17 February 2016. https://www.vatican.va/content/francesco/en/speeches/2016/february/documents/papa-francesco_20160217_messico-conferenza-stampa.html.
35. Benedict XVI, *Light of the World: The Pope, the Church, and the Signs of the Times - A Conversation with Peter Seewald* (San Francisco: Ignatius Press, 2010), 119.
36. Ibid., *Humanae vitae*, 13.

Bibliography

Benedict XVI, Pope. *Light of the World: The Pope, the Church, and the Signs of the Times; A Conversation with Peter Seewald*. San Francisco: Ignatius Press, 2010.
Dobbs v. Jackson Women's Health Organization, U.S. 597 (Breyer, Sotomayor, and Kagan, J.J., dissenting), 2022.
Eisenstadt v. Baird, 405 U.S. 438 (1972).
Francis, Pope. *Amoris laetitia*. 2015.
Griswold v. Connecticut, 381 U.S. 479 (1965).
John Paul II, Pope. *Evangelium vitae*. New York: Random House, 1995.
John Paul II, Pope. *Familiaris consortio*, 1981.
John Paul II, Pope. *Laborem exercens*, 1981.
John Paul II, Pope. *The Theology of the Body: Human Love in the Divine Plan*. Boston: Pauline Books and Media, 1997.
John Paul II, Pope. *Veritatis splendor*. 1993.

Jordan, Mark. *The Ethics of Sex*. Malden, MA: Blackwell Publishing, 2002.

Kaiser, Robert Blair. *The Politics of Sex and Religion: A Case History in the Development of Doctrine, 1962–1984*. New York: Sheed and Ward, 1985.

Kalbian, Aline H. *Sex, Violence, and Justice: Contraception and Catholicism*. Washington, DC: Georgetown University Press: 2014.

McClory, Robert. *Turning Point: The Inside Story of the Papal Birth Control Commission, and How* Humanae vitae *Changed the Life of Patty Crowley and the Future of the Church*. New York: Crossroad, 1995.

Miller, Richard. *Casuistry and Modern Ethics: A Poetics of Practical Reasoning*. Chicago: University of Chicago Press, 1993.

Noonan, John T. *Contraception: A History of Its Treatment by the Catholic Theologians and Canonists*. Cambridge, MA: Harvard University Press, 1966.

Paul VI, Pope. *Humanae vitae*. 1968.

Salzman, Todd, and Michael Lawler. "Following Faithfully: The Catholic Way to Choose the Good." *America* 212, no. 3 (February 3, 2015).

Salzman, Todd, and Michael Lawler. *The Sexual Person: Toward a Renewed Catholic Anthropology*. Washington, DC: Georgetown University Press, 2008.

Weinberg, Tessa. "Before the Spread of the Zika Virus, the Vatican Allowed Contraceptive Use in Limited Situations." *Los Angeles Times*, July 16, 2016.

Wojtyla, Karol (Pope John Paul II). *Love and Responsibility*, rev. ed. San Francisco: Ignatius Press, 1993.

CHAPTER 20

CONTRACEPTION
Protestant Evangelical Perspectives

DAVID B. FLETCHER

WHAT do evangelicals believe about the moral acceptability of contraception? Other church groups might have clearly defined beliefs about this matter, whether or not their laity always truly believes in and follows them. Evangelicals, unlike Roman Catholics, do not share a teaching office of the church, nor are there authority structures to commend teachings to the faithful. There is no office that would be accepted as legislator over controversial moral or theological questions across the evangelical movement. Evangelicals belong to a wide variety of denominations and nondenominational churches, some of which offer teachings to members of that group, but there is no official "evangelical view" on questions of personal or social morality. This is as true of global evangelicalism as it is of the movement in the United States. However, the bioethical views of many American evangelicals are expressed by organizations such as the National Association of Evangelicals, the Christian Medical and Dental Society, and other organizations that span denominational divides. Because none of the deliberations of these organizations are binding on those who think of themselves as evangelical, we can at best discern major streams of evangelical thought through the expressed views of such groups when they speak on such matters. Individual evangelical ethicists also write on a variety of ethical topics, often published by evangelical publishing houses, and these writings are intended not merely to express the authors' own evangelical convictions but to commend their conclusions to other evangelicals.

Until recently evangelicals have moved with the general society in accepting contraception morally, although this position is being challenged in many quarters for a variety of reasons. Evangelicals who accept contraception nearly always insist that sex, reproduction, and family planning are reserved for married heterosexual couples only.[1] Evangelicals also typically believe that marriage should be fruitful in reproduction, they accept the permissibility of sexually active married couples delaying reproduction for family planning purposes, and they assert the sovereignty of God over human reproduction.

Evangelicals today generally accept the "pro-life" or anti-abortion view to be all but definitive of Christian orthodoxy. According to that view, the worth of the life of the fertilized ovum is that of a human being and the embryo shares in the sanctity and inviolability of human life. Thus, reproductive techniques will be tested by the standard of whether they protect the embryo or subject it to danger and death. Most evangelicals will evaluate contraceptive techniques based on whether they believe they prevent fertilization or rather jeopardize or harm the human embryo. They will find themselves able to accept contraception within marriage when they are convinced that the method of contraception is not what they might consider "abortifacient," that is, preventing the embryo from implantation.

Evangelical views of contraception vary widely. We will review the positions from the most permissive to the most conservative, taking note of the reasons offered for each position. We will take note of the recent revolt, widely covered in news media, among evangelical institutions from the federal contraception mandate that was included in the Affordable Care Act and the specific forms of contraception that these institutions found problematic.

1. *Strong Acceptance.* While the strong acceptance view is no doubt a minority viewpoint in published writings, it has been commended in the mainstream evangelical magazine *Christianity Today* by Jenell Paris, professor of anthropology and sociology at Messiah College. Paris highlights the failure of evangelical abstinence-only moral teaching on sex for singles. Having been a participant in a Q Conference held in Washington, DC in 2012 in a discussion of abortions among those within the church, she gained insight into current beliefs and practices of younger single evangelicals. At the conference, a poll was taken of the young attendees with the question, "Do you believe churches should advocate contraception for their single twentysomethings?" Perhaps surprisingly, 70 percent agreed.[2] She observes that "4 out of 5 Christians aged 18–29 have had sex, many within the last year,"[3] implying though not explicitly stating that these are unmarried. This is comparable to the findings of Rachel K. Jones and Joerg Dreweke, who find that 75 percent of never-married young adult evangelical women have had sex, shockingly high to evangelicals, although it is a lower number than for Roman Catholics and mainline Protestants.[4] They also find that for those evangelical women who have not had sex, religious and moral reasons predominate in influencing their decisions.

As shocking as the statistic of sexual experience may be to evangelicals, she also notes even more disturbingly that "about 1 in 3 unplanned pregnancies among evangelicals end in abortion," despite the fervent opposition to abortion in evangelical churches. Paris laments that the reality among younger evangelicals is that they are *not* "just not doing it," and their activity can have severe consequences.

In light of this reality, she advocates that "churches take a both-and approach to abortion reduction: both uphold premarital chastity as the Biblical ideal, and encourage and educate unmarried singles about the effective use of contraception."[5] Paris presumably accepts contraception for married couples, which is consistent with the mainstream view, but what makes her position daring among evangelicals is that she is even willing to countenance its use among single Christians, advisable in light of their actual sexual activity, notwithstanding the teachings about abstinence to which they are exposed in the church setting.

In light of the stark reality of single Christian sexual activity, Paris advocates a "compromise" in ministry with Christian singles, advocating contraception for those who will miss the mark of celibate abstinence, all the while maintaining the ideal of chastity in the church. While Paris by no means endorses sexual activity among singles, she wishes for singles to find in the church to be a place of a love that might well lead to repentance. "Right loving—full of compromise, compassion, and companionship—is the best encouragement for right living."

It would be surprising if the Strong Acceptance view did not meet with firm resistance by many other evangelicals, and in fact, it does. Matthew Lee Anderson, in an article offered as a direct counterpoint to Paris, expresses his own concern for the abortions that seem to happen in the midst of the church and for those who have those abortions. He admits that "advocating for contraception for sexually active single people in our churches . . . may temporarily reduce abortions," but at the same time it would "further engrain into our communities the broken understanding of sex and community that is at the heart of our predicament."[6] He sees offering contraception as "little more than a tacit rejection of the power of the gospel to transform lives and bring people to a repentance that is genuine and genuinely holistic," reinforcing their "infantile faith." Much as the church needs to reduce abortions, "We are not called to reduce abortions by any and every means available to us." Anderson wants the church to "call people to repentance for our sins and exhort us toward the holiness that ought to mark us off as the people of God."

The idea of "both chastity and contraception" is not a "sacred compromise." "It is a scandalous capitulation to the unfettered sexual mores of twenty-first century American society," according to Trevin Wax in a vigorous attack of this position. While it tries to "maintain the 'ideal' of chastity in singleness alongside the 'compromise' of contraception," it is unsuccessful in Wax's view.[7] Rather, he says, "it devalues the struggle to remain chaste while legitimizing sexual expression among Christian singles as something unavoidable." To him, this is a "gospel-denying" position. Wax confesses to being "flabbergasted that evangelicalism has come to the place where such a scandalous capitulation to a sexualized culture could be considered a 'sacred compromise.'" He agrees with author Matthew Lee Anderson that contraception for unmarried evangelicals is a "pragmatic concession" that "actually contributes to the conditions where Christians can sin without consequences for themselves or their community."

Neither Anderson nor Wax fully addresses address Paris's concern, however, that unmarried evangelicals are in fact sexually active and having unplanned pregnancies. Anderson seems to think that it is better to accept that some abortions will occur than to accept contraception for the unmarried when he opposes contraception that he admits would "temporarily reduce abortions." Wax argues that "telling singles they ought to turn toward Jesus and contraception is an implicit denial that repentance is integral to the Christian life. It's like Jesus telling the woman caught in adultery: 'Neither do I condemn you. Go and sin some more.'" Like Wax, Anderson's sole advice is to preach "repentance," which they believe Paris's view fails to do with conviction.

To be sure, Paris certainly rejects the idea that sex before marriage is acceptable for the Christian, as her article makes clear. There may well be those even in the evangelical camp who advocate contraception based on the belief that traditional Christian sexual morality is outdated, overly legalistic, or constraining, and an obstacle to reaching young singles with the Gospel. Paris advocates no such position and no less than her critics, clearly believes that premarital sexual activity is sinful and demands repentance. However she is attentive to the ecclesial context for receiving and acknowledging that repentance; it must be within a community that welcomes and upholds repentant sexual sinners rather than shuns and shames them. Paris as well as Anderson bemoan that the current church environment is lacking in its ability to minister to sexual sins. With her apprehension about the actual state of the facts of evangelical sexual practice, Paris is quite concerned about consequences that may severely impact lives and she seeks a solution that is practical while maintaining the strong commitment to proper sexual behavior. Her "both-and approach to abortion reduction" still maintains chastity as the Biblical ideal, but recognizes that there are those who will need to be encouraged and educated "about the effective use of contraception. Encouraging, not pushing. Educating, not affirming."

Anderson raises an interesting question about what it is that churches are actually being asked to do in this "sacred compromise." The poll referred to earlier from the Q conference asked, "Do you believe churches should advocate contraception for their single twentysomethings?" Anderson then asks, "Advocate how? From the pulpit? Which twentysomethings? All of them?" The questions I believe Anderson is asking can be developed further. What exactly would be expected of churches when they are asked to "advocate contraception for young Christian singles"? What it is to "advocate contraception," or to "educate" about it? I doubt that contraception would be addressed in sermons. Neither would it be somehow prescribed for all evangelical singles. It seems most reasonable to construe "advocacy" as permission to address issues of contraception in the pastoral context, in one-on-one conversations between a minister and a single, sexually active parishioner. In all likelihood, that parishioner is uncomfortable with his or her sexual practice to a greater or lesser degree in light of his or her religious convictions. Personal, pastoral counsel that a minister might offer such a parishioner might not be the sort of thing that is spoken about in meetings of the entire church. It is possible to imagine a minister recommending contraception to this particular evangelical single person in his or her particular life situation.

But what is envisioned as "educating" about contraception? It seems unlikely in the twenty-first century that ignorance of contraception among twenty-somethings would be common. Those parishioners who received public school education would surely, by their twenties and early thirties, understand the various methods of contraception and would know how to access them. That is no doubt true in the suburban, perhaps urban, population that seems to be presupposed by these writers. Employed women would normally be offered medical coverage for such care in their employer-sponsored insurance plans. There would surely be no need for group instruction about the methods of contraception that are available. Pastoral counseling about methods of contraception would probably build upon that knowledge in helping the parishioner to determine which method would be most suitable.

Although the Strong Acceptance view will meet with vigorous theological resistance in the evangelical world, it remains true that despite church teaching, young evangelicals are having sex, dealing with pregnancy, abortion, and sexual diseases. I suspect that this view is held more widely than is publicly acknowledged in the evangelical community.

2. *Covenantal Acceptance.* We might give this name to the mainstream, traditional understanding, as seen in the statement of the National Association of Evangelicals:

> Sex is by nature procreative, and children should be recognized as a blessing from the Lord (see Psalm 127). This does not mean that a couple must intend with every sexual act to have children. From the beginning, God established multiple purposes for sex and granted humans a stewardship role over his creation, so there is legitimacy (sic) in family planning and the use of ethical means of contraception.[8]

The NAE recognizes that there are "four primary reasons for sexual intimacy: 1. God gives us sex as a one-flesh union that consummates a marriage. 2. God gives us sex for procreation. 3. God gives us sex as a way to express love to our spouse in the covenant relationship of marriage. 4. God gives us sex for enjoyment and pleasure." Evangelicals in this camp would agree with this statement by Stanton Jones of Wheaton College,

> I embrace the view that a marital sexual relationship should have life-giving potential; something is relationally and morally off-target if there is not openness toward producing children. Nevertheless, there is nothing wrong with the use of morally acceptable and effective methods that prevent conception in order to temporarily prohibit the possibility of getting pregnant.[9]

A relatively early statement of this position was offered by the evangelical professional organization, the Christian Medical Society, with the title, "A Protestant Affirmation on the Control of Human Reproduction."[10] This statement emerged from a 1970 conference including physicians, theologians, and other scholars. The CMS states, "The prevention of conception is not in itself forbidden or sinful providing the reasons for it are in harmony with the total revelation of God for married life." They mention a variety of considerations that must be included when contemplating contraception use, including "disease, psychological debility, the number of children already in the family, and financial capability," which are "among the factors determining whether pregnancy should be prevented." The CMS believes that the acceptable methods of contraception are determined medically rather than theologically. Apparently any of the available contraceptive methods are acceptable theologically and morally. The physician is counseled to recognize that "the partners in marriage should have the privilege of determining the number of children they wish to have in their family. The physician should cooperate by providing counselling, taking into consideration both medical and moral factors." There are a variety of contraceptive methods available, but the document notes without evident disapproval that "in some countries, the intrauterine device (IUD) is expected to be the contraceptive method of choice for some time."

The Covenantal Acceptance view is the de facto position of evangelicals at large. In 2010, the National Association of Evangelicals cited polls of evangelical leaders and found them "overwhelmingly open to artificial methods of contraception." The Evangelical Leaders Survey found that approval was nearly 90 percent of respondents. They also reported on a survey conducted by the NAE in partnership with Gallup, Inc., that showed that "90/91 percent of evangelicals find hormonal/barrier methods of contraception to be morally acceptable for adults."[11] They also noted that a number of leaders coupled their acceptance of contraception with a strong objection to abortion. In the pews, studies suggest that 74 percent of evangelicals rely on what the Guttmacher Institute refers to as "highly effective methods" of contraception, including "sterilization, the pill, or the IUD." Of all religious groups studied, at 40 percent, evangelicals rely on sterilization most frequently.[12]

Evangelical theologian and ethicist Dennis P. Hollinger notes that up until the 1930s evangelicals and other Protestants disapproved of contraception, although it was "not paramount in their thought," but came to accept it after it was approved by the Lambeth Conference of the Anglican Communion. The arrival of the Pill, an oral contraceptive with a high degree of effectiveness, made the change complete.[13] What he finds significant "about this change is not that it happened, but that there was so little theological reflection in the process." This lack of reflection is often seized upon by evangelical foes of contraception as an indication that it should not have been accepted at that time. Nonetheless, Hollinger believes that evangelicals were correct in accepting contraception for use by married couples in planning their families. He claims, "that it is possible to give a defense of family planning using contraceptive devices if those devices are not intrinsically immoral." The "two theological constructs that are most significant in the debate" are "our understanding of human stewardship in relationship to divine Providence (especially as it relates to nature), and our understanding of the meaning and purposes of sex." Stewardship, given to humans at creation, includes careful husbandry of our reproductive potential. "We can utilize non-natural means of contraception to work with nature just as we steward many dimensions of natural life through technology and human knowledge."

Sex, Hollinger tells us, has multiple functions in marriage. First, it is a "one flesh" consummation of marriage. Hollinger describes this in metaphysical terms. "Something ontological happens to the man and the woman and they are never the same again through their physical union." Second is procreation, the carrying on of humanity into the next generation. Third is to express love in a physical way, expressed clearly in the Song of Solomon. Fourth is pleasure, a good gift of God to be enjoyed in the marital context. He notes that God has endowed the sexes with organs that serve no function but pleasure, such as the clitoris and the glans penis. Hollinger believes that only in marriage can the four purposes of sex be realized. Nature places limits on the reproductive potential of sexual intercourse, since conception has a small window of time in the monthly cycle, and many individuals either never had or have lost their ability to reproduce but can still enjoy sexual union. Stewardship allows us to further limit conception within marriage for the good of the family. With this theological grounding, the Covenantal Acceptance group can comfortably accept contraception, at least within marriage.

Another statement of the Covenantal Acceptance view is offered by John S. Feinberg and Paul D. Feinberg. John and Paul Feinberg offer a careful and vigorous defense of contraception for Christian couples. They assert, "We believe contraception is morally permissible, though not all forms of birth control can be justified,"[14] They would exclude "any birth control method that is equivalent to abortion," and cite the IUD as an example of this.[15] With this caveat, they proclaim that "In sum, nothing Scriptural or otherwise prohibits all forms of birth control."[16]

Feinberg and Feinberg recognize that contraception is important for women to achieve their life goals in addition to motherhood. They note with no evident disapproval that "increasingly, women have found great fulfillment in careers outside the home" and recognize that many women are "very competent" and want to "make a mark," and also that "many of these women want to have children and raise a family." The solution of course is to postpone childbearing. The authors assert that abstinence is "contrary to Scripture and cannot be a morally justifiable means of continuous birth control."[17]

Since contraception is necessary for women to achieve the full range of their goals, a supportive theological rationale is necessary. After reviewing arguments against birth control, Feinberg and Feinberg assert, "We think there are stronger arguments favoring birth control."[18] They list six Scriptural purposes for sex within marriage, more than other writers: procreation, companionship, unity, pleasure (citing Ecclesiastes 9:9, "Enjoy life with the wife that you love"), to raise up a godly seed, and to curb fornication and adultery. "In order to avoid pregnancy while fulfilling one of the other purposes, a birth control device may be necessary. Given the many purposes of marital sex," and abstinence is unacceptable, "that seems morally permissible."[19]

Feinberg and Feinberg steadfastly refuse to allow the abuse of contraception to disallow its appropriate use, and they counter arguments based on negative social consequences that have followed the introduction of contraceptive methods. They also note that as some couples may be at risk of passing on genetically transmitted diseases, and since birth control is not forbidden, those couples are allowed to forgo reproduction altogether to avoid transmitting these diseases.[20]

Covenantal Acceptance evangelicals are concerned that some methods of contraception might prevent pregnancy but not fertilization. Jay Barnes of Bethel University says that contraception is acceptable for Christians to use under a set of conditions, one of which is that "the method prevents fertilization rather than implantation."[21] However, even the staunchly conservative evangelical group, Focus on the Family, in answer to a question about contraception in marriage, acknowledges questions about the potential of some methods to allow fertilization yet nevertheless does not offer a strict condemnation. It simply advises, "We would suggest that contraception is an issue that should be approached with generous amounts of prayer and plenty of wise counsel from friends, parents, older adults, pastors, and trusted medical professionals."[22]

3. *Conditional Covenantal Acceptance.* While all evangelicals writing on contraception are careful to avoid permitting methods that they fear might "cause abortions," some are modifying their covenantal stance to object more strenuously to certain forms of birth control, even among married couples. I will call this Conditional Covenantal Acceptance. This is a departure from the Christian Medical Society's position of 1970, that did not differentiate morally between types of contraception and that accepted the IUD. They differ from Covenantal Acceptance not in principle, since both reject methods that might prevent fertilized ovum from survival, but in degree, first of all, because of their relatively stronger concern and emphasis on this risk. Second, they more vigilantly police contraceptive methods that are widely accepted, looking for any possibility that they might function in this way.

Evangelicals as well as the general public have no doubt been surprised at the phenomenon of evangelical leaders joining forces with Roman Catholics in opposition to contraception. Jacob Lupfer says, "Evangelical leaders are tripping over themselves in the rush to stand with Roman Catholic bishops."[23] "Most associate evangelicals with Catholics in their steady leadership in pro-life advocacy, and rightly so," said Leith Anderson, president of the NAE. "But it may come as a surprise that unlike the Catholic church, we are open to contraception."[24]

Since evangelicals and Roman Catholics traditionally have had little in common, this event demands explanation. A recent development has moved many evangelicals toward a more conservative position, one that objects to some common methods of birth control that have not concerned them in the past. Along with Roman Catholics whose long-standing opposition to contraception are well known, many evangelicals have recoiled against the Patient Protection and Affordable Care Act of 2010. This act famously makes health insurance coverage available to previously uninsured patients and has been credited with adding 24 million people to the insured,[25] adding immensely to their well-being. Among its various provisions, the Act followed the recommendations of the Institute of Medicine to provide all medically available contraception to insured women at no cost to them. This might have been expected to disturb evangelicals, as it did not differentiate between married and unmarried women in who would receive the contraceptives, but surprisingly there is scant evidence of an evangelical reaction to this aspect of the mandate.

The concern among some prominent evangelicals is that some of the mandated contraceptive methods were incompatible with their view of the sanctity of life as found in the embryo. In particular, the morning-after pill, the hormone levonorgestrel, available in many brands including Plan B, along with ulipristal acetate, available as Ella, got their attention, because they believed that their mechanisms of operation were to prevent the implantation of the embryo already created by sexual intercourse rather than to prevent fertilization. In that respect they considered it an "abortifacient." A number of evangelical Christian colleges reacted strongly against the mandate that their employee insurance plans would have to offer such "abortifacients," in light of their view that life begins at conception. Evangelical colleges joined lawsuits pursued by the Roman Catholic group the Beckett Legal Fund against the Department of Health and Human Services brought by the University of Notre Dame, the Little Sisters of the Poor, and the evangelical-owned retail chain Hobby Lobby.

The argument offered by evangelicals and Roman Catholics was that it would be a violation of their exercise of religion if they were forced to participate in any way in providing the entire package of contraceptives to employees. Along the way as this struggle went along, these evangelicals came to classify the IUD as an abortifacient as well. After a number of legal battles and a change in presidential administrations, these institutions as well as Hobby Lobby obtained the relief that they had sought. The evangelicals among the litigants had won the right to withhold contraception altogether, but nonetheless continued to offer the contraceptives they deemed acceptable while refusing to be involved in any way in providing those they found objectionable.[26]

Are some contraceptive methods actually abortifacient? If there is a statistically tiny chance that a method might fail to prevent conception but instead interfere with implantation, should that method be thought of as abortifacient and therefore unacceptable? As the acceptance of the IUD, a form of long-term reversible birth control, by the Christian Medical Society indicates, evangelicals in the Covenantal camp traditionally have not had moral concerns with the use of that device. This attitude is now being challenged by those who support the Conditional Covenantal position, who appear to have a "zero tolerance" position regarding the possibility that a method might allow fertilization but prevent implantation. The key question for them is whether the IUD prevents fertilization or rather prevents implantation and the subsequent growth of the embryo. The Magee-Women's Hospital, University of Pittsburgh

School of Medicine, disputes what it calls "the mythological mechanism" that the IUD prevents fertilized eggs from implanting and cites research that shows "the IUD acts primarily as a contraceptive device by preventing fertilization. Copper-containing IUDs release free copper and copper salts.... The resulting changes in the intrauterine environment and cervical mucus act to immobilize sperm or prevent their migration to the fallopian tubes."[27] According to this medical group, there is evidence of fertilization in only 0.7 percent of women using a copper-containing IUD.

Even the slight, lower than one percent, chance that the IUD might prevent fertilized eggs from implanting seems to be a higher chance than Conditional Covenantal people are willing to accept. This is evidenced by this method being included in the evangelical colleges' lawsuit. Evangelicals judge contraception as acceptable for Christians to use if it prevents fertilization. While the IUD certainly does just that, Conditional Covenantal evangelicals argue that even the less than one percent chance that things are otherwise would exclude the IUD from acceptable use.

The zero tolerance view has the advantage of standing on a principle, but is it realistic? If an activity has a one percent chance of causing the death of an embryo, is it wrong to do that activity? Does a one percent chance that a method allows conception but prevents implantation, thereby leading to the death of the fertilized egg, make that method an abortifacient? Much could be said about this matter, but I will simply suggest that this shows a great deal concern for the one percent and completely disregards the fact that couples find contraception necessary for a number of important reasons, not least of which is the woman's career as well as her care for existing children.

The strongly risk-averse, zero tolerance attitude of the Conditionals bears a degree of scrutiny. First, the only way to ensure that one is not fertilizing ovum that might not survive is to avoid sexual intercourse entirely. This is so because of the high rate of fertilized eggs that will not implant and survive, even with no methods in place. The sad fact is that half of all fertilized eggs fail to implant.[28] It is unclear why it is acceptable for a couple to engage in unprotected intercourse leading to the loss of fertilized eggs, but not to have sex while using a birth control method that has a statistically small chance of losing the fertilized egg. A convincing argument for the difference is essential.

Do we insist on the zero tolerance policy toward risk in other areas of life? We find it acceptable regularly to run significant risks as we go about our lives, risks to ourselves and to others. It is reported that base jumping carries a one in 2,300 chance of dying, while driving 100 miles in a car imposes a risk of death of one in 877,000,[29] yet neither is regarded as immoral. One has a yearly risk of drowning in a pool at one in 450,511.[30] According to the Centers for Disease Control and Prevention, there is one crash-related pedestrian death every 1.5 hours in the United States, using 2016 figures. In fact, pedestrians are more likely to be killed in a car crash than vehicle occupants, one and a half times more.[31] Apparently in most areas of life we go about our business and attempt to meet our various obligations, despite the fact that we do impose risks of injury and death not merely on ourselves but on others.

The Opposition View. The Conditional Covenantal Acceptance view invites further abandonment of the traditional Covenantal Acceptance view, as some evangelicals move further away from approval of the methods of contraception advocated by that latter view. Let us call the view that emerges from this abandonment the Opposition View. Opposition View supporters object to contraception, even for married couples, for one or both of two reasons. One reason is their claim that the standard, acceptable methods of hormonal contraception and the IUD may in some cases be abortifacient in that statistically small range of cases. This leaves only a few contraceptives and Natural Family Planning, the so-called rhythm method. The other reason, and the one most at odds with the Covenantal Acceptance view, stems from moral objections to contraception in principle, as a violation of God's standards. It is here that the confluence of evangelical and Roman Catholic thinking about contraception is most evident and the reasons given by Opposition evangelicals borrow significantly from Roman Catholic thinking about contraception.

Opposition to contraception in principle, rather than for technical reasons having to do with implantation, was in fact evangelicals' past position, according to Allan C. Carlson. He argues that the history of the Church to the earliest times, and through the Reformation, demonstrates the complete rejection of contraception. Carlson outlines the theological objections to the practice as they developed over time. Carlson emphasizes with approval that nineteenth-century evangelicals strongly objected to contraception and attempted to control it through legislation. Carlson laments the changes as he outlines the fateful movement first within mainline Protestantism and then evangelical thought to approve of the practice, leading to today's quiet acceptance of contraception. He hopes that "the issue of birth control use by evangelicals may be opening up again in the first decades of this, the twenty-first Christian century. Indeed he has reason for hope, as the Oppositional View has been developed by a number of evangelical writers who break decisively with the Covenantal Acceptance position.

Bryan C. Hodge believes that the Church's historic opposition to contraception should incline today's evangelicals to reject the practice. Hodge does not exclude Natural Family Planning (NFP) from condemnation, seeing it as a method of contraception that is "contradictory to the historic Christian position."[32] Writers such as Hodge and Carlson cite the early Church's opposition to birth control appeal to history to make a normative point for evangelicals today.

This view is not unproblematic. For one, evangelicals seldom are convinced by arguments from Church tradition, insisting that traditional sources might have erred in light of Scriptural understanding. Another problem is that one must carefully assess the methods that were being considered historically, the philosophical assumptions made centuries ago, and the conditions of modern living. A Christian wife in the early centuries, probably employed in farming, might have had very different reasons for turning to birth control than one in the twenty-first century, who must balance postgraduate education, career, care and education needs of existing children, finances, and other concerns. It is far from obvious that early objections to contraception would sway evangelicals unless they recognize within it reasons that resonate with our Scriptural and theological understandings.

Christopher L. Penner and Joyce J. Penner respect the moral concerns faced by many evangelicals when considering contraception. They note, "Over the years, the Church has struggled with the issue of contraception. The concern has been that taking reproduction into our own hands is interfering with God's plan for our lives. In other words, we are in some way interrupting the work of the Creator.... Each of you must come to grips with the religious and moral issues of contraception, then the two of you must work through these issues together."[33] They seem to assume that the result of this process will be to approve contraception, because most of the book is a detailed discussion of all available contraceptive methods. They conclude that NFP, rather than an alternative to contraception, is in fact an attempt at contraception.

Sam Torode and Bethany Torode were young evangelical newlyweds who considered thoughtfully the purposes of sex in their marriage and began to question the acceptance of contraceptives that is prevalent among evangelical couples. They came to believe that an "open embrace" in sexual intercourse must not involve efforts to prevent conception. Borrowing heavily from the Roman Catholic version of natural law ethics, they concluded that there are three goods in marital sex: procreative, unitive, and sacramental. They viewed these three goods as "a package deal," and determined that it would be wrong to seek one good while deliberately frustrating another. They lamented that today we have attempted "to tear them apart. It doesn't work; they are fused by God's natural and supernatural design, and what God has joined, no man can put asunder."[34]

In light of that claim, it seems inconsistent that they said, "We aren't concerned here with the question of whether contraception ... is intrinsically evil or sinful. We would say that it's not *ideal*."[35] Yet it would seem by their reasoning that it is indeed intrinsically sinful, since it would be to work against God's purposes. Like many Roman Catholic ethicists, they saw a link between the acceptance of contraception and abortion, participating alike in a "culture of death." "In a culture of death, married Christians must reclaim the true meaning and beauty of sex, not only by bearing and rearing children, but by forsaking contraception and embracing purity, chastity, and restraint."[36] In light of their convictions, they criticized evangelical leaders Tim and Beverly LaHaye, James Dobson, Tony Campolo, and others who believe that the functions of marital sex include pleasure, arguing that this leads to selfish hedonism. The Torodes accepted and relied on NFP alone, also known as the rhythm method, as an appropriate way to attempt to limit pregnancy while respecting the purposes of sexuality.

It is worth noting with regret that Sam Torode and Bethany Patchin, who had four children, wrote in 2006 that they no longer believed in NFP and the anticontraception position, and in fact divorced in 2009. Reflecting on their earlier views, in 2006 Sam Torode said, "Wanting to make love to your spouse often is a good thing, but NFP often lays an unfair burden of guilt on men for feeling this." He also called it "a theological attack on women to always require . . . abstinence during the time of the wife's peak sexual desire (ovulation) for the entire duration of her fertile life, except for the handful of times when she conceives."[37]

Perhaps the most extreme evangelical reaction to contraception in principle is seen in the view that contraception is a form of homicide. Royce Dunn has written that contraception represents an "'abortifacient holocaust' gripping America," killing up to 8 million or more preborn U.S. citizens annually, after their conception.[38] He sees it as a bigger killer than abortion. Dunn evaluates the major forms of contraception and believes that rather than prevent pregnancies, they often prevent fertilized eggs from implanting. He believes it is a "devious intruder" into "God's domain" and "bears homage to the spirit world," that is, is an area of active Satanic influence in the world. His generation, he believes, has "yielded to contraception" because "the portion of our hearts ordained for children has found other interests."

Dunn goes on to link contraception to other practices to which he objects. "America bears the shame God assigns to nations that reject chastity, fidelity, and procreation—the badge of Sodom." He argues that "we who claim to know Christ have joined the grim coalition against children. Contraception has served to steal our affection for them and, thereby, our will to seriously defend them." Dunn provides no evidence that accepting contraception causes people to lose affection for children, however. He implies that evangelicals will support abortion as well as contraception, since they have lost the will to protect children, although the evidence strongly contradicts his claim at present. Certainly an objection to Dunn can be raised that couples use contraception precisely because of their affection for the children they will bear and their desire to provide them with effective nurture and support. Dunn also perceives a linkage between acceptance of contraception and approval of homosexuality, presumably because homosexual acts are non-procreative; "little should we marvel that homosexuality" and legalization of same-sex marriage are now becoming acceptable in society. Evidence that evangelicals support homosexuality is not given, and seems contrary to contemporary evangelical attitudes.

Clearly the debate between evangelical positions on contraception stem from different ideas about the divine purposes of human sexuality, from the three recognized by the Torodes to the six identified by the Feinbergs. They also vary in their recognition of the importance of other factors. The Feinbergs alone among the writers we have considered respect the legitimacy of the pursuit of careers by women, and they are also unique in their concern for preventing genetic disease in children. They along with Hollinger value pleasure among the divine purposes of sexuality, ignored or decried by other authors. Hollinger cites as evidence that God has ordained sexual pleasure the fact that males and females have bodily features designed solely for that purpose, the clitoris in the woman and the glans penis in the man. Among these writers, only Paris shows concern for preventing unwanted pregnancy and possible abortion among the growing population of single young evangelicals, many of whom are professionals putting off marriage and parenthood. In all our writers show the wide diversity one might expect among evangelicals, and all are seeking to follow Scripture and honor God in their various ways.

There is clearly a wide variety among evangelicals on contraception, unlike on abortion, reflecting quite different understandings of the purpose of sex, the relevance of historical positions, the nature of modern life, and their varied level of tolerance toward risk. Evangelicals on the matter of birth control exhibit a range of various positions not unlike their views on other social issues, such as war, the responsibility of government to care for the poor, proper treatment of the environment, and other social issues.

Notes

1. "Although no single entity claims to speak on behalf of U.S. evangelicals on the issue of contraception, there is evidence that most Evangelical leaders and church members are open to the use of contraception, including hormonal methods and sterilization, for married women as a matter of personal conscience. However, most Evangelical leaders strongly oppose sexual activity—and contraceptive use—among unmarried women of all ages." R. K. Jones and J. Dreweke, *Countering Conventional Wisdom: New Evidence on Religion and Contraceptive Use* (New York: Guttmacher Institute, 2011), 3.
2. M. L. Anderson, "Why Churches Shouldn't Push Contraceptives to Their Singles," *Christianity Today*, April 25, 2012. Christianitytoday.com.
3. Paris, "Both Chastity and Contraception."
4. Jones and Dreweke, *Countering Conventional Wisdom*, 4.
5. Paris, "Both Chastity and Contraception."
6. Anderson, "Why Churches Shouldn't Push Contraceptives."
7. Trevin Wax, "Both Chastity and Contraception: A Scandalous Capitulation," *Gospel Coalition*, May 1, 2012. thegospelcoalition.org.
8. "Is Contraception Acceptable for Evangelicals to Use?" National Association of Evangelicals, May 19, 2015. https://www.nae.net/is-contraception-acceptable-for-evangelicals-to-use/.
9. National Association of Evangelicals, "Is Contraception Acceptable?"
10. Christian Medical Society, "A Protestant Affirmation on the Control of Human Reproduction," *Journal of the American Scientific Affiliation* 22 (June 1970): 46–47.
11. "Evangelical Leaders Are Okay with Contraception," National Association of Evangelicals, May 19, 2015, https://www.nae.net/evangelical-leaders-are-ok-with-contraception/.
12. "Contraceptive Use Is the Norm Among Religious Women," Guttmacher Institute, April 21, 2011, https://www.guttmacher.org/news-release/2011/contraceptive-use-norm-among-religious-women.
13. D. P. Hollinger, "The Ethics of Contraception: A Theological Assessment," *Journal of the Evangelical Theological Society* 56, no. 4 (2013), https://www.etsjets.org/JETS/56_4.
14. John S. Feinberg, and Paul D. Feinberg., *Ethics for a Brave New World*, 2nd ed. (Wheaton, IL: Crossway, 2010).
15. Ibid., 305.
16. Ibid., 306.

17. Ibid., 290 and 296.
18. Ibid., 299.
19. Ibid., 301–302.
20. Ibid., 306.
21. National Association of Evangelicals, "Is Contraception Acceptable?"
22. "Use of Contraceptives in Marriage." Focus on the Family, n.d., https://www.focusonthefamily.com/family-qa/use-of-contraceptives-in-marriage.
23. J. Lupfer, "Commentary: The Evangelical Unease over Contraception," *Religion News Service*, January 2, 2014, https://religionnews.com/2013/12/30/commentary-evangelical-unease-contraception.
24. National Association of Evangelicals, "Evangelical Leaders Are Okay with Contraception."
25. "Federal Subsidies for Health Insurance Coverage for People Under Age 65: 2016 to 2026," Congressional Budget Office, March 24, 2016. https://www.cbo.gov/publication/51385.
26. Nicole Fisher, "Battle Between HHS And Christian College Comes To Dramatic End," *Forbes*, March 5, 2018, https://www.forbes.com/sites/nicolefisher/2018/03/05/battle-between-hhs-christian-college-comes-to-dramatic-end/#2be1597c4641.
27. Magee-Women's Hospital, University of Pittsburgh School of Medicine, "Intrauterine Devices: Separating Fact from Fallacy," *Medscape*, October 14, 1996, https://www.medscape.com/viewarticle/718183_3.
28. UCSF Health, "Conception: How It Works," October 31, 2019, https://www.ucsfhealth.org/education/conception_how_it_works/.
29. Spencer Greenberg, "Which Risks of Dying Are Worth Taking?" *Optimize Everything blog*, November 7, 2013. https://www.spencergreenberg.com/2013/10/which-risks-of-dying-are-worth-taking/.
30. "Facts Statistics: Mortality Risk," III, https://www.iii.org/fact-statistic/facts-statistics-mortality-risk.
31. Centers for Disease Control and Prevention, "Pedestrian Safety," May 24, 2017, https://www.cdc.gov/motorvehiclesafety/pedestrian_safety/index.html.
32. Bryan C. Hodge, *The Christian Case against Contraception: Making the Case from Historical, Biblical, Systematic, and Practical Theology & Ethics* (Eugene, OR: Wipf & Stock Publishers, 2010).
33. Clifford Penner, and Joyce Penner, *Getting Your Sex Life off to a Great Start: a Guide for Engaged and Newlywed Couples* (Dallas: Word Pub., 1994).
34. Sam Torode and Bethany Torode, *Open Embrace: A Protestant Couple Rethinks Contraception* (Grand Rapids, MI: Eerdmans, 2002).
35. Ibid., 8.
36. Ibid., 71.
37. Mark Oppenheimer, "An Evolving View of Natural Family Planning," *New York Times*, July 9, 2011. https://www.nytimes.com/2011/07/09/us/09beliefs.html.
38. Royce Dunn, "Contraception: The Tragic Deception." https://web.archive.org/web/20110803195838/http://www.lifeandlibertyministries.com/archives/000165.php.

Bibliography

Anderson, M. L. "Why Churches Shouldn't Push Contraceptives to Their Singles." *Christianity Today*. April 25, 2012. https://www.christianitytoday.com/ct/2012/aprilweb-only/churches-contraception.html

"Contraceptive Use Is the Norm Among Religious Women." Guttmacher Institute. April 21, 2011. https://www.guttmacher.org/news-release/2011/contraceptive-use-norm-among-religious-women.

Royce Dunn, "Contraception: The Tragic Deception." http://www.lifeissues.net/writers/dun/dun_01contraception.html.

"Evangelical Leaders Are Okay with Contraception." National Association of Evangelicals. May 19, 2015. https://www.nae.net/evangelical-leaders-are-ok-with-contraception/.

"Facts Statistics: Mortality Risk." III. 2023. https://www.iii.org/fact-statistic/facts-statistics-mortality-risk.

"Federal Subsidies for Health Insurance Coverage for People Under Age 65: 2016 to 2026." Congressional Budget Office. March 24, 2016. https://www.cbo.gov/publication/51385.

Feinberg, J. S., and P. D. Feinberg. *Ethics for a Brave New World*. 2nd edition. Wheaton, IL: Crossway, 2010.

Fisher, Nicole. "Battle Between HHS And Christian College Comes to Dramatic End." *Forbes Magazine*. March 5, 2018. https://www.forbes.com/sites/nicolefisher/2018/03/05/battle-between-hhs-christian-college-comes-to-dramatic-end/#2be1597c4641.

Greenberg, Spencer. "Which Risks of Dying Are Worth Taking?" *Optimize Everything blog*, November 7, 2013. https://www.spencergreenberg.com/2013/10/which-risks-of-dying-are-worth-taking.

Hodge, Bryan C. *The Christian Case against Contraception: Making the Case from Historical, Biblical, Systematic, and Practical Theology & Ethics*. Eugene, OR: Wipf & Stock Publishers, 2010.

Hollinger, D. P. "The Evangelical Theological Society." *Journal of the Evangelical Theological Society* 56, no. 4 (2013). https://www.etsjets.org/JETS/56_4.

"Is Contraception Acceptable for Evangelicals to Use?" National Association of Evangelicals. May 19, 2015. https://www.nae.net/is-contraception-acceptable-for-evangelicals-to-use/.

Lupfer, J. "Commentary: The Evangelical Unease over Contraception." *Religion News Service*. January 2, 2014. https://religionnews.com/2013/12/30/commentary-evangelical-unease-contraception.

Magee-Women's Hospital, University of Pittsburgh School of Medicine. "Intrauterine Devices: Separating Fact From Fallacy." *Medscape General Medicine* 1, no. 1 (1996). https://www.medscape.com/viewarticle/718183_3.

Oppenheimer, Mark. "An Evolving View of Natural Family Planning." *New York Times*. July 9, 2011. https://www.nytimes.com/2011/07/09/us/09beliefs.html.

Paris, J. "Both Chastity and Contraception: A Sacred Compromise." *Christianity Today*. April 27, 2012. Christianitytoday.com. https://www.christianitytoday.com/ct/2012/aprilweb-only/chastity-contraception.html.

"Pedestrian Safety." Centers for Disease Control and Prevention. May 24, 2017. https://www.cdc.gov/motorvehiclesafety/pedestrian_safety/index.html.

Penner, Clifford, and Joyce Penner. *Getting Your Sex Life off to a Great Start: A Guide for Engaged and Newlywed Couples*. Dallas: Word, 1994.

Torode, Sam, and Bethany Torode. *Open Embrace: A Protestant Couple Rethinks Contraception*. Grand Rapids, MI: Eerdmans, 2002.

UCSF Health. "Conception: How It Works." UCSF Health. October 31, 2019. https://www.ucsfhealth.org/education/conception_how_it_works/.

"Use of Contraceptives in Marriage." Focus on the Family. n.d. https://www.focusonthefamily.com/family-qa/use-of-contraceptives-in-marriage.

Wax, Trevin. "Both Chastity and Contraception: A Scandalous Capitulation." *Gospel Coalition*, May 1, 2012. www.thegospelcoalition.org.

CHAPTER 21

ABORTION IN THE JEWISH TRADITION OF RELIGIOUS HUMANISM

NOAM ZOHAR

THE DIVINE IMAGE: BIBLICAL AND RABBINIC FOUNDATIONS OF RELIGIOUS HUMANISM

MUCH has been written in recent decades about abortion in the Jewish tradition; this includes *halakhic responsa*, essays promoting a particular position or arguing for a specific methodological approach, encyclopedia entries, and notably a comprehensive monograph by Daniel Schiff (2002). In this chapter, I will seek to elucidate the central sources and tendencies from a theological perspective and thereby to offer an integrated view of the diverse teachings and debates.

The Jewish tradition is by no means monolithic; rather, it contains a plurality of voices. Yet overall, it can be characterized as endorsing religious humanism, that is, a supreme valuation of humanity and of human life grounded in a religious worldview. Starting from its roots in the Hebrew Bible, this tradition perceives the value of human life in terms of the Divine Image. The six days of creation culminate in the majestic pronouncement: "And God created man in His image, in the image of God He created him; male and female He created them" (Genesis 1:27).[1] Somewhat jarringly, this serves also as the ground for insisting on capital punishment for murder: "Whoever sheds the blood of man, By man shall his blood be shed; For in His image Did God make man" (Genesis 9:6). The paradoxical nature of this edict was fully appreciated by the rabbis, who taught that in effect capital punishment must be abolished.[2]

Indeed, this mode of valuing the human person extends beyond people who are alive, and thus does not completely depend on whether the interests of any person are at stake. Generalizing from the Biblical law which forbids exposure of an executed criminal's body and demands instead burial "that same day" (Deuteronomy 21:22–23), the rabbis established an injunction against "anyone who leaves his dead [relative unburied] overnight" (Mishnah, Sanhedrin 6:5). The requirement of proper treatment of a human cadaver, focused on a timely burial, is perceived as expressing "respect for the dead"; its significance is illuminated in a parable (as is common in rabbinic parables, God is represented by a king):

> Two brothers, identical twins, [lived] in the same city.
> One was appointed king, while the other became a highwayman;
> the king ordered him hanged.
> Everyone who saw him exclaimed: "The king is hanged!";
> the king ordered him taken down. (BT Sanhedrin, 46b)[3]

The description of "identical twins" expresses the belief that humans are made "in God's image," extended here to the dead human body, which retains a measure of that resemblance. Yet it is clear that disgracing—or even brutally disfiguring—a cadaver does not violate the Divine Image to the same degree, or rather in the same manner, as shedding the blood of a live person. The dead body is but a secondary reflection of the divine, a human form but no longer a living person.

The rabbis likewise applied the idea of the Divine Image to the beginning of human life—indeed, to express the value of procreation itself:

> Rabbi Elazar ben Azaria said:
> Anyone who does not engage in procreation is considered as though he had diminished the [divine] image. (Tosefta, Yevamot 8:7)

Surely, failing to procreate cannot constitute harm to the interests of those people not created, since as long as a person is not created, there is no one to have the interest in coming to exist. But Rabbi Elazar is speaking of harm not to unborn people but to the Divine Image. His statement is hyperbolic, for it equates failure to enhance the image with actually diminishing it, but the idea itself is perfectly understandable, given the grounding of human value in a sphere that transcends the interests of human beings.

Thus the idea of the Divine Image yields religious obligations (*mitzvot*;—singular: *mitzvah*) both to produce new humans and to show respect for human remains. These are, however, clearly distinct from the supreme duty to respect human life (i.e., the prohibition of killing and the obligation to rescue); this is evident from the fact that these obligations are set aside in the face of critical interests of living persons. For the purposes of the present discussion, it is pertinent to illustrate this with regard to the obligation to procreate, which may be set aside to engage in years of study or in order to first secure the means of making a living.[4]

Abortion and the Status of the Embryo: From *Aggadah* to *Halakhah*

What, then, of abortion? Is the fetus regarded as a manifestation of the Divine Image—rendering its destruction tantamount to murder? Or is it no more than a secondary reflection of the divine, somewhat akin to a cadaver—a human form but not yet a living person?

A large part of the discourse in Jewish bioethics draws upon *halakhah*—the Jewish tradition of normative discourse (often translated as "Jewish Law"). This may seem reasonable, insofar as what is being sought is normative guidance. Yet the central Judaic texts, from the Hebrew Bible to the Talmud, contain far more than legal instructions. The various non-legal components of the Talmud—including extensive interpretations of the non-legal parts of the Bible, rabbinic homilies, stories and parables, folk wisdom, and more—are collectively known as *aggadah*. Since our inquiry is essentially about the nature and status of the fetus, does it not make sense to peruse *aggadic* texts about fetal life, seeking direct evidence regarding the kind of existence it is thought to have? In fact, however, such an approach yields insufficient clarity, as will become evident by examining a preeminent example.

The most prominent aggadic text of this kind is a homily drawing upon a Biblical paragraph in which the suffering Job expresses longing for a long-gone serene and protected existence:

> O that I were as in months gone by, In the days when God watched over me,
> When His lamp shone over my head, When I walked in the dark by its light,
> When I was in my prime, When God's company graced my tent . . .
>
> (Job 29:2–4)

Strikingly, this is taken as referring to the condition of the embryo:

> Rabbi Samlai expounded: The embryo in its mother's womb lies folded. . . . A candle burns above its head, and it looks and beholds from one end of the world to the other, as written, "When His lamp shone over my head, When I walked in the dark by its light"; and do not marvel [at this], for a person sleeping here beholds a dream in Spain.
>
> There are no days in which a person enjoys well-being more than those days, as written, "O that I were as in months gone by . . ." [which alludes to] the months of gestation; and [the embryo] is taught the entire Torah. . . . Once it emerges into the air of

the world, an angel comes and delivers a blow above its mouth, causing it to forget the entire Torah.

(BT Nidah 30b)

How are we to understand this depiction of the embryo as possessing cosmic awareness and as achieving mastery of the entire Torah? At face value, this might be read as showing that the rabbis (or at least some of them) considered a human fetus as capable of both high-level cognition and broad powers of imaginative apprehension. But the sensible reader will realize, of course, that these aspects of the homily can hardly be taken more literally than the burning candle (or lamp), which facilitates the limitless vision.

No doubt, the impact of this fine homily might give pause to anyone contemplating the destruction of an embryo. But even the unfanciful kernel of Rabbi Samlai's picture—the unsurpassed, wondrous well-being of protected fetal existence in the womb—seems more a projection of adult yearning than a straightforward embryological postulate. The power of *aggadah*, as it speaks explicitly of things unknowable, implies also its limitations, for as in any worthy work of art, it induces even deeper perplexity than the reality which serves as its inspiration.

Hence, like most participants in the discourse of Jewish bioethics, we should indeed turn our attention to the tradition's legal teachings.[5]

INTERPRETING BIBLICAL LAW: RABBINIC VS. HELLENISTIC JUDAISM

For ancient Judaic discourse on the status of the embryo, the point of departure is undisputedly this pivotal text from Exodus:

> When men fight, and one of them pushes a pregnant woman and a miscarriage results,[6] but no disaster ensues, the one responsible shall be fined according as the woman's husband may exact from him, the payment to be based on reckoning. But if disaster ensues, the penalty shall be life for life, eye for eye, tooth for tooth, hand for hand, foot for foot, burn for burn, wound for wound, bruise for bruise.
>
> (Exodus 21:22–25)

The Hebrew word *ason* appears in the Bible in only one other context, but its three occurrences there suffice to warrant its translation as "disaster."[7] The plain meaning is that harming the woman's life or limb is regarded as a severe crime, punishable under the strict *lex taliones*. Fetal death, in contrast, is not that kind of "disaster"; causing it is regarded as a matter for monetary compensation payable to the husband, who is deemed the stakeholder with regard to the economic value of the lost children.

This straightforward interpretation was endorsed in the rabbinic tradition. But although their heritage eventually became the classical core of mainstream Judaism, the rabbis were by no means the only voice among the Jews of late antiquity. Other Jewish groups took a more severe view of destroying an embryo.[8] The best illustration of this view is found in the traditions of Hellenistic Judaism (based primarily in Alexandria), which explicitly offer an alternative interpretation of the verses from Exodus, as reflected in the ancient Greek translation of the Torah, the Septuagint:

> And if two men strive and smite a woman with child, and her child be born imperfectly formed, he shall be forced to pay a penalty: as the woman's husband may lay upon him, he shall pay with a valuation.
> But if it be perfectly formed, he shall give life for life, eye for eye, tooth for tooth, hand for hand, foot for foot, burning for burning, wound for wound, stripe for stripe.[9]

The unique Greek word employed here is *exeikonismenon*, a construction from *eikon* (the origin of the English "icon"). Richard Freund has argued that this reading evidently involves a substitution of a Greek word that sounds like *ason* (a homophone), without regard for the word's meaning in Hebrew.[10] Such far-fetched interpretive ploys were an accepted practice both in Hellenistic Alexandria and among the rabbis, who utilized them in molding the meaning of the sacred text to yield valid religious instruction.[11] The theological stance informing this rendition derives from the central idea described above: grounding the value of human life in the Divine Image. In the tradition of Hellenistic Judaism, the image inheres in the physical form of the embryo. According to the above translation, once it is "fully formed" it has become a divine *eikon* and destroying it is deemed murder.[12] Likewise, Philo—commenting on the law as rendered in the Septuagint—explains that a fully formed fetus—i.e., a fetus that has completed its physical development—"is a human being ... like a statue lying in a studio requiring nothing more than to be conveyed outside."[13]

In contrast, rabbinic sources overall reject the equation of feticide with murder, and contain an explicit denial of the possibility that the "disaster" entailing capital punishment refers to the fate of the embryo. It is instructive to note how the Mishnah—the core text of rabbinic Judaism—explicates the law of causing miscarriage:

> If a person, aiming [to strike] his fellow, strikes a woman and a miscarriage results,[14] he must pay compensation for the embryos.
> How is payment of compensation for the embryos [determined]? An assessment is made of the woman—[comparing] her value before she gave birth with her value after giving birth ... and [the difference] is given to the husband; if she no [longer] has a husband, it is given to his heirs.
>
> (Mishnah, Bava Kama 5:4)

The Mishnah clearly follows the plain meaning of the law in Exodus, stipulating monetary compensation for feticide, and there is no mention of any distinction with respect to gestational stage or fetal formation. A significant feature of this text is revealed once we look beyond the clause itself and consider its placement within the mishnaic tractate. One would expect this law to be included in the chapter devoted to assault, battery and maiming (Bava Kama Chapter 8). Instead, it is found within a section devoted to harm to property by a goring ox. The connection to that section is facilitated by means of a brief contrasting rule, excluding [the owner of] an ox from compensation for miscarriage it has caused.

Indeed, there are strong indications that this clause detailing the mode of compensation for feticide was originally located within the discourse on assault and battery. The principle itself ("compensation for embryos") is mentioned there, without the detailed instructions—yet other clauses in that chapter provide detailed instructions in remarkably similar style. Moreover, in the Mishnah's complementary work, the Tosefta, the entire discussion of compensation for feticide is in fact located in the chapter devoted to assault and battery (Tosefta Bava Metsia 9:20). Although the Tosefta was compiled [shortly] after the Mishnah, it often reflects an earlier phase of the material's arrangement—this being, I believe, a poignant case in point.

Strikingly, in its present location the clause in question is juxtaposed with a clause (5:1) involving the causing of miscarriage in a cow. It is scarcely credible that these two clauses—among the relatively few mentions of embryos in the Mishnah, and the only two in the entire tractate at hand—have been placed close by each other by mere happenstance. The clause regarding compensation for feticide was evidently detached from the context of penalties for assault upon persons and inserted in the context of payment for damage caused to chattel. This serves to emphasize the import of the Biblical law itself, according to its plain meaning as endorsed by the rabbis, and in opposition to the contrary view of feticide conveyed in other Jewish circles.

Fully consonant with this is the oft-cited mishnaic rule regarding maternal-fetal conflict in a situation of crisis during childbirth:[15]

> If a woman has difficulty in giving birth, the embryo should be cut up in her belly and removed limb by limb, since her life has precedence over its life. Once most of it has emerged, however, it may not be harmed, for one life [*nefesh*] may not be set aside for the sake of another life [*nefesh*].
>
> (Mishnah Ohalot 7:6)

In Biblical usage, the word *nefesh*—which I translated here as "life"—has the concrete (and likely original) meaning of "throat"; but it mostly signifies person, life, psyche, self and perhaps soul (the latter usage clearly attested in rabbinic Hebrew).[16] In any event, and in all strata of the language, it clearly signifies that whose destruction constitutes murder. Once the baby is deemed born, it is a *nefesh*, co-equal with the mother. As stated bluntly by the classical Talmudic commentator *Rashi*, the embryo—even if it is full-term—"as long as it has not emerged into the air of the world is not a *nefesh*"; which in modern terms means: "is not a person."[17]

How is this to be understood from the perspective of religious humanism, focused on the Divine Image, as described above? Certainly, the rabbis knew that long before birth, a fetus attains well-defined physiological human form. Unlike the view of Hellenistic Judaism, however, they did not regard this as endowing it with the Divine Image in the crucial sense of implying the supreme valuation and protection of human life. Philo likened a fully formed embryo to a finished statue awaiting transport from the studio; it thus differs from a born infant merely by location. The rabbis, in contrast, clearly believed that the Divine Image, although associated with human form, involves some aspect (or aspects) pertaining to a live-born infant and not yet present in an embryo. After all, nothing is more characteristic of Jewish faith than denying that God's image can be found in an inanimate statue! We can speculate regarding the specific nature of this crucial aspect: Is it independently breathing (which facilitates also communication, at least—from the very beginning—in the form of crying)? Or being situated outside the womb, enabling interaction with human society?[18] I do not know of convincing evidence for any particular explanation; yet for the purpose of the current discussion, it need not be resolved. With regard to abortion, the decisive fact is that for the rabbis, an embryo (even in an advanced stage of gestation, and regardless of its physical form) is qualitatively and crucially different from a person, and its destruction is not murder, but rather calls for monetary compensation.

Before moving on to post-Talmudic discussions and thence to contemporary debates, it is important to take note of two additional Talmudic sources.

First, there is a source reporting an apparently dissenting view, linking feticide to murder, found in the context of a large Talmudic segment devoted to the "Noahide Laws." These laws (enumerated by some rabbis as "seven commandments") constitute the rabbis' effort to define, from a monotheistic perspective, the minimal duties incumbent upon all humankind, as distinct from the full range of commandments obligating the Jewish people, who are bound by the covenant of Torah they accepted at Sinai. Since the rabbis lacked jurisdiction over the Gentiles, exposition of the Noahide laws was mostly an exercise in hypothetical (not to say, fantastical) jurisprudence. This may account for the draconian character of the stated criminal sanctions, which uniformly call for capital punishment for all offenses.[19]

Within this context, it is reported that the School of Rabbi Ishmael taught that "a Noahide is to be put to death even for [destroying] an embryo" (BT Sanhedrin 57b). It is possible to see this teaching as echoing anti-abortion policies in the Roman Empire. Even so, this teaching cannot simply be seen as irrelevant for intra-Judaic guidance, since it stands to reason that whatever norms apply to Noahides must apply to Jews as well. Moreover, we should not disregard the accompanying derivation by means of an ingenious (if ungrammatical) interpretation of Genesis 9:6 (cited above), in which capital punishment for murder was grounded in the idea of the Divine Image. Thus we have evidence of a minority position among the rabbis, endorsing the perspective attested in Hellenistic Judaism that includes embryos (at least once they have attained human form) in the scope of the Divine Image.

Second, there is an illuminating Talmudic exchange related to the concluding line of the mishnah (Ohalot 7:6) cited above, "Once most of [the baby] has emerged, however, it may not be harmed, for one life [*nefesh*] may not be set aside for the sake of another life [*nefesh*]." According to the Jerusalem Talmud, Rabbi Yirmiya juxtaposed this with another teaching of the Mishnah (Sanhedrin 8:7) which decrees that a person posing a lethal threat to another (a "pursuer") should be killed in defense of the victim. The sense of his question seems to be: Why should the not-fully-emerged baby not be regarded as a "pursuer" of its mother—and thus be killed to save her life? The reply is offered by Rabbi Yose the son of Rabbi Avun, citing Rav Hisda: "That [case] is different, for you do not know who is killing whom!" (JT Sanhedrin 26c). A similar, though distinct, retort is cited in the Babylonian Talmud (BT Sanhedrin 72b): "That is different, for she is pursued by heaven." The Jerusalem Talmud emphasizes the issue of mutual endangerment, whereas the Babylonian Talmud emphasizes the issue of the baby's innocence. Common to both versions of the exchange is the affirmation that the rule of the "pursuer"—that is, the justification of killing an attacker in defense of the victim—is not relevant to the situation of a woman endangered in childbirth.

As we shall see presently, these Talmudic exchanges carry special significance for the subsequent Jewish discourse on abortion—in particular, as the backdrop to a problematic pronouncement in the Code of Maimonides, which in turn serves as a basis for a more prohibitive stance among some later authors. Before proceeding to explore that issue, it is worth spelling out the significance of this Talmudic position in the terminology of contemporary moral philosophy. Several contemporary authors have linked the debate about abortion to discussions of killing in self-defense or in the defense of others. This linkage depends on regarding the fetus as posing a threat to the life (or perhaps, to the bodily integrity) of the gestating woman; for this to come under the self-defense justification, the latter must be extended to so-called "innocent threats." The rabbis here, however, preclude the use of lethal force against the embryo, precisely because of its innocence.

Medieval Teachings: Valuing the Full-Term Embryo

For mainstream medieval Judaism, the Talmud came to be regarded as the authoritative source of normative guidance. Nevertheless, it seems that many rabbis found it difficult to accept the dichotomous demarcation between a newborn (or even a mostly born baby)—regarded as a person—and a full-term embryo, who is "not a *nefesh*."

An important source for valuing the life of an embryo in late gestation involves a case in which a woman carrying an advanced pregnancy has died. The Talmud teaches that the Shabbat prohibitions should be set aside in saving such an embryo, by extracting it from the womb of the deceased woman (BT Arakhin 7b). Since the general rule is that violating the Shabbat is warranted only for the sake of saving a life (and not, for example, for rescuing property), this teaching seems to indicate that the same supreme value inheres in a late-term embryo. How can this be squared with the Mishnah cited above (regarding a crisis in childbirth), which sharply distinguishes between the newborn, who immediately attains the full protections of personhood, and the not-yet-born embryo, who is "not a *nefesh*"?

Nahmanides (13th century, Girona) strongly resists any suggestion that the teaching regarding rescue on Shabbat implies that an embryo at full term—or, as some argue, at least once labor has begun—should be regarded as a person (*nefesh*), pointedly citing the law of monetary compensation for feticide, which allows no such distinctions. Instead, he offers a justification for violating the Shabbat in terms of the future value of this human life once it is delivered. This is a cogent form of the problematic argument from potential which appears in contemporary debates about abortion. In its faulty form, the argument seeks to ascribe value to embryonic life here and now, based on its potential to become a full-flung human being. Nahmanides, however, emphasizes that at present the embryo is not a person, and thus one who destroys it is not culpable of murder. Nevertheless, the value of future human life—which can be promoted by rescuing the embryo—warrants violation of the Shabbat (Nahmanides, Commentary on BT Nidah 44b).

An alternative approach might be to regard an embryo as a living person once labor has begun, thus providing a direct justification for the teaching about violating the Shabbat to save it, without adducing its potential future. This need not conflict with the main biblical and Rabbinic stance, reflected in the law about causing miscarriage, which rejects the ascription of Divine Image to an embryo throughout gestation. Rather, it is only a matter of shifting the point of transition to a slightly earlier time—the onset of labor as opposed to near completion of delivery.

It is possible that this approach was adopted by Maimonides, as in codifying the rule regarding a crisis in childbirth, he eschews the accepted justification for destroying the embryo. Unlike Rashi and virtually all other commentators, he refrains from asserting that the not-yet-born embryo is not a *nefesh*. Instead, he justifies its destruction, when necessary to save the woman, by comparing it to "a pursuer"—that is, in terms of defending a victim from one who is threatening her life.

A widely noted puzzle with respect to this statement of Maimonides is whether it can be reconciled with the pertinent Talmudic discussions cited above, which explicitly deny that an emerging baby can be deemed a "pursuer" of its mother. Moreover, if—*pace* the Talmudic arguments to the contrary—the maternal-fetal conflict is construed as "pursuit," why does the same perspective not equally mandate killing the mostly-born baby to rescue the woman?

Many scholarly efforts have been invested in trying to answer these questions, and I shall not attempt to tackle them here. However the puzzle is to be resolved, it seems right to say that in some important sense, Maimonides extended the status of protected human life to an embryo, once the birth process has begun. Clearly, this cannot extend to embryos at earlier stages of gestation, whose destruction is unquestionably a matter for monetary compensation alone. It seems most plausible to limit Maimonides's position to its specific context, where labor has already begun. Still, since he does not provide an explicit demarcation, it is possible to ascribe to him an extension of human status to an embryo at some earlier stage as well, e.g., to a full-term embryo even before the beginning of labor.

Having described the main theological and textual sources for the halakhic discussion of abortion, we can conclude by portraying the salient features of modern discourse on the issue.

Modern Jewish Debates: *Halakhah*, Ethics, and Gender

As a backdrop for modern *halakhic* discourse on abortion, it is important to keep in mind the decidedly pronatalist character of the Judaic tradition as a whole. In the opening section of this chapter, we noted the theological aspect of the imperative to procreate: humanity constitutes the Divine Image. This is accompanied by a consciousness of historical calling: the People Israel carry the mission of preserving and promoting the Torah across the generations; and this cannot be fulfilled unless these generations are born.

The duty to procreate, in its traditional formal definition, involves a curious feature: according to the majority view, only men are obligated, whereas women are exempt. Since no man can procreate without enlisting a woman, it is clear that this formal structure implicitly assumes a gender hierarchy. Thus women—although formally free to neither marry nor procreate—are nevertheless strongly induced to mate and produce the requisite offspring. In fact, in traditional Jewish society the value of procreation was generally internalized by most individuals, men and women alike; and women in particular saw it as a significant aspect of their identity and purpose.

In traditional Jewish culture, infertility is regarded as a severe misfortune. Central Biblical texts, read in the synagogue in a repeating annual cycle, both reflect and convey this attitude. In Isaiah's poetry, redemption for the long-suffering Zion is heralded: "Sing out, O barren one/ You who bore no Child! . . . For the children of the desolate one will be more . . ." (Isaiah 54:1). In the foundational narratives of Genesis, the matriarchs suffer greatly by their initial lack of offspring; thus Rachel exclaims to Jacob, "Give me children, or I shall die" (Genesis 30:1). In such a setting contraception is a problematic issue;[20] all the more so abortion, which interrupts the process of procreation when it is already underway.

Hence in *halakhic* discourse, the overall stance toward abortion has been negative, independently of determining what specific transgression (if any) is involved in aborting a fetus. In practice this means that if a woman contemplating abortion seeks Judaic guidance, the response will generally be a query about her reasons: abortion, as it were, goes against the basic grain of this religious culture.

What counts as a valid reason will depend in part upon the strength of the aversion to abortion. This in turn depends on the extent to which the developing embryo is regarded as embodying the Divine Image. As we saw, in contrast with Philo's analogy to a finished statue, the rabbis considered physical human form—not yet delivered into the world as a living infant—as lacking some essential aspect of the Divine Image. Yet we also saw that a dead human body demands respect as reflecting the Divine Image, and the same would seem to hold for an embryo, at least from some point in the pregnancy onward. If we focus on physical form, the earliest candidate for this point seems to be at forty days, in light of the explicit Talmudic statement that prior to that "it is mere fluid" (BT Yevamot 69b); perhaps more plausibly, it should be some later point, when the semblance of human form is more definitely present. Alternatively, we might consider modes of representation akin to writing, less oriented toward visible shape. From that perspective, the imagined homunculus of old might be replaced by the genetically defined early embryo of contemporary science.[21]

Thus from a theological perspective, the embryo possesses some not-clearly-defined value as a reflection of the Divine Image, starting from some point in gestation and up to actual birth, when it emerges as a full-status person. This ambiguity allows for a wide array of approaches in contemporary Judaic discourse. These range from assessment of abortion as only marginally more problematic than contraception, all the way to describing it as "bloodshed," only slightly less severe than outright murder.[22]

Formally, this is often expressed by the technical characterization of the posited prohibition, following the accepted categories of *halakhic* norms. Numerous *halakhic* discussants here ask: Is the prohibition Biblical or rabbinic? Does abortion involve transgressing a "negative commandment" (i.e., a prohibition) or only failure to perform a "positive commandment"? Or perhaps it involves no formal *halakhic* violation of any kind, but rather only exhibits less than perfect piety?

Against this backdrop, it is not surprising that the reasons that have been contemplated and recognized by various *halakhic* authors as warranting abortion vary across a rather wide spectrum. At one end is the obligation to destroy a full-term (and even partly born) embryo when the life of the birthing woman is at stake. This explicit and uncontested ruling of the Mishnah sets Judaic teaching clearly apart from those religious traditions that regard such an embryo (or, for that matter, embryos at much earlier stage of gestation) as a person who may not be killed to save another. A few halakhists believe that this is the only reason that justifies abortion; anything less than a clear and present danger to the woman's life is insufficient. At the other end of the spectrum are reasons such as preserving the woman's emotional well-being when this is threatened either by the pregnancy itself or by the prospect of being mother to the expected child.[23]

In light of the theological ambiguity and the concomitant wide array of halakhic options, it is hardly surprising that some halakhists (in this context, so it seems, more than elsewhere) are explicitly conscious of the value dimensions of the stance they advocate, above and beyond its formal grounding. Given the obvious sensitivity of discourse on abortion to gender perspectives, it will be instructive to conclude this chapter by comparing the positions taken by two prominent twentieth-century rabbis. This is intended, of course, as no more than a poignant illustration of contemporary applications of the tradition.

Rabbi Aharon Lichtenstein was a leading advocate of recognizing the force of moral considerations beyond the requirements of formal *halakhic* norms. In a discussion of abortion, he first grants that on formal *halakhic* grounds it is possible to adopt certain lenient instructions. But he proceeds to argue on moral grounds for a stricter position: "the humane and ethical element [in Halakha] ... rises up in indignation against the torrent of abortions."[24] While the commitment to moral obligations beyond formal, "legal" requirements is certainly laudable, it is striking how he takes it for granted that morality calls simply for valuing embryonic life—and how little weight he seems to give to the woman's interests.[25]

An opposite position is indicated in a comprehensive essay entitled "Regarding the Question of Abortion Where There Is Concern That the Fetus Has a Severe Malformation," composed by Rabbi Shaul Yisraeli (1966). The scenario as described seems to involve Thalidomide, and Yisraeli's discussion addresses the interests of the future child; yet strikingly, his concluding remarks give significant weight to the interests of the prospective parents. Having reiterated the mainstream *halakhic* view that a fetus is not a person (*nefesh*), he cites a Talmudic source to establish that "it is right to also take into consideration the parents' anguish, as they stand to witness their offspring's great suffering."[26] Thus above and beyond regard for the woman's (physical) health, preventing her emotional suffering may well outweigh whatever prohibition normally attaches to performing an abortion.

Yisraeli's position makes it possible to formulate an alternative to Lichtenstein's moral perspective. After all, halakhic culture—part and parcel of the Jewish tradition overall—is permeated by a gender hierarchy, which routinely discounts the interests of women. Emphasizing the emotional costs sometimes entailed by carrying a pregnancy to term and becoming a parent allows recognition and validation of the (non-physical-health-related) reasons a woman might have for seeking an abortion. In weighing her interests against the value of the fetus, it seems right to be guided by the idea of the Divine Image, which (as we have seen) underlies this tradition's discourse on these issues.

According to the Judaic-Hellenistic view, a fully formed fetus has attained the Divine Image status of a human being, and its destruction amounts to homicide. But according to the rabbinic tradition, that status is attained only by a born infant.

The pregnant woman, by contrast, is herself a fully constituted person, sharing in the Divine Image, as written: "And God created man in His image, in the image of God He created him; male and female He created them" (Genesis 1:27).

Abbreviations

BDB   Francis Brown, Samuel R. Driver, and Charles A. Briggs, *A Hebrew and English Lexicon of the Old Testament* (Oxford, Clarendon Press 2006).
BT   Babylonian Talmud
JPS   Jewish Publication Society

Notes

1. For Biblical translations, I have generally followed the New Jewish Publication Society version (1985), but have made some alterations as seemed advisable.
2. The paradox was noted by Moshe Greenberg in his classical essay, "Some Postulates of Biblical Criminal Law," in his *Studies in the Bible and Jewish Thought* (Philadelphia: Jewish Publication Society, 1995), 25–41. Greenberg likewise noted that the Rabbis moved to effectively abolish capital punishment; cf. Walzer et al., *The Jewish Political Tradition: Vol 3—Community*, chapter 23 (New Haven, CT: Yale University Press, forthcoming).
3. All translations of rabbinic materials are my own (NZ).
4. See Jeremy Cohen, *Be Fertile and Increase, Fill the Earth and Master It": The Ancient and Medieval Career of a Biblical Text* (Ithaca: Cornell University Press, 1989).
5. A similar point is made by Immanuel Jakobovits, in *Jewish Medical Ethics*, 2nd ed. (New York: Bloch, 1975), in his discussion of "Abortion in Jewish Law," 182–191 (cf. 182–183).
6. Literally: "and her children emerge." A few translations take this to indicate a live birth, but if the children are alive and well, what is the harm that requires compensation?- Moreover, survival of premature newborns, especially when the pregnancy was cut short by violence, seems a highly unlikely outcome in pre-modern times.
7. In the story of Joseph and his brothers, Genesis 42:4, 38; 44:29. In all those instances, NJPS employs "disaster," and its choice of the bland "other damage" here seems misguided.
8. For a thorough presentation of scholarly views regarding the Biblical passage itself and its rival interpretations in late antiquity, see Daniel Schiff, *Abortion in Judaism* (Cambridge University Press, 2002), 1–26.
9. *Septuagint* (Brenton translation 1851)
10. See Richard Freund, "The Ethics of Abortion in Hellenistic Judaism," in his *Understanding Jewish Ethics*, 241–254 (San Francisco: EMText, 2002). Freund believes the homophonic Greek word is *soma*; but it could be the word *eikon* itself, arguably closer in its sound to *ason*.
11. Freund provides additional examples; more generally, see Menachem Elon, *Jewish Law: History, Sources, Principles*, trans. Bernard Auerbach and Melvin J. Sykes (Philadelphia:

The Jewish Publication Society, 1994), vol. I, chapter 9: "Exegetical Interpretation of the Torah," 281–399.
12. Freund himself translates *exeikonismenon* as "made from the image." This leaves out the issue of its being "fully" formed, but reflects essentially the same idea: at some point in the pregnancy, the embryo comes to share the essential human status of Divine Image.
13. Philo, *The Special Laws* III: 108–109, trans. F. H. Colson (Harvard University Press, 1958), vol. VII: 545.
14. The precise wording is identical to the biblical phrase: "and her children emerge" (cf. note 6 above).
15. See also Mishnah Arakhin 1:4, and the related discussion in BT Arakhin 7a (advocating killing the fetus of a woman awaiting execution in order to spare her mental anguish or indignity). For a comprehensive discussion, see Schiff, *Abortion in Judaism*, chapter 2, "Evaluating Life: Rabbinic Perspectives on Fetal Standing," 27–57.
16. Cf. BDB, 659–661.
17. Rashi's commentary to BT Sanhedrin 72b, S.V. *yatsa rosho*.
18. The Conservative movement has put forward a convincing case for regarding the embryo as a part of the pregnant woman rather than an independent being, citing the Talmudic teaching that "an embryo is its mother's limb." For this argument in context, see the two statements approved by the Rabbinical Assembly Committee on Jewish Law and Standards, by D. M. Feldman and Isaac Klein, in *Life and Death Responsibilities in Jewish Medical Ethics*, edited by Aaron L. Mackler (New York: Jewish Theological Seminary, 2000), at 196 and 208 (respectively). As far as I can see, the RA position has not been argued in terms of the Divine Image.
19. For a detailed discussion, see Michael Walzer, Menachem Lorberbaum, Noam J. Zohar and Madeline Kochen, *The Jewish Political Tradition, Vol 2: Membership* (Yale University Press, 2003), 451–463.
20. See David M. Feldman, *Birth Control in Jewish Law* (New York: NYU Press, 1968).
21. See Noam Zohar, "Divine Representations and the Value of Embryos: God's Image, God's Name, and the Status of Human Nonpersons," in *Jews and Genes: The Genetic Future in Contemporary Jewish Thought*, ed. Elliot N. Dorff and Laurie Zoloth, 55–67 (JPS—Nebraska University Press, 2015).
22. For a survey of the range of (Orthodox) *halakhic* teachings regarding abortion, indicated here and in the ensuing paragraphs, see Avraham Steinberg, "Abortion and Miscarriage," *Encyclopedia of Jewish Medical Ethics* 1 (2003): 7–13.
23. For a survey and discussion of various attempts to provide methodological, second-order grounds for reaching more definitive *halakhic* guidance on this issue, see Schiff, *Abortion in Judaism*, 227–269.
24. Aharon Lichtenstein, "Abortion: A Halakhic Perspective," *Tradition* 25, no. 4 (1991): 12.
25. For an extensive and illuminating analysis of *halakhic* discourse on reproductive ethics from a feminist perspective, see Ronit Irshay, *Fertility and Jewish Law* (Waltham, MA: Brandeis University Press, 2012); regarding abortion, cf. chapters 3 and 4, 111–200.
26. Shaul Yisraeli, *Amud Ha-Yemini* (Torah Temimah Institute, 1966);, 32:9; cf. the discussion by Ronit Irshay, *Fertility and Jewish Law* (Waltham, MA: Brandeis University Press, 2012), 175–176;. For the pertinent Talmudic source, see note 15 in this chapter, and Schiff, *Abortion in Judaism*, 37–39.

Bibliography

Cohen, Jeremy. *"Be Fertile and Increase, Fill the Earth and Master It": The Ancient and Medieval Career of a Biblical Text*. Ithaca: Cornell University Press, 1989.

Colson, Francis Henry (translator). *Philo: The Special Laws*. Vol. VII. Harvard University Press, 1958.

Elon, Menachem. *Jewish Law: History, Sources, Principles*, trans. Bernard Auerbach and Melvin J. Sykes. Philadelphia: Jewish Publication Society, 1994.

Feldman, David M. *Birth Control in Jewish Law*. New York: NYU Press, 1968.

Freund, Richard. "The Ethics of Abortion in Hellenistic Judaism." In his *Understanding Jewish Ethics*, 241–254. San Francisco: EMText, 1990.

Greenberg, Moshe. "Some Postulates of Biblical Criminal Law." In *Studies in the Bible and Jewish Thought*, 25–41. Philadelphia: Jewish Publication Society, 1995.

Irshay, Ronit. *Fertility and Jewish Law*, Waltham, MA: Brandeis University Press, 2012.

Jakobovits, Immanuel. *Jewish Medical Ethics*, 2nd ed. New York: Bloch, 1975 (1959).

Lichtenstein, Aharon. "Abortion: A Halakhic Perspective," *Tradition* 25, no. 4 (1991): 3–12.

Mackler, Aaron L., ed. *Life and Death Responsibilities in Jewish Medical Ethics*, New York: Jewish Theological Seminary, 2000.

Schiff, Daniel. *Abortion in Judaism*. Cambridge University Press, 2002.

Steinberg, Avraham. "Abortion and Miscarriage." In Encyclopedia of Jewish Medical Ethics, vol. 1, 1–29.

Yisraeli, Shaul. *Amud Ha-Yemini*, Torah Temimah Institute, 1966.

Zohar, Noam. "Midrash: Amendment through the Molding of Meaning." In *Responding to Imperfection: New Approaches to the Problem of Constitutional Amendment*, edited by S. Levinson, 307–318. Princeton University Press, 1995.

Zohar, Noam. "Divine Representations and the Value of Embryos: God's Image, God's Name, and the Status of Human Nonpersons." In *Jews and Genes: The Genetic Future in Contemporary Jewish Thought*, edited by Elliot N. Dorff and Laurie Zoloth, 55–67. JPS—Nebraska University Press, 2015.

CHAPTER 22

THE ROMAN CATHOLIC POSITION ON ABORTION

PATRICK LEE

THE Catholic Church has always taught that the life of every human being, from conception on, is to be respected and reverenced, that the intentional killing of an innocent human being, no matter at what stage of development, is gravely wrong. From the early teaching on this issue in the Didache (second century), to the Fathers of the Church in the next few centuries, on through to the teachings of the popes, from Stephen V (ninth century) to that of all of the popes in the last century and a half, the Catholic Church has taught that every human life is intrinsically valuable and that abortion and infanticide are grave sins.

This teaching was recently reaffirmed explicitly by Pope St. John Paul II in the Encyclical *Evangelium Vitae* (The Gospel of Life) in 1995. There Pope John Paul stated that:

> I declare that direct abortion, that is, abortion willed as an end or as a means, always constitutes a grave moral disorder, since it is the deliberate killing of an innocent human being.[1]

The teaching that every human being at every stage of his or her life is to be protected and cared for is, Catholics claim, an integral part of the Gospel handed on from Christ and the apostles. Central to the Gospel is the truth that God loves all human beings, that every human being, no matter what his or her circumstances—including those of size, age, degree of development—is made in the image and likeness of God and has an intrinsic dignity.[2]

Reading attentively, one can see that Scripture affirms the life of the human being developing in the womb. For example, referring to the New Testament, Pope John Paul teaches:

> The New Testament revelation confirms the indisputable recognition of the value of life from its very beginning. The exaltation of fruitfulness and the eager expectation of life resound in the words with which Elizabeth rejoices in her pregnancy: "The Lord has looked on me . . . to take away my reproach among men" (Luke 1:25). And even more so, the value of the person from the moment of conception is celebrated in the meeting between the Virgin Mary and Elizabeth, and between the two children whom they are carrying in the womb.[3]

The Church reaffirmed this teaching in clear terms in the Second Vatican Council. It condemns: "Whatever is opposed to life itself, such as any type of murder, genocide, abortion, euthanasia or willful self-destruction," and said that such acts were "infamies indeed."[4]

The Church also teaches that this proposition can be known by the light of natural reason. Thus Pope John Paul says, "This doctrine [that abortion is always a grave wrong] is based upon the natural law [as well as] upon the written Word of God, and is transmitted by the Church's Tradition and taught by the ordinary and universal Magisterium."[5]

The basic principles regarding our duties to respect the lives of unborn human beings are the same as our duties toward any fragile and needy human being. However, issues specific to abortion arise because of questions on the personhood of the unborn, and on the application of norms to difficult cases, or on how to harmonize respect for the lives of both the child and the mother in various cases.[6]

It is true that Catholic teachers and theologians in earlier times—before the significant advances in the science of embryology in the late nineteenth century—had varying positions concerning when the human rational soul is infused into the developing embryo. The standard view was that the rational soul was probably not infused at conception but at some time later during gestation. Many of Church Fathers as well as St. Thomas Aquinas—who followed Aristotle on this point—held that the rational soul was not created and infused into the body until the body had developed to the stage where it was sufficiently organized to participate in the actions specific to a rational being.[7]

However, embryological facts discovered and made widely known in the nineteenth century—in particular, the existence of the ovum and the sperm, how they unite in fertilization, and details of the embryo's apparently internally directed multicellular growth in its first days of development—challenged that earlier view. And so after these developments, Catholic thinkers more and more concluded that human ensoulment occurred at conception.

Still, the earlier uncertainty about the time of creation and infusion of the rational soul never led Catholic teachers to hold that direct abortion could be morally right. As the *Declaration on Procured Abortion* explained:

> In the course of history, the Fathers of the Church, her Pastors and her Doctors have taught the same doctrine—the various opinions on the infusion of the spiritual soul did not introduce any doubt about the illicitness of abortion. It is true that in the Middle Ages, when the opinion was generally held that the spiritual soul was not present until after the first few weeks, a distinction was made in the evaluation of the sin and the gravity of penal sanctions. Excellent authors allowed for this first period more lenient case solutions which they rejected for following periods. But it was never denied at that time that procured abortion, even during the first days, was an objectively grave fault. This condemnation was in fact unanimous.[8]

The Catholic Church's position that abortion it is objectively immoral, then, does not depend on settling the issue of the time of ensoulment.

> In reality, respect for human life is called for from the time that the process of generation begins. From the time that the oocyte is fertilized, a life is begun which is neither that of the father nor of the mother, it is rather the life of a new human being with his own growth. It would never be made human if it were not human already.[9]

Most important, if one doubts that what one is choosing to bring about is the killing of a human being, one must proceed on the assumption that it is a human being: "From a moral point of view this is certain: even if a doubt existed concerning whether the fruit of conception is already a human person, it is objectively a grave sin to dare to risk murder." The one who will be a man is already one."[10] To choose to kill what one thinks might be a human being is to consent to the killing of a human being as a means of bringing about one's end.

It is worth seeing the rationale that led some in earlier times to conclude that the rational soul is not present from conception, and how it is affected (refuted) by the advances in embryology that began in the late nineteenth century. Before then philosophers and theologians thought that in higher animals the efficient cause of generation is the male, and that the female is only the material cause, providing the material for the formative action provided by the male. What she contributes to the generative process—they reasoned—is relatively unformed blood, while the male contributes semen, which is the active principle.

Since the generative process occurs outside the male's body, Aristotle and Aquinas proposed that the father acts through a medium, the semen, and so the semen is an instrumental cause. The semen, they held, had within it a force from the father, a "*virtus formativa.*" They reasoned that the semen, acting as an instrumental cause, organized the matter provided by the female in the menstrual blood, first to form a being with vegetative life, then a being with lower sensitive life, then a being with a higher sensitive life, and so on, until the organization produced is sufficient for an animal of the same species as the parents. The active part of the semen (called "the animal spirit") remains until the generative process is completed.

Since on their view the distance between the beginning point of the generative process (the material out of which the human being is generated, the relatively unformed menstrual blood) and its end point (a body organized sufficiently to receive a rational soul) is very great, it was reasonable to conclude that traversing that distance required time and so the generative process must be temporally extended.

Following Aristotle, they held that the human soul was related to the human body as form to matter, that is, that the human soul specifies the human body to be the kind of body it is. And the matter must be proportionate to the form. The matter, or that out of which something comes to be, must be apt for receiving that specific type of form; it must be a body capable of participating in the actions specific to the species in question—somewhat as the materials from which one makes a knife must be apt for being sharpened or the materials from which one makes a house must be stable enough to support a roof. And so Aristotle and Thomas Aquinas, for example, held that in the generative process of a human being the body was not apt for reception of a rational, human soul until it possessed sense organs—and thus capable of acts of sensation as prerequisites for rational consciousness.[11]

However, modern embryology shows that the female provides a gamete (the ovum) which is already a highly organized living cell, containing highly complex, specific information, in the genetic structure of the nuclear chromosomes. This information (together with that provided by the genetic structure in the chromosomes of the male sperm) helps guide the development of the new living organism formed by the fusion of the sperm and the ovum. Hence the ovum is actually very close to readiness for rapid embryological development; it only requires union with the sperm and the activation that occurs with that union. To a certain extent the gradual transition from the simple to the complex that earlier thinkers (Aquinas for example) expected actually occurs during gametogenesis (of which, of course, he was unaware).

Moreover, we now know that nothing from the semen remains as a distinct agent in the process of the embryo's development. The result of the fertilization process is a distinct organism. After fertilization neither the sperm nor the ovum remains. What exists is a distinct organism which then apparently begins a process of self-development oriented to the stage of a mature human adult. Nothing of the semen-a fortiori no "vital spirit"-remains attached to the developing embryo. While constituents from the sperm and the ovum (chromosomes and cytoplasm) enter into the makeup of this new organism, they become its parts or organs, they are not distinct agents. So if one holds that the embryo is only gradually formed to the point that it becomes apt for the emergence of a sensitive soul and then (the infusion) of a rational soul, one is faced with a complex, organized process which occurs with regularity, but with no apparent cause. If there is no extrinsic agent responsible for the regular, complex development, then the obvious conclusion is that the cause of the process is within, that it is the embryo itself. Thus, the process is not an extrinsic formation, but an instance of growth or maturation, i.e., the active self-development of a whole, though immature organism that is already a member of the human species, the mature stage of which it is developing toward.[12]

While it is true that the organs are not present in the developing embryo from the conception (fertilization) stage onward, nevertheless we now know that from fertilization on the embryo has the internal potential to develop for herself all of the organs needed for the mature actions specific to human nature. All the embryo needs to develop herself to the mature stage of the human organism is appropriate environment and nutrition, and so the embryonic body seems to satisfy the requirement that the body be proportioned to the soul: it has the internal, specific instructions and active disposition for developing human sense organs, including a brain apt to be the substrate for conceptual thought. And so, many philosophers and theologians have argued that applying Aquinas's metaphysical principles to the embryological facts uncovered since his time leads to the conclusion that the human being is present from fertilization on.[13]

The issue of the soul arises usually only because of historical considerations. Logically, the question of whether the embryo or fetus is a human organism does not depend on first determining whether there is a rational soul present. Rather, the direction is the reverse: one first should look for criteria that might mark the embryo or fetus as a human organism and, if there are such marks, that would be evidence that the human soul—given that human beings are composed of soul and body—is at that time present.[14]

Nowadays the standard scientific texts on this issue—in embryology, developmental biology, and genetics—explicitly affirm that a human being at the earliest stage of development comes to be at fertilization. Here are three of many examples:

> Human life begins at fertilization, the process during which a male gamete or spermatozoon unites with a female gamete or oocyte (oocyte) to form a single cell called a zygote. This highly specialized, totipotent cell marked the beginning of each of us as a unique individual. . . . A zygote is the beginning of a new human being (i.e., an embryo).[15]
>
> Fertilization is the process by which male and female haploid gametes (spermatozoon and egg) unite to produce a genetically distinct individual.[16]
>
> Although life is a continuous process, fertilization (which, incidentally, is not a "moment") is a critical landmark because, under ordinary circumstances, *a new, genetically distinct human organism is formed* when the chromosomes of the male and female pronuclei blend in the oocyte [emphasis added].[17]

The underlying science seems clear. At fertilization a sperm unites with an ovum, each of them ceases to be, and a new entity is generated. This is a new beginning: neither the sperm nor the ovum survives and so one cannot say that a sperm or an ovum becomes a mature human, or that a sperm or an ovum has the potential to become a mature human being. For ingredients do not become what they enter into, whereas an immature human being—an embryo, fetus, or infant—does become an adult human being simply by maturing. This new human embryo is a *distinct* entity, not a part of the mother or a part of the father. For unlike body cells, tissues, or organs, the embryo does not function as part of its mother. The one-cell embryo (zygote) develops by dividing into two cells, then four, then eight and so on. While these divisions occur, all of the cells continue to be enclosed within a thin membrane called the *zona pellucida*, which is inherited from the ovum.

Sometimes it is claimed the embryo at this stage is merely a bundle of disparate cells. But the evidence shows that these cells inter-communicate and seem to function together as parts of a whole in a regular and predictable manner. As a result, they perform an ordered, differentiated growth and constitute a stable body. For as the embryo travels down the uterine tube into the uterus during the first four or five days, the different cells begin differential gene expression (modifications of different parts of the DNA within the cells' nuclei in order to generate different types of new cells that can function in different ways).

On day three or four, at the transition from the eight-cell stage to the sixteen-cell stage, the embryo differentiates into trophoblastic cells (precursors of the placenta) on the one hand, and inner cell mass cells (precursors of the permanent part of the embryo and fetus), on the other hand. This is the first overt functional differentiation that occurs, but the cells have been preparing for this differentiation since day one.

So from the zygote stage onward the cells are functioning as parts of a whole, and there is inner coordination toward the next step in a developmental trajectory that eventually involves a clear development of a body plan and distinct organs. The material constitution of the embryo from the one-cell stage onward helps to provide the embryo an active disposition to develop itself to the mature stage of a human being. This is a new and distinct multi-cellular organism. It is developing itself in a predictable direction. And obviously it is *human* since its cells have the genetic structure characteristic of humans.

Still, one might ask whether the embryo is at this stage a *whole* human organism. For human tissue and separate human cells have the human genome in their nuclei, but they are not whole human organisms—for example, an isolated skin cell or a heart before it's implanted into a recipient. Each of these is human but neither is a whole organism. However, unlike separate cells, tissue or organs, the human embryo has within itself all of the internal resources and the active disposition to develop itself to the mature stage of a human being. The direction of its growth is internally coordinated—what it receives from outside itself is only a suitable environment and nutrition. The organizational information for its growth comes from within.

Also, at no stage after fertilization does there occur a fundamental change in the direction of growth. None of the changes that occur to this being afterward—as long as this being stays alive—qualify as producing a fundamental change in its interiorly directed growth, so as to involve the coming to be of a new organism. Rather, everything that happens after fertilization either assists or retards its interiorly directed self-development. So a new, whole human organism comes to be at fertilization, albeit at an immature stage of development.

Still, some philosophers admit that human embryos and fetuses are human beings but object that they are not *persons*. It is wrong to kill persons, they argue, but not necessarily human beings, that is, human organisms. Only persons deserve moral respect; that is, only persons are intrinsically worthwhile, are beings whose interests we should take account of. But human embryos or fetuses, they argue, are not persons.[18]

This argument has some initial plausibility. It seems obvious that it is morally permissible to kill some things (such as lettuce, vicious dogs, etc.) but not others. Where does one draw the line between those things it is permissible to destroy or kill, and those it is not? A long tradition says the line should be drawn at *persons*. But what is a person, if not a thing that has self-consciousness and other mental functions?

However, this objection is mistaken. It implicitly identifies the human person with an entity—a self-conscious subject—that inhabits or uses a body. The self is thought of as one thing or subject, and the body as something else. And so proponents of this position concede that the human organism comes to be at conception, but they claim that the human person—you or I—comes to be only much later, perhaps when self-consciousness appears. But if this human organism came to be at one time, and *I* came to be at a later time, it would follow that I am one thing and this human organism is another thing.

Catholic teaching rejects this position on the basis both of faith and of reason. The Church teaches that a human being is not a soul possessing or inhabiting a body, but a body-soul composite. While teaching on abortion Pope John Paul criticizes a dualistic position on the human person that views the body as an extrinsic tool of the self:

> Within this same cultural climate, the body is no longer perceived as a properly personal reality, a sign and place of relations with others, with God and with the world. It is reduced to pure materiality: it is simply a complex of organs, functions and energies to be used according to the sole criteria of pleasure and efficiency.[19]

According to Catholic teaching the body is part of what a human being is.

The central importance of the resurrection of the body to Catholic teaching, the teachings on marriage, on one's duty to take care of one's health, on the absolute duty to adopt ordinary means to preserve one's life and health—these all are rooted in the firm belief that human beings are bodily in nature—as well as having a spiritual component, an immortal soul.

> The human body shares in the dignity "image of God": it is a human body precisely because it is animated by a spiritual soul, and it is the whole human person that is intended to become, in the body of Christ, a temple of the Spirit.[20]

Thus, while human beings possess rational and immortal souls, distinguishing them from other animals, they also *are* particular types of organisms.

> The unity of soul and body is so profound that one has to consider the soul to be the "form" of the body: i.e., it is because of its spiritual soul that the body made of matter

becomes a living, human body; spirit and matter, in man, are not two natures united, but rather their union forms a single nature.[21]

And so human beings are human organisms—particular types of human organisms—and come to be when the organisms they are come to be.

The unity of body and soul is attested to by reason as well as by faith. We seem to have an immediate awareness of the truth that we are living bodies. When I take a shower I say that I am washing *myself*. If you strike my face I do not say, "You hit my body," but: "Why did you hit *me*?" If while walking past a vase on a coffee table I accidentally knock it to the floor and it shatters, I do not say, "My body did that," but: "I am so sorry, *I* accidentally broke your vase."

In addition, various strong philosophical arguments—based for example on facts of sensation, human understanding, language, difficulties raised by alternative positions—have been advanced against such body-self dualism.[22]

Another attempt to deny that human embryos and fetuses have rights is to argue that, even though you and I once were embryos or fetuses, we were not valuable as subjects of rights at that time. On this view, being identical to the entity that has basic rights at a later time is not sufficient to ground having rights now. Thus, on this view, in addition to being the same kind of thing or substance as you and I are, to have basic rights a being must possess some accidental attribute, such as self-consciousness or a capacity for self-consciousness.[23]

Again, this position can have an initial plausibility. What grounds rights, it is sometimes argued, is *having interests*, and a being can have interests only if its desires for an object would be frustrated. Newspapers and bicycles have no interests, whereas developed human beings do. The relevant difference between them seems to be that the "harm" one does to a newspaper cannot matter *to* the newspaper, and this difference seems to be grounded in the fact that newspapers have no desires that can be frustrated, whereas developed humans do.[24]

Catholic teaching firmly rejects this position. Human beings are valuable in virtue of what they are, that is, in virtue of being human beings. All human beings are made in the image and likeness of God and therefore possess equal and inherent fundamental rights. Pope St. John Paul reiterated this teaching in *The Gospel of Life*:

> Looking at the situation from this point of view, it is possible to speak in a certain sense of a war of the powerful against the weak: a life which would require greater acceptance, love and care is considered useless, or held to be an intolerable burden, and is therefore rejected in one way or another. A person who, because of illness, handicap or, more simply, just by existing, compromises the well-being or lifestyle of those who are more favored tends to be looked upon as an enemy to be resisted or eliminated. In this way a kind of "conspiracy against life" is unleashed.[25]

There also are serious philosophical problems for the position that we are persons (have basic rights) at only certain stages during our lives. The basis for having fundamental rights must be either (a) the fundamental kind of thing or substance one is, or (b) an accidental attribute (or attributes), that is, an attribute one may acquire or lose at different stages of one's life. But the position that the basis for having fundamental rights is an accidental attribute seems inevitably to involve arbitrary line-drawing.

To distinguish those beings that have basic rights from those that do not, one will have to point in some way to some mental function—the mental functions most often proposed being self-consciousness and self-conscious desires. Also, the relevant attribute will have to be a *capacity* or *potentiality* of some sort. For there does not seem to be any mental action that is at all times being performed by all of those who are obviously bearers of fundamental rights. Otherwise, even those who are asleep, for example, would not qualify as having rights. But human embryos and fetuses do have, in some sense, the same capacities for mental functions as other humans. Although they cannot *now* perform such functions, they are actively developing themselves to the stage at which they will do so. They have the structure or nature such that, provided the right environment, nutrition, and absence of violence, they *will* perform such actions—something not true, for example, of an unborn dog or cat. So to provide a justification for abortion, this position (namely, that basic rights must be grounded in an accidental attribute) will have to specify that the capacity needed to have rights must be an immediately exercisable one, or exercisable in response to a stimulus. If the position is to allow for abortion it must hold that having a radical, natural capacity (i.e., one that someone possesses in virtue of one's nature, and that may take time to actualize) is not sufficient for having basic rights. But why require an immediately exercisable capacity rather than only a radical capacity? The choice seems at best arbitrary.

Moreover, there are strong reasons against such a requirement. What is referred to as an "immediately exercisable capacity" is actually only a *degree of actualization or development* of the same basic capacity for mental functions that exists in the human being from the beginning. A capacity such as that for self-consciousness is a power to perform a specific type of action. It is grounded in some way in the constitution of the organism. With maturation the organism gradually develops its basic capacities toward the point where it performs the relevant action in the appropriate circumstances or environment. Thus, the transition from having only the radical capacity for performing an action, on the one hand, to the proximate or immediately exercisable capacity for that action, on the other, is only the development of the same basic power that the organism possessed from its beginning. And so to base the right to life on an immediately exercisable capacity, as opposed to the living being's nature and natural capacities—is a selection of a certain degree of development of a given capacity, an arbitrary selection. It is more reasonable to base the right to life on the *substantial nature* of the entity—the fundamental kind of being one is—rather than on developed immediately exercisable capacities, such as for self-consciousness or self-conscious desires. Human beings possess basic rights *in virtue of what* (i.e., *the kind of being*) *they are*. And so *all* human beings—not just some, and certainly not just those who have advanced sufficiently along the developmental path as to be able immediately (or almost immediately) to exercise their capacities for characteristically human mental functions—possess basic rights, including a basic right to life.

Second, consider a person in a coma. A comatose human being is still a person, but he does not have a capacity, in the sense of an immediately exercisable capacity, for self-consciousness, or rationality. Yet he surely has a right to life.

Why is this so? The clearest reason is that, what is ethically decisive is not what a being can do right now, or even in the immediate future. Rather what is ethically decisive is the nature of the being, the kind of being one is. The comatose human being is still a person with rights because, even if he cannot *right here and now, or in the immediate future,* have self-consciousness, conceptual thought, and so on, still he is the *kind of being* that can and will perform such actions, given time, adequate good health, and the right environment.

But this same point is true also of the human embryo or fetus. The human embryo or fetus is a being with a rational nature; she is a being with the radical capacity to actively develop herself to the point where she will shape her life by rational deliberation and choice, even though it will take her several months, indeed years, to do so. Since human beings are intrinsically valuable and deserving of full moral respect in virtue of what they are, it follows that they are intrinsically valuable from the point at which they come into being. Even in the embryonic stage of our lives, each of us was a human being and, as such, worthy of concern and protection.

This point is confirmed when we examine how in our everyday life we come to understand our basic responsibility to promote and protect the well-being of others, and not just our own well-being. When we deliberate about what to do, we begin by apprehending that some objects or activities are worthwhile pursuing for their own sake, and not as mere means toward other conditions. We apprehend, for example, that life and health, knowledge, aesthetic experience, harmony with other people, and other conditions are worth pursuing. Each of us recognizes that the conditions or activities that are genuinely fulfilling of oneself and of others like oneself are worthwhile in themselves. At the same time I apprehend that I have a *responsibility* specified by these goods as opportunities—a responsibility, basically, to do something with my life, something worthwhile, responsive somehow to opportunities such as these.[26] For I apprehend these goods not just as things I would *like to do,* but as conditions that are worthwhile. Further, in understanding there are goods worth pursuing when I deliberate about what to do I apprehend that I myself am an agent and I am someone whose being and fulfillment are worthwhile.

Now, I also apprehend that the persons next to me, for example, the persons sitting with me at the dinner table, the kids playing games with me outdoors, are similarly situated toward these same basic human goods: I understand that the possibilities I view are also possibilities that these other persons view, and I understand that the basic responsibility I apprehend they also apprehend. And so I understand that the goods worthy of pursuit include not just those that fulfill my own self but also are at least the possible fulfillments of those who are presented (or can be presented) with the same type of view, and who see (or can see) the same type of responsibility.

And as I apprehend that I am a person persisting through time, and am worthwhile, I see that *in just the same way* the human beings next to me are also persons persisting through time and are worthwhile.[27] As *my* life, health, knowledge and so on *matter*—are worth pursuing—in the same way, the life, health, truth and so on, of others who are similarly related to such goods are worth pursuing, and the persons themselves are worthwhile.[28]

The responsibility specified by goods understood as to-be-pursued extends to the goods—that is, the being and fulfillment—of all those who either do or can—now or in the future—understand these goods as worth pursuing. Thus, while animal urges, or sheer desires, do not ground or justify the choice-worthiness of their objects, *being a fulfillment that someone's practical reason can apprehend as a good worth pursuing* does ground and enable one to understand the intrinsic good and worthiness of the well-being of other agents.

We also grasp that others are in essentially the same practical position we are in when we actively co-operate with others to pursue goods in common. I then understand that some other beings are related to me as *co-subjects*, and others of course as *potential* co-subjects. If I cooperate with others in pursuing the good of health or understanding, then I directly apprehend both myself and these others as subjects, as worthwhile in ourselves, and as persons for whom such goods as health, understanding and so on, are worth pursuing. These co-subjects are distinct in kind from other beings, some of which also are alive, the natural (not free or deliberate) causality of which may assist or impede one's projects, but which are not (either actually or potentially) co-subjects.

The beings that a person should care for—herself and all others similarly situated toward these intelligible goods—are agents, beings who persist through time, in other words, in philosophical language, substances. And an agent ought to care about what happens to her and to beings like her, not only when they are actually conscious, but also during those periods of their lives when they are unable to respond to commands, to painful stimuli, and the like. The beings that a person cares for—the beings whose welfare matters for her—are *particular kinds* of substantial entities, and these substantial entities exist before their basic *natural capacities* for self-conscious acts and deliberate choice have developed to the stage where these capacities are immediately exercisable. And these substantial entities are valuable during those periods when, because of injury or illness, their capacities for rationality are not immediately exercisable.[29] Hence the basis for distinguishing between those beings a person should treat always as ends and never as mere means, and those she can use as mere means, is the possession of a rational nature; every human being is a person.

Thus, just as it is wrong to kill a human being today, it would also have been wrong to kill that human being ten years ago, or twenty years ago, or at any point in her existence. It would have been wrong to kill her when she was an infant, but also when she was a fetus, and it would have been wrong to kill her when she was an embryo—because at each point she was the same human being.

Finally, some supporters of abortion object that the real issue is a clash between the rights of women and the rights of the unborn, and they argue that the rights of the women should prevail. Even granted, they argue, that a human embryo or fetus is a human person, the woman's right to her bodily autonomy supersedes the human embryo's or fetus's right to life. They conclude that the woman has a right to expel the fetus from her womb—and thereby regain her bodily autonomy—even though this means that the fetus (child) will die as a result.[30]

There are many problems with this argument. No one has a right directly to kill another innocent human being in order to protect one's own autonomy or any aspect of his or her well-being. So a choice to kill (or have someone else kill) the embryo or fetus as a means of extricating oneself from difficulties is morally wrong.

However, one might object to this reply that many abortions are not direct killing, that the choice (often) is to refrain from allowing the child the use of the woman's body, a choice to expel the child from the mother's womb and the child's death is a side effect. Although the language of direct and indirect killing may not be used, those who argue in this way are claiming that many abortions are justified because they are indirect killing.[31]

Catholic philosophers and theologians have taken different positions on how to respond to this objection. Some reply that the bodily rights objections in fact must rely on the position that direct killing of the unborn can be justified, while others say that even if some abortions are indirect killing they are not justified.[32]

Let us grant, at least for the sake of argument, that in some abortions the baby's death is a side effect. Still, it does not follow that these are morally justified. It is true that in some cases causing death as a side effect is morally permissible. For example, in some cases it is morally right to use force to stop a potentially lethal attack on one's family or country, even if one foresees that the force used will also result in the assailant's death. Similarly, there are instances in which it is permissible to perform an act that one knows or believes will, as a side effect, cause the death of a child in utero (more on this point in a moment).

But it also is clear that not every case of causing death as a side effect is morally right. For example, if a child has a serious respiratory disease and her father is told that his continued smoking in her presence will cause her death, it would obviously be immoral for him to continue the smoking. Similarly, if a man works for a steel company in a city with significant levels of air pollution, and his child has a serious respiratory problem and so the air pollution endangers her life, certainly he should move to another city. He should move, we would say, even if that meant he had to resign a prestigious position or make a significant career change.

Surely, this is partly because parents have special responsibilities to their children. One has some responsibilities to all other people (for example, not to kill them, and to take them into account whenever one's actions bear on them), but one has a greater responsibility to those people to whom one has a closer unity or connection. The unity of a person to his children is very great. And so, while one may have a certain degree of responsibility to all children, one has a special and intense responsibility to one's own children. In the cases mentioned above—the smoker and the father working in the steel company—the parent has a special responsibility to his child.

Moreover, in each of those cases the act would cause a harm to the child that is significantly worse than the harm the parent would be avoiding for him or herself. And so, even if the harm done is a side effect, in these cases the act that causes the death would be an *unjust* act, and morally wrongful *as such*. The special responsibility of parents to their children requires that they *at least* refrain from performing acts that cause terrible harms to their children in order to avoid significantly lesser harms to themselves. In sum, unless the mother's life is in proximate danger, the burden of carrying a baby to term is significantly less than the harm the baby would suffer by being killed; the mother and father have a special responsibility to the child; therefore, even if in some cases the baby's death is a side effect, abortion is unjust and therefore objectively immoral.

It is worth noting that if the bodily rights objection were correct, one could argue in the same way about a two-year-old child, or about one's aging parents when they become dependent on one. Suppose a woman births a baby, takes her home from the hospital, and everything goes well for the first two years. But at two years old the baby becomes very sick, suffers severe brain damage, and develops other problems, with the result that now taking care of the baby is more burdensome than she (and her husband, say) anticipated. Suppose also finding someone to adopt the child is not possible, or that it would take several months to arrange. So either they shoulder the responsibility to care for this child, or the child will die. Clearly, killing the child or abandoning the child in the woods (even if that was the only way to ensure the child was not returned to the parents) would be morally wrong. But causing the baby's death by abortion—even if that death is a side effect rather than intended—is in the relevant respects similar to these cases. Again, the parents have a special responsibility to their children (true of the father as well as of the mother), and the harm caused to the unborn child by abortion is much worse than the burdens of pregnancy that would be avoided. A mother or father of a child at least has a duty not to cause the death of the child in order to avoid difficulties that are far less than death.

The claim that the abortion issue is essentially a clash between the rights of women and the rights of the unborn is misleading: it does not help women to persuade them to have their child killed, but harms them perhaps as much as it harms the unborn children killed. And the experiences of many, many women confirm that doing so only exacerbates what may be already a very critical situation.[33]

Finally, it is Catholic teaching that there are some situations where the mother's life is in proximate danger and a procedure that results in the unborn child's death *as a side effect* is morally permissible. For example, if a pregnant woman is discovered to have a cancerous uterus, and this is a proximate danger to the mother's life, it can be morally right to remove the cancerous uterus with the baby in it, even if the child will die as a result. A similar situation can occur in ectopic pregnancies. And in some cases, where the mother's life is threatened, it can be morally right to induce labor early on, foreseeing that the baby will die. These are not direct abortions. *What is done* (the means) is the correction of a pathology (such as a cancerous uterus, or a ruptured uterine tube), and the end is the saving of the mother's life. The baby's death is neither a means nor an end but a by-product (side effect) of what is directly done. So these are *indirect* or *non-intentional* abortions.

This position on indirect abortions is an application of a more general principle of morality, often called "the principle of double effect." According to this principle, it can be morally permissible to do something that causes a grave harm—including death—but only if it is a side effect of what one does (that is, it is neither one's end nor one's means), and only if there is a proportionate reason for causing the bad side effect. It is this principle that justifies lethal self-defense. According to this principle one might hold that it can be morally right to use force to stop a potentially lethal attack on one's family or country, even if one foresees the force used will also result in the assailant's death. It is always morally wrong to intend a grave harm (for example to kill, maim, sterilize) whether as end or as a means; but it is not always wrong to cause a bad side effect. Thus, procedures aimed at alleviating a pathological condition to save the mother's life, where the death or harm to the child is a side effect, can be morally permissible. In such cases the harm avoided is comparable to the harm caused as a side effect, that is, there is proportionate reason for doing what causes the grave harm as side effect.

Notes

1. Pope John Paul II, Evangelium vitae *(The Gospel of Life)*, #62, http://w2.vatican.va/content/john-paul-ii/en/encyclicals/documents/hf_jp-ii_enc_25031995_evangelium-vitae.html.
2. Ibid., #2.
3. Ibid., #45
4. Vatican Council II, Gaudium et spes *(Constitution of the Church in the Modern World)*, #27, http://www.vatican.va/archive/hist_councils/ii_vatican_council/documents/vat-ii_const_19651207_gaudium-et-spes_en.html Two important works on the Catholic Church's development of teaching on abortion are John Connery, *Abortion: The Development of the Roman Catholic Perspective* (Chicago: Loyola University Press, 1977); Germain Grisez, *Abortion: The Myths, the Realities, and the Arguments* (New York: Corpus Books, 1970).
5. Evangelium vitae, #62.
6. Germain Grisez, *The Way of the Lord Jesus, Volume 2: Living a Christian Life* (Quincy, IL: Franciscan Press, 1993), 488.
7. St. Thomas Aquinas, *Summa Theologiae*, Part I, Question 118, article 1.
8. Congregation for the Doctrine of Faith, *Declaration on Procured Abortion*, #7, http://www.vatican.va/roman_curia/congregations/cfaith/documents/rc_con_cfaith_doc_19741118_declaration-abortion_en.html.

9. Ibid., #12.
10. Ibid., #13.
11. On this point see John Haldane and Patrick Lee, "Aquinas on Human Ensoulment, Abortion and the Value of Life," *Philosophy* 78 (2003): 255–278.
12. Someone might propose that even though nothing of the semen or ovum remains as a distinct agent, nevertheless a formative power persists, somewhat in the way one might conceive an impetus being imparted to a projectile. On this view an extrinsic force would remain for a time within the body, moving it in a direction contrary to that to which its intrinsic tendencies incline it. But there is no reason in the case of the embryo to think that the DNA—which provides the essential directive instruction for the embryo's development—is an extrinsic agent. Unlike the forces operative in a projectile body, for example, the factors responsible for the direction of the embryo's growth are not transitory, but remain in the developing organism until it dies.
13. Haldane and Lee, "Aquinas on Human Ensoulment," 255–278; Stephen Heaney, "Aquinas and the Presence of the Human Rational Soul in the Early Embryo," in *Abortion: A New Generation of Catholic Responses*, edited by Stephen J. Heaney, 43–72 (Braintree, MA: Pope John Center, 1992).
14. Some important contemporary works on abortion that defend the position that human beings have basic rights from conception on are: Francis Beckwith, *Defending Life: A Moral and Legal Case Against Abortion Choice* (New York: Cambridge University Press, 2007); Christopher Kaczor, *The Ethics of Abortion, Women's Rights, Human Life, and the Question of Justice* (New York: Routledge, 2011); Patrick Lee, *Abortion and Unborn Human Life*, 2nd ed. (Washington, DC: Catholic University of America Press, 2010).
15. Keith L. Moore and T. V. N. Persaud, *The Developing Human: Clinically Oriented Embryology*, 7th ed. (Philadelphia, PA: Saunders, 2003), 16, 16.
16. J. Signorelli, S. Diaz, P. Morales, "Kinases, Phosphatases and Proteases during Spermatozoon Capacitation," *Cell and Tissue Research* 349, no. 3 (March 20, 2012): 765.
17. Ronan O'Rahilly and Fabiola Mueller, *Human Embryology and Teratology*, 3rd ed. (New York: John Wiley & Sons, 2000), 8. (Many other examples could be cited, some of which may be found here: http://clinicquotes.com/list-of-quotes-from-medical-textbook sscientists-proving-life-begins-at-conception/)
18. Examples are: Mary Anne Warren, "On the Moral and Legal Status of Abortion," in *Bioethics: Principles, Issues and Cases*, 2nd ed., edited by Lewis Vaughn, 333–342 (Oxford, UK: Oxford University Press, 2012); Michael Tooley, "On Abortion," in *Abortion: Three Perspectives*, ed. Michael Tooley, Celia Wolfe-Devine, Philip E. Devine, and Allison Jaggar (Oxford, UK: Oxford University Press, 2009).
19. *Evangelium vitae*, #23
20. *Catholic Catechism of the Catholic Church*, #364.
21. Ibid., #365; see also Vatican Council II, *Gaudium et spes*, #14.
22. Some examples: Peter Geach, *God and the Soul* (New York: Schocken, 1969); Patrick Lee and Robert P. George, *Body-Self Dualism in Contemporary Ethics and Politics* (New York: Cambridge University Press, 2008).
23. Examples are Judith Thomson, "Abortion," *Boston Review*, 1995, at: http://new.bostonreview.net/archives/BR20.3/thomson.phpbostonreview.mit.edu/BR20.3/thomson.html; Ronald Dworkin, *Life's Dominion: An Argument about Abortion, Euthanasia, and Individual Freedom* (New York: Knopf, 1993); Bonnie Steinbock, "Moral Status, Moral Value, and Human Embryos," in *Oxford Handbook for Bioethics* (Oxford, UK: Oxford

University Press, 2009); David Boonin, *A Defense of Abortion* (New York: Cambridge University Press, 2003).
24. Judith Thomson makes this type of argument in Thomson, "Abortion."
25. *Evangelium vitae*, #12.
26. This responsibility need not be conceived of as moral responsibility in the full sense, but perhaps as part of or the root of moral responsibility. Speaking of the basic goods as in themselves worthwhile, Joseph Boyle says: "The options supported by judgments of value make a kind of demand on the acting person, not necessarily the unconditional obligation of morality, but surely something more than the urgency of desire." Joseph Boyle, "Reasons for Action: Evaluative Cognitions That Underlie Motivations," *American Journal of Jurisprudence* 46 (2001): 195. The demand he refers to there is what I am calling a responsibility that is not necessarily yet moral.
27. For more discussion of this position: John Finnis, "Personal Identity in Aquinas and Shakespeare," in *Collected Essays, Volume 2: Intention and Identity*, ed. John Finnis, chapter 2 (New York: Oxford University Press, 2011); Patrick Lee and Robert P. George, *Body-Self Dualism in Contemporary Ethics and Politics* (New York: Cambridge University Press, 2008), chapter 1. Also see Bernard Williams, "The Self and the Future," *Philosophical Review* 79 (1970): 161–180, reprinted in *Problems of the Self* (Cambridge University Press, 1976); Eric Olson, *What Are We?* (Oxford: Oxford University Press, 2007).
28. John Finnis, *Collected Essays, Volume 3: Human Rights and Common Good* (NY: Oxford University Press, 2011), 5.
29. To say that it is rational beings that are worthwhile—the being and fulfillment of which I should respect as I respect my own—is to take the word *ration* as denoting a type of substance, not an ability conceived of as an accidental attribute that can come to be at some time after the rational individual herself comes to be, and can cease to be before this individual ceases to be.
30. Judith Thomson, "A Defense of Abortion," reprinted in many places, for example, Vaughn, *Bioethics: Principles, Issues and Cases*, 307–316; Boonin, *A Defense of Abortion*.
31. Thomson, "Defense of Abortion," 307–316.
32. Cf. Kaczor, *The Ethics of Abortion*; Lee, *Abortion and Unborn Human Life*.
33. Ryan Anderson and Alexandra DeSanctis, *Tearing Us Apart: How Abortion Harms Everything and Solves Nothing* (Washington, DC: Regnery Publishing, 2022).

Bibliography

Anderson, Ryan, and Alexandra DeSanctis. *Tearing Us Apart: How Abortion Harms Everything and Solves Nothing*. Washington, DC: Regnery Publishing, 2022.

Beckwith, Francis J. *Defending Life: A Moral and Legal Case Against Abortion Choice*. New York: Cambridge University Press, 2007.

Boonin, David. *A Defense of Abortion*. New York: Cambridge University Press, 2002.

Boyle, Joseph. "Reasons for Action: Evaluative Cognitions That Underlie Motivations." *American Journal of Jurisprudence* 46 (2001): 177–197.

Catechism of the Catholic Church. 2nd edition. 2258–2275, Vatican website. http://www.vatican.va/archive/ccc_css/archive/catechism/p3s2c2a5.htm, 2000.

Condic, Maureen L. *When Does Life Begin?: A Scientific Perspective*. Westchester Institute. White Paper 1. 2008.

Congregation for the Doctrine of the Faith. *Quaestio de abortu* [*Declaration on Procured Abortion*]. Vatican Website. http://www.vatican.va/roman_curia/congregations/cfaith/documents/rc_con_cfaith_doc_19741118_declaration-abortion_en.html, 1974.
Connery, John, S. J. *Abortion: The Development of the Roman Catholic Perspective.* Chicago: Loyola University Press, 1977.
Dworkin, Ronald. *Life's Dominion: An Argument about Abortion, Euthanasia, and Individual Freedom.* New York: Knopf, 1993.
Finnis, John. *Collected Essays, Volume 2: Intention and Identity.* New York: Oxford University Press, 2011.
Finnis, John. *Collected Essay, Volume 3: Human Rights and Common Good.* New York: Oxford University Press, 2011.
Geach, Peter. *God and the Soul.* New York: Schocken, 1969.
George, Robert P., and Christopher Tollefsen. *Embryo: A Defense of Human Life.* New York: Doubleday, 2008.
Grisez, Germain. *Abortion: The Myths, the Realities, and the Arguments.* New York: Corpus Books, 1970.
Grisez, Germain. *The Way of the Lord Jesus, Volume 2: Living a Christian Life.* Chicago, Franciscan Press, 1993.
Haldane, John, and Patrick Lee. "Rational Souls and the Beginning of Life." *Philosophy* 78 (2003): 532–540.
Haldane, John, and Patrick Lee. "St. Thomas Aquinas on Human Ensoulment." *Philosophy* 78 (2003): 255–278.
John Paul II, Pope. *Evangelium vitae* [*Encyclical on The Gospel of Life*]. Vatican Website. http://w2.vatican.va/content/john-paul-ii/en/encyclicals/documents/hf_jp-ii_enc_25031995_evangelium-vitae.html, 1995.
Kaczor, Christopher. *The Ethics of Abortion: Women's Rights, Human Life, and the Question of Justice.* New York: Routledge, 2014.
Langman, Jay. *Langman's Medical Embryology.* 7th edition. Baltimore: William & Saunders, 1995.
Larsen, William J. *Human Embryology.* 3rd edition. Philadelphia: Churchill Livingstone, 2001.
Lee, Patrick. *Abortion and Unborn Human Life.* 2nd edition. Washington, DC: Catholic University of America Press, 2010.
Lee, Patrick and Robert P. George. *Body-Self Dualism in Contemporary Ethics and Politics.* New York: Cambridge University Press, 2008.
Little, Margaret Olivia. "Abortion, Intimacy, and the Duty to Gestate." *Ethical Theory and Moral Practice* 2 (1999): 295–312.
Moore, Keith, and T.V.N. Persaud. *The Developing Human: Clinically Oriented Embryology*, 7th edition. New York: W. B. Saunders, 2003.
O'Rahilly, Ronan, and Fabiola Mueller. *Human Embryology and Teratology.* 3rd edition. New York: John Wiley & Sons, 2000.
Olson, Eric. *What Are We?* Oxford, UK: Oxford University Press, 2007.
Signorelli, J., S. Diaz, and P. Morales. "Kinases, Phosphatases and Proteases during Spermatozoon Capacitation." *Cell and Tissue Research* 349, no. 3 (March 20, 2012): 765.
Singer, Peter. *Practical Ethics.* 3rd edition. New York: Cambridge University Press, 2011.
Steinbock, Bonnie, "Moral Status, Moral Value, and Human Embryos." In *Oxford Handbook for Bioethics*, edited by Bonnie Steinbock, 416–440. Oxford, UK: Oxford University Press, 2009.
Thomson, Judith. "A Defense of Abortion." In *Bioethics: Principles, Issues and Cases*, 2nd edition, edited by Lewis Vaughn, 307–316. Oxford: Oxford University Press, 2012.

Thomson, Judith. "Abortion: Whose Right." *Boston Review*, 20, no. 3 (1995), 11–15. http://new.bostonreview.net/archives/BR20.3/thomson.php

Tooley, Michael. *Abortion and Infanticide*. New York: Oxford University Press, 1983.

Tooley, Michael, Celia Wolfe-Devine, Philip E. Devine, and Allison Jaggar, eds. *Abortion: Three Perspectives*. Oxford: Oxford University Press, 2009.

Vatican Council II. *Gaudium et spes* [*Constitution of the Church on the Modern World*]. Vatican website. http://www.vatican.va/archive/hist_councils/ii_vatican_council/documents/vat-ii_const_19651207_gaudium-et-spes_en.html, 1965.

Warren, Mary Anne. "On the Moral and Legal Status of Abortion." In *Bioethics: Principles, Issues and Cases*, 2nd edition, ed. Lewis Vaughn, 333–342. Oxford, UK: Oxford University Press, 2012).

Williams, Bernard, "The Self and the Future." *Philosophical Review* 79 (1970): 161–180, reprinted in *Problems of the Self* (Cambridge University Press, 1976).

CHAPTER 23

TALK LESS

Why Protestants Will Never Agree on Abortion (and That's OK)

KATHRYN D. BLANCHARD

An ironically large number of books and articles on abortion begin with some indication that there is not much purpose in talking about it. Abortion debates are "intractable," we are told, because participants are generally self-selected from far ends of the spectrum: "Most people who write about this subject do so to shore up agendas that are strongly pro-choice or strongly pro-life," while folks who are ambivalent or indifferent just don't bother.[1] "The clash in these ideologies has resulted in an impasse so great," remarks one author, "so deeply entrenched and the arguments so routine, that one can accurately forecast the course of an argument about abortion based on an individual's first few words."[2] Others aren't quite so sure: "It seems that both sides already know and can refute all arguments of the other side, as if nothing new could be said on the subject."[3] This may be because certain voices have been excluded from previous conversations. Nevertheless, the addition of a greater variety of voices in recent decades has done nothing to "depolarize," "end," or take us "beyond" the culture wars over abortion.

History suggests that it is *not*, in fact, a mere "illusion that we have a hopeless stalemate in the abortion debate."[4] Regardless of how many Americans are truly middle-of-the-road on the issue, the stalemate is real and rests on a basic disagreement over the status of fetal life, vis-à-vis a pregnant person's life. There is simply no "principled middle ground"[5] if a fertilized egg is already an innocent and vulnerable human person; this is a binary position—on or off—and if on, fetal personhood must be protected at all costs. "Cliché though it may be, there really are abortion wars raging in the United States, wars fought on numerous fronts,"[6] not only between popes, activists, and politicians seeking votes. On one side—about 8 percent of American adults—abortion is murder and therefore always wrong.[7] On the other side is everyone else, for whom abortion is something other than outright murder, at least in the early months, and therefore is sometimes right or morally neutral. In any case, "Abortion is not a peripheral issue for Christian theology" for anyone who takes it seriously, because it "stands at the center of some very important questions about what it means to be a creature made in the image of God."[8]

But perhaps it's time to de-center the abortion debate in Christian theology and ethics. If there is no conclusive argument yet to be made, "nothing new under the sun" to be said, the present reader and writer are hereby relieved of the responsibility to solve an insolvable problem. There will be no figuring out of abortion once and for all. There is still value, however, in retracing old ground—which is the whole point of a tradition. In doing so, we have an opportunity to walk the well-trodden path with our full attention and a "beginner's mind," rather than the mind of an "expert" who already has all the answers.[9]

It should go without saying (though it rarely does) that *the* Protestant view of abortion *does not exist*. This means any given Protestant has no choice but to speak "on no other authority at all other than my own, which is no authority at all."[10] Protestantism is a fractured tradition because it began with fracture. Among the favorite motifs of Martin Luther, John Calvin, and other Reformers of the sixteenth century was an emphasis on *freedom*: freedom from having to earn one's salvation with good works, freedom from coercion, and freedom to relate to God directly through prayer, faith, and Scripture without help from ordained clergy.[11] Out of these spiritual declarations of independence grew countless other iterations of Protestant Christianity over the next centuries—Puritans and Quakers, Mennonites and Baptists, African Methodist Episcopalians and the Salvation Army—as Protestants struggled to figure out how best to be disciples of Jesus. At upwards of 20,000 denominations and counting, Protestant unity is utterly beyond the realm of possibility. Still, Protestants do share, along with Catholic and Orthodox Christians, a primary fidelity to Jesus the Christ, whom we know and relate to by a few well-established means—namely Scripture, church tradition, natural reasoning, and experience.[12] In what follows we will examine each of these four sources of Christian thought, thinking generally about what it means to think "Protestantly," and specifically about what being Protestant means for abortion.

Source One: Scripture

A frequent refrain of Luther and other early Protestant reformers was *sola Scriptura*— the idea that "Scripture alone" was the final arbiter of Christian truth, that *only*

Scripture was needed to know Christ. As it turned out, however, this simple rule wasn't actually simple. Things Luther found perfectly obvious (like infant baptism, or fighting wars in the prince's army when ordered to do so) were not at all obvious to the Anabaptists of his time, according to *their* readings of Scripture. Almost within seconds of Luther's ninety-five theses, there were "radical reformers" accusing him and other magisterial reformers of being "papist," or too much in the thrall of Catholic tradition. The sixteenth century knew no end of Christians martyring other Christians over the so-called plain meaning of Scripture.

Today's inheritors of *sola Scriptura* can be found among Evangelical and fundamentalist Christians who present "the Bible" as the infallible, even literal, word of God.[13] As the Southern Baptist Convention (SBC) puts it,

> The Holy Bible was written by men divinely inspired and is God's revelation of Himself to man [sic]. It is a perfect treasure of divine instruction. It has God for its author, salvation for its end, and truth, without any mixture of error, for its matter. . . . It reveals the principles by which God judges us, and therefore is, and will remain to the end of the world the true center of Christian union, and the supreme standard by which all human conduct, creeds, and religious opinions should be tried.[14]

From this perspective, Scripture is of foremost authority in informing Christians how to live, think, and prepare themselves to stand before the eternal judge of the universe.

The main trouble with using Scripture to talk about abortion is that the Bible never mentions it. Yet "pro-life" Christians note that the God of Genesis 1 creates humankind out of nothing, "in our image," both male and female, and tells them to "be fruitful and multiply" (1:27–28). They also note that the author of Psalms attributes to God alone the power of "knitting together" (139:13) and "numbering the days" of (39:4) each human life. According to the Southern Baptist reading, despite its silence the Bible could not be clearer that "children, from the moment of conception, are a blessing and heritage from the Lord" and that human life is sacred "from conception to natural death," thus prohibiting abortion "except in those very rare cases where the life of the mother is clearly in danger."[15] (We can be grateful for this modern concession; Luther, in contrast, suggested women should be honored to die in childbirth.)

Other Protestants, however, find very different messages in Scripture. The United Church of Christ (UCC), which locates itself in the mainstream of "Hebrew-Christian tradition," affirms that humans are made "in God's image." But rather than taking this as a self-explanatory mandate to protect fetal rights, they interpret the verse to mean that humans are charged with responsibility, freedom, and discernment.[16] With Jewish readers, some Protestants look to Exodus 21:22–25 which treats a fetus as less than fully human in the case of injury to a pregnant woman. This lower status is even more pronounced in rabbinic interpretations of Torah, which generally agree that "Jewish tradition does not regard the fetus as a person independent of the mother."[17] The UCC asserts that, while human life is sacred, "an ethical view does not necessarily require an *undifferentiated* concern for life," and that many people "find it difficult, if not impossible, to attribute anything more than the *potentiality* of human personhood to the embryo in its *early* stages."[18]

Scripture, it seems, even for *sola Scriptura* Protestants, is not a simple matter of picking isolated verses and stamping them onto individual test cases. To insist that the Bible supplies its own meaning is to ignore the reality that all reading takes place in communities of tradition—such as the "conservative" SBC or the "liberal" UCC, each of which has its own distinct history, social location, and priorities. It is not that one denomination reads Scripture and the other doesn't, but rather that each tradition *reads Scripture differently*, emphasizing and relativizing different parts, leading them to different conclusions. (Indeed, it may be more accurate to say that we choose Scripture verses that bolster the primitive gut instincts to which we are already committed.[19]) Protestants are people who wrestle with the Bible in order to reach a set of teachings and practices that enable them to "lead a life worthy of the calling to which they have been called, with all humility and gentleness, with patience, bearing with one another in love, making every effort to maintain the unity of the Spirit in the bond of peace" (Ephesians 4:1–3).

The inevitable failure of Scripture to provide a foolproof set of rules by which all Christians everywhere can live is precisely why the sixteenth-century Roman Catholic hierarchy was so horrified by the idea of "Scripture alone." Far from providing a unifying standard, naked Scripture unmoored from tradition was a Pandora's jar of gifts easily abused. The ineluctable diversity of interpretation is why the Catholic Church insisted upon a final correct reading, approved by one spiritual head. There is simply no unity to be had if individual Christians can read the Bible by and for themselves. And yet this freedom to interpret Scripture is precisely what makes Protestants Protestant.

Source Two: Tradition

Luther and Calvin (both of whom grew up Catholic) were well aware of the dangers inherent in individuals interpreting Scripture on their own. They therefore both relied heavily on the corrective power of—wait for it—tradition. For them, the teachings of church fathers and early church practices and creeds were Scripture's much-needed anchors. While Christian tradition sometimes provides conflicting messages on certain matter, such as on questions of pacifism and just war, it is fairly consistent (before the twentieth century) in its stance against abortion.

As early as the second century, Christians like Clement of Alexandria felt it was evil to "kill, by various means of a perverse art, the human offspring, born according to the designs of divine providence" by using "abortive drugs which expel the child completely dead."[20] More than a thousand years later, none of the Protestant Reformers saw fit to question the status quo. In his commentary on Exodus Calvin wrote:

> the foetus, though enclosed in the womb of its mother, is already a human being ... and it is almost a monstrous crime to rob it of the life which it has not yet begun to enjoy. If it seems more horrible to kill a man in his own house than in a field, because a man's house is his place of most secure refuge, it ought surely to be deemed more atrocious to destroy a foetus in the womb before it has come to light.[21]

Unlike Jewish rabbis, Calvin does hold a man responsible for homicide if he kills a fetus when injuring a pregnant woman. For all its emphasis on freedom, older Protestant tradition offers as little support for women's reproductive liberty as its Catholic counterpart.

The trouble with Christian tradition, as feminist and other theologians have pointed out, is it has often been openly sexist and even brutally misogynist, much like the cultures around it.[22] "Most Christian thought and practice has reverted to cultural norms about gender," writes Lisa Sowle Cahill; "Women have been more or less confined to domestic space, and men expected to take responsibility in the economic and political realms."[23] Beverly Harrison put it even more strongly: one cannot talk about abortion "without reference to contemporary scholarly evidence that the disvaluation of women [as something less than full, morally competent members of the human species] is deeply embedded in Western culture and constitutes an unacceptable moral heritage that requires correction."[24] This moral heritage is still very much with us, even decades after Mary Daly said, "Theology which is overtly and explicitly oppressive to women is by no means a thing of the past," just before offering a litany of horrible things male theologians have written about women that would be entertaining had they not been put to such devastating effect.[25] But even the most brazen evidence of Christianity as a glorified He-Man Woman-Haters Club does not render all of its tradition worthless to Protestants today, and we can be thankful that most conservatives now teach that "women are equal in value to men"—even if in perpetual need of men's protection and guidance.[26] Christian history nevertheless serves as a painful warning that theological tradition is a human learning process, highly susceptible to the power of cultural suggestion.

Tradition—a long-standing insiders' argument that reaches into the past—offers no bridge between sides on the matter of abortion. It will always offer more leverage for opponents of abortion, not because the fetus has always been sacred, but because women have always been suspect among male Christians. When Protestant abortion opponents seek to make pro-woman arguments, the best they can usually do is infantilize women, presenting them as helpless victims rather than as human beings with agency, who weigh options and make choices just as men do. For example, according to the SBC, *Roe v. Wade* "was an act of injustice against innocent unborn children as well as against vulnerable women in crisis pregnancy situations, both of which have been victimized by a 'sexual revolution' that empowers predatory and irresponsible men and by a lucrative abortion industry."[27] In (admirably) seeking to shift blame for unwanted pregnancies away from women alone, the SBC and other self-identified "pro-life feminists" often fail to see women as full human adults.

To make a pro-choice argument from tradition therefore calls for—even requires—heterodoxy, along with a concomitant willingness to be dismissed by Christians who think it impossible to think or do anything "Christianly" that hasn't been pre-approved by Augustine, Aquinas, Luther, Calvin, Barth—or preferably all of the above. Feminist theologians remind us that *women's tradition has always existed alongside men's religion*, though it has rarely found a home in men's spaces and is therefore not well preserved in Christian texts.[28] This is no less true regarding abortion than any other aspect of human life.[29] Women inherit unwritten "fruits" from their foremothers' gardens that enable them to find liberation and "claim our life-giving power."[30] These supplementary resources, in addition to the Bible and (men's) Christian tradition, are necessary for "expanding our Christian identity and developing a more inclusive theology" that includes not only ancient Jewish, Greco-Roman, and European texts but also stories from people on the underside of history who found unorthodox ways to survive and to walk with God.[31]

SOURCE THREE: NATURE AND REASON

Since, as it turns out, Protestant Christians agree neither about the interpretation of Scripture, nor about the relative importance of traditions set by earlier Christians, some also turn to nature, apprehensible by human reason, as the final arbiter of Christian behavior. But as readers can now predict, Protestants do not agree on what constitutes "reasonable" readings of the book of "nature," any more than they agree on how to read Scripture or tradition. Reason and natural law are the theological areas most often neglected by Protestants, who have often seen human reason as thoroughly corrupted by sin, in contrast with Catholics who have held that humankind retains an important natural capacity to grasp many important truths. While Catholics have spent centuries perfecting their natural law reasoning, Protestants have largely neglected it and are now out of practice (think: "It's Adam and Eve, not Adam and Steve").[32]

Protestants with historical consciousness are wisely skeptical of arguments based on nature or natural reason. It once seemed "natural" to white Christians that they should enslave Africans. It once seemed "natural" that women were intellectually and physically susceptible to the devil's witchcraft because of defects in their creation.[33] What seems natural or reasonable to one set of folks is often nonsensical to others, since reason is worked out within cultures. What people call *natural* morality is in fact *social* or *cultural*, "forged by people over time through trial and error," leading some Protestant thinkers to deny "that there are available to any rational agent standards of truth sufficient to resolve fundamental moral, scientific, and metaphysical disputes in a definitive way."[34] This is not to say that anything goes (by no means!), but to acknowledge that *human understanding is always provisional and in need of constant reformation*—preferably with the input of as many diverse members of the community as possible.

After the Enlightenment, it was natural (so to speak) that abortion opponents "began to discuss abortion not merely as a failure to understand and obey the will of God but also as a form of ignorance about the workings of nature."[35] Since the 1970s, the scientific understanding of fetal development has included photographs of fetuses floating like astronauts in space. Critics note that these images are anything *but* natural and are fundamentally distorted. "By making [dead] fetuses into autonomous 'babies,'" writes one author, "fetal imagery has masked the interdependent and consequential nature of pregnancy."[36] It creates an illusion of an individual person, when in fact a living fetus is entirely dependent upon a host body. Such images render women and pregnant people invisible, fostering a sense of separateness (and even hostility) between parasite and host. "Once the fetus could be individualized, the idea that a woman and her fetus could have contrasting interests was easier to imagine."[37] Autonomously floating fetuses make visceral sense to many of us because we are steeped in a culture of individualism and rights and can imagine ourselves in their place. Illusory though it is, the independent fetus as "miniature celebrity is a product not only of a voyeuristic medical culture ... but also of a society saturated with liberal individualist political discourses. The fetus represents 'man' in his natural condition," all alone against the world.[38] Now that fetal images have taken root in our collective imagination, it is difficult to "recontextualize the fetus," to "place it back into the uterus, and the uterus back into the woman's [sic] body, and her body back into its social space."[39]

While the science of prenatal health has brought some improvements to women's lives in the last century, "the overlapping boundaries between media spectacle and clinical experience" make it excessively difficult to discern a line between scientific truth and cultural production.[40] The trouble with "nature" is that it has never been as natural as it seems, namely because (as Protestants have always argued) our "reason" is limited, flawed by sin and always incomplete. In the case of fetal life, science can tell us a few things—such as what lies in its DNA, or when its organs make it possible to survive outside the womb—but "personhood" is not a concept science can define. There are, as Wendell Berry puts it, "questions of ultimate seriousness and importance: questions of life and death that exceed the competence of human intelligence and are forever veiled in mystery."[41] In the absence of a final answer provided by nature, humans have no option but to *reason together* about what personhood is, understanding that we may get it wrong or at best only partially right, and may at some points have to leave reason behind and let intuition, compassion, or other factors take the lead.

Source Four: Experience

Experience is the final and perhaps most controversial leg of the theological table, although as we have seen the first three legs are themselves rather shaky, precisely because they depend so much on . . . experience. What each of us finds in Scripture, tradition, and nature—what seems "reasonable" to us as rational beings—has everything to do with who we are, where and when we live, and who our communities are. For many centuries, educated men had the luxury of assuming their experiences were "normal," neutral, untouched by feminine weakness or savage passions, and therefore normative. But as theological conversations have expanded to include people of color and women of all kinds, it has become more apparent that what used to pass for natural was every bit as contingent as "women's theology" or "Black theology." Scholar Brittney Cooper highlights the importance of experience this way: "It's easy when you are young and ain't been through nothing, or when you are white and straight and Christian and been married since you were twenty-five (as so many of my high school friends were) to believe the world works a certain way."[42] John Calvin may not have noticed that his experiences (e.g., growing up a wealthy Frenchman amid the terrors of plague and warfare, or losing his only child in infancy) had anything to do with shaping his theology, but it is certain that they did. Experience is an ineluctable part of Christian ethics, whether we acknowledge it or not.

To that point, experience shapes this essay. Just before turning forty I had a miscarriage (not for the first time). It was a wanted pregnancy; my only son was almost five and we were hoping he could have a sibling. But at my ten-week appointment, when there should have been a heartbeat, I learned that I was carrying a dead fetus. I then had a choice: undergo dilation and curettage ("D and C") in a hospital, or go home and take pills (misoprostol) that would encourage my body to expel the embryo on its own. Opting for the latter, I proceeded to bleed heavily off and on over the next month. In one incident that I can only describe as mini-labor, I painfully pushed something out of my cervix into the toilet. With sadness and some relief, I flushed it away.

This may seem like too much information, but it is necessary to making my point.[43] As I was losing my fetus, a neighbor was too; she had to give birth to a five-month stillborn. She grieved this baby enough to give him a name and tattoo it on her body. Soon thereafter, another neighbor's six-year-old died suddenly of an infection that went to his heart, and yet another neighbor's daughter, a recent college graduate, died suddenly of a blood clot. These two mothers became heavily involved in charities to commemorate their dead children. Living in proximity to such losses, I contextualized and relativized my own grief, real as it was. I would *never* liken my experience in the bathroom to the trauma of a mother who gave birth to a dead baby in a hospital, much less to the grief of parents whose living children had died, leaving them with six or twenty-four years' worth of memories and the intense loss of their bodily presence. I would never post pictures of my "baby" on social media to commemorate its life. In context, I discerned that my miscarriage represented, at most, the *hope* of a child. I suspect most readers instinctively agree that my loss was of a different character than these others.

The experience of grieving a dead embryo is not uncommon, since anywhere from 10 to 25 percent of pregnancies end in miscarriage in the first trimester. Bereavement may influence people's stances on abortion. One researcher found that many anti-abortion activists struggled with abortion as "tragic death," such that their activism became a "ritualized" way to mourn publicly: "Emotional response to 'individual deaths' brought about by abortion was one of the most powerful motives to direct action."[44] Moreover, activist groups often include women who have had abortions, who express the kind of "anguish and remorse" that reinforces pro-life narratives.[45] In short, the main problem with experience is its sheer variety, which is partly why Christian thinkers have often tried to push it aside as a source of wisdom.

Experience has other drawbacks as a source of ethics, the most important being that we do not always know *ourselves* as well or in as straightforward a manner as we might think. Experience is conditioned, as is our narration of experience. We shape our life stories in context, so it is wise to "view narratives as politically, historically, and socially constructed and situated rather than as a reflection of an inherently true experience;" to be careful when we "deploy experience as a form of evidence" since "subjects are constructed *through* social movements."[46] An emphasis on experience can also tend toward individualism in a way that is decidedly un-Christian. "The pro-choice celebration of the autonomous self is plainly antithetical to the ethics of Reformed Protestantism," as one author puts it; "Celebration of the self and its independence of any obligation not voluntarily assumed elevates the human being to the place of God at the center of the normative universe and epitomizes the alienation from God's will that is the essence of sin."[47]

It is here, in the realm of experience, that the mediating power of *community* comes to the forefront. It is in churches that we learn how to read Scripture and engage our traditions, so both liberal and conservative Protestants see an important role for "the church." For Southern Baptists it is "an autonomous local congregation of baptized believers, associated by covenant in the faith and fellowship of the gospel . . . under the Lordship of Christ through democratic processes. In such a congregation each member is responsible and accountable to Christ as Lord."[48] The United Church of Christ shares the sense that baptism forms them into one body with a "promise of 'love, support and care' . . . no matter where your journey leads you."[49] Likewise, in communion, "the many people of God, are made one in the body of Christ, the church. . . . In the breaking of bread, we remember and celebrate Christ's presence among us along with a 'cloud of witnesses'—our ancestors, family and friends who have gone before us."[50] Though the SBC and UCC lay out differently-nuanced guidelines for what it means to be part of the church, both come to their self-understandings and narrate their experiences in the context of a church community.

Talk Less, Act More

The foregoing exploration of Scripture, tradition, reason, and experience seems to affirm what so many have said before: there is really not much left for Protestants to say to each other about abortion. Everyone's individual experiences are, to some degree, "new" to conversations about abortion and therefore worth talking about. But even our own life stories must be read with a hermeneutic of suspicion, since our narrations of ourselves are shaped by Scripture, tradition, and community-approved reason, with all the edifying dignity and negative baggage these things entail. We not only narrate but *are narrated by* those around us, both those we love and those we don't. Thus, I am obliged to conclude—after lo these many words—that the best thing for Protestants to say to each other about abortion is . . . as little as possible.[51]

This is not an original idea. Monastic Christians have often called for silence around mysterious things. Erasmus of Rotterdam satirically rebuked "the theologians" of his era, whom he saw as too certain of their own understanding on matters about which Scripture was silent.[52] Another call for silence came from Marguerite Porète (eventually burned for heresy), who wrote that pretty much *any* talk about an ineffable God "is as much lying as it is telling the truth."[53] While it is certain that Christian Scripture and tradition affirm the *general* worthiness of human life, God's *specific* will for any given pregnancy is not as obvious. Sometimes it's best to admit what we cannot possibly know.

More recently, the poet-theologian Wendell Berry has suggested it is time to stop fighting about abortion. Although nothing humans do in life is truly private, choices about abortion are "more personal than public" and therefore better decided by individuals, with those they love and trust.[54] While not saying abortion is good, he acknowledges that abortion is a matter best handled by pregnant people. He writes, "the inexpressibly intimate involvement of her own body in a woman's decision to have an abortion is a real and urgent consideration, and for a man it is a special one. That it does not involve, and could never have involved, my body does not invalidate my belief that abortion is wrong, but it does require me to be carefully aware of the bodily difference."[55]

Widespread mistrust of women makes it difficult for many theologians to stop talking about abortion, which they see as proof of a "cavalier and rebellious attitude toward human sexuality," "economic irresponsibility," or a "cover-up for evil."[56] (Men's role in the matter is usually exempted from judgment or consequence.) "In the overwhelming majority of cases," goes one Anglican argument, "a woman who elects to terminate her pregnancy is seeking to avoid or reject the consequence of her [sic] sexual sin."[57] According to one Mennonite argument, "permissive attitudes toward abortion teach us that we get to pick our obligations and avoid the burdens and suffering that we did not explicitly choose."[58] The harm from negative views about women falls especially hard on women of color, who, in "an act of historical amnesia," are held to *individual* consequences of *communal* problems; the system "disguises its historical antecedents in order to obviate recognition of former injustices, such as social structures" of slavery, segregation, and intersectional oppression.[59] Black women are five times more, and Latina women twice as likely to have abortions than white women, in part because they tend to be lower-income, and "low-income women . . . are less likely to have health insurance or consistent access to health care, and therefore birth control."[60]

My call to talk less goes out especially to *white* Protestants, who have historically dominated the conversation. Women of color have pointed out the ways in which their oppression has often been at the hands of educated white women "leaning in" to their educations or careers. Even higher-income Black women have more abortions than the national average; they and their babies also die in childbirth at disproportionately high rates—two to three times that of white women.[61] America's history of "neglect of Black infants," writes Dorothy Roberts, "casts doubt on the professed concern for the welfare of the fetus. When a nation has always closed its eyes to the circumstances of pregnant Black women, its current expression of interest in the health of unborn Black children must be viewed with distrust."[62] Indeed, Black women's reproduction is often treated as a social disease in need of remedy.[63]

Women of color have thus broadened the necessary scope of the topic from abortion alone to *reproductive justice* (RJ), a paradigm that tries to comprehend the big picture—systems, socio-economic conditions, cultural and political context—instead of an overly simplified, hyper-individualized "right to choose."[64] It is true that "WOMEN DESERVE BETTER" than abortion, as the pro-life slogan goes, but "only in a society that provided what is now lacking in contemporary America—affordable housing, living wages, better child care, better domestic violence programs, and above all universal health care" would women and children actually have a shot at something better.[65] Meanwhile, in the absence of these things, safe and legal abortion has been a blessing for countless women, some of whose lives it has literally saved.

Very few Protestants are on record saying that widespread abortion is the ideal state of things (#ShoutYourAbortion hashtags notwithstanding).[66] No one aspires to have an abortion, any more than they aspire to have a failed pregnancy. Abortion is a short-term, individual solution—whether to an immediate individual problem or to long-term, systemic, communal problems—but it is a solution, nonetheless. "Legalizing abortion didn't just save women from death and injury and fear of arrest," writes Katha Pollitt, "it didn't just make it possible for women to commit to education and work and free them from shotgun marriages and too many kids. It changed how women saw themselves: as mothers by choice, not fate"; this kind of "existential freedom is not always welcome—indeed, is sometimes quite painful—but that has become part of what women are."[67]

Reproductive justice is not a settled matter and requires constant contextualizing, lest it fixate on symptoms to the exclusion of causes. "The dominant view of liberty reserves most of its protection only for the most privileged members of society," since it doesn't address underlying problems; this preserves the unjust social structure that benefits the "choices" of the dominant, while making it "impossible for some people to make a choice in the first place."[68] Abortion opponents will be quick to point out that fetuses—not poor women—are the least privileged members of society, which brings us back to the stalemate with which we began.

To say (white) Christians should stop debating abortion is not about avoiding a "sensitive topic" so as not to "offend anyone."[69] Instead it does two things. First, in not *talking* about abortion, we are forced to *act*. And second, in not talking about *abortion*, we expand the field of things we do talk about. Rather than focusing only on an individual right, we can imagine genuine economic and social justice, and "oppose multiple and interlocking inequalities simultaneously."[70] We may rightly grieve over lost human potential, but the deaths of early-term fetuses that can be flushed down a toilet (around 90 percent of abortions)[71] are inherently no more grievous than any number of other human evils we tolerate every day, in order to maintain our sanity and ability to function—such as 70,000 poor women, many of them already mothers, who die annually as a result of illegal abortions.[72]

Scripture reports Jesus himself suggested motherhood might not always be worth the pain, and that it might be better for some people not to be born.[73] And Israel's God reportedly caused or allowed any number of infants to be killed for the sake of blessing his chosen people, suggesting that not all infants are created equal.[74] It would certainly be foolish to take any of these verses out of context and make a universal ethic out of them. Given all that we cannot know about God's purposes, Christians are better off dealing with the "planks in our own eyes" than the specks in our neighbors' wombs. However much we might wish Christians didn't have quite so many abortions (and for the record, this *is* what I wish), they do. Of the nearly one million people who had abortions in the United States in a recent year, about a third were Protestants.[75] Whatever else they *believe*, the fact remains: Protestants have abortions.

If it is "theoretically impossible" (to paraphrase James Alison) for a Christian woman to have an abortion without telling her story as "a somewhat penitential account," then it is time for Christians to "attempt to find the shape of a new story that starts to emerge when there is a rupture in impossibility."[76] Christian women *do* have abortions, with full awareness that God is watching. Some may even believe that abortion is murder, and yet feel confident that their decision was justified.[77] Christian churches are marked indelibly by women who have had abortions, who go on to be pillars of their communities as well as devoted parents, edifying teachers, and compassionate pastors. There is no reason this should surprise anyone who reads the Gospels. "God likes the impure people," and "wants them to be on the inside of God's story just as they are."[78] Better Protestant conversations over abortion will take place the more Protestants come to understand ourselves as *forgiven*, rather than primarily as *forgivers*. Christians are "part of the unrepentant hard-hearted block that is in need of forgiveness" rather than innocent people who stand in self-righteous judgment of others' sins.[79]

It would be a strong act of faith—both faith *in* Christ and faithfulness *to* Christ—to stop talking about abortion as such, in favor of *being* the kinds of people who create a world in which abortion is less "intelligible."[80] But we mustn't be naive about it. Abortion has always been. It is ancient, older than both Christianity and the sexual revolution, and it will most certainly exist as long as there are people who get pregnant. To say "talk less" is not to be callous but rather to acknowledge, as Christians must, the brokenness of human social life. The task of theological ethics is not to "set out how everything in the world actually ought to be but unfortunately is not,"[81] which leads to despair, but rather to shape and support real-live humans who make decisions under less-than-perfect conditions. Laws come into existence as reluctant provisions for imperfect people whose "hardness of heart" warrants help (Mark 10:5, Matthew 19:8).

Those for whom fetal personhood from the moment of fertilization is non-negotiable (about 10 percent of Americans) will have difficulty compromising in the slightest, as will those who cannot permit any restrictions whatsoever on women's bodily autonomy (less than 20 percent).[82] The best we can hope for is to act in good faith, with vulnerability and uncertainty. As one author puts it, "we need to open our hearts and not always let our intellects prevail. Opening our hearts might allow us to develop abortion policies that show compassion for women, for fetuses as they develop, for poor women, for young women, and for the disabled."[83]

In Protestant terms, the most just and loving stance may be to emphasize Christian freedom: freedom from the need to justify oneself under the law, freedom from sin, freedom from coercion, freedom to do the right thing willingly, freedom to relate to God directly and with delight rather than fear. Freedom has been at the heart of Protestant Christianity since its inception, and virtue cannot exist without it, which is why Luther (like Paul before him) was so insistent on the limits of the law. This emphasis on freedom makes Protestantism messy and often much less satisfying than a clean set of universal rules; it leaves Protestants open to accusations of libertinism, individualism, sloppy reasoning, and modernist relativism, all of which are indeed Protestant temptations. Genuine Christian freedom therefore takes great courage—the courage to fail and admit when we fail, as well as to stand confidently in grace, even when others deem us failures.

How Not to Talk About Abortion

I end with a few proposals for Protestants going forward, all of which extend from Jesus' command to treat others as we ourselves wish to be treated. The list is overly simple, but points toward ways of *doing* better and *being* better while *talking* about abortion less—or at least less confidently—than usual.

First, Protestants will limit speech about the "sanctity of human life" to already-born persons including sick people, people in prison, hungry people, homeless people, immigrants or strangers, poor people, other people's children, and our most hated enemies and feared persecutors.[84]

Second, Protestants will not talk about "choice" without also acknowledging that, to quote Calvin, "We are not our own."[85] If we claim to be members of God's family, we must also consider our neighbors and the common good in even our most "private" decisions.[86]

Third, Protestants will proactively reject and work to break down the culture of toxic masculinity that rewards men for violence, aggression, sexual conquest, and paternal and domestic uselessness.

Fourth, Protestants will work for high-quality health care for all our neighbors, regardless of ability to pay. This health care will include contraceptives for those who want them, as well as prenatal, obstetric, and pediatric care.[87]

Fifth, Protestants will work for high-quality education for all our neighbors, regardless of income, starting with infant childcare. This will not only prepare children for constructive participation in democratic processes and the economy in which they must live, and free up their parents to do the same, but will also include comprehensive sex education of the sort proven to reduce instances of unintended pregnancy.

Sixth, Protestants will work to create conditions for lives of flourishing, including safe and decent housing, nourishing food, clean water, soil, and air, and dignified work for all, on the understanding that these things are necessities rather than luxuries.

Seventh, understanding that poor people and people of color are disproportionately punished for crimes that wealthy and/or white people commit in similar numbers, Protestants will work against the economy and culture of mass incarceration and state-sponsored violence.

Finally, in awareness of the dangerous political precedent of forcing women to undergo pregnancy and childbirth,[88] Protestants will turn our theological attention away from restricting other people's abortions and toward our own roles in the economy, the environment, education, sexuality, and other areas in which we may be contributing to a culture that is hostile to new life. We will do our part, wherever we are, to create a world in which unwanted and unsafe pregnancies are rarer.

I am inclined to agree with my Catholic counterparts that "there should always be a presumption against taking human life."[89] But only once we have virtually eliminated real evils like hunger and thirst, homelessness, maternal and infant mortality, sexism, job discrimination, ignorance, human trafficking, environmental racism, and all forms of violence from our communities and our nation, can we turn our attention back to abortion in good conscience. Until that time, Protestant Christians may "ponder all these things in our hearts," relying on the promise of God's grace—for fetuses, children, pregnant women, deadbeat dads, and ourselves—just as we are, utterly imperfect and yet loved by God, right here in the midst of a fallen world.

Notes

1. Elizabeth Mensch and Alan Freeman, *The Politics of Virtue* (Durham, NC: Duke University Press, 1993), 2.
2. Phillip B. Levine, *Sex and Consequences: Abortion, Public Policy, and the Economics of Fertility* (Princeton, NJ: Princeton University Press, 2003), 1.

3. Beverly Wildung Harrison, *Our Right to Choose: Toward a New Ethic of Abortion* (Boston: Beacon, 1983), 6. She goes on to note that, in fact, women's experience was, at the time of her writing, still new to the conversation.
4. Charles C. Camosy, *Beyond the Abortion Wars* (Grand Rapids, MI: Eerdmans, 2015), 3.
5. Michael W. McConnell, "Religion and the Search for a Principled Middle Ground on Abortion," Michigan Law Review 1895 (1994).
6. Carole Joffe, *Dispatches from the Abortion Wars* (Boston: Beacon Press, 2009), xi.
7. "America's Abortion Quandary," Pew Research Center (May 6, 2022): https://www.pewresearch.org/religion/2022/05/06/americas-abortion-quandary/.
8. Ruben Rosario Rodriguez, "A Voice for the Voiceless: Discussing Abortion from a Hispanic Perspective," *Apuntes* 22, no. 3 (Fall 2002): 115.
9. This is a term borrowed from Zen Buddhism about meeting familiar things with curiosity: "In the beginner's mind there are many possibilities, but in the expert's there are few." Shunryu Suzuki, *Zen Mind, Beginner's Mind* (Shambhala, 2011).
10. James Alison, *On Being Liked* (New York: Crossroad, 2003), 78.
11. For a more extensive treatment of the history of Protestant thought on abortion, see Gloria Albrecht, "Contraception and Abortion within Protestant Christianity," in *Sacred Rights: The Case for Contraception and Abortion in World Religions*, ed. Daniel C. Maguire, 79–103 (New York: Oxford, 2003).
12. This is sometimes called the "Wesleyan Quadrilateral," though John Wesley himself never used this term and the idea is not unique to him.
13. That "the Bible" doesn't exist except as an ancient mash-up of sources, translated over thousands of years with countless interpretive editorial choices incorporated into it, with no independent existence apart from the communities that honor it, is not for this article to address.
14. "Basic Beliefs," Southern Baptist Convention website. http://www.sbc.net/aboutus/basicbeliefs.asp.
15. "On the Sanctity of Human Life" (2015 resolution), Southern Baptist Convention website, http://www.sbc.net/resolutions/2256/on-the-sanctity-of-human-life.
16. United Church of Christ, *General Synod Statements and Resolutions Regarding Freedom of Choice*, 1971 http://d3n8a8pro7vhmx.cloudfront.net/unitedchurchofchrist/legacy_url/2038/GS-Resolutions-Freedon-of-Choice.pdf?1418425637.
17. Leila Leah Bronner, "Is Abortion Murder? Jews and Christians Will Answer Differently," Bible and Jewish Studies website. http://bibleandjewishstudies.net/articles/abortion.htm. See also Laurie Zoloth, "'Each One an Entire World': A Jewish Perspective on Family Planning," in *Sacred Rights: The Case for Contraception and Abortion in World Religions* (New York: Oxford University, 2003), 21–53.
18. United Church of Christ, *General Synod Statements*, 2 (emphasis original).
19. Psychologists debunk the "rationalist delusion," suggesting that human ethical reasoning exists "not to reconstruct the actual reasons why *we ourselves* came to a judgment," which is mostly an intuitive process, but rather "to find the best possible reasons why *somebody else ought to join us* in our judgment." Jonathan Haidt, *The Righteous Mind* (New York: Vintage, 2012), 34, 52, emphasis original.
20. Clement of Alexandria, *Paedagogus* II, cited by Michael J. Gorman, "Abortion in the Early Church," *In Communion* (November 2004), http://incommunion.org/2004/11/28/abortion-and-the-early-church/.
21. John Calvin, *Commentary on Exodus* (21:22): http://biblehub.com/commentaries/calvin/exodus/21.htm.

22. When the Supreme Court overturned *Roe v. Wade*, it did so on grounds that a right to abortion was not "deeply rooted in this Nation's history and tradition" as established by the white male landowners who had nearly exclusive control over the nation in its tradition-shaping years. *Dobbs v. Jackson Women's Health Organization* (2022).
23. Lisa Sowle Cahill, "Gender and Christian Ethics," in *The Cambridge Companion to Christian Ethics*, ed. Robin Gill, 117 (New York: Cambridge, 2001).
24. Harrison, *Our Right to Choose*, 7–8.
25. Mary Daly, "The Women's Movement: An Exodus Community," *Religious Education* 67, no. 5 (September/October 1972): 229–330.
26. "Position Statements," Southern Baptist Convention website. http://www.sbc.net/aboutus/positionstatements.asp.
27. "Resolution 8: On Thirty Years of *Roe v. Wade* (2003)," Southern Baptist Convention website: http://www.johnstonsarchive.net/baptist/sbcabres.html. Outside investigators have since found the SBC to have a pattern of empowering predatory and irresponsible men through widespread sexual abuse and cover-ups; see Guidepost Solutions, *The Southern Baptist Convention Executive Committee's Response to Sexual Abuse Allegations and an Audit of the Procedures and Actions of the Credentials Committee* (Washington, DC: May 15, 2022).
28. Leila Ahmed writes of the "women's Islam" of her upbringing, which took place entirely outside mosques and apart from Quranic scholarship: "A Border Passage: From Cairo to America—A Woman's Journey," excerpted in *Women's Studies in Religion*, ed. Kate Bagley and Kathleen McIntosh, 35 (Upper Saddle River, NJ: Pearson, 2007).
29. One historian concludes, "Regardless of whether abortion was legal, or how many people believed fetuses had rights or what physicians thought or anything else really, women have always had abortions." In other words, abortion is itself part of tradition. Lauren MacIvor Thompson, "Women Have Always Had Abortions," *New York Times* (December 13, 2019).
30. Chung, Hyun Kyung, "Following Naked Dancing and Long Dreaming," in Bagley and McIntosh, *Women's Studies in Religion*, 31.
31. Kwok, Pui-Lan, "Mothers and Daughters, Writers and Fighters," in Bagley and McIntosh, *Women's Studies in Religion*, 69. Her focus is on Chinese women who willingly combine indigenous traditions with Western Christianity.
32. Zach Schonfeld, "The Surprising History of the Phrase 'Adam and Eve, Not Adam and Steve,'" *Newsweek* (July 1, 2015), http://www.newsweek.com/2015/07/24/surprising-history-phrase-adam-and-eve-not-adam-and-steve-348164.html. While on the surface this is a Biblical argument, it works only because it relies on an exclusively procreative understanding of "natural" sexual intercourse.
33. Jacob Sprenger and Heinrich Kramer, "*Malleus maleficarum* (1486)," in *Women and Religion: The Original Sourcebook of Women in Christian Thought*, ed. Elizabeth A. Clark and Herbert Warren Richardson, 126 (New York, NY: HarperCollins, 1996).
34. Stanley Hauerwas, "The Virtues of Alasdair MacIntyre," *First Things*, October 2007, https://www.firstthings.com/article/2007/10/the-virtues-of-alasdair-macintyre.
35. Laurie Shrage, *Abortion and Social Responsibility: Depolarizing the Debate* (New York: Oxford, 2003), 88.
36. Ann Neumann, "The Patient Body: Visual Politics of Abortion," *The Revealer* (March 8, 2017): https://wp.nyu.edu/therevealer/2017/03/08/the-patient-body-visual-politics-of-abortion/.
37. Lisa Wade, "How Fetal Photography Changed How We Think about Motherhood," *Sociological Images* blog: https://thesocietypages.org/socimages/2014/11/07/visualizing-the-fetus/.

38. Shrage, *Abortion and Social Responsibility*, 92.
39. Ibid., 89. Here I wish to acknowledge that not *only* women have uteruses, and not *all* women have uteruses. That said, the vast majority (well over 99 percent) of pregnant people and those seeking abortions are still women. For details see "United States Abortion Demographics," Guttmacher Institute: https://www.guttmacher.org/united-states/abortion/demographics.
40. Rosalind Pollack Petchesky, "Fetal Images: The Power of Visual Culture in the Politics of Reproduction," *Feminist Studies* 13, no. 2 (Summer, 1987): 265.
41. Wendell Berry, "Caught in the Middle: On Abortion and Homosexuality," *Christian Century* (March 20, 2013): https://www.christiancentury.org/article/2013-03/caught-middle.
42. Brittney Cooper, "I remember this brief period in high school when I was a pro-lifer," Facebook post, June 26, 2022: https://www.facebook.com/Dr.BrittneyCooper/posts/pfbid02KheLCqsGLHppryvxYT8PwT15CSK7QEckN90Lu843s1GaTb2FjfNthaBqu23ccgE2l.
43. For an excellent discussion of why our individual experiences are relevant to our perspectives on abortion, I recommend the introduction of Rebecca Todd Peters, *Trust Women: A Progressive Christian Argument for Reproductive Justice* (New York: Beacon Press, 2019).
44. Carol J. C. Maxwell, *Pro-Life Activists in America: Meaning, Motivation, and Direct Action* (New York: Cambridge, 2002), 122 and 143.
45. Maxwell, *Pro-Life Activists in America*, 144. It is reasonable to ask where the women are when all-male groups of lawmakers propose or pass legislation to make women pay for funerals or even go to prison when they miscarry (Karissa Haugesberg, "'How Come There's Only Men up There?': Catholic Women's Grassroots Anti-Abortion Activism," *Journal of Women's History* 27, no. 4 (Winter 2015): 38–61). E.g., Amanda Terkel, "Donald Trump Signs Anti-Abortion Executive Order Surrounded By Men," *Huffington Post* (January 23, 2017), and "Room Full of Men Decides Fate of Women's Health Care," *Huffington Post* (March 23, 2017).
46. Carly Thomsen, "The Politics of Narrative, Narrative as Politic: Rethinking Reproductive Justice Frameworks through the South Dakota Abortion Story," *Feminist Formations* 27, no. 2 (Summer 2015): 20. Emphasis original.
47. McConnell, "Religion and the Search," 1905.
48. "Basic Beliefs," http://www.sbc.net/aboutus/basicbeliefs.asp.
49. "What We Believe," http://www.ucc.org/about-us_what-we-believe.
50. Ibid.
51. Author's note: This article was originally drafted in 2017, when *Roe v. Wade* was still settled law. As I revise in 2022, a week after the *Dobbs* decision, I note that political discussion and activism around *abortion laws* are still necessary, even if Christian theological debates about *abortion as such* are all but pointless.
52. They were "so blessed by their self-love as to be fully persuaded that they themselves dwell in the third heaven, looking down from high above on all other mortals as if they were earth-creeping vermin almost worthy of their pity," and dared to "explicate sacred mysteries just as arbitrarily as they please." Desiderius Erasmus, "In Praise of Folly" (1510), in *A Reformation Reader*, ed. Denis R. Janz, 57–58 (Minneapolis: Augsburg Fortress, 1999).
53. Marguerite Porète, *Mirror of Simple Souls*, trans. Ellen Babinsky (Paulist, 1993), chapter 119.
54. Berry, "Caught in the Middle."
55. Ibid. On gender, see Carol Maxwell's book which includes an important study of "gender differences in motivation" among pro-life activists; she finds that women, in general, act

more out of a sense of relationship, while men, in general, act upon a sense of duty. See *Pro-Life Activists in America*, 238–239.
56. Lindsey Disney and Larry Poston, "The Breath of Life: Christian Perspectives on Conception and Ensoulment," *Anglican Theological Review* 92, no. 2 (Spring 2010): 294.
57. Ibid.
58. Joseph J. Kotva Jr., "The Question of Abortion: Christian Virtue and Government Legislation," *Mennonite Quarterly Review* 79, no. 4 (October 2005): 496. Even he eschews state-sponsored coercion: "Using moral persuasion, through the example of our lives and the power of our words, to change people's minds about abortion is more in keeping with Anabaptist convictions regarding both violence and the state" (p. 502).
59. Steven Martinot, "Motherhood and the Invention of Race," *Hypatia* 22, no. 2 (Spring 2007): 81. In blaming an individual woman, he argues, the state is able "to sanctify its withholding of humane conditions" (p. 95). We will end up with mostly Black women in prison, "yet another form of a historical structure reappearing in the present that requires the condemnation and sacrifice of Black bodies and Black personhood in the service of the purity of whiteness" (p. 96).
60. Zoe Dutton, "Abortion's Racial Gap," *Atlantic* (September 22, 2014).
61. Center for Disease Control and Prevention, "Working Together to Reduce Black Maternal Mortality," April 6, 2022, https://www.cdc.gov/healthequity/features/maternal-mortality/index.html.
62. Dorothy Roberts, *Killing the Black Body* (New York: Vintage, 1997), 183.
63. E.g., "to reduce the number of children born to women receiving public assistance." Ibid., 209.
64. On reproductive justice see National Asian Pacific American Women's Forum, "Reproductive Health," http://www.napawf.org/reproductivejustice.html; and Loretta Ross and Rickie Solinger, *Reproductive Justice: An Introduction* (University of California Press, 2017). For an African American male doctor's point of view, see Willie Parker, *Life's Work* (New York: Atria/37 INK, 2017).
65. Joffe, *Dispatches from the Abortion Wars*, 103.
66. See http://shoutyourabortion.com/.
67. Katha Pollitt, *Pro: Reclaiming Abortion Rights* (New York: Picador, 2014), 3.
68. Roberts, *Killing the Black Body*, 294.
69. Natalia Deeb-Sossa and Heather Kane, "Not Avoiding a 'Sensitive Topic': Strategies to Teach about Women's Reproductive Rights," *NWSA Journal* 21, no. 1 (Spring 2009): 151.
70. Ibid., 170. Making a similar, Catholic-oriented argument, theologian Emily Reimer-Barry writes, "The pro-life movement must detach from patriarchal power dynamics, reject oversimplified discourse, and refocus our efforts away from making abortion illegal and instead foster a culture and society that empowers pregnant women to choose life": "Another Pro-Life Movement Is Possible," *Proceedings of the Catholic Theological Society of America* 74 (2019): 41.
71. CDC, "Abortion Surveillance—United States, 2019," *Surveillance Summaries* 70, no. 9 (November 26, 2021), https://www.cdc.gov/mmwr/volumes/70/ss/ss7009a1.htm#T10_down.
72. Susan A. Cohen, "Facts and Consequences: Legality, Incidence and Safety of Abortion Worldwide," *Guttmacher Policy Review* 12, no. 4 (November 2009).
73. Luke 23:28–29; Mark 14:21.
74. Matthew 2:13–18; Exodus 12:29–30; Deuteronomy 20:16–18.
75. "Seventeen percent identified as mainline Protestant, 13 percent as evangelical Protestant and 24 percent as Roman Catholic, while 8 percent identified with some other religion.

Thirty-eight percent of patients did not identify with any religion." Jenna Jerman, Rachel K. Jones, and Tsuyoshi Onda, "Characteristics of U.S. Abortion Patients in 2014 and Changes Since 2008," *Guttmacher Institute Report*, May 2014, https://www.guttmacher.org/report/characteristics-us-abortion-patients-2014#full-article.
76. James Alison, *On Being Liked*, xi. Alison's book deals mainly with the supposed theoretical "impossibility" of gay and lesbian Christians, which contrasts with the reality of them.
77. In Karen McCarthy Brown, *Mama Lola* (Berkeley: University of California, 2001), 241, abortion is seen by the Catholic-Vodou priestess as an evil, but one in which she has nevertheless partaken: "You know, human being do everything. That's life! Right?"
78. Alison, *On Being Liked*, x.
79. Alison, *On Being Liked*, 38.
80. Alasdair MacIntyre, "The Intelligibility of Action," in *Rationality, Relativism, and the Human Sciences*, ed. Joseph Margolis, Michael Krausz, and Richard Burian, 63–80 (Boston: M. Nijhoff, 1986).
81. The quotation is attributed to Bonhoeffer, via Barth, in Mensch and Freeman, *The Politics of Virtue*, 57.
82. Pew, "America's Abortion Quandary."
83. Shrage, *Abortion and Social Responsibility*, 138.
84. Matthew 19:14; 25:41–44.
85. John Calvin, *Institutes of the Christian Religion*, ed. John T. McNeill, trans. Ford Lewis Battles, Library of Christian Classics (Philadelphia: Westminster, 1960 [1559]), 3.7.1.
86. See Harrison, *Our Right to Choose*, 52.
87. "Where contraceptive use increased the most, abortion rates dropped the most. . . . Where contraceptive use is high, abortion can be legal and widely available, and still relatively rare. The lowest abortion rates in the world can be found in western and northern Europe, where abortion has been legal for decades but access to contraception is widespread." Cohen, "Facts and Consequences."
88. Tyrene White, *China's Longest Campaign: Birth Planning in the People's Republic, 1949–2005* (Ithaca, NY: Cornell University Press, 2006), 72. China's precedent is a cautionary tale. To jump-start its policies, the government employed "shock attacks," including traveling and local teams of educators and medical professionals to conduct "intimidation meetings" and institute the widespread use of IUDs, abortions (even late-term), and sterilizations for both men and women (pp. 108–109).
89. Reimer-Barry, "Another Pro-Life Movement Is Possible," 23.

Bibliography

Ahmed, Leila. "A Border Passage: From Cairo to America—A Woman's Journey." *Women's Studies in Religion*, edited by Kate Bagley and Kathleen McIntosh, 35–47. Upper Saddle River, NJ: Pearson, 2007.

Alison, James. *On Being Liked*. New York: Crossroad, 2003.

Albrecht, Gloria. "Contraception and Abortion within Protestant Christianity." *Sacred Rights: The Case for Contraception and Abortion in World Religions*, edited by Daniel C. Maguire, 79–103. New York: Oxford, 2003.

Berry, Wendell. "Caught in the Middle: On Abortion and Homosexuality." *Christian Century* (March 20, 2013): https://www.christiancentury.org/article/2013-03/caught-middle.

Bronner, Leila Leah. "Is Abortion Murder? Jews and Christians Will Answer Differently." Bible and Jewish Studies website. http://bibleandjewishstudies.net/articles/abortion.htm.

Brown, Karen McCarthy. *Mama Lola*. Berkeley: University of California, 2001.

Cahill, Lisa Sowle. "Gender and Christian Ethics." In *The Cambridge Companion to Christian Ethics*, edited by Robin Gill. New York: Cambridge, 2001.

Calvin, John. *Commentary on Exodus*. 1563. http://biblehub.com/commentaries/calvin/exodus/21.htm.

Calvin, John. *Institutes of the Christian Religion*. Edited by John T. McNeill. Translated by Ford Lewis Battles. Philadelphia: Westminster, 1960 (1559).

Camosy, Charles C. *Beyond the Abortion Wars*. Grand Rapids, MI: Eerdmans, 2015.

Center for Disease Control and Prevention. "Working Together to Reduce Black Maternal Mortality." April 6, 2022. https://www.cdc.gov/healthequity/features/maternal-mortality/index.html

Center for Disease Control and Prevention. "Abortion Surveillance—United States, 2019," *Surveillance Summaries* 70, no. 9 (November 26, 2021). https://www.cdc.gov/mmwr/volumes/70/ss/ss7009a1.htm.

Cohen, Susan A. "Facts and Consequences: Legality, Incidence and Safety of Abortion Worldwide." *Guttmacher Policy Review* 12, no. 4 (November 2009).

Cooper, Brittney. 2022. "I remember this brief period in high school when I was a pro-lifer." Facebook post. June 26, 2022. https://www.facebook.com/Dr.BrittneyCooper/posts/pfbid02KheLCqsGLHppryvxYT8PwT15CSK7QEckN9oLu843s1GaTb2FjfNthaBqu23ccgE2l.

Daly, Mary. "The Women's Movement: An Exodus Community." *Religious Education* 67, no. 5 (September/October 1972): 227–233.

Deeb-Sossa, Natalia and Heather Kane. "Not Avoiding a 'Sensitive Topic': Strategies to Teach about Women's Reproductive Rights." *NWSA Journal* 21, no. 1 (Spring 2009): 151–177.

Disney, Lindsey and Larry Poston. "The Breath of Life: Christian Perspectives on Conception and Ensoulment." *Anglican Theological Review* 92, no. 2 (Spring 2010): 271–295.

Dutton, Zoe. "Abortion's Racial Gap." *Atlantic*. September 22, 2014. https://www.theatlantic.com/health/archive/2014/09/abortions-racial-gap/380251/

Erasmus, Desiderius. "In Praise of Folly." (1510). *A Reformation Reader*, edited by Denis R. Janz, 63–73. Minneapolis: Augsburg Fortress, 1999.

Gorman, Michael J. "Abortion in the Early Church." *In Communion*. November 2004. http://incommunion.org/2004/11/28/abortion-and-the-early-church/.

Guidepost Solutions. *The Southern Baptist Convention Executive Committee's Response to Sexual Abuse Allegations and an Audit of the Procedures and Actions of the Credentials Committee*. Washington, DC: May 15, 2022.

Haidt, Jonathan. *The Righteous Mind*. New York: Vintage, 2012.

Harrison, Beverly Wildung. *Our Right to Choose: Toward a New Ethic of Abortion*. Boston: Beacon, 1983.

Hauerwas, Stanley. "The Virtues of Alasdair MacIntyre." *First Things*. October 2007. https://www.firstthings.com/article/2007/10/the-virtues-of-alasdair-macintyre

Haugesberg, Karissa. "'How Come There's Only Men Up There?': Catholic Women's Grassroots Anti-Abortion Activism." *Journal of Women's History* 27, no. 4 (Winter 2015): 38–61.

Jerman, Jenna, Rachel K. Jones, and Tsuyoshi Onda. "Characteristics of U.S. Abortion Patients in 2014 and Changes Since 2008." *Guttmacher Institute Report* (May 2014). https://www.guttmacher.org/report/characteristics-us-abortion-patients-2014

Joffe, Carole. *Dispatches from the Abortion Wars*. Boston: Beacon Press, 2009.

Kaplan, Sarah. "Indiana Woman Jailed for 'Feticide.' It's Never Happened Before." *Washington Post*. April 1, 2015. https://www.washingtonpost.com/news/morning-mix/wp/2015/04/01/indiana-woman-jailed-for-feticide-its-never-happened-before

Kotva, Joseph J., Jr. "The Question of Abortion: Christian Virtue and Government Legislation." *Mennonite Quarterly Review* 79, no. 4 (October 2005): 439–480.

Kwok, Pui-Lan. "Mothers and Daughters, Writers and Fighters." In Bagley and McIntosh, *Women's Studies in Religion*, 65–73.

Kyung, Chung Hyun. 2007. "Following Naked Dancing and Long Dreaming." In Bagley and McIntosh, *Women's Studies in Religion*, 23–34.

Levine, Phillip B. *Sex and Consequences: Abortion, Public Policy, and the Economics of Fertility*. Princeton, NJ: Princeton University Press, 2003.

MacIntyre, Alasdair. "The Intelligibility of Action." In *Rationality, Relativism, and the Human Sciences*, edited by Joseph Margolis, Michael Krausz, and Richard Burian, 63–80. Boston: M. Nijhoff, 1986.

Marcotte, Amanda. "Texas Will Now Require Funeral Services Whenever a Woman Has an Abortion." *Salon*. November 30, 2016. http://www.salon.com/2016/11/30/texas-will-now-require-funeral-services-whenever-a-woman-has-an-abortion/

Martinot, Steven. "Motherhood and the Invention of Race." *Hypatia* 22, no. 2 (Spring 2007): 79–97.

Maxwell, Carol J. C. *Pro-Life Activists in America: Meaning, Motivation, and Direct Action*. New York: Cambridge, 2002.

McConnell, Michael W. "Religion and the Search for a Principled Middle Ground on Abortion." *Michigan Law Review* 1895 (1994).

Mensch, Elizabeth, and Alan Freeman. *The Politics of Virtue*. Durham, NC: Duke University Press, 1993.

National Asian Pacific American Women's Forum. "Reproductive Health." NAPAWF.org: http://www.napawf.org/reproductivejustice.html.

Neumann, Ann. "The Patient Body: Visual Politics of Abortion." March 8, 2017: https://wp.nyu.edu/therevealer/2017/03/08/the-patient-body-visual-politics-of-abortion/.

Parker, Willie. *Life's Work*. New York: Atria/37 INK, 2017.

Petchesky, Rosalind Pollack. "Fetal Images: The Power of Visual Culture in the Politics of Reproduction." *Feminist Studies* 13, no. 2 (Summer 1987): 263–292.

Peters, Rebecca Todd. *Trust Women*. Boston: Beacon, 2018.

Pew Research Center, "America's Abortion Quandary." May 6, 2022. https://www.pewresearch.org/religion/2022/05/06/americas-abortion-quandary/.

Pollitt, Katha. *Pro: Reclaiming Abortion Rights*. New York: Picador, 2014.

Porète, Marguerite. *Mirror of Simple Souls*. Edited by Ellen Babinsky. Mahwah, NJ: Paulist, 1993.

Reimer-Barry, Emily. "Another Pro-Life Movement Is Possible." *Proceedings of the Catholic Theological Society of America* 74 (2019): 41.

Roberts, Dorothy. *Killing the Black Body*. New York: Vintage, 1997.

Rodriguez, Ruben Rosario. "A Voice for the Voiceless: Discussing Abortion from a Hispanic Perspective." *Apuntes* 22, no. 3 (Fall 2002).

Ross, Loretta and Rickie Solinger. *Reproductive Justice: An Introduction*. University of California Press, 2017.

Schonfeld, Zach. "The Surprising History of the Phrase 'Adam and Eve, Not Adam and Steve.'" *Newsweek*. July 1, 2015. http://www.newsweek.com/2015/07/24/surprising-history-phrase-adam-and-eve-not-adam-and-steve-348164.html.

Sheppard, Kate. "Mississippi Could Soon Jail Women for Stillbirths, Miscarriages." *Mother Jones*. May 23, 2013. http://www.motherjones.com/politics/2013/05/buckhalter-mississippi-stillbirth-manslaughter/.

Shrage, Laurie. *Abortion and Social Responsibility: Depolarizing the Debate*. New York: Oxford, 2003.

Southern Baptist Convention. "Basic Beliefs." SBC.net. http://www.sbc.net/aboutus/basicbeliefs.asp.

Southern Baptist Convention. "On the Sanctity of Human Life" (2015 resolution). SBC.net. http://www.sbc.net/resolutions/2256/on-the-sanctity-of-human-life.

Southern Baptist Convention. "Position Statements," SBC.net. http://www.sbc.net/aboutus/positionstatements.asp.

Southern Baptist Convention. "Resolution 8: On Thirty Years of *Roe v. Wade* (2003)," SBC.net: http://www.johnstonsarchive.net/baptist/sbcabres.html.

Sprenger, Jacob and Heinrich Kramer. "*Malleus maleficarum* (1486)." In *Women and Religion: The Original Sourcebook of Women in Christian Thought*, edited by Elizabeth A. Clark and Herbert Warren Richardson, 126. New York, NY: HarperCollins, 1996.

Suzuki, Shunryu. *Zen Mind, Beginner's Mind*. Shambhala, 2011.

Terkel, Amanda. "Donald Trump Signs Anti-Abortion Executive Order Surrounded by Men." *Huffington Post*. January 23, 2017. http://www.huffingtonpost.com/entry/donald-trump-abortion-men_us_5886369be4b0e3a7356a7910.

Terkel, Amanda. "Room Full of Men Decides Fate of Women's Health Care." *Huffington Post*. March 23, 2017. https://www.huffpost.com/entry/room-men-maternity-coverage_n_58d416e6e4b02d33b749b713.

Thomsen, Carly. "The Politics of Narrative, Narrative as Politic: Rethinking Reproductive Justice Frameworks through the South Dakota Abortion Story." *Feminist Formations* 27, no. 2 (Summer 2015): 1–26.

Thompson, Lauren MacIvor. "Women Have Always Had Abortions." *New York Times*. December 13, 2019.

United Church of Christ. *General Synod Statements and Resolutions Regarding Freedom of Choice* (1971): http://d3n8a8pro7vhmx.cloudfront.net/unitedchurchofchrist/legacy_url/2038/GS-Resolutions-Freedon-of-Choice.pdf?1418425637.

United Church of Christ. "What We Believe." http://www.ucc.org/about-us_what-we-believe.

Wade, Lisa. "How Fetal Photography Changed How We Think about Motherhood." *Sociological Images* blog: https://thesocietypages.org/socimages/2014/11/07/visualizing-the-fetus/.

White, Tyrene. *China's Longest Campaign: Birth Planning in the People's Republic, 1949–2005*. Ithaca, NY: Cornell University Press, 2006.

Zoloth, Laurie. "'Each One an Entire World': A Jewish Perspective on Family Planning." In Maguire, *Sacred Rights*, 21–53.

CHAPTER 24

ISLAMIC PERSPECTIVES ON ABORTION

THOMAS EICH

In contemporary parlance, abortion is regularly understood as induced abortion rather than spontaneous abortion, which is often equated with the term *miscarriage*. The most important criterion to differentiate between the two is the aspect of intention. Looking at texts of Islamic normativity, which constitute a discursive tradition reaching over more than a millennium, it has to be kept in mind that the distinction between abortion and miscarriage was historically very difficult to make and often not pivotal. Also, the Muslim religious scholars did not separate clearly *legal* and *moral* assessments as belonging to entirely different areas of scholarly reflection. Rather, they considered both to belong to their professional activities.

For the sake of clarity, three text corpora can be distinguished with which Muslim religious scholars (*'ulamā'*) started working overtime when deriving normative statements. 1) The Qur'an, which Muslim dogma considers to be the verbally inspired word of God. This text reached closure during the seventh century. It does not contain passages relating directly to abortion. However, several passages describe prenatal development and others denounce infanticide and murder. 2) Sayings, many attributed to the Prophet, others to his companions. In many instances sayings originally ascribed to the companions eventually became attributed to the Prophet himself—a process unmistakenly noted and analyzed by the Muslim tradition itself. They are summarily called Hadith here, a term literally meaning "speech, saying," which also points to the fact that the transmission of these Hadiths was originally oral. During the eighth century writing started to play a more common role, though more in the form of an aide-memoire for the oral transmission. In a process stretching well into the early tenth century, the habit became widely accepted to rely on certain written collections of Hadith, many of which arrange the material according to topic. Through their structuring and the inclusion or elimination of variant material these collections can reflect legal debates of their time. 3) Texts written by Muslim thinkers over time who were trying to deduce their normative statements from Qur'an and Hadith (arab. *fiqh*).

This article will mostly analyze material from the source groups of Hadith and *fiqh*. Where necessary, Qur'an passages will also be incorporated for clarification. Analyzing these sources separately aims at a diachronical approach, situating them in their respective historical context and identifying interpretational processes. This approach also helps to show how different foci of discussion existed at different times, what was *not* discussed, and to what extent the source material is difficult to interpret.

Terminology

Does the corpus of Hadith know a technical terminology in the sense of consistent use of a specific noun and correspondent verb forms? There is only one specific term describing the act of causing a premature end of a pregnancy: *imlāṣ*, with only miniscule traces of usage of an accompanying verb form. There are indications that the term had fallen out of use by the ninth century, eventually was not understood anymore and was explained with *siqṭ* ("abort") (Ibn Māja II:882, Abū Dawūd VI:627). The implied shift from the act of abortion to the result of the act probably reflects jurisprudential concerns about possible ways to prove that an abortion had occurred at all. The nowadays common terminology of *isqāṭ* and *ijhāḍ* for abortion is not attested in Hadith. However, usage of the verb-form *asqaṭa(t)* in that sense can be found. For *ijhāḍ* there is no verb-form in the Hadith.

The *Hadith* material knows several terms to describe the unborn in the context of induced abortion or premature delivery: abort (*siqṭ*), embryo (*janīn*), sometimes "what was in her belly" (*mā kāna fī baṭnihā*) or similar expressions. *Janīn* is overwhelmingly used in material discussing scenarios of ending a pregnancy prematurely, be it an induced abortion or the situation that a pregnant woman is killed and the unborn dies with her. In this material the scenario of an *intended* induced abortion is touched upon but does not receive much attention. *Siqṭ* is more often used in chapters devoted to the discussion whether (parts of) funerary rites should be applied to deceased small children or fatal premature deliveries.

Positions in Sunni Hadith from the Eighth to Tenth Centuries

In my characterization of the material I provide an analysis of two collections from the eighth century containing prophetic Hadith as well as statements of other early authorities, the *Muwaṭṭa'* of Mālik b. Anas (d.795) and especially the *Muṣannaf* of ʿAbd al-Razzāq al-Ṣanʿānī (d.827). Against the background of these earlier sources I will refer to later collections from the ninth and tenth centuries in order to point out continuities and differences. Within these sources I analyze primarily the chapters on blood money (*diya*), which contain a subchapter on ending a pregnancy prematurely. Where appropriate I add analysis of the chapter on funerary rites (*janā'iz*) which also covers the scenario of spontaneous late abortions. These sources emphasize legal rather than moral or ethical aspects in their discussions about abortion. In the eighth century Sunni sources three approaches concerning legal consequences can be identified, which are to be considered as independent of each other at this time. I label them as gradualist approach, binary approach, and expiation approach.

The *gradualist approach* computes the fine for an abortion (*ghurra*) according to the developmental stages of the unborn. In defining these stages, a linguistic link to Qur'anic descriptions of prenatal development is clearly visible. For example, Q 23:12–14 reads:

> Man We did create from a quintessence of clay. Then We placed him as a sperm-drop (*nuṭfa*) in a place of rest, firmly fixed. Then We made the fluid-drop into a clot of congealed blood (*ʿalaqa*); then of that clot We made a little lump of flesh (*muḍgha*); then we made out of that little lump bones (*ʿiẓām*) and clothed the bones with flesh (*fa-kasawnā al-ʿiẓām laḥman*); then we developed out of it another creature (*khalq ākhar*). So blessed be Allah, the best to create!

ʿAbd al-Razzāq's *Muṣannaf* records three opinions discussing abortion with reference to this terminology. In one of them, Qatāda (d.736?) states that two third of the *ghurra* are due if the unborn has reached the *muḍgha*-stage and one third for the *ʿalaqa*-stage (ʿAbd al-Razzāq X:56). The approach to divide the fine according to developmental stages is also visible in a practice recorded for the Umayyad caliph ʿAbd al-Malik (d.705) which is also ascribed to ʿAlī b. Abī Ṭālib (d.661) (ʿAbd al-Razzāq X:55f):

> He ruled for the embryo if he slipped out (*immalaṣa*) as an *ʿalaqa* with 20 dinar. If it is a *muḍgha*, 40 dinar. If it is bones, 60. If the bone has been clothed with flesh, 80. And if its forming (*khalquhu*) is completed and its hair has taken root (*nabata shaʿruhu*), it is 100.

Note that this description does not use any technical term for the fine and simply states absolute numbers.

In a third statement, ʿAṭā' (d.732) says that blood money (*nadhar*) is due even before the *muḍgha*-stage and before the forming is completed (ʿAbd al-Razzāq X:56). This statement can be interpreted in different ways. In isolation, it could be understood to mean that *full* blood money has to be paid already for an early abortion. On the other hand, the statement is grouped together with other material (the only material in 'Abd al-Razzāq's chapter using the Qur'anic term *mudgha*) expressing the view that the blood money is broken down according to developmental stages of the unborn. Put into this context 'Aṭā's statement could thus be interpreted to reiterate the point that *at least something* of the blood money is due before the *mudgha*-stage.

This material is not present in later major Hadith collections. It also did not influence Sunni *fiqh* texts to adapt the scheme of a concrete graded fine, though the material remained known to at least some *fiqh* authorities (Ibn Qudāma XII: 64).

The *binary approach* does not differentiate according to several developmental stages of the unborn and focuses on the question of whether a fine is due or not. It is most elaborately expressed in a story describing a quarrel between two women (variants as to detail exist). One woman beat the other, who was pregnant and died after the blow. Muḥammad was asked for a ruling and he decreed that the full blood money (*diya* or *'aql* according to version) had to be paid for the mother and a *ghurra* was due for the embryo (*janīn*). The *ghurra* is specified as "a male or female slave" (*'abd aw ama* ['Abd al-Razzāq 56–59, 61f (5 variants)] or *'abd aw walīda* ['Abd al-Razzāq X:60, Mālik IV:195] or *ghulām . . . jāriya* ['Abd al-Razzāq X:61]). In many instances somebody objects concerning the *ghurra*: "How can somebody be subsumed under the legal category of blood money who has not eaten, not drunk, not spoken, or cried?" or a similar expression ('Abd al-Razzāq X:56f). Muḥammad rejects this critique as talk from soothsayers of pre-Islamic times. (See also Holmes-Katz, 27; Stewart 1990) In some material the *ghurra* was explicitly broadened beyond a slave to other living beings in the possession of the culprit: a horse or a certain number of sheep or camel ('Abd al-Razzāq X:59, 62f; see also Abū Dawūd VI:635). However, the variants defining *ghurra* as a slave had the strongest impact on later abortion debates (Holmes-Katz, 27–29, Ibn Qudāma XII:64). Beside this group, other material equates the *ghurra* with 50 dinar. In all likelihood this material—not ascribed to the Prophet—was originally an independent contribution which implicitly linked the *ghurra* more directly to the *diya* of a born human which is expressed in money ('Abd al-Razzāq X:63, Mālik IV:196).

The material on abortion also reflects the ambiguity that is specific to cases of intentional killing for which Q 2:178 knows the capital sentence, but offers the possibility to replace the retaliation with paying blood money (Lange 2011). Now, sources from the eighth century include into the abortion chapter the statement that if somebody intentionally killed a pregnant woman, the perpetrator must be executed. (Mālik IV: 197) Later Hadith collections integrate this aspect into variants of the two quarreling women by stating that the female perpetrator had to pay the *ghurra* "for the embryo" (*fī l-janīn*) and was sentenced to death "for the killing of [the woman]" (*tuqtal bi-hâ*) (Abū Dawūd VI:629; Ibn Māja II:882; Dārimī, 568). Possibly this Hadith material is in the background of variants of the story where the female perpetrator dies afterward and the question is settled who receives her inheritance and who is responsible for paying the blood money (*'aql*) after her demise (e.g., Bukhārī, 1200). Therefore, some Hadith collections document in their abortion chapters reverberations of early Islamic legal discussions about capital punishment.

All of this material shares the concept that if a case of ending a pregnancy prematurely occurred, it had to be fined with one amount of money or one article of value without any grading according to the actual developmental state of the unborn—therefore being labeled as the *binary approach* here. It became foundational for Sunni *fiqh* texts (Holmes-Katz, 27–29).

In this group of material about recompensation—binary and gradualist approach alike—the idea of expiation (*kaffāra*) is never hinted at, the third of the above-mentioned three approaches. But a group of four different traditions in 'Abd al-Razzāq's *Muṣannaf* does (X:63f). In the text, 'Aṭā' states that the person who killed an unborn who did not scream (*istahallā*) should emancipate a slave or fast. Mujāhid (d.722) is quoted with a similar opinion concerning a woman who massaged a pregnant woman's belly leading to fetal loss. Both statements do not mention a *ghurra*. Rather, they use a technical terminology (*'itq raqaba*), which makes a strong cross-reference to Qur'an 4:92, where *kaffāra*—defined either as freeing a slave or a two months fast—is spelled out for cases of accidental killing. This terminology does not overlap with the material discussed above under *binary approach* where slaves are also mentioned but with clearly different terminologies not resonating with Q 4:92. One statement ascribed to al-Zuhrī (d.742) about a husband beating his pregnant wife causing fetal loss, combines *ghurra* and *kaffāra* and stipulates that he cannot be among the recipients of the *ghurra*. The more elaborate structure of this statement in comparison to the two others makes it likely that it is later than them. A fourth and final statement is ascribed to Ibrāhīm (d.715), who is asked about a woman drinking a medicine or inserting something into herself "so that her child falls" (*fa-yasquṭ waladuhā*). Ibrāhīm's answer in the printed edition seems to indicate that he equates the *kaffāra* with the *ghurra*, which could either be genuine (and thus reflect a sort of confusion whether *kaffāra* and *ghurra* are one and the same thing) or a writing mistake by a copyist (compare the disambiguate version in Ibn Ḥazm XI: 240). At any rate, the material indicates that in the time of 'Abd al-Razzāq al-Ṣan'ānī around 800 CE the two approaches of *ghurra* (aiming at social recompensation) and *kaffāra* (addressing the relationship between culprit and God) were not necessarily linked to each other. This forms a contrast to later Sunni *fiqh* sources, where the two are almost always discussed together. (Holmes-Katz, 28).

To sum up so far, the Sunni sources from the eighth century document three approaches in the abortion debate: First, a gradualist approach, computing a fine in relation to developmental stages of the unborn. Second, a binary approach, which does not differentiate according to embryological development. The first clearly resonates linguistically with the Qur'an, while the second does not. Both positions aim at the social level of compensation for the unborn's kin group. The third position primarily aims at expiation and restoring the relation between the culprit and God. It is clearly derived from the Qur'an.

Ensoulment and Late Antiquity

The later sources from the tenth century onward built their legal reasoning about abortion on material analyzed so far. In these later developments—and especially since the 1980s—ensoulment became paramount. Interestingly, this is not the case in the early sources from the seventh and eighth centuries CE. Generally speaking, we know very little about how Muslim authors imagined individual ensoulment in that time—and whether it was an issue at all. The Qur'an does not mention ensoulment explicitly except for Adam (15:29, 32:9, 38:72; Rahman 1980, 112). The key reference for individual ensoulment in Islamic sources is a prophetic Hadith transmitted by Ibn Mas'ūd. However, already early Muslim Hadith experts considered its ensoulment section to be a later addition (see below). Against this background it is not surprising that early Islamic legal discussions about abortion mentioned ensoulment only rarely. But this does not mean, of course, that these authors did not have any implicit notions of ensoulment that surface in their discussions and that can be gleaned from the larger intellectual milieu of Late Antiquity in which they operated.

Late antiquity discussed three models of ensoulment, which put forward three differing emphases concerning the point in time of pregnancy considered to be the most decisive: conception (e.g., Tertullian), a later stage of the pregnancy when the unborn reached bodily shape (e.g., Galen), and birth with the first breath (e.g., Porphyrius). For all of those thinkers, Plato and Aristotle were major references, among other things with the differentiation between three different sorts of souls: vegetative, animal, rational. The basic idea was that all three shared the aspect of being a sort of energy of life but differed as to the set of capacities linked to them (for example, the capacity of willing movement differentiates animals from plants, while humans are set apart from animals through mental/rational capacities among other things). In this view, humans are the only beings having in themselves all three souls together, which had been manifested in them during pregnancy and birth one after the other (Wilberding).

Against this background, let us look again at the chapters about ending a pregnancy prematurely in Mālik's *Muwaṭṭa'* and 'Abd al-Razzāq's *Muṣannaf*. They are unanimous concerning the scenario, if the abortion took the form of a premature delivery leading to a live birth after which the newborn soon dies. In this case the full blood money is due. Ways were discussed how to establish that the aborted child actually had lived. Here *istihlāl*, the screaming of the newborn, became the mostly discussed criterion (Mālik IV: 197, 'Abd al-Razzāq X: 56, 57f, 60, 63). In this context al-Zuhrī was also remembered to have stated that in these issues "the sneezing (*'aṭs*) has for me the same position as the screaming (*istihlāl*)" ('Abd al-Razzāq X: 58, 63). Again, it is difficult to interpret this material. It is possible that the debate was simply about finding a standard for legal proof for life and thus drew its inspiration from practical experience ("newborns scream, often they sneeze"). But it is also possible that this discussion was influenced by imaginations of ensoulment. For example, several descriptions ascribed to early Islamic authorities exist depicting the creation of Adam, into whom God infused the soul, and then Adam sneezed (Firyābī, 19, 24). Therefore, a link to other text material rather than life experience is perceivable. This text material would point to imaginations of ensoulment.

The argument that the discussions on *istihlāl* possibly reflect an underlying idea of ensoulment is further strengthened by the material that it is included in the chapters on funerary rites of 'Abd ar-Razzāq's *Muṣannaf*. There, the contents are arranged according to terminologies and scenarios: first the new-born (*maulūd*), then the aborted child (*siqṭ*), then again a born child (*maulūd, abnā'*), and finally the "ensouled" (*manfūs*). A major topic of the chapter is the screaming of the respective being (mostly *istihlāl*). This is hardly a coincidence. If put into the late antique context of debates about ensoulment, one finds that the neonatal scream was used as a yardstick to distinguish between the unborn and the neonatal infant concerning the ways both react toward pain. From this, conclusions were drawn concerning ensoulment and to argue for ensoulment at birth (Wilberding, 47).

What is more, the *janā'iz*-chapter in the *Muṣannaf* mentions the soul (*rūḥ*) twice—a considerable contradistinction to the chapter on abortion, which does not mention it at all. Both statements are positioned in the sections discussing the *maulūd* and the *siqṭ* respectively. Although they clearly refer to two different legal scenarios, they offer precious insights into their ensoulment theories. The first statement, ascribed to Qatāda (d.736?), reads: "If the soul stays in it [the *maulūd*] 'as three' (*thalāthan*), it does not inherit until it screams" ('Abd al-Razzāq III: 530). This can be interpreted as a reference to the concept of three consecutive souls and the scream is likely a proof for ensoulment, though it is not clear whether it happened before or during birth. In the other statement, Qatāda reports that he heard from two of his teachers: "If its [the *siqṭ*'s] forming is completed and the soul is blown into it, a prayer is said over it even if it did not scream" ('Abd al-Razzāq III: 531). This statement clearly equates the soul with the completion of shape during pregnancy, which can be read as a counter-statement to the first concept.

Taken together, this material can be interpreted in the following way: The debate about *janā'iz* strongly focused on infant death and neonatal death and was likely extended to premature deliveries. In this specific context *siqṭ* unambiguously depicts the "prematurely delivered" or spontaneous late abortions. Here, *istihlāl* became a major topic as a possible yardstick for the decision of legal consequences. Very likely the scream was read as a sign that ensoulment had taken place, as is indicated in the statement "The ensouled (*al-manfūs*) inherits if its voice is heard" ('Abd al-Razzāq III: 533). However, the *istihlāl* does not indicate whether ensoulment was imagined to happen prenatally or during birth. In the chapter on *janā'iz* this distinction did not matter anyway. In contradistinction to this debate, the chapter on blood money focused on induced early and late abortions, mostly using the term *embryo* (*janīn*) and often indicating that the embryo left the mother's body dead or died with her. The term *siqṭ* is used more rarely: the respective chapter in Mālik's *Muwaṭṭa'* does not use it and 'Abd al-Razzāq's *Muṣannaf* uses it only twice (X: 56, 59), in one case arguably replacing *janīn*. In the context of the *diya*-chapters on abortion, both works discuss *istihlāl*, though not systematically and the formulations clearly indicate that it was a contested issue. This strongly suggests that the debate about *istihlāl* had its primary locus in the discussion about neonatal death and premature delivery (linked to the term *siqṭ* there) and only entered the debate about induced abortion in a secondary step. This also explains its somewhat surprising positioning within the debate in the abortion chapters which are very often about scenarios where the unborn dies with the mother or leaves the mother's body dead.

Against this background, the different positions on abortion, fetal loss, and neonatal death of early Muslim authorities can be situated in the landscape of ensoulment theories in late antiquity. For example, the idea that ensoulment occurs during or after birth with the first breath is likely at the bottom of al-Zuhrī's statements about *istihlāl* and sneezing of the embryo. The idea to link ensoulment to the completing of the unborn's formation during pregnancy can be seen in 'Abd al-Malik's statement "And if its forming (*khalquhu*) is completed and its hair has taken root (*nabata sha'ruhu*), it is 100 [dinar]" (see above), which echoes Hippocrates' position about ensoulment during pregnancy almost verbally (Wilberding, 33). The abovementioned statement by Qatāda goes in a similar direction: "If its [the *siqṭ*'s] forming is completed and the soul is blown into it, a prayer is said over it even if it did not scream." ('Abd al-Razzāq III: 531) Within the broader panorama of late antique ensoulment theories, it is also noteworthy then, that none of the positions mentions early pregnancy (the *nuṭfa*-stage in the Qur'anic tripartite *nuṭfa-'alaqa-muḍgha*-scheme), which is a strong indication that the Tertullian position was not considered in the debate.

The Hadith of Ibn Mas'ūd

Eventually this plurality of imaginations of ensoulment vanished and the idea that it takes place on the 120th day of pregnancy became the overarching paradigm in Sunni Islamic abortion debates. This development can be linked to a growing importance of a prophetic Hadith, which was transmitted by Ibn Mas'ūd, in the debate. In its first half according to the version in the chapter on predestination (*qadar*) in the authoritative Hadith collection (*Ṣaḥīḥ*) of Muslim b. al-Ḥajjāj (d.875) the Hadith reads:

> One of you, his creation is gathered in the belly of his mother for forty days, then it is in this a blood-clot (*'alaqa*) likewise, then it is in this a lump of flesh (*muḍgha*) likewise, then the angel is sent to him and he breathes into him the soul (*rūḥ*), and he is ordered

to write down four words: his sustenance, his time of death, his deeds and whether he will be wretched or blessed.

This specific phrasing can only be found in Muslim's collection; other collections present different specific phrasings (such as the four versions to be found in the Ṣaḥīḥ of Bukhārī [d.870]). Some variants contain the reference to ensoulment while others do not and the ensoulment passage might occur in different places of the text depending on the variant (van Ess). This means that it was very likely added to the Hadith, possibly during the eighth century, a view also proposed by early Muslim Hadith experts (Ṭaḥāwī IX:484; Ibn ʿAsākir I:235).

Read together with Q 22:5 and especially 23:12–14—the only two Qur'an passages describing prenatal development with the lexicon of "blood-clot" and "lump of flesh" in a tripartite formula *nutfa-ʿalaqa-muḍgha*—this Hadith was eventually understood to state that the unborn goes through three consecutive developmental stages, each lasting forty days, before being ensouled on the 120th day. In later *fiqh* texts this became a standard view structuring the discussion about abortion, no matter the considerable differences in all remaining areas of the debate (Eich 2009). Note, however, that in the Sunni Hadith collections this Hadith explicitly mentioning individual ensoulment is usually not included in the chapters discussing fetal loss, which forms a considerable contrast to Shiite Hadith collections.

Shiite Hadith

The Shiite (here always meaning 12er Shiite) by and large developed a different system of authorizing norms than the Sunnis. While the Sunnis considered only Muhammad and a specific group of his companions and early followers as potential normative authorities, Shiites developed a concept of inherited charismatic authority in a line starting from Muhammad and continuing through his daughter Fatima and her husband ʿAlī b. Abī Ṭālib. In this line of the so-called imams only one representative of this charismatic authority could exist at any given time. This line came to an end in the first half of the tenth century, according to 12er Shiite belief. This means that only toward the end of this period of the imams did the Shiite community start to consider it necessary to put down authoritative statements into writing in an organized effort. For this reason the major collections of authoritative sayings of the Shiites were composed during the tenth and eleventh century, which is considerably later—up to two centuries—than the Hadith collections of the Sunnis. Here, the works of Kulaynī (d.941), Qummī (d.991), and Ṭūsī (d.1067) are consulted.[1]

The chapters about ending a pregnancy prematurely (*diyat al-janīn*) in these Shiite collections also know the two approaches of societal recompensation (gradualist and binary approach) but they do not contain any material mentioning the *kaffāra*. The binary approach is present in material that can be found in similar form in the earlier Sunni collections (*ghurra* defined as slave (Kulaynī 3, 4, 7; Qummī 5319; Ṭūsī 1125–1127) or as 50 dinar (Kulaynī 13; other material speaks about 40 dinar [Kulaynī 6 & 16; Qummī 5321; Ṭūsī 1130]).

The material with the gradualist approach shows a clear orientation toward Qur'an 22:5 and 23:12–14 and can be divided into two sub-groups. In one group, the material is very similar to the statement ascribed to the Umayyad caliph ʿAbd al-Malik in ʿAbd al-Razzāq's *muṣannaf* quoted above, where it already had been ascribed to ʿAlī b. Abī Ṭālib as well. Yet, after the exposition of the gradualist scheme of five developmental stages corresponding with fines of 20, 40, 60, 80, and 100 dinar, some (later) Shiite versions add that if ensoulment occurred, the full *diya* would have to be paid (Kulaynī 1, 2; and Ṭūsī 1123, 1124). However, very similar material does not mention ensoulment here rather than *istihlāl* (Kulaynī 9; Qummī 5316; Ṭūsī 1122). For this group of material it is very difficult to tell whether the ensoulment-versions "correct" the *istihlāl*-version and can be read as indications that ensoulment was understood to happen during pregnancy, or if they explain each other, i.e., that *istihlāl* actually means ensoulment, which would then happen at birth.

The other group of the material develops a scheme of the three Qur'anic stages *nuṭfa-ʿalaqa-muḍgha* corresponding with a 20, 40, and 60 dinar fine, postulating that the full *diya* is due in the stage of bones, which is defined as a stage where limbs become visible and the capacity to hear and see starts. (Kulaynī 8, 10) In probably a further development of this scheme the three stages are computed at forty days each, which clearly resonates with the ideas expressed in the Ibn Masʿūd-ḥadīth. After the 120th day the aborted child is described this way: "If she ejects him and he is a formed person (*nasama mukhallaqa*), he has bones and flesh, the limbs are established and the rational soul (*rūḥ al-ʿaql*) is infused, [the perpetrator] has to pay the complete *diya*" (Kulaynī 15). The term *rational soul* and the following discussion in this passage clearly resonate with the Aristotelian concept of three consecutive souls (vegetative, animal, rational) during pregnancy and birth and therefore might express that some sort of soul is present from the start.

Both groups of material systematically include the *nuṭfa*-stage into their deliberations—a noteworthy contrast to the earlier Sunni Hadith collections. This is likely a reflection of the Shiite position to forbid contraceptive measures, including coitus interruptus (Kulaynī 1, 2; Qummī 5394).

To sum up: The Shiite Hadith collections address abortion exclusively on the level of societal recompensation. They contain the two approaches (binary and gradualist) as well, but the gradualist approach is present to a much greater extent and also includes the earliest stages of pregnancy. Finally, the material clearly shows that the explicit element of ensoulment had become integrated into the presentation of the abortion debate. Yet, it is not always clear which concept of ensoulment underlay the respective statements. The one case where this is unambiguously clear is very likely later than the other material. This specific case adds a significant element to the debate: the point in time of the pregnancy when the abortion had occurred. Most of the Hadith material on abortion either does not define criteria *at which time* a fine or punishment is due or it uses the criteria of outer shape or post-natal reactions respectively. Here the element of time (120 days) is integrated into the catalogue of criteria and as such resembles one other passage in the Shiite material stating "when the five months have passed, life has started in [the unborn] and the [full] *diya* is obligatory" (Kulaynī 11, Qummī 5318). This is a decisive development in the discussion because it allows for shifting the focus of the legal debate away from the specific developmental form of the aborted child to the criterion of the point in time of the pregnancy at which the abortion happened.

Sunni *Fiqh*-Debates Ninth until Thirteenth Centuries

The Sunni sources show a similar development that in a longer process after 800 CE a specific point in time of the pregnancy became the decisive cut-off criterion, largely a four-month period. Partly this was linked to the Ibn Mas'ūd-ḥadīth (see below), but other developments factored in as well. For example, around 800 CE, Qatāda was quoted as having said: "If [an aborted child's] shape was completed and the soul was blown into him, a prayer is said over him even if it did not scream" ('Abd al-Razzāq III: 531). A few years later this statement was remembered as "If the soul was blown into him, a prayer is said over him and this is the case after four months" (Ibn Abī Shayba IV: 465). This number of four months was very likely derived from Q 2:234 where a waiting period for widowed women before remarriage is defined as "four months and ten [days or nights]." Qatāda was remembered to explain the ten days or nights as the period of ensoulment (Ṭabarī II: 540). Only in a process stretching out well into the twelfth century did the Ibn Mas'ūd-ḥadīth with its concept of ensoulment on the 120th day become the major explanatory reference in Sunni Muslim legal discussions about abortion under which other material such as the exegesis of Q 2:234 was subsumed (Ṭaḥāwī IX: 484–486; Eich 2009, 329–331).

The centuries after 800 CE were also the time when the so-called four legal schools in Sunni Islam finally formed: the Mālikīya, Ḥanafīya, Shāfi'īya, and Ḥanbalīya. Only the Mālikīya developed a discussion about early abortion, the *nuṭfa*-stage from the tripartite Qur'anic formula *nuṭfa-'alaqa-muḍgha* (Q 22:5 and 23:12–14), which was not an issue in the early discussions as noted above. *Nuṭfa* literally means "drop," which could mean semen. However, in the exegesis, especially of 22:5, the following statement by 'Abd Allāh b. Mas'ūd was quoted:

> When the *nuṭfa* [i.e., the semen] enters the uterus and God wants to create a human out of it, it [viz., the *nuṭfa*] moves in the woman's skin beneath every fingernail and

hair. Then it establishes itself, then it turns into blood in the uterus. This is its "gathering" and this is the time when it is [i.e., has become] a blood-like clot (*'alaqa*). (e.g., Qurṭubī 1967, XII: 7)

'Abd Allāh b. Mas'ūd's statement was understood as explaining the *Hadith* about the 120 days, which only contained the terms *'alaqa* and *muḍgha* from the tripartite Qur'anic formula, but not *nutfa*. Against the background of this statement, leading Mālikī jurists of the twelfth and thirteenth centuries such as al-Qurṭubī (d.1273) drew conclusions for the legal arena that until the fortieth day an abortion did not have legal consequences:

> Beyond a doubt, the semen-stage (*nutfa*) has no [legal significance], and no legal consequences ensue if the woman expels it, because it has not [yet] been gathered in the uterus; it is as if it were [still] in the loins of the man. When it turns into a blood-like clot (*'alaqa*) we know for sure that the *nutfa* has established itself and has been gathered. (Qurṭubī 1967, XII: 9)

This passage also shows explicitly that here the *nutfa* was understood as semen which had not yet merged with the female contribution to procreation. The legal position expressed here was also shared by the Ḥanbalīs (Shaumān, 55).

Other Mālikī scholars argued for protection rights at a much earlier stage such as al-Qāḍī Ibn al-'Arabī (d.1148), who stated that the process of procreation should not be interrupted externally even in the earliest stages of prenatal development. He argued that the merging process of male and female procreational contributions had started but not yet reached its end (Ibn al-'Arabī II: 763). In this sense the major difference between the two groups of Maliki scholars did not lie in disagreements about the conceptualization of the *nutfa* stage as a process. Rather, the two groups differed on the question whether the beginning or the end of that process should be taken as a cut-off point. Contemporary bioethical discussions regard the latter view as *the* Mālikī position.

A second major discussion emerged about the question of the status of the unborn either as an independent being or a part of the pregnant woman's body. This legalistic debate ensued around Hadith material computing the *ghurra* as 50 dinar and the question why the Prophet had decided on this precise sum. Mālik had argued that 50 dinars are 10 percent of 500 dinars, the *diya* for the killing of a free woman. He concluded that the *ghurra* is one-tenth of the *diya* of the mother and thus to consider the unborn as a part of the pregnant woman's body (Mālik IV:196). The Ḥanafīs took issue with this interpretation for reasons of juridic systematization in the scenario of induced fetal loss of a slave mother. They concluded that the underlying principle of setting the *ghurra* at 50 dinars must be the concept of treating the unborn as a being independent of the mother's body (Eich 2009, 317–318). However, these conceptual differences were of deductory nature and therefore did not significantly impact legal statements on abortion beyond this specific discussion.

In their general assessments of abortion, the four legal schools developed considerable differences resulting from different interpretations of specific Qur'anic and Hadith statements and the way they related to each other. In addition, the schools had different ideas which of the three stages of the Qur'anic tripartite formula could already fulfill criteria of proof. As a result, a considerable range of opinions whether and until what stage of pregnancy an abortion should go unpunished existed side by side for most of the history of Islamic law. The idea of forbidding any interfering with a pregnancy after conception was expressed by the Shiites and a group of Mālikīs. Another group of Mālikīs and the Ḥanbalīs allowed such interference in early pregnancy, the *nutfa* stage of the first forty days. The Shāfiʿī position is not as clear, because the school's namegiver al-Shāfiʿī was remembered to take the end of the *ʿalaqa*-stage after eighty days as cut-off point while later authors of the school also extended the argument to both earlier and later stages (Holmes-Katz, 42; Shaumān, 53, 55). The Ḥanafīs stated that abortion before ensoulment could go unpunished especially if a justifying cause existed. (Shaumān, 51, 53) Historically, the standard scenario to define this justifying cause was the situation when a breastfeeding mother got pregnant again and would cease to lactate. If the family could not afford a wet nurse, abortion was considered a justified option.

However, it has to be reiterated that the *ʿulamā'* did not separate clearly *legal* and *moral* assessments as belonging to entirely different areas of scholarly reflection considered both to belong to their professional activities. As a result, often the same scholars of the different schools who opted for a later cut-off point in the legal discussion about abortion clearly considered the act as morally reprehensible already before that point (Holmes-Katz, 42; Eich 2009, 333–334). Possibly, the historical precursors of this view can be found in the gradualist position of the early sources described above.

Twentieth and Twenty-First Centuries

The plurality of approaches in the debate about abortion has prevailed in Islamic history well into the twentieth century. Especially in the 1980s this changed for two reasons: first, the rise of natural sciences to leading fields of knowledge production since the nineteenth century. In previous discussions relating to the unborn, it had been an entirely legitimate and widely accepted option for religious scholars to reject medical knowledge of their respective times (Weisser 1981). In the second half of the twentieth century this approach became less and less of an option for the *ulamā*. The development of modern diagnostic technologies in the medical field such as ultrasound imaging, especially during the 1970s, brought about landmark changes in the diagnosis of prenatal life. This considerably narrowed down one variable which had allowed legal pluralism in the past, i.e., the different positions concerning proof of life in the unborn.

The second aspect was the emergence of new international forums in the Islamic world entitled to the debate of legal matters since the 1970s. In these forums medical scholars participate together with religious scholars, mostly from Arabic countries. They discuss the respective issues at hand such as abortion, and constantly renegotiate the demarcation lines between their two fields of expertise (Eich 2010; Ghaly 2015). The decisions or recommendations of these forums—qua being issued by international bodies—have no immediate legal binding effects, since the legislative is situated on the national level. However, these texts can become points of reference in public debate and they do command a degree of authoritativeness, because they are issued by international committees that are freer to work independently from the pressures of one specific nation-state than other, national committees. In addition, they are staffed with high-ranking representatives especially from the Muslim religious scholars. When these committees addressed the question of abortion in the 1980s, the discussion quickly zoomed in on the question of ensoulment. This debate was carried out entirely as an exegetical discussion about the correct interpretation of the Hadith of Ibn Masʿūd. To the common interpretation that the text described ensoulment after 120 days was now added a reading that put it on the fortieth day. This latter opinion was a minority position from the beginning and was soon pushed aside. Partly this was so because within the larger debates of the time, a link was established between this question and findings of recent embryological research in order to argue for a scientific proof of ensoulment on the 120th day. In this line of argumentation certain cerebral changes in the unborn on that day would allow for *willing* movement and thus indicate ensoulment. The major reason for this marginalization, though, was the simple fact that the historical precedent of juridic pluralism could not continue in the new structure of the international forums, which had to reach a clear position on a given topic in order to be able to formulate decrees and recommendations. It is the forum's job to formulate *Islamic* positions, not Mālikī or Ḥanafī positions.

Once the 120th day had been established as the most important cut-off point in contemporary Sunni Islamic debate, the discussion soon turned to the question of possible indications legitimating an induced abortion. During the 1980s, it quickly began to focus on disabilities and inherited diseases, which became to be considered as a possible medical indication in 1990 (Eich 2008). A similar process can be witnessed in 12er Shiite Iran after 1979, where the 120th day also became the overarching criterion determining the abortion discussion—in a complete reversal from historical precedence in which Shiite jurisprudence had argued for protection rights of the unborn since conception. Iran also implemented laws allowing for abortion in case of inherited diseases (Eich 2005).

Around 2000 the question of abortion for social indications became an issue with reference to abortion after rape. Initially this discussion focused on the situation of systematical mass-rape of Muslim women by non-Muslims in the Balkan wars. Here, the religious scholars mostly allowed abortion. Eventually the focus became more general and it became possible to speak about cases of rape in Muslim majority countries. In this context, the *'ulamā'* became more reluctant concerning abortion, often referring to the essentially sexist slippery slope-argument, that immoral behavior (i.e., pre- or extra-marital sex) would spread within society if women could simply claim afterward to have been raped in order to get an abortion. No overall consensus emerged on the question whether ensoulment of the unborn child would preclude it from being aborted. The lineage issue did not play a significant role in all these discussions of unborn conceived in rape. (Eich 2005). After the political and social upheavals in Arabic countries starting in 2011 these discussions entered a new phase, the outcome of which is difficult to speculate for each Muslim majority country in the Mediterranean. However, in 2017 Tunisia passed significant reforms in its legal framework concerning rape, which was generally praised as a significant step forward for women's rights. On the other hand, although possible repercussions for similar legislative processes in other countries such as Jordan have been foretold, one should not generalize from the Tunisian example to other countries, each of which has its own mix of social and political internal and external dynamics.

Note

1. For the sake of transparency and clarity, in this section the references refer to the Hadith-numbers within the respective chapters, not to page numbers.

Bibliography

'Abd al-Razzāq, Abū Bakr b. Hammām al-Ṣan'ānī. *Muṣannaf*. 12 vols. Edited by Ḥabīb al-Raḥmān al-A'ẓamī. Beirut, 1983.
Abū Dawūd Sulaymān al-Ash'ath al-Sijistānī. *Sunan*. Edited by Shu'ayb al-Arnā'ūṭ et al. Damascus, 2009, 7 vols.
Bukhārī, 'Abd Allāh b. Ismā'īl b. Ibrāhīm. *Ṣaḥīḥ al-Bukhārī*. Sidon/Beirut, 2015.
Dārimī, 'Abd Allāh b. 'Abd al-Raḥmān al-. *Al-Musnad al-Jāmi'*. Edited by Nabīl b. Hāshim b. 'Abd Allāh al-Ghamrī Āl Bā 'Alawī. Mecca, 2013.
Eich, Thomas. *Islam und Bioethik. Eine kritische Analyse der modernen Diskussion im islamischen Recht*. Heidelberg: Reichert Verlag, 2005.
Eich, Thomas. "Decision Making Processes among Contemporary *'ulamā'*: 'Islamic Embryology' and the Discussion about 'Frozen Embryos.'" In *Muslim Medical Ethics. From Theory to Practice*, edited by Jonathan E. Brockopp and Thomas Eich, 61–77. Columbus, SC: University of South Carolina Press, 2008.
Eich, Thomas. "Induced Miscarriage in Early Maliki and Hanafi *fiqh*." *Islamic Law and Society* 16 (2009): 302–336.

Eich, Thomas. "Islamische Bioethik: Determinanten und Elemente der Meinungsbildung und Entscheidungsfindung." In *Religion in bioethischen Diskursen. Interdisziplinäre, internationale und interreligiöse Perspektiven*, edited by Friedemann Voigt, pp. 245–266. Berlin/New York: de Gruyter, 2010.

Firyābī, Jaʿfar b. Muḥammad b. al-Ḥasan b. al-Mustfād al-. *Kitab al-Qadar*. Edited by ʿAmr b. ʿAbd al-Munʿim Salīm. Beirut, 2000.

Ghaly, Mohammed. "Biomedical Scientists as Co-Muftis: Their Contribution to Contemporary Islamic Bioethics." *Die Welt des Islams* 55 (2015): 286–311.

Holmes Katz, Marion. "The Problem of Abortion in Classical Sunni Fiqh." In *Islamic Ethics of Life: Abortion, War, and Euthanasia*, edited by Jonathan E. Brockopp, 25–50. Columbus, SC. University of South Carolina Press. 2003.

Ibn Abī Shayba, Abu Bakr ʿAbd Allāh b. Muḥammad b. Ibāhīm. *Al-Muṣannaf*. Edited by Abū Muḥammad Usāma b. Ibrāhīm b. Muḥammad. Cairo, 2008. 15 vols.

Ibn al-ʿArabī, Abū Bakr. *Kitāb al-qabas fī sharḥ Muwaṭṭaʾ Mālik b. Anas*. Edited by Muḥammad ʿAbd Allāh Walad Karīm. Beirut, 1992. 3 vols.

Ibn al-ʿAsākir, Abū al-Qāsim ʿAlī b. al-Ḥasan. *Muʿjam al-shuyūkh*. Edited by Wafāʾ Taqī al-Dīn. Damascus 2000. 3 vols.

Ibn Ḥazm, Abū Muḥammad ʿAlī b. Aḥmad b. Saʿīd. *Al-Muḥallā bi-l-āthār*. Edited by ʿAbd al-Ghaffār Sulaymān al-Bandārī. Beirut, 1984. 14 vols.

Ibn Mājah, Abū ʿAbd Allāh Muḥammad b. Yazīd al-Qazwīnī. *Sunan*. Edited By Muhammad Fuʾād ʿAbd al-Bāqī. 2 vols. Cairo, 1954.

Ibn Qudāma, ʿAbd Allāh b. Aḥmad. *Al-Mughnī*. Edited by ʿAbd Allāh b. ʿAbd al-Muḥsin al-Turkī / ʿAbd al-Fattāḥ Muḥammad al-Ḥulw. Riyad, 1999. 15 vols.

Kulaynī, Abū Jaʿfar Muḥammad b. Yaʿqūb b. Isḥāq al-. *Furūʿ al-kāfī*. Beirut, 2008.

Lange, Christian. "Capital Punishment." In *Encyclopaedia of Islam THREE*, edited by Kate Fleet, Gudrun Krämer, Denis Matringe, John Nawas, and Everett Rowson. Leiden et al. http://dx.doi.org.encyclopaediaofislamonline.emedien3.sub.uni-hamburg.de/10.1163/1573-3912_ei3_COM_25344. First published online 2011.

Mālik b. Anas. *al-Muwaṭṭaʾ bi-riwāyātihi*. Edited by Salīm b. ʿĪd al-Hilālī al-Salafī. Dubai, 2003. 5 vols.

Qummī, Abū Jaʿfar Muḥammad b. ʿAlī b. al-Husayn Bābawayh al-. *Kitāb man lā yaḥḍuruhu al-faqīh*. Beirut, 1986. 4 vols.

Qurṭubī, Abū ʿAbd Allāh b. Aḥmad al-Anṣārī al-. *al-Jāmiʿ li-aḥkām al-Qurʾān*. Cairo.

Rahman, Fazlur. *Major themes of the Qurʾān*. Minneapolis/Chicago 1967/1980. 10 vols.

Shaumān, ʿAbbās. *Ijhāḍ al-ḥaml*. Cairo 1999.

Ṭabarī, Abū Jaʿfar Muḥammad b. Jarīr al-. *Tafsīr: jāmiʿ al-bayān fī taʾwīl al-Qurʾān*. Beirut, 1992. 19 vols.

Ṭaḥāwī, Abū Jaʿfar Aḥmad b. Muḥammad al-. *Sharḥ mushkil al-āthār*. Edited by Shuʿayb al-Arnaʾūṭ. Damascus, 1994. 16 vols.

Ṭūsī, Abū Jaʿfar Muḥammad b. al-Ḥasan. *Al-Istibṣār fīmā ukhtulifa min al-akhbār*. Edited by Ḥasan al-Mūsawī. Tehran, 1390 [1970?]. 4 vols.

Van Ess, Josef. *Zwischen Ḥadīṯ und Theologie: Studien zum Entstehen prädestinatianischer Überlieferung*. Berlin, 1975.

Weisser, Ursula. "Ibn Qaiyim al-Ğauziya über die Methoden der Embryologie." *Medizinhistorisches Journal* 16 (1981): 227–239.

Wilbdering, James, trans. *Porphyry: To Gaurus on How Embryos are Ensouled and on What Is in Our Power*. London et al., 2011.

CHAPTER 25

PUBLIC OPINION AND ATTITUDES TOWARD ABORTION

Patterns across Religious Traditions

TED G. JELEN

THE circumstances under which a woman may legitimately terminate a pregnancy have long been a source of controversy in national and international politics. As old as human awareness of sexuality (the practice of abortion was addressed by Aristotle), the abortion issue stands at the intersections of the public and the private, the sacred and the profane, and the spiritual and the pragmatic. As such, the question whether, or under what circumstances, abortion is morally or legally acceptable continues to animate political conflict at virtually all levels, and across nearly all cultures.

Abortion is a moral issue, on which a variety of spiritual and ethical considerations converge. Abortion involves ultimate questions of human life, as well as issues of sexual morality and appropriate gender roles. As such, the abortion issue has powerful moral and emotional components, which often raise the importance of the issue above and beyond more mundane practical and policy considerations. Indeed, abortion is an issue with profound implications within a variety of religious traditions, which provides the question of reproductive freedom with a transcendent dimension.

Abortion is a political issue. Despite the efforts of some activists to frame abortion as a private matter of "choice," abortion is the subject of public policy. The possibility of an independent "humanity" of the fetus, if nothing else, makes abortion at least a potentially "other-regarding issue," which cannot easily be relegated to a personal or private sphere of activity. Abortion involves law, which in turn involves government, which entails at least the possibility of legal enforcement and coercion. Abortion policy, regardless of the content of that policy in a particular jurisdiction, thus involves the public and authoritative enactment (or suppression) of citizens' deepest moral and theological values.

My purpose in this chapter is to summarize a large and growing literature about public opinion and abortion. More specifically, I will attempt to describe empirical research on the distribution of abortion attitudes, as well as the reasons people come to approve or disapprove of reproductive freedom, and to compare these patterns across diverse religious traditions in a variety of countries. To anticipate the course of the chapter, my analysis suggests that there does exist substantial variation about the abortion issue across difference global and national religious traditions. However, despite cross-denominational religious differences in the *level* of approval or disapproval of abortion, the *reasons* people come to favor or oppose reproductive choice are remarkably similar across traditions. For example, to characterize a restrictive position on abortion as "pro-life" is as apt a description for an adherent of Buddhism or Hinduism as it is for a Roman Catholic. Even if adherents of different religious hold different beliefs and attitudes about abortion, they seem to share a subjective understanding of the nature of the issue.

The empirical claims of this study are based on studies of public opinion conducted over the past two decades by many scholars. Public attitudes toward abortion are among the most analyzed opinions in existence. The chapter that follows draws heavily on a non-technical summary of the state of the evidence regarding public attitudes toward abortion, and on my 2014 article "The Subjective Bases of Abortion Attitudes: A Cross-National Comparison of Religious Traditions."[1] The 2014 study consists of statistical analyses of the reasons people who adhere to diverse religious traditions hold different attitudes concerning the justifiability of abortion.

The Social and Political Bases of Abortion Policy

In other words, the general cognitive orientations associated with mass attitudes toward abortion, as well as their relative weight, do not vary across different religious traditions. This would seem somewhat surprising, given the variety of abortion policies and practices throughout the world. Even a cursory glance at abortion policy in various nations of the world suggest that there are important differences in the availability of legal abortion in diverse national and international settings. Abortion policy ranges from permissive and supportive, in cases such as Sweden,[2] to virtual prohibition in nations such as El Salvador. Previous research has suggested that variations in national abortion policy are largely a function of several variables. These would include the religious composition and level of religiosity of a country's population.[3] Restrictive abortion policies are associated with a high percentage of Roman Catholics citizens, as well as a highly religious population.[4] Thus, devout, Catholic Poland has more restrictive abortion policies than Protestant, secular Sweden. At the macro (country) level, relatively high levels of female participation in public life (such as business or government) are correlated with relatively permissive abortion policies, in which access to the procedure is often facilitated by government.[5]

Further, nations that have experienced a history of communist domination often have relatively easy access to abortion (Poland being a prominent exception). The combination of official atheism, economic mobilization, and a desire for medical efficiency may have rendered communist nations supportive of access to abortion.[6]

Thus, a comparison of abortion policies across nations suggests that such differences are consistent with what might be expected if abortion policy were consistent with public opinion. Highly industrialized countries (in which children may lack economic value), and nations in which a high percentage of women participate in the public sphere tend to have relatively permissive (or even supportive) abortion policies. Conversely, nations with highly religious populations, or in which a high percentage of citizens identify with religious traditions opposed to abortion (such as Roman Catholicism), tend to have abortion policies that are relatively restrictive. In one sense, this is not particularly surprising. At the level of the mass public, abortion might be considered an issue that is not particularly cognitively demanding, but rather "easy."[7] Further, studies in the United States and in emerging democracies with Catholic majorities have shown a moderately strong relationship between mass opinion on abortion and abortion policy.[8]

The suggestion of correspondence between public opinion and public policy on the abortion issue provides at least one compelling rationale for attending to mass attitudes on reproductive freedom. At least in some settings, what ordinary citizens think about abortion matters, and may have consequences for electoral politics and public policy.

The Morality of Abortion: Religious Differences

There are differences across religious traditions in the level of acceptability of abortion. When respondents in the World Values Surveys (WVSs) taken in the first decade of the twenty-first century were asked to rate abortion (along with other practices) on a scale from 1 to 10, in which 1 was "never justifiable" to 10 as "always justifiable," the mean responses for respondents from different religious traditions varied from a high of 4 (for members of Eastern Orthodox Churches) to a low of 2.1 (for Muslim respondents). Buddhists, Hindus, Protestants, and (perhaps surprisingly) Roman Catholics exhibit intermediate levels of disapproval for abortion. This suggests that, although abortion is not a popular practice for any religious tradition (all means are below 5 on a 1–10 scale), there does exist substantial interreligious variation on the acceptability of abortion.

The Subjective Sources of Abortion Attitudes

However, as will be shown below, the reasons people come to regard abortion as morally permissible or impermissible are remarkably uniform across religious traditions. Attitudes toward abortion represent a combination of beliefs about the sanctity of human life, sexual morality, and (much less importantly) appropriate social, economic, and political roles for women. Further, across religious traditions, higher levels of religious observance are associated with lower levels of acceptance of abortion.

Religiosity

Across five of the religious traditions examined in this research, people who engage in more frequent religious behavior are more likely to disapprove of abortion. Since adherents of different religions engage in diverse religious practices, the behavior sources of religious opposition to abortion vary. Frequent attendance at religious services is significantly related to disapproval of abortion for Roman Catholics, while frequency of prayer is an important source of anti-abortion attitudes for Orthodox Christians and Hindus. Public and private religious observance (attendance at religious services and prayer) appear to occasion opposition to abortion among Protestants[9] and Muslims, while religious observance does not appear to affect abortion attitudes among Buddhist respondents. The effects of religious behavior persist even when attitudes toward human life, sexual morality, and gender roles are held constant. This result is, of course, consistent with previous research.[10]

Ontology and Fetal Life

In any discussion of religion and abortion, the first point to be made is that all religious traditions are multivocal.[11] Doctrines regarding abortion differ across and within religious traditions. Thus, even the Roman Catholic Church—perhaps the staunchest public voice opposing abortion—contains (in the United States) a monthly publication, *Conscience*, which is an explicitly Catholic, explicitly "pro-choice" magazine.

Second, as noted above, most specifically religious teaching on abortion addresses the life or potential life of the fetus. For many opponents of abortion, the practice of terminating a pregnancy intentionally is literally a matter of life and death. Although precise theological accounts of participation in *ummahk*, *atman*, or "ensoulment" differ, most theological analyses of abortion ultimately address the question of when human life begins, and whether, or at what point, abortion represents homicide.

To what extent does mass opinion on abortion reflect differences in beliefs about the nature of human life? Empirically, this is an extraordinarily difficult question to answer. A general question about the value of human life (e.g., "Do you regard human life as sacred?") would not likely create much variance. Most people would state that they in fact place a high value on human life. Conversely, when mass publics in Western societies are asked questions about specific issues involving "life issues" (e.g., capital punishment, military spending, etc.) few ordinary citizens take consistently pro-life positions on diverse issues such as military spending, the death penalty, or abortion. Despite the elegance and moral clarity of Cardinal Bernardin's "consistent ethic of life,"[12] which he characterized as a "seamless garment," there does not appear to exist a consistently and generally pro-life constituency in any mass public.[13] In other words, abortion opponents are no more or less likely than other citizens to take positions opposing nuclear weapons, capital punishment, or any other issue that would seem to involve questions of "life and death."

Faced with this measurement dilemma, in my own work, I have operationalized "respect for life" as a variable tapped by asking respondents about their attitudes toward euthanasia.[14] This approach, while controversial, has two general advantages. First, if abortion and euthanasia are regarded as forms of homicide, the "life" to be taken is presumably innocent, and not morally deserving of ending (unlike condemned murderers or enemy soldiers). Second, attitudes toward euthanasia and abortion are empirically related in mass publics in a variety of nations, which suggests that many respondents subjectively regard the issues as related.

As it happens, attitudes toward euthanasia are strongly and significantly related to abortion attitudes in all six religious traditions considered here. Respondents who disapprove of euthanasia are approximately 20 percent less likely to regard abortion as justified, when the effects of other variables are held constant. One important difference across religious traditions is the fact that the percentage of people who approve of euthanasia differs widely across religious traditions. While the differences among Christian traditions (Orthodox, Catholic, and Protestant) and between Christians and Hindus are quite small, Buddhists are relatively tolerant of killings designed to end suffering (mean = 4.67 on a 1–10 scale) and Muslims much lower than other respondents (mean of 2.14). Thus, across a number of different religious traditions, people with strong reservations about the euthanasia are also less likely to approve of abortion. Acceptance of euthanasia does not differ across most traditions, but Buddhists and Muslims represent significant outliers (in opposite directions).[15]

Sexual Morality

At the level of mass opinion, the most important subjective sources of abortion attitudes are attitudes toward nonmarital sex. Numerous analysts have noted that the possibility of pregnancy under circumstances in which the birth of a child is not sanctioned is a powerful deterrent to sexual activity.[16] The unavailability of legal or safe abortion increases the potential costs of nonmarital pregnancy, and, therefore, increases the risks associated with sex outside of marriage.

My own empirical research[17] shows that the importance of the relationship between attitudes toward nonmarital sex and approval of abortion is consistently the strongest of any relationships I have examined. If we are to ask why some mass publics disapprove of the practice of abortion, the simplest and empirically most accurate answer is because some people oppose intimate sexual relations between persons unmarried to each other.

There are several different aspects to this point. First, in my examination of mass attitudes of members of various religious traditions (Catholic, Orthodox, Protestant, Muslim, Buddhist, Hindu) this pattern does not vary at all. A person who is morally opposed to sex outside of marriage is 40 to 50 percent less likely to regard abortion as justified than one who is open to alternative sexual relationships. Across all the religious traditions I have considered, considerations of sexual morality are nearly twice as important in determining abortion attitudes as those concerning human life. Moreover, at the level of mass opinion, this pattern is remarkably uniform across countries. A similarly high ratio of effects of sexual traditionalism to disapproval of euthanasia is observed in Catholic Poland, Switzerland, and Columbia, as well as in Muslim Malaysia and Jordan.[18]

This finding renders differences among religious traditions more readily understandable. For example, although Islam allows for the nuanced, gradual attainment of "personhood" of the fetus, empirically, Muslims are the least likely to approve of abortion of any of the groups I have considered. The importance of sexual conservatism in accounting for abortion attitudes makes this apparent contradiction intelligible. The interests of the fetus are not the only consideration, but legal abortion may be considered both a potential cause and consequence of sexual promiscuity, which may in turn have disruptive familial and social consequences beyond the ontological status of the unborn.

This set of findings also sheds some light on one possibly anomalous finding. Given the vociferous opposition of the Catholic hierarchy to abortion, why are lay Catholics so moderate on the issue? One partial answer is that Catholics seem to hold relatively permissive attitudes on matters of sexual morality (defined here as attitudes toward homosexuality and prostitution). While an explanation of relative Catholic liberalism on questions of sexual conduct is beyond the scope of this chapter, the empirical results of the research on which this chapter are based suggests that at least some Catholics are relatively nonjudgmental with respect to the nonmarital sexual conduct of others.

Thus, the political characterization of a restrictive position on abortion as "pro-life" may be something of a misnomer, or at least incomplete. As the analysis of the relationship between attitudes toward abortion and euthanasia suggests, considerations of human life *do* matter when it comes to abortion. Nevertheless, the status of the fetus is typically not the only, or even the primary consideration for many members of the mass public in different nations, or who are members of different religious communities. Sexual values and self-images are central to the belief systems of many, if not most people, and such attitudes can have powerful effects when given political expression.

Gender Roles

At the level of public rhetoric and political discourse, abortion is, in many nations and jurisdictions, a "women's issue." Perhaps the most compelling argument for allowing women access to safe, legal, abortions is the simple notion that reproductive freedom is necessary for women to gain full political, economic, and social equality. That is, pregnancy, childrearing, and motherhood are potentially disruptive to the engagement of other pursuits, and in order to pursue careers or other lifestyle choices, women must be allowed to choose the number and timing of children.[19] Conversely, opponents of abortion often argue that more traditional gender roles are more consistent with different intrinsic natures between the sexes, and that women are particularly well-suited for nurturing tasks associated with motherhood.[20]

However, the empirical evidence linking abortion policy and opinion to women's politics is somewhat mixed. As noted above, at the aggregate level, more permissive abortion policies are related to female participation in government institutions, and in the paid labor force. In other words, nations that have relatively high percentages of women engaged in business and politics are likely to have relatively permissive abortion policies. This tendency seems particularly pronounced in countries that were formerly governed by communist regimes.[21] Further, at the level of individual mass opinion, women who are employed in the paid labor force are significantly more likely to favor legal abortion, and to regard abortion as justified.[22]

However, the relationship between egalitarian gender role beliefs and values and attitudes toward abortion is generally weak and inconsistent. Relative to values such as religiosity, respect for human life, and traditional attitudes toward sexual morality, *attitudes* about the appropriate social, economic, and political roles of women have surprisingly little to do with public attitudes toward abortion.[23] Put simply, once demographic and situational factors are taken into account, "feminists," or persons who do not believe in ascribed differences between men and women, are no more likely to support a woman's right to terminate a pregnancy than citizens who hold more "traditional" beliefs about gender differences. This result seems to persist whether respondents are asked about the competence of women to engage in activities in business or politics, or about special female characteristics relating to nurturing or childrearing.

This "non-finding" represents something of an anomaly. Three possible explanations for the virtual irrelevance of gender role attitudes to beliefs about abortion seem possible. First, it may be the case that the links between beliefs about gender and beliefs about abortion are cognitively demanding. It may be difficult for some people to make the link between "fairness" in politics or the workplace and a medical procedure. Further, some citizens may overestimate the reliability of contraception, and may not regard access to abortion as necessary for reproductive freedom.[24]

Second, women who might otherwise hold "pro-choice" attitudes may well experience emotional or cognitive cross-pressures. In particular, it is widely accepted that, in most societies, women are more religious than men, and an impressive body of research (cited above) shows that religiosity is often related to restrictive preferences with respect to abortion. Elsewhere I have shown that both of these hypotheses receive limited empirical support in cross-national surveys.[25]

Finally, many women may simply not regard themselves as the potential beneficiaries of permissive abortion policies. The doctrinal emphases placed in most religious traditions on the ontological status of the fetus may well have placed a stigma on women who have had abortions, and women who have not undergone the procedure may not identify as potential consumers of abortion products. Other groups (e.g., sexual and racial minorities) who have been historically stigmatized have, in some instances, come to regard their status as representing positive group identities. For example, the designation of homosexuals as "queer" has passed in public rhetoric from the expression of a hideous prejudice to an assertion of militant pride in one's sexual orientation. It seems unlikely that any similar process or rhetorical shift has characterized women who have undergone illicit or legal abortions.

Thus, the strong cognitive associations related to attitudes toward abortion may suppress what would seem to be a natural connection between gender role egalitarianism and the availability of abortion. Even if the connection between the general value of human life and approval of abortion does not represent the strongest empirical relationship in public opinion, the persistence of the perception of the fetus as human may render abortion an "other-regarding issue" (as John Stuart Mill might put it) and make value judgments about the importance of privacy, personal freedom, or equality seem less compelling. While approval of abortion seems related to the *interests* of women who seek control over their reproductive choices, the translation of such interests into *values* supporting reproductive freedom is much weaker and more tenuous.

Across religious traditions, there are few differences in the importance of gender role beliefs as sources of abortion attitudes, but those differences are potentially intriguing. At one end of the spectrum, gender role egalitarianism has its greatest effect on attitudes toward abortion among adherents of Eastern Orthodoxy, which is also the tradition in which aggregate abortion approval is highest. I examined the effects of "public feminism" (belief in the equal competence of men and women to engage in business or politics) and "private feminism" (a belief in the enhanced fitness of women to engage in childrearing). Among the religious traditions considered in my 2014 piece, the effects of private feminism are only statistically significant among the Orthodox. This finding, as well as the relatively high level of abortion approval among the Eastern Orthodox, may reflect the legacy of communist regimes among countries with Orthodox majorities.[26]

Among Catholics, Protestants, and Hindus, only the effects of public feminism matter. Perhaps surprisingly, gender role attitudes are empirically unrelated to abortion approval among Buddhists and Muslims. Despite a body of academic and popular opinion linking Islam to inegalitarian attitudes toward men and women,[27] Muslim opposition to abortion is not related to gender role traditionalism at the level of mass opinion.

Conclusion: Do Religious Differences Matter?

The abortion controversy is indeed fascinating. The question of whether women should be allowed to terminate pregnancies intentionally poses intriguing questions in the areas of theology, ethnics, psychology, politics, and law. Beliefs, policies, and practices about abortion vary across nations, across religious traditions, and within traditions and political jurisdictions.

Therefore, it may be somewhat surprising that, across these diverse sources of variations, ordinary citizens appear to understand the abortion issue in very similar ways. Regardless of whether one is male or female, Protestant, Catholic, Muslim, or Hindu, the same sets of considerations appear to underlie attitudes toward abortion and reproductive freedom.

Again, the most important of these seems to be citizen attitudes toward nonmarital sex. Research has consistently shown that the strongest predictor of abortion attitudes relates to approval or disapproval of sex outside traditional, monogamous, heterosexual relationships. The possibility of pregnancy outside of marriage is, for many, a strong deterrent to "adulterous" sex, and the availability of abortion substantially reduces the SOCIAL risk of such a pregnancy. In one sense, this general finding is not surprising, in that sexual values are quite central to the personalities of many (if not most) people, and the political expression of sexuality seems likely to be quite powerful.

Second, attitudes about abortion seem strongly related to beliefs about the ontology of the fetus. Indeed, most religious doctrine relating to abortion across religious traditions involves questions of the humanity of the unborn entity carried by a pregnant woman. Although direct and noncontroversial evidence to this point is quite difficult to come by, the direct effects of euthanasia attitudes on beliefs about abortion are quite suggestive. Again, for many, abortion is literally "a matter of life or death."

Although the relationship between attitudes toward euthanasia and those concerning abortion attitudes are usually weaker (typically about half as strong) as those associated with attitudes toward sexual morality, the "human life" consideration may have indirect effects not easily measured with the analysis of survey data.[28] The possibility that the fetus is an independent entity, bearing such characteristics as rights, a soul, or the possibility of an individual existence may allow abortion opponents to regard abortion as an "other-regarding act," which is not subsumed by claims of individual autonomy, privacy, or choice. In individualist political cultures, such as the United States and Western Europe, assertions about the humanity of the fetus may license public discussion (and, indeed, regulation) of a practice that might otherwise be considered a private, personal, matter. Further, beliefs about the humanity of the fetus may suppress the effects of other attitudes, such as support for gender equality, population control, or other considerations.

Third, the role of changing gender roles is arguably important, but rather poorly understood. Permissive policies and attitudes about abortion are more common in settings, and among people, whose interests might be served by reproductive freedom. Abortion policies are generally more permissive in nations in which relatively high numbers of women serve as government officials, or participate in the paid labor force. Approval of abortion is generally stronger among people who are potential beneficiaries of relatively easy access to reproductive services. However, these relationships do not seem to extend to a connection between egalitarian gender role *values* and approval of abortion. Consistently, and anomalously, the relationships between "feminist" values and support for legal abortion are weak and inconsistent, despite the close connection between the two in public discourse.

It is not clear why this is the case. This is an area that cries out for innovative (perhaps qualitative or experimental) research. It might be hypothesized that the empirical link between abortion attitudes and gender role egalitarianism is suppressed by other values, such as religiosity, a belief in the humanity of the fetus, or the value of chastity and monogamy.

Finally, religiosity matters. Across different religious traditions, frequent religious behavior is associated with relatively restrictive abortion attitudes. What counts as normative religious behavior (whether attendance at public religious services or private prayer) varies across variations of Christianity, Hinduism, Buddhism, or Islam, but such behavior is empirically related to relatively high levels of disapproval of abortion. This relationship, while not usually very strong, persists even after the effects of the attitudinal variables described above are taken into account. Again, the reasons for this consistent finding are not clear. Perhaps religious behavior is associated with a moral general trait of communal integration and involvement, which suppresses individualism and unconventional sexual behavior. That is, people who are more religiously active may be more attuned to community norms, which may in turn decrease the value placed on individual autonomy.

The main point of this chapter is that the considerations that occasion restrictive or permissive abortion attitudes do not appear to differ across religious traditions. "Pro-life" Catholics (for example) are likely to bring the same subjective considerations to bear on judgments about abortion as their Muslim or Orthodox counterparts. Indeed, the consistency of the importance of considerations of sexual morality and respect for life, as well as the relative unimportance of gender role attitudes, is quite remarkable.

Given this uniformity of the structure of abortion attitudes across cultures and religious traditions, how can the variation among abortion policies, practices, and beliefs be understood? If abortion is understood in the same way in (highly restrictive) El Salvador as it is in (relatively permissive) Japan, why do abortion politics differ so drastically? Three explanations seem to suggest themselves.

First, at the level of mass opinion, the marginal distributions of predictor variables may differ across religious traditions. In less technical language, this means that differences in abortion attitudes among adherents of different creeds may be attributable to differences in the attitudes associated with beliefs about abortion. Some religions may (and, indeed, appear to) inculcate different attitudes about sexual morality or human life than do others. For example, a member of an Eastern Orthodox Church and a Muslim who disapprove of sex outside of marriage seem about equally likely to oppose legal abortion. However, opposition to nonmarital sex is significantly more common among adherents of Islam than among the Orthodox. Indeed, one reason that lay Catholics are not particularly distinctive on abortion, despite the Church's intensive efforts at religious socialization, is that Catholics seem to hold relatively permissive attitudes about nontraditional sexual relationships. Of course, explaining the reasons for interdenominational differences with respect to variables that predict abortion attitudes is a promising topic for future research.

Second, religious traditions may have other resources to bring to bear on public policies besides the aggregation of mass opinion. If the concept of representation is more broadly defined as the translation of public opinion into public policy, it seems clear that the translation of the preferences of ordinary citizens into authoritative laws is usually indirect, and is likely to involve some distortion. Some political actors, such as religious organizations, may be able to influence the actions of government officials beyond the simple aggregation and mobilization of potential voters. One obvious example of this phenomenon is the Roman Catholic Church. Although the empirical research cited in this chapter suggests that lay Catholics are no more "pro-life" than adherents of other religious traditions, the Church often has political resources at the elite level that render its institutional preferences disproportionately influential in the formulation of public policy. In many societies, perhaps especially those in which Catholics are particularly numerous, the Church is likely to have an extensive infrastructure, including mass communication media, social networks, educational institutions, and access to elite recruitment via bureaucratic means or political parties.[29] In such jurisdictions, the "official" Catholic position on abortion is likely to have greater influence on policy outcomes than are the preferences of lay Catholics. It is also possible that the hierarchical organization of the Roman Catholic Church allows it to claim one "official" position, which is not possible in other religious traditions, such as Buddhism or Islam. This point can be generalized. Not all opinions are created equal, nor are all opinions equally influential. Political arenas may be biased to favor or suppress the enactment of certain preferences into policy.

Finally, religious values must interact with other, secular aspects of national political cultures in order to produce responses to issues of reproductive freedom. Abortion politics are contested in political contexts in which religion is but one consideration. In the United States, a "rights" culture, in which the very legitimacy of abortion legislation is occasionally contested, as well as the radical centralization of policy making institutions, ensures that abortion politics will often be contested in legal institutions such as courts of law.[30] Similarly, the Catholic Church seems to enjoy special prestige in such nations as Ireland and Poland,[31] while the legitimacy of Catholic-based political action may be contested in such nations as France or Spain.[32] Concerns about the political consequences of differential levels of fertility among different religious or ethnic groups have occasionally animated abortion policy in Israel and could conceivably have similar effects in the future in Western Europe. Fears of an emerging "Eurabia" may occasion a demand for more restrictive abortion policies in nations whose policies are relatively permissive. That is, fears among ethnic Europeans that "natives" of nations such as France, Germany, or the Netherlands may eventually be outnumbered by the descendants of immigrants from Muslim-majority nations, owing to permissive immigration policies and (more importantly for present purposes) greater fertility among Muslim immigrants.[33] Such demographic concerns may occasion a demand for public policies that encourage large families, and which would discourage abortion and contraception.

Jose Casanova has suggested that an important aspect to secularization is compartmentalization, in which the areas of social and political life in which religion is perceived as relevant may be shrinking.[34] Abortion is a moral and religious issue, to be sure, but abortion is not *simply* an issue of personal or public morality. Considerations of economics, demography, and foreign policy may have a role.[35]

However, the results of empirical work (mine and others) suggest that abortion politics are organized around frames of reference that do not differ greatly across nations or religious traditions. The issue of abortion may be an important component of a "culture war," or a "clash of civilizations," but the moral and intellectual weapons in such political conflict seem well-defined and commonly understood. The politics of abortion represents an area in which differences in practices and policies conceal shared understandings about the stakes of the struggle.

Notes

1. Ted G. Jelen, "The Subjective Bases of Abortion Attitudes: A Cross-National Analysis of Religious Traditions," *Politics and Religion* (2014): 550–567.
2. Yael Yashivi, "Public Ideas and Public Policy: Abortion Attitudes in Four Democracies," *Comparative Politics* 25 (1993): 207–228.
3. Mala Hutu and S. Laurel Weldon, "When Do Governments Promote Women's Rights? A Framework for the Analysis of Sex Equality Policy," *Perspectives on Politics* 8 (2010): 207–216, and Achim Hildebrandt, "What Shapes Abortion Law? A Global Perspective," *Global Policy* 6 (2015): 418–428.
4. Francis Castles, "The World Turned Upside Down: Below Replacement Fertility, Changing Preferences, and Family-Friendly Policies in 21 OCD Countries," *European Journal of Social Policy* 12 (2003): 209–227; and Michael Minkenberg, "Religion and Public Policy: Institutional, Cultural, and Political Impact on the Shaping of Abortion Policy in Western Democracies," *Comparative Political Studies* 35, no. 29920; 221–247.
5. Michele Dillon, "Cultural Differences in the Abortion Discourse of the Catholic Church: Evidence From Four Countries," *Sociology of Religion* 57 (1996): 25–46; and, "Public Ideas and Public Policy," 207–228.
6. Hildebrandt, "What Shapes Abortion Law?" In some settings, abortion has been regarded as a more cost-effective means of contraception than preventive devices or medications. See Ted G. Jelen and Clyde Wilcox, "Attitudes Toward Abortion in Poland and the United States," *Social Science Quarterly* 78 (1997): 907–921.
7. Edward G. Carmines and James A. Stimson, "The Two Faces of Issue Voting," *American Political Science Review* 74 (1980): 78–91.
8. Matthew Wetstein, *Abortion Rates in the United States: The Influence of Opinion and Policy* (Albany, NY: State University of New York Press, 1996); and T. G. Jelen and J. D. Bradley, "Abortion opinion in emerging democracies: Latin America and Central Europe," *Politics, Groups and Identities* 2, no. 1 (2014): 52–65.
9. Unfortunately, the World Values Surveys do not permit more precise distinctions among varieties of Protestants. In the analysis described here, there were too few Jews to permit detailed analysis.
10. See Amy Adamczyk, "The Effect of Personal Religiosity on Attitudes Toward Abortion, Divorce, and Gender Equality," *EurAmerica* 43 (2013): 213–251; and Elizabeth Adell Cook, Ted G. Jelen, and Clyde Wilcox, *Between Two Absolutes: Public Opinion and the Politics of Abortion* (Boulder, CO: Westview). Of course, it is impossible to establish causality in data gathered at a single point in time, but it seems likely that a specific policy opinion (such as abortion) is a consequence, rather than a cause, of general orientations such as attitudes toward sexual morality or respect for human life. However, an emerging literature suggests that abortion attitudes may be sufficiently salient to affect more general moral or political orientations. See especially Mitchell Killian and Clyde Wilcox, "Does Abortion Lead to Party Switching?" *Political Research Quarterly* 61 (2008): 561–573.
11. Michael Driessen, *Religion and Democratization: Framing Religious and Political Indentities in Muslim and Catholic Societies* (New York: Oxford University Press, 2014); and Cherian George, *Hate Spin: The Manufacture of Religious Offense and Its Threat to Democracy* (Cambridge, MA: MIT Press, 2016).
12. Joseph Bernardin, *A Consistent Ethic of Life* (Chicago: Sheed and Ward, 1988).

13. Ted G. Jelen, "Religious Belief and Attitude Constraint," *Journal for the Scientific Study of Religion* 29 (1990): 118–125.
14. See Ted G. Jelen, "Gender Role Beliefs and Attitudes Toward Abortion: A Cross-National Exploration," *Journal of Research in Gender Studies* 5 (2015): 11–22; Jelen, "The Subjective Bases of Abortion Attitudes," and Cook et al., *Between Two Absolutes*. See also Catherine I. Bolzendhal and Daniel J. Mays, "Feminist Attitudes and Support for Gender Equality: Opinion Change in Women and Men, 1974–1988," *Social Forces* 83 (2004): 759–789.
15. Again, for the purposes of this study, the WVS contains too few Jews for analysis. The WVS item measuring attitudes toward euthanasia is a simple ten-point scale asking whether "euthanasia" is "Never acceptable" (1) to "always acceptable" (10). Thus, the measure is rather crude, and does not capture distinctions among various circumstances under which someone may intentionally end one's own life (with or without assistance).
16. See especially Kristin Luker, *Abortion and the Politics of Motherhood* (Berkeley: University of California Press, 1985).
17. Jelen, "The Subjective Basis of Abortion Attitudes," and Luker, *Abortion and the Politics of Motherhood*. The assertion of causality is, of course, not definitive, but seems quite plausible, in that attitudes toward sexual conduct seem basic and relatively stable. I call the reader's attention to the fact that it is not possible definitively to establish causality with data gathered at a single point in time.
18. Jelen, "The Subjective Bases of Abortion Attitudes."
19. See Luker, *Abortion and the Politics of Motherhood*. See also Eileen McDonagh, *Breaking the Abortion Deadlock: From Choice to Consent* (New York: Oxford University Press); Myra Marx Farere, "Resonance and Radicalism: Feminist Framing in the Abortion Debates in the United States and Germany," *American Journal of Sociology* 109 (2003): 304–344; and Ruth Colker, "Feminism, Theology, and Abortion: Toward Love, Compassion, and Wisdom," *California Law Review* 77 (1989): 1011–1075.
20. See Luker, *Abortion and the Politics of Motherhood*; see also Carole Gilligan, *In A Different Voice: Psychological Theory and Women's Development* (Cambridge, MA: Harvard University Press, 1988).
21. Hildebrandt, "What Shapes Abortion Law?"
22. Jelen, "Gender Role Beliefs and Attitudes Toward Abortion"; Cook et al., *Between Two Absolutes*.
23. John Lynxwiler and David Gay, "The Abortion Attitudes of Black Women, 1978–1991," *Journal of Black Studies* 2 (1996): 260–277; Jennifer Strickler and Nicholas I. Danigelis, "Changing Frameworks in Attitudes Toward Abortion," *Sociological Forum* 17 (2002): 187–201; and Blozendhal and Mays, "Feminist Attitudes and Support for Gender Equality."
24. Cook et al. *Between Two Absolutes*. For general accounts of the cognitive limitations of ordinary citizens, see Phillip E. Converse, "The Nature of Belief Systems in Mass Publics," in *Ideology and Discontent*, ed. David Apter (New York: Free Press): 206–261; John R. Zaller, *The Nature and Origins of Mass Opinion* (New York: Cambridge University Press); Jelen, "Gender Role Beliefs and Attitudes Toward Abortion."
25. Jelen, "Gender Role Beliefs and Attitudes Toward Abortion."
26. See Hildebrandt, "What Shapes Abortion Law?" and Daniela Kalkandjieva, "A Comparative Analysis of Church-State Relations in Eastern Orthodoxy: Concepts, Models, and Principles," *Journal of Church and State* 53 (2011): 587–614.
27. Ronald Inglehart and Pippa Norris, *Rising Tide: Gender Equality and Cultural Change Around the World* (New York: Cambridge University Press, 2003).

28. Again, the reader is reminded that it is difficult to assess causality in cross-sectional survey data. I hypothesize that attitudes toward euthanasia and abortion are both specific instances of a more general attitude toward the sanctity of human life, which seems to vary across respondents. The idea of a general "respect for life" is difficult to measure directly.
29. Anna Grzymala-Busse, *Nations under Gods: How Churches Use Moral Authority to Influence Policy* (Princeton, NJ: Princeton University Press, 2014).
30. Laurence Tribe, *Abortion: The Clash of Absolutes* (New York: Norton, 1992).
31. Timothy A. Byrnes, "The Challenge of Pluralism: The Catholic Church in Democratic Poland," in *Religion and Regimes: Support, Opposition, or Separation*, edited by Mehran Tamadonfar and Ted G. Jelen, pp. 27–44 (Lanham, MD: Lexington, 2014); and Michele Dillon, "The Orphaned Irish: Church and State in Neo-Liberal Ireland," in Tamadonfar and Jelen, *Religion and Regimes*, 187–211.
32. Ahmet Kuru, *Secularism and State Policy Toward Religion: The United States, France, and Turkey* (New York: Cambridge University Press, 2009); Paul Christopher Manuel, "The Roman Catholic Church and Political Regimes in Portugal and Spain," in Tamadonfar and Jelen, *Religion and Regimes*, 141–156; and Ramazan Kilinc, "International Context and State-Religion Regimes in France and Turkey," in Tamadonfar and Jelen, *Religion and Regimes*, 97–120.
33. See especially Bat Ye'Or, *Eurarabia: The Euro-Arab Axis* (Madison, NJ: Fairleigh-Dickenson University Press, 2005).
34. Jose Casanova, *Public Religions in the Modern World* (Chicago: University of Chicago Press, 1994).
35. For example, It has been suggested that abortion policy has often been contested in European Union institutions. See Brent Nelsen and James L. Guth, *Religion and the Struggle for European Union* (Washington, DC: Georgetown University Press, 2015).

PART V
PRENATAL DIAGNOSIS

CHAPTER 26

PREGNANCY AND PIETY

The Situated Ethics of Prenatal Diagnostic Technologies for Ultra-Orthodox Jewish Women

ELLY TEMAN AND TSIPY IVRY

> *I was part of a conversation that focused on asking a rabbi for a* psak *(ruling) on taking any kind of (prenatal) test, even amnio. . . . I remember thinking then, well, there lies the answer as to why we don't take these tests—what would you do? The life of the mother takes precedence over the life of the unborn, and that's the only case in which an action would be deemed halachically advisable. Our* emunah *(faith) and* bitachon *(certainty) guide us— every* neshama *(soul) that is sent to this world is precious, even or perhaps especially so, a specially-abled baby. Fast forward to the seventh child born to us, and my ninth pregnancy [she had miscarried twice]. I was thirty-seven when she was born, and my doctor only said it in the negative, "You're not doing the amnio, right?" Right.*

THE quote above from Miriam, forty-one, an Ultra-Orthodox Jewish mother of seven, was made in regard to her decision to refuse her doctor's offer of amniocentesis, a prenatal test that is used to detect congenital anomalies in the sixteenth to twentieth week of pregnancy. Age thirty-seven during that pregnancy, Miriam was already in the "high-risk" category of "advanced maternal age" in which American and Israeli women are routinely offered prenatal tests, including amniocenteses. Yet Miriam's doctor, who works primarily with Ultra-Orthodox Jewish women, knew before she had even answered his question that Miriam would not be interesting in doing this prenatal test because so many of his Orthodox patients routinely refused it.

There are plenty of possible explanations for refusal of amniocentesis, as well as other prenatal tests, as the rich ethnographic literature on prenatal diagnostics and testing (PND) has illustrated.[1] Apart from the prohibition on abortion, there are also many additional reasons why Ultra-Orthodox Jewish women might refuse these tests.[2] Some of these reasons Miriam speaks of directly: rabbis from different sectors of the Ultra-Orthodox community direct their followers to use or to refuse particular tests, and doctors working with Ultra-Orthodox Jewish women make assumptions about which tests their clientele will agree to take and thus may shape the women's responses in the way they offer these options.

Since termination of pregnancy is prohibited in Jewish law other than under very specific circumstances, doing tests to discover fetal anomalies might be considered useless as there is often not much one can do with the information from the tests other than terminate the pregnancy. Yet it is significant that Miriam's explanation about her decision regarding amniocentesis also reveals a prevailing discourse in her community about the souls of "specially-abled babies" and about the need to be guided by one's faith and certainty in God to make reproductive decisions.

In this study we attempt to understand the attitudes, experiences, and decisions of Ultra-Orthodox women regarding prenatal diagnosis and testing. First, we include a short overview of the PND scholarship, particularly in anthropology, as well as a brief introduction to the Haredi communities. After outlining the basic concepts of their worldview, we look at the way our interviewees employed faith-based concepts in explaining their decisions regarding PND. In the conclusion we suggest that the women's negotiations of PND can be conceptualized as a form of "situated ethics" that may be viewed as a gendered folk interpretation and vernacular religious application of Jewish ethics.

Prenatal Diagnostic Screening and Testing

Prenatal diagnosis and testing refers to an array of tests offered routinely to women in Israel and in the United States during pregnancy. These tests can largely be divided into invasive and non-invasive tests. The non-invasive tests include maternal serum screening, which predicts the probability of a fetus being affected by neural tube defects or Down syndrome, and ultrasound screening, which is used for confirming the due date, weighing and measuring the fetus, and diagnosing various fetal anomalies. The invasive tests include amniocentesis and chorionic villus sampling, which can accurately diagnose genetic malformations, but these carry up to a 2 percent chance of inducing miscarriage. A relatively new test, NIPT, is now available in both countries as an alternative to the invasive tests while also achieving a high level of accuracy.

What is important to note about these tests is that there are few options to correct fetal anomalies that are diagnosed, and pregnant women and their partners who receive a positive diagnosis will face what has been called a "burden of choice"[3] or an illusory "forced choice"[4] between terminating the pregnancy or carrying the baby to term. It is in light of this situation that prenatal testing has been theorized as subjecting pregnant women to a discourse of "risk," defined by medical experts, and creating a situation in which women who refuse prenatal tests are marked often as "irresponsible" mothers.[5]

Prenatal testing has also been discussed in the scholarship as increasing the uncertainty women experience in pregnancy, and as making women and couples facing these life and death decisions into "ethical gatekeepers" or "moral pioneers."[6] As Davis (2010) argues, the more that new genetic tests become part of routine prenatal care, the more quick decisions patients are forced to make on "uncharted ethical ground" where straightforward guidelines are not necessarily forthcoming. A root paradigm guiding medical professionals who counsel these patients is that patients should have autonomy to make independent decisions free of coercion about their bodies and futures.[7] But how do women think about prenatal diagnosis when they are devoutly religious and believe that only God has the right to decide?

As White has noted, there has been relatively little research that examines the impact of religious and spiritual values on decision-making about genetic issues, and the few studies that have been conducted are difficult to draw conclusions from.[8] These studies do suggest in general that religious and spiritual beliefs shape risk perceptions and decisions of persons with a high risk of developing certain genetic conditions, such as breast cancer and Huntington's disease.[9] However, most of the studies are based on quantitative empirical data or focus group discussions and do not account for the depth of religious commitment of the study participants.[10]

While several anthropological studies of assisted reproduction have looked at the ways in which religion and local moral economies shape understandings and use of the new reproductive technologies,[11] few anthropological studies have looked particularly at the role of faith in women's decisions about PND.[12] Our interest in Ultra-Orthodox Jewish women and prenatal diagnosis stems from the unique circumstances in which these women experience pregnancy and make decisions regarding PND. A core understanding of this group is that only God controls the universe and choice is not determined by autonomous individuals, so rabbis are consulted on all matters related to the interpretation and application of Jewish Law in everyday life and all major decisions are made through rabbinical mediation. Yet the women we met from these communities made decisions despite giving up control, and exercised a set of religious concepts to aid them in those decisions.

Ultra-Orthodox Jewish Women and PND

The particular religious group that we refer to here as "Ultra-Orthodox" are also customarily referred to with the term *Haredi* (meaning God-fearing) Jews. This population follows a deeply religious lifestyle in accordance with the five books of Moses (the Torah) as well as a broad spectrum of rabbinic literature, commentary, and rulings. Distinguished from the larger and more liberally oriented Reform and Conservative branches of Judaism by their more strict interpretation of Jewish Law, Haredi Jews also distinguish themselves from the modern Orthodox, who are typically more open to Israel's statehood, secular knowledge, and modern society.[13]

Haredi society actually refers to a plurality of communities, each with its own religious leaders or rabbis and style of religious observance.[14] In each of these groups, a particular rabbi or group of rabbis serve as "community gatekeeper."[15] Rabbis are consulted on all matters related to the interpretation and application of Jewish law in everyday life, including medical issues. Haredi society can be roughly divided into the Lithuanian Yeshiva (Torah learning) communities and the Hassidic dynasties; among their many differences, the latter embrace Jewish mysticism (Kabala) and follow the leadership not only of rabbis but also of spiritual advisors. Haredi communities may be visually distinguished by their dress code of black hats and dark suits for men and long skirts and covered hair for women.[16]

What unifies these communities for our purposes is their rapidly growing birth rate and cultural attitudes toward reproduction. The estimated birth rate in the United States of 6.6 for the Lithuanian population and 7.8 for the Hassidic population differentiates the reproductive practices of Haredi Jewry from the modern Orthodox (at 3.3) and from the declining fertility levels of the non-Orthodox Jewish population (Wertheimer 2005). The case of Haredi women is particularly interesting to consider in terms of prenatal diagnosis because of the high number of pregnancies among the women of this population and their tendency to continue bearing children up until the time of menopause when the risk for having a child with a chromosomal anomaly increases significantly.[17]

All Haredi communities practice arranged marriages, usually within their specific sect, which results in a high rate of consanguinity. Having children is believed to be a divine commandment, so birth control is not encouraged and women tend to begin reproducing shortly after marriage. Women normally continue having children at short intervals up until menopause, often reaching a family size of ten or more children by their forties. Consanguineous marriages, the possibility of being a carrier for the genetic diseases that have been traced among Ashkenazi Jews, and advanced maternal age increase the risk that babies will be born with congenital anomalies or genetic disorders.[18]

Within the Haredi communities, there is one program in place to reduce the risk of bearing children with a genetic disorder. A majority of individuals that enter into arranged marriages are screened before matchmaking for genetic incompatibility by the Dor Yeshorim Institute, an international genetic testing program operating within these communities that aims to prevent arranged marriages between Orthodox persons who are carriers of the same disease.[19] However, this screening cannot address a long list of genetic conditions, including Down syndrome. Although no data on rates of affected births could be found for the US population, a study of all Down syndrome births in Israel between 1997 and 2004 showed that there was a substantially higher rate of babies born with Down syndrome among the Haredi population (1.81 per 1,000 live births) compared to the non-Orthodox Jewish population (0.31 per 1,000 live births).[20] The growing number of programs for special needs children among the Haredi communities in the United States also point in this direction.[21] It is with this background in mind that we turn to our study on the women's decisions regarding PND.

METHODS

This study included twenty interviews in Israel in 2007–2009 with Haredi women aged twenty-one to forty-five in Jerusalem and the surrounding Haredi enclaves and an additional twenty-five interviews in the Northeastern United States with Haredi women aged twenty-one to forty-eight in 2009–2010. Four additional interviews were undertaken in Israel in the spring of 2013 with women aged thirty to sixty from an additional Haredi enclave in the Netanya area of Israel. What unifies the women from these samples for our purpose in this study is their reproductive habitus of raising notably large families and the fact that Haredi women in both countries spend most of their married life pregnant and caring for children.[22]

To account for the differences among Haredi groups within Israel and the United States, and to account for the plurality of Hassidic sects and Lithuanian Yeshiva communities, we included women who identified themselves with as many different sectors of Haredi society as possible, including Lithuanian and several Hasidic groups. The Israeli sample also included the Mizrahi-Haredi affiliation (Sephardic Jews formerly from Islamic countries). Contact with interviewees was facilitated through personal social networks: the first author was able to contact women in Israel through a Haredi woman she met during her research on gestational surrogacy, and in the United States by establishing rapport with one central contact person in each Haredi community studied. The second author was able to network through women she had met when she lived for eight years in a neighborhood in Jerusalem populated by several Haredi sects. In Israel and in the United States additional interviewees were recruited in each Haredi community through snowball sampling.[23]

All of the women interviewed in the Israeli sample were mothers of two to eleven children, including one mother raising a child with Down syndrome; the women in the US sample were mothers of two to twelve children, including four mothers of children with special needs. All interviews were open-ended, lasting one and a half to three hours, audiotaped and transcribed. The interviews in Israel were conducted in Hebrew and the US interviews in English, but all interviews were peppered with Yiddish terms. In both segments of the study women were asked to describe their experiences of pregnancy, prenatal care, and prenatal diagnosis beginning with their first pregnancy. Specific prenatal tests, communication of religious beliefs to their obstetrician, and the role of their faith in decision-making about prenatal care were probed.[24]

The participants were given the choice of being interviewed at home, at the workplace, or by telephone. In the Israeli sample, the majority of the interviews were conducted in the woman's home; in the US sample, five of the interviews were conducted in the women's homes, two at their place of work, and eighteen by telephone. The verbatim transcripts were coded for emergent themes by the grounded theory approach. All the names given are pseudonyms. The Israeli sample of this research was reviewed and approved by the ethics committee of the Faculty of Social Sciences at the University of Haifa and the US sample was approved by the IRB of the University of Pennsylvania.

In our study, at first glance, there was no basic recipe for predicting whether women would refuse or accept prenatal testing. All of the women in the Israeli sample and most in the US sample refused maternal serum screening—a test which is based upon probabilities which looks for neural tube defects and Down syndrome in the fifteenth to seventeenth week of gestation—yet seven of the women in the US sample did accept the offer of this test in at least one of their pregnancies. All of the women in both samples refused amniocentesis, including those over age thirty-five ("advanced maternal age"), yet two of the women received rabbinical permission to do chorionic villus sampling (CVS) because they were known carriers of a genetic condition.

In these samples, the women's acceptance of the offer of ultrasound was all across the board. Most of our interviewees agreed to ultrasounds, but their number and timing varied among women and from one pregnancy to another. Some agreed to do an early scan to date the pregnancy but refused diagnostic scans, such as the nuchal scan or anatomy scan. Some refused all ultrasounds in accordance with a custom in their community not to do scans, but all of these women except for one did agree to an ultrasound in at least one pregnancy because of "medical necessity." These findings concur with Mittman's (2005) survey and interviews with members of the Lithuanian Yeshiva community in Baltimore, which showed a widespread use of ultrasound in pregnancy among women in the community but low uptake of amniocentesis, CVS, and maternal serum screening.[25] This selective uptake of prenatal diagnosis is echoed in findings from several other studies that have included the Haredi population in Israel as well.[26] How can one explain this selective uptake of PND? What is the logic behind acceptance of some tests and refusal of others?

The Soul and its Mission

The first reason we suggest for the women's selective uptake of PND derives from their discourse of the soul and its mission. The women in this study described a worldview based on the central idea that God oversees the universe and humans are not in control of their fate. Using the concept of Divine Providence [*hashgacha pratis*] to explain how this relates to reproduction, the women explained that only God has control over reproductive outcomes, maternal and fetal health. As Shaini, age twenty-seven and a mother of four explained: "We are not God. God chooses to make things happen. Who knows what he chooses? Who knows why he chooses? So for us to say, 'I need to find this out so that I can decide what to do.'... It's not something we really have the right to get involved in." In accordance with this belief system, only God autonomously makes choices, according to His overarching divine plan and the unique mission [*tafkid*] He has envisioned for every soul [*neshama*].

Along these lines, most of the women in our study spoke of having children as their most important role and purpose [*tafkid*] in life. Raising a family was viewed as their "mission" [*shlichut*] from God and their way of worshipping God and expressing piousness.[27] Shimona, twenty-six, mother of four explained:

> It is a wonderful experience. I am fulfilling my role, the reason I came into this world [*tafkid*]. It is a very idealistic feeling. Because for us, each pregnancy and birth are not some kind of accident of nature, not something I planned exactly so that it accords with my conditions. When I am pregnant, I am doing the role for which I was brought here. When I am pregnant, I am doing what I am supposed to [be doing]. It is a feeling of fulfilling a divine mission [*shlichut*] because it is my purpose [*tafkid*], not because nature did it to me. There is an expression in Judaism: "There are three partners in (the creation of) man: the Lord, blessed be He, his father and his mother." The Lord, the mother and the father create the child together. It is as if I am now His partner. He chose me to bring another person into the world.

Like Shimona, most of the women spoke about regarding pregnancy as *being a partner or helper of God* in carrying out his divine plan for the people of Israel. Bringing children into the world was not rationalized as an individual pursuit, and never viewed as an egoistic choice, as it may be rationalized among some less pro-natalist persons. Instead, the women expressed the sincere view that bringing children into the world was an important and positive contribution to society. Rachel, twenty-seven, mother of two, explained the meaning of bearing children in her view:

> It is in this matter that the people of Israel will be redeemed. The mission and role [*tafkid*] of the daughters of Israel is to bear offspring. The messiah will not come until all of the souls have been born. We have the Torah, which guides us. God commanded us to bring children into the world. We don't do it because we feel like it or it is good for us or bad for us, it is a commandment, the first mitzvah in the Torah. . . . It is all in the hands of God.

Rachel's view of childbearing as a divine mission from God was also expressed in the word she used throughout the interview to refer to the moment she had become pregnant using the Hebrew verb *nifkaditi*. The verb *pakad* is used in the Bible to describe conception. For instance, it is used to describe Sarah conceiving Isaac in Genesis 21:1. Yet it is also widely used in the Bible to convey an authoritative order, either divine or human. The double meaning of the verb attests to the wide association between pregnancy and God's mission more generally, while Rachel's choice to describe her pregnancies with this term suggests that she views childbearing as divine service.

When the women spoke of the possibility of having a baby with special needs, it was within this framework of the divine mission. Batsheva, forty-seven, mother of twelve children, one with Down syndrome, stated: "Does anybody really think that we came here (to earth) to indulge in the Garden of Eden? Just to enjoy ourselves? No! We are here on a mission. We have a purpose [*tachlit*] to our existence." Rejecting the American doctrine of the pursuit of happiness, Batsheva's words convey that difficulties and suffering are inextricable parts of life, parts that have meaning and purpose. The women in our study were personally familiar with babies, children, and adults with disabilities, and their families. Women in their communities bear up to six children after age forty, so statistically more babies are born with Down syndrome,[28] one of the conditions most often mentioned in our interviews. Moreover, children with disabilities are becoming more visible in the Haredi public sphere, and many women mentioned the growing visibility of children with Down syndrome in their communities.

Quite strikingly, their references to children with Down syndrome all shared an identical pattern. They began with appreciative comments on the unique characteristics of these children, such as their talent for praying and reciting prayers by heart. These children were especially warm and loving, and were deeply loved and appreciated by their families and all who knew them. Some women said these souls had been incarnated in this form to teach us something and to correct a single karmic issue.[29] Yet this recognition of the cosmological meaning and role of children with Down syndrome was always accompanied by acknowledgment of the difficulty caring for them. Nevertheless, the women unequivocally stated that diagnosis of Down syndrome during pregnancy was not grounds for interrupting a divine mission. Toby, twenty-seven, mother of three explained: "Just because a child has Downs doesn't mean that they don't have a meaning in life.... there is a divine purpose why this child is being born the way he is being born. No, a child being Downs is not a reason to terminate a pregnancy."

Unlike the secular mothers in studies by Landsman in the United States[30] and Ivry in Israel,[31] who were indirectly blamed for personally "allowing" a disabled baby into the world, the Haredi women in our study did not view mothers as personally responsible for their fate. Instead, it was believed that disabled children were special "souls" [neshamot] and that it was a divine privilege [zchut] if God chose you to raise such a child. Of course, this did not mean that women were not concerned with the possibility that they would be "chosen" or that any of them actively wanted such a "mission." However, if they were chosen, they could find purpose in their role. One doctor who was interviewed for this research, who has a largely Ultra-Orthodox, Lithuanian clientele in New Jersey, spoke about how he was able to comfort couples for whom he diagnosed an affected pregnancy: "I tell them about the souls and they were chosen and by the end you almost want to have an affected pregnancy."

Women who *were* chosen and were able to carry out their mission successfully were regarded as particularly righteous. Baila, age fifty-six, mother of eight, referred to special needs children as "gifted" and their mothers as more highly evolved than other mothers who were not chosen for this mission: "[My friend] told me that these children are considered gifted, they are highly evolved souls [neshamas]. It is considered by people that you are on a spiritual [ruchniyus] basis high enough to accept it [mekabel]. It's considered really a divine privilege [zchut]. You have to be on a very high level to embrace it that way."

Within the context of this divine cosmology, Zeesy, age twenty-eight, mother of two, expressed both the difficulties she encountered raising her disabled kindergartener and how she wished sometimes that she had not been deemed worthy of this mission, but at the same time she felt proud for having been chosen:

> And I feel like obviously God thought I was—my husband and I were strong enough to deal with this and to raise this special child, you know.... There's a famous saying that God doesn't give more than he thinks you can handle. So in a way I feel, you know, proud.... it gives me strength to think that obviously God thinks I'm a strong enough person. What I say very often, I wish I wasn't so strong that God didn't think I have to, that I could handle this.... As much as I want to know why and it's not fair and I wish it didn't happen, it's not really up to me to question.... There's a God in this world and He has a plan and you know.... He's gonna carry out his plan whether we like it or not.

The discourse of reproduction as a divine mission, of disabled children as "special souls" with a purpose to their lives and of mothers of disabled children as "chosen" for this role frame prenatal tests as measures that might undercut—rather than support—the plan that God has devised for a particular woman, for her offspring, and for the people of Israel. But as we shall see below, there are other discourses at work in the women's decision-making regarding PND; for a person of faith, accepting or refusing these tests can reflect the measure of one's own devotion.

Faith and Certainty

The second reason we suggest for the women's selective uptake of PND derives from their discourse of faith and certainty. In everyday life, the practice of conceding control to God is expressed in not only having faith [*emunah*] in God but also having certainty [*bitachon*] that God will take you on the right path, even if that path is not what you would have envisioned for yourself. Along these lines, prenatal screening tests are based on probabilities. Relying on these tests shows that you do not have full certainty in God, while refusing the tests proves your faith and certainty. Accordingly, Baila explained that she refused prenatal diagnostic tests, including ultrasounds, during all eight of her pregnancies because she had "a different mindset," which she perceived as the opposite of that represented by probability-based prenatal tests:

> It's like this.... Everything is in the hands of God. We are not going by probabilities and statistics.... It is going against rational thinking. You are not looking at cause and effect anymore. You are looking at a different principle of what runs the universe. It's not easy.... everybody should be blessed with faith [*emunah*].

As Baila's words impart, prenatal tests were conceptualized as the antithesis to full faith and certainty, for they are based on probabilities, on risk medicine and uncertainty and on attempts of humanity, using technology, to control their fate. Raizy, age thirty-one, mother of six, explained that she is tempted to have ultrasounds during her pregnancies because she is curious and believes that the sonogram will ease her uncertainty. Still, she tries to keep from giving in to this temptation as a testament to her faith:

> RAIZY: Everybody wants to know that the heart is beating properly and that the arms and legs are okay and that the head is good. I'm curious and for me it is more of a curiosity thing than anything else. I mean, curiosity that I think is gonna bring me peace of mind [*menuhah*], but it's probably not going to.... I mean it does, but it doesn't mean it's not false *menuhah*. Anything could happen, so ...
> INTERVIEWER: But you still choose not to do the sonogram?
> RAIZY: [The doctor] can do the sonogram; nobody said you shouldn't do it, but why should I do it? ... Curiosity is not a good enough reason.

Goldie, age thirty-eight, mother of nine, discussed how she aimed to go through her pregnancies without needing an ultrasound because to truly trust God means one does not need a "picture" of the fetus. Still, the refusal of this token of reassurance remained a struggle, especially as she got older and realized the higher risk of giving birth to a disabled child:

> The truth is that once you have it [the ultrasound], it's very calming.... It is 'cuz you see the picture. You know, thank God [*Baruch Hashem*], everything is going normally and you're like [relieved].... You know, on the other hand, I struggle with the idea that you are supposed to have trust in God and trust that everything's gonna be good, and confidence that God is gonna do the right thing. So would I need to have a picture to prove that to me, you know? But it does calm you down. I guess as you get older also its more nerve-wracking.

Goldie's experience of pregnancy represents a struggle with faith and certainty. While she is attracted to the idea of prenatal tests, particularly ultrasound, to ameliorate her uncertainty, she strives to express her faith and certainty in God by refusing routine ultrasound examinations unless the doctor has given specific medical reasons and her rabbi has given his permission. Goldie is concerned about the impact a disabled child would have on her life, but this does not lead her to take the tests. Instead, she feels scared and worried throughout her pregnancy while struggling to "keep the faith."

Many of the women imparted stories in the interviews about misdiagnosis from prenatal tests, particularly sonograms. These stories circulated among women as testimonies to the risk of trusting prenatal diagnosis instead of trusting God. The stories relay the message that prenatal testing is seductive but uncertain, tempting but antithetical to having full certainty in God's plan. As a result, to give in to one's fears and to accept the offer of prenatal tests was understood as a weakness in faith and certainty, and one that women struggled with.

Doing Their Obligatory Effort

The third reason we suggest for the women's selective uptake of PND derives from their discourse of obligatory effort [*hishtadlut*, also pronounced *hishtadlus*], a concept that refers to the practical effort people make in order to help themselves find solutions to their problems while still showing faith and certainty. It is the idea that a person can take action to help their situation even as they understand that ultimately these actions may not alter God's plan; it is through *hishtadlut* that one can create the vessel or mechanism through which God can grant blessings if He wills. Orthodox Jews must figure out the fine balance for themselves between making their obligatory effort and having enough certainty to leave the rest in God's hands. Nechamie, a forty-two-year-old mother of seven, explained how balancing faith, certainty, and obligatory effort has a significant impact upon her life:

> There are no absolutes. The more a person sees God's hand open and clear.... the less obligatory effort [*hishtadlus*] a person is gonna feel necessary to make.... I am going

to make my obligatory effort [*hishtadlus*] in life but I am going to know every second of the way that the outcome is totally in God's hands.

Degrees of *hishtadlut* may vary, but there is a certain amount of basic action that an individual is *obligated* to take in order to facilitate God's plan coming to fruition. Some actions of *hishtadlut* are widely agreed upon: it is normal *hishtadlut* to eat, or one will starve to death, and it is normal *hishtadlut* to go to the doctor and take medicine, or one will become ill. Pursuing second and third medical opinions or pursuing technologically assisted medical treatments are generally not seen as extraneous efforts [*Hishtadlut Yitera*]; In fact, to rely solely on God to restore one's health without pursuing medical diagnosis may be understood to be a sin of hubris [*Chet Hayohara*]. The boundary between what is considered basic *hishtadlut* versus what is considered action that extends beyond natural means is not written in stone: there is a variation in the ways that different rabbis, communities, and individuals interpret degrees of endeavor.

The concept of hishtadlut was thus reconciled in a variety of contradictory ways in our interviews with Haredi women. Doing prenatal tests was seen by some as part of their obligatory effort, and for others, to do one's *hishtadlut* was to refrain from doing these tests. All of our interviewees believed that the prevention of an arranged marriage between carriers of the same genetic condition through the Dor Yeshorim program was a necessary effort, as Toby explained: "It just prevents so much heartbreak. We all recognize that we're walking around with a lot of baggage in our blood and we might as well clear it before it's even an issue." Sima, age twenty-six, mother of two, saw complying with Dor Yeshorim as a basic duty: "Our responsibility is to prevent whatever can be prevented."

Yet once pregnancy had commenced, the women differed in their views of what constituted their necessary effort in terms of PND. Some women saw doing prenatal tests as part of their *hishtadlut*. This was especially the case with ultrasound, which some of the women believed could provide information that might prevent the surprise of a breech birth, diagnose placenta previa, or save the mother or the baby's life. Leah, age forty-two, mother of ten, explained: "There are some rabbis that say, 'Do the ultrasound' so that, God forbid, if there is a problem with the baby then you can have a cardiologist at the birth, you can induce the birth, you can see if the baby is too big or . . . small." Other women reconciled prenatal tests into the realm of *hishtadlut* to help themselves, as mothers, prepare mentally and emotionally for any eventuality. Nechamie accepted all tests offered except for amniocentesis in most of her seven pregnancies:

> I wouldn't have aborted if I had found out there was something wrong. It was rather to have the information, to have the time to prepare. I myself felt that it's good to (to avoid) surprises at birth, but emotionally to be prepared, rather than going through the pregnancy experience expecting something and then find out something else.

While Nechamie justified a positive purpose for prenatal testing, to do tests without a defendable reason was designated extraneous *hishtadlut*; ultrasounds for identifying fetal sex or for curiosity's sake were not justifiable. Nevertheless, some of our interviewees explained that although a prenatal test might originally be viewed as outside the realm of *hishtadlut*, it could become part of one's obligatory effort if a doctor deemed that test to be "medically necessary" and not simply routine. Sari, age twenty-seven, mother of four, explained that she had refused all prenatal tests during her first pregnancy but later conceded to a full diagnostic anatomy scan after her doctor convinced her through this logic: "That's what I needed to hear. . . . that it is medically necessary."

While accepting the offer of prenatal tests could be interpreted as part of one's obligatory effort, a majority of the women in our study stated that doing any type of PND just to find out if the fetus had Down syndrome was futile, because "it wouldn't change anything" and because "We don't believe in terminating pregnancies, so it won't help if you tell. . . . It's not gonna make a difference." Some of the women, in fact, believed that it was their duty to protect the fetus by refraining from tests that might harm it, such as amniocentesis: "You can miscarry because of that one, right? So I wouldn't do it."

Some of the women refused ultrasounds on these grounds, believing sonograms to be harmful to the fetus, stating that "it's radiation" and that it "disturbs the baby" or that "ultrasound has risks." Other women avoided ultrasounds altogether or minimized the number of ultrasounds they allowed because of a belief, based on the Talmud, that "a blessing is found only in what is hidden from the eye." Accordingly, a certain element of concealment was necessary for God to be able to perform a miracle if needed. Limiting the visibility of the fetus could thus be considered a positive measure of promoting fetal health. Refusing prenatal tests, as part of one's *hishtadlut*, was therefore actively creating the space for a miracle to happen.[32] Refraining from routine PND as part of one's *hishtadlut* was also partly fueled by "misdiagnosis stories" about the technologies, as we discuss below.

A Slippery Slope to a God-Sent Ordeal

The final reason we suggest for the women's selective uptake of PND stems from the discourse of God-sent ordeals and tests of faith. The women believed that every person's faith is tested in various ways during one's life, and they prayed routinely that their faith should not be tested. Toby explained her understanding of this concept:

> A test of faith is when you're given something that you would normally, not necessarily want. And your faith is tested to be able to understand how this is really for the best. [. . .] When you are faced with a situation that's not necessarily the situation that you think is best, suddenly you have to understand your faith. Like, "One second—this is not what I thought I wanted. And I know everything God does is for the best." How can

I rationalize that in my faith? And if your faith is tested, let me believe that the situation I'm faced with right now is really for the best and that's what it is. And so where I might think that I'd like to have, God willing, only healthy children, I don't want to be tested by something that I guess God might think that that's for my best interest. But hopefully God will think everything that is in my best interest is something that I clearly see for the good.

Pregnancy, in general, was viewed as both exciting and scary for its potential to lead a woman to be "chosen" for a task she did not necessarily want. Shimona, who spoke earlier of pregnancy in idealized terms, appended her idealized description saying that "Of course, for me pregnancy means a lot of anxiety." She then explained that pregnancy could introduce a God-sent ordeal:

> I hope the Lord will always choose me to have healthy and good children, but if once He chooses me for something else then it is probably my fated duty. Pregnancy for me is a God-given duty [*tafkid*] so I will do the task that has been prescribed for me. . . . If I am chosen I must be suitable for the task and I can handle it. I pray a lot that this won't happen. There is a special prayer that we say: "Please do not test my faith."

Later in our interview, Shimona relayed that during one of her pregnancies a routine ultrasound inadvertently became a pathway for a test of faith to enter her life. In an instant, a simple scan became a God sent ordeal when the doctor told the fetus had claw-foot locked feet. "And I said to him, 'Why are you telling me this? Why are you giving me this information? You know that I can do nothing except walk around for twenty more weeks being depressed.'" Shimona described the anxiety and uncertainty that followed this diagnosis as she turned both to her rabbi and to a second medical opinion. Even Shimona's much admired rabbi, the spiritual advisor (*admor*) of her small Hassidic sect, whom she consulted on every important issue in her life, could not relieve her uncertainty. The biomedical diagnosis overpowered her emotional health and spiritual allegiance, and made her feel inadequate for worrying:

> I was at war within myself. I said: "Everything will turn out fine. Why are you worried? You've received a blessing." On the other hand I wanted it to be over with, to know that everything was all right and I needn't worry. . . . I knew I was doing what I had to do. I would prefer everything to turn out okay, but if not we'll live with whatever happens. I didn't even consider terminating the pregnancy. . . . I prayed a lot. . . . I said, "I'm so young. I want to bring healthy children into the world and I feel unfit to deal with anything more complicated than that."

The idea that prenatal tests might be a slippery slope toward a God-sent ordeal was widespread among our interviewees and fueled by what Rapp has referred to as "community epidemiology"—a type of lay epidemiology based on local knowledge circulating among community members, which may not conform to scientific knowledge[33]—and by the circulation of what we have called "misdiagnosis stories" about the technologies.[34] As Eti, age thirty-eight, mother of eleven explained: "They [doctors] say things that are not correct. There are a lot of these stories about ultrasounds, and that is another reason some don't do it."

Each of our interviewees relayed at least one story that had happened to them or to someone they knew within the community in which a prenatal test, most often an ultrasound, led to prolonged anxiety and uncertainty. Often these stories conveyed that the test created unnecessary worry when false positive results led women to believe they were carrying an affected fetus. In most of these stories, the baby was born healthy or the woman chose to keep it anyway but suffered from the terrifying ordeal she endured. The point of these stories, discussed elsewhere,[35] was to mark prenatal tests as possibly leading women into a "test of faith" [*nisayon*]. Avoiding them could be seen as a self-protective measure in the hopes of not being "chosen" by God for such an ordeal. To do one's *hishtadlut*, in this light, was to protect one's own mental health by avoiding these risk-laden tests.

Conclusion

In this chapter, we have discussed the way Haredi women make decisions regarding prenatal diagnostic testing and screening using concepts drawn from religious texts but formulated in their own gendered, folk interpretation in dialogue with both doctrinal religion and reproductive technologies. What do the women's decision-making practices say about ethics of reproductive choice? Rapp's ethnography of amniocentesis in New York provides evidence toward the impact of language and culture on individual women's ethics of reproductive choice.[36] As "ethical gatekeepers," the women in Rapp's study constructed Down syndrome differently depending on their language and culture, thus affecting their choices regarding amniocentesis based partially on whether Down syndrome was constructed as an abnormality in their culture or whether there was even a word for it in their language. The Haredi women in our study also negotiate ethical decision-making partially based on cultural mores and values within a local moral economy.

For Haredi women, this local moral economy is situated between two bodies of authoritative knowledge—medical and rabbinical—linked with powerful institutions and worldviews that struggle to define how ethical decisions should be made regarding PND.[37] The "ethical gatekeeping" of the Haredi women we interviewed occurs in negotiation with these two distinct cultural systems in which ethics are defined differently. At one end is the medical terrain in which reproductive ethics are formulated in terms of the Euro-American core values of individual choice and autonomous control of an autonomous rational self. At the other end are the rabbinical doctrinal texts of Jewish ethics, which rabbinical experts interpret in relation to everyday life.

In this realm, devotees are not supposed to make autonomous choices or assume individual control over moral decisions, but are supposed to turn to rabbis who assume the burden of these moral decisions upon themselves in accordance with the Jewish religious texts. As Ivry has suggested,[38] when these two systems meet, the "moral pioneering" assumed by many of Rapp's interviewees—the necessity of making moral decisions about doing amniocentesis and terminating an affected pregnancy alone as an individual choice—is ideally replaced in Orthodox Judaism by the "moral relief" of turning to a rabbinical expert to advise, and to give a rabbinical ruling on what decision to make according to Jewish law.

However, as our study of Haredi women's decisions regarding PND reveals, the women's "ethical gatekeeping" does not blindly follow either of these two competing spheres. In their collective interpretation of faith, certainty, and obligatory effort, the women do not necessarily follow doctrinal religious texts word for word. Indeed, the women applied these concepts and others drawn from Jewish moralistic texts, even as they were not necessarily familiar with the thousands of moralistic texts that have debated these concepts. They may have encountered rabbinic discussions of these concepts in the Haredi education system, and in religious ethics books, such as the *Path of the Just*, that line the bookshelves of their homes, but they did not necessarily apply the concepts in the way that rabbinic sources have interpreted them.

Instead, the women in this study seemed to be drawing upon widely circulated ideas drawn from the rabbinic literature that have become part of everyday discourse in their communities, drawing particularly from the shared knowledge that circulated among the women in their community—ideas circulating among sisters, sisters-in-law, cousins, and friends—rather than strictly upon texts written and interpreted by male rabbis. At least in the gendered sphere of reproduction, in which issues particular to women's reproductive lives were central, the women's discourse can be viewed as a gendered folk-religious interpretation of theological concepts and their application to women's particular reproductive-related experiences.

Accordingly, as Seeman warns us,[39] the women's "ethical gatekeeping" should not be reduced into theological formulations, because the messiness of lived experience of devotees and the emic explanatory models devotees may call upon often veer from official religious doctrine. It follows that Haredi women's collective and individual interpretation and application of theological concepts in their own emic terms may be viewed as a type of "situated ethics." Ong suggests in her conceptualization of "situated ethics" that anthropologists must look at "the primacy of context and situation in thinking through ethical problems, an examination of their culturally specific meanings as part of lived, contested, and negotiated relations."[40] Following Ong's lead, Whittaker calls on anthropologists to address both the structural conditions and local moral economies within which moral reasoning over reproductive practices take place.[41] In the case of surrogacy in Thailand, Whittaker has discussed how a local moral economy based on the Buddhist notion of merit-making has led to a local conceptualization of surrogacy as an ethical practice despite official sanctions against it.

Along these lines, Haredi women draw on the concepts of faith, certainty, and obligatory effort in order to determine when PND should be refused or accepted and whether that choice is interpreted as an act of devotion or heresy. They may turn to rabbis in cases of dramatic moral decision-making in order to achieve some "moral relief,"[42] but in their everyday lives in which pregnancy is a "way of life"[43] they practice "ethical gatekeeping" according to a gendered "situated ethics" in which it is their mothers and sisters and their selves who have expertise, even though the women would most likely not acknowledge themselves as experts. This "situated ethics," which diverts both from the individual choice discourse and from doctrinal sources of Jewish ethics, thus etches out a space between religion and technologies of procreation in which women make ethical decisions about their reproductive lives within a predetermined patriarchal world, interpret reproductive experiences through a gendered, folk application of doctrinal concepts, and create a humble space for expertise while acknowledging God's control of the universe and the hierarchies of authoritative knowledge that structure their everyday lives.

Notes

1. T. M. Gammeltoft, *Haunting Images: A Cultural Account of Selective Reproduction in Vietnam* (Berkeley: University of California Press, 2014); Susan Markens, Carole H. Browner, and H. Mabel Preloran, "Interrogating the Dynamics between Power, Knowledge and Pregnant Bodies in Amniocentesis Decision Making," *Sociology of Health & Illness* 32, no. 1 (2010): 37–56; N. Press and C. Browner, "Characteristics of Women Who Refuse an Offer of Prenatal Diagnosis: Data from the California Maternal Serum Alpha Fetoprotein Blood Test Experience," *American Journal of Medical Genetics* 78 (1998): 433–445; R. Rapp, *Testing Women, Testing the Fetus: The Social Impact of Amniocentesis in America* (New York: Routledge, 1999); J. Taylor, *The Public Life of the Fetal Sonogram: Technology, Consumption, and the Politics of Reproduction* (New Brunswick, NJ: Rutgers University Press, 2008).
2. See, for instance, S. E. Gross and J. T. Shuval, "On Knowing and Believing: Prenatal Genetic Screening and Resistance to 'Risk Medicine,'" *Health Risk and Society* 10 (2008): 549–564; Tsipy Ivry, Elly Teman, and Ayala Frumkin, "God-Sent Ordeals and Their Discontents: Ultra-Orthodox Jewish Women Negotiate Prenatal Testing," *Social Science & Medicine* 72, no. 9 (2011): 1527–1533; Elly Teman, Tsipy Ivry, and Barbara A. Bernhardt, "Pregnancy as a Proclamation of Faith: Ultra-Orthodox Jewish Women Navigating the Uncertainty of Pregnancy and Prenatal Diagnosis," *American Journal of Medical Genetics: Part A* 155, no. 1 (2011): 69–80; E. Teman, T. Ivry, and H. Goren, "Obligatory Effort [*Hishtadlut*] as an Explanatory Model: A Critique of Reproductive Choice and Control," *Culture, Medicine and Psychiatry* (2016): 1–21; Ilana S. Mittman, "Most Studied Yet Least Understood: Perceptions Related to Genetic Risk and Reproductive Genetic Screening in Orthodox Jews" (Johns Hopkins University, 2005); Ilana S. Mittman, Janice V. Bowie, and Suzanne Maman, "Exploring the Discourse between Genetic Counselors and Orthodox Jewish Community Members Related to Reproductive Genetic Technology," *Patient Education and Counseling* 65, no. 2 (2007): 230–236.
3. Sarah Donovan, "Inescapable Burden of Choice? The Impact of a Culture of Prenatal Screening on Women's Experiences of Pregnancy," *Health Sociology Review* 15, no. 4 (2006): 397–405.
4. Barbara Katz Rothman, *The Tentative Pregnancy: Prenatal Diagnosis and the Future of Motherhood* (New York: Viking, 1986).

5. Landsman 2008; Tsipy Ivry, *Embodying Culture: Pregnancy in Japan and Israel*. New Brunswick, NJ: Rutgers University Press, 2010.
6. Rayna Rapp, "Refusing Prenatal Diagnosis: The Meanings of Bioscience in a Multicultural World," *Science, Technology & Human Values* 23, no. 1 (1998): 45–70.
7. Dena Davis, *Genetic Dilemmas: Reproductive Technology, Parental Choices, and Children's Futures* (Oxford University Press, 2010).
8. M. T. White, "Making Sense of Genetic Uncertainty: The Role of Religion and Spirituality," *American Journal of Medical Genetics: Part C* 151C (2009): 68–76, 71.
9. See, for instance, M. D. Schwartz, C. Hughes, J. Roth, C. Kavanagh, and C. Lerman, "Spiritual Faith and Genetic Testing Decisions among High-Risk Breast Cancer Probands," *Cancer Epidemiology, Biomarkers & Prevention* 9 (2000): 381–385; S. Ahmed, K. Atkin, J. Hewison, and J. M. Green, "The Influence of Faith and Religion and the Role of Religious and Community Leaders in Prenatal Decisions for Sickle Cell Disorders and Thalassaemia Major," *Prenatal Diagnosis* 26 (2006): 801–809; White, "Making Sense of Genetic Uncertainty."
10. White, "Making Sense of Genetic Uncertainty."
11. Aditya Bharadwaj, "Sacred Conceptions: Clinical Theodicies, Uncertain Science, and Technologies of Procreation in India," *Culture, Medicine and Psychiatry* 30, no. 4 (2006): 451–465; Marcia Inhorn, *Local Babies, Global Science: Gender, Religion and In Vitro Fertilization in Egypt* (New York: Routledge, 2003); Elizabeth F. S. Roberts, *God's Laboratory: Assisted Reproduction in the Andes* (Berkeley: University of California Press, 2012); Andrea Whittaker, "Merit and Money: The Situated Ethics of Transnational Commercial Surrogacy in Thailand," *International Journal of Feminist Approaches to Bioethics* 7, no. 2 (2014): 100–120; Tsipy Ivry, "Kosher Medicine and Medicalized Halacha: An Exploration of Triadic Relations among Israeli Rabbis, Doctors, and Infertility Patients," *American Ethnologist* 37, no. 4 (2010): 662–680.
12. See, for instance, Ivry et al., "God-Sent Ordeals and Their Discontents"; Teman et al., "Pregnancy as a Proclamation of Faith"; Teman et al., "Obligatory Effort"; Michal Raucher, *Conceiving Agency: Reproductive Authority among Haredi Women* (Bloomington: Indiana University Press, 2020).
13. Menachem Friedman, *The Haredi Ultra-Orthodox Society: Sources Trends and Processes* (Jerusalem: Jerusalem Institute for Israel Studies, 1991); Teman et al., "Pregnancy as a Proclamation of Faith."
14. J. Comenetz, "Census-Based Estimation of the Hasidic Jewish Population," *Contemporary Jewry* 26 (2006): 35–74.
15. Mittman, Bowie, and Maman, "Exploring the Discourse."
16. Teman et al., "Pregnancy as a Proclamation of Faith."
17. Ibid.
18. Ibid.
19. Mittman, Bowie, and Maman, "Exploring the Discourse"; Barbara Prainsack and Gil Siegal, "The Rise of Genetic Couplehood? A Comparative View of Premarital Genetic Testing," *Biosocieties* 1, no. 1 (2006): 17–36.
20. J. Zlotogora, Z. Haklai, and A. Leventhal, "Utilization of Prenatal Diagnosis and Termination of Pregnancies for the Prevention of Down Syndrome in Israel," *Israeli Medical Association Journal* 9, no. 8 (2007): 600–602
21. Teman et al., "Pregnancy as a Proclamation of Faith."
22. Teman et al., "Obligatory Effort."
23. Ibid.

24. Ibid.
25. Mittman, "Most Studied Yet Least Understood."
26. C. Sher, O. Romano-Zelekha, M. S. Green, and T. Shohat, "Factors Affecting Performance of Prenatal Genetic Testing by Israeli Jewish Women," *American Journal of Medical Genetics: Part A* 120A (2003): 418–422; Zlotogora et al., "Utilization of Prenatal Diagnosis."
27. Ivry et al., "God-Sent Ordeals"; Teman et al., "Pregnancy as a Proclamation of Faith."
28. Zlotogora et al., "Utilization of Prenatal Diagnosis."
29. Cf. A. Shaw, *Negotiating Risk: British Pakistani Experiences of Genetics* (Oxford: Berghahn Books, 2009).
30. G. Landsman, *Reconstructing Motherhood and Disability in the Age of "Perfect" Babies* (New York: Routledge, 2008).
31. Ivry, *Embodying Culture*.
32. Teman et al., "Obligatory Effort."
33. R. Rapp, *Testing Women, Testing the Fetus: The Social Impact of Amniocentesis in America* (New York: Routledge, 1999).
34. Teman et al., "Pregnancy as a Proclamation of Faith."
35. Ivry et al., "God-Sent Ordeals"; Teman et al., "Pregnancy as a Proclamation of Faith."
36. Rapp, "Refusing Prenatal Diagnosis," 67–68.
37. Ivry, "Kosher Medicine and Medicalized Halacha."
38. Tsipy Ivry, "The Predicaments of Koshering Prenatal Diagnosis and the Rise of a New Rabbinic Leadership," *Ethnologie Française* 45, no. 2 (2015): 281–292; Ivry, "Kosher Medicine and Medicalized Halacha."
39. Don Seeman, "Ethnography, Exegesis, and Jewish Ethical Reflection: The New Reproductive Technologies in Israel," in *Kin, Gene, Community: Reproductive Technology among Jewish Israelis*, ed. Daphna Birenbaum-Carmeli and Yoram Carmeli, 340–360 (Oxford, UK: Berghahn Books, 2010); Don Seeman, "Subjectivity, Culture, Life-World: An Appraisal," *Transcultural Psychiatry* 36, no. 4 (1999): 437–445. doi:10.1177/136346150003700306; Don Seeman, Iman Rushy-Hammady, Annie Hardisan-Moody, Winnifred Thompson, and Carol J. Rowland Hogue, "Blessing Unintended Pregnancy: Religion, Agency and the Discourse of Public Health," *Medicine, Anthropology Theory* 3, no. 1 (2016): 29–54.
40. Aihwa Ong, "Introduction: An Analytics of Biotechnology and Ethics at Multiple Scales," in *Asian Biotech: Ethics and Communities of Fate*, ed. Aihwa Ong and Nancy N. Chen, 1–51 (Durham, NC: Duke University Press, 2010), 102.
41. Whittaker, "Merit and Money."
42. Ivry, "The Predicaments of Koshering Prenatal Diagnosis."
43. Elly Teman and Tsipy Ivry, "Pregnancy and the Reproductive Habitus," *Medical Anthropology* 40, no. 8 (2021): 772–784.

Bibliography

Ahmed, S., K. Atkin, J. Hewison, and J. M. Green. "The Influence of Faith and Religion and the Role of Religious and Community Leaders in Prenatal Decisions for Sickle Cell Disorders and Thalassaemia Major." *Prenatal Diagnosis* 26 (2006): 801–809.

Bharadwaj, Aditya. "Sacred Conceptions: Clinical Theodicies, Uncertain Science, and Technologies of Procreation in India." *Culture, Medicine and Psychiatry* 30, no. 4 (2006): 451–465.

Comenetz, Joshua. "Census-Based Estimation of the Hasidic Jewish Population." *Contemporary Jewry* 26 (2006): 35–74.

Davis, Dena. *Genetic Dilemmas: Reproductive Technology, Parental Choices, and Children's Futures.* Oxford University Press, 2010.

Donovan, Sarah. "Inescapable Burden of Choice? The Impact of a Culture of Prenatal Screening on Women's Experiences of Pregnancy." *Health Sociology Review* 15, no. 4 (2006): 397–405.

Friedman, Menachem. *The Haredi Ultra-Orthodox Society: Sources Trends and Processes.* Jerusalem: Jerusalem Institute for Israel Studies, 1991.

Gammeltoft, Tina M. 2014. *Haunting Images: A Cultural Account of Selective Reproduction in Vietnam.* Berkeley: University of California Press.

Gross, Sky E., and T. Shuval Judith. 2008. "On Knowing and Believing: Prenatal Genetic Screening and Resistance to 'Risk Medicine.'" *Health Risk and Society* 10: 549–564.

Inhorn, Marcia. *Local Babies, Global Science: Gender, Religion and In Vitro Fertilization in Egypt.* New York: Routledge, 2003.

Ivry, Tsipy. *Embodying Culture: Pregnancy in Japan and Israel.* New Brunswick, NJ: Rutgers University Press, 2010.

Ivry, Tsipy. "Kosher Medicine and Medicalized Halacha: An Exploration of Triadic Relations among Israeli Rabbis, Doctors, and Infertility Patients." *American Ethnologist* 37, no. 4 (2010): 662–680.

Ivry, Tsipy. "The Predicaments of Koshering Prenatal Diagnosis and the Rise of a New Rabbinic Leadership." *Ethnologie Française* 45, no. 2 (2015): 281–292.

Ivry, Tsipy, Elly Teman, and Ayala Frumkin. "God-Sent Ordeals and Their Discontents: Ultra-Orthodox Jewish Women Negotiate Prenatal Testing." *Social Science & Medicine* 72, no. 9 (2011): 1527–1533.

Landsman, Gail. *Reconstructing Motherhood and Disability in the Age of "Perfect" Babies.* New York: Routledge, 2008.

Markens, Susan, Carole H. Browner, and H. Mabel Preloran. "Interrogating the Dynamics Between Power, Knowledge and Pregnant Bodies in Amniocentesis Decision Making." *Sociology of Health & Illness* 32, no. 1 (2010): 37–56.

Mittman, Ilana S. "Most Studied Yet Least Understood: Perceptions Related to Genetic Risk and Reproductive Genetic Screening in Orthodox Jews." Dissertation, Department of Health Policy and Management, Johns Hopkins University, Baltimore, MD, 2005.

Mittman, Ilana S., Janice V. Bowie, and Suzanne Maman. "Exploring the Discourse between Genetic Counselors and Orthodox Jewish Community Members Related to Reproductive Genetic Technology." *Patient Education and Counseling* 65, no. 2 (2007): 230–236.

Ong, Aihwa. "Introduction: An Analytics of Biotechnology and Ethics at Multiple Scales." In *Asian Biotech: Ethics and Communities of Fate*, edited by Aihwa Ong and Nancy N. Chen, 1–51. Durham, NC: Duke University Press, 2010.

Prainsack, Barbara, and Gil Siegal. "The Rise of Genetic Couplehood? A Comparative View of Premarital Genetic Testing." *Biosocieties* 1, no. 1 (2006): 17–36.

Press, Nancy, and Carole Browner. "Characteristics of Women Who Refuse An Offer of Prenatal Diagnosis: Data From The California Maternal Serum Alpha Fetoprotein Blood Test Experience." *American Journal of Medical Genetics* 78 (1998): 433–445.

Rapp, Rayna. "Refusing Prenatal Diagnosis: The Meanings of Bioscience in a Multicultural World." *Science, Technology & Human Values* 23, no. 1 (1998): 45–70.

Rapp, Rayna. *Testing Women, Testing the Fetus: The Social Impact of Amniocentesis in America.* New York: Routledge, 1999.

Raucher, Michal. *Conceiving Agency: Reproductive Authority among Haredi Women.* Bloomington: Indiana University Press, 2020.

Roberts, Elizabeth F. S. *God's Laboratory: Assisted Reproduction in the Andes.* Berkeley: University of California Press, 2012.

Rothman, Barbara Katz. *The Tentative Pregnancy: Prenatal Diagnosis and the Future of Motherhood.* New York: Viking, 1986.

Schwartz, M. D., C. Hughes, J. Roth, C. Kavanagh, and C. Lerman. "Spiritual Faith and Genetic Testing Decisions among High-Risk Breast Cancer Probands." *Cancer Epidemiology, Biomarkers & Prevention* 9 (2000): 381–385.

Seeman, Don. "Subjectivity, Culture, Life-World: An Appraisal." *Transcultural Psychiatry* 36, no. 4 (1999): 437–445.

Seeman, Don. "Ethnography, Exegesis, and Jewish Ethical Reflection: The New Reproductive Technologies in Israel." In *Kin, Gene, Community: Reproductive Technology among Jewish Israelis*, edited by Daphna Birenbaum-Carmeli and Yoram Carmeli, 340–360. Oxford, UK: Berghahn Books, 2010.

Seeman, Don, Iman Rushy-Hammady, Annie Hardisan-Moody, Winnifred Thompson, and Carol J. Rowland Hogue. "Blessing Unintended Pregnancy: Religion, Agency and the Discourse of Public Health." *Medicine, Anthropology Theory* 3, no. 1 (2016): 29–54.

Shaw, Alison. *Negotiating Risk: British Pakistani Experiences of Genetics.* Oxford: Berghahn Books, 2009.

Sher, C., O. Romano-Zelekha, M. S. Green, and T. Shohat. "Factors Affecting Performance of Prenatal Genetic Testing by Israeli Jewish Women." *American Journal of Medical Genetics: Part A* 120A (2003): 418–422.

Taylor, Janelle. *The Public Life of the Fetal Sonogram: Technology, Consumption, and the Politics of Reproduction.* New Brunswick, NJ: Rutgers University Press, 2008.

Teman, Elly, Tsipy Ivry, and Barbara A. Bernhardt. "Pregnancy as a Proclamation of Faith: Ultra-Orthodox Jewish Women Navigating the Uncertainty of Pregnancy and Prenatal Diagnosis." *American Journal of Medical Genetics: Part A* 155, no. 1 (2011): 69–80.

Teman, Elly, Tsipy Ivry, and Heela Goren. "Obligatory Effort [*Hishtadlut*] as an Explanatory Model: A Critique of Reproductive Choice and Control." *Culture, Medicine and Psychiatry* (2016): 1–21.

Teman, Elly, and Tsipy Ivry. "Pregnancy and the Reproductive Habitus of Ultra-Orthodox Jewish Women." *Medical Anthropology* 40, no. 8 (2021): 772–784.

Teman, Elly, Tsipy Ivry, and Barbara A. Bernhardt. "Pregnancy as a Proclamation of Faith: Ultra-Orthodox Jewish Women Navigating the Uncertainty of Pregnancy and Prenatal Diagnosis." *American Journal of Medical Genetics: Part A* 155, no. 1 (2011): 69–80.

Wertheimer, J. "Jews and the Jewish Birthrate." *Comment Magazine* (2005).

White, M. T. "Making Sense of Genetic Uncertainty: The Role of Religion and Spirituality." *American Journal of Medical Genetics: Part C* 151C (2009): 68–76.

Whittaker, Andrea. "Merit and Money: The Situated Ethics of Transnational Commercial Surrogacy in Thailand." *International Journal of Feminist Approaches to Bioethics* 7, no. 2 (2014): 100–120.

Zlotogora, J., Z. Haklai, and A. Leventhal. "Utilization of Prenatal Diagnosis and Termination of Pregnancies for the Prevention of Down Syndrome in Israel." *Israeli Medical Association Journal* 9, no. 8 (2007): 600–602.

CHAPTER 27

CHRISTIAN PERSPECTIVES ON PRENATAL DIAGNOSIS

KAREN PETERSON-IYER

For you created my inmost being; you knit me together in my mother's womb. I praise you because I am fearfully and wonderfully made; your works are wonderful, I know that full well.

—Psalm 139:13–14

People's stories are marked by paradox and complexity. They are messy. We will not have fruitful conversations about disability, reproduction, screening and choice until we learn to make such stories the starting point of conversation.

—Ellen Painter Dollar

As a human experience, pregnancy encompasses some of the highest of highs and the lowest of lows. That a living, breathing, thinking, feeling, small human being is gradually formed in the dark depths of a person's uterus is surely one of life's deepest and most powerful mysteries. And yet most people who have been through the often-messy process of a pregnancy know that a single, fairy-tale version of events does not constitute the whole story. The hope and joy, and sometimes the fear and even dread that accompany the discovery that one is pregnant; the retching nausea, exhaustion, and all manner of discomforts and dangers that can characterize the physical state; the pleasure of hearing the fetal heartbeat for the first time; and the mixture of thrill, delight, searing pain, and, at times, terror and disappointment—these are the poles that characterize the real, lived experiences of pregnant people.

With the development of technologies of prenatal testing and diagnosis, including amniocentesis, chorionic villus sampling, ultrasound, and, most recently, cell-free fetal DNA testing, the experience of pregnancy has become even more complex. Over thirty-five years ago, sociologist Barbara Katz Rothman described the way in which prenatal diagnostic technology can elicit from a pregnant woman a more "tentative" or conditional posture toward her pregnancy—at times placing additional burdens and a heightened sense of responsibility upon her for its outcome.[1] A few decades later, Rayna Rapp, in her seminal study of the experiences of pregnant women from a wide variety of sociocultural backgrounds, argued that these women and their supporters "express heterogeneous and complex responses" to these prenatal technologies, dependent primarily on both their social location and individual experiences of pregnancy.[2] Being pregnant in today's technologized society is a genuinely complex experience, where access to scientifically based knowledge about the fetus's physical condition is increasingly taken for granted.

It is not easy to construct a nuanced moral response to technologies of prenatal diagnosis, one that speaks meaningfully to the diverse experiences of pregnant people even as it develops moral guideposts. In the market-driven US economy, use of these technologies has primarily been understood as a matter of personal choice, with individual autonomy as the core driving moral value. In the present chapter, I examine this response in light of certain key Christian convictions that provide a slightly different perspective on prenatal diagnosis. It is my contention that affording individual autonomy *too* much emphasis causes us to lose sight of certain critical insights, insights about both the individual human person and the collective human community. Along these lines, several important themes emerge from the Christian tradition, directing our attention to the limitations of a response that overly privileges individual choice above all other concerns. By examining these, I hope to indicate the broad outlines of an adequate response to prenatal diagnostic technologies, one that errs neither by drawing conclusions that inordinately downplay the importance of human freedom nor by failing to speak meaningfully into the relational, embodied, social complexity of human experience.

Prenatal Screening, Diagnostic, and Related Technologies

In contrast to a century ago, a person who is pregnant today is offered a host of screening and diagnostic tools designed to increase the knowledge about the fetus. Beginning with carrier screening, which can be done before or during pregnancy, potential parents can learn whether or not either carries genetic variants for diseases such as cystic fibrosis, Tay-Sachs disease, or sickle cell anemia. During pregnancy itself, people typically undergo several ultrasounds and blood tests that screen for a statistical likelihood of various fetal conditions—for example, Down syndrome, Trisomy 18, or neural tube defects such as spina bifida or anencephaly. These screening tests, while essentially noninvasive, also indicate only the relative *probability* of fetal abnormality; they are generally not considered accurate enough to be used as definitive diagnostic tools.

If prenatal screening tests reveal a heightened risk of fetal conditions, or if a pregnant person is at risk for some other reason (age or family history, for example), more invasive forms of testing are typically offered; most common among these include chorionic villus sampling, done at ten to thirteen weeks gestation, and amniocentesis, done at fifteen to twenty weeks. Amniocentesis, a widely available diagnostic test in use for many years, relies on a sample of amniotic fluid retrieved using a needle inserted into the amniotic sac and then tested in the laboratory for various genetic and chromosomal anomalies. In chorionic villus sampling, a needle is used to extract a small piece of the placenta for chromosomal testing. Both procedures are generally considered safe but do slightly increase the risk of miscarriage. Both can test definitively for Down syndrome and certain other genetic and chromosomal abnormalities. Amniocentesis can also detect certain neural tube defects, including spina bifida.

More recently, cell-free fetal DNA (cffDNA) testing has grown dramatically in prominence. Often referenced as NIPT, or Non-Invasive Prenatal Testing, this testing is now available in over sixty countries, with a global market of roughly $3.9 billion in 2019.[3] It is usually performed at or near nine weeks gestation and is used to determine fetal sex (including diagnosis of x-linked disorders, such as Duchenne muscular dystrophy or hemophilia), to establish *rh*-compatibility, and to diagnose some single-gene disorders, such as achondroplasia, thalassemia, and cystic fibrosis. It is also currently used as a screening test for aneuploidies, including Down syndrome, but some in the scientific community expect that it will eventually achieve diagnostic status for that purpose.[4] As the name suggests, NIPT is noninvasive, accomplished using a simple maternal blood sample, and thus avoids the safety risks of other techniques. According to manufacturer claims, NIPT is highly accurate and potentially takes place very early in a pregnancy. Thus, NIPT presents several advantages to pregnant persons, even as it further complicates the ethical landscape.

Making matters even murkier is the practice of preimplantation genetic diagnosis (PGD), used in conjunction with in vitro fertilization (IVF). Here, typically, embryos created in vitro are tested prior to transfer to a person's uterus. This allows for the selection of embryos of a particular sex or thought to be free of genetic or chromosomal disorders or propensities. Hence, while other forms of prenatal diagnosis typically raise the question of whether or not to terminate a pregnancy, PGD bypasses the issue of abortion by placing the locus of choice at an earlier stage—that is, before a viable pregnancy is ever achieved.

Finally, several related scientific techniques have been developed in recent years—or loom on the horizon. Whole genome sequencing (WGS) is anticipated to allow for increasingly quick and accurate analysis of the full genome, including every base pair as well as mitochondrial DNA.[5] This of course could considerably increase the number of conditions for which prenatal or preimplantation genetic diagnosis could test. Moreover, a trend toward direct-to-consumer (DTC) marketing of genetic tests will no doubt amplify many of the ethical issues related to the interpretation of murky test results (prenatal or otherwise) by ordinary consumers.[6]

Beyond the realm of genetic testing, several newer techniques would potentially allow genetic intervention not just to diagnose but rather to alter "defective" embryonic DNA. For instance, mitochondrial replacement therapy (MRT) targets the mitochondria in the ova of someone who may be a carrier for mitochondrial-related disease mutations, replacing the problematic mitochondria with "healthier" mitochondria from a second female donor.[7] Even more newsworthy of late is CRISPR (standing for Clustered Regularly Interspaced Short Palindromic Repeat), a revolutionary tool for editing DNA (human or otherwise) derived from bacterial immune systems.[8] CRISPR has re-ignited scientific hopes for the possibility of repairing "defective" DNA, something that was accomplished years ago in mice, and, in 2018, apparently led to three live human births (in China).[9] The development of CRISPR technologies is sure to spur on the field of gene therapy.

These newer techniques push the scientific and ethical conversations about genetic intervention beyond the *diagnosis* of genetic abnormality and further into the realm of gene therapy and enhancement—that is, the altering of genes to *shape* the characteristics of specific and future persons. The current chapter will focus more squarely on prenatal diagnosis, thus addressing only peripherally these more proactive interventions. Yet while scientifically and ethically distinct, these latter interventions do provide important moral and cultural context for the present inquiry.

Autonomy and the Limits of Individual Choice

Professional organizations closely connected to the implementation of these technologies have responded with an ethical posture that emphasizes enhanced genetic counseling, thus aspiring to improve the information available to pregnant people in the service of individual choice. In 2016 the American Congress of Obstetricians and Gynecologists (ACOG) and the Society for Maternal-Fetal Medicine (SMFM) offered a revised set of recommendations on genetic screening and testing, followed by ACOG's continued guidance in 2020. Taken as a whole, these recommendations prioritize the informed choice of the pregnant patient as well as the patient's risks, reproductive goals, and preferences. Further, these societies maintain a sharp awareness of the limitations of screening tests in particular, resolving difficulties by calling for care providers to deliver better information, thus amplifying informed individual choices: "It is important that obstetrician–gynecologists and other obstetric care providers be prepared to discuss not only the risk of aneuploidy but also the benefits, risks, and limitations of available screening tests."[10] In similar fashion but specifically addressing preimplantation genetic diagnosis, the American Society of Reproductive Medicine (ASRM) urges increased access to genetic counseling *before* the procedure is undertaken. This counseling should "ensure understanding" both of the risk of having an affected child and of the impact of the disease(s) in question, in addition to clarifying available options. Also attentive to problems of testing accuracy, the ASRM calls for prenatal diagnostic testing to confirm falsely negative PGD results.[11] In this way, maximizing the accuracy of information again serves the reproductive autonomy of the individual or couple.

If there is one theme to extract from the above interpretations of prenatal diagnostic techniques, it is that their use is seen as a matter of fully informed individual choice. This approach of course fits well with a general American cultural ethos. Particularly in the public sphere, Americans prize freedom, understood as independence, self-sufficiency, and control over one's own destiny. Life's core values are seen as largely individually determined, and medicine should serve the individual in executing these values. In this light, the choices opened up by the technological developments of prenatal diagnosis are most appropriately framed as a matter of individual deliberation. That is, each individual (or couple) should be equipped—by way of bolstered informed consent, enhanced genetic counseling, or some other means—to make educated personal choices regarding prenatal diagnosis.

Upon closer inspection, however, the limitations of this strongly individualistic paradigm surface quickly. While undeniably raising up crucial values, this worldview can blind us to other important dimensions of human existence, dimensions such as our interdependence, vulnerability, and fundamental lack of control.[12] This blindness becomes particularly evident when facing matters related to disability. Philosopher Hans Reinders argues persuasively that social responsibility for disabled persons derives not primarily from contractual relationships or cooperative exchange, but rather from the nature of the moral self discovering itself within a network of social relationships.[13] Relationality is fundamental to the moral self; humans are not simply free-floating choice-makers, but rather creatures bound up intricately with each other in the *messiness* of life. People are complex: our choices collide, our allegiances are divided, and our choice-making ability is often compromised for one reason or another. Hence, navigating technologies of prenatal diagnosis *solely* in the terms of personal choice is an insufficiently nuanced framework, causing us to overlook other vital moral considerations.

In fact, for real (and complex) people, the development of newer prenatal diagnostic techniques—and especially noninvasive techniques such as NIPT—may actually undermine reproductive freedom in unanticipated ways. For instance, the routinization of early prenatal testing may amplify the pressure to test that pregnant people experience. In other words, the more common and easy to obtain such tests are, the less free pregnant people may feel to opt out. As sociologist Barbara Katz Rothman has pointed out, purely free, unstructured choices are an illusion, since our choices are always shaped and guided by social forces; she cites biologist Ruth Hubbard's words, "as 'choices' become available, they all too rapidly become compulsions to 'choose' the socially endorsed alternative."[14] Moreover, the growth of direct-to-consumer marketing of testing kits will most certainly augment this trend. Bioethicist Christian Munthe argues that such marketing incentivizes people to seek prenatal testing for increasingly vague reasons, distorting their expectations about the results and ultimately *decreasing* patient autonomy.[15]

The prospect of earlier and easier testing, often without the interface of genetic counseling, may also carry a certain expectation (and pressure) to act upon that information by terminating the pregnancy. Hence, some fear that the choice *not* to abort a fetus with a chromosomal abnormality will become increasingly difficult to make.[16] Inflated claims by screening test companies magnify the problem, since false positives may lead to increased abortion of basically healthy fetuses.[17] Additionally, as the list of tested disorders grows, so might the pressure to terminate fetuses with conditions that have genetic variants of unclear significance. Especially in the absence of high-quality genetic counseling, the increased information such testing yields may in fact *decrease* reproductive autonomy and genuine freedom.

Not only is the freedom of prospective parents potentially undermined by certain uses of prenatal diagnostic technologies; so too is the future *child's* autonomy. Here, the work of bioethicist Dena Davis is particularly instructive. Drawing on Joel Feinberg's philosophical concept of a child's right to an open future, Davis contends that an overly narrow focus on parental reproductive autonomy in genetic counseling inappropriately excludes the autonomy-related claims of the (future) child. In her words, "by privileging client autonomy and by defining the client as the person or couple who has come for counseling, there seems no space in which to give proper attention to the moral claims of the future child who is the endpoint of many counseling interactions."[18] In this way, prospective parents—in part led by prenatal and preimplantation technologies—may fixate on particular characteristics of children-to-be, thereby inadvertently objectifying their (future) children. The technologies may thus pave the way for legitimate hopes to become expectations or even entitlements, compromising children in the process.[19]

Organized Religious Responses to Prenatal Diagnosis

Religious—and specifically Christian—responses to prenatal diagnostic technologies, while sometimes maintaining a strong place for reproductive autonomy, have also raised a wide swath of moral concerns. Among official church documents, the most extensive ethical writings come from the Roman Catholic tradition. These have been articulated through various channels, most notably in 1987 through the

Congregation for the Doctrine of the Faith's *Donum vitae* and subsequently *Dignitas personae* in 2008. Additionally, Pope John Paul II in 1995 addressed prenatal diagnosis in his encyclical *Evangelium vitae*, building on earlier documents in the 1980s discussing genetic manipulation more generally. In the United States, the Church succinctly addresses these topics in the US Conference of Catholic Bishops' *Ethical and Religious Directives for Catholic Health Care Services*.

The most prominent theme driving official Roman Catholic teaching about prenatal diagnosis—as well as about genetic manipulation more generally—is the affirmation of human dignity and the unqualified value of respect for human life. Because official Roman Catholic teaching affirms the full value of life "from the moment of conception," intentional abortion beyond that point is prohibited.[20] Accordingly, *Donum vitae* explicitly forbids abortion even of the severely disabled, affirming prenatal diagnosis only if it might enhance therapeutic, medical, or surgical procedures to benefit the embryo/fetus.[21] The *Ethical and Religious Directives* hold that prenatal diagnosis is permitted *only* when it does not threaten the life or physical integrity of the fetus or mother and does not subject them to disproportionate risks. Genetic counseling is acceptable insofar as it promotes responsible parenthood by preparing parents for the treatment and care of children with genetic "defects," not as a tool that enables the termination of a pregnancy.[22] *Dignitas personae* problematizes not just prenatal diagnosis but also PGD, insofar as the latter expresses a "eugenic" mentality.[23] Further, PGD generally depends upon other procedures such as in vitro fertilization and embryo transplantation, which are themselves considered problematic in the Catholic tradition.[24]

Importantly, this Roman Catholic view does not outright *deny* human freedom as a tool to serve human health and welfare. In fact, several early addresses of Pope John Paul II affirm genetic research insofar as it promises new tools to fight genetic and chromosomal disease. This exercise of human freedom must be done, however, without reducing life to an "object," without treating children (or embryos/fetuses) as anything less than full human beings, and without creating new categories of marginalized groups within society.[25] The freedom affirmed here is best understood as a situated freedom, contained by a certain understanding of human dignity and the proper limits that human finitude imposes upon purely individual choice.

In contrast to the Roman Catholic magisterium, Protestant tradition speaks with no such unified voice. Still, several relevant documents have emerged from ecumenical fellowships such as the World Council of Churches (WCC) and the National Council of the Churches of Christ (NCC). In many cases these Protestant bodies have been concerned not only with prenatal diagnostic technologies, but also with broad technological developments that enable genetic manipulation. For instance, in 1982 the WCC published a report entitled "Manipulating Life," in which it addressed then-burgeoning recombinant DNA technologies that, when applied to prenatal diagnosis, were seen to open up vast possibilities for diagnosing "most" genetic conditions. The report acknowledges the power of such technologies to increase human health and well-being, but it also raises questions about how the technologies might lead us to treat other human beings as merely composite objects of interchangeable elements. This propensity could fundamentally alter our human self-understanding; the report asks, "In what way do we, by manipulating our genes in other than simple ways, change ourselves into something less than human?"[26]

An awareness of the social context of prenatal diagnosis and genetic manipulation emerges strongly in later WCC reports. In 1989, for instance, the WCC's Subunit on Church and Society acknowledged both a faith in God's work as sustainer of creation and also a human tendency to grasp inappropriately at the forces of power. While this document includes a generally positive attitude toward the possibilities of "genetic engineering," it also identifies the danger of "eugenic judgments" by way of selective abortion and the danger that women may feel guilty if they do *not* use such procedures. The document calls for a prohibition on genetic testing for sex selection or other forms of "social engineering"; attention to the possibility of unfair genetically based discrimination; and increased pastoral counseling for persons faced with difficult reproductive choices.[27] Here, the ethical concern derives not directly from the moral status of the human embryo as much as from the economic, political, and cultural injustice that the technologies may exacerbate. Similarly, a 2005 report flags the context of unequal resource distribution, where genetic technologies are generously funded even as some children's most basic health needs remain unmet. This report also questions a medical model in which genetic abnormalities are understood as needing "correction" through intervention, as well as the danger of "eugenic" judgments about the relative worth of lives. Like the Roman Catholic magisterium, the WCC affirms the dignity of life; but the WCC acknowledges that a range of views exists among churches as to the moral status of the human embryo—with some taking the view that a life of full moral value begins at conception, and others taking a more developmental approach.[28] Its policy recommendations, reminiscent of Catholic conclusions, include opposition to: the intentional destruction of embryos, prenatal tests to facilitate the selective implantation of embryos, techniques that allow for the selection of genetic traits in offspring, and PGD wherein cells are removed in order to test for disease or sex. Prenatal testing is affirmed insofar as it helps parents know how best to care for their children, and it should be accompanied by genetic counseling.[29]

In the United States, the NCC has been the largest ecumenical Protestant voice responding to prenatal diagnosis and genetic technologies. Here, one finds a deep awareness of the complexity of ethical concern that these technologies raise. On the one hand, the NCC affirms that life is a gift from God, that it has sacred worth, and that humans are charged with exploring life's possibilities, caring for creation, and supporting that worth through our creative (including scientific) action. On the other hand, the NCC recognizes that science can be flawed, that humans are often tempted to overreach their natural limits, and that, while we should work to reduce suffering, there is also value in learning from it.[30] In a 1986 report, the Council affirms several guiding themes: the sacred worth of human life; the value of fairness, justice, and love; and human responsibility vis-à-vis God's creation. From these it derives a diverse set of affirmations, including the value of "genetic modification" to reduce suffering, cure disease, and enhance life; the need to guarantee equal access to beneficial technologies; and a call to resist the notion that human worth is genetically determined. In the end, the NCC here takes a rather vague posture of cautious optimism, acknowledging the awesome power of genetic science to achieve worthy goals but also warning that some limits do need to be recognized.[31]

While each of the above church bodies approaches prenatal technologies with its own distinctive emphases, taken together they emphatically expand the ethical conversation beyond the protection and promotion of full information and individual choice. Freedom is certainly an important value in both Catholic and Protestant thought, but both traditions are quick to situate that freedom in the context of broader social concerns, including justice and the common good, a duty to relieve human suffering where possible, a respect for the worth of all human life, and an alertness to human shortcoming and tendency toward a will to power. Differing views of the moral status of the human embryo distinguish these approaches from one another; but, in their own ways, both Catholics and Protestants complicate the moral landscape of prenatal diagnosis by raising up concerns beyond individual choice.

Expanding the Autonomy Paradigm: Christian Theological Themes

The responses of religious bodies outlined above encompass a variety of theological and moral perspectives that together serve to challenge a monolithic focus on personal autonomy as an adequate response to prenatal diagnosis. While these concerns are profoundly intertwined, it is nevertheless helpful to tease them apart where possible, thereby lifting out insights from various strands within the Christian tradition. Ultimately, my goal here is to indicate a perspective that represents the best insights of the tradition while also respecting the complex and diverse interests of the individuals most deeply affected by these technologies.

Respect for Human Life and the Moral Status of the Embryo

One of the biggest tripping points for the Christian tradition as it responds to prenatal diagnosis has to do with respect for human life in its earliest forms. Disagreement over the moral status of the human embryo has of course led to enormously divisive conflicts about abortion in the United States.[32] Selective abortion, as one possible response to prenatal diagnosis, complicates such conflict by introducing new concerns about potential suffering of the child-to-be, or of the difficulty prospective parents may experience in caring for that child. Further, views about the status of human embryos impinge upon PGD, since the practice ordinarily entails the cryopreservation and/or destruction of non-selected embryos. Such concerns have led some, including the Roman Catholic magisterium, to reject not only abortion of any sort (including the selective abortion of embryos/fetuses with chromosomal or genetic abnormalities), but also the practice of embryo selection in PGD; these are all understood as a profound mistreatment of human life.[33]

Not all Christian groups hold to this understanding of the moral status of the human embryo. In particular, more liberal and/or mainline Christian teaching is apt to acknowledge moral complexity with regard to the stages of embryonic and fetal development. Bioethicist Cynthia B. Cohen, for example, insists that there are important moral differences between an embryo five to six days after fertilization and a born human being. Although early embryos should not be treated arbitrarily, abortion may be morally justifiable under some circumstances, for example, to avoid bringing a person into the world with a "serious" inherited disease.[34] Other Protestant bioethicists take a more abstract approach, describing "personhood" as a theological category that resists both biological definition and easy moral conclusions.[35]

There does indeed exist an empirical link between prenatal diagnosis and abortion. While the vast majority of those who undergo prenatal testing end up choosing to continue the pregnancy following a negative test result, termination remains by far the most common choice following positive test results, especially for conditions such as Down syndrome.[36] This figure, of course, does not account for pregnant persons who elect to forego prenatal testing such as amniocentesis in the first place; that is, some who would ultimately choose *not* to abort a fetus with Down syndrome would presumably opt out of prenatal testing procedures that carry even a small risk of miscarriage. By contrast, NIPT entails less risk, and the earlier diagnoses which it enables also allow for earlier (and thus safer) abortion. Yet some opponents of abortion worry that this easier availability may subtly guide conflicted pregnant people toward abortion, gradually making the choice *not* to terminate less socially acceptable.

Clearly, the disagreement is wide among Christians about the moral status of the human embryo as well as about selective implantation or abortion following prenatal diagnosis. It *is* possible to generalize that Christianity on the whole affirms the deep value of human life, both born and unborn. However one understands the human embryo, it carries the potential for life, and that alone demands that we take it seriously and regard it as more than a simple mass of cells. Yet if the issue ended there, there would be little disagreement among Christians about the implications of prenatal diagnosis. For many Christians, respecting a human embryo does not necessarily mean bringing it to term, particularly when it is known to carry a serious genetic abnormality.[37] To arrive at greater clarity regarding prenatal diagnosis, we must therefore turn to other sources of insight.

The Relief of Suffering and a Posture of Radical Hospitality

A second Christian theme that bears upon the question of prenatal diagnosis is the mandate to relieve human suffering, even while simultaneously heeding a call for radical hospitality toward all persons. The most widely espoused justification for prenatal diagnostic technologies is the idea that they can function to prevent unnecessary suffering. As Francis S. Collins, former head of the NIH and one of the principle architects of the Human Genome Project, and a Christian himself, has stated, "[t]he mandate to alleviate human suffering is one of the most compelling of all expectations of humanity."[38] In the context of Christian faith, such relief of suffering is of paramount moral importance. Jesus himself lived a life characterized by the effort to relieve suffering, healing the sick, and ministering to the broken. Physical or mental disability can indeed be linked to profound suffering, both for the afflicted as well as for those who care for them. This is particularly true of disorders that cause extreme physical pain or early death, such as Tay-Sachs disease or certain neural tube defects. Accordingly, prenatal testing can here seem like a logical extension of good prenatal care.[39]

The problem, however, is that the argument to prevent suffering often takes the form of an argument to prevent the birth of people who might suffer. This seems—at least to some—to tread dangerously close to an argument against the full worth and humanity of disabled individuals. As medical ethicist Daniel Wikler has stated, "It takes considerable rhetorical agility to urge the public to support screening programs so as to prevent the conception of handicapped individuals while at the same time insisting that full respect be paid to such developmentally disabled adults as are already among us."[40] At issue here is what one might call a posture of radical hospitality toward all persons, including the least powerful among us. The biblical theme of "welcoming the stranger" is prevalent in both Old and New Testaments and figures prominently in the life of Jesus in the Gospels. Jesus befriended the poor, the weak, and the marginalized—and he called his followers to do the same. Even Jesus' acceptance of his own death provides a portrait of humanity that recognizes the primacy of our human vulnerability and weakness, defining God not foremost as a powerful fix-it deity but rather as standing in profound solidarity with a suffering humanity.[41]

In sharp contrast to this theme of welcoming people into full community, modern technologies of prenatal diagnosis can seem like they in fact function to define and rule persons *out* from such community. As Christian ethicist Mary Jo Iozzio has put it, these technologies identify deviant "others" in our midst before they are even born, threatening not only their very existence but also the presence of genuine human diversity.[42] In the face of such "othering" of disabled persons, Iozzio calls for an appreciation of disability as one of the many ways that God is revealed in the human community, in a form of human frailty that should engender in us a posture of humility.[43]

Those who would privilege an attitude of radical hospitality argue not that we should affirm suffering as a norm, but rather that suffering can function to teach and transform us. Christian community is called to *care* for those who cause us discomfort—not eliminate them. Christian ethicist Stanley Hauerwas, for instance, challenges any given society's ability to do away with disability while simultaneously affirming the full worth of those classified as disabled. He instead calls for Christian communities to find ways fully to welcome persons with disability: "Too often the suffering we wish to spare them is the result of our unwillingness to change our lives so that those disabled might have a better life."[44]

In fact, an argument along these lines has emerged from the disability community itself, making a case for the social construction of disability rather than a purely medical understanding. For instance, in recent years many in the "Deaf" community have argued that deafness is better characterized as a particular *culture* than as a *disability*, one in which those who claim membership take both pride and joy.[45] According to this view, conditions ordinarily thought of as "disabling" should be viewed in a broader social context; instead of trying to reduce the number of disabled persons in society, we should focus on changing society so that it is more welcoming to those who possess these conditions.

It seems that the relief of suffering is perhaps not as straightforward a concept as it first seems, in the context of a posture of radical hospitality toward persons with disability. *Who* suffers and *what* exactly it means to suffer with a disability within a particular social context complicate the picture and deserve further exploration. Moreover, an erosion of social supports available to disabled persons over recent decades provides important moral context for the question; the burden of caring for disabled persons is likely to fall disproportionately on individual parents—and, to be sure, especially on the individual mothers, who perform the lion's share of caregiving in general as well as for disabled children.

Paying attention to the experiences of those closest to this issue—that is, parents of disabled children, or people pregnant with fetuses known to carry genetic or chromosomal abnormalities—is instructive here. Many such parents have articulated profound transformational experiences of allowing disabled children to change their lives, including their self-understandings, in a positive direction.[46] For example, in *Expecting Adam*, Harvard-trained sociologist Martha Beck movingly describes the transformation she underwent in learning to accept and love Adam, her child with Down syndrome: "Slowly, slowly . . . I realized that I was not looking for information to transform my child into a prize every parent would envy. I needed to transform myself into a parent who could accept her child, no matter what." She goes on to discover the many wonderful qualities that Adam possesses:

> The immediacy and joy with which he lives his life makes rapacious achievement, Harvard-style, look a lot like quiet desperation. Adam has slowed me down to the point where I notice what is in front of me, its mystery and beauty, instead of thrashing my

way through a maze of difficult requirements towards labels and achievements that contain no joy in themselves. Adam takes his joy straight-up, in purer form than most of us can handle.[47]

Here, Adam brings unique gifts to the world, gifts that are perhaps less common in children classified by the world as "normal."

While it is important to see the positive assessments of disability, one also must bear in mind that some parents of children with disabilities might tell a different story. For instance, Ellen Painter Dollar, who has a child with osteogenesis imperfecta (OI)—a painful and debilitating genetic disease—sees as enormously problematic the oversimplified narratives that describe genetic illness as tragic (on the one hand) or as part of a "good diversity" (on the other). Dollar criticizes views in particular that call only for social hospitality, absent a genuine recognition of the pain and difficulty of disability: "These realities are not a challenge to be overcome; they are terrible wounds that cry out for healing, not mere hospitality."[48]

The diversity of experience embodied in these stories is apparent; they are, indeed, "messy."[49] As does any child, a child with mental or physical disability brings both joys and struggles, rewards and challenges. Many parents of disabled children are quick to say that they would heal or correct the disability if they were given the chance, and yet they nonetheless profoundly love their children. Simply issuing a call toward radical hospitality, while ideologically powerful, ignores the ambiguity of their experience. This is particularly true in the context of a world with waning social supports for persons with disabilities and for their caregivers.

In the end, a Christian approach must affirm both a posture of hospitality *and* the instinct to heal or minimize the genuine suffering that is part and parcel of certain forms of disability. Disability, while profoundly socially constructed, is not infinitely so. It is possible to make *some* normative judgments about what counts as genuine human flourishing, and to hold that certain kinds of disability do indeed profoundly compromise such flourishing.[50] However, in our rush to avoid suffering, we also must take care not to bypass too quickly the often profound lessons that reside within the transformational stories of disability, stories which may alert us to truths not readily apparent in our "normalized," fast-paced world.

The Meaning of Parenthood

This leads to a related set of Christian moral concerns associated with prenatal diagnosis: that which constitutes an adequate understanding of parenthood. In Western society today, there exists a tension between two conceptions of parenthood. First is the view whereby a child is the product of a conscious individual decision, someone for whose growth and development parents are responsible and thus over whom those parents should exert some degree of control. This approach privileges parental privacy as they make individual choices conducive to the well-being of "their" child. Accordingly, prenatal diagnosis becomes a matter of parental autonomy as they seek to protect and advance the interests of their families.

In tension with this view is a second perspective, one that understands a child not as the product of the wills of two parents, but rather as a "gift" or trust from God. Here, children "belong" to God and are commended into the care of loving parents. These parents are charged with promoting children's best interests, but within a larger understanding of the child not as a *choice*, but rather as an *unchosen gift*. Anglican theologian Oliver O'Donovan undertakes this perspective, contrasting the "begetting" and "making" of children. O'Donovan worries that the tendency to understand children as a project of parental will undermines parents' ability to love children for the mysterious selves that they are. "When we start making human beings," he holds, "we necessarily stop loving them."[51] Catholic moral theologian Maura Ryan highlights this fundamentally *given* quality of parental obligation:

> The common expression, "This child has a face only a mother could love" speaks ... about acceptance and fidelity to children, even to those whose looks or gender or genetic characteristics are not what the parent would have desired or what meets society's standards. We have accepted the fact that, unlike a product in the market, children cannot be returned or exchanged if found to be other than what was expected.[52]

Parents thus love children for their own sake, not primarily as instruments to satisfy parental need or desire.

The bulk of the Christian tradition leans toward the latter view. The Hebrew Bible understands childlessness as a burden and children as a blessing from God—like all persons, in possession of a sublime dignity that resists instrumentalization. In the New Testament Gospels, there persists the theme of children as beloved gifts from God. Jesus in his teaching in fact relativized the biological ties of family, indicating that loyalty to God precedes family bonds and implying that children are best understood as belonging not to parents but rather to God.[53] Moreover, he was known for his care and concern for children, gathering them around him and dwelling upon their special relationship to God's kingdom.[54] Finally, later Christian theological tradition has understood parenthood not as purely a matter of individual choice, much less a form of ownership over children. Rather, parenthood is closely connected to one's life before God, a holy vocation carried out as an act of faithfulness to the divine.[55]

A deep love for children echoes and expresses the larger theological affirmation of God's profound and unconditional love for humanity—a fundamental Christian conviction. Moreover, it ties into the desire of most parents to nurture and help improve the lives of their children. Few would dispute that this desire is a natural part of parenthood, whether biological, genetic, or social. The problem, from a Christian point of view, is when that desire transforms into a more self-serving tendency to treat a child primarily as an extension of oneself, loveable not for the child's own sake but rather for the ability to satisfy parental aspirations. In effect, to do this would be to trade in the unconditional love that Christians prize for an acceptance of children conditioned upon their instrumental value—upon whether they are beautiful enough, smart enough, or have the "right" kinds of abilities.

Of course, there is no easy way to know or identify when a parent has crossed the line from responsible nurture to unhealthy objectification. But certainly the possibility of utilizing prenatal diagnosis for the "quality control" of offspring paves the way, even as it enhances the opportunity for genuine, loving care. As Bridget Burke Ravizza points out, prenatal testing for all pregnant women is now accepted by many as standard to good prenatal care; quoting Rapp, she highlights how this puts pregnant women into the awkward position of being "forced to judge the quality of their own fetuses, making concrete and embodied decisions about the standards for entry into the human community."[56] Such a posture of judgment operates against the unconditional parental love and acceptance advanced by a Christian perspective.

The best insights of the tradition lie in balancing the care, nurture, and hopeful desires of parents to support their children's well-being with the caution against overly instrumentalizing these same children, thus losing sight of their intrinsic and unique worth. Here again, reality is far messier than one might like. Simply maximizing individual parental choice in response to prenatal diagnostic technologies does not do justice to this messiness. Neither does denying that choice altogether, and in particular denying the instinct that most parents have to care for and support their children.

Concretely, what does such a balance look like? On the one hand, Christian thought urges us to resist the "routineness" of prenatal diagnosis without examining its purposes and goals vis-à-vis the child-to-be. Insofar as prenatal diagnosis subtly pressures prospective parents to envision offspring as deliberately created objects, it can be damaging. Insofar as its use—especially in the absence of robust genetic counseling—leads to a false idea that parenting itself can somehow be "risk-free," it is dangerous. And insofar as prenatal diagnosis encourages prospective parents toward a reductionist view of their (future) children, understanding these children primarily in terms of their genetic propensities rather than their sublime value before God, it is harmful.[57]

Yet to the extent that such technologies provide a tool for promoting health at the prenatal level, they indeed may enhance human well-being and neighbor-love. For Christians who embrace a developmental view of the early embryo, PGD (and selective implantation) or even prenatal diagnosis (and selective termination) offer a means of preventing deep suffering in cases of severe disease or disability.[58] Indeed, some parents who make use of prenatal diagnostic technologies may already have one child with a profound disability and wish to spare subsequent children similar challenges. Further, prenatal diagnosis may help prepare and psychologically ease the path of parents who learn of disability but who choose to continue the pregnancy; in this way it can certainly contribute toward the well-being of both parent and child. In the midst of our important affirmation that God loves all persons unconditionally, we must simultaneously acknowledge and affirm that God's cause is life and flourishing, not disease and death.[59]

The Common Good and Distributive Justice

An often overlooked set of Christian concerns that further impacts an evaluation of prenatal diagnosis has to do with the notions of the common good and distributive justice. Much of this ground has already been covered above, in the discussions of welcoming persons with disability and caring for children. But other considerations remain, largely related to the costs of prenatal diagnosis for those being tested, as well as the social resources that are funneled into development of the technologies themselves.

Crucial to an adequate moral understanding of prenatal diagnosis is the social and economic context in which it takes place. In some Christian spheres, a prominent focus on the moral status of the embryo has eclipsed conversations regarding justice and the dynamics of power. Moreover, the Western tendency to frame such matters in terms of individual rights takes our focus away from broader social patterns such as the socioeconomic bases of disease, lack of resources devoted to basic forms of healthcare, or unequal access to these technologies themselves. If justice in this context generally signifies equal access to the goods of human well-being, we may rightly ask how the benefits and the burdens of prenatal diagnosis are *socially* distributed, as well as how harmful patterns of power and privilege may be exacerbated by these technologies. Such common good considerations constitute a persistent theme within Christianity, one that includes a special concern—and a "preferential option"—for those who are economically, socially, or otherwise marginalized.

Prenatal diagnostic technologies—especially more expensive ones—are not available to all pregnant persons; those with less social power, on the whole, do not share equal access. Writing specifically about the newer, noninvasive technologies, Christian ethicist Aana Marie Vigen points out that cffDNA is pricey and often not covered by insurance; thus it is less available to those of limited financial resources who may in fact lack access to far more basic forms of prenatal care.[60] The problem exists both nationally and globally; for many poorer women worldwide, clean water, food, basic healthcare, perinatal care, and pandemic disease are far more pressing concerns than genetic technologies.[61] This is not to argue that such technologies are unimportant, but rather that we must evaluate them within a larger context and in a way that recognizes issues of disproportionate access. As prenatal diagnosis is targeted and utilized by these populations, therefore, it is not unreasonable to worry that disability itself may become increasingly concentrated in poorer populations already socially marginalized.

From the perspective of a Christian concern for justice and the common good, such a trend would be highly problematic. Do genetic technologies such as these inadvertently foster a "survival of the fittest" social ethic,[62] one in which the common good and the well-being of those with less social power take a moral back seat? In this regard, the liberal market considerations driving technological development in the West, alongside a US tendency to privilege individual (and especially consumer) choice, are troubling. A Christian approach demands greater *fairness* of access to genetic technologies, even as it continues to wrestle with the complex and ambiguous moral status of the technologies themselves.

Perhaps even more importantly, an adequate Christian perspective mandates that society more broadly shoulder the burdens associated with disability, so that they do not fall disproportionately upon isolated individuals, particularly those with few resources. Vigen calls communities of faith to step in: "Rather than place all the burden on a woman, a couple, or a family to welcome a child with disabilities, we all need to keep looking in the mirror. What, as people of faith, are we doing to ensure that our society makes competent childcare, various therapies, and educational resources readily available to all?"[63] Only when justice is supported in these ways can Christians with integrity claim to support the common good.

Individual Freedom, Co-Creation, and the Givenness of Nature

Many of the above tensions—between, for instance, the call to prevent human suffering and also to affirm radical hospitality; or between promoting the well-being of children and also an unconditional acceptance of them—point the way toward a more fundamental Christian theological theme: the place of human freedom as it coexists alongside the givenness of nature. Indeed, this concern draws us squarely back to the questions raised at the start of this chapter regarding how centrally we should value free choice in responding morally to prenatal diagnostic technologies.

Much of Christian thought affirms a crucially important role for human freedom. Among the more well-known Christian advocates of freedom, understood in the terms individual choice and genetic control, was Protestant ethicist Joseph Fletcher. Fletcher believed that humans, qua humans, are fundamentally free; and that this freedom allows them to control their future: "Control is human and rational," he writes. "[A] basic ethical principle of medicine and healthcare is . . . the minimization of human suffering, by deliberate control. . . . Not to control when we can is immoral."[64] This belief led Fletcher to affirm nearly every reproductive and genetic intervention he envisioned and to advocate for strong versions of genetic screening, testing, and engineering, including selective abortion to "control for quality."[65]

Most Christians have not embraced genetic control with Fletcher's zeal. But the tradition does retain the idea that autonomy partially constitutes what it means to *be human*. Sometimes this has taken on a particularly feminist hue. Protestant ethicist Beverly Wildung Harrison spent her lengthy career arguing persuasively for a robust version of women's procreative choice, including not only access to safe abortion but also safe contraception, economic and social security, stronger support for childrearing, a lessening of racial brutality, and a reduction of violence against women.[66] Here, "choice" constitutes not simply a negative form of liberty but rather a substantive good, one foundational to human—and here, women's—well-being. Such choice is best understood in the context of broader human qualities that in fact *complicate* choices, qualities such as our embodied vulnerabilities, our relational allegiances, and the vagaries of our social context.

Coming from a Roman Catholic perspective, moral theologian Cathleen Kaveny defends individual autonomy, yet she too critiques the veneration of purely negative freedom. Kaveny advocates for framing autonomy as *positive* freedom, freedom that engenders solidarity with others and offers the opportunity to become "part-author" of one's own life.[67] Applying this understanding to the explosion of genetic information, Kaveny calls for social supports and consumer protections that promote individual and social flourishing. She rejects direct consumer access to genetic tests unlikely to provide practical helpful information to parents or likely to encourage parents to treat their children as instruments for their own goals.[68]

Theologically speaking, a Christian affirmation of human freedom often manifests in the concept of *co-creation*, describing the God-gifted creative power (and responsibility) of human beings to promote God's purposes. Themselves created by God, human beings are also active participants in the ongoing process of creation and must exercise their ability to shape, direct, even redesign nature. To be a co-creator lies at the very heart of what it means to bear God's image.[69] Enacting neighbor love by seeking medical ways to heal or prevent suffering is an expression of this co-creative posture.

In tension with a strongly co-creationist theological approach is one that instead places the accent on the *createdness* of human beings and the primacy of God's natural order. Humans are properly charged with caring for creation, but this includes the humility to recognize the limits to our creative power. Here, respecting the dictates of nature leads to a cautious posture toward scientific advances. In the last century, Protestant theologian Paul Ramsey was a visible example of this approach; he called for a respect for biological "givens" and stressed that the distinctively "human" includes not simply human freedom but also human sexual, bodily nature.[70] Lutheran Gilbert Meilaender similarly emphasizes in his work that human freedom is tempered by embodiment. He maintains that Christians must retain the virtue of humility before the mystery of human personhood, resisting the temptation to overextend our control over the qualities of our children.[71] In the context of this approach, Meilaender's opposition to both abortion and embryo research would seem to imply a similar cautiousness about prenatal diagnostic technologies, insofar as they would conduce to selective abortion, the destruction of human embryos, or to the veneration of individual choice over respect for the dignity of each individual child.

It is certainly difficult to resolve the tension between these various views, all held by those claiming a Christian identity. Perhaps the most accurate way to generalize about Christian understandings of freedom in the context of prenatal diagnosis is to say that Christianity affirms that human beings are both free and finite, co-creators but also limited by nature. On one hand, an approach that privileges only individual autonomy is insufficient, for it undervalues the complexity of human relational and embodied existence and conduces to an inordinately "thin" understanding of human good. On the other hand, to shy away entirely from the use of prenatal technologies as a responsible exercise of freedom would be to shirk the responsibilities of neighbor-love and the call to minimize human suffering. In the end, what seems to be called for is some limited embrace of the possibilities of prenatal diagnostic technologies to ward off unnecessary suffering—whether by preparing prospective parents for the challenges that lie ahead, or by enabling an authentic choice to avoid the birth of a child destined to suffer profoundly and whose care needs would themselves prove overwhelming. Yet this embrace must be accompanied by a genuine willingness to expand the boundaries of the human community and to recognize the contribution of persons whom society is otherwise tempted to disregard or undervalue.

Conclusion

From a Christian perspective, there are no neat or easy lines delineating when prenatal diagnosis is acceptable or desirable, and when it is not. The world that we live in is messy, and prenatal diagnosis, as a response to the ambiguities of pregnancy, participates in this messiness. Yet the Christian tradition does not leave us without guidance. Rather, the road forward is to hold in creative tension the best insights that the tradition has to offer, bridging goods that may appear to compete with each other.

The great twentieth-century Jesuit theologian Karl Rahner provides an instructive example of this ability to bridge perspectives. Rahner lifted up both poles of human nature—freedom and finitude—when he addressed the development of genetic technologies over a half-century ago. He affirmed human freedom understood as radical human self-determination, enabling self-manipulation in the service of neighbor-love; and yet he also advocated a certain Christian "cool-headedness" toward these technologies, opposing the anxious desire to over-determine our human future.[72] Rahner's effort to navigate the rift in this way indicates a fruitful pathway forward through the various, and sometimes competing, strands of Christian tradition as it addresses prenatal diagnosis.

Notes

1. Barbara Katz Rothman, *The Tentative Pregnancy: Prenatal Diagnosis and the Future of Motherhood* (New York: Viking, 1986).
2. Rayna Rapp, *Testing Women, Testing the Fetus: The Social Impact of Amniocentesis in America* (New York: Routledge, 1999), 24.

3. Vardit Ravitsky, Marie-Christine Roy, Hazar Haidar, Lidewij Henneman, John Marshall, Ainsley J. Newson, Olivia M. Y. Ngan, and Tamar Nov-Klaiman, "The Emergence and Global Spread of Noninvasive Prenatal Testing," *Annual Review of Genomics and Human Genetics* 22 (2021): 309–338, https://doi.org/10.1146/annurev-genom-083118-015053.
4. Rebecca Daley, Melissa Hill, and Lyn S. Chitty, "Non-Invasive Prenatal Diagnosis: Progress and Potential," *Archives of Disease in Childhood* 99, no. 5 (2014): F426–F430. See also Vardit Ravinsky's November 2014 address at Harvard Law School, "Law and Ethics of Noninvasive Prenatal Testing," accessed July 11, 2022, https://vimeo.com/111444284.
5. Christian Munthe, "A New Ethical Landscape of Prenatal Testing: Individualizing Choice to Serve Autonomy and Promote Public Health: A Radical Proposal," *Bioethics* 29, no. 1 (2015): 37.
6. To date, FDA regulation of genetic tests has been incomplete and generally aimed at tests sold to laboratories, and although the FDA announced in 2010 its intention to expand such regulation to all genetic tests, it has yet to do so. See National Human Genome Research Institute, "Regulation of Genetic Tests," https://www.genome.gov/10002335/regulation-of-genetic-tests/. See also Ravitsky et al., "The Emergence and Global Spread of Noninvasive Prenatal Testing," 325. Kits marketed directly to consumers are now readily available over the internet, though their accuracy is often considered to be unreliable. See Cathleen Kaveny, *Law's Virtues: Fostering Autonomy and Solidarity in American Society* (Washington, DC: Georgetown University Press, 2012), 127; and, as a more recent example, Michael Mezher, "FDA Warns Three Companies Over DTC Genetic Tests," http://www.raps.org/Regulatory-Focus/News/2015/11/09/23563/FDA-Warns-Three-Companies-Over-DTC-Genetic-Tests/.
7. Hitika Sharma, Drishtant Singh, Ankush Mahant, Satwinder Kaur Sohal, Anup Kumar Kesavan, and Samiksha, "Development of Mitochondrial Replacement Therapy: A Review," *Heliyon* 6, no. 9 (2020), https://doi.org/10.1016/j.heliyon.2020.e04643.
8. Carl Zimmer, "Breakthrough DNA Editor Born of Bacteria," *Quanta Magazine*, February 6, 2016, https://www.quantamagazine.org/20150206-crispr-dna-editor-bacteria/; and Jennifer Kahn, "Life, Edited," *New York Times Magazine*, November 15, 2015, 62–66 and 82–83.
9. The 2018 genetic engineering of human embryos, leading to three live births, was conducted by Chinese researcher He Jiankui. The work has thus far been roundly condemned by the international bioethics community. See Antonio Regalado, "Chinese Scientists Are Creating CRISPR Babies," and "A Third CRISPR Baby May Already Have Been Born in China," both in *MIT Technology Review*, last modified November 25, 2018 and July 3, 2019 (respectively), https://www.technologyreview.com/s/612458/exclusive-chinese-scientists-are-creating-crispr-babies/?fbclid=IwAR0OXaU1jkbQ3sDhSmnG7DYS_N8Q9wurywHZko2Eb_CPHxU5L6RLEk6UHcY and https://www.technologyreview.com/s/613890/a-third-crispr-baby-may-have-already-been-born-in-china/. For a helpful (albeit older) discussion of Chinese human embryonic research using CRISPR, see David Cyranoski and Sara Reardon, "Chinese Scientists Genetically Modify Human Embryos," *Nature*, http://www.nature.com/news/chinese-scientists-genetically-modify-human-embryos-1.17378; and Ewen Callaway, "Second Chinese Team Reports Gene Editing in Human Embryos," *Nature*, http://www.nature.com/news/second-chinese-team-reports-gene-editing-in-human-embryos-1.19718.
10. American Congress of Obstetricians and Gynecologists, "Practice Bulletin No. 163: Screening for Fetal Aneuploidy" and "Practice Bulletin No. 162: Prenatal Diagnostic Testing for Genetic Disorders," *Obstetrics & Gynecology* (May 2016); and "Practice Bulletin

No. 226: Screening for Fetal Chromosomal Abnormalities," *Obstetrics & Gynecology*, October 2020. As for cffDNA testing, ACOG considers the tests still to be of screening, not diagnostic, levels of accuracy.
11. American Society of Reproductive Medicine, "Preimplantation Genetic Testing: A Practice Committee Opinion," *Fertility and Sterility* 90, Suppl. 3 (November 2008): S136–S143.
12. See Hans S. Reinders, *The Future of the Disabled in Liberal Society: An Ethical Analysis* (Notre Dame, IN: University of Notre Dame Press, 2000), esp. 203–204.
13. Ibid., 17.
14. Barbara Katz Rothman, "The Meanings of Choice in Reproductive Technology," in *Test Tube Women: What Future for Motherhood?* ed. Rita Arditti, Renate Duelli Klein, and Shelley Minden (Boston: Pandora Press, 1984), 32 and 27; in the second page reference, Rothman is quoting Ruth Hubbard.
15. See, for instance, Munthe, "A New Ethical Landscape," 36–45.
16. Ibid. Munthe does not oppose prenatal testing altogether, but he does call for its downscaling such that it targets a narrowly selected range of particularly severe conditions and is accompanied by improved social supports for sick and disabled persons.
17. Manufacturer claims of over 99 percent accuracy have been the subject of much controversy. See, for instance, a series of *Boston Globe* articles: Beth Daley, "Oversold Prenatal Tests Spur Some to Choose Abortions," *Boston Globe*, December 14, 2014, https://www.bostonglobe.com/metro/2014/12/14/oversold-and-unregulated-flawed-prenatal-tests-leading-abortions-healthy-fetuses/aKFAOCP5NoKr8S1HirL7EN/story.html; and Beth Daley, "When Baby Is Due, Genetic Counselors Seen Downplaying False Alarms," March 6, 2016, https://www.bostonglobe.com/metro/2016/03/05/when-baby-due-genetic-counselors-seen-downplaying-false-alarms/bBCoKAFVidJASkkOiMg6DI/story.html.
18. Dena Davis, *Genetic Dilemmas: Reproductive Technology, Parental Choices, and Children's Futures*, 2nd ed. (New York: Oxford University Press, 2010), 25.
19. Dena S. Davis, "The Parental Investment Factor and the Child's Right to an Open Future," *Hastings Center Report* 39, no. 2 (March 2009): 24–27. Others have echoed this concern, particularly as it relates to prenatal sex selection; see, for example, Audrey R. Chapman and Peter A. Benn, "Noninvasive Prenatal Testing for Early Sex Identification: A Few Benefits and Many Concerns," *Perspectives in Biology and Medicine* 56, no. 4 (Autumn 2013): 530–547.
20. Congregation for the Doctrine of the Faith, "Instruction *Dignitas personae* on Certain Bioethical Questions," #4, http://www.vatican.va/roman_curia/congregations/cfaith/documents/rc_con_cfaith_doc_20081208_dignitas-personae_en.html. One should be quick to note that this view is not shared by all Catholics; some more liberal Catholics dissent from the official teaching. See John H. Evans and Kathy Hudson, "Religion and Reproductive Genetics: Beyond Views of Embryonic Life?" *Journal for the Scientific Study of Religion* 46 no. 4 (2007): 565–581. See also the work of Catholics for Choice, a nonprofit organization: https://www.catholicsforchoice.org/.
21. Congregation for the Doctrine of the Faith, "Instruction on Respect for Human Life in Its Origin: Replies to Certain Questions of the Day," ("*Donum vitae*"), http://www.vatican.va/roman_curia/congregations/cfaith/documents/rc_con_cfaith_doc_19870222_respect-for-human-life_en.html.
22. United States Conference of Catholic Bishops, *Ethical and Religious Directives for Catholic Health Care Services* (Washington DC: United States Conference of Catholic Bishops, 2009), #50 and #54.

23. *Dignitas personae*, #22.
24. Kevin D. O'Rourke, O.P., "Catholic Principles and In Vitro Fertilization," *National Catholic Bioethics Quarterly* (Winter 2010): 720–721.
25. See, for example, John Paul II, "Biological Experimentation: Address to Members of the Pontifical Academy of Sciences," October 23, 1982, https://w2.vatican.va/content/john-paul-ii/en/speeches/1982/october/documents/hf_jp-ii_spe_19821023_pont-accademia-scienze.html; and John Paul II, "The Ethics of Genetic Manipulation," *Origins* 13 (November 17, 1983): 386–9.
26. World Council of Churches, "Manipulating Life: Report on Ethical and Social Issues in Genetic Engineering and the Ownership of New Living Organisms," *Church and Society* 73 no. 1 (Sep-Oct 1982): 37.
27. World Council of Churches, "Biotechnology," 1989, https://www.oikoumene.org/en/resources/documents/wcc-programmes/justice-diakonia-and-responsibility-for-creation/science-technology-ethics/biotechnology; see Ronald Cole-Turner, *The New Genesis: Theology and the Genetic Revolution* (Louisville: Westminster/John Knox Press, 1983), 71. Protestant theologian Cole-Turner interprets the 1989 WCC document as taking a generally positive stance towards technologies of genetic manipulation and biotechnology.
28. By this I refer to the view that the embryo's moral claim to protection increases gradually as it develops.
29. Ibid., 23–25.
30. National Council of the Churches of Christ, *Human Life and the New Genetics* (New York: National Council of the Churches of Christ, 1980), 41, 44; cited in Cole-Turner, *The New Genesis*, 71–72.
31. National Council of the Churches of Christ, "Genetic Science for Human Benefit," 1986, http://nationalcouncilofchurches.us/common-witness/1986/biotech.php.
32. Ethical debates about abortion, including its legal accessibility, have substantially increased in the wake of 2022 US Supreme Court case *Dobbs vs. Jackson*.
33. A Roman Catholic rejection of prenatal genetic diagnosis also derives from the procedure's necessary connection to in vitro fertilization (IVF); IVF is seen wrongly to depersonalize human procreation, separating reproduction from sexual intercourse. See, for example, *Dignitas personae*, #16.
34. Cynthia B. Cohen, "The Moral Status of Early Embryos and New Genetic Interventions," in *A Christian Response to the New Genetics: Religious, Ethical, and Social Issues*, ed. David H. Smith and Cynthia B. Cohen (Lanham, MD: Rowman & Littlefield, 2003), 105–130; see also Cynthia B. Cohen and Mary R. Anderlik, "Creating and Shaping Future Children," 75–103 in the same volume.
35. For a good example of one such approach, see Ronald Cole-Turner and Brent Waters, *Pastoral Genetics: Theology and Care at the Beginning of Life* (Cleveland: The Pilgrim Press, 1996), 120–122.
36. According to Ellen Painter Dollar, 75–80 percent of those receiving a Down syndrome diagnosis while pregnant elect to abort the pregnancy. See Ellen Painter Dollar, "Messy Stories," *Christian Century* (November 13, 2013), accessed July 11, 2022, http://www.christiancentury.org/article/2013-10/messy-stories. Special Olympics founder Eunice Kennedy Shriver places the figure higher, at 90 percent; see "Prenatal Testing," *America* (May 14, 2007), accessed July 11, 2022, http://americamagazine.org/issue/614/other-things/prenatal-testing.

37. In fact, it should be noted that, in some cases, the advance knowledge provided by PGD, combined with selective implantation, may actually *enable* a genetically at-risk couple (for example, two carriers of the Tay-Sachs gene) to consider parenthood—giving them the assurances they desire in order to choose to become pregnant in the first place.
38. Francis S. Collins, "Forward," in *Playing God: Genetic Determinism and Human Freedom*, ed. Ted Peters, 2nd ed. (New York: Routledge, 2003), ix.
39. Erik Parens and Adrienne Asch, "The Disability Rights Critique of Prenatal Genetic Testing: Reflections and Recommendations," in *Prenatal Testing and Disability Rights*, ed. Erik Parens and Adrienne Asch (Washington DC: Georgetown University Press, 2007), 4.
40. As philosopher Hans Reinders writes, citing bioethicist Daniel Wikler in Reinders, *The Future of the Disabled*, 1.
41. Amy Julia Becker, "Babies Perfect and Imperfect," *First Things* (November 2008): 9–11.
42. Mary Jo Iozzio, "Genetic Anomaly or Genetic Diversity: Thinking in the Key of Disability on the Human Genome," *Theological Studies* 66 (2005): 862–863.
43. Ibid., 879.
44. Stanley Hauerwas, *Suffering Presence: Theological Reflections on Medicine, the Mentally Handicapped, and the Church* (Notre Dame, IN: University of Notre Dame Press, 1986), 163 and 173.
45. The capitalization of the term designates cultural identity versus a physical condition. For a nuanced moral analysis of these arguments, see Parens and Asch, esp. pages 23–26. See also Dena S. Davis, "Choosing for Disability," in *Genetic Dilemmas*.
46. Reinders, *The Future of the Disabled*, 175–192.
47. Martha Beck, *Expecting Adam: A True Story of Birth, Rebirth, and Everyday Magic* (Times Books/Random House, 1999), 195 and 313. A similar memoir, though focusing more on the agonizing process of decision-making when receiving a prenatal diagnostic result for Down syndrome, may be found in Mitchell Zuckoff, *Choosing Naia: A Family's Journey* (Boston: Beacon Press, 2003).
48. Dollar, "Messy Stories," 23.
49. Ibid. See also Rapp, *Testing Women*.
50. See, for instance, Karen Peterson-Iyer, *Designer Children: Reconciling Genetic Technology, Feminism, and Christian Faith* (Cleveland: Pilgrim Press, 2004), 154–168. For a nuanced philosophical account of human flourishing and disability that takes a roughly similar view, see Jonathan Glover, *Choosing Children: Genes, Disability, and Design* (Oxford: Clarendon Press, 2006), especially 4–36.
51. Oliver O'Donovan, *Begotten or Made?* (Oxford: Clarendon Press, 1984), 65.
52. Maura A. Ryan, "The Argument for Unlimited Procreative Liberty: A Feminist Critique," *Hastings Center Report* 20, no. 4 (1990): 10.
53. See, for example, Matthew 12:46–50.
54. One well-known example can be found in Mark 10:13–16.
55. This understanding is present throughout the history of the tradition but is particularly apparent in the writings of Martin Luther. See Martin Luther, "The Estate of Marriage," in *Luther's Works*, vol. 45, ed. Walther I. Brandt (Philadelphia: Fortress, 1962), 12–49. See also "A Sermon on the Estate of Marriage," in *Luther's Works*, vol. 44, ed. James Atkinson (Philadelphia: Fortress, 1966), 3–14.
56. Bridget Burke Ravizza, "Ministering to Moral Pioneers: Prenatal Testing and Christian Parenting," *New Theology Review* 23 no. 3 (August 2011): 63–64; and citing Rapp, *Testing Women*, 3.

57. Here I draw upon some of the conclusions of Ronald Cole-Turner and Brent Waters in *Pastoral Genetics*, chapter 8.
58. It should be clarified here that I am not suggesting the abortion of all fetuses shown to carry a disability. Rather, difficult judgment calls must be made about the likelihood and specific details of any given disability, including its degree of severity, associated life span, and impact on the prospective parents in the context of a society that generally provides insufficient support for disabled persons.
59. Allen Verhey, "'Playing God' and Invoking a Perspective," *Journal of Medicine and Philosophy* 20 (1995): 361.
60. Aana Marie Vigen, "Prenatal Genetic Testing & the Complicated Quest for a Healthy Baby: Christian Ethics in Conversation with Genetic Counselors" (unpublished paper presented at the Society of Christian Ethics, Seattle, Washington, January 2014), 7. Vigen also highlights how linguistic, cultural, and educational barriers can serve as a further challenge for genetic counselors who seek to convey prenatal diagnostic results to patients. See also Vigen, "Neglected Voices at the Beginning of Life: Prenatal Genetics and Reproductive Justice," in *Catholic Bioethics and Social Justice: The Praxis of US Health Care in a Globalized World*, ed. M. Therese Lysaught and Michael McCarthy (Collegeville, MN: Liturgical Press Academic, 2018), 97–112.
61. Lisa Sowle Cahill, "Biotechnology, Genes, and Justice," in *Theological Bioethics: Participation, Justice, and Change* (Washington DC: Georgetown University Press, 2005), 218.
62. See Maura Ryan, "Feminist Theologies and the New Genetics," in *The Ethics of Genetic Engineering*, ed. Maureen Junker-Kenny and Lisa Sowle Cahill (Maryknoll: Orbis, 1998), 98.
63. Vigen, "Neglected Voices at the Beginning of Life," 21.
64. Joseph Fletcher, *The Ethics of Genetic Control: Ending Reproductive Roulette* (Buffalo, NY: Prometheus Books, 1988), 157–158.
65. Ibid., 156.
66. Beverly Wildung Harrison, *Our Right to Choose: Toward a New Ethic of Abortion* (Boston: Beacon Press, 1983), 4.
67. Kaveny, *Law's Virtues*, 7.
68. Ibid., 111–140.
69. Peterson-Iyer, *Designer Children*, 123. Some examples of theologians who might be categorized as co-creationists with respect to genetic technologies generally include Philip Hefner, Ted Peters, and Ronald Cole-Turner, among others. See, for instance, Philip Hefner, "The Evolution of the Created Co-Creator," in *Cosmos as Creation: Science and Theology in Consonance*, ed. Ted Peters (Nashville: Abingdon, 1989), 211–233; Ted Peters, *For the Love of Children: Genetic Technology and the Future of the Family* (Louisville: Westminster John Knox, 1996); Peters, *Playing God? Genetic Determinism and Human Freedom* (New York: Routledge, 1997); Cole-Turner, *The New Genesis*; and Cole-Turner, "Is Genetic Engineering Co-Creation?" *Theology Today* 44 (October 1987): 338–49.
70. Paul Ramsey, *Fabricated Man: The Ethics of Genetic Control* (New Haven: Yale University Press, 1970), 31.
71. Gilbert Meilaender, *Body, Soul, and Bioethics* (Notre Dame: University of Notre Dame Press, 1995), 84–85. See also *Bioethics: A Primer for Christians* (Grand Rapids, MI: Eerdmans, 2005).
72. Karl Rahner, *Foundations of Christian Faith: An Introduction to the Idea of Christianity*, trans. William V. Dych (New York: Crossroad, 1994), 97; "The Dignity and Freedom of

Man," in *Theological Investigations*, vol. 2, trans. K. H. Kruger (Baltimore: Helicon, 1963), 247; "The Experiment with Man: Theological Observations on Man's Self-Manipulation" and "The Problem of Genetic Manipulation," in *Theological Investigations*, vol. 9, trans. D. Bourke (New York: Herder & Herder, 1972), 205–24 and 225–252 (respectively).

Bibliography

American Congress of Obstetricians and Gynecologists. "Practice Bulletin No. 162: Prenatal Diagnostic Testing for Genetic Disorders." *Obstetrics & Gynecology* 127, no. 5 (May 2016): e108–e122. https://doi.org/10.1097/AOG.0000000000001405.

American Congress of Obstetricians and Gynecologists. "Practice Bulletin No. 163: Screening for Fetal Aneuploidy." *Obstetrics & Gynecology* 127, no. 5 (May 2016): e123–e137. https://doi.org/10.1097/AOG.0000000000001406.

American Congress of Obstetricians and Gynecologists. "Practice Bulletin No. 226: Screening for Fetal Chromosomal Abnormalities." *Obstetrics & Gynecology* 136, no. 4 (October 2020): e48–e69. https://doi.org/10.1097/AOG.0000000000004084.

American Society of Reproductive Medicine. "Preimplantation Genetic Testing: A Practice Committee Opinion." *Fertility and Sterility* 90, suppl. 3 (November 2008): S136–S143.

Beck, Martha. *Expecting Adam: A True Story of Birth, Rebirth, and Everyday Magic*. Times Books/Random House, 1999.

Becker, Amy Julia. "Babies Perfect and Imperfect." *First Things*, no. 187 (November 2008): 9–11.

Burke Ravizza, Bridget. "Ministering to Moral Pioneers: Prenatal Testing and Christian Parenting." *New Theology Review* 23, no. 3 (August 2011): 63–74.

Cahill, Lisa Sowle. "Biotechnology, Genes, and Justice." In *Theological Bioethics: Participation, Justice, and Change*. Washington DC: Georgetown University Press, 2005.

Callaway, Ewen. "Second Chinese Team Reports Gene Editing in Human Embryos." *Nature*. Last modified April 8, 2016. http://www.nature.com/news/second-chinese-team-reports-gene-editing-in-human-embryos-1.19718.

Chapman, Audrey R., and Peter A. Benn. "Noninvasive Prenatal Testing for Early Sex Identification: A Few Benefits and Many Concerns." *Perspectives in Biology and Medicine* 56, no. 4 (Autumn 2013): 530–547.

Cohen, Cynthia B. "The Moral Status of Early Embryos and New Genetic Interventions." In *A Christian Response to the New Genetics: Religious, Ethical, and Social Issues*, edited by David H. Smith and Cynthia B. Cohen, 105–130. Lanham, MD: Rowman & Littlefield, 2003.

Cohen, Cynthia B., and Mary R. Anderlik. "Creating and Shaping Future Children." In Smith and Cohen, *A Christian Response to the New Genetics*, 75–103. Lanham, MD: Rowman & Littlefield, 2003.

Cole-Turner, Ronald. "Is Genetic Engineering Co-Creation?" *Theology Today* 44 (October 1987): 338–349.

Cole-Turner, Ronald. *The New Genesis: Theology and the Genetic Revolution*. Louisville: Westminster/John Knox Press, 1983.

Cole-Turner, Ronald, and Brent Waters. *Pastoral Genetics: Theology and Care at the Beginning of Life*. Cleveland: Pilgrim Press, 1996.

Collins, Francis S. "Foreword." In *Playing God: Genetic Determinism and Human Freedom*, edited by Ted Peters, ix–xi. 2nd ed. New York: Routledge, 2003.

Congregation for the Doctrine of the Faith. "Instruction *Dignitas Personae* on Certain Bioethical Questions." September 8, 2008. http://www.vatican.va/roman_curia/congregations/cfaith/documents/rc_con_cfaith_doc_20081208_dignitas-personae_en.html.

Congregation for the Doctrine of the Faith. "Instruction on Respect for Human Life in Its Origin: Replies to Certain Questions of the Day" (*"Donum vitae"*). February 22, 1987. http://www.vatican.va/roman_curia/congregations/cfaith/documents/rc_con_cfaith_doc_19870222_respect-for-human-life_en.html.

Cyranoski, David, and Sara Reardon. "Chinese Scientists Genetically Modify Human Embryos." *Nature*. Last modified April 22, 2015. http://www.nature.com/news/chinese-scientists-genetically-modify-human-embryos-1.17378.

Daley, Beth. "Oversold prenatal tests spur some to choose abortions." *Boston Globe*. December 14, 2014. https://www.bostonglobe.com/metro/2014/12/14/oversold-and-unregulated-flawed-prenatal-tests-leading-abortions-healthy-fetuses/aKFAOCP5N0Kr8S1HirL7EN/story.html;

Daley, Beth. "When Baby Is Due, Genetic Counselors Seen Downplaying False Alarms." *Boston Globe*. March 5, 2016. https://www.bostonglobe.com/metro/2016/03/05/when-baby-due-genetic-counselors-seen-downplaying-false-alarms/bBC0KAFVidJASkkOiMg6DI/story.html.

Daley, Rebecca, Melissa Hill, and Lyn S. Chitty. "Non-Invasive Prenatal Diagnosis: Progress and Potential." *Archives of Disease in Childhood* 99, no. 5 (2014): F426–F430.

Davis, Dena S. *Genetic Dilemmas: Reproductive Technology, Parental Choices, and Children's Futures*. 2nd ed. New York: Oxford University Press, 2010.

Davis, Dena S. "The Parental Investment Factor and the Child's Right to an Open Future." *Hastings Center Report* 39, no. 2 (March 2009): 24–27.

Dollar, Ellen Painter. "Messy Stories." *Christian Century* 130, no. 23 (November 13, 2013). http://www.christiancentury.org/article/2013-10/messy-stories.

Evans, John H., and Kathy Hudson. "Religion and Reproductive Genetics: Beyond Views of Embryonic Life?" *Journal for the Scientific Study of Religion* 46, no. 4 (2007): 565–581.

Fletcher, Joseph. *The Ethics of Genetic Control: Ending Reproductive Roulette*. Buffalo, NY: Prometheus Books, 1988.

Glover, Jonathan. *Choosing Children: Genes, Disability, and Design*. Oxford: Clarendon Press, 2006.

Harrison, Beverly Wildung. *Our Right to Choose: Toward a New Ethic of Abortion*. Boston: Beacon Press, 1983.

Hauerwas, Stanley. *Suffering Presence: Theological Reflections on Medicine, the Mentally Handicapped, and the Church*. Notre Dame, IN: University of Notre Dame Press, 1986.

Hefner, Philip. "The Evolution of the Created Co-Creator." In *Cosmos as Creation: Science and Theology in Consonance*, edited by Ted Peters, 211–233. Nashville: Abingdon, 1989.

Iozzio, Mary Jo. "Genetic Anomaly or Genetic Diversity: Thinking in the Key of Disability on the Human Genome." *Theological Studies* 66 (2005): 862–863.

John Paul II. "Biological Experimentation: Address to Members of the Pontifical Academy of Sciences." October 23, 1982. https://w2.vatican.va/content/john-paul-ii/en/speeches/1982/october/documents/hf_jp-ii_spe_19821023_pont-accademia-scienze.html.

John Paul II. "The Ethics of Genetic Manipulation." *Origins* 13 (November 17, 1983): 386–389.

Kahn, Jennifer. "Life, Edited." *New York Times Magazine*. November 15, 2015, 62–66 and 82–83.

Kaveny, Cathleen. *Law's Virtues: Fostering Autonomy and Solidarity in American Society*. Washington, DC: Georgetown University Press, 2012.

Luther, Martin. "A Sermon on the Estate of Marriage." In *Luther's Works*, vol. 44, edited by James Atkinson, pp. 3–14. Philadelphia: Fortress, 1966.

Luther, Martin. "The Estate of Marriage." In *Luther's Works*, vol. 45, edited by Walther I. Brandt, 12–49. Philadelphia: Fortress, 1962.

Meilaender, Gilbert. *Bioethics: A Primer for Christians*. Grand Rapids, MI: Eerdmans, 2005.

Meilaender, Gilbert. *Body, Soul, and Bioethics*. Notre Dame, IN: University of Notre Dame Press, 1995.

Mezher, Michael. "FDA Warns Three Companies Over DTC Genetic Tests." *Regulatory Focus*, November 9, 2015. https://www.raps.org/news-and-articles/news-articles/2015/11/fda-warns-three-companies-over-dtc-genetic-tests /.

Munthe, Christian. "A New Ethical Landscape of Prenatal Testing: Individualizing Choice to Serve Autonomy and Promote Public Health: A Radical Proposal." *Bioethics* 29, no. 1 (2015): 36–45.

National Council of the Churches of Christ. "Genetic Science for Human Benefit." 1986. http://nationalcouncilofchurches.us/common-witness/1986/biotech.php.

National Council of the Churches of Christ. *Human Life and the New Genetics*. New York: National Council of the Churches of Christ, 1980.

National Human Genome Research Institute. "Regulation of Genetic Tests." https://www.genome.gov/10002335/regulation-of-genetic-tests/.

O'Donovan, Oliver. *Begotten or Made?* Oxford: Clarendon Press, 1984.

O'Rourke, Kevin D., O.P. "Catholic Principles and In Vitro Fertilization." *National Catholic Bioethics Quarterly* 10, no. 4 (Winter 2010): 720–721.

Parens, Erik, and Adrienne Asch. "The Disability Rights Critique of Prenatal Genetic Testing: Reflections and Recommendations." In *Prenatal Testing and Disability Rights*, edited by Erik Parens and Adrienne Asch, 3–43. Washington DC: Georgetown University Press, 2007.

Peters, Ted. *For the Love of Children: Genetic Technology and the Future of the Family*. Louisville: Westminster John Knox, 1996.

Peters, Ted. *Playing God? Genetic Determinism and Human Freedom*. New York: Routledge, 1997.

Peterson-Iyer, Karen. *Designer Children: Reconciling Genetic Technology, Feminism, and Christian Faith*. Cleveland: Pilgrim Press, 2004.

Rahner, Karl. "The Dignity and Freedom of Man." In *Theological Investigations*, vol. 2, 235–263. Translated by K. H. Kruger. Baltimore: Helicon, 1963.

Rahner, Karl. "The Experiment with Man: Theological Observations on Man's Self-Manipulation." In *Theological Investigations*, vol. 9, 205–224. Translated by D. Bourke. New York: Herder & Herder, 1972.

Rahner, Karl. *Foundations of Christian Faith: An Introduction to the Idea of Christianity*. Translated by William V. Dych. New York: Crossroad, 1994.

Rahner, Karl. "The Problem of Genetic Manipulation." In *Theological Investigations*, vol. 9, 225–252. Translated by D. Bourke. New York: Herder & Herder, 1972.

Ramsey, Paul. *Fabricated Man: The Ethics of Genetic Control*. New Haven, CT: Yale University Press, 1970.

Rapp, Rayna. *Testing Women, Testing the Fetus: The Social Impact of Amniocentesis in America*. New York: Routledge, 1999.

Ravinsky, Vardit. "Law and Ethics of Noninvasive Prenatal Testing." Address at Harvard Law School, November 2014. https://vimeo.com/111444284.

Ravitsky, Vardit, Marie-Christine Roy, Hazar Haidar, Lidewij Henneman, John Marshall, Ainsley J. Newson, Olivia M. Y. Ngan, and Tamar Nov-Klaiman. "The Emergence and Global

Spread of Noninvasive Prenatal Testing." *Annual Review of Genomics and Human Genetics* 22 (2021): 309–338. https://doi.org/10.1146/annurev-genom-083118-015053.

Regalado, Antonio. "Chinese Scientists Are Creating CRISPR Babies." *MIT Technology Review*. Last modified November 25, 2018. https://www.technologyreview.com/s/612458/exclusive-chinese-scientists-are-creating-crispr-babies/?fbclid=IwAR0OXaU1jkbQ3sDhSmnG7DYS_N8Q9wurywHZko2Eb_CPHxU5L6RLEk6UHcY.

Regalado, Antonio. "A Third CRISPR Baby May Already Have Been Born in China." *MIT Technology Review*. Last modified July 3, 2019. https://www.technologyreview.com/s/613890/a-third-crispr-baby-may-have-already-been-born-in-china/.

Reinders, Hans S. *The Future of the Disabled in Liberal Society: An Ethical Analysis*. Notre Dame, IN: University of Notre Dame Press, 2000.

Rothman, Barbara Katz. "The Meanings of Choice in Reproductive Technology." In *Test Tube Women: What Future for Motherhood?* edited by Rita Arditti, Renate Duelli Klein, and Shelley Minden, 23–33. Boston: Pandora Press, 1984.

Rothman, Barbara Katz. *The Tentative Pregnancy: Prenatal Diagnosis and the Future of Motherhood*. New York: Viking, 1986.

Ryan, Maura A. "The Argument for Unlimited Procreative Liberty: A Feminist Critique." *Hastings Center Report* 20, no. 4 (1990): 6–12.

Ryan, Maura A. "Feminist Theologies and the New Genetics." In *The Ethics of Genetic Engineering*, edited Maureen Junker-Kenny and Lisa Sowle Cahill, 93–101. Maryknoll: Orbis, 1998.

Sharma, Hitika, Drishtant Singh, Ankush Mahant, Satwinder Kaur Sohal, Anup Kumar Kesavan, and Samiksha. "Development of Mitochondrial Replacement Therapy: A Review." *Heliyon* 6, no. 9 (2020): 1–7. https://doi.org/10.1016/j.heliyon.2020.e04643.

Shriver, Eunice Kennedy. "Prenatal Testing." *America* 196, no. 17 (May 14, 2007). http://americamagazine.org/issue/614/other-things/prenatal-testing.

United States Conference of Catholic Bishops. *Ethical and Religious Directives for Catholic Health Care Services*. Washington DC: United States Conference of Catholic Bishops, 2009.

Verhey, Allen. "'Playing God' and Invoking a Perspective." *Journal of Medicine and Philosophy* 20 (1995): 347–364.

Vigen, Aana Marie. "Neglected Voices at the Beginning of Life: Prenatal Genetics and Reproductive Justice." In *Catholic Bioethics and Social Justice: The Praxis of US Health Care in a Globalized World*, edited by M. Therese Lysaught and Michael McCarthy, 97–112. Collegeville, MN: Liturgical Press Academic, 2018.

Vigen, Aana Marie. "Prenatal Genetic Testing & the Complicated Quest for a Healthy Baby: Christian Ethics in Conversation with Genetic Counselors." Unpublished paper presented at the Society of Christian Ethics, Seattle, Washington, January 2014.

World Council of Churches. "Biotechnology." Geneva: World Council of Churches, August 1989. https://www.oikoumene.org/en/resources/documents/wcc-programmes/justice-diakonia-and-responsibility-for-creation/science-technology-ethics/biotechnology.

World Council of Churches. "Manipulating Life: Report on Ethical and Social Issues in Genetic Engineering and the Ownership of New Living Organisms." *Church and Society* 73 no. 1 (September/October 1982): 29–51.

Zimmer, Carl. "Breakthrough DNA Editor Born of Bacteria." *Quanta Magazine*, February 6, 2016. https://www.quantamagazine.org/crispr-natural-history-in-bacteria-20150206/.

Zuckoff, Mitchell. *Choosing Naia: A Family's Journey*. Boston: Beacon Press, 2003.

CHAPTER 28

EVANGELICAL PERSPECTIVES ON PRENATAL TESTING

PAIGE COMSTOCK CUNNINGHAM

ONE of the marks of Christian fidelity is outward evidence of inner transformation, expressed through concern for the marginalized, compassion for the vulnerable, and hospitality for the stranger. The impulse for this response appears first in the Old Testament, and is repeated in the second of the two Great Commandments in the New Testament: "Love your neighbor as yourself."[1] Obedience to this divine direction has varied over time and in culturally distinct ways. Conclusions about Christian responsibility and moral imperatives frequently are at odds with the surrounding culture, from earliest times to the present day. Arguably, nowhere has this been more distinct than in how Christians regard early human life and people with disability, two of the most vulnerable groups both then and now. Early Christians were known for their sacrificial care for those abandoned by society: infants, especially girls, the disabled, and the plague-stricken. The church became the only organization that systematically cared for the abandoned, the sick, and the dying, marked by compassion and personal sacrifice, including one's own death, which was absent from the Greco-Roman culture.[2] All early Christian thinkers opposed abortion, but were nonetheless confronted with cultural pressures to regard the fetus as a lesser kind of human being.[3]

Caring for the vulnerable historically has been understood both affirmatively and negatively. Loving one's neighbor pointed toward the positive path of choosing life, and the blessings that would redound to the people of God. The negative path, choosing death, led to curses and separation from God, a fate to be earnestly avoided. The essential argument about abortion rested on both positive and negative concepts: 1) abortion was considered to be murder and a violation of the Sixth Commandment, "Thou shalt not kill",[4] 2) those who participated were guilty and accountable to God, and 3) the fetus is the object of God's care as a living human being, and thus merits equal care as those already born.[5] Not unlike Christians in the early church, Christians today encounter cultural pressures to regard the fetus in the womb or the embryo in the petri dish as less than fully human; Christian regard for the embryo and fetus as a person is sharply and increasingly at odds with dominant nonreligious perspectives.

The fate of the fetus and people with disability is joined in the context of reproductive technologies, in particular those used to identify potential anomalies. Except where used to identify gestational age and sex, ultrasound and other prenatal tests are not used primarily for therapeutic purposes to benefit the fetus, but for diagnostic purposes to detect fetal anomalies with the likely outcome of termination of the pregnancy. Preimplantation genetic diagnosis is performed on embryos created via in vitro fertilization (IVF), for the purpose of identifying those that have a genetic anomaly to ensure they are not transferred to the mother's womb. Whether resident in a womb or petri dish, the developing human being is at risk of losing his or her life if found to have an unacceptable disability. The tests may also be used to reject an embryo or fetus of the undesired sex, usually female. Evangelical attitudes about, and uses of, these technologies are shaped by their beliefs about embryonic human life and abortion. This chapter attempts to describe the perspectives of evangelicals about these intersecting technologies and the values conflicts they entail.

Evangelicals

The definition of both "evangelical" and "evangelicalism" are contested, whether examined through the lens of history, sociology, or doctrine.[6] Regardless of the approach one takes, evangelicals place themselves in continuity with the earliest Christian tradition. Contemporary evangelicalism, as discussed below, grew largely out of concerns for the authority and reliability of the Bible. Today, evangelicals are a significant religious group, with estimates ranging from 300 to 550 million worldwide.[7] In the early twentieth century, most evangelicals lived in North America or Europe. Today, Latin America, Africa, and Asia are home to the largest numbers of evangelicals. These demographic realities should be placed in the context of the wide variation in defining who is an "evangelical."

Those who self-identify as "evangelical" in the United States in the twenty-first century represent 25 to 38 percent of the population.[8] When nine factors that refer to more formal doctrinal beliefs are applied, that number decreases.[9] The National Association of Evangelicals (NAE), America's largest coalition of evangelicals, includes many denominations, including Reformed, Holiness, Anabaptist, Pentecostal, Charismatic and other traditions. The NAE describes "evangelical" in terms of adherence to the

NAE Statement of Faith, and four distinctive characteristics: (1) *Conversion*, a personal and active experience of God; (2) *Biblicism*, regard for the Bible as the ultimate authority for faith and practice; (3) *Activism* in expressing the gospel through missionary efforts and works of charity; and (4) *Crucicentrism*, an emphasis on Christ's death on the cross, sealed by his resurrection, that made possible the redemption of humanity.[10]

In the last fifty years, there has been a noticeable flowering of evangelical theology in the academy.[11] Beyond dogmatics or systematic theology, evangelical theologians are working in hermeneutics, historical theology, public theology, Christian ethics, and theology of culture, while denominations, parachurch leaders, and pastors are on the front lines of testing and living out applied theology. One challenge with bioethics is that applied theology often moves far ahead of systematic theological reflection. Changes in medical technology, therefore, frequently outpace the ability—and interest—of evangelical theologians to articulate foundational Biblical and theological concepts. In addition, evangelicals do not recognize an ultimate teaching authority, in contrast to the Roman Catholic *magisterium*; thus there is no consensus on what is the official teaching of "evangelical theology." This does not leave evangelical bioethics bereft of resources. Confidence in the Bible as authoritative for faith and practice, and confidence in the inherited Christian tradition as a God-given, secondary authority support drawing ethical conclusions that are relevant for decision-making, and this includes making decisions about prenatal testing (PNT) and preimplantation genetic diagnosis (PGD). PNT assesses functional and structural abnormalities in utero. In the discussion that follows, both modes (PNT and PGD), including genetic diagnosis and genetic screening, will be treated for convenience as PNT, except where the difference is relevant.

THEOLOGICAL ANTHROPOLOGY

For the evangelical, as would be true for Christians in general, attempting to answer the question of the permissibility of using pre-implantation and prenatal tests begins with Christian theological anthropology, for this answers the question of who we are and how we are to live in this world. The debate about the proper uses of these and all other technologies, for that matter, is a debate about human nature, and the implications of being contingent, finite, and limited creatures.

Understanding who is a person and what it means to be human begins, in an evangelical account,[12] with a prior understanding of who God is. As Cherith Fee Nordling explains, rather than building a theological anthropology from the "bottom up," that is, based on human experience and self-understanding, a Christian theology begins "top down," with an understanding of who God is and his relationship with the human beings he created. "The Christian story assumes that human being and personhood reflect a prior Reality—the triune God—through whom humanity derives its being, personhood, identity, and purpose as divine image-bearers."[13] Thus, the inquiry does not place human beings at the center, but the triune God of Father, Son, and Holy Spirit, in eternal self-giving relationship of perfect love, who freely created and entered into relationship with his creation, and most particularly with the only creatures he made *imago Dei*, in God's own image.

Image of God

Theologians have wrestled for over two millennia with the meaning of *imago Dei*. Being made in the image of God "has a small textual base, yet its importance in the Scriptures and Christian thought far exceeds this."[14] Indeed, it is the foundation for belief that human beings are exceptional, that they have intrinsic dignity and incommensurable worth, and thus merit compassionate respect.

In the Biblical account of Genesis, the creation of humankind is the climax of the six-day creation narrative. Of all living things that God created, only human beings are made in his image.[15] Humankind was given dominion over, and responsibility for, all the rest of creation, and was directed to "be fruitful and multiply."[16] In the Genesis narrative, human beings are positioned in three relationships: toward God in obedience and praise; toward each other as male and female, expressing diversity within unity; and toward the rest of creation, in dominion and stewardship.

The foundational doctrine of *imago Dei* is paired in Christian anthropology with the doctrine of the incarnation of Jesus. Jesus's human life did not begin with the Nativity, but at the Annunciation, when he was "conceived by the power of the Holy Spirit," as the Apostles' Creed affirms. His voluntary and complete dependence upon and confinement in the womb of a woman dignifies our bodily existence, and, specifically, when it begins: at conception. Not only did the Son take on a human body, he did not shed it at the end of his life on earth, but is seated in his glorified body for all time at the right hand of God the Father. This "serves as a lynchpin of Christology since it establishes the continuity of [the] Lord's human nature in time and eternity."[17]

Evangelical theology has high regard for the child in the womb. From the moment of conception, the newly formed individual human being is a member of the human species, the species that God honored, and is a person whose life should not be harmed, instrumentalized, or cut short by others. Contemporary moral objections to abortion are consistent with the history of the Christian church.[18] Early Christian thinkers made distinctions about the age of the fetus for purposes of determining punishment, but agreed that in all cases it was a sin.[19] In the Roman Catholic tradition, the careful working out of theological and moral judgments over centuries culminated in the conclusion that "the fetus [is] possessed of equal rights with other humans," animated by the conviction that "the fetus as human was a neighbor" whom Christians are enjoined by Scripture to love.[20] An evangelical theologian, working from Biblical principles, similarly states that "there is a clear Scriptural warrant for affirming the sacredness of all human life at every stage of biological development," and that the ethically responsible thing to do is "treat developing human life as personal at every stage of prenatal development."[21]

Evangelical perspectives on prenatal life were articulated most recently during the abortion debates in the latter part of the twentieth century. In 1973, *Roe v. Wade* provoked evangelical theologians and ethicists to wrestle with the newly legalized practice of abortion. Some denominations revised their views, illustrated most notably in the Southern Baptist Convention's reversal of its 1971 approval of abortion in limited circumstances, to its 1976 affirmation of the sacredness of fetal life and rejection of "abortion as a means of birth control," and their 1980 resolution calling for a constitutional amendment prohibiting abortion except to save the life of the mother.[22] The greatest influence on evangelicals was a trio of two theologians and a surgeon: Harold O. J. Brown, a Harvard trained historian and theologian; Francis Schaeffer, a theologian, philosopher, and pastor; and C. Everett Kopp, a pediatric surgeon who would go on to become US surgeon general in 1982. Koop and Schaeffer produced *Whatever Happened to the Human Race?* which was widely viewed in churches. The project is a book and film series on threats to human dignity posed by such practices as abortion, infanticide, and euthanasia.[23] Their efforts roused and energized evangelicals, to the point that evangelical identity became synonymous with being pro-life.[24]

Being pro-life in principle, meaning the fetus's life is acknowledged to be equal in value to the mother's, did not necessarily equate with demanding that public policy align 100 percent with that principle. While most evangelicals opposed abortion except where the mother's life was at stake, some reluctantly accepted the possibility of abortion as the least evil option in rare cases. Writing for an evangelical audience, anatomy professor D. Gareth Jones addressed the issue of abortion for genetic reasons. Although he expressed sympathy for the "absolute protection" view of the fetus based on sanctity of life principles, he aligned with the "potentiality" view, declining to draw a line between non-personhood and personhood. "Throughout the whole of its development the fetus is potentially an actual person, and deserves the respect and treatment due to a being with this sort of potential."[25] One of his major objections to genetic abortion was that it violated the principle of justice, "because defective individuals are being selected for destruction."[26] Nonetheless, he conceded that when taking into account family considerations, some dilemmas are so "appalling" that "abortion for medical reasons"[27] provides the only resolution.[28] Jones's views were controversial at the time his book was published, and continue to represent a minority view within the evangelical perspective.

Even if evangelicals have differences about the morality of a small number of abortions, they do agree that abortion as a practice is not a good, and should be avoided. The primary reason is that the unborn child is a member of the human family and a person made in God's image. Evangelicals believe that a child is ideally born into a family consisting at least of a mother and father who are married to each other.

Coupled with their firm convictions about abortion and the equal value of unborn life, evangelicals would resist genetic testing of the embryo and fetus that could ultimately harm the child through discarding, in the case of an embryo, or abortion of a fetus in the womb. The result would be the death of the actual child, not a potential child.

Marriage, Family, and Children

Evangelical views on marriage begin, like so much of theology, in Genesis. Jesus himself said that marriage was the norm from the beginning, quoting from Genesis (Matthew 19:4–6). Marriage is established by God, and is a gift from God. Marriage is designed by God as a voluntary, exclusive, and lifelong commitment between one man and one woman. Sexual relations outside of marriage are proscribed because they violate the unity of marriage. The "one flesh" union, or sexual intercourse, is both unitive, expressing and strengthening the couple's love, and procreative, for bearing children and ensuring the continuation of the human race (Genesis 1:28).

Traditionally, family consists of a husband and wife and their children by birth or adoption, and may include, secondarily, other people related by blood or marriage.[29] Some who describe themselves more broadly as evangelical might disagree, but this is not consistent with normative standards. Others may be welcomed into the household, modeling the new family Christians join when they become part of the "household of faith."[30] The married couple is open to the gift of children as living evidence of their self-giving love.[31] Children are regarded as a blessing from God (Psalm 27:5), persons of inestimable value who have an eternal destiny, and are entrusted to parental care. They bring not only happiness, but pain and suffering, which teaches parents patience, endurance, and sacrificial love. Evangelicals' love for children is evidenced by their higher birth rate, which is exceeded only by that of historically black Christian traditions and Mormons.[32]

Whether or not children are born, the couple's faithful, loving relationship has purposes beyond procreation. Monogamous fidelity bears witness by making and keeping promises, in loving response to a promise-making and promise-keeping God. A married couple may express their life-giving purposes through other relationships such as adoption, mentoring, or acting as surrogate grandparents. A proper understanding of children as gifts and not achievements "will affect our motivation for having children and may free us from inordinate anxiety about *whether* we have children and *what* children we have."[33] It frees couples and parents to be courageous in the face of technologically driven decisions about children, and to welcome children, if they do come, for as long as they live.

Marriage, then, as the first institution in society, supports all other societal institutions. Healthy marriages support healthy children—regardless of physical or mental capacities—and families. Healthy families promote healthy institutions, and virtuous institutions promote families where cultivation of many virtues can flourish.[34]

Theological Reflection on Procreation and Reproductive Technologies

Theological reflection, while speaking to current cultural shifts, often lags behind in offering analysis and response. This is particularly evident in the context where medical technologies intersect with procreation. Evangelical theology, while attending to marriage, family, and children, is less robust in its work on reproductive technologies. Physician and bioethicist Megan Best notes, "it is difficult to find a comprehensive [Reformed] theology of the issues surrounding human procreation."[35] The lay evangelical may rely on a naive Biblicism or "proof-texting," searching for Bible verses for explicit direction. In the absence of applicable Scripture, some may assume that silence equates with divine assent. The answer according to theologians Kevin Vanhoozer and Daniel Treier is "a *critical (evangelical) Biblicism* that situates Biblical authority in a broader pattern of authority, one that recognizes the purpose for which the Scriptures have been sent."[36]

Evangelical theology has not been extensively applied to bioethical questions, but as medical technologies become more complex, scholars are taking note[37] and engaging bioethics for the church. Christian ethicist James Thobaben, writing within the Wesleyan tradition, points out that the church has a central responsibility in providing moral guidance in bioethics. Christians hold a view of human flourishing that is not concerned merely with one's own ultimate good, but also with "assist[ing] others toward that true Good to the greatest extent possible," in marked contrast with culturally dominant hyperindividualism.[38] Working within the Reformed tradition, David VanDrunen proposes that Christian bioethics denotes not simply the bioethics practiced by Christians, but distinctively Christian ways of moral reflection on life, health, and death shaped by "what is unique to the Christian experience—that is, salvation in Christ."[39] It is a "moral way of life both respecting the goodness of the original creation and reflecting the achievement of the original creation's *telos* in Christ."[40] Accordingly, Christian bioethics affirms both the goodness and finitude of human beings, eschewing efforts to expand upon or "improve" God's original design.

Both views paint a distinct picture, one where Christians have a different understanding of what it means to be human than does the broader culture. They are called to a higher moral standard, worked out within the faith community that sees a greater purpose for human existence than maximizing individual choice. Bioethical autonomy over reproductive decisions is thus limited and guided by beliefs about procreation, the status of the unborn child, the cultural mandate, the commandment to love one's neighbor, the sovereignty and Providence of God, and the meaning of suffering.

Procreation, for Christians, is the act of begetting, rather than of making, that is, when we "give existence to another human being, not by making him [or her] the end of a project of our will, but by imparting to him [or her] our own being, so that he [or she] is formed by what we are and not by what we intend."[41] Whether marriage is seen primarily as procreative or as relational, separating procreation from the physical union of husband and wife presents the risk of loosening the mystical bond of marriage. Reproduction becomes an act of the will, rather than the fruit of spiritual, emotional, and physical union. Yet, a Christian understanding of human dignity points toward how people live, rather than whether their desires are fulfilled, as central to human dignity and flourishing.[42] In assisted reproduction, fertilization of egg by sperm becomes an object of technical skill, subject to carefully controlled conditions. Giving birth to a child comes to depend upon the techniques and skills of others, and subject to calculated odds of success. The very nature of assisted reproduction tends toward treating the potential child as a project, accomplished with a high financial, physical, and emotional cost. The assumptions behind PNT, and particularly preimplantation genetic testing, instrumentally assess the child. Evangelical understanding of the child as a person in her own right rejects such instrumentalization. Neither embryo de-selection nor abortion for fetal anomaly is an ethical option. To put it crudely, "What parents would think, that is, that if a better version were available, they would be well advised to eliminate their present child, in order to upgrade to a better model?"[43] Yet, the language of IVF suggests the disposability of embryos, with its references to "spares" and embryos in storage, and subjectively grading their quality.[44]

Cultural Mandate

Generally speaking, reproductive technologies are not held by evangelicals to be intrinsically evil, but may be regarded as one instance of humanity's creative powers. Christians are not surprised by contemporary expressions of the stewardship mandate: "Then God blessed them [the male and female], and God said to them, 'Be fruitful and multiply; fill the earth and subdue it; have dominion over the fish of the sea, over the birds of the air, and over every living thing that moves on the earth.'"[45] Also described as the cultural mandate, it is the foundation for creative endeavors in medicine, science, and technology. "Doing technology—the forming and transforming of natural creation with the aid of tools and procedures—is part of human beings' activity as formers of culture," for purposes and by means that are consistent with God's normative will.[46] When understood in the light of Jesus's ministry of healing, the cultural mandate is expressed in compassionate responses to physical suffering, through innovations in all manner of medical technologies. Normative boundaries of those technologies are contested. Non-therapeutic uses of technologies that discriminate against human beings based on actual or potential disability fall outside morally permissible uses. This is consistent with one of the essential limits on human freedom: the power one human being exercises over another, which is "explicitly not given to human beings over one another."[47]

Evangelicals accept this limitation on human freedom that forbids exercise of life and death power over another human being. Both the embryo created via IVF and the unborn child in the womb are human beings, and must be respected as such. The employment of pre-implantation and prenatal tests is a prohibited "dominion" of one human being over another, if the outcome is to prevent the implantation or birth of a child. Prenatal tests administered for benefit of the child would not violate this limitation.[48]

Love Your Neighbor

Christians are commanded to care in practical ways for the least of these as if they were caring for Christ himself (Matthew 25:40), to welcome the stranger in their midst (Exodus 23:9, 12), and to love their neighbor as themselves (Leviticus 19:18; Matthew 22:39; Mark 12:31; Luke 10:27; 1 John 4:11, 20–21). Jesus's instruction regarding children is clear: "Whoever welcomes one of these little children in my name welcomes me."[49] The obligation to welcome and care for the stranger is not contingent upon how similar the stranger is to us. How much more does this obligation apply to the neighbor who is known to us, that is, our own offspring? Children, whether in the womb or the laboratory, are owed, as philosopher and Christian ethicist Agneta Sutton phrases it, "unconditional welcome."[50] The quality of their DNA is not a basis for turning them away at the door. Cameron and DeBaets point out that "as we welcome the strangers of the next generation, they are our guests and not our creatures."[51] Sondra Ely Wheeler similarly states, "Parenting is the most routine and socially essential form of welcoming the stranger."[52]

Sovereignty and Providence of God

While the doctrine of creation accounts for what God did in making the universe and all it contains, the doctrine of God's Providence explains God's continuing and active presence in the world and in our lives. He sustains and maintains his creation, the natural order, not from a remote distance, but as a personal God who offers intimacy to his creatures:

> It means that we are able to live in the assurance that God is present and active in our lives. We are in his care and can therefore face the future confidently, knowing that things are not happening merely by chance. We can pray, knowing that God hears and acts upon our prayers. We can face danger, knowing that he is not unaware and uninvolved.[53]

Confidence in God's loving Providence deepens understanding and appreciation for God's sovereignty, that is, his authority over all creation, including human beings. Whether one believes in general sovereignty, the belief that in giving persons free will, God grants them freedom to make choices, or specific sovereignty, the belief that God brings about all things,[54] both agree that God "causes all things to work together for good to those who love God, to those who are called according to His purpose."[55] God's limitations on human freedom are not signs of divine displeasure, but are safeguards understood in the light of God's character and unfathomable love for human beings. The New Testament contains one of the most profound statements about this love:

> For I am convinced that neither death nor life, neither angels nor demons, neither the present nor the future, nor any powers, neither height nor depth, nor anything else in all creation, will be able to separate us from the love of God that is in Christ Jesus our Lord.[56]

Not even the unexpectedly sad results of a genetic test. The posture of dependence upon God, acknowledgment of his sovereignty, and confidence in his loving care, are particularly poignant in the face of deep suffering and dying,[57] and the suffering of anticipation—finding out that the child one dearly longs for may not be healthy after all. Prenatal testing occurs in the context of an ongoing pregnancy, when the possibility of a genetic or physical defect surfaces. Pre-implantation genetic diagnosis (PGD) most often occurs in the context of infertility, or the desire to avoid transmitting a serious genetically linked disease. Both of these scenarios bring to the surface the question of, and concern about, human suffering.

Suffering

Evangelical perspectives on suffering are at odds with contemporary trends. Those who wish to completely avoid suffering seem to believe "suffering has no purpose and needs to be eradicated," which is consistent with the twin values of Western civilization: relief of suffering and "progress."[58] Suffering is not the same thing as physical pain. As Peterman and Schmutzer describe it,

> Pain is primarily *objective*, external, and typically social or physical as opposed to personal and mental.... Suffering is primarily *internal*, and typically mental or emotional as opposed to physical or social.[59]

One can experience pain without suffering, as in childbirth, and one can suffer without experiencing physical pain, as in grief. One can suffer in anticipation of physical pain, whether one's own or that of a child yet to be born. Parents suffer because they care about their children, and because they want to spare them physical and emotional pain. Discarding embryos that carry genetic mutations for diseases, or terminating pregnancy after a positive prenatal diagnosis could be understood as avoiding the suffering associated with the disease, both for the child and his or her parents.[60]

Christians understand suffering in the context of not only this present earthly life, but ultimate realities. In marked contrast with the dominant contemporary Western view, evangelical views of suffering draw from a deep well of Christian reflections on the subject. These understandings of suffering place it at the center of their faith, pre-eminently, in the suffering and death of Jesus as atonement for the sins of all humankind. People are not left to suffer alone and abandoned, but identify with Christ in his suffering, and are comforted by God in their own suffering (2 Corinthians 1:3–5).

Human suffering is not part of God's original design, but is a result of the curse and sin that infected the world with the fall of Adam and Eve. Christians, like non-Christians, experience physical and emotional suffering, but their response is framed in light of their relationship with Christ. They "suffer in union with Christ (Romans 8:17), who first suffered and then was raised to glory, never to suffer again."[61] Christians believe that suffering is not meaningless, is not endless, and is not solitary. Suffering may be a means of personal refinement to become more like Christ (James 1:2–4; 1 Peter 1:6–7). It can cause us to admit our weakness and dependence upon God's strength (2 Corinthians 1:8–10; 4:7–12). Beyond and through the suffering, there is always hope. Christians live in the belief and knowledge that this fallen physical life is temporary, and that after death, they will be united with Christ in glorified bodies, living with him and fellow believers forever. Thus, the sufferings of this present life are understood within the perspective of eternity (2 Corinthians 4:17; Romans 8:17–27).

Suffering often occurs in the context of infertility. Although there may be other reasons for pursuing IVF, parents who consider PGD most likely are an infertile couple. Prior to considerations of genetic testing, the couple has had to resolve the pain of infertility. Understood in the light of evangelical faith, childlessness is not a meaningless tragedy, to be endured in autonomous isolation. The focus instead is turned toward the larger Christian family, the fellowship or *koinonia*. Christian believers are joined together as one spiritual body, with Jesus Christ as the head. This places the natural family in a new context. As VanDrunen points out, while natural family relationships are important, Christian identity is primarily as members of Christ's body the church, and these supercede family relationships when they conflict (Matthew 10:37; Luke 14:26).[62] These extended spiritual relationships provide that Christians do not suffer alone. Their local church community is a primary source of support, comfort, and encouragement for the couple walking through the issues of infertility. Beyond that, the community is present for the parents who choose to implant their embryos regardless of their genetic imperfections. Some parents who reject PGD altogether will have a child born with a disability. They can anticipate the spiritual, emotional, and practical support of their church family as they welcome the baby and adjust to their new reality. Parenting a child with a disability is not synonymous with lifelong suffering.

Belief and disposition to accept that suffering is an expected part of life turns the focus away from the external specific outcomes, such as ensuring the birth of a healthy child, to the internal matters of the heart. The Christian life is a walk of faithfulness and obedience, oriented not toward external measures of success, but toward growth in character, maturity, and virtue, as evidenced, for example, by the fruit of the Spirit.[63] Suffering in the present life is understood as temporary and passing away, while life to come after death is eternal. That eager anticipation of the time when every tear will be wiped away, and there will be no more sorrows,[64] is especially poignant for those who live with their own, or parent a child with, disability. Although the reasons for a child's disability may never be understood, God's Providence, sovereignty, and unbreakable love for that child are a reality more powerful than life itself. This belief is lived out by families with disability in faithful, hard won, often heartbreaking, honest witness to a reality that the present life is not about the pursuit of perfection or escape from unhappiness and sorrow, but about trusting the loving God of the universe who one day *will* make everything new (Revelation 21:5).

Disability crosses a wide spectrum. Much of the pain experienced by people with disabilities and their families is not physical; it is social, arising from the attitudes of and rejection by others. As someone who lives with and writes about disability, Christopher Ralston describes disability as the negative mismatch between the individual and their surrounding environment.[65] However, people with disabilities do suffer, and the ways we talk about and respond to that can gloss over the complexities. Amy Julia Becker, who has written about faith, family, and disability, and whose first child was born with Down syndrome, explains: "Disability and suffering are not one and the same, and yet a theological response to genetic testing and disability must affirm life's goodness while also taking into account the real pain experienced by families and individuals with disabilities"[66] In Becker's assessment, evangelicals exhibit greater receptivity to disability and the elderly than the culture at large.[67] Evangelical commitment to respecting people with disability is expressed in practical ways.[68] Even so, Becker suggests that there is a gap in how the church equips people to choose and act in accordance with their beliefs. Pastors are needed to help guide couples in thinking how their theological views inform whether and how they would use prenatal testing. Finally, she observes that the same theological and ethical questions that are asked of prenatal testing should also be posed for IVF and PGD.[69]

EVANGELICAL PERSPECTIVES ON PRENATAL TESTING

Evangelical attitudes about prenatal testing logically connect with attitudes about abortion. Their pro-life convictions include respecting the dignity of the unborn child who has functional or structural abnormalities, which would bar abortion for those reasons (which would manifest as a physical disability or genetic disease) Instead, the couple encountering this can anticipate the presence of a loving, caring community of faith who surrounds them with spiritual resources such as fervent prayer, and practical resources such as caring for the baby's siblings. If the baby survives, family and friends will welcome the new arrival, for as long as he or she lives. The neonate with disability may also be cared for via perinatal hospice,[70] helping the couple to be the best parents they can, for as long as they can. The death of their child is commemorated through a funeral or memorial service. This contrasts with an abortion decision, particularly of a wanted but genetically anomalous child, which may be carried out in secrecy, with no burial or public acknowledgment of the loss of a child, and which may carry higher levels of grief and post-traumatic stress.[71]

Testing of IVF embryos raises slightly different considerations than abortion. A confirmed pregnancy has not begun, the woman's body has not begun bonding with the child, and the emotional attachments between parent and child may be different. The couple struggling with infertility is less likely to bond with embryos in a petri dish, and the desire for a child at any cost understandably may overwhelm all other considerations. Whether or not pregnancy will occur seems to be in the hands of the doctor. The medical and technological nature of the process is far removed from the preferred context of procreation, potentially rendering the child as an abstraction. The couple may simply follow the doctor's advice regarding preimplantation testing, without considering the moral implications for the fate of their embryos. The reality often sets in after an unsuccessful pregnancy attempt, after the birth of one or more children, or after they decide their family is complete. These events may trigger grief, guilt, or a sense of loss of their embryonic children. They may struggle, sometimes painfully so, with a decision about any cryopreserved embryos.[72]

Theological and ethical considerations for PGD are similar to those regarding the use of embryos in stem cell research. Theologically, embryos are creatures made in God's image, intrinsically valued and eternally loved by him. Ethically, as biologically human beings, embryos should not be subjected to lethal experimentation. Simply because a vast number exist in cryopreservation does not justify regarding them as a resource for medical research. Evangelicals oppose human embryonic stem cell (HESC) research more than does the general population, driven by the belief that human life should be protected from harm from the moment of conception.[73] Opposition to HESC research would be consistent with opposition to discarding embryos after PGD or donating them for research.

Both prenatal and preimplantation testing are rapidly becoming routine. The offer of prenatal testing is standard care for older mothers, who are at higher risk of chromosomal abnormalities. With the development of the noninvasive tests, the offer of both diagnostic and screening PNT is rapidly becoming routine for all pregnancies.[74] The protocol may lead women to view their pregnancy with hesitancy, not bonding with their child until all results are in, contributing to the modern phenomenon of the "tentative pregnancy."[75]

The pressure only increases with IVF. The couple has already invested financial, physical, and emotional resources directed toward "producing" a child and testing invites the pursuit of not just any child, but of a particular kind of child. The temptation of such choices is that the language and habits of commodification can overtake the procreative impulse. The pursuit of a healthy child, while understandable and desirable, is uncomfortably close to the eugenics impulses of the early twentieth century. More than twenty-five years ago, Sutton warned that "it will be found that the logic behind selective abortion and prenatal diagnosis, with a view to abortion of fetuses affected by illness or malformation, is the logic of negative eugenics."[76]

Eugenic Concerns

Evangelicals have historically rejected efforts to improve human beings through science, in their concerns over eugenics. In her account of the involvement of American religious leaders in the eugenics movement of the late nineteenth and early twentieth centuries, Christine Rosen observes that leaders of nearly every Protestant denomination, Jews, and Catholics became involved in eugenics, "and they overwhelmingly represented the liberal wings of their respective faiths."[77] Evangelical Protestants, however, stood in marked contrast to their liberal and modernist counterparts, focusing on salvation and the eternal destiny of their fellow creatures, rather than on bringing about God's kingdom on earth through progressive reform and confidence in the temporal perfectibility of humankind.

Religious leaders who advocated eugenics were motivated by "compassion, empathy, and a deep sense of social responsibility," even as they were blind to the devastating and genocidal implications of eugenics.[78] They embraced the idea of scientific control that would improve the social conditions of humanity by encouraging breeding among the healthiest, but also by the forced sterilization of the less desirable classes, which overwhelmingly included more recent immigrants and the feeble-minded.

The eugenicists' understandable motivations of "compassion, empathy, and a deep sense of social responsibility," seem to have resurfaced. This time, they are not directed toward discouraging procreation among the "unfit," but toward parental autonomy and choice. With the advent of genetic technologies, options have expanded beyond contraception and sterilization. Indeed, through PNT and the option to terminate or discard, parents may exercise control after conception, in the lab and in the womb. It can be argued that instead of the "hard eugenics" of governmental control, we are in the era of the "soft eugenics" of parental choice. The assumption of autonomous decision making, however, may one day be limited by eugenic goals, as reflected in ethicists' admonitions to parents about their reproductive choices and responsibilities.

Some ethicists have argued that the availability of genetic technologies implies an obligation to employ them in furtherance of the goals of eliminating genetic disease. In 2011, a group of geneticists, fertility experts, and ethicists recommended that where IVF is publicly funded, objective criteria be imposed, "regardless of the preferences of the couple," restricting parental choice over their embryos.[79] Ethicist Julian

Savulescu argues for the principle of "procreative beneficence," obligating parents, where reasonably possible, to select an embryo that is most likely to have the best life; he accepts selecting for sex and for intelligence as ethical, "even if this maintains or increases social inequality."[80] Worries about coercion after positive test results are not unfounded. Women have recounted their experiences of being pressured to abort following an unexpected prenatal diagnosis.[81] Pressures may be even harder to resist when the embryo resides in a petri dish. The consequences of their decision may be difficult. Evangelical couples are finding their suffering in welcoming a child with disability is compounded by the puzzlement, ostracism, penly expressed critical judgments, or even hostility of others.

Parents' Experiences with Positive Findings

An analysis integrating the findings of qualitative research studies of parents who received a positive prenatal diagnosis of any fetal impairment characterized their unique experiences: they are "distinctive among catastrophic perinatal events by virtue of the chosen losses and lost choices it engenders."[82] A positive diagnosis was a traumatic life event and devastating for women. Researchers Sandelowski and Barroso admitted that their study could be read to "showcase the negative consequences of advances in reproductive technology."[83] All the studies they reviewed suggested that a positive finding forces parents into an array of decisions: about continuing the pregnancy, whether to view the remains of their child, how to handle those remains, and whether and what to tell others. Couples struggled with the conflict between a wanted pregnancy and *not* wanting the particular child they conceived, due to genetic impairment. The outcomes for couples who continue pregnancy, particularly minority couples "who are often prominent among expectant parents continuing pregnancy after positive fetal diagnosis," are not well studied.[84] Minority couples might be included among evangelical couples who reject termination after an unexpected diagnosis.

Although the experiences and behaviors of couples facing disappointing PNT results are not well studied, there is some research regarding attitudes among all evangelicals. For example, evangelicals were among respondents to a survey on Christian attitudes about assisted reproductive technologies.[85] Open-ended comments in response to genetic screening in several hypothetical situations expressed sympathy for parents trying to avoid a serious disability, affirmation of the child's right to live, and concerns that genetic screening might increase discrimination against the disabled. Another study reported that attitudes toward abortion for genetic defect became less favorable over time (1990–1996); the study identified but did not define "Protestant Fundamentalist" respondents, which might include "evangelical."[86] The study found that those with a higher frequency of church attendance, which would include evangelicals, were less likely to accept abortion for a positive test.[87] A subsequent study

(1996–2004) found that the increase in those who would not choose abortion was "about twice as large as that between 1990 and 1996," and particularly noticeable among "those who categorized their religion as fundamentalist."[88] One researcher who included evangelicals, fundamentalists, and Pentecostals as "largely conservative Protestants," found that many do not want to use reproductive genetic technologies to eliminate suffering.[89] They reasoned that it is wrong "to eliminate suffering by ending the life of the sufferer," and that genetic tests imply "that those who have genetic qualities that lead to suffering are somehow less valuable to society."[90]

Regardless of research about attitudes of evangelicals, many evangelical women who are pro-life simply decline prenatal tests. Dr. John Thorpe, director of women's healthcare at the University of North Carolina, states that ultrasound exams are adequate for identifying fetuses that will require urgent care at birth, obviating the need for invasive testing.[91] Some couples do go ahead with testing, but with non-lethal intentions for their child. Becker identifies three purposes for prenatal testing other than selective abortion: time to prepare to welcome their child, time to learn about their child's disability and support services, and time to grieve for the child they had hoped to have.[92] Her conclusions are in line with beliefs about loving one's neighbor, the Providence of God in caring for their baby, and the community of faith who surrounds the couple in their grief and in the new reality of their life parenting a child with disability.

Commodification Concerns

Apart from decisions about whether to discard an affected embryo, PNT raises additional concerns for evangelicals. A negative test may yield a false sense of confidence that all is well. Birth of a child with an undetected anomaly may understandably trigger intense disappointment, grief, or even anger. The desire for one's child to be healthy is good, and distress over a positive genetic test is natural. PGD and PNT reveal the child's sex, and for many evangelical parents, ultrasound is desired for that reason alone, not to reject a son or daughter via sex selective abortion, but to more intimately personalize their relationship with their unborn child, often naming the baby during pregnancy.

The average cost for one IVF cycle is $15,000; PGD adds up to $6,000(which insurance may not cover).[93] The costs raise concerns about wise stewardship of financial and medical resources. The financial implications cause couples to question the wisdom of pursuing IVF cycles coupled with PGD. Instead, like many evangelicals couples who are not infertile, they opt for adoption, caring for children who are already born. Evangelical attitudes about disability extend beyond children that are genetically or biologically connected. They extend to welcoming children through adoption, whether ethnically similar or not, and whether or not the child has a disability.

Adoption

Adoption provides the context for introducing one more theological theme, the great reversal, most fully developed in the teachings of Jesus and in other New Testament writings. Those who are deemed unimportant in this life will be honored in the next. Jesus said, "But many who are first will be last, and many who are last will be first."[94] Later, he taught that those who invited the stranger to come in were not only caring for that person, but that "whatever you did for one of the least of these brothers and sisters, you did for me."[95] Although the commendation was couched in tender love, he coupled it with a warning, that in ignoring or rejecting "one of the least of these," they rejected him and eternal life with him, choosing instead eternal punishment. One way that Christians care for the stranger and the "least of these" is through adoption.[96] Adoption invites a reversal of attitude about children. Theological ethicist Gilbert Meilaender describes it:

> When we remember again the number of needy children who go unadopted precisely because of their needs, when we consider the degree to which new reproductive technologies have—in a very short time—begun to teach our society to think of reproduction as a right to which everyone is entitled, when we ponder the implications of these technologies for our society's understanding of children, we must ask whether Christians should not call a halt—at least for themselves.[97]

In rejecting the implications and consequences of PNT, and perhaps all reproductive technologies, evangelicals embody their countercultural beliefs. Indeed, their concern for children who need a stable home outpaces the rest of society. Evangelicals are "more than twice as likely to adopt as the general population, and 50 percent more likely to foster."[98] Adoption is even more common among evangelical leaders, where 30 percent have adopted members in their immediate family; 14 percent were children with special needs.[99]

Adoption, then, is a hospitable alternative to PNT, an example of the "great reversal" of welcoming the child who presently exists, rather than pursuing a genetically acceptable "child of one's own."[100]

Conclusion

Evangelical theological teaching and personal expression of attitudes about prenatal testing might best be illustrated by the life experience of one couple, Erik and Cristina.[101] Early in the pregnancy of their second child, Erik and Cristina learned of a potential problem with their baby. Prenatal testing revealed that they were having a girl, and that she had Trisomy 13, a serious untreatable chromosomal anomaly usually lethal within the first year. Stunned by the news, they shared it with their local Christian community. The community surrounded them with fervent prayers, in faith, for healing. Cristina suffered for most of the pregnancy, knowing that unless God chose to intervene she was carrying a daughter who would be born dying. Jane Ellen was born, and she had not been healed. Cristina, supported by Christian friends, devoted herself to loving Jane Ellen every day she lived. One month later, the baby died. Again, their church community enveloped Erik and Cristina with love and prayer; hundreds attended the memorial service. At no time during their entire ordeal were they or their daughter alone or unloved. Despite their anguish and pain, they trusted in God's sovereignty, Providential care, and ultimate purposes for them and the life of their daughter. They mourn, but they do not despair. They live each day in the confident, bitterly tested hope that they will be reunited with their daughter in her glorified, perfect body, for eternity, in the presence of God and rejoicing with the entire family of faith.

Not only did this couple's experience of grief give witness to the gracious presence of God through the Spirit and in his church, it also confirms that—unlike the dominant pro-abortion strategies today—prenatal testing can be used within a prayerful, life-affirming, and God-honoring framework. This, in sum, is the evangelical perspective on prenatal testing.

Notes

1. Leviticus 19:18; Mark 12:31, New International Version (NIV).
2. Gary B. Ferngren, *Medicine and Health Care in Early Christianity* (Baltimore, MD: Johns Hopkins University Press, 2009).
3. Michael J. Gorman, *Abortion and the Early Church* (Eugene, OR: Wipf and Stock, 1998).
4. Exodus 20:13, King James Version (KJV).
5. Gorman, *Abortion and the Early Church*.
6. See, e.g., Mark Hutchinson and John Wolffe, *A Short History of Global Evangelicalism* (Cambridge: Cambridge University Press, 2012); Mark A. Noll, *A History of Christianity in the United States and Canada* (Grand Rapids, MI: Eerdmans, 1992); Douglas A. Sweeney, *The American Evangelical Story: A History of the Movement* (Grand Rapids, MI: Baker, 2005).
7. "Number of Evangelicals Worldwide," Lausanne Global Analysis, https://www.lausanne.org/lgc-transfer/number-of-evangelicals-worldwide.
8. See, e.g., 25.4 percent as reported by "Religious Landscape Study," Pew Research Center, http://www.pewforum.org/religious-landscape-study/; or 38 percent as reported by "Survey Explores Who Qualifies as an Evangelical," Barna Group, January 18, 2007, https://www.barna.com/research/survey-explores-who-qualifies-as-an-evangelical/.
9. Barna Group. See also, "Evangelical Beliefs and Practices," Pew Research Center, Religion & Public Life, http://www.pewforum.org/2011/06/22/global-survey-beliefs/
10. "What Is an Evangelical?" National Association of Evangelicals, https://www.nae.net/what-is-an-evangelical/. The NAE explicitly relies on historian David Bebbington's

characterization of the four evangelical distinctives. David W. Bebbington, *Evangelicalism in Modern Britain: A History from the 1730s to the 1980s* (London: Unwim Hyman, 1989).

11. Gerald R. McDermott, "Introduction," in *The Oxford Handbook of Evangelical Theology*, ed. Gerald R. McDermott (Oxford: Oxford University Press, 2010), 3–18. But, see Mark Noll, Cornelius Plantinga, Jr. and David Wells, "Evangelical Theology Today," *Theology Today* 51, no. 4 (1995): 495–507.

12. As there is no single evangelical theological perspective, in what follows I shall frequently refer to "the evangelical account," "evangelical theology," or "evangelical perspective." These are descriptive of a mainstream evangelical perspective. Contrasting evangelical theological views are noted.

    For the purposes of this chapter, *evangelical* may be used interchangeably with *Christian*, particularly in discussions that are broadly applicable to confessional Christianity.

13. Cherith Fee Nordling, "The Human Person in the Christian Story," in *The Cambridge Companion to Evangelical Theology*, ed. Timothy Larsen and Daniel J. Treier (Cambridge, UK: Cambridge University Press, 2007), 65.

14. Charles Sherlock, *The Doctrine of Humanity* (Downers Grove, IL: InterVarsity Press, 1997), 29.

15. Genesis 1:26–27.

16. Genesis 1:28, New King James Version (NKJV).

17. Nigel M. de S. Cameron and Amy Michelle DeBaets, "Germline Gene Modification and the Human Condition before God," in *Design and Destiny: Jewish and Christian Perspectives on Human Germline Modification*, ed. Ronald Cole-Turner (Cambridge, MA: MIT Press, 2008), 104.

18. Gorman, *Abortion and the Early Church*.

19. John T. Noonan, Jr. "Abortion and the Catholic Church: A Summary History," *Natural Law Forum*, Paper 126 (1967): 85–131, http://scholarship.law.nd.edu/cgi/viewcontent.cgi?article=1125&context=nd_naturallaw_forum.

20. Ibid., 130–131.

21. John Jefferson Davis, *Abortion and the Christian: What Every Believer Should Know* (Philipsburg, NJ: Presbyterian and Reformed Publishing, 1984), 61.

22. "Resolutions," Southern Baptist Convention, accessed July 28, 2023, https://www.sbc.net/resource-library/resolutions/resolution-on-abortion-2/ (1971). https://www.sbc.net/resource-library/resolutions/resolution-on-abortion-3/ (1976) https://www.sbc.net/resource-library/resolutions/resolution-on-abortion-6/ (1980). In a 2022 resolution, the Souther Baptist Convention referenced its more than twenty resolutions supporting "abortion-vulnerable women." https://www.sbc.net/resource-library/resolutions/on-anticipation-of-a-historic-moment-in-the-pro-life-movement/ .

23. See, e.g., Matthew Miller, "How the Evangelical Church Awoke to the Abortion Issue: The Convergent Labors of Harold O. J. Brown, Francis Schaeffer, and C. Everett Koop," *Reformation 21*, March 2013, http://www.reformation21.org/articles/how-the-evangelical-church-awoke-to-the-abortion-issue-the-convergent-labors-of.php; Albert Mohler, "Whatever Happened to the Human Race?—A 25th Anniversary," Albertmohler.com, January 26, 2004, http://www.albertmohler.com/2004/01/26/whatever-happened-to-the-human-race-a-25th-anniversary/.

24. C. Ben Mitchell, "Theological Approaches to Contemporary Life," *The Oxford Handbook of Evangelical Theology*, ed. Gerald R. McDermott (Oxford: Oxford University Press, 2010), 492.

25. D. Gareth Jones, *Brave New People: Ethical Issues at the Commencement of Life* (Grand Rapids, MI: Eerdmans, 1985), 162.
26. Ibid., 183.
27. Ibid., 150.
28. Ibid., 183.
29. See, e.g., Andreas J. Kostenberger and David W. Jones, *God, Marriage, and Family: Rebuilding the Biblical Foundation* (Wheaton, IL: Crossway Books, 2010).
30. In the Episcopal order of service for baptism, the newly baptized is greeted with these words: "We receive you into the household of faith." Episcopal Church, *The Book of Common Prayer and Administration of the Sacraments and Other Rites and Ceremonies of the Church: Together with the Psalter or Psalms of David According to the Use of the Episcopal Church* (New York: Seabury Press, 1979), 308.
31. This is not gift in the sense of conferring ownership, but stewardship. "We receive children in trust from God, and with the gift always come the claim of God." Hessel Bouma III, Douglas Diekema, Edward Langerak, Theodore Rottman, and Allen Verhey, *Christian Faith, Health, and Medical Practice* (Grand Rapids, MI: Eerdmans, 1989), 198.
32. "America's Changing Religious Landscape," Pew Research Center on Religion and Public Life, May 12, 2015, http://www.pewforum.org/2015/05/12/americas-changing-religious-landscape/; Sarah Eekhoff Zylstra, "Pew: Evangelicals Stay Strong as America Crumbles," *Christianity Today*, May 11, 2015, http://www.christianitytoday.com/gleanings/2015/may/pew-evangelicals-stay-strong-us-religious-landscape-study.html.
33. Bouma et al., *Christian Faith, Health, and Medical Practice*, 204.
34. David Van Drunen, "What Is Christian about Christian Bioethics?" *Christian Bioethics* 21, no. 3 (2015): 334–355.
35. Megan Best, *Fearfully and Wonderfully Made* (Kingsford, Australia: Matthias Media, 2012), 12.
36. Kevin J. Vanhoozer and Daniel J. Treier, *Theology and the Mirror of Scripture: A Mere Evangelical Account* (Downers Grove, IL: IVP Academic, 2015), 85 (emphasis in original).
37. Dennis Hollinger, "Can Bioethics Be Evangelical?" *Journal of Religious Ethics* 17, no. 2 (1989): 161–79; Edwin Hui, *At the Beginning of Life: Dilemmas in Theological Bioethics* (Downers Grove, IL: InterVarsity Press, 2002); Patrick T. Smith and Fabrice Jotterand, "Toward a Common Grace Christian Bioethics: A Reformed Protestant Engagement with H. Tristram Engelhardt, Jr.," *Christian Bioethics* 20, no. 2 (2014): 229–245; James R. Thobaben, "Bioethics After Christendom is Gone: A Methodist Evangelical Perspective," *Christian Bioethics* 21, no. 3 (2015): 282–302; Van Drunen, "What Is Christian about Christian Bioethics?" 334–355.
38. Thobaben, "Bioethics after Christendom is Gone," 297.
39. Van Drunen, "What Is Christian about Christian Bioethics?" 335.
40. Ibid., 346.
41. Oliver O'Donovan, *Begotten or Made?* (Oxford, UK: Clarendon Press, 1964), 15.
42. Gilbert Meilaender, *Neither Beast nor God: The Dignity of the Human Person* (New York: Encounter Books, 2009).
43. Ryan T. Anderson and Christopher Tollefsen, "Biotech Enhancement and Natural Law," *New Atlantis* 20 (2008): 79–103, 90.
44. Allison E. Baxter Bendus, Jacob F. Mayer, Sharon K. Shipley, and William H. Catherino, "Interobserver and Intraobserver Variation in Day 3 Embryo Grading," *Fertility and Sterility* 86, no. 6 (2006): 1608–1615.

45. Genesis 1:28, New King James Version (NKJV).
46. Stephen V. Monsma, ed., *Responsible Technology: A Christian Perspective* (Grand Rapids, MI: Eerdmans, 1986).
47. Cameron and DeBaets, "Germline Gene Modification," 98.
48. Theological conclusions about marriage, procreation, and the value of the embryo would preclude IVF that uses donor gametes or creates more embryos than will be transferred in one cycle (thereby necessitating discarding or cryopreservation). In actual practice, however, evangelical couples often end up with "excess" embryos, perhaps unwittingly, that were cryopreserved. The dilemma of how to preserve the lives of these embryos was the primary impetus behind the movement toward embryo donation and adoption. Hannah Strege, the first child born through embryo adoption, is now eighteen years old, and will be attending an evangelical university. Shannon M. Hoffman, "'Snowflake' Baby: 'I Feel Lucky That I Was Given A Chance At Life.'" *Reporter-Herald*, June 24, 2017, http://www.reporterherald.com/news/loveland-local-news/ci_31091141/i-feel-lucky-that-i-was-given-chance.
49. Mark 9:37, New International Version (NIV).
50. Agneta Sutton, "The Case against Genetic Perfection," *Catholic Medical Quarterly* 61, no. 3 (2011): 30–35.
51. Cameron and DeBaets, "Germline Gene Modification," 93–118.
52. Sondra Ely Wheeler, "Making Babies? Genetic Engineering and the Character of Parenthood," *Sojourners* 28, no. 3 (May/June 1999): 14.
53. J. Millard Erickson, *Christian Theology*, 3rd ed. (Grand Rapids, MI: Baker Academic, 2013), 359.
54. Erickson, *Christian Theology*.
55. Romans 8:28, New King James Version (NKJV).
56. Romans 8:38–39, New International Version (NIV).
57. Darrell W. Amundson, "Suffering and the Sovereignty of God: One Evangelical's Perspective on Doctor-Assisted Suicide," *Christian Bioethics* 1, no. 3 (1995): 285–313.
58. John H. Evans, *Contested Reproduction: Genetic Technologies, Religion, and Public Debate* (Minneapolis, MNL Fortress Press, 2010).
59. Gerald W. Peterman, *Between Pain and Grace: A Biblical Theology of Suffering* (Chicago, IL, Moody Publishers, 2016), n.p.
60. Ibid.
61. Van Drunen, "What Is Christian about Christian Bioethics?" 350.
62. Ibid., 334–355.
63. "But the fruit of the Spirit is love, joy, peace, patience, kindness, goodness, faithfulness, gentleness, self-control; against such things there is no law." Galatians 5:22–23, New American Standard Bible (NASB).
64. "And God will wipe away every tear from their eyes; there shall be no more death, nor sorrow, nor crying. There shall be no more pain, for the former things have passed away." Revelation 21:4, New King James Version (NKJV).
65. C. Christopher Hook and D. Christopher Ralston, "Hope, Suffering, and Disability" (Paper presented at The Center for Bioethics and Human Dignity's 2016 Academy of Fellows Consultation, Trinity International University, Deerfield, IL, February 5–6, 2016), https://cbhd.org/content/hope-suffering-and-disability.
66. Amy Julia Becker, "The Good Life," *First Things*, December 31, 2008, https://www.firstthings.com/web-exclusives/2008/12/the-good-life.
67. Interview with Amy Julia Becker, October 25, 2016.

68. Examples include a global ministry that provides wheelchairs, family retreats, training resources, disability training and awareness, and scholarly research (Joni and Friends); overnight respite and day programs for children (Jill's House); residential living arrangements and related services for adults with intellectual disabilities (STARS Family Services); and other support (Stephen Ministries, Fetal Hope Foundation).
69. Interview with Amy Julia Becker, October 25, 2016.
70. Byron C. Calhoun, Peter Napolitano, Melissa Terry, Carie Bussey, and Nathan J. Hoeldtke, "Perinatal Hospice: Comprehensive Care for the Family of a Fetus with a Lethal Condition," *Journal of Reproductive Medicine* 48, no 5 (2003): 343–348.
71. Marijke J. Korenromp, Godelieve C. M. L. Page-Christiaens, Jan van den Bout, Eduard J. H. Mulder, and Gerard H. A. Visser, "Adjustment to Termination of Pregnancy for Fetal Anomaly: A Longitudinal Study in Women at 4, 8, and 16 Months," *American Journal of Obstetrics and Gynecology* 201, no. 2 (2009): 160. e1–160.e7, doi:10.1016/j.ajog.2009.04.007
72. Tamar Lewin, "Industry's Growth Leads to Leftover Embryos, and Painful Choices," *New York Times*, June 17. 2015.
73. John Bryant and Mary Gudgin, "Attitudes amongst Young Adults to Use of Embryonic Stem cells in Research and Therapy: Comparison of Evangelical Christian Students with Non-Christian Students," *Science and Christian Belief* 20, no. 1 (2008): 91–104. But see "Abortion Viewed in Moral Terms: Fewer See Stem Cell Research and IVF as Moral Issues," Pew Research Center on Religion & Public Life, August 15, 2013, http://www.pewforum.org/2013/08/15/abortion-viewed-in-moral-terms/.
74. Mark Wheach, "ACOG Issues New Prenatal Testing Guidelines," Prenatal Information Consortium, April 29, 2016, https://prenatalinformation.org/2016/04/29/acog-issues-new-prenatal-testing-guidelines/.
75. Barbara Katz Rothman, *The Tentative Pregnancy: How Amniocentesis Changes the Experience of Motherhood* (New York: Norton, 1993).
76. Agneta Sutton, *Prenatal Diagnosis: Confronting the Ethical Issues* (London: Linacre Centre, 1990), 47–48.
77. Christine Rosen, *Preaching Eugenics: Religious Leaders and the American Eugenics Movement* (Oxford, UK: Oxford University Press, 2004), 14.
78. Ibid., 23.
79. Kristien Hens, Wybo Dondorp, Alan H. Handyside, Joyce Harper, Ainsley J. Newson, Guido Pennings, Christoph Rehmann-Sutter, and Guido de Wert, "Dynamics and Ethics of Comprehensive Preimplantation Genetic Testing: A Review of the Challenges," *Human Reproduction Update* 19, no. 4 (2013): 366–375.
80. Julian Savulescu, "Procreative Beneficence: Why We Should Select the Best Children," *Bioethics* 15, no. 5–6 (2001): 413.
81. See, e.g., Melinda Tankard Riest, *Defiant Birth: Women Who Resist Medical Eugenics* (North Melbourne, Vic.: Spinifex Press, 2006); Margarete Sandelowski and Julie Barroso, "The Travesty of Choosing after Positive Prenatal Diagnosis," *JOGNN: Journal of Obstetric, Gynecologic & Neonatal Nursing* 34, no. 3 (2005): 307–318; Jennifer Guon, Benjamin S. Wilfond, Barbara Farlow, Tracy Brazg, and Annie Janvier, "Our Children Are Not a Diagnosis: The Experience of Parents Who Continue Their Pregnancy after a Prenatal Diagnosis of Trisomy 13 or 18," *American Journal of Medical Genetics Part A* 164, no. 2 (2014): 308–318.
82. Margarete Sandelowski and Julie Barroso, "The Travesty of Choosing after Positive Prenatal Diagnosis," *Journal of Obstetric, Gynecologic, & Neonatal Nursing* 34, no. 3 (2005): 315, doi:10.1177/0884217505276291.

83. Ibid., 316.
84. Ibid.
85. Megan Best, Principal Investigator, "Attitudes toward Assisted Reproductive Technologies," March 12, 2013–July 13, 2013, sponsored by the Center for Bioethics & Human Dignity, unpublished findings. The online survey garnered 1599 responses (not all completed). Cross-tabs for male/female, and denominations are not available.
86. Eleanor Singer, Amy D. Corning, and Toni Antonucci, "Attitudes toward Genetic Testing and Fetal Diagnosis, 1990–1996," *Journal of Health and Social Behavior* 40, no. 4 (1999): 429–445.
87. Ibid.
88. Eleanor Singer, Mick P. Couper, Trivellor E. Raghunathan, John Van Howeyk, and Toni C. Antonunucci, "Trends in U.S. Attitudes toward Genetic Testing, 1990–2004," *Public Opinion Quarterly* 72, no. 3 (2008): 446–458, doi:10.1093/poq/nfn033.
89. John H. Evans, "Religious Belief, Perceptions of Human Suffering, and Support for Reproductive Genetic Technology," *Journal of Health Politics, Policy and Law* 31, no. 6 (2006): 1069.
90. Ibid.
91. Amy Julia Becker, "Should Christians Pursue Prenatal Testing?" *Christianity Today*, January 2013, http://www.christianitytoday.com/women/2013/january/should-christian-women-pursue-prenatal-testing.html.
92. Ibid.
93. "The Costs of Infertility Treatment," *Resolve*, http://www.resolve.org/family-building-options/making-treatment-affordable/the-costs-of-infertility-treatment.html?referrer=https://www.google.com/.
    Marissa Conrad and James Grifo, "How Much Does IVF Cost?" *Forbes*, accessed July 28, 2023, https://www.forbes.com/health/family/how-much-does-ivf-cost/.
    "The Cost of IVF by City," Fertility IQ, accessed July 28, 2023, https://www.fertilityiq.com/topics/ivf/the-cost-of-ivf-by-city.
94. Matthew 19:30, New International Version (NIV).
95. Matthew 25:40, New International Version (NIV).
96. See, e.g., Aaron Halbert, "My Wife and I Are White Evangelicals. Here's Why We Chose to Give Birth to Black Triplets," *Washington Post*, April 21, 2016, https://www.washingtonpost.com/news/acts-of-faith/wp/2016/04/21/my-wife-and-i-are-white-evangelicals-heres-why-we-chose-to-give-birth-to-black-triplets/?utm_term=.f7180c678244.
97. Gilbert Meilaender, "A Child of One's Own: At What Price?" in *The Reproduction Revolution*, ed. John F. Kilner, Paige C. Cunningham and W. David Hager (Grand Rapids, MI: Eerdmans, 2000): 45.
98. Kelly Rosati, "How to Address America's Foster Care Crisis? It Takes a Village," *Christianity Today*, May 2016, http://www.christianitytoday.com/women/2016/may/why-churches-are-key-to-addressing-americas-foster-care-cri.html; see also Ethics Daily Staff, "Christians More than Twice as Likely to Adopt a Child," *Ethics Daily*, November 8, 2013, http://www.ethicsdaily.com/christians-more-than-twice-as-likely-to-adopt-a-child-cms-21267.
99. "Adoption Among Evangelicals," National Association of Evangelicals, November 2015, https://www.nae.net/adoption-among-evangelicals/.
100. Meilaender, "A Child of One's Own," 36–45.
101. While the details of this narrative are true, derived from a firsthand account by the couple, pseudonyms are used to protect the privacy of the family.

Index

For the benefit of digital users, indexed terms that span two pages (e.g., 52–53) may, on occasion, appear on only one of those pages.

'Abd al-Barr, Ibn, 184, 186
'Abd al-Razzāq al-Ṣan'ānī, *Muṣannaf*, 444–46, 448–50
abortifacient, evangelical views on, 373, 380–81, 384
abortion
    binary approach, 446–47, 451–52
    Catholic views on, 213–14, 215, 403–16, 461, 462–63, 464–65, 504
    Christian tradition and views, 213, 424–26, 526–27
    contraceptive use and, 439n.87
    death of fetus as side effect and, 414, 415–16
    debate, 459
    evangelical views of, 373–74, 530–31
    fetus images and, 427
    gradualist approach, 445–46, 447, 451–53
    indirect or non-intentional, 415–16
    induced vs. spontaneous, 443
    international Islamic forums and, 456
    intractable opinions on, 421
    Islamic views and rulings on, 65, 75–76, 214, 455–57
    John Paul II on, 403, 404
    Judaism and Jewish views on, 18, 122, 212, 390–91, 395, 397–400
    language of direct and indirect killing and, 414
    in Latin America, 211
    moral debates and, 459, 461–62
    parents' special responsibility to their child and, 414–15
    as political issue, 459–60
    prenatal diagnostic screening and testing and, 503, 507, 519n.36, 521n.58
    Protestant views of, 47, 422, 427–29, 433–34
    public opinion and, 459–70
    rape and, 456–57
    relevance of religious differences in, 467–70
    reproductive justice and, 431
    respectable debate on, 215
    rights of women vs. rights of embryos, 414–15
    Shiite sources and, 451–53
    stalemate in debate, 421–22, 431
    Sunni sources and, 444–47, 453–55
    Supreme Court rulings on, 369n.5
    terminology in Islamic sources, 444
    women an, 430–31, 432
    See also miscarriage; souls and ensoulment
abortion policy
    demographic concerns and, 470
    public opinion and, 460–61
    secularism and, 470
    social and political bases of, 460–61
    variations in national, 460–61, 469–70
Abraham, 178–79, 289, 309–10
abstinence, 373, 374, 378–79
activism, evangelicals and, 527–28
Act to Provide for the Adoption of Children (Massachusetts Adoption Act), 250–51
Acts of the Apostles, 301
Aderet, Rabbi Solomon ben, 224, 235n.38
adoption
    biblical contexts for, 284–306
    Canadian ban on Pakistani, 253–54n.3
    in Christian Scriptures, 284–96
    closed records and, 305–6
    conversion of minor children to Judaism and, 230–31
    definitions of, 240
    Esther in Old Testament, 287–88

adoption (*cont.*)
  evangelical views on, 542
  exploitation of the poor and the widow, 304–5
  gay couples/parents and, 192, 199–200
  in Greco-Roman context, 295–96
  intercountry, 304–5
  Islamic conceptions vs. modern Western conceptions, 250–51
  in Islam and Islamic law and, 239, 240–41, 242–49, 338–39
  Jewish law vs. American law, 221–22, 226–27, 231–32
  in Judaism and Jewish law and, 125–26, 223, 225–27, 231–32, 232n.4
  as long-term foster care, 221–22
  natural law theory and, 101
  in New Testament, 289–96
  in Old Testament, 284–89
  open vs. closed, 229–30
  in pre-modern or classical Islamic law, 242–49
  rabbinic views on, 230–31
  relationship with natural family and, 305–6
  as relative good, 304
  religion and, 239
  "right to know" and, 226–27
  in Roman law, 292–96
  in US, 221–22, 226–27, 231–32, 250–51, 305–6
  See also embryo adoption
adultery
  and assisted reproductive technology in Jewish context, 321, 327, 340
  and assisted reproductive technology in Islamic context, 339, 341
  and embryo adoption in Catholic context, 271
Affordable Care Act. *See* Patient Protection and Affordable Care Act
aggadah, 390–91
ahadith (collections of traditions), 241, 245
Alexander III, 140–41
al-Ḥaffār, Abū ʿAbd Allah Muḥammad, 185
Alison, James, 432
Allen, John, 261–62
Alpert, Rebecca, 198–99
American Congress of Obstetricians and Gynecologists (ACOG), 501–2

American Eugenics Society, 165–66
American Society of Reproductive Medicine (ASRM), 501–2
amniocentesis, 477–79, 500
Amoris laetitia, 149, 358
Anderson, Leith, 379
Anderson, Matthew Lee, 374, 375
Andolsen, Barbara Hilkert et al., 38, 46
Anglican Church, 85, 356
Anthropocene, 207
antigay initiatives and groups, 193, 201n.10, 202n.12
Apostles' Creed, 42
"Apostolic Exhortation on the Family, An" (*Familiaris consortio*), 147–48
apotropos (guardianship of children), 126
Aquinas, Thomas. *See* Thomas Aquinas, Saint
Arctic ice, melting of, 208
Aristotle
  natural law theory and, 91–92
  Politics, 205–6
  on population control, 205–6
  on the soul, 96, 212, 405–6, 452
artificial insemination
  Islamic views on, 82n.19, 343–44
  Jewish law and, 222
  Protestant ethics and, 47
artificial insemination with donor sperm (AID)
  Islamic views on, 65–66, 76–77, 78–79, 80, 340
  Judaism and Jewish views on, 264–65, 321–23, 331
  Protestant views on, 163–64
artificial insemination with husband's sperm (AIH)
  Islamic views on, 65–66, 76–77, 340
  in Jewish law, 322
Asher ben Yehiel, Rabbi, 224–25, 234n.30
assisted reproduction technology (ART), 337
  adultery and, 341
  Catholic views on, 25, 33
  concerns about, 337–38
  evangelical views on, 533
  fatwas issued on, 340–41
  heterologous and homologous, 100, 101, 102
  Islamic law and, 347–48
  Islamic views on, 61–62, 65–68, 337–44, 349
  Judaism and Jewish views on, 122–23

New Natural Law Theory and, 101
number of births with, 349n.2
Protestant views on, 47, 162–63, 164–65
Shiite Islam and, 346–47
Association du marriage Chretien, 146
Augustine, Saint, 43, 213, 215
  on marriage, 138–39, 140, 143, 158
authority
  in bioethics, 84
  Christianity and, 85–87
  Islam and, 87–88
  Judaism and, 84–85
  questions of, 84
  reception by faith community, 88
  role in religious ethics, 83–84
autonomy, prenatal diagnostic screening and testing and, 501–3, 514–16
  See also freedom
Azaria, Rabbi Elazar ben, 389

Bacon, Sir Francis, 158–59, 164
"Baconian project," 159–60, 162
Bargach, Jamila, 248–49
Barnes, Jay, 379
Barroso, Julie, 540
Barth, Karl, 41, 43–44, 163
Barzelatto, Jose, 210–11
basic goods, in natural law theory, 94, 101, 103–4
Beck, Martha, 509–10
Becker, Amy Julia, 537, 541
Beckett Legal Fund, 380
Ben Azzai, 117
Benedict XVI, 86, 91, 148–49, 368
Bernardin, Joseph, 463
Berry, Wendell, 427, 430
Best, Megan, 532
"best interests of the child"
  in American law, 250–51
  in Jewish law, 223–24
Bible, the. *See* Hebrew Bible (Old Testament); New Testament; Scripture
Bible and Morality, The (Pontifical Biblical Commission), 26–27
Biblicism, 527–28
  critical (evangelical), 532
binary approach, to abortion
  in Shiite Hadith, 451–52
  in Sunni Hadith, 446–47

Birch, Bruce C., 39, 40
birth control. *See* contraception; Pill, the; intrauterine device (IUD)
birth rates, population policy and control of, 205–6
bishops (Catholic)
  authority of, 31
  doctrine of infallibility and, 86–87
Black women, abortion and, 430–31
bodily experience, 46
body, the, in natural law theory, 95
body-soul composite, 409–10
  See also dualism
Boesak, Allan Aubrey, 41
Bonhoeffer, Dietrich, 41, 43–44, 46, 48–49
"born gay" rhetoric, 192, 194–95
Bouma, Hessel, III, 39, 41
Bradley, Gerard V., 101–2
breastfeeding, 345
  See also *radaah/raadah* (suckling)
brit milah (covenant of circumcision), 198–99
Brown, Harold O. J., 530
Brown, Lester R., 209
Brown, Louise Joy, 163, 264, 340
Brown, Peter, 211–12
Brunner, Emil, 40, 43–44, 45
Bryant, Anita, 192–94
Budziszewski, J., 100
burial of the dead, 389
Burtchaell, James Tunstead, 42
Bush, George W. and administration, 263, 264
Buxton, C. Lee, 355–56

Cahill, Lisa Sowle, 136, 148, 151, 425
Calvin, John
  experience and, 427–28
  on killing of fetus, 424–25
  on marriage, family, and sex, 47
  on reason, 43–44
  on Scripture, 39
  on tradition, 43
Cameron, Nigel M. de S., 534
Cameron, Paul, 196
Campbell, Courtney S., 38
capital punishment, 388–89, 394, 446–47
Carlson, Allan C., 382
carrier screening, 499–500
carrying capacity of earth, 206–7

Casanova, Jose, 470
Cassandra moment, 207
Casti connubii, 30, 136, 142–44, 146, 151–52
Castle-DeGette stem cell bill, 104–5
casuistry, 10–11, 69, 262
Catholic Answers, 196
Catholic Charities, 199
Catholic Church and Catholicism. *See* Roman Catholic Church
celibacy, 138, 157–58, 276
cell-free fetal DNA (cffDNA) testing, 500, 513
Central Conference of American Rabbis, 117
Chapman, Audrey R., 37–38, 40
Charo, R. Alta, 98
chastity, 271
 contraception and, 374–75
child custody (ḥaḍāna), in Islamic jurisprudence, 172–73, 182–87
 child custody and the child ward, 182–83
 child's right to safety and security and, 185–86
 concern over unrelated stepfathers and, 184–85
 gendering of rules at puberty, 186–87
child custody, in Jewish law, 222–23
childlessness, 40, 47, 511, 536
 See also infertility
children
 Augustine on, 141
 conversion to Judaism through adoption, 230–31
 evangelical views on, 531
 gendering in Islamic jurisprudence, 187
 Jewish guidance on number of, 118–19
 Jewish responsibilities and guidance for one's own, 123–25
 in Judaism, 333
 in New Testament, 137–38
 Protestantism and, 47
 in Qur'anic narratives, 181
 rights in Islamic jurisprudence, 182–83, 185–86, 187
 Thomas Aquinas on, 141
 and welcome in Christian tradition, 534
children's education
 Catholic views of, 143, 148–49
 Judaism and Jewish views of, 125, 126, 127–28, 236n.56
 Protestant action for, 434
child welfare, in Islamic jurisprudence, 249–51
"Child Welfare Provider Inclusion Act," 199–200
China, population management in, 206, 439n.88
choice
 abortion and, 433–34
 prenatal diagnostic screening and testing and, 501–3, 514–15, 539–40
 reproductive, 1–2
chorionic villus sampling, 478–79, 482, 500
Christianity and Christian tradition
 abortion and, 424–26, 526–27
 authority in, 85–87
 care for vulnerable people, 526–27, 534
 categories within, 85
 children and parenting in, 510–12
 common good and distributive justice in, 513
 embryo adoption and, 275–76
 emergence in Roman Empire, 157
 family, notions of, 164, 165
 human suffering in, 535–37
 natalism and, 211–12
 population justice and, 213–14
 sexism and misogyny in, 425
 See also Protestantism; Roman Catholic Church
Christian Medical and Dental Society, 372
Christian Medical Society, 379, 380–81
"Christians for Socialism," 46
Chrysostom, Saint John, 139–40, 146–47, 151, 211–12
Church of Jesus Christ of Latter-Day Saints (Mormons), 85–86
Clarke, Victoria, 191, 196
Clement of Alexandria, 424
coastline erosion, in California, 208–9
co-creation, 48, 515
Code of Maimonides, 395
Cohen, Cynthia B., 507
Cohen, Hermann, 14
coitus interruptus, 25, 214, 452
Cole-Turner, Ronald, 42, 48

Collins, Francis, S., 508
Committee on Jewish Law and
    Standards, 329–30
common good, prenatal diagnostic screening
    and testing and, 513–14
community
    consensus and, 87
    marriage and, 101
    parenting in Judaism and, 126–28
    prenatal diagnosis and, 508–9
    in Protestant ethics, 42, 46, 429
    suffering and, 536
community epidemiology, 490
compassion for the couple, and artificial
    insemination, 326
Comstock Act, 355–56
concubinage, 18–19, 157–58, 308, 309
concupiscence, 139
conditional covenantal acceptance view, of
    contraception, 379–81
condoms, 25, 122, 367–68
Cone, James, 41, 46
Congar, Yves, 358–59
conjugal acts, embryo adoption and, 271–72, 273
    See also sexual intercourse and sexuality
conscience, in Protestant ethics, 45
consensus, conscience vs., 33
contraception
    abortion and use of, 439n.87
    ancient beliefs about, 26
    artificial and natural, 356–57, 359, 360, 361–62, 364–66
    Catholic Church on, 28, 29–31, 88, 195–96, 262, 356–57, 358, 359, 360, 361–62, 364–65, 367–68
    Christian views of, 213, 356
    conditional covenantal acceptance
        view, 379–81
    covenantal acceptance view of, 376–79
    distributive justice and, 210
    evangelical views on, 372–85
    in *Humanae vitae*, 147, 149, 360–63
    Islamic views on, 65, 214
    Jewish views on, 18, 121–22
    John Paul II on, 29–30
    in medical circumstances, 367

    natural law theory and, 99–100
    opposition view of, 382–84
    Protestant views on, 47, 356
    religious support for, 212
    respectable debate on, 215
    strong acceptance view of, 373–76
    Supreme Court rulings on, 355–56
Cooper, Brittney, 428
Council of Trent, 141–42, 151–52
covenant, 41, 43–44, 47
covenantal acceptance view of
    contraception, 376–79
CRISPR (Clustered Regularly Interspaced
    Short Palindromic Repeat), 501, 517n.9
crucicentrism, 527–28
cryopreserved embryos, 263, 264–65,
    276–77nn.5–6
cultural relativism, 61–63, 361
Curran, Charles, 86–87
Curran, Charles, 33–34

Daly, Mary, 425
Darwin, Charles, 93
Davis, Dena, 479, 503
Dawkins, Richard, 93
Deaf community, 509
DeBaets, Amy Michelle, 534
Decalogue, moral theology in, 26, 27
Declaration on Procured Abortion, 404–5
Dei verbum, 23, 24
delayed ensoulment/animation, 96, 212, 213
Deltete, Robert, 213
Department of Human and Health Services
    (HHS), 264, 380
depopulation, humans and, 204
DeRogatis, Amy, 194
Deuteronomy
    4:9, 124
    6:7, 124
    6:18, 13
    levirate marriage in, 117
Dignitas personae (2008), 503–4
disabilities, children and people with
    evangelical views on, 536–38, 539–40
    parenting and, 509–10
    radical hospitality and, 508–9
    suffering and, 508, 536–37

distributive justice, 210, 513–14
Divine Image, in Judaism, 388–90, 392, 394, 397, 398, 399–400
divorce, 26, 120, 125, 137, 222
diya (blood money), for fetal death, 444–45, 446, 452–53, 454
Dollar, Ellen Painter, 498
Dombrowski, Daniel, 213
Doms, Herbert, 144, 145
Donum vitae, 33, 270, 503–4
Dorn, Harold F., 204
Dor Yeshorim Institute, 481
double effect, principle of, 416
Down syndrome
  Haredi Jewish women on children with, 484–86
  screening and testing for, 478–79, 481, 482, 489, 499–500, 507, 519n.36
Dreweke, Joerg, 373
dualism, 138, 161, 162, 409–10
Dunn, Royce, 384

earth
  carrying capacity of, 206–7
  orbital path around the sun, 204
Eastern Orthodox Church, 85
Ecclesiastes 11:6 119
Edels, Rabbi Samuel Eliezer, 225–26
Edwards, Jonathan, 44
egg donation
  confidentiality and, 321, 332
  health risks and, 326–27, 332
  identity of the mother in Judaism and, 328
  Judaism and Jewish views of, 326–28, 332
  moral and psychological issues in, 327
  obligation to procreate in Judaism and, 328
  sibling donors and, 327
  See also in vitro fertilization (IVF)
Egypt, 62, 347–48
Eisenstadt v. Baird, 355–56
Ella contraceptive, 380
Elyashiv, Rabbi, 230–31
embryo(s)
  in *aggadah*, 390–91
  basic rights of, 410–12
  Catholic views on, 404, 410–12
  cell development and differentiation and, 408
  at conception (fertilization) and, 404, 406–8, 505
  dignity of, 104–5
  Divine Image and, 388–90, 398
  evangelical views on, 538
  generative process and, 405–6
  genetic uniqueness argument, 97
  in Jewish law (*halakhah*), 390, 398–400
  as human in potency, 97
  Islamic terminology and, 444
  John Paul II on, 95
  in medieval Jewish teachings, 395–97
  natural law theory and status of, 91, 95–99, 104–5
  nature of pregnancy and implantation and, 98–99
  as organism, 97
  personhood and, 104, 266, 408–9
  potentiality (capacity) and, 97, 98, 411–12, 530
  prenatal diagnostic screening and testing and, 506–7
  procreative teleology of sex and, 104
  produced through IVF, 264
  Protestant views of, 423–24, 505
  Rabbinic vs. Hellenistic Judaism, 391–95
  for research, 104–5, 538
  soul and, 96
  "twinning" and, 96, 97–98
  as whole human organism, 408
  See also embryo adoption
embryo adoption
  as acceptable but problematic, 273–74
  as adoption, 266, 267, 268–69, 274
  Catholic debate over, 261–63, 265–66, 275–76
  Christian beliefs and, 275–76
  as cooperation with IVF industry, 273, 274
  evangelical Protestants and, 262, 546n.48
  further moral considerations, 274–76
  good of children and, 272
  historical-medical background and, 264–65
  initial scholarly debate, 265–66
  initiative to promote and publicize, 264
  number of, 262
  origin of issue, 263–64
  paradigmatic moral descriptions of, 266–67

perspectives on parents involved in, 274–75
as procreative infidelity, 266, 267, 271–73, 279–80n.36
relationship between woman and embryo in, 268–69, 271, 279n.26, 279n.30, 279n.34
relationship between woman and husband in, 271
as rescue, 266, 267–68, 278–79n.23
responses in debate, 266–67
as source of scandal, 273–74
as surrogacy, 266, 267, 270–71
as term, 266–67
woman's agency and choice in, 266–67, 272
embryo transfer (ET), 264, 267, 271–72
heterologous, 266–67
Enlightenment, the, 11, 84–85, 103
ensoulment. *See* souls and ensoulment
Ephesians, 41
5:22,–38 26
Erasmus of Rotterdam, 430
eschatology, 26, 45, 47
"Estate of Marriage, The" (Luther), 158
Esther (in Old Testament), 287–88, 300
Ethical and Religious Directives for Catholic Health Care Services, 503–4
ethical monotheism, 12
eugenics and eugenic mentality
evangelical views on, 539–40
"hard" and "soft," 539
Islamic Tradition and, 77
artificial insemination with donor's sperm and, 326
prenatal testing and, 538–39
Protestantism and, 165–67
euthanasia, public opinion and, 463–64, 468
Evangelical Leaders Survey, 377
evangelicals and evangelical Protestants, 535
on abortion, 373, 530–31
on adoption, 542
authority and, 372
bioethics and, 528
characteristics of, 527–28
conditional covenantal acceptance view of contraception, 379–81
on contraception, 372–85

covenantal acceptance view of contraception, 376–79
cultural mandate and, 533–34
embryo adoption and, 262
on family, marriage, and children, 531
on the fetus, 529–31
on gay parenting, 191–92, 193–94
on gender complementarity, 194
high birth rate of, 531
on marriage, 194, 372–73
number of, 527–28
organizations, 372
overview of, 527–28
Patient Protection and Affordable Care Act and, 379–80
on prenatal testing, 537–42
Scripture and, 39–42, 423
on sovereignty and Providence of God, 534–35
strong acceptance view of contraception, 373–76
on suffering, 535–37
theological anthropology and, 528–31
theological reflection on procreation and reproductive technologies, 532–37
Evangelium vitae, 95, 366, 403, 503–4
evolutionary theories, 93
Exodus, 41
20:13, 41
21:22–25, 122, 391–93, 423–24
experience
as source of Protestant moral knowledge, 37–39, 45–47
as source of Protestant views on abortion, 427–29
Ibn Ezra, Rabbi Abraham, 223

Fadel, Mohamed, 242, 248
family
Catholicism and, 138–41
Catholic Scripture and, 137–38
domestic church metaphor in Catholicism, 148
evangelical views on, 531
Jewish notions of, 197–98
Protestant views of, 164, 165
Religious Right views of, 193

"family circles," 146
family planning, 356
  Catholic views on, 213, 367
  Islamic views on, 214
  natural, 156, 361–62, 370n.16, 382, 383
  See also contraception
Farley, Margaret, 33–34, 86
*fatawa/fata>wa/*fatwa, 61, 81n.5, 88, 252
  on assisted reproductive technology, 340–41, 347–48
fatherless, the
  in New Testament, 300–3
  in Old Testament, 297–300
fathers and fatherhood
  Islamic views of adoption and, 244
  Islamic views of lineage and, 79–80
  in Judaism and Jewish law, 124–25, 321–23
  in Qur'an, 180–81
  in Roman law, 292
Fei, Hans, 205
Feinberg, John S., 378–79, 384–85
Feinberg, Paul D., 378–79, 384–85
Feinstein, Rabbi Moses (Moshe), 119–20, 122, 123, 229, 230, 231
Felder, Rabbi Gedalya, 229
feminism and feminist perspectives
  of Christian tradition and, 425
  prenatal diagnostic screening and testing and, 514–15
  Protestant ethics and moral knowledge and, 38, 40, 46, 48
  public opinion on abortion and, 465–67, 468
  "public" and "private," 466–67
fetal death/feticide, in Jewish tradition, 391–95
Fetner, Tina, 193
fetus, status of, 213
  basic rights of, 410
  Catholic views of, 529–30
  in Christian tradition, 529–30
  Divine Image and, 399–400
  evangelical views of, 529–31, 533
  Judaism and Jewish views of, 122, 212, 395, 396
  Maimonides on, 396–97
  public opinion on abortion and, 463, 468
  See also embryo(s)
Finnis, John, 101

fiqh (derivative Islamic rules), 87, 240–41, 254n.11, 443–44
  on abortion, 446, 447, 451, 453–55
  on *radaah*, 245
firash principle, 247
First Vatican Council (1868–1870), 86–87
Fletcher, Joseph, 44, 160–63, 514
Focus on the Family, 193–94, 379
fossil fuels, 209
Francis (Pope), 196–97, 358
  on abortion, 213–14
  on contraception, 367–68
  on marriage and family, 149
fratricide, in Qur'an, 181
freedom
  as American value, 502
  Catholic views on, 504, 506, 515
  in Christian tradition, 514, 515–16
  co-creation and, 515
  evangelical views on, 533–34, 535
  Protestant views on, 422, 433, 506
  See also autonomy

gamete donation
  fatwas issued on, 340–41
  in Islamic context, 339–40, 341, 345–47, 349
  legislating in Muslim countries, 347–48
  New Natural Law Theory and, 102
  Protestantism and, 47
  statements of Islamic institutions on, 343–44
gamete intra-fallopian transfer (GIFT), 65, 67–68, 80
Gaudium et spes, 32, 146, 147
gay men and lesbians
  antidiscrimination protections for, 192–93
  stereotypes of, 191–92, 193–94
  See also gay parenting
gay parenting
  adoption and, 192, 199–200
  brit milah and, 198–99
  Catholic perspectives on, 195–97
  evangelical views of, 191–92
  familial formations and, 200–1
  Judaism and Jewish views on, 192, 197–99
  Pope Francis on, 196–97
  Protestant views on, 192–95
  religious perspectives on, 191, 199–201

Geach, M., 271–72, 273
Gellman, Rabbi Marc, 329
gender, in Jewish law, 223
gender complementarity
    Catholic views of, 147, 196–97, 368–69
    evangelical views of, 194
gender roles, public opinion on abortion and, 465–67, 468
Genesis, Book of
    creation stories in, 42, 137, 529
    control of human fertility in, 205
    narratives on parenting in, 123–24
    story of Hagar, Bilhah, and Zilpah in, 306–10
    1:1–2:3, 8
    1:27–28, 25, 116, 137, 320, 365, 366, 388–89, 399–400, 423, 529
    2:18–25, 137
    3:16, 124
    5:2, 118
    9:1, 116
    9:6, 41, 388–89
    19, 25–26
    35:11, 116
    38:6–10, 25, 121
genetic counseling, 501–2, 504, 505
genetic testing, 500–1, 502–3, 517n.6
genocide, of Israelite male children, 285–86
George, Robert P., 97–99, 101–2
gestational surrogacy, 78–79, 80, 329, 342–43, 345–47
ghurra, 445, 446–47, 454
global warming, 208–9
Gnosticism, 138
Gordis, Rabbi Daniel, 329, 330
gospels
    absence of reference to adoption, 290
    on divorce, 26
gradualist approach, to abortion
    in Shiite Hadith, 451–53
    in Sunni Hadith, 445–46, 447
"great extinctions," 207–8
Greek law, 294–95
Green, Ronald M., 85, 88
Greenfield, Dorothy A., 325
Gregory, Brad S., 156–57
Grenholm, Carl-Henric, 44

Grisez, Germain, 102
Griswold, Estelle, 355–56
Griswold v. Connecticut, 355–57
Grodzinsky, Rabbi Chaim Ozer, 231
Gudorf, Christine, 213
Guenin, Louis, 98
Gundry-Volf, Judith M., 137–38
Gushee, David P., 40
Gustafson, James M., 40–41, 48, 86
Guttmacher Institute, 88, 377

Hadith
    abortion in, 444–47, 450–53
    ensoulment in, 448, 450–51
    of Ibn Mas'ūd, 450–51
    radaah (suckling) in, 245
    Shiite, 451–53
    as source for normative statements, 443–44
    as source of law in Islam, 87
Hagar, 306–7
halakhah. See Jewish law (*halakha/halakhah*)
Hall, Amy Laura, 164–65, 166–67
Hamilton, Clive, 208
Hanafi School/Ḥanafīya, 183, 184, 186, 187, 241, 246–47, 248, 453, 454, 455
Hananel, Rabbenu, 223
Hanbali School/Ḥanbalīya, 183, 184, 187, 241, 246–47, 248, 453, 454, 455
Handel, William, 330
Haredi Jews, 480–81
    arranged marriages in, 480, 481
    birth rate of, 480
    Down syndrome among, 481
    rabbinic advice and, 480, 491–92
    See also Ultra-Orthodox (Haredi) Jewish women
Haring, Bernard, 144
harm and harassment, rule in Islamic ethics, 73–76
Harrison, Beverly, 425, 514–15
Hassidic Jews, 480
Hauerwas, Stanley, 41, 42, 48, 509
health insurance, Patient Protection and Affordable Care Act and, 379–80
Hebrew Bible (Old Testament), 84–85
    adoption in, 125–26, 284–89
    childlessness in, 116–17, 511

Hebrew Bible (Old Testament) (*cont.*)
  children and parenting in, 511
  commentaries to, 9–10
  communal parenting responsibilities in, 127
  Elijah and Elisha (in Old Testament), 299–300
  foundation of Jewish ethics and, 7–8, 9
  humans created in image of God in, 388–90
  intimate relationships in, 137
  levirate marriage in, 117
  marriage in, 137
  "master narratives" in, 15–16
  orphans, fatherless, and widows in, 297–300
  parenting in, 123–24
  story of Hagar, Bilhah, and Zilpah in, 306–10, 328–29
  surrogacy in, 18–19
Hebrews, Letter to the, 13:4 26
Hefner, Philip, 43
Heiene, Gunnar, 38
Hemings, Sally, 309–10
Henkin, Rabbi Joseph Eliyahu, 229
heterologous embryo transfer (HET), 266–67
Himalayan glaciers, melting of, 208–9
HIV/AIDS, 368
Hodge, Bryan C., 382
Hollinger, Dennis P., 377–78, 384–85
Holocene, 205, 207, 208
homosexuality, 194–95, 196–97, 206, 223, 384
homunculus, 26
hospitality, radical, prenatal diagnostic screening and testing and, 508–10
House of Hillel, 118–19
huiothesia, 290, 291–92
Humanae vitae, 28, 33, 86–87, 147
  Catholic views of contraception after, 363–67
  on contraception, 28, 29–31, 99–100, 149, 359, 360–63, 367
  on dominion over nature, 366–67
  on IVF, 101
  on marriage and family, 147
  response from American Catholic theologians to, 363–64
human beings
  basic rights of, 410–12
  as body-soul composites, 162, 408–10
  fertility of population and, 205, 209–10
  "in God's image," 389, 423–24, 515
  goods worthy of pursuit and, 411–13
  personhood and, 408–10
human cloning, 75–76, 97–98, 101, 222
human embryonic stem cell (HESC) research, 538
Human Fertilisation and Embryology Act (UK), 263
human life
  at conception/fertilization, 404, 406–8, 433, 505
  sanctity or sacredness of, 423, 433
  valuing of, 388–90, 463–64, 468, 505–7
human nature, 160–61

Ibn al-'Arabī, al-Qāḍī, 454
Ibn al-Qāsim, 'Abd al-Raḥmān, 183, 185–86
Ibn Hajar al-Asqalani, 248
Ibn Mas'ūd, 448
  Hadith of, 450–51, 456
Ibrahim, Ahmed Fekry, 187
ice ages, 204
ijma' (consensus), 87, 241, 253
ijtihad (independent reasoning or intellectual effort), 87, 241, 252, 253
illness, as source of Protestant moral knowledge, 45
imago Dei, 160–61, 388–89, 529–31
immediately exercisable capacities, 411–12, 413
incest
  and adoption in Jewish law, 228, 238n.93
  and artificial insemination in Islamic law, 80
  and artificial insemination in Jewish law, 321
individualism, 149, 166–67, 427, 429, 468, 502, 532
infallibility, doctrine of, 31, 86–87
infanticide, 175–76, 303
infertility
  in Hebrew Bible and, 116, 124
  Islamic ethics and, 61–62, 67, 76–77, 79, 80
  in Judaism and Jewish tradition, 116, 122–23, 326, 397
  natural law theory and, 100
  perceptions of, 337
  suffering and, 536
inheritance, 245–46, 249, 251, 292, 293, 294, 322

Institutes of the Christian Religion (Calvin), 43
interglacials, 204
International Energy Agency, 208–9
International Islamic Center for Population Studies and Research, 340–41
International Islamic Fiqh Academy (IIFA), 343–44
International Theological Commission, 27–28
intrauterine device (IUD), 376–77, 378, 379, 380–81, 382
in vitro fertilization (IVF), 65, 326
   Catholic views on, 100, 519n.33
   costs of, 541
   early days of, 264
   evangelical views on, 533, 546n.48
   Islamic views and rulings on, 60, 65–68, 78, 79, 80, 341, 343–44
   Judaism and Jewish views on, 123
   natural law theory and, 101
   number of births with, 337–38
   preimplantation genetic diagnosis and, 500, 527
   prenatal testing and, 538–39
in vitro fertilization embryo transfer (IVF-ET), 264–65, 277n.9
Iozzio, Mary Jo, 508
Iran, 62, 72, 81–82n.9, 346–47, 348, 456
Isaiah 45:18 119
islah (reform), 252
Islam and Islamic ethical discourse
   abortion and, 214, 444–47
   adoption and, 285, 338–39
   assisted reproduction technology and, 61–62, 339–44
   authority and, 63–64, 87–88
   biomedical ethics in, 62, 77–78
   contraception and, 214
   cultural relativism and, 61–63
   divine commands in, 64–65
   gamete donation and surrogacy in, 80, 345–48
   infertility and, 67
   international forums and, 456
   IVF and, 65–68
   lineage in, 59, 60, 62–63, 66, 76–77, 78, 80, 338–39
   medical practice, 78
   nature of, 60, 63–68
   new reproductive technologies and, 65
   obligation to promote good, 75
   paradigmatic cases and rulings, 63, 68, 69–70
   population justice and, 214
   rationale for rulings in, 63, 64, 68
   reason in, 61, 63, 69, 72, 75–76, 241
   reproductive genetics and, 76–80
   sex selection and, 72
   status of fetus in, 214, 448–50
   use of frozen embryos and, 67–68
   women's modesty, 65–67, 78–79
Islamic Fiqh Council (IFC), 343–44, 345, 347–48
Islamic law
   acknowledgement of paternity, 244, 246–48
   adoption per se, 242–49
   on child conceived through adultery, 62–63
   gamete donation and surrogacy, 347–48
   jurists and, 61–62, 68–69, 73, 74–76, 172, 182, 241, 250–51
   kafala, 248–49
   overview of, 240–41
   reformation of adoption and child welfare law, 251–53
   schools of, 241
   tabanni in, 242–44
   tabanni alternatives in, 244–49
   Western conceptions of adoption and child welfare and, 249–53
   See also Shari'a
Islamic premodern jurisprudence
   child custody (*ḥaḍāna*) in, 182–87
   child custody and child ward in, 182–83
   childhood and parenting in Qur'an, 175–82
   child's right to safety and security, 185–86
   concern over unrelated stepfathers, 184–85
   gendering of *ḥaḍāna* rules at puberty, 186–87
   parent-child relationships in, 172–73
   theological perspectives on procreation, 173–75
Islamic principles and rules, 68–69
   principle of "juristic preference," 70
   principle of proportionality, 76
   principle of public (common) good, 71–72

Islamic principles and rules (*cont.*)
   principles applied to bioethics and, 69–72
   rule of "Action depends on intention," 73
   rule of "Custom determines course of action, 73
   rule of "Hardship necessitates relief," 70, 73, 74–75, 76–77
   rule of "Harm must be rejected," 73, 74
   rule of "No constriction, no distress," 71, 75, 79
   rule of "No harm, no harassment," 71–72, 73–76, 81n.7
   rules for rulings in interpersonal relations, 73, 74–75
Islamic Organization for Medical Sciences (IOMS), 341, 342, 343–44, 347–48
Islamic Research Council, 340–41
Islam's Attitude Toward Family Planning, 214
Israel, twelve tribes of, 285, 288–89, 307, 309–10, 322–23
Isserles, Moshe, 120
istihlāl, 448–50, 452
Ivry, Tsipy, 485, 491–92

Jackelen, Antje, 44–45
Jacob (in Old Testament), 285, 288–89, 309–10, 322–23
Jād al-Ḥaqq, ʿAlī Jād al-Ḥaqq, 340–41
Jaʿfari School, 241
Jain, Anrudh, 210–11
Jakobovits, Rabbi Immanuel, 324, 329, 330
Jakobsen, Janet, 191, 194–95
James, Book of, orphans, fatherless, and widows in, 300–1
janāʾiz, 444–45, 449–50
janīn (embryo), 444, 446, 449–50
Janssens, Louis, 32–33
Jefferson, Thomas, 309–10
Jesus Christ
   in Catholic Tradition, 27
   in Christian anthropology, 529
   Father-Son relationship with God and, 289
   human suffering and, 536
   Protestants and, 422
   welcoming the stranger and, 508
   widow assistance and, 301–2

Jewish ethics
   abortion and, 18
   approaches to, 14–17
   as casuistic, 10–11
   contemporary challenges to tradition, 11–13
   contraception and, 18
   core beliefs and, 7–8
   covenantal approach to, 15, 16–17
   egg donation and, 332
   legal approach to, 15, 16
   liturgy of Jewish practice and, 8
   "master narratives" in, 15–16
   meta-issues in, 19
   narrative approach to, 8, 13, 15–16, 17
   parenting issues and, 18–19
   problem of interpretation in, 17–19
   rabbis addressing moral issues in, 10
   reproductive issues and, 18
   sperm donation and, 331–32
   surrogacy and, 18–19
   textual sources, 9–11
   theological foundations, 7–9
   unprecedented moral issues, 17–18
Jewish law (*halakha/halakhah*), 13–14, 84–85, 390
   abortion and, 397–400
   adoption and, 225–27
   adoption, no legal category of, 221–23, 231–32
   artificial insemination with donor sperm and, 321–23
   basic family law status, no authority over, 222–23
   "best interests of the child" and, 125, 223–25, 231–32
   egg donation and, 327
   incest in, 228
   levirate marriage in, 285
   Mishnah and, 10
   parental custody in, 223–25
   quasi-adoption in, 224–26, 227–29, 284–85
   on termination of pregnancy, 478
Jewish tradition
   blessings of children and, 333
   medieval teachings on status of embryo, 395–97

religious humanism in, 388–89
status of fetus in, 390–95
Jews and Jewish population
  birth rates, 118, 120
  civil rights and, 11–12
  identity and, 197–98, 201n.9, 321
  population and demographics, 117, 120, 197–98, 326
  relationship with God, 9
  religious commandments and, 8–9
  "secular" Jews, 85
Job, Book of, 29:2–4 390
John, Gospel of, 23, 41
John Paul II, 86, 364–66
  "An Apostolic Exhortation on the Family" (*Familiaris consortio*), 147–48
  on contraception, 29–30, 362
  on dualism, 409
  Evangelium vitae of, 366, 403
  on inherent value of human life, 410
  Laborem exercens of, 365
  on marriage and family, 147
  natural law theory and, 94–95
  on ordination of women, 86–87
  on prenatal diagnosis, 503–4
John XXIII, 30–31, 147, 359, 360
Jones, D. Gareth, 530
Jones, L. Gregory, 41, 42
Jones, Rachel K., 373
Jones, Stanton, 376
Jordan, Mark, 193, 196, 199
Joseph (in New Testament), 289–90
Judah of Regensberg, Rabbi, 228
Judaism
  abortion and, 122, 212
  assisted reproduction in, 122–23
  authority in, 84–85
  ceremony of "release" in, 117
  children, guidance on number of, 118–20
  children, responsibilities and guidance for one's own, 123–25
  communal parenting responsibilities in, 126–28
  Conservative tradition, 84–85, 119, 121–22, 123, 197, 198
  contraception and, 121–22
  conversion of minor children in course of adoption, 230–31
  diversity in, 115–16, 128
  divorce in, 120
  egg donation and, 326–28
  focus on children and, 197–98
  gay parenting and, 192, 197–99
  gender and parenting in, 124
  Haredi tradition, 197
  Hasidic tradition, 197
  instruction and discipline of children and, 127–28
  law and ethics in, 13–14
  levirate marriage in, 121, 322–23, 335n.25
  obligation to procreate, 115, 116–21, 197–98, 225–26, 302–3, 320, 328, 389–90, 397
  Orthodox tradition, 84–85, 121–22, 123, 197
  parenting and, 123–28
  parenting through adoption in, 125–26
  physician-assisted death and, 88
  population justice and, 212
  procreation and, 116–23
  protection of Jewish infants, 302–3
  Reconstructionist tradition, 122, 197, 198
  Reform tradition, 12, 84–85, 119, 121–22, 126, 197–98
  same-sex marriage and, 197–98
  Scripture in, 84–85
  status of fetus in, 122, 212
  subgroups within, 12–13
  on surrogacy, 328–30
  Ultra-Orthodox, 84–85
  on value of life, 88
  See also Jewish ethics; Jewish law (*halakha/halakhah*); Jewish tradition; Jews and Jewish population; Ultra-Orthodox (Haredi) Jewish women
judges and legislators, role in moral issues, 215
justice, 207
  population control and, 207, 210

kafala (fostering or sponsorship), 244, 248–49, 252
kaffāra, 447, 451–52
Kaplan, Benjamin, 156–57
Kass, Leon, 101
Kaveny, Cathleen, 515

Keenan, James, 33–34
Kellner, Menachem M., 84–85
Kelsay, John, 87
Keown, John, 90
Kepler, Johannes, 159
Khamene'i, Ayatollah Ali Hussein, 346–47
King, Martin Luther, Jr., 46, 90, 310
Klum, Mattias, 209
knowledge, new biological and scientific, 26, 38–39
Kohlberg, Lawrence, 33
Kolbert, Elizabeth, 207–8
Kook, Rabbi, 230–31
Kopp, C. Everett, 530
Krauthammer, Charles, 104–5
Krempel, Bernard, 144–45

Laborem exercens, 365
lakits (foundlings), 246, 247–48, 250
Landsman, Gail, 485
Lauritzen, Paul, 324–25
Lawler, Michael G., 33–34, 150, 358–59
Lee, Patrick, 101–2
Leo XIII, 142, 143
Leviticus 19:17 14
levonorgestrel, 380
liberation theology, 38, 40, 43, 46
licentiousness, and moral concerns with artificial insemination, 323–24
Lichtenstein, Rabbi Aharon, 399
life expectancy, in Roman Empire, 211–12
Lightman, Alan, 208–9
lineage
    Islamic conceptions of, 59, 60, 62–63, 65, 76–77, 78, 79, 80, 244, 338–39, 344
    in Law of Moses, 285
Lithuanian Yeshiva, 480, 482–83
Locht, Pierre de, 145
Lot, story of (in Genesis), 25–26
Lupfer, Jacob, 379
Luther, Martin, 39, 43, 45, 94
    on marriage, family, and sex, 47, 158
    "orders of creation," 43
    on *Sola Scriptura*, 39, 85–86, 422–23
Lutheran tradition, 45, 46, 158

McGrath, Alasdair, 103–4
MacIntyre, Alasdair, 103–4
McKenny, Gerald, 159, 162, 166–67
Mahlstedt, Patricia P., 325
Maimonides, 14, 118–19, 396–97
Majma' al-fiqhi> al- isla>mi> (the Islamic Juridical Council), 71–72
Mālik b. Anas, 182, 450
    Muwaṭṭa' of, 444–45, 448–50
Mālikī School/Mālikīya, 241, 246, 248
    child custody and, 182, 184–85
    child's right to safety and security and, 185–86
Manicheans, 138–39
"Manipulating Life" (World Council of Churches), 504–5
marriage
    artificial insemination with donor's sperm and, 324–25
    Augustine on, 158
    in *Casti connubii*, 142–44
    Catholic views of, 30, 31, 140–41, 142, 195–96
    in Christian Scripture, 26
    as contract, 140–42, 151–52
    "ends" of, 140, 141, 143–45, 151–52
    evangelical views on, 194, 372–73, 378, 531, 533
    Gnosticism and, 138
    "goods" of, 102, 138–39, 140, 143, 151–52, 383
    Jewish law and, 222
    levirate, 117, 121, 285, 322–23, 335n.25
    "modified consent theory" and, 140–41
    New Natural Law Theory and, 101–2
    personalism and, 144–45
    Protestant views of, 193
    in Roman law, 292
    as sacrament of Catholic Church, 140, 141–42, 151–52, 195–96
    same-sex, 192, 195–96, 197–98, 199–201, 384
    in Scripture (Catholic), 137–38
    temporary *mut'ah*, 346–47, 349
    Thomas Aquinas on, 141
al-Marwazi, Abu Ishaq, 247
Mary, mother of Jesus, 289–90, 296
Massachusetts Adoption Act, 250–51
Massachusetts Bay Colony, 86
masturbation, 25, 92

maternal serum screening, 478–79, 482
maternity, defined in Islamic context, 346–47
Matthew 22:35–40, 39
Meilaender, Gilbert, 38, 40, 41, 47, 48, 160–61, 162, 515, 542
Messner, Johannes, 205–6
Methodist Church, 165
Meyers, Helene, 197–98
"middle axioms," 41, 43–44
Miguez Bonino, Jose, 46
Miles, Jack, 205
miscarriage, 428–29, 443
Mishnah, 10, 84–85
    birth prevention in, 212
    on crisis in childbirth, 393
    on fetal death, 392–93
    specifics of procreation in, 118
Mishneh Torah, 118–19, 124–25, 128
mitochondrial replacement therapy (MRT), 501
Mittman, Ilana S., 482–83
mitzvot/mitzvah, 231, 389–90
modified consent theory, 140–41
Mohd, Azizah, 245
mokh, prevention of conception with, 121, 122
Moon, Dawne, 194–95
moral issues, respectable debate on, 215
morning-after pill, 380
Moschella, M., 102
Moses, 182, 285–87
mothers and motherhood
    assisted reproductive technology in Islamic context and, 342–43
    child custody in Islamic jurisprudence and, 182–83, 184–85
    egg donation in Judaism and, 328
    embryo adoption and, 268, 269, 273
    in Judaism, 124
    in Qur'an, 180–81
    See also surrogacy
Mott, Stephen Charles, 40, 41, 44–45
Munthe, Christian, 502–3
Muslim Women's Shura Council, 252–53

Nahmanides, 396
National Association of Evangelicals (NAE), 372, 376, 377, 379, 527–28

National Council of Churches (NCC), 504–6
natural family planning (NFP), 361–62, 382, 383
natural law theory
    bioethics and, 90
    Catholicism and, 22, 28–31, 90
    contraception and, 29–30, 361
    failure of, 102–3
    natural sciences vs., 93–94
    normative content of, 92–93
    objectivity and, 91
    ongoing relevance to reproductive ethics, 102–5
    ontological status of embryo and, 91, 95–99
    origins of, 91–95
    personalism and, 99–100
    procreative teleology of sex and, 99–102
    Protestant views of, 43, 44, 426–27
    questioning, 30–31
    reason and practical reason, 91–93, 94, 361
    reproductive ethics and, 91
    response to *Humanae vitae* and, 364
    structures of society and, 30
    two meanings of, 29
natural methods of contraception, 365–66
nature/creation, dominion over, 137, 159, 205, 357, 362, 363, 364–65, 366–67, 369
neural tube defects, 499–500, 508
new genomics, 166
New Jerome Biblical Commentary, The, 25
New Natural Law Theory, 91, 94, 97, 101–2, 103–4
New Organon, The (Bacon), 158–59
New Testament
    adoption in, 289–96
    children and parenting in, 137–38, 511
    marriage and intimate relationships in, 137
    orphans and fatherless in, 300–1, 302–3
    on value of life, 404
    widows in, 300–2
Noahide Laws, 394
Non-Invasive Prenatal Testing (NIPT), 478–79, 500, 502–3, 507
nonmarital sex, 464, 467, 469
Noonan, John, 144, 145, 213
Nordling, Cherith Fee, 528–29
Novak, David, 97, 103

Nussbaum, Martha, 48
nutfa (drop or semen), 445, 450, 453–54

Obama, Barack, 88, 213
Obergefell v. Hodges, 192, 199–200
objective culture, 32
O'Donovan, Oliver, 511
Old Testament. *See* Hebrew Bible (Old Testament)
onah ("season") for procreation, 118, 119–20
Onan (in Genesis), 25
Ong, Aihwa, 492
opposition view, of contraception, 382–84
organ donation, 93–94
original sin, 139
orphans and foundlings
    exploitation and, 304–5
    in Islamic jurisprudence, 249–50, 251–52
    in New Testament, 300–3
    in Old Testament, 297–300
Ostnor, Lars, 38
overpopulation
    as crisis, 165, 205, 206–7
    as worldwide justice issue, 209–10
Oxnam, G. Bromley, 165

Papal Commission on Family Planning and Population, 359, 360
Papo, Eliezer, 120–21
parental custody, in Jewish law
    best interests of the child approach, 223–25
    parental rights approach, 223–25
parent-child relationships
    Islamic perspectives on adoption and, 240
    Judaism and artificial insemination with donor's sperm in, 324–25
    in premodern Islamic jurisprudence, 182–87
    in Qur'an, 173–82
parenting and parenthood
    assisted reproductive technology in Islamic context and, 342–43, 344
    Catholic views of, 136, 139–40, 143, 148–49, 151
    of children with disabilities, 509–10
    in Christian tradition, 510–12
    embryo adoption and, 274–75
    Judaism and Jewish perspectives on, 18–19, 123–28, 222–23
    in premodern Islamic jurisprudence, 172–73, 182–87
    prenatal diagnostic screening and testing and, 510–12
    in Qur'an, 173–81, 187
    single parenthood, 331
    Thomas Aquinas on, 141
Paris, Jenell, 373–74, 384–85
Paris accords, 208–9
Patchin, Bethany, 383–84
pater familias, 292
Patient Protection and Affordable Care Act, 88, 213, 373, 379–80
patria potestas, 292
Paul, letters of, adoption in, 290–92, 293–96
Paul VI, 29–31, 360
    Humanae vitae of, 99–100, 147, 360–63, 366–67
Pelagians, 139
Pellegrini, Ann, 191, 194–95
Penner, Christopher L., 383
Penner, Joyce J., 383
personalism, 99–100, 144–45
"personal is political," 46
Peters, Ted, 41, 42, 45, 47, 48
Peterson-Iyer, Karen, 48
Philo, 392, 398
physician-assisted death, Judaism on, 88
pietistic movement, 13, 20n.13
Pill, the, 30–31, 122, 356, 377–78
    See also contraception
Pius XI, 145
    Casti connubii of, 142–44
    on marriage, 143, 144
    on women, 143
Pius XII, 145, 213
Plan B contraceptive, 380
Planned Parenthood, 355–56
Pleistocene, 204, 205
Pollitt, Katha, 431
Pontifical Biblical Commission, 26–27
Pontifical Commission on Birth Control, 147
pope(s)
    authority of, 31, 85, 358
    doctrine of infallibility and, 86–87
    encyclical letters of, 360

population justice, 207–8
  Christianity and, 213–14
  Islam and, 214
  Judaism and, 212
  limiting fertility and, 209–10, 211
  religion and, 210–12
population momentum, 209–10
population policy, early history of, 205–6
Porète, Marguerite, 430
Postman, Neil, 159
potentiality, of embryo or fetus, 97, 98, 411–12, 530
practical reason, natural law theory and, 92, 94, 103
pragmatism, influence on Protestant moral knowledge, 39
Pratt, Minnie Bruce, 193
pregnancy
  experience of, 498
  prenatal testing and diagnosis and, 498–99
  "tentative," 538
pregnancy termination. *See* abortion
preimplantation genetic diagnosis (PGD), 77, 500, 501–2, 527, 528
  Catholic views of, 504
  costs of, 541
  evangelical views on, 528–31, 538–39
  status of embryo and, 506–7
  suffering and, 535, 536
prenatal development
  in Hadith of Ibn Masʿūd, 450–51
  in Qurʾan, 451
  in Shiite Hadith, 452
  in Sunni Islam, 453–55
prenatal diagnostic screening and testing (PND), 478–79
  autonomy and limits of choice, 501–3
  "burden of choice" and, 479
  common good and distributive justice in, 513–14
  cost and access to, 513
  "eugenic" mentality and, 504, 505
  experience of pregnancy and, 498–99, 502–3
  faith and certainty, Haredi women and, 486–87
  God-sent ordeals, Haredi women and, 489–91
  Haredi (Ultra-Orthodox) Jewish women and, 477–93
  human freedom and autonomy and, 514–16
  invasive tests, 478–79, 500
  meaning of parenthood and, 510–12
  non-invasive tests, 478–79, 499–500, 538
  obligatory effort, Haredi women and, 487–89
  organized religious responses to, 503–6
  overview of technologies, 499–501
  relief of suffering and posture of radical hospitality, 508–10
  respect for human life and moral status of embryo, 506–7
  soul and its mission, Haredi women and, 483–86
prenatal testing (PNT), 528
  commodification concerns, 541
  evangelical views on, 528–31, 533, 537–42
  experience of one couple, 542–43
  experiences with positive findings and, 540–41
Presbyterian Church, 194–95
President's Council on Bioethics, 97–98
priestly status, in Jewish law, 321–22
primum non nocere, 211
printing press, invention of, 85–86
"pro-choice" attitudes, 466
procreation
  evangelical views on, 533
  Judaism and Jewish views, 116–23
  personalism and, 144–45
  Protestantism and, 156, 157
  theological perspectives in Islamic jurisprudence, 173–75
procreative infidelity, 271–73, 280n.37
procreative integrity, 271
Prohibition, 215
"pro-life" attitudes, 211, 423, 460, 463, 465, 469
  evangelicals and, 373, 379, 537–38
Prophet Muhammad, 179–81, 245, 250
  adoption of Zayd b. Haritha and marriage to Zaynab b. Jahsh, 242–44, 256n.29
"Protestant Affirmation on the Control of Human Reproduction, A," 376–77

Protestantism, 85
  abortion and, 47, 422–27
  Bible as authority accessible by individuals, 85–86
  church as source of moral knowledge, 42–43
  community in, 429
  on contraception and planned parenting, 47, 356
  debate over sources of moral knowledge in, 37–38
  debates about authority, 84
  diminished juridical role of, 86
  diversity within, 37–38, 422
  ethical principles or axioms in, 43–44
  eugenics and, 165–67
  experience as source of moral knowledge, 37–39, 45–47
  experience as source of views on abortion, 427–29
  fissility and, 156–57, 166–67
  freedom and, 422, 433
  fundamental challenge to ethics, 48–49
  gay parenting and, 192–95
  goods or purposes of human sexuality, 47
  group documents vs. individual thinkers, 38
  imago Dei in, 160–61
  marriage and family, 158, 193–94
  moral thinking, influences on, 38
  moral thinking in US, 39
  natural law theory and, 94
  nature and reason and, 426–27
  prenatal diagnostic screening and testing and, 504–6
  procreation and parenting and, 156–67
  range of traditions and views, 43
  reason as source of moral knowledge, 37, 38–39, 43–45
  Reformed tradition, 48, 94, 158
  reproductive ethics and, 47–49
  reproductive technology and, 47
  Scripture and, 39, 85–86, 422–24
  Scripture as source of moral knowledge, 37–38, 39–42, 45
  sources of moral knowledge, 37–39
  tradition as source of moral knowledge, 37, 39, 42–43, 424–26
  ways to not talk about abortion, 433–34
  See also evangelicals and evangelical Protestants
Protestant Reformation, 47, 85–86, 142
Proverbs
  13:24, 124
  22:6, 125
Providence/Divine Providence, 92, 483, 534–35
Psalms
  19:7, 14
  39:4, 423
  139:13,–14 423, 498
public opinion, on abortion
  gender roles and, 465–67, 468
  national abortion policy and, 460–61
  ontology and fetal life and, 462–64, 468
  religiosity and, 462, 468–69
  sexual morality and, 464–65, 467
  subjective sources and, 462–67
  World Values Surveys and, 461–62

Qatāda, 450
qiyas (analogical reasoning), 241
Quakers, 45, 84
quasi-adoption, in Jewish law, 224–25, 229–30
  open versus closed, 229–30
  parental rights and, 227–29
Qur'an
  adoption in, 242
  care of orphans in, 250
  children, childhood, and siblings in, 177, 181–82
  division of inheritance in, 176
  God as disciplinarian in, 173–74
  God's appellations in, 173–74
  God's nurturing and caretaking roles in, 173–74
  God without offspring in, 173, 188n.1
  human life cycle in, 174–75
  inability to procreate in, 177–78
  Islamic ethical discourse and, 64, 69
  lineage in, 65, 338–39
  motherhood and fatherhood in, 180–81
  overview, 241
  parent-child relationships in, 172–75, 177–78, 187
  parents and parenting in, 175–80
  prenatal development in, 451

procreation in, 173
prohibitions against incest in, 176
protection of vulnerable persons in, 176
as religious authority behind moral-legal rulings, 63–65
on sexual modesty ("guarding of the private parts"), 65–66
sibling relationships in, 181–82
as source of Islamic law, 87, 241
Sūrat al-Kahf, 177
Qur'an verses
  2:124, 178
  2:233, 180
  3:195, 180
  4:9, 176
  4:23, 245, 256n.30
  4:75, 176
  4:124, 180
  6:74, 178–79
  6:98, 173–74
  6:151, 214
  7:51, 182
  7:190, 177–78
  8:28, 177
  9:55, 177
  11:42–43, 178
  11:45–46, 178
  13:8–9, 173
  13:23, 175
  14:30, 178
  15:46, 175
  16:58–59, 175–76
  16:70, 174–75
  16:78, 173
  17:31, 175
  17:111, 173
  18:39–41, 176–77
  18:46, 177
  19:4–6, 177
  22:5, 174, 451
  23:12–14, 445, 451
  28:26, 179
  31:13–20, 179
  33:4–5, 242–43, 338–39
  33:37–40, 242–44
  36:68, 174–75
  37:102, 179
  42:11, 173
  43:3–4, 180–81
  58:2, 242
  60:4, 178–79
  81:8–14, 176

racism, and artificial insemination with donor's sperm in Judaism, 325
radaah/raadah (suckling), 244, 245–46, 252
Rahner, Karl, 516
Ralston, Christopher, 537
Rambam, 119, 121, 122
Ramsey, Paul, 41, 43–45, 47, 160–61, 162, 163–64, 515
rape, Islamic perspectives on abortion and, 456–57
Rapp, Rayna, 491–92, 498–99, 512
Rashi, 393
Rasmussen, Larry L., 39, 40
rational soul, 96, 404, 405, 406, 407, 452
Ratzinger, Joseph, Cardinal, 91
  See also Benedict XVI
Ravizza, Bridget Burke, 512
al-Ra>zi>, Fakhr al-Di>n, 66
reason
  cogency of argument and, 44–45
  in Islamic ethical discourse, 63–65, 69–70, 75–76
  natural law theory and, 91–92, 361
  Protestantism and, 426
  as source of Protestant moral knowledge, 37, 38–39, 43–45
reasoning, analogical, 61, 72, 87, 241
Reformers (Protestant)
  on marriage, family, and parenting, 157, 158, 159, 164
  rejection of celibacy, 157–58
  schism and, 156–57
  See also Protestantism
Reinders, Hans, 502
religiosity, public opinion on abortion and, 462, 468–69
religious freedom, 192, 199–200, 214–15
religious humanism, in Jewish tradition, 388–89
Religious Right, 193
remarriage, 184–85, 298, 301

reproductive genetics, Islamic ethics and, 76–80
reproductive integrity, 271
reproductive justice, 431
reproductive technology. *See* assisted reproductive technology (ART)
respectable debate, on moral issues, 215
revelation, 9–10, 69
rhythm method, 213, 356, 382, 383
Rivers, Daniel, 200–1
Roberts, Dorothy, 431
Rockstrom, Johan, 209
Roe v. Wade, 425, 436n.22, 530
Roiphe, Anne, 120
Roman Catholic Church, 85
    abortion and, 213–14, 215, 403–16, 464–65, 469–70, 504
    assisted reproduction and, 33
    authority and, 31–32, 85–86, 358
    authority/hierarchy vs. consensus/community in, 358–59
    code of law (canon law), 86
    commissions and committees in, 32
    communication with God, 23, 27
    conscience and, 22, 32–33
    contemporary debate on reproductive issues, 33–34
    contraception and, 29–31, 88, 195–96, 262, 356–57, 362–63, 368–69
    contraception, in *Humanae vitae*, 147, 360–63
    contraception, after *Humanae vitae*, 363–67
    contraception, dominion over nature and, 359, 361, 362, 364–65, 369
    contraception, natural vs. artificial means, 361–62, 365–66
    contraception, practical considerations and, 367–68
    contraception, response to Zika virus and, 367–68
    contraception, in Scripture, 137, 361
    debate on reproductive issues, contemporary, 33–34
    dualism in, 138
    embryo adoption and, 261–64, 273–74
    "ends" of marriage and, 31
    family ethics in, 136, 138–40
    family planning and, 213, 367
    fetus, status of, 529–30
    gay parenting and, 195–97, 199
    gender and gender complementarity, 196, 368–69
    on "intrinsic evil," 29
    laity in, 28, 85–86, 145, 151–52
    magisterium, teachings of, 27–28, 100, 149, 265–66, 358, 361, 404, 506–7, 528
    marriage and, 30
    marriage, legal views of, 142, 151–52
    marriage and family, 136, 138–40, 149, 151–52
    marriage and family, *Casti connubii* to Vatican II, 142–46
    marriage and family, in early Church, 138–40
    marriage and family, *Humanae vitae* and, 147
    marriage and family, in Middle Ages, 140–41
    marriage and family, Reformation to twentieth century, 141–42
    marriage and family, revisionist theology since *Humanae vitae*, 150
    marriage and family, in Scripture, 137–38, 151–52
    marriage and family, traditionalists vs. revisionists, 150, 151
    marriage and family, in twentieth century, 151
    marriage and family, Vatican II and, 146–47
    marriage and sex and, 195–96
    medical interventions and, 367
    natural law theory and, 22, 28–31, 90, 93–94, 361
    official teaching in, 22
    ordinary magisterium, 32
    organ donation and, 93–94
    prenatal diagnostic screening and testing and, 503–4, 518n.20, 519n.33
    official teachings of, 357–59
    Scripture as source of moral theology, 22, 23–27, 424
    seven sacraments, 141
    sexual ethics in, 30–31, 33–34, 149
    sources of moral theology, 22
    See also Tradition (Catholic)

Roman emperors
    historical record of adoptions, 293–94
    claims of divinity, 294
Roman Empire
    fertility in, 211–12
    life expectancy in, 211–12
Roman law
    adoption in, 291, 292–96
    family law and, 292
    male line and family name in, 292–93
Romans, Book of
    9:4 290–92
    11 291–92
Rosen, Christine, 166, 539
Rothman, Barbara Katz, 498–99, 502–3
Rubin, Gayle, 193
Rubio, Julie Hanlon, 136, 151
Ruth narrative, 298–99
Ryan, Maura, 511

Sadik, Nafis, 210
Sait, M. S., 244
Saliers, Don E., 46–47
Salzman, Todd A., 33–34, 150, 358–59
same-sex marriage, 199, 200–1
    evangelical views of, 384
    Jewish views of, 198
    legally recognized in US, 199–200
    See also gay parenting
Samlai, Rabbi, 390–91
Sanchez, Thomas, 213
Sandelowski, Margarete, 540
Sandys, Edwina, 46–47
Sanger, Margaret, 165–66
"Save Our Children" campaign, 191–93
Savulescu, Julian, 539–40
Schaeffer, Francis, 530
Schiff, Daniel, 388
Scholem, Gershom, 9
Schroedel, Jean Reith, 211
Schtisel (television series), 1
scientific knowledge
    abortion debate and, 427
    Catholic position on abortion and, 404
    Islamic perspectives on abortion
        and, 455–56
    Protestant ethics and, 45, 48

Scripture
    in Abrahamic traditions, 84
    Catholic moral theology and, 22, 23–27
    Protestantism and, 37–38, 39–42, 45, 85–86, 422–24
    See also Hebrew Bible (Old Testament); New Testament; Qur'an
sea levels, rising, 208–9
Second Vatican Council (Vatican II, 1962–1965), 22, 31, 85–86, 262
    on abortion, 404
    on Bible as "inspired," 23
    on marriage, sex, and family, 146–47, 195–96
    new ecclesiological model and, 358–59
    "signs of the times," 28, 33
    See also *Gaudium et spes*
Seeman, Don, 492
semen, role in generative process, 405, 406
Sensus fidei in the Life of the Church (International Theological Commission), 27–28
Serreze, Mark, 208
sex change (reassignment) surgery, 223
sex selection/screening, 72, 505, 541
sexual intercourse and sexuality
    Augustine on, 139
    Biblical prohibitions and, 26
    in *Casti connubii*, 143–44
    Catholic views of, 30–31, 33–34, 149, 361, 364–65, 368–69
    in Catholic Scripture, 25–26
    evangelical views of, 373, 374–75, 376, 378–79, 383, 531
    procreative teleology of, 99–102, 104
    Protestant views of, 47
    within marriage, 195–96
sexual morality, and public opinion on abortion, 464, 467
Sha'arei Uziel, 126
Shafi'i School, 241, 246, 248
Shaikh, Sadiyya, 214
Shaltūt, Maḥmūd, 340
Shari'a
    assisted reproductive technology and, 339–40
    defining and overview, 87, 240–41, 254n.11
    family status issues and, 347–48

Shari'a (cont.)
   gamete donation and surrogacy, 345
   harm and harassment in, 73–74
   human and child welfare in, 249–50
   incest in, 62–63, 80
   IVF and, 59, 60, 62–63, 66–67, 78, 80
   language of obligation in, 70
   social interactions and, 78
al-Shaybānī, Muhammad, 186
shevet, 119–20
Shiite Islam
   assisted reproduction technology and, 339, 349
   authority and, 63–64, 451
   binary approach to abortion, 451–52
   on contraception, 452
   gradualist approach to abortion, 451–53
   Hadith of, 451–53
   Ja`fari School, 241
   jurists in, 72
   principles and rules in, 69–70
   reason and divine judgments in, 69–70
   schism from Sunni Islam, 255n.19
   sources for normative statements and, 451
   surrogacy and gamete donation and, 346–47
Shulchan Arukh, 118–19, 121, 122, 124–25, 126
siblings
   egg donation and, 327
   in Qur'anic narratives, 181–82
single parenthood
   and artificial insemination in Jewish law, 331
   See also parenting and parenthood
siqt, 444, 449–50
"situated ethics," 478, 492–93
situation ethics, 41, 43–44
slavery, and surrogacy in Old Testament, 309–10
social justice, 210
Society for Maternal-Fetal Medicine (SMFM), 501–2
sociobiology, 93
Sofer, Rabbi Moses, 229
Sola Scriptura, 39, 85–86, 156–57, 422–23, 424
Soloveitchik, Rabbi Joseph B., 221, 226, 230, 231–32

somatic-cell nuclear transfer (SCNT, the "Dolly technique"), 59, 76–77
sonograms, 486, 487, 489
souls and ensoulment
   Aristotle and Aquinas on, 405–6
   Catholic position on, 404–5, 406–7
   in Hadith of Ibn Mas'ūd, 450–51, 456
   Islamic views of, 448–50, 455–57
   natural law theory and, 96
   in Shiite Hadith, 452
   types of, 448, 452
Southern Baptist Convention (SBC), 423, 424, 425, 530
special needs children, Haredi Jewish women with, 477, 478, 484–86
sperm banks, 321, 326, 340–41
sperm donation, Jewish ethics and, 331–32
Spitz, Rabbi Elie, 329–30
Stanton, Glenn, 194
state, population policy and, 206
Steinberg, Rabbi Mair, 229
stem cell research, 67, 95, 103, 104–5, 538
stepfathers, in Islamic jurisprudence, 184–85
stewardship, 48, 377–78, 533–34
Stout, Jeffrey, 42
strong acceptance view, of contraception, 373–76
subjective culture, 33
subjectivism, conscience and, 32, 33
suffering
   evangelical views on, 535–37
   prenatal diagnostic screening and testing and relief of, 508–10, 515–16
   as source of Protestant moral knowledge, 45
Sunna of the Prophet, 87, 241, 242, 250, 338–39
Sunni Islam
   on assisted reproductive technology, 349
   binary approach to abortion, 446–47
   expiation for fetal death in, 447
   fiqh and, 87
   fiqh debates on abortion in ninth until thirteenth centuries, 453–55
   gamete donation and surrogacy and, 339
   gradualist approach to abortion, 445–46, 447
   Hanafi School/Ḥanafīya, 453, 454, 455
   Hanbali School/Ḥanbalīya, 453, 455

Mālikī School/Mālikīya, 453, 454, 455
methodological stratagems used by jurists, 72
position on abortion in Hadith from eighth
    to tenth centuries, 444–47
principles and rules in, 70
on reason, 69
on religious authority behind rulings
    in, 63–64
schism and, 255n.19
schools in, 241, 453, 455
Shāfiʿī School/Shāfiʿīya, 453, 455
supererogation, 13
Supreme Court, rulings on contraception and
    abortion, 355–56, 369n.5
surrogacy
    agreements, 330
    altruistic, 270–71
    Biblical stories of, 306–11
    Catholic views of, 263
    as commodification, 329
    contemporary, 311
    disintegrative, 270–71
    embryo adoption as, 270–71
    gainful, 270–71
    gestational, 329, 345
    in Islamic context, 61–62, 78–79, 339–40,
        341, 345–47, 349
    Islamic institutions on, 343–44
    Islamic law and, 347–48
    Judaism and Jewish law, 18–19, 123,
        222, 328–30
    natural law theory and, 101
    Protestant ethics and, 47
    social effects of, 329
    traditional or ovum, 328–29
    transitory, 270–71
Sutton, Agneta, 534

tabanni (adoption), 242–45, 251–52
tajdid (renewal), in Islamic tradition, 252
Talmud, 10–11, 84–85, 395
    aggadah of, 390
    Babylonian, 20n.6, 117, 124, 395
    contraception in, 121
    on education of children, 128
    extralegal norms in, 13
    health risks of egg donation and, 332

Jerusalem, 20n.6, 395
on parenting, 124
on parenting through adoption, 126
specifics of procreation in, 118
status of embryo in, 394–96
Tana Devei Eliyahu Zuta 14, 117
Tate, Julia J., 306–9
teleology, 91–92, 93
Ten Commandments, 43–44
Thalidomide, 399
Thatcher, Adrian, 149–50
"theology of the cross," 45, 46
Thobaben, James R., 102, 532
Thomas Aquinas, Saint, 24, 213, 215
    on children, 141
    on human sexuality, 99
    on marriage, 141
    on natural law, 29, 92–93, 94
    on nature of ethics, 213
    on parental responsibilities, 141
    on population control, 205–6
    on soul of embryo, 96, 405–6
Thorpe, John, 541
1 Timothy, 301
Tollefsen, Christopher, 97, 98–99
Tonti-Filippini, N., 266
Torah
    covenantal ethicists and, 16–17
    interpretation and, 10
    Jewish ethics and, 7–8, 10–11, 13, 84–85
    narrative approach and, 17
    practice of reading, 8
    Reform movement and, 12
Torode, Sam, 383–85
Torode, Bethany, 383, 384–85
Tosefta, 121, 393
totality, principle of, 362
Tradition (Catholic)
    God's revelation in, 27
    role of laity in moral teaching, 28
    as source of moral theology, 22, 27–28, 32
    teaching in, 27–28
Tradition (Islamic)
    authority behind rulings, 63–65
    child's lineage in, 65, 66
    eugenics in, 77
    in Islamic ethical judgments, 69

tradition (Protestant), as source of moral knowledge, 37, 39, 42–43
Treier, Daniel, 532
Troeltsch, Ernst, 43
tubal ovum transfer with sperm (TOTS), 102
Tunisia, legal framework concerning rape in, 456–57

ulama (interpreters), 87, 443–44, 450, 455–57
ulipristal acetate, 380
Ultra-Orthodox (Haredi) Jewish women
  babies with Down syndrome and special needs, 484–86, 491
  decisions regarding prenatal testing and, 491–93
  "ethical gatekeeping" and, 491, 492
  faith and certainty and, 486–87
  God-sent ordeals and, 489–91
  methodology of study, 481–83
  obligatory effort and, 487–89
  pregnancy and childbearing and, 480, 483–84
  prenatal diagnostic screening and testing and, 477–78, 479, 480–81, 491–93
  soul and its mission and, 483–86
ultrasound screening, 478–79, 482–83, 486–87, 488–89, 490–91, 499–500, 541
Umar (classical Muslim jurist), 247
United Arab Emirates (UAE), legislating assisted reproductive technology, 348
United Church of Christ (UCC), 48, 194–95, 423–24
United Nations Paris Conference (2015), 207, 208–9
United Nations Population and Development Conference (Cairo, 1994), 210
United States
  adoption and adoption law in, 221–22, 226–27, 231–32, 250–51, 305–6
  embryo adoption in, 263–64
  live births from IVF-ET or ET of frozen embryos, 265
Universal Declaration of Human Rights (UDHR), 81n.3
urf (custom), 241
US Conference of Bishops, 503–4

Vacek, Edward Collins, S. J., 100
values, human, 23, 26
VanDrunen, David, 532, 536
Vanhoozer, Kevin, 532
Vatican II. *See* Second Vatican Council (Vatican II)
Vaux, Kenneth L., 47
Veatch, Robert M., 38
Verbum Domini, 148–49
Verhey, Allen, 40, 42
Veritatis splendor, 29–30
Viefhues-Bailey, Ludger, 193–94
Vigen, Aana Marie, 513, 514
virtue ethics, 13
von Hildebrand, Dietrich, 144, 145

Waldenberg, Eliezer Yehudah, 123
al-Wansharīsī, Aḥmad b. Yaḥyā's, 185
Waters, Brent, 40
Watt, H., 268–69, 271, 272, 273, 280n.46, 280n.48
Wax, Trevin, 374–75
Wesley, John, 45
West, Traci C., 38, 41, 43, 46
Whatever Happened to the Human Race (Koop and Schaeffer), 530
Wheeler, Ely, 534
White, Heather, 194–95
Whittaker, Andrea, 492
whole genome sequencing (WGS), 500–1
widows, 297–98, 300–3
Wikler, Daniel, 508
Wilson, E. O., 93
Winkel, Eric, 87
Wisdom literature, 137
Wogaman, J. Philip, 38, 42, 43–44
Wojtyla, Karol, Cardinal, 147, 365–66
  See also John Paul II
women
  and abortion in Christian tradition, 425–26, 430–31, 432, 433
  in *Casti connubii*, 143
  Catholicism and, 30, 33–34
  Catholic ordination and, 86–87
  economic and educational empowerment of, 210
  evangelical views of contraception and, 378–79

experience as source of moral knowledge and, 427–28
modesty in Islam and, 66–67
as mothers in Qur'an, 180–81
in public life, 460–61
public opinion on abortion policy and, 465–67
role in reproduction, 26
women of color, abortion debate and, 431
Women's Consciousness, Women's Conscience (Andolsen et al.), 38
work, in *Laborem exercens*, 365
World Alliance of Reformed Churches, 37–38
World Council of Churches (WCC), 165, 504–5
World Values Surveys (WVSs), 461–62

Yehoshua, Rabbi, 119
Yisraeli, Rabbi Shaul, 399
Yoder, John Howard, 41, 42
Yosef, Rabbi Ovadiah, 231

Zachariah, 177–78
Zamudio, Lucero, 211
"zero-tolerance" view, of contraception, 380–81
Zika virus, Catholic views of contraception and, 367–68
Zoloth, Laurie, 212
al-Zuhrī, 448–49, 450
Zwally, Jay, 208
zygote intra-fallopian transfer (ZIFT), 65, 80